C000319139

Congratulations on choosing the most comprehensive guide to Bed & Breakfast in Ireland. This guide is all you will need to find the accommodation you require in any part of the entire island of Ireland, as we now have members in every county in Ireland.

There are 1,700 homes in this guide and all have been inspected and approved by the Tourist Boards. Whether you are looking for accommodation in the hustle and bustle of the large cities, in quaint seaside villages or out in the quiet and peaceful countryside, this guide will give you full details of exactly the type of accommodation you are looking for throughout the entire island of Ireland. Each home is unique in it's own individual style and taste, but the one thing that is found in all our homes is a warm friendly welcome. What better way to meet the Irish than as a guest in the comfort of their home!

This year, we in Town & Country Homes Association are celebrating 30 years in business and we are committed to ensuring that you enjoy your stay with us. Our Association motto is "The Personal Touch" and is your guarantee of the very best hospitality and service while staying in our homes.

Bed & Breakfast in a Town & Country Home continues to be the most sought after, value for money accommodation in Ireland and the large number of guests who return year after year are proof of this. In order to maintain our high standard of accommodation and hospitality, we would welcome your comments as we are constantly striving to improve the service we offer to you.

Over 70% of our homes can now be booked through email and we recommend that you book your first and last night accommodation in advance. Our members will be only too happy to assist you in making onward reservations before you leave their home, thus assuring you of the very best accommodation throughout your holiday.

We hope you enjoy your stay in Ireland and that you too will continue to return to Town & Country Homes again and again.

Fiona Byrne

Fiona Byrne, Chairperson

Tourist Regions of Ireland

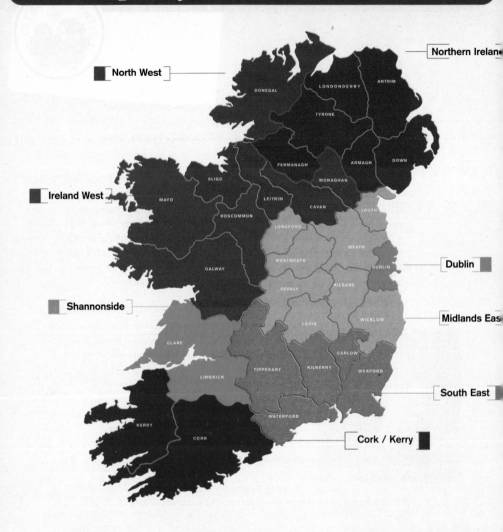

- Northern Ireland
- North West
- Ireland West
- Dublin
- Shannonside
- Midlands East
- South East
- Cork / Kerry

DONEGAL
LONDONDERRY
ANTRIM
TYRONE
FERMANAGH
ARMAGH
DOWN
SLIGO
MONAGHAN
MAYO
LEITRIM
CAVAN
ROSCOMMON
LOUTH
LONGFORD
MEATH
WESTMEATH
GALWAY
DUBLIN
OFFALY
KILDARE
LAOIS
WICKLOW
CLARE
CARLOW
LIMERICK
TIPPERARY
KILKENNY
WEXFORD
KERRY
WATERFORD
CORK

Approved Accommodation Signs
This sign will be displayed at most premises which are approved to Irish Tourist Board Standards.

Plakette für Geprüfte Unterkunft
Diese Plaketten werden an den meisten Häusern angezeigt, die von auf die Einhaltung der Normen der irischen Fremdenverkehrsbehörde überprüft und zugelassen wurden.

Borden voor goedgekeurde accommodatie
Deze borden vindt u bij de meeste huizen die zijn goedgekeurd door voor de normen van de Ierse Toeristenbond.

Simbolo di sistemazione approvata
Questi simboli saranno esposti nella maggior parte delle case approvate (associazione dei Bed & Breakfast approvati per qualità), rispondenti agli standard dell'Ente del Turismo Irlandese.

Símbolo de alojamiento aprobado
Estos símbolos se muestran en los establecimientos que han sido aprobados por bajos los estandars de la Oficina de Turismo Irlandesa.

Skyltar för Godkänd logi
Dessa skyltar finns vid de flesta gästhus som har godkänts (Föreningen för kvalitetsgodkända gästhus AB), enligt irländs turisföreningens normer.

Panneaux d'homologation des établissements
Ces panneaux sont affichés dans la plupart des établissements homologués selon les normes de l'Office du tourisme irlandais.

Contents

HEAD OFFICE
Belleek Road, Ballyshannon, Co. Donegal.
Tel: 00353 72 22222   Fax: 00353 72 22207
(Monday-Friday 9am-5pm)
Email: admin@townandcountry.ie
Web: www.townandcountry.ie
WAP: www.bandbireland.com

Head Office and Officers of Association

Head Office

Please forward all correspondence & enquiries to:
**Mrs Margaret Storey, Chief Executive,
Town & Country Homes Association Ltd.**
Belleek Road, Ballyshannon, Co. Donegal.
Tel: 00353 72 22222. Fax: 00353 72 22207.
Email: admin@townandcountry.ie
Web: www.townandcountry.ie
WAP: www.bandbireland.com

Chairperson
Mrs Fiona Byrne, Glen na Smole, Ashtown Lane
Marlton Road, Wicklow, Co. Wicklow
Tel: 0404 67945, Fax: 0404 68155
Email: byrneglen@eircom.net
Web: http://homepage.eircom.net/~byrneglen

Vice-Chairman
Mrs Carol O'Gorman, Ashfort, Galway/Knock Rd,
Charlestown, Co. Mayo
Tel: 094 54706, Fax: 094 55885
Email: ashfort@esatclear.ie
Web: www.mayobandb.com

Secretary
Mrs Noreen McBride, 3 Rossmore Grove,
off Wellington Lane, Templeogue, Dublin 6W.
Tel: 01 490 2939, Fax: 01 492 9416
Email: denismb@iol.ie

Treasurer
Mrs Tess Haughey, Rathnashee, Teesan, Donegal Road (N15), Sligo, Co. Sligo
Tel: 071 43376, Fax: 071 42283

IRELAND
Bord Failte
Bord Failte Eireann
Baggot Street Bridge
Dublin 2
Tel: 1850 23 03 30
Fax: 01 602 4100

NORTHERN IRELAND
BELFAST
Bord Failte
53 Castle Street
Belfast BT1 1GH
Tel: 028 9032 7888
Fax: 028 9024 0201

DERRY
Bord Failte
44 Foyle Street
Derry
BT48 6AT
Tel: 028 71369501
Fax: 028 71369501
* if dialing Northern Ireland from
Republic of Ireland dial 048
instead of 028

EUROPE
AUSTRIA
Irische Fremdenverkehrszentrale
Libellenweg 1
A-1140 Vienna
Tel: 01- 501596000
Fax: 01 -911 3765

BELGIUM
Irish Tourist Board – Bord Failte
Avenue Louise 327 Louizalaan
1050 Brussels
Tel. 02 –275 01 71
Fax : 02 – 642 98 51

BRITAIN
Irish Tourist Board
Ireland House
150 New Bond Street
London W1S 2AQ
Tel: 0800 039 7000
Fax: 20 - 7493 9065

DENMARK
Det Irske Turistkontor
"Klostergaarden"
Amagertorv 29B,3
DK 1160
Copenhagen K
Tel: 33 - 15 8045
Fax: 33 - 93 6390

FINLAND
Irlannin Matkailutoimisto
Embassy of Ireland
Erottajankatu 7A
PL33, 00130 Helsinki
Tel: 09 - 608 966/961
Fax: 09 - 646 022

FRANCE
Office National du Tourisme
Irlandais
33 rue de Miromesnil
75008 Paris
Tel: :   01 -7020 00 20
Fax: 01 - 4742 01 64

GERMANY
Irische Fremdenverkehrszentrale
Untermainanlage 7
D-60329 Frankfurt am Main
Tel   069 - 66 800950
Fax: 069 – 923 18588

ITALY
Ente Nazionale del Turismo
Irlandese
Via Santa Maria Segreta 6
20123 Milano
Tel   02 – 4829 6060
Fax: 02 – 869 0396

THE NETHERLANDS
Iers Nationaal Bureau voor
Toerisme
Spuistraat 104
1012 VA Amsterdam
Tel: 20 - 504 0689
Fax: 20 - 620 8089

NORWAY
Irlands Turistkontor
Postboks 6691 St. Olavs Plass
N-0129 OSLO
Tel: +47 22 20 26 40
Fax: +47 22 20 26 41

PORTUGAL
Delegacao de Turismo Irlandesa
Embaixada da Irlanda
Rua da Imprensa a Estrela 1-4∫
1200 Lisboa,Portugal
Tel: 21 - 3929440
Fax: 21 - 397 7367

SPAIN
Oficina de Turismo de Irlanda
Paseo de la Castellana 46, 3ᵀᴹ
Planta 28046 Madrid
Tel: 91 - 745 6420
Fax: 91 - 577 6934

SWEDEN
Irlandska Turistbyran,
Stora Nygatan 40,
SE-11127 Stockholm,
Sweden.
Tel: 00 46 8 662 8510
Fax: 0046 8 233 727

SWITZERLAND
Ireland Mailing House
CH-5634 Merenschwand
Switzerland
Tel: 01 – 210 4153
Fax: 056 675 75 80 - Ireland

USA
Irish Tourist Board
345 Park Avenue
New York
NY 10154
Tel: 1800 223 6470
Fax: 212 371 9052

SOUTH AFRICA
(Postal Address)
PO Box 30615
Braamfontein 2017
Johannesburg
Tel: 11 - 339 4865
Fax: 11 - 339 2474

NEW ZEALAND
Irish Tourist Board
Dingwall Building
2nd Floor
87 Queen Street
Auckland
Tel: 09 – 379 8720
Fax: 09 – 302 2420

AUSTRALIA
Irish Tourist Board
5th Level
36 Carrington Street
Sydney
NSW 2000
Tel: 02 - 9299 6177
Fax: 02 - 9299 6323

JAPAN
Irish Tourist Board
Ireland House 4f
2-10-7 Kojimachi
Chiyoda-ku
Tokyo 102-0083
Tel: 03 - 5275 1611
Fax: 03 - 5275 1623

Using This Guide

The guide is divided into eight geographical regions which are subdivided into counties (see page 2 for map of regions and counties). The regions are: **Ireland West, Midlands East, North West, Northern Ireland, Dublin, South East, Cork/Kerry, Shannonside.**

Booking Procedure
It is advisable to **book first and last night's accommodation** in advance at all times.

Room Availability in Dublin
Rooms in Dublin City and County can be difficult to find unless accommodation is pre-booked. If visiting the capital city, we strongly advise pre-booking all accommodation **well in advance.** Never count on finding rooms at short notice in Dublin. Always reserve in advance.

Onward Reservations:
During peak season, should problems arise finding accommodation when in Ireland, contact any Tourist Information Office, or seek advice and assistance from your host/hostess in Town & Country Homes. She/he will assist in booking subsequent night/nights for the cost of a telephone call. We recommend securing your following nights accommodation before leaving the B&B.

Credit Card Bookings
Credit cards are accepted in homes with the [cc] symbol.
Telephone reservations may be guaranteed by quoting a valid credit card number. Check terms and conditions when booking.

Travel Agents Vouchers
Please present your voucher on arrival. Vouchers are only valid in homes displaying Ⓥ.
Standard Vouchers cover B&B in room without private facilities. To **upgrade to ensuite** rooms, the maximum charge is **€2.00 per person.** The maximum charge for 3 or more sharing should **not exceed €5.00 per room.**
Ensuite vouchers cover a room with full private facilities. No extra charge is payable

Dublin Supplement:
A room supplement for Dublin city and county of €7.50 applies for the months of **June, July August & September** on Travel Agency Vouchers. This charge is paid directly to the accommodation provider and is not included in the voucher.

Cancellation policy
When a reservation has been confirmed, please check cancellation policy with establishment at the time of booking. The person making the reservation is responsible for the agreed cancellation fee.
Please telephone immediately in the event of a cancellation. Should it be necessary to cancel or amend a booking without sufficient prior notice, a financial penalty applies.
- 7-14 days notice – 25% of the 1st night
- 2-6 days notice – 50% of the 1st night
- 24 hours notice /failure to show – 75% of the 1st night.

Late Arrivals
Please note that late arrival – **estimated after 6pm is by Special Agreement with home.** It would be much appreciated if time of arrival were given to your host/hostess.

Advance Bookings
For advance bookings, a cheque or Credit Card number may be requested to guarantee arrival. Check Terms and Conditions.

Check In/Out
Please advise of early arrival.
- Rooms available between 2pm and 6pm.
- Check out should be no later than 11am.
- Reservations should be taken up by 6pm.

Reduction for Children
Applies where children share with a parent or three or more children share one room. Full rate applies when one or two children occupy separate rooms. Please check that the home is suitable for children when booking. Cots 🛏 are available in some homes – there may be a nominal charge.

Evening Meals
Book in advance preferably before 12 noon on the day. Light meals ☒ available on request.

Pets
With the exception of Guide Dogs, in the interest of hygiene pets are not allowed indoors.

Disabled Persons/Wheelchair Users
Premises will only be listed with homes that have been approved by Comhairle or in the past by the National Rehabilitation Board.

Colour Coded Bar for each Region

Family Name
NAME OF TOWN OR
COUNTRY HOME
Address
Description of Town & Country Home

Area

TEL: FAX:
EMAIL:
WEB:
BUS NO:

B&B	#	Ensuite	Min€/Max€	Dinner	€
B&B	#	Standard	Min€/Max€	Partial Board	Min€/Max€
Single Rate			Min€/Max€	Child reduction	%

Nearest Town distance in km

Facility Symbols:

B+B PPS: Bed & Breakfast per person sharing
PARTIAL BRD: Bed & Breakfast, Evening meal for seven days.
No of rooms.

Open:

Child Reduction % for Children sharing parents room or where three or more children share one room
SINGLE RATE: : Single Rate for Room

Symbols

cc	Credit Cards accepted	🍼	Cot available
♿	Access for disabled with helper.	✗	Light meals available
	Comhairle approved.	🍷	Wine Licence
S	Single Room	🚶	Walking
P	Private off-street parking	🚲	Cycling
☘	Irish spoken	⛳	Golf within 5kms.
	Facilities for Pets	🐎	Horse riding within 5kms.
⊗	No smoking house	🐟	Facilities for Fishing
⌀	No smoking bedrooms	🐟 L	Lake fishing within 15km.
▢	TV in bedrooms	🐟 S	Sea Fishing within 15km.
☏	Direct dial telephone in bedrooms	🐟 R	River fishing within 15km.
☕	Tea/Coffee facilities in bedrooms	V	Travel Agency Vouchers Accepted.
👶	Babysitter, normally to 12 midnight	⊗	Travel Agency Vouchers Not Accepted

Compliments and Comments

Complaints should always be brought to the attention of the proprietor before departure. Failing satisfaction and in the case of alleged overcharging, your receipt should be sent with your complaint to: **Customer Care, Town & Country Homes, Belleek Road, Ballyshannon, Co. Donegal.**

To maintain the high standards which the Association is renowned for, all comments on the general level of service and the standards you have experienced are welcome. All constructive criticisms will be taken seriously to ensure continued service improvement.

Errors and Omissions

Every care has been taken to ensure accuracy in this publication in compliance with the Consumer Protection Laws of Ireland. The Town & Country Homes Association Ltd. cannot accept responsibility for errors, omissions or inaccurate particulars in material supplied by members for inclusion in this publication, or for any loss or disappointment caused by dependence on information contained herein. Where such are brought to our attention, future editions will be amended accordingly. There may be changes after going to press where properties are sold, and the home changes ownership.

Page 390
Page 391
Page 392
Page 393
Page 394
Page 395

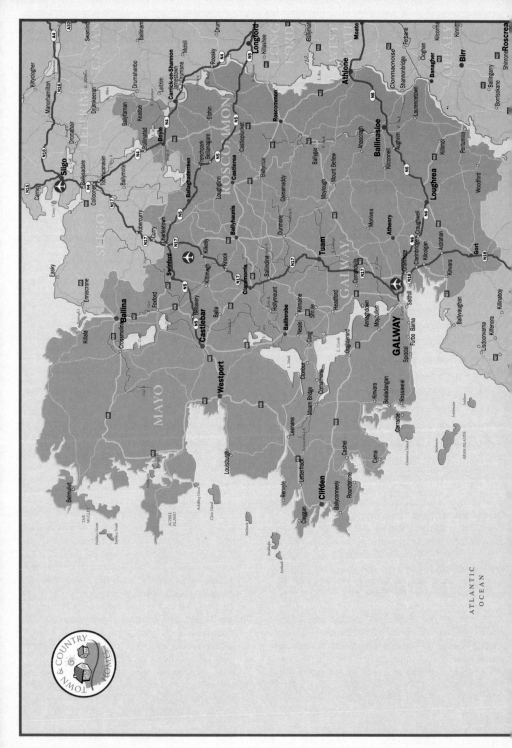

Ireland West

Ireland West

There is a special quality about these three beautiful Counties in the West of Ireland that is unique in Europe. The welcome is heartwarming, the quality of life, people and land-scape is all there for our visitor to share.

The spectacularly beautiful countryside, the coast that has been etched by the Atlantic, rambling hills and mountains and the lovely lakes and bays that mirror that special light from the clear skies over the countryside. Each County has its own special attractions and rich in all that is best in Irish folklore, music and song. There is something here for everyone, you will not be disappointed.

Connemara National Park

Area Representatives

GALWAY
Ms Bernadette Donoghue, Kiltevna, 24 Grattan Park, Coast Rd, Galway, Co Galway Tel: 091 588477   Fax: 091 581173
Mrs Bernie McTigue, Abbey View, Bushy Park, Galway, Co Galway Tel: 091 524488
Mrs Mary Noone, Ashbrook House, Dublin Road, Oranmore, Co Galway Tel: 091 794196 Fax: 091 794196
MAYO
Mrs Mary O'Dowd, Cnoc Breandain, Quay Road, Ballina, Co Mayo Tel: 096 22145
Mrs Carol O'Gorman, Ashfort, Galway/Knock Road, Charlestown, Co Mayo Tel: 094 54706 Fax: 094 55885
Mrs Maureen Daly, Woodview Lodge, Breaffy (Breaghwy), Castlebar, Co Mayo Tel: 094 23985   Fax: 094 23985
ROSCOMMON
Mary Cooney, Cesh Corran, Abbey Tce, Sligo Rd, Boyle, Co Roscommon Tel: 079 62265 Fax: 079 62265

Tourist Information Offices

OPEN ALL YEAR

Galway City
Forster Street
Off Eyre Square
Tel: 091 537700

Oughterard
Main Street
Tel: 091 552808

Westport
James St
Tel: 098 25711
Website: www.ireland.travel.ie

9

Galway - A vibrant University City renowned for its Festivals, Music and Theatre. Archeological sites, Golf courses, Rivers, Lakes and the Aran Islands combine to make this county a magical place. Connemara dominated by the Twelve Pins is a delight to explore.

Mrs Veronica Marley
SILVER BIRCH
Clonboo, Annaghdown,
Co Galway

Annaghdown
TEL: **091 791036**
EMAIL: **jmarley@eircom.net**

Friendly home. Main route Cong/Connemara on N84. Walking distance Pub/Restaurant - Clonboo Riding School, Galway City 9km, Lough Corrib 4km.

B&B	4	Ensuite	€25.50	Dinner	-
B&B	-	Standard	-	Partial Board	-
Single Rate			€38.50	Child reduction	25%

Galway City 9km

Open: 1st April-31st October

Mrs Bridie Conneely
BEACH VIEW HOUSE
Oatquarter, Kilronan,
Inis Mor, Aran Islands
Co Galway

Aran Islands (Inismore)
TEL: **099 61141**   FAX: **099 61141**
EMAIL: **beachviewhouse@eircom.net**

Situated in middle of island near Dun Aengus. Scenic and tranquil surroundings. Ideal for Cliff walk's with views of Cliff's of Moher. Blue flag Beach, Restaurants and Pubs nearby.

B&B	-	Ensuite	-	Dinner	-
B&B	6	Standard	€23/€23	Partial Board	-
Single Rate			€36/€36	Child reduction	25%

Kilronan   4.5km

Open: 20th May-16th September

Mrs Margaret Conneely
CREGMOUNT HOUSE
Creig-An-Cheirin, Kilronan,
Inis Mor, Aran Islands,
Co Galway

Aran Islands (Inismore)
TEL: **099 61139**

Spectacular sea panorama from house set in unspoilt location. Historic monuments easily accessible. Qualified Cook/London City and Guilds Diploma.

B&B	2	Ensuite	€26.66/€26.66	Dinner	€21.59
B&B	1	Standard	€24.13/€24.13	Partial Board	-
Single Rate			-	Child reduction	-

Kilronan   6km

Open: 1st April-31st October

Cait Flaherty
ARD MHUIRIS
Kilronan, Aran Islands,
Co Galway

Aran Islands
TEL: **099 61208**   FAX: **099 61333**
EMAIL: **ardmhuiris@eircom.net**

5-7 minutes from Ferry - turn right, then left. View of Galway Bay, peaceful area. Walking distance from Restaurants, Pubs, Beaches.

B&B	6	Ensuite	€26/€30	Dinner	-
B&B	-	Standard	-	Partial Board	-
Single Rate			€38.50/€44.50	Child reduction	-

In Kilronan

Open: 1st March-1st November

Bridie & Patrick McDonagh
AN CRUGAN
Kilronan, Inis Mor,
Aran Islands, Co Galway

Aran Islands (Inismore)

TEL: **099 61150**   FAX: **099 61468**
EMAIL: **ancrugan@eircom.net**
WEB: **www.ancrugan.com**

Situated in Kilronan, the principal port and village of Inishmore. Convenient to Restaurants, Pubs, Beaches. Visa accepted. Hairdryers in bedrooms.

B&B	5	Ensuite	€30	Dinner	-
B&B	1	Standard	€25	Partial Board	-
Single Rate			€45	Child reduction	50%

In Kilronan

Open: 1st April-30th September

Mrs Rita McDonagh
PORT ARAN HOUSE
Upper Kilronan, Inismore,
Aran Islands, Co Galway

Aran Islands (Inismore)

TEL: **099 61396**

Friendly welcome awaits you at Portaran House overlooking Galway Bay, Connemara Coast and Clare Hills. Situated within walking distance of all amenities.

B&B	3	Ensuite	€30	Dinner	-
B&B	3	Standard	€25	Partial Board	-
Single Rate			€40/€45	Child reduction	50%

In Kilronan

Open: April-October

Joe & Maura Wolfe
MAN OF ARAN COTTAGES
Kilmurvey, Inish Mor,
Aran Islands, Co Galway

Aran Islands

TEL: **099 61301**   FAX: **099 61324**
EMAIL: **manofaran@eircom.net**
WEB: **homepage.eircom.net/~manofaran**

This historic thatched cottage on an acre of organically grown vegetables and herbs was built by Robert Flaherty as a set for his film "The Man of Aran".

B&B	1	Ensuite	€32	Dinner	-
B&B	1	Standard	€28	Partial Board	-
Single Rate			€37/€41	Child reduction	-

Kilronan 6.5km

Open: 17th March-31st October

Ms Marion E McDonagh
TEACH AN GHARRAIN
Ballygarraun, South Athenry,
Co Galway

Athenry

TEL: **091 844579**   FAX: **091 845390**
EMAIL: **mcdhaus@eircom.net**
WEB: **www.mcdonaghsbandb.com**

Hotel Quality, B&B prices. Tranquil scenic location. Heritage town, train service. Galway City-15 mins. Great base for touring West. Take N6 to R348. Payphone/Internet.

B&B	4	Ensuite	€27.50/€30	Dinner	-
B&B	-	Standard	€39/€39	Partial Board	-
Single Rate			€39/€39	Child reduction	-

In Athenry

Open: All Year

Ms Mary Thompson
ARD RI
Swangate, Athenry,
Co Galway

Athenry

TEL: **091 844050**

Galway city 12km. Train station Dublin-Galway line. Ideal for touring Connemara, Burren, Aran Islands, Heritage Town. Fishing, Golfing.

B&B	4	Ensuite	€25.50/€25.50	Dinner	-
B&B	-	Standard	€38.50/€38.50	Partial Board	-
Single Rate			€38.50/€38.50	Child reduction	50%

In Athenry

Open: 1st January-21st December

Ballinasloe 3km

Angela Lyons
NEPHIN
Portumna Road,
Kellygrove, Ballinasloe,
Co Galway

Ballinasloe
Tel: **0905 42685**

Spacious house on landscaped gardens overlooking Golf Course. Complimentary Tea/Coffee. Hairdryers. Le Guide du Routard recommended. 1 mile off N6.

B&B	2	Ensuite	€25.50	Dinner	-
B&B	1	Standard	€23	Partial Board	-
Single Rate			€36	Child reduction	25%

Open: 1st April-31st October

Clifden 8km

Ms Bernadette Keogh
MURLACH LODGE
Ballyconneely Village,
Clifden, Co Galway

Ballyconneely Connemara Area
Tel: **095 23921**   Fax: **095 23748**
Email: **murlachlodge@eircom.net**
Web: **www.keoghs-murlachlodge.com**

Modern family home in quiet location. 1 min walk to local Pub, Restaurants and Shops etc. Convenient to Connemara, Golf Club, Beaches, Fishing, Horse Riding.

B&B	6	Ensuite	€25.50/€26.50	Dinner	-
B&B	-	Standard		Partial Board	-
Single Rate			€38.50/€38.50	Child reduction	25%

Open: All Year

Ballyconneely 1km

Bernie O'Neill
MANNIN LODGE
Mannin Road,
Ballyconneely, Co Galway

Ballyconneely Connemara Area
Tel: **095 23586**   Fax: **095 23861**
Email: **boneillmanninlodge@eircom.net**

Family run home. Convenient to Beaches, Golf Club, Pony Trekking. All with TV and Hairdryers. Clifden 10 minutes drive. Near Restaurants.

B&B	6	Ensuite	€25.50	Dinner	-
B&B	-	Standard		Partial Board	-
Single Rate			€38.50	Child reduction	25%

Open: 1st April-1st November

Galway 8km

Mrs Irene Carr
VILLA DE PORRES
Barna,
Galway, Co Galway

Barna Village
Tel: **091 592239**   Fax: **091 592239**

Off Coast Road. Close to sea food Restaurants. Beaches, Fishing, Barna Golf Club, Pony trekking. Private carpark. All rooms with TV, Hairdryers, Electric blankets. Tea/Coffee facilities.

B&B	4	Ensuite	€28/€30	Dinner	-
B&B	1	Standard	€25/€28	Partial Board	-
Single Rate			€40/€40	Child reduction	25%

Open: 17th March-31st October

Galway City 8km

Mrs Joan Codyre
FREEPORT HOUSE
Barna Village, Co Galway

Barna
Tel: **091 592199**   Fax: **091 592199**

Coast road R336. Seafront in Village. Overlooking Galway Bay. Breakfast menu, Home baking. Beside village Restaurants, Pubs, Barna Golf Club, Connemara, Aran Islands.

B&B	5	Ensuite	€28/€30	Dinner	-
B&B	1	Standard		Partial Board	-
Single Rate			€40/€40	Child reduction	25%

Open: 17th March-1st November

Barna

Bernadette Ryan
ABBEYVILLE
Freeport, Barna,
Co Galway

TEL: **091 592430**
EMAIL: **ryanbearna@eircom.net**

Attractive modern home. TV, Orthopaedic beds. Private Car parking. 200 meters Restaurants, Pubs. Located off the R336 to Barna and Connemara. Barna Golf Club.

B&B	4	Ensuite	€28/€30	Dinner	-
B&B	-	Standard		Partial Board	-
Single Rate			€38.50/€38.50	Child reduction	50%

Galway City 6km

Open: All Year

Beal A Daingin Connemara

Colm & Una Conneely
RADHARC NA NOILEAN
Annaghvane, Bealadangan,
Co Galway

TEL: **091 572137**

A friendly family home with sea and mountain views. Tea/Coffee, Scones on arrival. Aran Islands nearby, also Fishing, Walks, Golf.

B&B	3	Ensuite	€25.50/€25.50	Dinner	-
B&B	-	Standard		Partial Board	-
Single Rate			€38.50/€38.50	Child reduction	33.3%

Bealadangan 1km

Open: All Year Except Christmas

Beal A Daingin Connemara

Padraic & Angela O'Conghaile
TEACH ANACH MHEAIN
Anach Mheain, Beal a Daingin
Connemara, Co Galway

TEL: **091 572348/572212** FAX: **091 572214**
EMAIL: **padraicoc@eircom.net**

Modern family house. All bedrooms with Sea and Mountain view. Convenient to Aran Islands, Ferry, Golf, Fishing ,Walks, Beaches etc.

B&B	4	Ensuite	€25.50/€25.50	Dinner	-
B&B	-	Standard		Partial Board	-
Single Rate			€38.50/€38.50	Child reduction	33.3%

Lettermore 3km

Open: April-30th September

Carna

Aine Collins
SANDY BEACH B&B
Mweenish Island, Carna,
Connemara, Co Galway

TEL: **095 32870**

3km over bridge from Carna. Luxury home 50m to Beach. Spectacular views. Nature unspoilt - wild flowers, birds, shore life. Relaxing and very quiet.

B&B	3	Ensuite	€25.50/€27	Dinner	-
B&B	-	Standard		Partial Board	-
Single Rate			€38.50/€38.50	Child reduction	-

Carna 3km

Open: 1st June-31st August

Carna Connemara

Mrs Barbara Madden
HILLSIDE HOUSE
Kylesalia, Kilkieran, Carna,
Connemara, Co Galway

TEL: **095 33420** FAX: **095 33624**
EMAIL: **hillsidehouse@oceanfree.net**
WEB: **www.connemara.net/hillside/**

Modern home between mountains and sea. Off route R340 near Kilkieran Village, 15km east of Carna. Stunning views, hill walks, beaches, Aran Islands. AA ◆◆◆◆.

B&B	4	Ensuite	€25.50/€30	Dinner	-
B&B	-	Standard		Partial Board	-
Single Rate			€38.50/€44	Child reduction	-

Kilkieran 3km

Open: 1st March-11th November

Carraroe 1km

Mrs Tina Donoghue
DONOGHUE'S
Carraroe, Connemara,
Co Galway

Carraroe

Tel: **091 595174**   Fax: **091 595174**
Email: **donoghuec@esatclear.ie**

Comfortable family home on spacious grounds. Beaches and Country Walks; daily trips to Aran Islands nearby. Credit Cards accepted.

B&B	2	Ensuite	€25.50	Dinner	-
B&B	1	Standard	€23	Partial Board	-
Single Rate			€36	Child reduction	50%

Open: 17th March-30th October

Galway 40km

Mrs Mary Lydon
CARRAROE HOUSE
Carraroe, Connemara,
Co Galway

Carraroe Connemara

Tel: **091 595188**
Email: **carraroehouse@oceanfree.net**

Modern family home on outskirts of village. Ideal for touring Connemara, Aran Islands, near Beaches-Coral Beach. R336 from Galway to Casla, R343 to Carraroe.

B&B	4	Ensuite	€25.50/€25.50	Dinner	-
B&B	1	Standard	€23/€23	Partial Board	-
Single Rate			-	Child reduction	33.3%

Open: 7th January-20th December

Clifden 18km

Mrs Margaret McDonagh
GLEN-VIEW
Cashel Bay, Connemara
Co Galway

Cashel Bay Connemara Area

Tel: **095 31054**

A tranquil setting overlooking Mountains in the heart of Connemara. Ideal for Walking, Cycling, Fishing. Tea/Coffee and Homemade scones, beside the turf fire on arrival. Breakfast menu.

B&B	-	Ensuite	-	Dinner	€17
B&B	3	Standard	€23	Partial Board	-
Single Rate			-	Child reduction	50%

Open: 1st February-20th December

Galway 7km

Maura Campbell
AVONDALE
Cregboy, Claregalway,
Co Galway

Claregalway

Tel: **091 798349**

Comfortable home on N17 Galway/Sligo road. Fishing and Horse riding nearby. 5km from Galway Airport. Ideal for touring Connemara/Clare.

B&B	2	Ensuite	€25.50/€26.77	Dinner	-
B&B	2	Standard	€23/€24.27	Partial Board	-
Single Rate			€38.50/€38.50	Child reduction	50%

Open: May-October

Claregalway 1km

Mary Gannon
CASTLEGROVE HOUSE
Tuam Rd, Claregalway,
Co Galway

Claregalway

Tel: **091 799169**
Email: **m_gannon45@hotmail.com**
Web: **www.castlegrove-house.com/**

Friendly family home on N17. Ideal touring base for Connemara and Clare. Lovely restaurants, lounge bars and other facilities 5 minutes walk. Galway City 9km.

B&B	4	Ensuite	€27/€29	Dinner	€19.05
B&B		Standard	-	Partial Board	-
Single Rate			€38.50	Child reduction	25%

Open: 1st June-1st October

Mrs Mary McNulty
CREG LODGE
Claregalway, Co Galway

Claregalway
Tel: **091 798862**
Email: **creglodge@eircom.net**

Luxury family home on the N17 Galway/Sligo Road. 10km from Galway City and 5km from Airport. Restaurants/Pubs within walking distance.

B&B	4	Ensuite	€25.50/€28	Dinner	-
B&B	-	Standard		Partial Board	-
Single Rate			€38.50/€38.50	Child reduction	25%

Galway City 10km

CC S P ⊗ ℞ ⌿ ▢ ⌣ ⋈ ⅈ ▲ ↩ ♪ ᵣ

Open: 1st January-20th December

Mr Niall Stewart
GARMISCH
Loughgeorge, Claregalway,
Co Galway

Claregalway
Tel: **091 798606**
Email: **garmisch@eircom.net**

Luxury dormer bungalow on N17. Adjacent to Central Tavern Bar and Restaurant. Convenient for Fishing, Golfing and Touring. Galway Airport 6km.

B&B	4	Ensuite	€26/€28	Dinner	-
B&B	-	Standard		Partial Board	-
Single Rate			€38.50/€38.50	Child reduction	-

Galway 12km

CC P ▢ ⌣ ⋈ ⅈ ▲ ↩

Open: All Year

Mrs Dympna Callinan
CLAREVILLE
Stradbally North,
Clarinbridge, Co Galway

Clarinbridge
Tel: **091 796248**
Email: **clareville@eircom.net**
Web: **homepage.eircom.net/~clareville/**

Luxurious spacious dormer home situated in the heart of Oyster Country. 0.5km off N18, within walking distance of Village, Sea. Central to Burren, Connemara.

B&B	4	Ensuite	€25.50/€30	Dinner	-
B&B	-	Standard		Partial Board	-
Single Rate			€38.50/€45	Child reduction	25%

In Clarinbridge

P ⊗ ℞ ⌿ ▢ ⌣ ⅈ ▲ ✈ ᵣ

Open: March-November

Mrs Bernie Diskin
ROCK LODGE
Stradbally Nth, Clarinbridge,
Co Galway

Clarinbridge
Tel: **091 796071**
Email: **johndiskin@eircom.net**

Home in quiet area, 0.5km off N18. Private walkway to seashore. Tea/Coffee facilities. Breakfast choice. Near Burren/Connemara. Guide du Routard recommended.

B&B	2	Ensuite	€25.50	Dinner	-
B&B	1	Standard	€23	Partial Board	-
Single Rate			€36/€38.50	Child reduction	33.3%

Clarinbridge 1km

P ℞ ⌿ ▢ ⌣ ⅈ ▲ ↩ ✈ ᵣ

Open: March-November

K Geraghty
INISFREE B&B
Slievaun, Clarinbridge,
Galway, Co Galway

Clarinbridge
Tel: **091 796655**

Conveniently located on the main N18. Within walking distance of Village and Restaurants. In the heart of Oyster Country and only 12 mins Galway.

B&B	3	Ensuite	€25.50/€25.50	Dinner	-
B&B	-	Standard	-	Partial Board	-
Single Rate			€38.50/€38.50	Child reduction	25%

In Clarinbridge

P ▢ ⌣ ⋈ ↩

Open: All Year

Clarinbridge 3km

Kathleen Healy
ST JUDES MEADOW
Ardrahan, Co Galway

Clarinbridge

TEL: **091 635010**
EMAIL: **stjudesmeadow@hotmail.com**

Spacious home on N18. Gateway to scenic West, Cliffs of Moher etc. Famous restaurants nearby. Comfortable rooms. Excellent home-cooked food.

B&B	3	Ensuite	€25.50/€28	Dinner	-
B&B	-	Standard		Partial Board	-
Single Rate			€38.50/€38.50	Child reduction	33.3%

Open: 1st January-23rd December

Clarinbridge 1km

Mrs Maura McNamara
SPRING LAWN
Stradbally, Clarinbridge,
Co Galway

Clarinbridge

TEL: **091 796045**   FAX: **091 796045**
EMAIL: **springlawn2@hotmail.com**
WEB: **www.surf.to/springlawn2**

Luxury family home on mature landscaped gardens. Located just off N18 near Village and Sea. Ideal base to visit Connemara, Aran Islands, Burren. Dillard Causin Guide recommended.

B&B	3	Ensuite	€25.50/€25.50	Dinner	-
B&B	-	Standard		Partial Board	-
Single Rate			€38.50/€40	Child reduction	25%

Open: 1st March-30th November

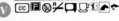

Clarinbridge 1km

Mrs Bernie Morrissy
RAHONA
Stradbally North,
Clarinbridge, Co Galway

Clarinbridge

TEL: **091 796080**
EMAIL: **rahona@gofree.indigo.ie**

Conveniently located off N18 in Clarinbridge, south of Galway City. This luxuriously appointed Guest House guarantees great Irish welcome.

B&B	4	Ensuite	€25.50/€30	Dinner	-
B&B	-	Standard	-	Partial Board	-
Single Rate			-	Child reduction	-

Open: 1st May-30th November

Clarinbridge 1km

Mrs Teresa O'Dea
KARAUN HOUSE
Stradbally, Clarinbridge,
Co Galway

Clarinbridge

TEL: **091 796182**
EMAIL: **tod_karaun@ireland.com**
WEB: **www.go.to/karaun**

Irish Times Recommended. 1km off N18. Walk to Sea. AA listed. Near Burren, Connemara, Aran Islands. Tea/Coffee, Hairdryers, Electric blankets. Visa, Master Cards accepted.

B&B	2	Ensuite	€25.50	Dinner	-
B&B	1	Standard	€23	Partial Board	-
Single Rate			€36/€36	Child reduction	-

Open: 1st March-31st October

Cleggan 1km

William & Bernie Hughes
COIS NA MARA
Cleggan, Clifden,
Co Galway

Cleggan Connemara Area

TEL: **095 44647**   FAX: **095 44016**
EMAIL: **coisnamara@hotmail.com**
WEB: **www.dirl.com/galway/cois-na-mara.htm**

Family home in scenic area. Daily boat trips to Inishbofin. Safe sandy Beaches and Pony trekking within walking distance. Access/Visa accepted.

B&B	4	Ensuite	€25.50	Dinner	-
B&B	1	Standard	€23	Partial Board	-
Single Rate			€36	Child reduction	33.3%

Open: 1st June-15th September

Mrs Mary King
CNOC BREAC
Cleggan, Co Galway

Cleggan Connemara Area
TEL: **095 44688**
EMAIL: **tking@gofree.indigo.ie**

Family home. Peaceful, scenic area. Beside sandy Beach. Fishing, Pony Riding. Bay Cruises arranged. Convenient for Inishbofin Ferry. Village 1km.

B&B	4	Ensuite	€25.50/€25.50	Dinner	-
B&B	-	Standard	-	Partial Board	-
Single Rate			€38.50/€38.50	Child reduction	25%

Clifden 10km

Open: 1st May-30th September

Mrs Loretta O'Malley
HARBOUR HOUSE
Cleggan, Co Galway

Cleggan Connemara Area
TEL: **095 44702**
EMAIL: **harbour.house@oceanfree.net**

Spacious family run home situated in pretty fishing Village of Cleggan from which to explore the wonderful land and seascapes.

B&B	4	Ensuite	€25.50	Dinner	-
B&B	-	Standard	-	Partial Board	-
Single Rate			€38.50	Child reduction	25%

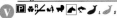

Clifden 9km

Open: 1st January-20th December

Ms Mary O'Malley
WILD HEATHER
Cloon, Cleggan,
Co Galway

Cleggan Connemara Area
TEL: **095 44617**   FAX: **095 44790**
EMAIL: **cloon@oceanfree.net**
WEB: **www.wildheather.org**

Dine in scenic splendour in conservatory overlooking Bay and Islands. Relax by peat fires. Rest well and enjoy Connemara. Information provided, Village 1.5km

B&B	4	Ensuite	€25.50	Dinner	€20
B&B	-	Standard	-	Partial Board	-
Single Rate			€38.50	Child reduction	25%

Cleggan 1.5km

Open: 1st April-31st October

Isabelle Pitorre
EMLOUGH HOUSE B&B
Cleggan, Connemara,
Co Galway

Cleggan Connemara Area
TEL: **095 44038**
EMAIL: **info@emloughhouse.com**
WEB: **www.emloughhouse.com**

Comfortable home overloooking Cleggan Bay and Inishbofin. Breakfast choice. You'll find us on the main road 2kms from the pier. "Gente Viaggi" recommended.

B&B	3	Ensuite	€25.50	Dinner	-
B&B	-	Standard	-	Partial Board	-
Single Rate			€38.50	Child reduction	25%

Cleggan 2km

Open: All Year

Mrs Christina Botham
LIGHTHOUSE VIEW
Sky Road, Clifden,
Co Galway

Clifden Connemara Area
TEL: **095 22113**
EMAIL: **cbotham@lighthouseview.buyandsell.ie**

Friendly home on scenic Sky Road, opposite Clifden Castle. Ideal base for touring Connemara or just relaxing. Home baking. Warm welcome assured.

B&B	4	Ensuite	€25.50/€28	Dinner	-
B&B	-	Standard	-	Partial Board	-
Single Rate			€38.50/€38.50	Child reduction	25%

Clifden 1.5km

Open: All Year

Mrs Noreen Conneely
BEN BREEN HOUSE
Tooreen, Moyard,
Co Galway

Clifden Connemara Area
Tel: **095 41171**
Email: **benbreenhouse@iolfree.ie**
Web: **www.connemara.net**

Comfortable well heated home. Peat fires. Magnificent view sea/mountain. Peaceful and tranquil location. Convenient to Connemara National Park.

B&B	6	Ensuite	€25.50/€25.50	Dinner	€19
B&B	-	Standard		Partial Board	€295
Single Rate			€38.50	Child reduction	25%

Clifden 8km

Open: 1st April 31st October

Mrs Anne Conroy
ROCKMOUNT HOUSE
Bayleek, Sky Road,
Clifden, Co Galway

Clifden Connemara Area
Tel: **095 21763**
Email: **rockmount@indigo.ie**
Web: **www.rockmounthouse.com**

Breathtaking views of scenic Sky Road. Convenient to Sandy Beaches, Fishing, Cliff Walks and Golf. Peaceful location, ideal touring base. Breakfast menu. Warm welcome assured.

B&B	3	Ensuite	€25.50	Dinner	€17
B&B	1	Standard	€23	Partial Board	
Single Rate			€36	Child reduction	25%

Clifden 5km

Open: April-30th September

John & Joan Coyne
SEA VIEW
Westport Road, Clifden,
Co Galway

Clifden Connemara Area
Tel: **095 22822**   Fax: **095 21394**
Email: **seaviewhse@eircom.net**
Web: **www.connemara.net/seaview.westportrd**

Modern bungalow in peaceful surroundings. Panoramic view of Streamstown Bay and Sky Road. Electric blankets, Orthopaedic beds. Ideal touring centre for Connemara. (N59).

B&B	5	Ensuite	€25.50	Dinner	-
B&B	-	Standard		Partial Board	-
Single Rate			-	Child reduction	33.3%

Clifden 2km

Open: All Year

Michael & Jane Delapp
HEATHER LODGE
Westport Road, Clifden,
Co Galway

Clifden Connemara Area
Tel: **095 21331**   Fax: **095 22041**
Email: **231@eircom.ie**

Warm friendly home. Breakfast menu, Home baking. Comfortable rooms and Guest lounge overlooking Lake and Mountains. Great touring base for Connemara.

B&B	5	Ensuite	€25.50/€28	Dinner	-
B&B	1	Standard	-	Partial Board	-
Single Rate			€36/€38.50	Child reduction	25%

Clifden 1.5km

Open: 1st March-31st October

Mrs Breege Feneran
LOUGH FADDA HOUSE
Ballyconneely Road, Clifden,
Co Galway

Clifden Connemara Area
Tel: **095 21165**
Email: **feneran@gofree.indigo.ie**
Web: **pages.zdnet.com/loughfaddahouse**

Spacious, well heated country home. Lovely quiet country walks in scenic area. Peat fires, Fishing & Pony Riding arranged. Credit Cards accepted.

B&B	6	Ensuite	€25.50	Dinner	-
B&B	-	Standard		Partial Board	-
Single Rate			€38.50	Child reduction	25%

Clifden 3km

Open: 27th March-1st November

Brendan & Ursula Flynn
WOODWINDS
Ardbear, Clifden,
Co Galway

Clifden Connemara Area
TEL: **095 21295**   FAX: **095 22899**
EMAIL: **woodwinds@clifden.ie**

Very private lakefront. All ensuite, TV, Car Park. Close to Lake, Beaches, Golf. Homely peaceful place to read, create and relax.

B&B	4	Ensuite	€27.93/€31.74	Dinner	-
B&B	-	Standard	-	Partial Board	-
Single Rate			€38.50	Child reduction	25%

Clifden 1.5km

Open: 30th June-1st September

Mrs Carmel Gaughan
ARD AOIBHINN
Ardbear, Ballyconneely Road,
Clifden, Co Galway

Clifden Connemara Area
TEL: **095 21339**
EMAIL: **ardbear@eircom.net**

Modern bungalow in scenic surroundings on Clifden - Ballyconneely Road convenient to safe Beaches and Golf Links. Excellent touring base.

B&B	2	Ensuite	€25.50	Dinner	-
B&B	1	Standard	€23	Partial Board	-
Single Rate			-	Child reduction	25%

Clifden 1km

Open: 1st April-31st October

Mrs Maureen Geoghegan
ROSSFIELD HOUSE
Westport Road, Clifden,
Co Galway

Clifden Connemara Area
TEL: **095 21392**

Family run home. Warm welcome. Convenient to safe Beaches & Golf Links. Excellent touring base. Orthopaedic beds and peaceful location.

B&B	2	Ensuite	€25.50/€25.50	Dinner	-
B&B	2	Standard	€23/€23	Partial Board	-
Single Rate			€36/€38.50	Child reduction	25%

Clifden 1km

Open: 1st April-1st November

Mrs Kathleen Hardman
MALLMORE HOUSE
Ballyconneely Road, Clifden,
Co Galway

Clifden Connemara Area
TEL: **095 21460**
EMAIL: **mallmore@indigo.ie**
WEB: **www.mallmorecountryhouse.com**

Lovingly restored Georgian home. 35 acre woodland grounds, spacious rooms, superb views, open fires and award-winning breakfasts. AA ✦✦✦✦.

B&B	6	Ensuite	€25/€30	Dinner	-
B&B	-	Standard	-	Partial Board	-
Single Rate			-	Child reduction	25%

Clifden 1.5km

Open: 1st April-1st October

Mrs Bridie Hyland
BAY VIEW
Westport Road, Clifden,
Co Galway

Clifden Connemara Area
TEL: **095 21286**   FAX: **095 22938**
EMAIL: **info@baview.com**
WEB: **www.baview.com**

Frommer recommended. Overlooking Streamstown Bay. View from house described "most spectacular view in Ireland". Orthopaedic Beds, Electric Blankets, hairdryers.

B&B	4	Ensuite	€25.50/€28	Dinner	-
B&B	-	Standard	-	Partial Board	-
Single Rate			€38.50	Child reduction	50%

Clifden 2km

Open: 1st February-30th November

Oliver Joyce
THE WILDERNESS
**Emloughmore,
Clifden, Co Galway**

Clifden Connemara Area

Tel: **095 21641**
Email: **thewilderness_b_b@hotmail.com**

Modern home located in peaceful scenic wilds of Connemara with mountain views, Turf fires. Warm friendly atmosphere. 8km from Clifden on N59 route.

B&B	4	Ensuite	€25.50/€27	Dinner	-
B&B	-	Standard	-	Partial Board	-
Single Rate			€38.50/€38.50	Child reduction	25%

Clifden 8km

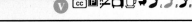

Open: 1st March-31st October

Mrs Margaret Kelly
WINNOWING HILL
**Ballyconneely Road, Clifden,
Co Galway**

Clifden Connemara Area

Tel: **095 21281**   Fax: **095 21281**
Email: **winnowinghill@eircom.net**

Situated on a tranquil hill overlooking the Twelve Bens, Clifden Town and Salt Lake. Views can also be enjoyed with a cup of tea from glass conservatory.

B&B	3	Ensuite	€25.50	Dinner	-
B&B	1	Standard	€23	Partial Board	-
Single Rate			-	Child reduction	33.3%

Clifden 1km

Open: 15th March-5th November

Mrs Maureen Kelly
FAILTE
**Ardbear, off Ballyconneely
Road, Clifden, Co Galway**

Clifden Connemara Area

Tel: **095 21159**   Fax: **095 21159**
Email: **kelly-failte@iol.ie**
Web: **www.connemara.net/failte**

Modern home overlooking Town and Bay. Breakfast award winner. AA ✦✦✦. "Le Guide du Routard" recommended.

B&B	2	Ensuite	€25.50/€25.50	Dinner	-
B&B	3	Standard	€23/€23	Partial Board	-
Single Rate			€36/€38.50	Child reduction	50%

Clifden 2km

Open: 1st April-30th September

Mrs Vera Kilkenny
WEST COAST HOUSE
**Westport Road, Clifden,
Co Galway**

Clifden Connemara Area

Tel: **095 21261**

Modern family run home N59. Good views, spacious en-suite bedrooms. Ideal touring base. Convenient to Beaches, Golf, Fishing, Horse Riding, Sports Centre.

B&B	4	Ensuite	€25.50/€25.50	Dinner	-
B&B	-	Standard	-	Partial Board	-
Single Rate			€38.50/€38.50	Child reduction	25%

In Clifden

Open: 31st March-31st October

Mrs Mary King
KINGSTOWN HOUSE
**Bridge Street, Clifden,
Co Galway**

Clifden Connemara Area

Tel: **095 21470**   Fax: **095 21530**

AA, RAC registered. Long established home in Town. Convenient to Beaches, Golf, Fishing, Riding. 2 mins walk Bus, 5 mins to Sea.

B&B	6	Ensuite	€25.50/€27	Dinner	-
B&B	2	Standard	€23/€24.50	Partial Board	-
Single Rate			-	Child reduction	25%

Open: All Year

Martin & Mary Kirby
LAKESIDE B&B
Goulane, Galway Road,
Clifden, Co Galway

Clifden Connemara Area

TEL: **095 21168**
EMAIL: **lakesideclifden@eircom.net**
WEB: **homepage.eircom.net/~lakesideclifden**

Spacious modern bungalow in quiet scenic surroundings on Galway/Clifden Rd (N59). Lake in front with views of the 12 Ben Mountains, Golf, Beaches nearby.

B&B	3	Ensuite	€26/€26	Dinner	-
B&B	1	Standard	€23/€23	Partial Board	-
Single Rate			€36/€36	Child reduction	-

Clifden 3km

Open: April-October

Odile LeDorven
KER MOR
Claddaghduff, Clifden,
Connemara, Co Galway

Clifden Connemara Area

TEL: **095 44954/44698** FAX: **095 44773**
EMAIL: **kermor@eircom.net**

Peaceful and friendly house on Streamstown Bay. Large bedrooms en-suite. Surprising healthy breakfast. Something special and different, Walking, Angling etc.

B&B	3	Ensuite	€25.50/€27.93	Dinner	-
B&B	-	Standard	-	Partial Board	-
Single Rate			-	Child reduction	33.3%

Clifden 8km

Open: All Year

Miss Catherine Lowry
AVE MARIA
Ballinaboy, Clifden,
Co Galway

Clifden Connemara Area

TEL: **095 21368**

Spacious 2 storey house located on the Clifden to Ballyconneely/ Roundstone Coast Road. 3km from Clifden. Scenic, tranquil location. Walks, Beaches, Horse riding, Golf, Fishing nearby.

B&B	1	Ensuite	€25.50/€25.50	Dinner	-
B&B	4	Standard	€23/€23	Partial Board	-
Single Rate			€36/€36	Child reduction	25%

Clifden 3km

Open: 1st May-30th September

Tina McDonagh
DOONHILL LODGE
Aillebrack, Ballyconneely,
Clifden, Co Galway

Clifden Connemara Area

TEL: **095 23726**

Warm comfortable home, situated 0.5km from Connemara Golf Club. Walking distance to Beaches and Pony Trekking. Hairdryer, Tea/Coffee facilities and TV in rooms. Ballyconneely 2km.

B&B	4	Ensuite	€25.50	Dinner	-
B&B	-	Standard	-	Partial Board	-
Single Rate			€38.50	Child reduction	25%

Clifden 10km

Open: 1st May-30th September

The McEvaddy Family
BAYMOUNT HOUSE
Seaview, Clifden,
Co Galway

Clifden Connemara Area

TEL: **095 21459** FAX: **095 21639**
EMAIL: **baymounthouse@eircom.net**
WEB: **www.baymount-connemara.itgo.com**

Spacious family home overlooking Clifden Bay. Magnificent Sea Views. Peaceful location. Hairdryers, Tea/coffee making facilities and TV in bedrooms.

B&B	10	Ensuite	€23/€26	Dinner	-
B&B	-	Standard	-	Partial Board	-
Single Rate			-	Child reduction	33.3%

In Clifden

Open: 1st March-31st October

Mrs Carmel Murray
OCEAN VILLA
Kingstown, Sky Road,
Clifden, Co Galway

Clifden Connemara Area

TEL: **095 21357**   FAX: **095 21137**
EMAIL: **oceanvilla@eircom.net**
WEB: **www.oceanvilla.com**

Modern bungalow overlooking sea with panoramic hill and sea views. Tranquil location on famous Sky Road. All outdoor activities arranged. Recommended.

B&B	4	Ensuite	€25.50/€30	Dinner	€20
B&B	2	Standard	€23/€28	Partial Board	€300
Single Rate			€36/€36	Child reduction	

Clifden 8km

Open: 1st March-31st October

Mrs Mary O'Donnell
CREGG HOUSE
Galway Road, Clifden,
Co Galway

Clifden Connemara Area

TEL: **095 21326**   FAX: **095 21326**
EMAIL: **cregghouse1@eircom.net**

On N59 landscaped garden. Spacious rooms, Breakfast menu. Owenglen River nearby. Ideal touring base. Recommended Elsie Dillard, Best B&B's Ireland.

B&B	5	Ensuite	€25.50	Dinner	-
B&B	1	Standard	€23	Partial Board	-
Single Rate			€36/€36	Child reduction	25%

Clifden 2km

Open: 25th March-1st November

Mrs Maureen O'Malley
HILLSIDE LODGE
Sky Road, Clifden,
Co Galway

Clifden Connemara Area

TEL: **095 21463**

Modern family home located on scenic Sky Road. Beside entrance to Clifden Castle. "Le Guide du Routard" recommended. Tea/coffee facilities. Hairdryers.

B&B	6	Ensuite	€25.50/€25.50	Dinner	-
B&B	-	Standard	-	Partial Board	-
Single Rate			€38.50	Child reduction	33.3%

Clifden 1.5km

Open: 1st March-31st November

Margaret & Orla Pryce
ATLANTIC VIEW
Letternoosh, Westport Road,
Clifden, Co Galway

Clifden Connemara Area

TEL: **095 21291**   FAX: **095 22051**
EMAIL: **info@atlantic-view.com**
WEB: **www.atlantic-view.com**

From home to home. All rooms with orthopaedic beds, Tea/Coffee, TV in rooms. Wonderful views of Atlantic. Turn right at Esso located on N59/Westport Road. Ideal touring base.

B&B	4	Ensuite	€25.50/€28	Dinner	€20
B&B	-	Standard	-	Partial Board	-
Single Rate			€38.50	Child reduction	50%

Clifden 2km

Open: All Year

Mrs Mary G Morrin
ISLAND VIEW HOUSE
Dooroy, Clonbur/Cong,
Co Galway

Clonbur Cong Connemara Area

TEL: **092 46302**   FAX: **092 46302**

Scenic setting overlooking Lough Corrib. Touring base for Connemara, West Mayo. Central to Restaurants, Angling Hill, Walking. Own Boats/Engines for hire.

B&B	4	Ensuite	€25	Dinner	-
B&B	-	Standard	-	Partial Board	-
Single Rate			€35	Child reduction	-

Clonbur 1km

Open: April-October

Cornamona 3km

Mrs Sorcha Peirce
GRASSHOPPER COTTAGE
Dooras, Cornamona,
Co Galway

Cornamona Connemara Area
TEL: **092 48165**   FAX: **092 48165**
EMAIL: **grasshopper@indigo.ie**
WEB: **www.troutfishingireland.com**

Lodge on shore of Lough Corrib off R345. Superb scenery. Angling centre (boat/ tackle hire). Ideal base for walking/touring Joyce Country and Connemara.

B&B	3	Ensuite	€26	Dinner	€22
B&B	1	Standard	€23	Partial Board	€300
Single Rate			€36/€39	Child reduction	25%

Open: 23rd March-28th October

In Craughwell

Mrs Peggy Gilligan
AHAVEEN HOUSE
Cappanraheen, Craughwell,
Co Galway

Craughwell
TEL: **091 846147**

Comfortable home on spacious grounds, just off N6 Galway - Dublin road. Excellent Restaurants, Hunting, Golf. Ideal touring base, Burren, Connemara.

B&B	4	Ensuite	€25.50/€25.50	Dinner	-
B&B	1	Standard	€23/€23	Partial Board	-
Single Rate			-	Child reduction	50%

Open: All Year

Mrs Colette Cawley
DUNGUAIRE
8 Lurgan Park, Murrough,
Dublin Road, Galway City,
(East) Co Galway

Galway City
TEL: **091 757043**
EMAIL: **ccawley@eircom.net**
BUS NO: **4E, 2E**

Warm friendly home. Convenient for touring Connemara, Burren and Aran Islands. Take Galway City east exit. House opposite Corrib Great Southern Hotel, GMIT, Merlin Park Hospital on N6.

B&B	2	Ensuite	€25.50/€32	Dinner	-
B&B	2	Standard	€23/€28	Partial Board	-
Single Rate			€36/€40	Child reduction	-

Galway City 2km

Open: All Year

Mrs Noreen Collins
ST ANTHONY'S
Terryland Cross,
Headford Road, Galway,
Co Galway

Galway City
TEL: **091 766477**
EMAIL: **fcollins@esatclear.ie**

Family run home. Warm welcome. Beside Shopping Centre. Cinema & Restaurants. Tea/Coffee facilities. Rooms ensuite. Private car park.

B&B	4	Ensuite	€25.50	Dinner	-
B&B	-	Standard	-	Partial Board	-
Single Rate			€38.50/€38.50	Child reduction	-

Galway City 1km

Open: 1st January-20th December

Galway City 2km

Mike & Orla Connolly
TARA LODGE
1 Barr Aille, Glenanail,
Galway City, Co Galway

Galway City
TEL: **091 771797**
EMAIL: **taralodge@eircom.net**
WEB: **homepage.eircom.net/~taralodge/**
BUS NO: **3**

New luxurious home, personally run. 3 mins drive, City Centre. Tea/Coffee, TV all rooms. From City (Eyre Square) take N17 at 2nd roundabout take left & sharp right.

B&B	3	Ensuite	€26/€32	Dinner	-
B&B	-	Standard	-	Partial Board	-
Single Rate			€38.50/€45	Child reduction	25%

Open: All Year

Ms Rita Conway
Galway City
MOYTURA
4 Ballybane Road, Ballybane,
Galway, Co Galway
Tel: **091 757755**
Bus No: **20, 51**

Beside Corrib Great Southern Hotel, GMIT, Merlin Park Hospital. Take Route 338 off N6 to "Galway City East". Lovely view of Galway Bay and Burren. Warm welcome.

B&B	3	Ensuite	€25.50/€38	Dinner	-
B&B	-	Standard	-	Partial Board	-
Single Rate			€38.50/€45	Child reduction	25%

Galway 2km

Open: All Year

Mrs Mary Corless
Galway City
COOLAVALLA
22 Newcastle Road,
Galway, Co Galway
Tel: **091 522415**

Family house beside Hospital and University, opposite Presentation School. 6 mins walk City, 15 mins Salthill. Close to all amenities. Ideal touring base.

B&B	1	Ensuite	€25.50/€28	Dinner	-
B&B	3	Standard	€23/€26	Partial Board	-
Single Rate			€36/€40	Child reduction	-

Galway City

Open: 1st February-30th November

Sean & Kathryn Cummins
Galway City
COIS NA TINE
2 Barr Aille, Glenanail,
Galway City, Co Galway
Tel: **091 758787**
Email: **scummins@indigo.ie**
Bus No: **3**

Luxurious family run home. Minutes to City Centre. Highly Recommended. Coming from Galway City take N17 route, on second roundabout, take N59 route, then immediate sharp right turn.

B&B	4	Ensuite	€26/€32	Dinner	-
B&B	-	Standard	-	Partial Board	-
Single Rate			€38.50/€45	Child reduction	25%

Galway City 2km

Open: All Year

Ms Frances Gallagher
Galway City
15 Beechmount Road,
Highfield Park, Galway,
Co Galway
Tel: **091 522078**
Bus No: **2**

Modern Semi-detached guesthouse overlooking open park. Conveniently located close to both Salthill and Galway. Excellent rates.

B&B	3	Ensuite	€25.50/€30.48	Dinner	-
B&B	1	Standard	€23/€27.94	Partial Board	-
Single Rate			€36	Child reduction	25%

Galway 1km

Open: 1st June-30th September

Helen Kathleen Hanlon
Galway City
CLOCHARD
4 Spires Gardens,
Shantalla Road, Galway
Co Galway
Tel: **091 521533**   Fax: **091 522536**
Email: **info@clochardgalway.com**
Web: **www.clochardgalway.com**

Warm friendly home. Quiet Historic Site within walking distance of City Centre and Beach. Close to University, Hospital and Shops. Hairdryers.

B&B	4	Ensuite	€26/€32	Dinner	-
B&B	-	Standard	-	Partial Board	-
Single Rate			€38.50/€45	Child reduction	-

Galway City

Open: All Year Except Christmas

Mrs Elizabeth Hassell
IVERNIA
41 Maunsells Park,
Taylors Hill, Galway,
Co Galway

Galway City
TEL: **091 523307**
EMAIL: **hasselle@indigo.ie**
BUS NO: **2**

Family home quiet area. 1km UCG and Hospital. Follow sign to Salthill. Right at Londis shop on Fr. Griffin Rd. Through next lights. Right into Maunsells Rd. 1st left.

B&B	1	Ensuite	€25.50/€29	Dinner	-
B&B	2	Standard	€23/€26.50	Partial Board	-
Single Rate			€36/€38.50	Child reduction	-

Galway 2km

Open: May-October

Mrs Maureen McCallion
VILLA NOVA
40 Newcastle Road,
Galway, Co Galway

Galway City
TEL: **091 524849**

Quiet bungalow off the main road. Beside Hospital & University & convenient to City Centre. Private car park.

B&B	4	Ensuite	€26/€32	Dinner	-
B&B	-	Standard	-	Partial Board	-
Single Rate			€38.50/€40	Child reduction	-

Open: 1st January-20th December

Miss Bridget Phil McCarthy
PETRA
201 Laurel Park, Newcastle,
Galway City, Co Galway

Galway City
TEL: **091 521844**
BUS NO: **4, 5**

Convenient to City Bus. Train/Aran Ferry, University, Hospital. Adjacent to Oughterard/Clifden Road N59. Second left Sioban McKenna Rd, first right.

B&B	3	Ensuite	€25.50/€25.50	Dinner	-
B&B	2	Standard	€23/€24.50	Partial Board	-
Single Rate			€36/€36	Child reduction	-

Galway 2km

Open: 1st February-30th November

Mrs Mary McLaughlin-Tobin
ARAS MHUIRE
28 Maunsell's Road,
Taylor's Hill, Galway,
Co Galway

Galway City
TEL: **091 526210**   FAX: **091 526210**
EMAIL: **mmtobin@eircom.net**
WEB: **www.galway.net/pages/arasmhuire**
BUS NO: **2**

Peaceful setting with a view of Galway's beautiful Cathedral. No.2 Bus. Recommended "Happy, homely warm atmosphere." Car park, walking distance Salthill and City.

B&B	2	Ensuite	€25.50/€40	Dinner	-
B&B	1	Standard	-	Partial Board	-
Single Rate			€36/€45	Child reduction	25%

In Galway

Open: 1st January-21st December

Mrs Marcella Mitchell
LIMA
Tuam Road, Galway City,
Co Galway

Galway City
TEL: **091 757986**
EMAIL: **limabb@ireland.com**
BUS NO: **3**

Detached bungalow adjacent to City Centre, close to all amenities of a vibrant City. Private parking. TV, Tea/Coffee facilities all bedrooms. Beside AIB bank.

B&B	2	Ensuite	€25.50/€27	Dinner	-
B&B	1	Standard	-	Partial Board	-
Single Rate			€36/€36	Child reduction	-

In Galway

Open: 1st January-20th December

Galway City 1.25km

Mary O'Brien
ANACH-CUIN HOUSE
36 Wellpark Grove,
Galway City, Co Galway

Galway City
TEL: **091 755120**
BUS NO: **2**

Town House, quiet and peaceful location as you enter City Centre, close to Restaurants and all amenities.

B&B	4	Ensuite	€25.50/€27	Dinner		-
B&B	-	Standard		Partial Board		-
Single Rate			€38.50	Child reduction		25%

Open: 1st March-30th November

Galway 3km

Mrs Phil Concannon
WINACRE LODGE
Bushy Park,
Galway, Co Galway

Galway City Dangan Area
TEL: **091 523459**
EMAIL: **winacrelodge@eircom.net**

Modern friendly home, spectacular views of River Corrib on N59. Near Glenlo Abbey and Westwood Hotels. Private parking. TV, Tea/Coffee in bedrooms. Visa.

B&B	5	Ensuite	€25.50/€33.50	Dinner		€21.50
B&B	-	Standard		Partial Board		€264
Single Rate			€38.50/€43.50	Child reduction		50%

Open: All Year

Galway 4km

Mrs Brenda Kelehan
LAKELAND HOUSE
Bushy Park, Galway,
Co Galway

Galway City Dangan Area
TEL: **091 524964**

Spectacular views of river Corrib/Glenlo Abbey, Golf Club. Adjacent to excellent Restaurants and Bars. On main route to Connemara.

B&B	5	Ensuite	€25.50/€33.50	Dinner		€21.50
B&B	1	Standard		Partial Board		-
Single Rate			€38.50/€43.50	Child reduction		-

Open: All Year

Galway 4km

Mrs Bernie McTigue
ABBEY VIEW
Bushy Park, Galway,
Co Galway

Galway City Dangan Area
TEL: **091 524488**

Frommer recommended. A warm welcome awaits you. View overlooks Glenlo Abbey Golf Course. Adjacent to Restaurants. Ideal for touring Connemara.

B&B	3	Ensuite	€25.50/€33.50	Dinner		€21.50
B&B	1	Standard		Partial Board		-
Single Rate			€38.50/€43.50	Child reduction		-

Open: All Year

Galway 3km

Mrs Annette O'Grady
KILBREE HOUSE
Circular Road, Dangan Upper,
Galway, Co Galway

Galway City Dangan Area
TEL: **091 527177**   FAX: **091 520404**
EMAIL: **info@kilbree.com**
WEB: **www.kilbree.com**

Welcoming luxurious home N59 with excellent food. En route Connemara. Overlooks City and Lake near Hotels and Pubs. TV, Tea/Coffee and Hairdryer in all rooms.

B&B	6	Ensuite	€25.50/€33.50	Dinner		€21.50
B&B	-	Standard		Partial Board		-
Single Rate			€38.50/€43.50	Child reduction		-

Open: All Year

Galway 6km

Mrs Bridie Ward
THE ARCHES
Woodstock, Bushy Park,
Galway, Co Galway

Galway City Dangan Area
Tel: **091 527815**
Email: **thearches@oceanfree.net**

Dormer style home on N59 enroute to Connemara. 3km from Glenlo Abbey Hotel. Golf, Fishing, Horse riding nearby. Private parking. Ideal touring base.

B&B	4	Ensuite	€26/€28	Dinner	-
B&B	1	Standard	€23/€25	Partial Board	-
Single Rate			€36/€39	Child reduction	50%

Open: 1st January-20th December

Galway 1.5km

Mary Beatty
SNAEFELL
6 Glenina Heights,
Galway, Co Galway

Galway City Glenina Heights
Tel: **091 751643**
Bus No: **2, 4,5**

Comfortable welcoming home with superb beds. Home made brown bread. Situated on N6 and main bus routes. Close to all amenities including Dog and Race Tracks.

B&B	3	Ensuite	€25.50/€30	Dinner	-
B&B	-	Standard		Partial Board	-
Single Rate			€38.50/€38.50	Child reduction	25%

Open: January-November

Galway 1.5km

Anne Smyth
10 Glenina Heights
Dublin Road, Galway,
Co Galway

Galway City Glenina Heights
Tel: **091 753327**
Bus No: **2, 4,5**

Friendly family modern home. Ideally beside Hotels, Leisure centres, Beach, Golf Clubs and main Bus routes. 1.5km east of City close to Galway Ryan Hotel.

B&B	2	Ensuite	€25.50/€30	Dinner	-
B&B	1	Standard	€23/€28.50	Partial Board	-
Single Rate			€36/€40	Child reduction	25%

Open: 1st February-30th October

Galway City 1km

Mrs Kathleen Burke
LISCARNA
22 Grattan Park Coast Road,
Galway, Co Galway

Galway City Grattan Park Area
Tel: **091 585086**

Modern detached home beside Beach on Coast Road, walking distance of City Centre, Leisureland. All rooms with shower/toilet, TV.

B&B	4	Ensuite	€27/€29	Dinner	-
B&B	-	Standard	-	Partial Board	-
Single Rate			-	Child reduction	-

Open: 1st February-1st November

Galway City 1km

Mrs Freda Cunningham
KYLE NA SHEE
37 Grattan Park,
Galway City, Co Galway

Galway City Grattan Park Area
Tel: **091 583505**
Email: **kylenashee@eircom.net**
Web: **homepage.eircom.net/~kylenashee**

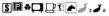

Detached home beside Beach on Coast road to Salthill. Quiet and close to all amenities. Walking distance of City Centre. Tea/Coffee & TV in all rooms.

B&B	3	Ensuite	€27/€29	Dinner	-
B&B	1	Standard	-	Partial Board	-
Single Rate			€36/€39	Child reduction	-

Open: April-October

In Galway City

Bernadette Donoghue
KILTEVNA
24 Grattan Park, Coast Road,
Galway, Co Galway

Galway City Grattan Park Area
TEL: **091 588477**   FAX: **091 581173**
EMAIL: **kiltevnahouse@eircom.net**

Modern detached home beside Beach, off Coast road. Within walking distance City, Leisureland. All rooms with bathrooms, TV, Hairdryers.

B&B	4	Ensuite	€27/€29	Dinner	-
B&B	-	Standard	-	Partial Board	-
Single Rate			-	Child reduction	25%

Open: 1st February-30th November

Galway City

Mrs Pat Greaney
HIGH TIDE
9 Grattan Park, Coast Road,
Galway City, Co Galway

Galway City Grattan Park Area
TEL: **091 584324/589470** FAX: **091 584324 (man)**
EMAIL: **hightide@iol.ie**

Panoramic views of Galway Bay. Frommer/Inside Ireland/Sullivan Guides recommended. 10 min. walk to City Centre. Also local Bus. Breakfast menu. Tours arranged.

B&B	4	Ensuite	€27/€29	Dinner	-
B&B	-	Standard	-	Partial Board	-
Single Rate			-	Child reduction	25%

Open: 1st February-1st December

Galway City 1km

Mrs Maureen Loughnane
DUNKELLIN HOUSE
4 Grattan Park, Salthill,
Galway, Co Galway

Galway City Grattan Park Area
TEL: **091 589037**
EMAIL: **maurel@unison.ie**

Panoramic views of Galway Bay. Walking distance of City & Salthill. Safe parking. Tours arranged. All rooms with TV, Hairdryers, Tea/Coffee. Breakfast menu.

B&B	3	Ensuite	€27/€29	Dinner	-
B&B	1	Standard	€25/€27	Partial Board	-
Single Rate			€36/€36	Child reduction	25%

Open: 1st January-15th December

Galway 1km

Ms Joan O'Dea
THE PERIWINKLE
14 Grattan Park, Grattan
Road, Galway, Co Galway

Galway City Grattan Park Area
TEL: **091 584885**
EMAIL: **periwinkle@eircom.net**

Tastefully renovated modern family home beside beach. 10 mins walk to City Centre or Salthill. Close to all amenities. Ideal touring base. Breakfast menu.

B&B	4	Ensuite	€27/€29	Dinner	-
B&B	-	Standard	-	Partial Board	-
Single Rate			-	Child reduction	25%

Open: 1st February-1st December

TELEPHONE

- Operator assisted calls within Ireland   Dial 10
- International telephone operator   Dial 11818
- Directory Enquiries   Dial 11811

FOR TROUBLE-FREE TELEPHONE CALLS FROM PUBLIC PAY PHONES IT IS ADVISABLE TO PURCHASE A TELEPHONE CALLCARD AVAILABLE IN POST OFFICES AND WHEREVER YOU SEE A CALLCARD SIGN.
TO DIAL IRELAND FROM ABROAD: Country Access Code + 353 + Area Code (omit first zero) + Local Number

Mrs Mary Murphy
WATERDALE
40 Grattan Park, Coast Road,
Galway, Co Galway

Galway City Grattan Park Area
TEL: **091 586501**   FAX: **091 586501**
EMAIL: **waterdale@ireland.com**

Modern detached home in quiet cul-de-sac. Beside Beach off Coast Road. Within walking distance of City Centre and Salthill. All rooms with TV.

B&B	2	Ensuite	€27/€29	Dinner	-
B&B	1	Standard	-	Partial Board	-
Single Rate			€36/€39	Child reduction	25%

Galway City 1km

Open: April-September

Mrs Dolores Bane
THE BRANCHES
13 Woodhaven, Merlin Park,
Galway, Co Galway

Galway City Merlin Park Area
TEL: **091 752712**
EMAIL: **branches13@eircom.net**
WEB: **www.branches.domainvalet.com**
BUS NO: **4**

New luxury accommodation 5 min City Centre beside Corrib Great Southern Hotel. Cable TV, Hairdryers all rooms. Car park. Enjoy Mikes Irish breakfast.

B&B	3	Ensuite	€26/€40	Dinner	-
B&B	1	Standard	€24/€36	Partial Board	-
Single Rate			€39/€50	Child reduction	-

Galway City 2km

Open: All Year

Mrs Olive Connolly
SEACREST
Coast Road, Roscam,
Merlin Park, Galway,
Co Galway

Galway City Merlin Park Area
TEL: **091 757975**   FAX: **091 756531**
EMAIL: **djcon@iol.ie**
WEB: **http://www.iol.ie/~djcon/**

Overlooking Galway Bay, Indoor Pool. Hairdryers, Radios, Bedrooms ground floor level, New York Times, Boston Globe, Le Guide du Routard recommended.

B&B	5	Ensuite	€26/€30	Dinner	-
B&B	1	Standard	€23/€25	Partial Board	-
Single Rate			€36/€36	Child reduction	-

Galway City 5km

Open: 10th February-10th November

Mrs Millie Forde
BAYSIDE
Coast Road, Curragreen,
Merlin Park, Galway,
Co Galway

Galway City Merlin Park Area
TEL: **091 794310**   FAX: **091 794310**
EMAIL: **mford@indigo.ie**
WEB: **http://indigo.ie/~mford**

Modern bungalow on Galway/Oranmore Coast road, 5 km from Galway. 1km from Galway Crystal, overlooking the Bay. No smoking.

B&B	4	Ensuite	€25.50/€28	Dinner	-
B&B	-	Standard	-	Partial Board	-
Single Rate			€38.50/€38.50	Child reduction	25%

Galway 5km

Open: 1st March-30th October

Ms Peggy Kenny
CLOONIFF HOUSE
16 Woodhaven, Merlin Park,
Galway, Co Galway

Galway City Merlin Park Area
TEL: **091 758815/582465**
BUS NO: **4**

Luxurious family run house beside Corrib Southern Hotel. City Centre 5 mins drive, private parking. Close to Beach and all amenities. Ideal touring base.

B&B	3	Ensuite	€25.50/€38.50	Dinner	-
B&B	1	Standard	-	Partial Board	-
Single Rate			€36.50/€38.50	Child reduction	33.3%

Galway City 2km

Open: 1st January-22nd December

Galway 3km

Peter & Gretta Kenny
WOODHAVEN LODGE
20 Woodhaven, Merlin Park,
Galway, Co Galway

TEL: **091 753806**
EMAIL: **woodhavenlodge@eircom.net**
WEB: **homepage.eircom.net/~woodhavenlodge**
BUS NO: **4**

AA recommended. Excellent family run B&B. Quiet cul-de-sac. Off R338 between Corrib Great Southern Hotel and Merlin Park Hospital. Warm welcome

B&B	4	Ensuite	€25.50/€38.50	Dinner		-
B&B	-	Standard	-	Partial Board		-
Single Rate			€38.50/€50	Child reduction		33.3%

Open: 1st January-21st December

Galway 3km

Matt & Marie Kiernan
ALMARA HOUSE
2 Merlin Gate, Merlin Park,
Dublin Road, Galway
Co Galway

TEL: **091 755345**   FAX: **091 771585**
EMAIL: **matthewkiernan@eircom.net**
WEB: **www.almarahouse.com**
BUS NO: **4**

Situated on N6 & N18. Tastefully appointed bedrooms furnished to highest standards. Hospitality tray, Radio alarms, Irons, Hairdryers. Extensive Breakfast menu.

B&B	4	Ensuite	€26/€40	Dinner		-
B&B	-	Standard	-	Partial Board		-
Single Rate			€38.50/€40	Child reduction		-

Open: All Year Except Christmas

Galway 3km

Juliette Manton
WOODVIEW B&B
10 Woodhaven, Merlin Park,
Galway, Co Galway

TEL: **091 756843**
EMAIL: **juliette2@eircom.net**
BUS NO: **4**

One of Galway City's finest B&B's, family run. Luxurious home, quiet cul de sac. Adjacent to Corrib Great Southern Hotel.

B&B	4	Ensuite	€26/€80	Dinner		-
B&B	-	Standard	-	Partial Board		-
Single Rate			€39/€50	Child reduction		-

Open: All Year Except Christmas

Galway City 4km

Mrs Ann McDonagh
AMBERVILLE
Coast Road, Roscam,
Merlin Park, Galway,
Co Galway

TEL: **091 757135**

Panoramic views of Galway Bay, Clare Hills and Championship Golf course. 1km from Galway Heritage. Coast Road N6. No Smoking.

B&B	4	Ensuite	€26/€30	Dinner		-
B&B	-	Standard	-	Partial Board		-
Single Rate			€38.50	Child reduction		25%

Open: April-October

Galway City 4km

Mrs Una McNulty
BEAUPRE
Coast Road (Oranmore),
Roscam, Galway,
Co Galway

TEL: **091 753858**

Overlooking the Burren, Galway Bay and Links Golf Course. Just off Coast Rd N6. 1km Galway Crystal Heritage Centre. Electric Blankets, Hairdryers. Reduction low season.

B&B	4	Ensuite	€25.50/€30	Dinner		-
B&B	-	Standard	-	Partial Board		-
Single Rate			€38.50	Child reduction		-

Open: 1st April-31st October

Liam & Yvonne O'Reilly
CORRIB VIEW B&B
12 Woodhaven, Merlin Park,
Galway, Co Galway

Galway City Merlin Park Area

Tel: **091 755667**
Email: **corribview@eircom.net**
Web: **www.corribview.com**
Bus No: **4**

Luxurious residence, quiet cul-de-sac. Recommended as one of the Best B&B in the West. Bus route. City Centre 3km. Adjacent Corrib Great Southern Hotel, GMIT.

B&B	3	Ensuite	€26/€40	Dinner	-
B&B	-	Standard		Partial Board	-
Single Rate			€39/€50	Child reduction	-

Galway City 3km

Open: 1st January-20th December

Maria Rabbitte
GRANGE HOUSE
15 Woodhaven, Merlin Park,
Galway, Co Galway

Galway City Merlin Park Area

Tel: **091 755470**　Fax: **091 755470**
Email: **mrabbitte@eircom.net**
Bus No: **4**

Luxurious home, personally run, quiet cul-de-sac. Convenient to City Bus Route. Adjacent Corrib Great Southern Hotel. Ideal touring base. Highly recommended.

B&B	4	Ensuite	€26/€40	Dinner	-
B&B	-	Standard		Partial Board	-
Single Rate			€39/€50	Child reduction	25%

Galway City 3km

Open: 1st January-20th December

Ms Mary Sweeney
CORRIGEEN B&B
4 Woodhaven, Merlin Park,
Dublin Road, Galway,
Co Galway

Galway City Merlin Park Area

Tel: **091 756226**　Fax: **091 756255**
Email: **corrigeen@eircom.net**
Web: **www.corrigeen.com**

Delightful purpose built B&B on main approach road to Galway City, adjacent Corrib Great Southern Hotel. One of the Best B&B's in the West.

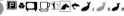

B&B	4	Ensuite	€26/€40	Dinner	-
B&B	-	Standard	-	Partial Board	-
Single Rate			€39/€50	Child reduction	-

Galway City 3km

Open: All Year

Mrs Teresa Burke
LYNBURGH
Whitestrand Road,
Lower Salthill, Galway,
Co Galway

Galway City Whitestrand Area

Tel: **091 581555**　Fax: **091 581823**
Email: **tburke@iol.ie**

Spacious residence overlooking Galway Bay. Beside Beach, walking distance to City Centre, Leisureland, University & Aran Ferry. TV, Hairdryers and Tea/Coffee facilities.

B&B	6	Ensuite	€27/€30	Dinner	-
B&B	-	Standard	-	Partial Board	-
Single Rate				Child reduction	25%

Galway 1km

Open: All Year

Mrs Esther Daly
GLENCAR
6 Beach Court, Off Grattan
Road, Lower Salthill,
Galway, Co Galway

Galway City Whitestrand Area

Tel: **091 581431**

Panoramic view Galway Bay beside Beach. Walking distance to Town, Aran Ferry, Restaurants. All rooms ensuite, TV, Tea facilities, Hairdryer. Warm quiet home.

B&B	4	Ensuite	€27/€29	Dinner	-
B&B	-	Standard	-	Partial Board	-
Single Rate				Child reduction	25%

Galway City 1km

Open: All Year Except Christmas

Mrs Sara Davy
ROSS HOUSE
14 Whitestrand Avenue,
Lower Salthill, Galway,
Co Galway

Galway City Whitestrand Area

TEL: **091 587431** FAX: **091 581970**
EMAIL: **rosshousebb@eircom.net**

Beside Galway Bay. All rooms en-suite, TV, Hairdryer, Hospitality tray. Ample safe offstreet parking. Ten minutes walking to City Centre. 5 minutes to Beach.

B&B	4	Ensuite	€27/€29	Dinner	-
B&B	-	Standard	-	Partial Board	-
Single Rate			-	Child reduction	-

Galway 1km   **Open:** All Year

Carmel Donoghue
ACHILL HOUSE
9 Whitestrand Road,
Galway, Co Galway

Galway City Whitestrand Area

TEL: **091 589149**

Family run home, 5 mins walk to City Centre and Beach. Ensuite rooms, Cable TV, Private Car Park. Complimentary Tea/Coffee available.

B&B	4	Ensuite	€27/€29	Dinner	-
B&B	-	Standard	-	Partial Board	-
Single Rate			-	Child reduction	25%

Galway City   **Open:** 7th January-22nd December

Stella Faherty
CONSILIO
4 Whitestrand Avenue,
Lower Salthill, Galway,
Co Galway

Galway City Whitestrand Area

TEL: **091 586450** FAX: **091 586450**
BUS NO: **1**

Friendly and comfortable home in quiet area between Galway and Salthill. Beside Beach and convenient to all City entertainment. No smoking house.

B&B	4	Ensuite	€27/€29	Dinner	-
B&B	-	Standard	-	Partial Board	-
Single Rate			€38.50/€40	Child reduction	-

Galway 1km   **Open:** All Year

Kathleen Melvin
LISKEA
16 Whitestrand Avenue,
Lower Salthill, Galway,
Co Galway

Galway City Whitestrand Area

TEL: **091 584318** FAX: **091 584319**

Beside Galway Bay. Beach 100 yds. Short walk to City Centre. All rooms ensuite, Television, Hairdryer, Tea/Coffee.

B&B	4	Ensuite	€27/€29	Dinner	-
B&B	-	Standard	-	Partial Board	-
Single Rate			-	Child reduction	-

Galway City 1km   **Open:** All Year

Mrs Maureen Nolan
GLENCREE
20 Whitestrand Avenue,
Lr Salthill, Galway City,
Co Galway

Galway City Whitestrand Area

TEL: **091 581061** FAX: **091 581061**

Beside Galway Bay. All rooms shower & toilet, TV, Hairdryers. Short walking distance City Centre, University, Aran Ferry etc. Beach 100 yds.

B&B	4	Ensuite	€27/€29	Dinner	-
B&B	-	Standard	-	Partial Board	-
Single Rate			-	Child reduction	25%

Galway City 1km   **Open:** 1st January-22nd December

Galway 1km

Tim & Carmel O'Halloran
RONCALLI HOUSE
24 Whitestrand Avenue,
Galway, Co Galway

Tel: **091 584159/589013** Fax: **091 584159**
Email: **roncallihouse@eircom.net**

Warm comfortable home beside Galway Bay. AA listed. Walking distance City Centre. Frommer, Lonely Planet, Ireland Guide, Birnbaum recommended. Breakfast Award.

B&B	6	Ensuite	€27/€29	Dinner	-
B&B	-	Standard	-	Partial Board	-
Single Rate			€38.50/€40	Child reduction	25%

Open: All Year

In Galway

Niamh Pender
NIDER HOUSE
37 Whitestrand Road,
Galway, Co Galway

Tel: **091 582313** Fax: **091 582313**
Email: **derek_pender@yahoo.co.uk**

Warm welcoming luxurious family run accommodation walking distance - 10 mins to City, 5 mins to Beach. Ensuite rooms, TV, Hairdryer, Tea/Coffee facilities.

B&B	4	Ensuite	€27/€31	Dinner	-
B&B	-	Standard	-	Partial Board	-
Single Rate			€38.50/€40	Child reduction	-

Open: 1st February-30th November

Galway 1km

Ms Maureen Tarpey
THE DORMERS
Whitestrand Road, Lr Salthill,
Galway, Co Galway

Tel: **091 585034** Fax: **091 585034**

Bungalow, conveniently situated within walking distance to City/Beach. All rooms with shower/toilet/TV/hairdryers. Some rooms on ground floor.

B&B	6	Ensuite	€27/€30	Dinner	-
B&B	-	Standard	-	Partial Board	-
Single Rate			-	Child reduction	33.3%

Open: All Year

In Galway

Mrs Bridie Thomson
ROCK LODGE
Whitestrand Road, Galway,
Co Galway

Tel: **091 583789** Fax: **091 583789**
Email: **rocklodgeguests@eircom.net**

Spacious residence beside Galway Bay. TV, Hairdryers, Tea/Coffee facilities. Private parking. 10 minutes walk City Centre. Beach 100 yds.

B&B	6	Ensuite	€27/€31	Dinner	-
B&B	-	Standard	-	Partial Board	-
Single Rate			€38.50/€40	Child reduction	25%

Open: All Year

In Galway

Kathleen Fahy
ABHOG
28 Grattan Court,
Fr Griffin Road, Galway,
Co Galway

Tel: **091 589528** Fax: **091 589528**
Email: **abhog@eircom.net**

Newly refurbished home centrally located in quiet residential area. Ensuite, TV, Tea/Coffee, Hairdryers in all rooms. Ground floor bedroom. Warm friendly atmosphere.

B&B	3	Ensuite	€25.50/€32	Dinner	-
B&B	1	Standard	-	Partial Board	-
Single Rate			€32/€39	Child reduction	25%

Open: 1st January-24th December

Mrs Berna Kelly
DEVONDELL
47 Devon Park, Lower Salthill,
Co Galway

Lower Salthill

TEL: **091 528306**
EMAIL: **devondel@iol.ie**
WEB: **www.devondell.com**
BUS No: **1**

Relaxed friendly home. Extensive Breakfast menu. Recommended by Lonely Planet, Jameson and Bridgestone 100 Best B&Bs. Overall Winner Galway AIB B&B Awards 1998.

B&B	4	Ensuite	€31/€38	Dinner	-
B&B	-	Standard		Partial Board	-
Single Rate			€31/€38	Child reduction	-

Galway 2km

Open: 1st March-31st October

Ita Johnstone
ST JUDES
110 Lower Salthill, Galway,
Co Galway

Lower Salthill

TEL: **091 521619**
EMAIL: **stjudes@indigo.ie**
WEB: **www.celtic-holidays.com/stjudes**
BUS No: **1**

Distinguished family residence, elegantly furnished. Private parking on City Bus route, short walk to Beach and all amenities. Breakfast menu.

B&B	6	Ensuite	€30/€35	Dinner	-
B&B	-	Standard		Partial Board	-
Single Rate			€40/€45	Child reduction	25%

Galway 1.5km

Open: 20th January-10th December

Mrs Christina Ruane
25 Grattan Court,
Fr Griffin Road, Lower Salthill,
Galway, Co Galway

Lower Salthill

TEL: **091 586513**

Modern detached house, quiet residential area. 10 mins walk Salthill, 5 mins Beach, Golf Club, 10 mins Hospital & University.

B&B	4	Ensuite	€25.50/€27	Dinner	-
B&B	1	Standard	€23	Partial Board	-
Single Rate			-	Child reduction	50%

Galway City

Open: All Year

Mrs Mary Barry
TRIESTE
12 Forster Park,
Off Dalysfort Road, Salthill,
Co Galway

Salthill

TEL: **091 521014**   FAX: **091 521014**
EMAIL: **maryba@indigo.ie**
BUS No: **1**

Bungalow, quiet cul-de-sac. Near Beach, Golf, Leisureland. Follow Salthill sign, turn first after roundabout/Rockland Hotel, up hill and 2nd turn right.

B&B	3	Ensuite	€25.50/€29	Dinner	-
B&B	1	Standard	€23/€26.50	Partial Board	-
Single Rate			€36/€38.50	Child reduction	25%

In Salthill

Open: May-October

Mrs Christina Connolly
CLARE VILLA
38 Threadneedle Road,
Salthill, Co Galway

Salthill

TEL: **091 522520**
EMAIL: **clarevilla@yahoo.com**

Spacious residence close to Beach, Tennis, Golf, Leisureland. On bus route. Complimentary Tea/Coffee 24 hours. Hairdryers. Lonely Planet recommended.

B&B	6	Ensuite	€27/€30	Dinner	-
B&B	-	Standard	-	Partial Board	-
Single Rate			€39/€45	Child reduction	25%

Galway 2km

Open: 1st Feburary-31st October

In Salthill

Noreen Cosgrove
MAPLE HOUSE
**Dr Mannix Road, Salthill,
Co Galway**

Salthill
TEL: **091 526136**

Purpose built luxury home. Peaceful location. Power showers. Adjacent Hotels, Golf, Tennis, Leisureland. Parking. Hairdryers. On bus route. Open all year.

B&B	4	Ensuite	€27/€30	Dinner	-
B&B	-	Standard		Partial Board	-
Single Rate			€38.50/€40	Child reduction	25%

Open: All Year Except Christmas

Galway 2km

Ms Marie Cotter
BAYBERRY HOUSE
**9 Cuan Glas, Bishop
O'Donnell Road, Taylors Hill,
Galway, Co Galway**

Salthill
TEL: **091 525171/525212**
EMAIL: **tcotter@iol.ie**
WEB: **www.galway.net/pages/bayberry**
BUS NO: **2**

A charming purpose built B&B conveniently located at the top of Taylors Hill. A stay at Bayberry combines a Georgian style elegance with a warm welcome.

B&B	4	Ensuite	€25.50/€35	Dinner	-
B&B	-	Standard		Partial Board	-
Single Rate			€38.50/€45	Child reduction	33.3%

Open: 1st February-30th November

Galway City 2km

Mrs Marian Coyne
COOLIN HOUSE
**11 Seamount,
Threadneedle Road, Salthill,
Co Galway**

Salthill
TEL: **091 523411**

Modern home. Beside Beach, Tennis Club, Leisureland. On bus route. Private parking. Tea/Coffee making, TV in all rooms.

B&B	4	Ensuite	€27/€30	Dinner	-
B&B	-	Standard	-	Partial Board	-
Single Rate			€39/€45	Child reduction	25%

Open: 1st April-30th September

Galway 2km

Phil Flannery
FLANNERY'S
**54 Dalysfort Road, Salthill,
Galway, Co Galway**

Salthill
TEL: **091 522048**　　FAX: **091 522048**
EMAIL: **phil.flannery@iol.ie**
WEB: **www.flannerysbedandbreakfast.com**
BUS NO: **1**

Award winning house with nice garden. German spoken. Follow signs to Salthill. On seafront between Waterfront Hotel and Leisureland, turn into Dalysfort Road.

B&B	3	Ensuite	€28/€32	Dinner	-
B&B	1	Standard	€26/€30	Partial Board	-
Single Rate			€36/€38	Child reduction	-

Open: All Year Except Christmas

Galway 2km

Mrs Mary Geraghty
MARLESS HOUSE
**Threadneedle Road, Salthill,
Galway, Co Galway**

Salthill Threadneedle Road Area
TEL: **091 523931**　　FAX: **091 529810**
EMAIL: **marlesshouse@eircom.net**
WEB: **www.marlesshouse.com**
BUS NO: **1**

Luxurious Georgian style home just steps from Beach. Frommer recommended. TV, electric blankets, hairdryers, Tea/Coffee facilities in all rooms.

B&B	6	Ensuite	€27/€30	Dinner	-
B&B	-	Standard		Partial Board	-
Single Rate			€39/€45	Child reduction	25%

Open: 1st January-20th December

Mrs Nora Hanniffy
ANNA REE HOUSE
**49 Oaklands, Salthill,
Galway, Co Galway**

Salthill

TEL: **091 522583**

Modern home. Private parking. Rear of Church by Sacre Coeur Hotel. 5 mins walk Beach, Leisureland and Bus route. Electric blankets.

B&B	5	Ensuite	€25.50	Dinner	-
B&B	1	Standard	-	Partial Board	-
Single Rate			€36	Child reduction	50%

Open: 1st March-1st Novembe

Mrs Phil Hough
ROSELAWN
**19 Carragh Drive, Salthill,
Galway, Co Galway**

Salthill

TEL: **091 529684**
EMAIL: **oheoca@oceanfree.net**
BUS NO: **2**

Luxurious new home overlooking Galway Bay. Friendly atmosphere in quiet location beside all amenities. West past golf course, 2nd right, 3rd left, 5th house L.H.S.

B&B	3	Ensuite	€25.50/€32	Dinner	-
B&B	-	Standard	-	Partial Board	-
Single Rate			€38.50/€45	Child reduction	25%

Galway 2km

Open: 1st March-31st Octobe

Mrs Catherine Lydon
CARRAIG BEAG
**1 Burren View Heights,
Knocknacarra Road, Salthill,
Galway, Co Galway**

Salthill

TEL: **091 521696**
BUS NO: **2**

Luxurious brick house. Convenient to Beaches, Golf, Tennis. Ideal base for touring Connemara, Aran Islands etc. Recommended by "Best B&B's in Ireland" and Rick Steve's.

B&B	4	Ensuite	€29/€34	Dinner	-
B&B	-	Standard	-	Partial Board	-
Single Rate			€38.50/€63	Child reduction	33.3%

Galway 2km

Open: All Year Except Christma

Mrs Mairead McGuire
WESTPOINT
**87 Threadneedle Rd, Salthill,
Galway, Co Galway**

Salthill

TEL: **091 521026/582152** FAX: **091 582152**
EMAIL: **westpointmac@netscape.net**
BUS NO: **1, 2**

Purpose built family run B&B near Ardilan and Galway Bay Hotel. Quality assured & multi recommendations. Sea view. Parking. Bus route, Beach, Leisureland, Tennis & Golf.

B&B	6	Ensuite	€25.50/€35	Dinner	€18
B&B	-	Standard	-	Partial Board	-
Single Rate			€38.50/€45	Child reduction	25%

Galway 2km

Open: All Year Except Christma

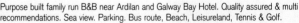

Marian Mitchell
CHESTNUT LODGE
**35 Rockbarton Road,
Salthill, Co Galway**

Salthill

TEL: **091 529988**

Luxurious home beside Galway Bay and Beach. Golf Club, Tennis Club and Leisureland. Ideal for touring Connemara, Aran Islands and the Burren.

B&B	3	Ensuite	€26/€28	Dinner	-
B&B	-	Standard	-	Partial Board	-
Single Rate			€38.50/€38.50	Child reduction	50%

Galway 2km

Open: 1st April-31st Septembe

John & Maureen Monaghan
MONTROSE HOUSE
3 Monksfield, Salthill,
Galway, Co Galway

Salthill

TEL: **091 525673**   FAX: **091 587862**
EMAIL: **monaghaj@gofree.indigo.ie**
BUS NO: **1**

Two storey house located quiet area. Central to amenities. Tea/Coffee/Snack on arrival. On Bus route. Convenient Leisureland, Aquarium, Beach. 15 mins City Centre, excellent Restaurants & Pubs.

B&B	6	Ensuite	€25.50/€28	Dinner	-
B&B	-	Standard		Partial Board	-
Single Rate			€38.50/€38.50	Child reduction	25%

Galway 2km

Open: 1st January-15th December

Mrs Nora O'Malley
ST KIERAN'S
33 Rockbarton Road, Salthill,
Galway, Co Galway

Salthill

TEL: **091 523333**
EMAIL: **michealomalley@hotmail.com**

Family run home beside all amenities. Within walking distance of Beach, Leisureland, Golf, GAA and Tennis Club. Home cooking. Tea or Coffee on arrival.

B&B	3	Ensuite	€25.50/€25.50	Dinner	-
B&B	1	Standard	€23/€23	Partial Board	-
Single Rate			€36	Child reduction	-

n Salthill

Open: 1st February-30th November

Mrs Ann O'Toole
CLYDAGH
Knocknacarra Road, Salthill,
Galway, Co Galway

Salthill

TEL: **091 524205**
EMAIL: **clydagh@ireland.com**
WEB: **www.dirl.com/galway/clydagh.htm**
BUS NO: **2**

Comfortable family home with private parking. Convenient to Beaches, Tennis, Golf. Bus route to City Centre. Ideal touring base for Connemara and Aran Island.

B&B	4	Ensuite	€25.50/€29.18	Dinner	-
B&B	-	Standard		Partial Board	-
Single Rate			€38.50/€38.50	Child reduction	33.3%

Galway City 2km

Open: 1st March-31st October

Mrs Ethna Regan
LISCARRA HOUSE
6 Seamount,
On Threadneedle Rd, Salthill,
Galway, Co Galway

Salthill Threadneedle Road Area

TEL: **091 521299**
EMAIL: **eregan@eircom.net**
WEB: **homepage.eircom.net/~gerregan**
BUS NO: **1**

Luxurious home just steps from Galway Bay, beside Beach, Tennis, Golf. TV, Tea/Coffee facilities, Electric blankets, Hairdryers all rooms. On bus route. R338

B&B	4	Ensuite	€27/€30	Dinner	-
B&B	1	Standard	€24/€27	Partial Board	-
Single Rate			€36.50/€43	Child reduction	25%

Galway City 2km

Open: 1st March-1st November

Mrs Evelyn Wrynn
FENAGH HOUSE
11 Rockbarton Green, Off
Rockbarton Road, Salthill,
Galway, Co Galway

Salthill

TEL: **091 522835**
EMAIL: **ewrynn@eircom.net**

Family home in tranquil setting beside Galway Bay. Ideal base for touring Connemara and the Burren. On bus route to City. Parking space.

B&B	3	Ensuite	€26/€28	Dinner	-
B&B	-	Standard		Partial Board	-
Single Rate			-	Child reduction	25%

Galway 1km

Open: 1st May-30th September

In Salthill

Mrs Georgianna Darby
MANDALAY BY THE SEA
10 Gentian/Blakes Hill,
Galway, Co Galway

Tel: **091 524177**   Fax: **091 529952**
Email: **mandalay@esatclear.ie**

Luxurious balconied residence panoramic view of Galway Bay. Recommended " Best B&B's in Ireland", Lonely Planet and Hidden Places of Ireland. Off 336 Coast road. 2 miles from Galway City.

B&B	4	Ensuite	€26/€38	Dinner	-
B&B	-	Standard		Partial Board	-
Single Rate			€52/€76	Child reduction	25%

Open: All Year

Salthill 2km

Mrs Mary Duggan
KNOCKMOY HOUSE
7 Westbrook, Barna Road,
Galway, Co Galway

Upper Salthill
Tel: **091 590674**
Bus No: **2**

Neo Georgian house overlooking Galway Bay. TV Lounge. Only 10 mins drive from Salthill, Golf, Tennis, Leisureland and Horse riding.

B&B	4	Ensuite	€28/€30	Dinner	-
B&B	-	Standard		Partial Board	-
Single Rate			€38.50/€38.50	Child reduction	50%

Open: 15th March-31st October

Galway 2km

Mrs Christina Fahey
CASHELMARA LODGE
Knocknacarra Cross, Salthill,
Galway, Co Galway

Upper Salthill
Tel: **091 520020**
Email: **cashelmara@eircom.net**
Web: **www2.wombat.ie/pages/cashelmara/**
Bus No: **2**

New luxury accommodation overlooking Galway Bay. Beside Beach, Golf, Horseriding, Surfing, Tennis, Leisureland. Breakfast menu. Power Showers in all rooms.

B&B	4	Ensuite	€26/€38	Dinner	-
B&B	-	Standard		Partial Board	-
Single Rate			€40/€50	Child reduction	25%

Open: February-November

Salthill 1km

Mrs Celine Glynn
DRUMLIN VIEW B&B
6 Cashelmara, Upper Salthill,
Galway, Co Galway

Upper Salthill
Tel: **091 529513**   Fax: **091 529513**
Email: **cglynn@iol.ie**

Luxurious home, overlooking Galway Bay. Breakfast Menu. Home Baking. One of the finest Breakfasts in Ireland - "Brooklyn Spectator". Near Leisureland.

B&B	6	Ensuite	€30/€50	Dinner	-
B&B	-	Standard		Partial Board	-
Single Rate			€45	Child reduction	33.3%

Open: 1st January-24th December

Salthill 2km

Tom & Colette Keaveney
THE CONNAUGHT
Barna Road, Salthill,
Galway, Co Galway

Upper Salthill
Tel: **091 525865**   Fax: **091 525865**
Email: **tcconnaught@eircom.net**
Bus No: **2**

Luxurious family home, purpose built. All amenities close by. Touring base Connemara. Recommended "Best B&B's in Ireland/Guide de Routard. Home from home. Breakfast menu, Chef owner.

B&B	6	Ensuite	€26/€30	Dinner	-
B&B	-	Standard		Partial Board	-
Single Rate			€38.50	Child reduction	25%

Open: 17th March-31st October

Salthill 2km

Mrs Caroline Larkin
KILBRACK HOUSE
2 Woodfield, Barna Road,
Galway, Co Galway

Upper Salthill
Tel: **091 590802**
Email: **kilbracklarkin@eircom.net**
Bus No: **2**

Luxurious home overlooking Galway Bay. Golf, Fishing, Horseriding, Leisureland, Aquarium, Tennis and good Restaurants nearby. Ideal touring base for Aran Islands.

B&B	6	Ensuite	€25.50/€32	Dinner	-
B&B	-	Standard	-	Partial Board	-
Single Rate			€38.50	Child reduction	50%

Open: March-November

Salthill 2km

David & Rita Lenihan
ATLANTIC SUNSET
Coast Road, Gentian Hill,
Salthill, Galway, Co Galway

Upper Salthill Gentian Hill Area
Tel: **091 521425**
Bus No: **2**

Luxurious comfortable home in scenic peaceful surroundings overlooking Galway Bay and Bird sanctuary. Award winning gardens 1998. Golf, Fishing, Beach, Leisureland closeby.

B&B	4	Ensuite	€26.00/€32	Dinner	-
B&B	-	Standard	-	Partial Board	-
Single Rate			-	Child reduction	50%

Open: 1st February-1st December

Galway 2km

Mrs Teresa McDonagh
ARD MHUIRE
Knocknacarra Road,
Upper Salthill, Galway,
Co Galway

Upper Salthill
Tel: **091 522344**   Fax: **091 529629**
Email: **teresa@ardmhuire.com**
Web: **www.ardmhuire.com**

Attractive, comfortable home within walking distance of the Seaside. Close to Leisureland, Golf, Tennis, Fishing, Horse riding etc.

B&B	6	Ensuite	€27/€30	Dinner	-
B&B	-	Standard	-	Partial Board	-
Single Rate			€38.50/€40	Child reduction	25%

Open: 1st January-20th December

Galway 3km

Mrs Mary McLoughlin
SAILIN
Gentian Hill, Coast Rd,
Upper Salthill, Galway,
Co Galway

Upper Salthill Gentian Hill Area
Tel: **091 521676**   Fax: **091 521676**
Email: **gentianhill@eircom.net**
Web: **homepage.eircom.net/~gentianhill**
Bus No: **2**

Located in bird sanctuary beside Galway Bay. Frommer recommended. Breakfast award. Secure parking. Hill walking information. 2nd left turn after Spinaker Hotel.

B&B	3	Ensuite	€26/€29	Dinner	-
B&B	-	Standard	-	Partial Board	-
Single Rate			€39/€39	Child reduction	50%

Open: 31st March-30th September

Galway 3km

Mrs Mary Meehan
SUMMERVILLE
4 Westbrook, Barna Rd,
Galway, Co Galway

Upper Salthill
Tel: **091 590424**   Fax: **091 591026**
Email: **meehanm@eircom.net**
Bus No: **2**

Luxury balconied home with panoramic views of Galway Bay. Breakfast menu. TV, Hairdryers, Tea/Coffee all rooms.Near Beaches, Leisureland, Horse-riding, Golf, Woods.

B&B	4	Ensuite	€26/€30	Dinner	-
B&B	-	Standard	-	Partial Board	-
Single Rate			€38.50/€40	Child reduction	-

Open: 1st May-30th September

Padraig & Maureen O'Donnell
Upper Salthill
SHAMROCK LODGE
4 Carragh Drive,
Knocknacarra Rd, Upper
Salthill, Galway, Co Galway

Tel: **091 521429**   Fax: **091 521429**
Email: **oods@eircom.net**
Bus No: **2**

Overlooking Bay, Beach, Golf, Tennis, Leisureland, TV, Hairdryers, Electric Blankets. Follow promenade, Golf Course, right at Spinnaker, 3rd left, 4th on right.

B&B	4	Ensuite	€25.50/€28	Dinner	-
B&B	-	Standard		Partial Board	-
Single Rate			€38.50/€38.50	Child reduction	25%

Galway 2km

Open: 1st March–31st October

Kevin & Maire O'Hare
Upper Salthill
ROSE VILLA
10 Cashelmara,
Knocknacarra Cross,
Salthill, Co Galway

Tel: **091 584200**   Fax: **091 584200**
Email: **kevin.ohare@ireland.com**
Web: **www.rosevilla.utvinternet.ie**
Bus No: **2**

New luxury accommodation overlooking Galway Bay and Bird sanctuary. Close to Golf, Fishing, Horse Riding, Surfing, Leisureland. Ideal touring base.

B&B	4	Ensuite	€25.50/€40	Dinner	-
B&B	-	Standard		Partial Board	-
Single Rate			€38.50/€45	Child reduction	25%

Galway 3km

Open: 1st January–20th December

Bernie Power
Upper Salthill
FOUR WINDS LODGE
Gentian Hill, Salthill, Galway,
Co Galway

Tel: **091 526026**
Email: **fourwindslodge@ireland.com**
Web: **www.galway.net/pages/fourwindslodge**
Bus No: **2**

Traditional home. Overlooking Galway Bay. Enjoy breakfast in conservatory. Net access. Private parking & gardens. 1st right after Statoil after Golf Club. 4 star AA approved. Car hire can be arranged.

B&B	4	Ensuite	€25.50/€40	Dinner	-
B&B	-	Standard		Partial Board	-
Single Rate			€38.50/€45	Child reduction	50%

Salthill 1.5km

Open: All Year Except Christmas

Mrs Patty Wheeler
Upper Salthill
WOODVILLE
Barna Rd, Salthill,
Galway, Co Galway

Tel: **091 524260**   Fax: **091 524260**
Email: **woodville@esatclear.ie**
Bus No: **2**

Friendly home on Coast road overlooking Galway Bay. Ideal touring base. Beaches, 3 Golf Clubs, Tennis, Horseriding, Windsurfing, Canoeing. Bird sanctuary closeby.

B&B	4	Ensuite	€25.50/€30	Dinner	-
B&B	-	Standard		Partial Board	-
Single Rate			€38.50/€40	Child reduction	50%

Salthill 2km

Open: 1st March–31st October

Mrs Kathleen O'Connor
Gort
THE ASHTREE
Glenbrack, Galway Road,
Gort, Co Galway

Tel: **091 631380**
Email: **katoconnor@eircom.net**

Comfortable home on N18. Galway and Ennis 30 mins. The Burren, Coole Park, Thoorballylee and 18 hole Golf course nearby. Shannon Airport 1 hr.

B&B	3	Ensuite	€25.50/€25.50	Dinner	-
B&B	-	Standard	-	Partial Board	-
Single Rate			€38.50/€38.50	Child reduction	25%

In Gort

Open: 1st April–31st October

John & Detta Murphy
ASHGROVE
Newtown, Kilcolgan,
Co Galway

TEL: **091 796047**
EMAIL: **ashgrovebandb@eircom.net**

Friendly comfortable home. Just off N18 Galway/Limerick rd, on N67 between Kilcolgan and Kinvara. Ideal touring base Burren/Connemara. Shannon Airport 1 hour drive.

B&B	3	Ensuite	€25.50/€25.50	Dinner	-
B&B	-	Standard	-	Partial Board	-
Single Rate			-	Child reduction	33.3%

Kilcolgan 1.3km

Open: 1st April-30th September

Mrs Maureen Fawle
HOLLYOAK
Kinvara Road, Ballinderreen,
Kilcolgan, Co Galway

TEL: **091 637165**
EMAIL: **maureenfawle@oceanfree.net**

Spacious, warm, country home on N67 between Kinvara - Kilcolgan. Central Burren, Cliffs of Moher, Connemara. Banquets nightly in Dunguire Castle. Fodor Guide recommended.

B&B	2	Ensuite	€25.50/€25.50	Dinner	-
B&B	1	Standard	€23/€23	Partial Board	-
Single Rate			€36/€36	Child reduction	25%

Kinvara 4km

Open: 1st April-31st October

Angela Larkin
BARN LODGE B&B
Kinvara Road, Toureen,
Ballinderein, Kilcolgan,
Co Galway

TEL: **091 637548**

Country home situated on N67. 50 yards off main road between Kilcolgan, Ballindereen and Kinvara. Scenic route to Burren, Cliffs of Moher, Aran Islands. Banquets in Dungaire Castle.

B&B	4	Ensuite	€25.50/€25.50	Dinner	-
B&B	-	Standard	-	Partial Board	-
Single Rate			€38.50/€38.50	Child reduction	25%

Kinvara 4km

Open: All Year Except Christmas

Nancy Naughton
KYLEMORE HOUSE
Kylemore, Connemara,
Co Galway

TEL: **095 41143**   FAX: **095 41143**
EMAIL: **kylemorehouse@eircom.net**
WEB: **www.connemara.net/kylemorehouse**

Impressive Georgian house on the shores of Kylemore Lake. Ideal base walking. Spacious bedrooms. Home cooking. Horse riding, Beaches nearby. Recommended B&B Guide. On N59.

B&B	6	Ensuite	€28/€34	Dinner	€25
B&B	-	Standard	-	Partial Board	-
Single Rate			€38.50/€45	Child reduction	-

Clifden 20km

Open: 1st March-30th October

Mrs Margaret Wallace
AVONDALE HOUSE
Leenane, Co Galway

TEL: **095 42262**

Friendly comfortable home in scenic area beside Village. Hillwalking, Adventure Centres, Angling, Pony Trekking, Restaurants in Village.

B&B	3	Ensuite	€25.50/€25.50	Dinner	-
B&B	-	Standard	-	Partial Board	-
Single Rate			-	Child reduction	25%

In Leenane

Open: 1st April-30th November

Loughrea 4km

Mrs Rose Plower
LA RIASC
**Clostoken, Loughrea,
Co Galway**

Loughrea
TEL: **091 841069**

Comfortable modern home, just off Dublin - Galway Road (N6). Galway side of Loughrea. Adjacent to award winning Restaurant "Meadow Court". Ideal touring base.

B&B	3	Ensuite	€25.50	Dinner	-
B&B	1	Standard	€23	Partial Board	-
Single Rate			€36	Child reduction	25%

Open: 10th January-20th December

In Moycullen

Aine Mulkerrins
ARD IOSEF
Moycullen, Co Galway

Moycullen
TEL: **091 555149**
EMAIL: **ardiosef@oceanfree.net**

Friendly comfortable home on N59, 10km from Galway City. Fishing, Golf, Excellent Restaurants nearby. Breakfast menu. Ideal base for touring Connemara.

B&B	3	Ensuite	€26/€29	Dinner	-
B&B	1	Standard	€24/€27	Partial Board	-
Single Rate			€36/€38.50	Child reduction	25%

Open: 1st April-31st October

In Oranmore

Mary Carney
ARDFINNAN HOUSE
**Maree Road, Oranmore,
Co Galway**

Oranmore
TEL: **091 790749**

Comfortable accommodation, orthopaedic beds, home baking, 5 mins from Galway City. Close to Restaurants, Beaches, Golf, Parks, Sailing. Heritage facilities

B&B	3	Ensuite	€27/€32	Dinner	€19.50
B&B	-	Standard	-	Partial Board	-
Single Rate			€38.50/€38.50	Child reduction	25%

Open: All Year

In Oranmore

Mrs Patricia Collins
CASTLE VIEW HOUSE
**Galway Coast Road,
Oranmore, Co Galway**

Oranmore
TEL: **091 794648**
EMAIL: **patcollins101@hotmail.com**
WEB: **www.geocities.com/pcollins100**

Quiet country home, spacious bedrooms. Overlooking Galway Bay, Burren Mountains. Golf course and Horse riding nearby. Galway 7 mins drive.

B&B	4	Ensuite	€26/€26	Dinner	-
B&B	-	Standard	-	Partial Board	-
Single Rate			-	Child reduction	25%

Open: All Year

Oranmore 1km

Mrs Mary Curran
BIRCHGROVE
**Dublin Rd, Oranbeg,
Oranmore, Co Galway**

Oranmore
TEL: **091 790238**
EMAIL: **birchgrove@eircom.net**
WEB: **homepage.eircom.net/~birchgrove/**

Comfortable modern bungalow off N6. Friendly relaxed atmosphere. Quality Restaurants/Pubs nearby. Ideal touring base. Quiet location. Galway 8 minutes.

B&B	4	Ensuite	€26	Dinner	€17
B&B	-	Standard	-	Partial Board	-
Single Rate			€38.50	Child reduction	33.3%

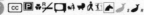

Open: All Year

In Oranmore

Teresa Dundon
MILLBROOK
**Dublin Road, Oranmore,
Co Galway**

Oranmore
TEL: **091 794404**
EMAIL: **teresadundon@eircom.net**

Dormer bungalow on Dublin road, 5 mins walk from Oranmore Village. Sailing, Windsurfing, Golf nearby. Ideal touring base for Connemara, Burren.

B&B	3	Ensuite	€27.50/€29	Dinner	-
B&B	1	Standard	€23/€25	Partial Board	-
Single Rate			€36	Child reduction	25%

Open: April-October

In Oranmore

Geraldine & Seamus Grady
SHANLIN HOUSE
**Maree Road, Oranmore,
Co Galway**

Oranmore
TEL: **091 790381**   FAX: **091 790381**
EMAIL: **ggrady@indigo.ie**
WEB: **www.shanlinhouse.com**

Friendly Georgian home. Walk to Village, Pubs, Restaurants, Irish Music. 5 mins to Golf Courses, Rinville Park. Galway City 10km. Centrally located to tour Connemara, Burren.

B&B	4	Ensuite	€27/€30	Dinner	€18
B&B	-	Standard	-	Partial Board	-
Single Rate			€38.50/€40	Child reduction	25%

Open: All Year

Oranmore 2km

Mrs Bridgie Hanley
FAIRWAY LODGE
**Renville, Oranmore,
Co Galway**

Oranmore
TEL: **091 790393**   FAX: **091 790393**
EMAIL: **info@fairwaysoranmore.com**
WEB: **www.fairwaysoranmore.com**

Charming residence at entrance to Galway Bay Golf & Country Club, Sailing Club.

B&B	4	Ensuite	€25.50/€38.10	Dinner	€31.75
B&B	-	Standard	-	Partial Board	-
Single Rate			€38.50/€44.45	Child reduction	-

Open: 16th January-16th December

Oranmore 1km

Mrs Maureen Kelly
COOLIBAH HOUSE
**Dublin Road,
Oranmore, Co Galway**

Oranmore
TEL: **091 794996**

Comfortable modern home on N6, 100 mts east N18 & N6 roundabout. Ideal base for touring. Friendly and relaxing. 1km to Village.

B&B	3	Ensuite	€26	Dinner	€17
B&B	-	Standard	-	Partial Board	-
Single Rate			€38.50	Child reduction	25%

Open: 2nd January-23rd December

Oranmore 1km

Mrs Kathleen McCarthy-Leyne
SON AMAR
**Coast Road, Oranmore,
Galway, Co Galway**

Oranmore
TEL: **091 794176**   FAX: **091 794176**
EMAIL: **sonamar@indigo.ie**

Georgian home, overlooking Galway Bay & Burren. SON AMAR offers peace, space, comfort in tranquil surroundings. A varied breakfast menu. Golf, Sailing, Walks, Horse Riding.

B&B	4	Ensuite	€27/€30	Dinner	-
B&B	2	Standard	-	Partial Board	-
Single Rate			€36/€38.50	Child reduction	-

Open: All Year

Ms Marian McVicker
THE BIRCHES
10 Carrowmoneash,
Oranmore, Co Galway

Oranmore
TEL: **091 790394**
EMAIL: **thebirches@eircom.net**

Friendly family home. Quiet road off N6. Oranmore Lodge/Quality Hotels 200m.
Pubs/Restaurants in Village. Galway 8km, Airport 3km. Ideal touring/golf base.

B&B	4	Ensuite	€25.50/€31	Dinner	-
B&B	-	Standard	-	Partial Board	-
Single Rate			€38.50/€38.50	Child reduction	25%

In Oranmore

Open: All Year Except Christmas

Maureen Murphy
HILLVIEW
Moneymore, Oranmore,
Co Galway

Oranmore
TEL: **091 794341**

Dormer bungalow on N18. View of Clare hills. Ideal touring base for the Burren and Connemara.
18 hole Golf course nearby. Galway Airport 5km. Galway City 7km.

B&B	3	Ensuite	€27/€29	Dinner	€17
B&B	1	Standard	€25/€26	Partial Board	-
Single Rate			€36/€36	Child reduction	25%

Oranmore 1km

Open: 1st February-30th November

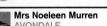

Mrs Noeleen Murren
AVONDALE
Renville West, Oranmore,
Co Galway

Oranmore
TEL: **091 790527**
EMAIL: **murrenwest@eircom.net**

Spacious warm Georgian house. Large ensuite bedrooms. Quiet location. Leisure Park, Sailing and
Golf 1km. Close to excellent Restaurants. Galway City/ Airport 10km.

B&B	3	Ensuite	€26/€31	Dinner	-
B&B	-	Standard	-	Partial Board	-
Single Rate			€38.50/€38.50	Child reduction	-

Oranmore 2km

Open: 1st April-1st December

Mrs Mary Noone
ASHBROOK HOUSE
Dublin Road, Oranmore,
Co Galway

Oranmore
TEL: **091 794196**　　FAX: **091 794196**
EMAIL: **mnoone@iol.ie**
WEB: **www.ashbrookhouse.com**

Purpose built house 1 acre of landscaped gardens. Opposite Water Tower N6. Tea/Coffee, TV,
Hairdryer all rooms. Golf, Sailing, Horse Riding nearby. Ideal touring Cliffs of Moher, Connemara.

B&B	4	Ensuite	€27/€30	Dinner	€22
B&B	-	Standard	-	Partial Board	-
Single Rate			€38.50/€38.50	Child reduction	25%

Oranmore 1km

Open: All Year

Edwina Bunyan
THE WESTERN WAY
Camp Street,
Oughterard, Co Galway

Oughterard Connemara Area
TEL: **091 552475**
EMAIL: **westernwaybb@hotmail.com**

Old style spacious town residence in picturesque Oughterard. Relaxed atmosphere. Walk to top
class Restaurants and Pubs. Ideal base to tour Connemara.

B&B	2	Ensuite	€26	Dinner	-
B&B	1	Standard	€24	Partial Board	-
Single Rate			€36/€39	Child reduction	-

In Oughterard

Open: 1st March-31st October

In Oughterard

Mrs Teresa Butler
CROSSRIVER
Glann Road, Oughterard,
Co Galway

Oughterard Connemara Area
Tel: **091 552676**
Email: **crossriver@eircom.net**

Superbly situated adjacent to Owen Riff River. 300 yards from Lough Corrib, famous for brown trout. Own boats available. 3 minutes walk from Village. Many first class Restaurants.

B&B	4	Ensuite	€25.50/€25.50	Dinner	-
B&B	2	Standard	€23/€23	Partial Board	-
Single Rate			€36/€36	Child reduction	**50%**

Open: 1st March-31st November

Oughterard 2km

Lal Faherty/Costelloe Family
LAKELAND COUNTRY HOUSE
Portacarron Bay, Oughterard,
Co Galway

Oughterard Connemara Area
Tel: **091 552121/552146** Fax: **091 552146**
Email: **mayfly@eircom.net**

Lakeshore lodge with private gardens to Lake. Complete Angling/Boating facility on site. 5 mins drive from Village. Golfing, Walking. Off the N59, 2nd right after Golf Club sign.

B&B	8	Ensuite	€28.57/€31.74	Dinner	€21.59
B&B	1	Standard	€24.13/€27.93	Partial Board	-
Single Rate			€38.50/€38.50	Child reduction	-

Open: 31st January-10th December

In Oughterard

Ms Deirdre Forde
CAMILLAUN
Eighterard, Oughterard,
Co Galway

Oughterard Connemara Area
Tel: **091 552678**   Fax: **091 552439**
Email: **camillaun@eircom.net**
Web: **http://homepage.eircom.net/~camillaunfishing**

Riverside setting. Lake boats moored in garden. A short walk to the Village by pedestrian way. Turn at the Lake Hotel, down street over bridge, next right.

B&B	4	Ensuite	€28/€32	Dinner	-
B&B	-	Standard		Partial Board	-
Single Rate			€41/€45	Child reduction	**33.3%**

Open: 1st April-31st October

Oughterard 1km

Carmel Geoghegan
RAILWAY LODGE
Canrower, Oughterard,
Co Galway

Oughterard Connemara Area
Tel: **091 552945**
Email: **railwaylodge@eircom.net**
Bus No: **191**

A real find! Delightful country home, individually decorated rooms. Antique furnishings. Relaxed atmosphere, enhanced by fine hospitality and good food.

B&B	4	Ensuite	€32	Dinner	-
B&B	-	Standard		Partial Board	-
Single Rate			€35/€41	Child reduction	-

Open: 15th January-15th December

Mrs Brenda Joyce
THE SUNSET
Killola, Rosscahill,Oughterard,
Co Galway

Oughterard Connemara Area
Tel: **091 550146**
Email: **thesunset@eircom.net**

Modern country home in route N59. Ideal base for touring Connemara. Golfing, Fishing, Horse Riding available locally. Excellent home cooking.

B&B	3	Ensuite	€27/€28	Dinner	€23
B&B	1	Standard	€26/€27	Partial Board	-
Single Rate			€36/€38.50	Child reduction	**25%**

Oughterard 4km

Open: 1st March-30th November

In Oughterard

Ann Kelleher
RIVER WALK HOUSE
Riverside, Oughterard,
Co Galway

Oughterard Connemara Area
TEL: **091 552788**   FAX: **091 557069**
EMAIL: **riverwalk@eircom.net**

Comfortable friendly home in peaceful setting. Ideal base to tour Connemara and Aran Islands. 3 minutes walk to Oughterard Village. Fishing, Golf, Walking tours all nearby.

B&B	5	Ensuite	€25.50/€29.28	Dinner	-
B&B	-	Standard		Partial Board	-
Single Rate			€38.50/€38.50	Child reduction	25%

Open: All Year Except Christmas

Oughterard 4km

Mrs Dolores Leonard
FOREST HILL
Glann Road, Oughterard,
Co Galway

Oughterard Connemara Area
TEL: **091 552549**
EMAIL: **lakeshoreroad@eircom.net**
WEB: **www.foresthillbb.com**

Quiet. Peaceful country home. Panoramic Connemara scenery. Ideal base for touring and walking. Central for exploring Irish National Park, Kylemore Abbey and Ashford Castle and Aran Islands.

B&B	6	Ensuite	€25.50/€25.50	Dinner	€17
B&B	-	Standard	-	Partial Board	-
Single Rate			€38.50/€38.50	Child reduction	50%

Open: 1st March-30th November

Oughterard 8km

Mrs Mary Maloney
PINE GROVE
Glann Lakeshore,
Hill of Doon Road, Oughterard,
Co Galway

Oughterard Connemara Area
TEL: **091 552101**
EMAIL: **annamal@gofree.indigo.ie**

Quiet family home on "Western Way". Overlooking Lough Corrib. Turf fires, Fishing, Golfing, Horseriding & Hill Walks nearby.

B&B	3	Ensuite	€25.50/€25.50	Dinner	€20
B&B	1	Standard	€23/€23	Partial Board	-
Single Rate			€36/€36	Child reduction	-

Open: 1st April-30th October

Oughterard 4km

Mrs Mary O'Halloran
LAKESIDE
Ardnasilla, Oughterard,
Co Galway

Oughterard Connemara Area
TEL: **091 552846**   FAX: **091 552846**

Superbly situated on the shores of Lough Corrib. Fishing, Boating, 18 hole Golf, Pitch & Putt, Aughnanure Castle 1km. Dillard Causin, Michele Erdvig Guides. First class Restaurants 4km.

B&B	4	Ensuite	€27/€30	Dinner	-
B&B	-	Standard		Partial Board	-
Single Rate			€38.50/€38.50	Child reduction	25%

Open: 1st March-30th November

Oughterard 1km

Miss Brid Tierney
GORTREVAGH HOUSE
Portacarron, Oughterard,
Co Galway

Oughterard Connemara Area
TEL: **091 552129**

Old style charm, beside Golf Course, 10 mins from Lough Corrib. Tennis and Horse Riding nearby. Traditional cooking, speciality vegetarian.

B&B	2	Ensuite	€25.50	Dinner	€17
B&B	3	Standard	€23	Partial Board	-
Single Rate			-	Child reduction	25%

Open: All Year

Mary & Tom Walsh
THE WATERFRONT
**Corrib View, Oughterard,
Connemara, Co Galway**

Oughterard Connemara Area

Tel: **091 552797**   Fax: **091 552730**
Email: **waterfront@indigo.ie**
Web: **http://indigo.ie/~waterfnt/**

Panoramic, Lakeside setting. Depart N59 at Golf course, towards Aughnanure Castle. Turn left, 0.5km. before the Castle towards Lake, drive along shore.

B&B	6	Ensuite	€26/€30	Dinner	-
B&B	-	Standard		Partial Board	-
Single Rate			€40/€44	Child reduction	25%

Oughterard 4km   [cc] 🅢🅟 symbols   **Open:** 3rd January-19th December

---

Sally Walsh
WOODSIDE LODGE
**Killola, Rosscahil,
Co Galway**

Oughterard Connemara Area

Tel: **091 550123**   Fax: **091 550123**

Warm friendly family home. Peaceful Mountain and Lake surroundings. Ideal walking/touring base. Charming Oughterard Village, Fishing, Golf within 5km.

B&B	4	Ensuite	€25.50/€25.50	Dinner	-
B&B	-	Standard		Partial Board	-
Single Rate			€38.50/€38.50	Child reduction	50%

Oughterard 5km   **Open:** 1st May-15th September

Michael & Bridie Dolan
SHANNON VILLA
**Bridge Road, Portumna,
Co Galway**

Portumna

Tel: **0509 41269**   Fax: **0509 41799**
Email: **shannonvilla@ireland.com**

Delightful family home, total relaxation in our peaceful conservatory. Ideal for all leisure activities, Angling, Boating, Walks, Equestrian. Central tour base for Clonmacnois, Clonfert, Birr Castle.

B&B	4	Ensuite	€25.50/€28.57	Dinner	€22.86
B&B	1	Standard	€24.13/€26.66	Partial Board	€355.53
Single Rate			€36/€36	Child reduction	25%

In Portumna   **Open:** All Year

Mrs Elizabeth Ryan
AUVERGNE LODGE
**Dominic Street,
Portumna, Co Galway**

Portumna

Tel: **0509 41138**   Fax: **0509 41138**
Email: **auvergnelodge@eircom.net**

Warm friendly family home. Quiet area close to River Shannon, Lough Derg, Castle, Golf, Angling, Go Karting, Equestrian, Pubs, Restaurants, Hotel. TV, Tea/Coffee.

B&B	4	Ensuite	€25.50/€25.50	Dinner	-
B&B	-	Standard		Partial Board	-
Single Rate			€38.50/€38.50	Child reduction	50%

In Portumna   **Open:** All Year

Conneely Family
SUNNYMEADE
**Tully, Renvyle,
Co Galway**

Renvyle Connemara

Tel: **095 43491**   Fax: **095 43491**
Email: **sunny@eircom.net**

Renvyle's longest established B&B. Deluxe accommodation, warm welcome, "Stress Free". Spectacular views of Atlantic Ocean. Walking, Horseriding, Bar, Food, Entertainment closeby.

B&B	4	Ensuite	€26	Dinner	-
B&B	-	Standard		Partial Board	-
Single Rate			€38.50	Child reduction	25%

Clifden 19km      **Open:** 1st January-20th December

Mrs Noreen Conneely
SEA BREEZE
Gurteen, Renvyle,
Co Galway

Renvyle Connemara

TEL: **095 43489** FAX: **095 43489**
EMAIL: **seabreezebandbrenvyle@eircom.net**
WEB: **www.connemara.net/seabreeze**

Luxury accommodation in scenic location. Convenient to Kylemore Abbey, Connemara National Park. Scuba Divewest, Oceans Alive, Golf, Fishing, Horse Riding nearby. Guest Conservatory.

B&B	3	Ensuite	€26/€26	Dinner	-
B&B	1	Standard	€26/€26	Partial Board	-
Single Rate			€38.50/€38.50	Child reduction	50%

Clifden 19km

Open: 1st January-20th December

Davin Family
OLDE CASTLE HOUSE
Curragh, Renvyle,
Connemara, Co Galway

Renvyle Connemara

TEL: **095 43460**

Traditional home situated in front of the sea beside 15th Century Renvyle Castle. Peaceful surroundings. House features in famous film Purple Taxi and Water Colour Challenge.

B&B	5	Ensuite	€25.50	Dinner	€17
B&B	1	Standard	€23	Partial Board	€264
Single Rate			€36	Child reduction	-

Clifden 20km

Open: 10th March-1st November

Mr John Diamond
DIAMONDS CASTLE HOUSE B&B
Tully, Renvyle, Co Galway

Renvyle Connemara

TEL: **095 43431** FAX: **095 43431**
EMAIL: **castlehouse@eircom.net**

Recently renovated 19th Century house, oozing olde-worlde charm and character. Comfortable bedrooms with spacious ensuites and magnificent sea views.

B&B	4	Ensuite	€25.50/€25.50	Dinner	€17
B&B		Standard	-	Partial Board	€264
Single Rate			€38.50/€38.50	Child reduction	33.3%

Clifden 19km

Open: All Year Except Christmas

Miss Sile Mullin
DERRYKYLE COUNTRY HOUSE
Casla/Costello,
Co Galway

Rossaveal

TEL: **091 572412**

Quiet home, peaceful location. Warm atmosphere. Great base for touring Connemara and the Aran Islands. Sea and fresh water Angling nearby. Home baking.

B&B	2	Ensuite	€25.50	Dinner	-
B&B	2	Standard	€23	Partial Board	-
Single Rate			-	Child reduction	25%

Spiddal 14km

Open: May-September

Catherine Burke
IVY ROCK HOUSE
Letterdyfe, Roundstone,
Co Galway

Roundstone Connemara Area

TEL: **095 35872** FAX: **095 35959**
EMAIL: **ivyrockhouse@eircom.net**

This newly refurbished Guesthouse overlooks the Sea and the Twelve Bens and is close to all amenities, Horseriding, Golf, Beaches.

B&B	5	Ensuite	€25.50/€30	Dinner	-
B&B	1	Standard	€25.50/€28	Partial Board	-
Single Rate			€36/€36	Child reduction	25%

Open: 1st March-1st November

In Roundstone

Christina Lowry
ST. JOSEPH'S
Roundstone, Connemara, Co Galway

TEL: **095 35865/35930** FAX: **095 35865**
EMAIL: **christinalowry@eircom.net**
WEB: **www.connemara.net/conemara.org**

Spacious, 19th Century town house overlooking Roundstone Harbour. Home from home. Repeat business. Traditional welcome. Bike shed, Hill, Beach & Island walks.

B&B	6	Ensuite	€25.50/€31.75	Dinner	-
B&B	-	Standard	-	Partial Board	-
Single Rate			€38.50/€44.50	Child reduction	25%

cc S P ❄ ☕ ⚡ 🏠 ♣ ⛵ 🚶 **Open:** All Year

In Roundstone

Linda Nee
RUSH LAKE HOUSE
Roundstone, Co Galway

TEL: **095 35915** FAX: **095 35915**
EMAIL: **rushlakeguests@eircom.net**
WEB: **www.connemara.net/rushlakehouse**

Peaceful setting overlooking Sea and Mountains, walking distance from Village. Friendly and relaxed atmosphere in a family run home.

B&B	4	Ensuite	€25.50/€30	Dinner	-
B&B	-	Standard	-	Partial Board	-
Single Rate			€38.50/€40	Child reduction	25%

cc P ☕ ⚡ 🏠 ♣ ⛵ 🚶 **Open:** 17th March-30th November

Brian Clancy
SUAN NA MARA
Stripe, Furbo, Spiddal, Co Galway

TEL: **091 591512** FAX: **091 591632**
EMAIL: **brian@suannamara.com**
WEB: **www.suannamara.com**

RAC ◆◆◆◆◆ Premier. National Winner Country Homes Award. Chef owned. Laundry. Internet. Gateway to Connemara, Aran Ferries. Beach, scenic walks. Route 336 west.

B&B	3	Ensuite	€32/€35	Dinner	€21
B&B	1	Standard	€32/€32	Partial Board	-
Single Rate			€45/€47	Child reduction	25%

Spiddal 5.5km

cc S P ❄ ⊗ ✂ 🖥 ☕ 🍴 ✕ ⚡ 🏠 ♣ ⛵ 🚶 **Open:** 1st January-23rd December

---

Mrs Alice Concannon
DUN LIOS
Park West, Spiddal, Co Galway

TEL: **091 553165**
EMAIL: **concass@indigo.ie**
WEB: **www.dunlios.8m.com**

Friendly family home with panoramic views of Galway Bay. Gateway to Connemara, Aran Islands. Restaurants, Traditional Music, Beach, Golf nearby. "Rough Guide" recommended.

B&B	4	Ensuite	€26/€30	Dinner	-
B&B	-	Standard	-	Partial Board	-
Single Rate			€38.50/€38.50	Child reduction	25%

Spiddal 3km

P ❄ ⊗ ✂ ✕ 🏠 ♣ ⛵ 🚶 **Open:** 1st May-31st October

Spiddal 5km

Mrs Maura Conneely (Ni Chonghaile)
CALADHGEARR THATCH COTTAGE
Knock, Spiddal, Co Galway

TEL: **091 593124**
EMAIL: **cgthatchcot@eircom.net**

Think old, friendly, traditional, find it in our thatch cottage, overlooking Galway Bay, on route 336 west of Spiddal Village. Recommended - Rough Guide to Ireland.

B&B	3	Ensuite	€25.50/€28	Dinner	-
B&B	-	Standard	-	Partial Board	-
Single Rate			€38.50/€40	Child reduction	50%

P ❄ ☕ ✕ 🍴 ♣ ⛵ 🚶 **Open:** 1st March-31st October

Mrs Phil Conneely
CLUAIN BARRA
Knock, Inverin,
Co Galway

Spiddal Connemara Area
Tel: **091 593140**
Email: **philconneely@hotmail.com**

Overlooking Clare Hills, Galway Bay, Aran Islands. Sandy Beaches, Aran Ferries and Inverin Airport nearby. Ideal for touring Connemara.

B&B	2	Ensuite	€25.50	Dinner	-
B&B	1	Standard	€23	Partial Board	-
Single Rate			€36/€38.50	Child reduction	25%

Spiddal 4km

Open: 1st May-31st October

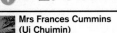

Mrs Frances Cummins
(Ui Chuimin)
BRISEADH NA CARRAIGE
Pairc, Spiddal, Co Galway

Spiddal Connemara Area
Tel: **091 553212**
Email: **frances@galwaybay.com**
Web: **www.galwaybay.com**

Guide du Routard recommended. Touring Connemara, Aran Islands, Galway Bay, Burren. Choice menu. Tea/Coffee arrival. Restaurants, Golf, Angling, Horse-riding, Beaches.

B&B	4	Ensuite	€26/€30	Dinner	-
B&B	-	Standard	-	Partial Board	-
Single Rate			-	Child reduction	-

Spiddal 3km

Open: February-December

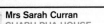

Mrs Sarah Curran
SLIABH RUA HOUSE
Salahoona, Spiddal (R336)
Galway, Co Galway

Spiddal Connemara Area
Tel: **091 553243**
Email: **sliabhrua@eircom.net**

Seaside dormer home on scenic Coast Road, west of Spiddal. Spacious, relaxing, peaceful, ocean view, Cliffs of Moher, bog walks, Aran Ferries. Tour Connemara.

B&B	4	Ensuite	€25.50	Dinner	-
B&B	-	Standard	-	Partial Board	-
Single Rate			-	Child reduction	-

Spiddal 1.5km

Open: 1st May-28th October

Patricia & William Farrell
IVERNA COTTAGE
Salahoona, Spiddal,
Co Galway

Spiddal Connemara Area
Tel: **091 553762**
Email: **ivernacottage@ireland.com**
Web: **ivernacottage.8m.com**

Recommended Sawdays "Special places to stay in Ireland". Welcome to join us here in spacious and interesting stone and wood cottage. Hope you love it too.

B&B	4	Ensuite	€25.50/€28	Dinner	-
B&B	-	Standard	-	Partial Board	-
Single Rate			-	Child reduction	33.3%

Spiddal 1.5km

Open: 15th March-15th November

Eamonn & Siobhan Feeney
TUAR BEAG
Spiddal, Co Galway

Spiddal Connemara Area
Tel: **091 553422**   Fax: **091 553010**
Email: **tuarbeagbandb@eircom.net**
Web: **www.tuarbeag.com**

Unique house built around 1831 thatched cottage. Bay view. Breakfast menu. Recommended Inside Ireland. Cooke/Rough guides. AA ◆◆◆◆ Award. West village R336.

B&B	6	Ensuite	€25.50/€28	Dinner	-
B&B	-	Standard	-	Partial Board	-
Single Rate			-	Child reduction	50%

In Spiddal

Open: 1st February-15th November

Mrs Moya Feeney
CALA 'N UISCE
Greenhill, Spiddal,
Co Galway

Spiddal Connemara Area

Tel: **091 553324**   Fax: **091 553324**
Email: **moyafeeney@iolfree.ie**
Web: **www.geocities.com/spiddalgalway**

Dillard Causin recommended. Modern home on Seaward side of R336. Just west of Spiddal. Close to all amenities. Ideal for touring Connemara and Aran Islands.

B&B	5	Ensuite	€27/€29	Dinner	-
B&B	-	Standard	-	Partial Board	-
Single Rate			€38.50/€38.50	Child reduction	-

Spiddal 1km

Open: 15th April-15th October

Mrs Rita Feeney
ARD MHUIRBHI
Aille, Inverin, Spiddal,
Co Galway

Spiddal Connemara Area

Tel: **091 593215**   Fax: **091 593326**
Email: **ardmhuirbhi@eircom.net**

"Dillard Causin Guide" recommended. Spacious seaside accommodation on Coast Road R336. Superb views, peaceful location, family suites, electric blankets.

B&B	4	Ensuite	€25.50/€27	Dinner	-
B&B	1	Standard	€23/€23	Partial Board	-
Single Rate			€36/€38.50	Child reduction	33.3%

Spiddal 5km

Open: 10th January-30th November

Bartley & Vera Feeney
ARDMOR COUNTRY HOUSE
Greenhill, Spiddal,
Co Galway

Spiddal Connemara Area

Tel: **091 553145**   Fax: **091 553596**
Email: **ardmor@ireland.com**
Web: **www.ardmorcountryhouse.com**

Country home enjoying superb views. Spacious rooms, comfort assured. Relaxed & friendly atmosphere. Breakfast awards. Recommended Frommer, Sullivan, Rough Guide. AA ♦♦♦♦ Selected.

B&B	7	Ensuite	€28/€30	Dinner	-
B&B	-	Standard	-	Partial Board	-
Single Rate			€40/€45	Child reduction	-

Spiddal 1km

Open: 1st March-December

Mrs Sarah Flaherty
COIS CAOLAIRE
Ballintleva, Spiddal,
Co Galway

Spiddal Connemara Area

Tel: **091 553176**   Fax: **091 553624**
Email: **sarah_flaherty@hotmail.com**
Web: **www.sarah_flaherty@hotmail.com**

"Cead Mile Failte". Enjoy Irish hospitality in a family run home on the Coast R336 to Connemara. Scenic view of Galway Bay, Aran Island, Burren. Home Baking.

B&B	3	Ensuite	€26/€28	Dinner	€20
B&B	3	Standard	€24	Partial Board	-
Single Rate			€36/€36	Child reduction	50%

Spiddal 2km

Open: 1st April-30th October

Mrs Mary Anne Flavin
TIGH NA MARA
Teach Mor, Inverin,
Co Galway

Spiddal Connemara Area

Tel: **091 593064**

Dormer bungalow, overlooking Galway Bay. Ideal for touring Connemara and Burren areas. Aran Ferries/Airport nearby. Peaceful location. Spiddal Village 6km.

B&B	2	Ensuite	€25.50/€27	Dinner	-
B&B	1	Standard	€23/€23	Partial Board	-
Single Rate			€38.50/€38.50	Child reduction	-

Spiddal 6km

Open: 1st March-30th September

Mary Joyce
ARD NA GREINE
**Cre Dhulah, Spiddal,
Co Galway**

TEL: **091 553039**
EMAIL: **mjoyce81@hotmail.com**

Modern friendly home, facing Atlantic. Near Restaurants, Pubs, Music, Bog walks, Golf, Beaches. Ferry for Aran Islands. Breakfast menu. Home cooking, TV.

B&B	4	Ensuite	€25.50/€26.67	Dinner	-
B&B	-	Standard	-	Partial Board	-
Single Rate			€38.50/€38.50	Child reduction	50%

Open: 1st April-30th September

Mrs Maureen Keady
(Ni Cheidigh)
COL-MAR HOUSE
**Salahoona, Spiddal,
Co Galway**

TEL: **091 553247**   FAX: **091 553247**

Peaceful country home. Set in private woods and colourful gardens. Warm hospitality, spacious, comfortable. Michelin, Guide du Routard, "Lonely Planets" recommended. 1.5km west Spiddal.

B&B	5	Ensuite	€25.50/€27	Dinner	-
B&B	-	Standard	-	Partial Board	-
Single Rate			€40	Child reduction	50%

Spiddal 1.5km

Open: May-September

Paul & Linda Murphy
COIS NA TRA
**Coast Road, Spiddal Village,
Connemara, Co Galway**

TEL: **091 553954**   FAX: **091 553954**
EMAIL: **coisnatra@eircom.net**
WEB: **www.coisnatra.com**

Country home beside beach, all rooms with sea views. Ideal for touring Connemara, Aran Islands. Restaurants/Traditional Music Pubs/Golf/Fishing/Horse Riding. Guide du Routard.

B&B	4	Ensuite	€29/€32	Dinner	-
B&B	-	Standard	-	Partial Board	-
Single Rate			€45/€45	Child reduction	25%

In Spiddal

Open: 1st April-31st October

Mrs Patsy McCarthy
(MacCarthaigh)
SAILIN
**Coill Rua, Spiddal,
Co Galway**

TEL: **091 553308**
EMAIL: **sailincoillrua@hotmail.com**

Bungalow overlooking Galway Bay & Cliffs of Moher. 5 mins sandy beach. Ideal for touring Connemara & Aran Islands. Canoeing, Angling & Horse-riding.

B&B	3	Ensuite	€25.50	Dinner	-
B&B	1	Standard	€23	Partial Board	-
Single Rate			€36/€38.50	Child reduction	33.3%

Spiddal 2km

Open: 1st April-31st October

Mrs Peg O'Connor
RADHARC AN CHLAIR
**Kellough, Spiddal,
Co Galway**

TEL: **091 553267**
EMAIL: **radharcanchlair@eircom.net**
WEB: **www.radharcanchlair.8m.com**

Bungalow tastefully decorated. Spacious rooms, overlooking Galway Bay, Aran Islands, Cliffs of Moher. Golf, beautiful Walks, Seafood Restaurants.

B&B	4	Ensuite	€28	Dinner	-
B&B	-	Standard	-	Partial Board	-
Single Rate			-	Child reduction	

Spiddal 1.5km

Open: April-October

Mrs Mairead O'Flaherty
DUN-CHAOIN HOUSE
Cor-na Ron East,
Inverin, Co Galway

TEL: **091 593302**
EMAIL: **dunchaoinbandb@hotmail.com**

Experience real comfort in a friendly, rural home, overlooking Galway Bay. Home-cooking, tranquil Bogwalks, Beaches. Aran Ferries, Airport nearby.

B&B	3	Ensuite	€25.50/€25.50	Dinner	€18
B&B	-	Standard		Partial Board	€265
Single Rate			€38.50/€38.50	Child reduction	25%

Spiddal 8km

Open: 1st June-30th September

Mrs Barbara O'Malley-Curran
ARD AOIBHINN
Spiddal, Connemara,
Co Galway

TEL: **091 553179**   FAX: **091 553179**
EMAIL: **aoibhinn@gofree.indigo.ie**

0.5km west Village. Multi Guidebook recommendations. Aran Ferry/Connemara/Burren. Tour bus pass door. Seafood Restaurants, Traditional music. Pubs, Bog. Seashore walks. AA ◆◆◆ award.

B&B	5	Ensuite	€25.50/€25.50	Dinner	-
B&B	-	Standard		Partial Board	-
Single Rate			€38.50/€38.50	Child reduction	50%

In Spiddal

Open: All Year

Mrs Gabrielle Hurst
FOUR SEASONS
Carrowmoneen, Dublin Road,
Tuam, Co Galway

TEL: **093 28375/25934** FAX: **093 25934**
EMAIL: **ghurst@oceanfree.net**

Spacious family residence in scenic, rural setting. Convenient for touring Galway Connemara and Cong. Golf, Fishing and Horse-riding.

B&B	3	Ensuite	€25.50	Dinner	-
B&B	-	Standard		Partial Board	-
Single Rate			€38.50	Child reduction	-

Tuam 2km

Open: 1st April-31st October

Mrs Josephine O'Connor
KILMORE HOUSE
Galway Road, Tuam,
Co Galway

TEL: **093 28118/26525** FAX: **093 26525**
EMAIL: **kilmorehouse@mail.com**
WEB: **ebookireland.com**

Spacious modern residence on farm. Warm hospitality. Frommer recommended. Peaceful rural setting. Knock, Connemara and Galway convenient. Restaurants, Pubs nearby.

B&B	7	Ensuite	€25.50	Dinner	€17
B&B	-	Standard		Partial Board	-
Single Rate			€38.50	Child reduction	25%

Tuam 1km

Open: All Year

RESERVATIONS

- Confirm phone bookings in writing without delay with agreed deposit.
- To avoid misunderstandings later, check rate on booking and
  clarify any additional changes which may apply to your booking.
- Give details of any special requirements.
- State clearly day, date of arrival and departure date.

Welcome to Mayo, "Ireland's best kept secret". Blue flag beaches, rivers, lakes and deep-sea fishing. Visitor attractions, great Golf courses, the most incredible Touring, Trekking and Walking countryside, but most of all the hospitality of the people of Mayo.

Michael G Lavelle
REALT NA MARA
Dooagh, Achill Island,
Co Mayo

Achill Island
TEL: **098 43005**   FAX: **098 43006**
EMAIL: **mglavell@gofree.indigo.ie**
WEB: **www.realtnamara.com**

On main road in Dooagh Village overlooking the Bay. New modern B&B. Family run with many facilities such as Snooker Room, Sauna, Gym, Jacuzzi, Laundry room, Drying, Freezing facilities.

B&B	6	Ensuite	€27/€35	Dinner	-
B&B	-	Standard	-	Partial Board	-
Single Rate			€38.50/€40	Child reduction	**50%**

Westport 55km

Open: All Year

Mrs Frances Masterson
ROCKMOUNT
Achill Sound, Achill Island,
Co Mayo

Achill Island
TEL: **098 45272**

Frommer Guide recommended. Scenic surroundings, adjacent to Bus Stop, House of Prayer, Village, Sea, Mountains, Electric Blankets. Tea making facilities.

B&B	5	Ensuite	€25.50	Dinner	-
B&B	1	Standard	€24	Partial Board	-
Single Rate			€36	Child reduction	-

In Achill Sound

Open: 1st January-1st December

Mrs Teresa McNamara
WEST COAST HOUSE
School Road, Dooagh,
Achill Island, Co Mayo

Achill Island
TEL: **098 43317**   FAX: **098 43317**
EMAIL: **westcoast@anu.ie**
WEB: **www.dirl.com/mayo/westcoasthouse**

AA ◆◆◆. Panoramic view, Tranquil setting. Orthopaedic beds. Hairdryer, Payphone, Breakfast menu, Drying room, Laundry service. Tours arranged. Fish Restaurant.

B&B	5	Ensuite	€25.50/€30	Dinner	€19
B&B	-	Standard		Partial Board	€300
Single Rate			€38.50/€40	Child reduction	**25%**

Keel 1km

Open: 1st March-5th November

Mrs T Moran
WOODVIEW HOUSE
Springvale, Achill Sound,
Co Mayo

Achill Island
TEL: **098 45261**

Modern bungalow in quiet scenic surroundings with panoramic view of Sea and Mountains, 1km from House of Prayer.

B&B	3	Ensuite	€25.50	Dinner	€17
B&B	3	Standard	€23	Partial Board	-
Single Rate			€38.50	Child reduction	-

Achill Sound 1km

Open: 1st January-30th November

Mrs Ann Sweeney
FINNCORRY HOUSE
Atlantic Drive, Bleanaskill Bay,
Achill Island, Co Mayo

Achill Island

TEL: **098 45755**   FAX: **098 45755**
EMAIL: **achill_island@hotmail.com**
WEB: **achill.mayo-ireland.ie/finncorry.htm**

Relax, enjoy traditional hospitality in luxuriously appointed modern home. Peaceful setting overlooking Bleanaskill Bay on spectacular Atlantic Drive. AA/RAC Approved-◆◆◆◆.

B&B	6	Ensuite	€25.50/€25.50	Dinner	-
B&B	-	Standard		Partial Board	-
Single Rate			€38.50/€38.50	Child reduction	33.3%

Achill Sound 3km

Open: March-October

Geraldine Best
GLENEAGLE HOUSE
Foxford Road, Ballina,
Co Mayo

Ballina

TEL: **096 70228**

Dormer bungalow, a home of genuine welcome. 10 mins walk from Town. Rooms ensuite with TV, Tea and Coffee facilities. Ideal for Fishing and Golfing.

B&B	3	Ensuite	€25.50/€26	Dinner	-
B&B	-	Standard		Partial Board	-
Single Rate			€38.50/€38.50	Child reduction	25%

In Ballina

Open: 1st March-30th November

Mrs Josephine Corrigan
GREEN HILL
Cathedral Close, Ballina,
Co Mayo

Ballina

TEL: **096 22767**

Comfortable home in quiet location at rear of Cathedral, within walking distance of River Moy, Ridge Pool and Town Centre.

B&B	3	Ensuite	€25.50/€28	Dinner	-
B&B	1	Standard	€23/€25.50	Partial Board	-
Single Rate			€36/€38.50	Child reduction	33.3%

In Ballina

Open: 1st January-20th December

Mrs Noelle Curry
EVERGREEN
Foxford Road, Ballina,
Co Mayo

Ballina

TEL: **096 71343**
EMAIL: **evergreen-curry@iol.ie**
WEB: **ballina.mayo_ireland.ie/evergreen.htm**

Welcome to our comfortable bungalow in peaceful location walking distance of Town. Rooms ensuite with TV, Private car park.

B&B	4	Ensuite	€25.50/€25.50	Dinner	-
B&B	-	Standard		Partial Board	-
Single Rate			€38.50	Child reduction	-

Ballina 1km

Open: All Year Except Christmas

Ms Dolores Jordan
RED RIVER LODGE
Iceford, Quay Rd,
Ballina, Co Mayo

Ballina

TEL: **096 22841**
EMAIL: **redriverlodge@eircom.net**
WEB: **homepage.eircom.net/~redriverlodge**

Friendly country home on 1 acre gardens overlooking Moy Estuary on Scenic Quay Road. 3km from Quay Village. Recommended by International Guides.

B&B	4	Ensuite	€25.50/€25.50	Dinner	-
B&B	-	Standard		Partial Board	-
Single Rate			€38.50/€38.50	Child reduction	25%

Ballina 6km

Open: April-October

Agnes & Brendan McElvanna
CLADDAGH HOUSE
Sligo Rd, Ballina, Co Mayo

Ballina

Tel: **096 71670**
Email: **brenclad@eircom.net**
Web: **homepage.eircom.net/~clad**

Modern home, excellent views. Comfortable and spacious. Guest TV Lounge, complimentary Tea/Coffee. Hospitable and friendly atmosphere. Full Fire Safety Certificate.

B&B	6	Ensuite	€25.50/€28.50	Dinner	-
B&B	-	Standard	-	Partial Board	-
Single Rate			€38.50/€43	Child reduction	33.3%

Ballina 4.8km

Open: 1st March-31st October

Mrs Carmel Murray
ASHLEY HOUSE
Ardoughan, Ballina, Co Mayo

Ballina

Tel: **096 22799**   Fax: **096 22799**
Email: **ashleyhousebb@hotmail.com**

Welcome to our highly recommended home off main Crossmolina Rd N59. All guests bedrooms ground floor. Award winning gardens. Walking distance to Town. Near Belleek Castle.

B&B	4	Ensuite	€25.50	Dinner	-
B&B	-	Standard	-	Partial Board	-
Single Rate			€38.50	Child reduction	33.3%

Ballina 1km

Open: All Year

Mary O'Dowd
CNOC BREANDAIN
Quay Road, Ballina, Co Mayo

Ballina

Tel: **096 22145**
Email: **nodowd@iol.ie**

Country home overlooking Moy Estuary. Noted for good food and hospitality. Many recommendations. Breakfast menu. 2km past Quay Village towards Enniscrone.

B&B	4	Ensuite	€25.50/€28	Dinner	-
B&B	-	Standard	-	Partial Board	-
Single Rate			€38.50	Child reduction	25%

Ballina 1km

Open: 1st May-31st August

Mrs Mary Reilly
BELVEDERE HOUSE
Foxford Rd, Ballina, Co Mayo

Ballina

Tel: **096 22004**

Modern Georgian style home on N26. Within walking distance from Town, Bus and Train. Ideal for Golf and Walking. Salmon Fishing on River Moy, Trout Fishing on Lough Conn.

B&B	4	Ensuite	€25.50	Dinner	-
B&B	-	Standard	-	Partial Board	-
Single Rate			€38.50	Child reduction	25%

In Ballina

Open: 1st January-22nd December

Mrs Helen Smyth
ASHLEAM HOUSE
Mount Falcon, Foxford Rd, Ballina, Co Mayo

Ballina

Tel: **096 22406**
Email: **helensmyth@eircom.net**
Web: **www.ashleambandb.ie**

Country home, half way between Ballina and Foxford N26. Beside River Moy. Near Lough Conn. Noted for hospitality. Ideal as a base for touring. Golfing.

B&B	4	Ensuite	€25.50/€25.50	Dinner	-
B&B	2	Standard	€23/€23	Partial Board	-
Single Rate			€36/€38.50	Child reduction	33.3%

Ballina 4km

Open: April-September

In Ballina

Mr & Mrs Breda & David Walsh | **Ballina**
SUNCROFT
3 Cathedral Close,
Ballina, Co Mayo

TEL: **096 21573**   FAX: **096 21573**
EMAIL: **suncroftbb@eircom.net**

Town house in quiet location behind Cathedral. Town Centre and River Moy, Ridge Pool 300 mtrs. Le Guide De Routard recommended.

B&B	4	Ensuite	€25.50/€27	Dinner	-
B&B	1	Standard	€23/€25	Partial Board	-
Single Rate			€38.50/€40	Child reduction	-

Open: 1st January-22nd December

In Ballinrobe

Martin & Breege Kavanagh | **Ballinrobe**
FRIARSQUARTER HOUSE
Convent Road, Ballinrobe,
Co Mayo

TEL: **092 41154**

Elegant house, period furnishings. Spacious gardens. Le Guide Du Routard recommended. 18 Champion Golf course. Touring Base. Connemara Knock N84.

B&B	3	Ensuite	€25.50/€25.50	Dinner	-
B&B	1	Standard	€25.39/€25.39	Partial Board	-
Single Rate			€36/€36	Child reduction	25%

Open: All Year Except Christmas

Ballinrobe

Anne Mahon | **Ballinrobe**
RIVERSIDE HOUSE
Cornmarket, Ballinrobe,
Co Mayo

TEL: **092 41674**
EMAIL: **annmahon@iol.ie**

Modern home in Lake District. Championship Golf Course, Scenic Walks. Easy driving distance Ashford Castle, Westport, Knock Shrine, Galway, Connemara, Fishing.

B&B	3	Ensuite	€25.50	Dinner	-
B&B	1	Standard	€23	Partial Board	-
Single Rate			€36	Child reduction	-

Open: All Year

Ballycastle 10km

Mrs Carmel Murphy | **Ballycastle**
THE HAWTHORNS
Belderrig, Ballina,
Co Mayo

TEL: **096 43148**   FAX: **096 43148**
EMAIL: **camurphy@indigo.ie**

Enjoy warm friendly hospitality in the picturesque Village of Belderrig. Beside Sea/Fishing Port. Hill/Cliff Walking. Ceide Fields nearby.

B&B	2	Ensuite	€25.50/€25.50	Dinner	€17
B&B	1	Standard	€23/€23	Partial Board	€264
Single Rate			€36/€38.50	Child reduction	50%

Open: All Year

Ballyhaunis 8km

Annette Fleming | **Ballyhaunis**
EASCAI
Lavallyroe, Clonfad,
Ballyhaunis, Co Mayo

TEL: **0907 46040**

Ideally situated on N83 for touring Galway, Westport, Sligo, Roscommon, all 1 hr drive. 18km from Knock, 25km from Knock Airport. Taxi service available.

B&B	4	Ensuite	€25.50/€25.50	Dinner	€19.05
B&B	-	Standard	-	Partial Board	-
Single Rate			€38.50/€38.50	Child reduction	25%

Open: All Year

Bangor Erris

Mrs Evelyn Cosgrove
HILLCREST HOUSE
Main Street, Bangor Erris,
Ballina, Co Mayo

Bangor Erris
TEL: **097 83494**
EMAIL: **hillcresthouse@eircom.net**
WEB: **homepage.eircom.net/~hillcresthouse**

Visit Ceide Fields. Recommended B&B Guide to Ireland. Walkers, Drying room facilities. Off Bangor Trail and Western Way. Ideal for Fishing, Cycling storage. Afternoon tea on arrival.

B&B	2	Ensuite	€26/€27	Dinner	€18
B&B	2	Standard	€23/€26	Partial Board	
Single Rate			€36/€39	Child reduction	33.3%

Open: All Year

Josephine Geraghty
BRU CHIANN LIR
Tirrane, Clogher,
Belmullet, Ballina, Co Mayo

Belmullet Peninsula
TEL: **097 85741**   FAX: **097 85741**
EMAIL: **bruclannlir@eircom.net**

Visit this unspoilt Peninsula location. Surrounded by Sea, Boat trips/Angling arranged. Quiet Blue Flag Beaches, Walks, Golf, Birdlife. We have it all.

B&B	5	Ensuite	€27	Dinner	-
B&B	-	Standard		Partial Board	-
Single Rate			€38.50	Child reduction	25%

Belmullet 13km

Open: 1st May-30th September

Ms Mairin Maguire-Murphy
DROM CAOIN
Belmullet, Co Mayo

Belmullet
TEL: **097 81195**   FAX: **097 81195**
EMAIL: **dromcaoin@esatlink.com**

Panoramic view of Blacksod Bay and Achill Island. AIB Best Food Award, Vegetarian option. Carne 18 hole Links, Sea Angling, Blue Flag Beaches, Ceide fields, Cycle storage, Drying room.

B&B	4	Ensuite	€30	Dinner	€19
B&B	-	Standard	-	Partial Board	
Single Rate			€38.50	Child reduction	33.3%

Belmullet 1km

Open: All Year

Anne Reilly
HIGHDRIFT
Haven View, Ballina Road,
Belmullet, Co Mayo

Belmullet
TEL: **097 81260**   FAX: **097 81260**
EMAIL: **anne.reilly@ireland.com**

Quiet scenic surroundings overlooking the Atlantic and Broadhaven Bay. Turf fires. 5 mins walk to Town. Visit Mullet Peninsula and Ceide fields. Warm welcome.

B&B	3	Ensuite	€25.50	Dinner	-
B&B	1	Standard	€24	Partial Board	-
Single Rate			€36	Child reduction	25%

Belmullet 1km

Open: 1st April-13th October

Veronica Reilly
CHEZ NOUS
Church Road, Belmullet,
Co Mayo

Belmullet
TEL: **097 82167**
EMAIL: **chez_nous_belmullet@esatclear.ie**

Old style house renovated to a high standard. Carne golf links, sea angling, blue flag beaches, ceide fields, walking.

B&B	3	Ensuite	€28/€30	Dinner	-
B&B	-	Standard		Partial Board	-
Single Rate			€38.50	Child reduction	25%

In Belmullet

Open: 1st March-31st December

Mrs Bernie Collins
DRUMSHINNAGH HOUSE
Rahins, Newport Road,
Castlebar, Co Mayo

Castlebar

Tel: **094 24211**   Fax: **094 24211**
Email: **berniecollins@oceanfree.net**

On Newport/Mulranny/Achill Island Road (R311). 300m off main road. Ideal for Touring, Fishing, Golfing. Boat & Wet room available.

B&B	4	Ensuite	€27	Dinner	-
B&B	-	Standard		Partial Board	-
Single Rate			€38.50	Child reduction	25%

Castlebar 3km   **Open:** 1st April-30th September

Mrs Maureen Daly
WOODVIEW LODGE
Breaffy (Breaghwy),
Castlebar, Co Mayo

Castlebar

Tel: **094 23985**   Fax: **094 23985**
Email: **woodviewlodge@eircom.net**

Luxurious country home, quiet peaceful location. N60 on Claremorris Road opposite Breaffy House Hotel. Rooms ensuite, Tea/Coffee, TV, Hairdryers.

B&B	6	Ensuite	€25.50	Dinner	-
B&B	-	Standard		Partial Board	-
Single Rate			€38.50	Child reduction	25%

Castlebar 4km   **Open:** All Year

Mrs Breeda Flannelly
FORT-VILLA HOUSE
Moneen, Castlebar,
Co Mayo

Castlebar

Tel: **094 21002**   Fax: **094 26827**
Email: **flanprop@eircom.net**

Old Georgian House, walking distance Town Centre. Touring centre. Outdoor activities, Fishing, Golf. Beside N5 roundabout. Rooms TV, Teasmaid. Friendly welcome.

B&B	5	Ensuite	€25.50/€25.50	Dinner	-
B&B	-	Standard		Partial Board	-
Single Rate			€38.50/€38.50	Child reduction	25%

Castlebar 1km   **Open:** 1st May-30th September

Mrs Margaret Lenehan
CORRICK HOUSE
Thornbrook, Pontoon Rd,
Castlebar, Co Mayo

Castlebar

Tel: **094 23313**
Email:**lenehanfamily@eircom.net**

Family home in quiet cul-de-sac, nice gardens. Within walking distance of Town Centre.

B&B	1	Ensuite	€25.50/€28.50	Dinner	-
B&B	2	Standard	€23/€25.50	Partial Board	-
Single Rate			€36/€36	Child reduction	25%

In Castlebar   **Open:** 1st April-1st November

Mrs Noreen McGinley
ASHLEIGH
Westport Rd, N5
Castlebar, Co Mayo

Castlebar

Tel: **094 24714**
Email: **ashleigh@iol.ie**

Cosy, welcoming, award winning B&B. Guest TV lounge. TV, Electric Blankets, Hairdryers, Tea/Coffee all rooms. Breakfast Menu. Superb touring base. Friendly welcome.

B&B	4	Ensuite	€25.50/€25.50	Dinner	-
B&B	-	Standard	-	Partial Board	-
Single Rate			€38.50/€38.50	Child reduction	33.3%

Castlebar 1km   **Open:** 15th January-15th December

Mrs Kay McGrath
WINDERMERE HOUSE
Westport Road, Islandeady, Castlebar, Co Mayo

Castlebar
TEL: **094 23329**
EMAIL: **windermerehse@eircom.net**

Luxurious spacious home. Bilberry Lake 1km. Home away from home. Brittany Ferries selected. Breakfast Menu. Trouser press, Hairdryers. Boat hire. Friendly and relaxed atmosphere.

B&B	4	Ensuite	€25.50	Dinner	€17
B&B	1	Standard	€23	Partial Board	
Single Rate			€36/€38.50	Child reduction	33.3%

Castlebar 6km

Open: All Year

Grainne McManus
BALLARD HOUSE
Aughaluskey, Windsor, Castlebar, Co Mayo

Castlebar
TEL: **094 26125** FAX: **094 26125**
EMAIL: **ballardhouse@eircom.net**

A warm welcome awaits you in our home. Peaceful country location off the Dublin Rd. N5. All home cooking. Ideal base for Golf, Fishing, Walking and Cycling.

B&B	2	Ensuite	€26	Dinner	-
B&B	1	Standard	€23	Partial Board	-
Single Rate			€36	Child reduction	50%

Castlebar 2km

Open: March-November

Rody & Mary McRandal
CARRAIG RUA
The Curragh, Castlebar, Co Mayo

Castlebar
TEL: **094 22103**
EMAIL: **mcrandal@iol.ie**

Comfortable town house home, within walking distance of Town Centre and all amenities. Touring centre.

B&B	3	Ensuite	€25.50	Dinner	-
B&B	-	Standard	-	Partial Board	-
Single Rate			€38.50	Child reduction	25%

Castlebar 1km

Open: 2nd January-24th December

Mrs Eileen Pierce
FOUR WINDS
Maryland, Breaffy Road, Castlebar, Co Mayo

Castlebar
TEL: **094 21767** FAX: **094 21767**
EMAIL: **epierce_fourwinds@esatclear.ie**

Spacious house. Quiet location. N60 walking distance Town. TV, Hairdryers in bedrooms. Convenient to Breaffy House Hotel, Train Station. Visit Knock Shrine. Ballintubber Abbey.

B&B	5	Ensuite	€25.50/€25.50	Dinner	€17
B&B	-	Standard	-	Partial Board	-
Single Rate			€38.50/€38.50	Child reduction	50%

In Castlebar

Open: 15th April-15th November

Mrs Teresa Quinn
NEPHIN HOUSE
Westport Road, Castlebar, Co Mayo

Castlebar
TEL: **094 23840** FAX: **094 23840**
EMAIL: **quinnnephin@eircom.net**

Comfortable home. Beside Westport road roundabout. Walking distance from Town. Travellers Friend Hotel, Hospital. TV, Tea/Coffee, Hairdryers in rooms. Ideal touring base.

B&B	3	Ensuite	€26/€28	Dinner	-
B&B	-	Standard	-	Partial Board	-
Single Rate			€38.50/€38.50	Child reduction	-

In Castlebar

Open: 1st May-31st October

Mrs Breege Scahill — Castlebar
MILLHILL HOUSE
Westport Road, Castlebar,
Co Mayo

TEL: **094 24279**
EMAIL: **millhill@eircom.net**
WEB: **homepage.eircom.net/~millhill**

Quality accommodation off main road. Easy to find. Take Westport Road N5 from Castlebar. Sign on left. Convenient to Westport. Guest lounge, TV, Tea/Coffee facilities.

B&B	2	Ensuite	€25.50	Dinner	€17
B&B	1	Standard	€23	Partial Board	-
Single Rate			€36/€36	Child reduction	50%

Castlebar 4km

Open: April-November

Mrs Bernadette Walsh — Castlebar
ROCKSBERRY B&B
Westport Road, Castlebar,
Co Mayo

TEL: **094 27254**   FAX: **094 27254**

Comfortable home on Castlebar/Westport road. Hairdryers, TV, Tea/Coffee in bedrooms. Boat hire for local Lakes.

B&B	4	Ensuite	€25.50 /€25.50	Dinner	-
B&B	-	Standard	-	Partial Board	-
Single Rate			€38.50/€38.50	Child reduction	25%

Castlebar 2km

Open: 1st February-30th November

Mrs Nora Ward — Castlebar
DEVARD
Westport Road, Castlebar,
Co Mayo

TEL: **094 23462**   FAX: **094 23462**
EMAIL: **devard@esatclear.ie**
WEB: **www.esatclear.ie/~devard**

Bungalow on N5 Westport road, 2 doors from Spar Foodstore. Electric Blankets, Hairdryers, TV, Tea/Coffee in bedrooms. Award winning gardens.

B&B	5	Ensuite	€26/€28	Dinner	-
B&B	-	Standard	-	Partial Board	-
Single Rate			€38.50/€38.50	Child reduction	50%

Castlebar 1km

Open: All Year

Philip & Carol O'Gorman — Charlestown
ASHFORT
Galway/Knock Road,
Charlestown, Co Mayo

TEL: **094 54706**   FAX: **094 55885**
EMAIL: **ashfort@esatclear.ie**
WEB: **www.mayobandb.com**

Spacious, comfortable home. Quiet, central location routes N17/N5. Personal attention, Route planning, Genealogy guidance. Knock Airport 5 mins. Knock Shrine 20 min. Frommer Guide.

B&B	5	Ensuite	€25.50/€28	Dinner	-
B&B	-	Standard	-	Partial Board	-
Single Rate			€38.50/€42	Child reduction	25%

Charlestown 1km

Open: 1st March-1st December

Mrs Rita Cleary — Claremorris
CASA MIA
Ballyhaunis Road, Claremorris,
Co Mayo

TEL: **094 71405**

Situated Claremorris/Ballyhaunis Road N60. Convenient Knock Shrine, Airport, Ballintubber Abbey Riding School. 18 hole Golf Course.

B&B	2	Ensuite	€25.50	Dinner	-
B&B	2	Standard	€23.50	Partial Board	-
Single Rate			€38.50	Child reduction	25%

In Claremorris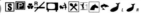

Open: 1st February-30th November

Claremorris 4km

Pat & Carmel Conway
CONWAYS B&B
Coilmore, Claremorris,
Co Mayo

Claremorris

TEL: **094 71117**
EMAIL: **coilmore@eircom.net**
WEB: **www.coilmore.com**

Set in mature secluded gardens on Ballyhaunis road N60. Close to Knock Shrine, Airport, Horse Riding, Golf, Swimming Pool. Home Baking. Welcome assured.

B&B	1	Ensuite	€25.50	Dinner	-
B&B	2	Standard	€23	Partial Board	-
Single Rate			€36/€38.50	Child reduction	33.3%

Open: All Year

Cong 1km

Mrs Ann Coakley
HAZEL GROVE
Drumshiel, Cong,
Co Mayo

Cong Connemara Area

TEL: **092 46060**   FAX: **092 46060**
EMAIL: **hazelgrovecong@eircom.net**

Warm friendly home, peaceful area between Lakes Corrib/Mask. Panoramic view of Connemara Mountains. Historic area. Ideal touring base for Connemara/Mayo.

B&B	4	Ensuite	€25.50/€25.50	Dinner	-
B&B	2	Standard	€23/€23	Partial Board	-
Single Rate			€36/€38.50	Child reduction	50%

Open: 1st February-30th November

Cong 2km

Christina Dunleavy
ASHFIELD HOUSE
Caherduff, Neale,
Co Mayo

Cong

TEL: **092 46759**   FAX: **092 46759**
EMAIL: **ashfield@mayo-ireland.ie**

Tastefully decorated home; close to Ashford Castle, Cong Abbey, Quiet Man Heritage cottage, Golf courses. Convenient for Fishing on Lough Corrib/Mask.

B&B	3	Ensuite	€25.50	Dinner	-
B&B	-	Standard	-	Partial Board	-
Single Rate			€38.50	Child reduction	25%

Open: 1st March-31st October

Cong 3km

Madge Gorman
DRINGEEN BAY B&B,
Cong, Co Mayo

Cong Connemara Area

TEL: **092 46103**
EMAIL: **dringeenbay@eircom.net**

Elegant home located off R345 Cong/Clonbur road. 300m from shore of Lough Mask. Scenic mountain views. Home baking. Forest walks, extensive gardens. Ideal base for touring Connemara.

B&B	2	Ensuite	€25.50	Dinner	-
B&B	1	Standard	€23	Partial Board	-
Single Rate			€36	Child reduction	50%

Open: 1st May-30th September

Cong 3km

Mrs Ann Holian
VILLA PIO
Gortacurra Cross,
Cong, Co Mayo

Cong Connemara Area

TEL: **092 46403**   FAX: **092 46403**
EMAIL: **villapiocong@hotmail.com**

Situated off R334 near Lough Corrib. Boat/Engine Hire. Ideal for walkers, cyclists and touring Connemara. Quiet Man film location and Ashford Castle. Taxi Service.

B&B	2	Ensuite	€25.50	Dinner	-
B&B	1	Standard	€23	Partial Board	-
Single Rate			€36	Child reduction	25%

Open: All Year

Kathy O'Connor
DOLMEN HOUSE
Drumsheel, Cong,
Co Mayo

Cong
Tel: 092 46466 Fax: 092 46466

Luxurious new house overlooking Connemara Mountains. Excellent touring base. Paradise for Anglers, Walkers, Golfers. Sauna available.

B&B	6	Ensuite	€25.50/€25.50	Dinner	-
B&B	-	Standard	-	Partial Board	-
Single Rate			€38.50/€38.50	Child reduction	25%

In Cong

Open: All Year

Maureen Varley
ROCKLAWN HOUSE
Drumshiel, Cong, Co Mayo

Cong
Tel: 092 46616

Family home on banks of Cong Canal. Excellent walks, tours steeped in local history. Angling, Boat trips locally. Drying room, Homebaking. 2km from Cong.

B&B	4	Ensuite	€25.50	Dinner	-
B&B	-	Standard	-	Partial Board	-
Single Rate			€38.50	Child reduction	-

Cong 2km

Open: 1st April-1st September

Mrs Nuala Gallagher-Matthews
LAKE VIEW HOUSE
Ballina Road, Crossmolina,
Co Mayo

Crossmolina
Tel: 096 31296
Email: lakeviewhouse@oceanfree.net

Country home. Close to Lough Conn. Family Research/Archaeological Centres and Ceide Fields. Boat/Ghillie hire. Fishing arranged. Tea/Coffee facilities. Ideal touring base.

B&B	6	Ensuite	€25.50/€25.50	Dinner	-
B&B	-	Standard	-	Partial Board	-
Single Rate			€38.50	Child reduction	33.3%

In Crossmolina

Open: 1st April-31st October

Mrs Nora Naughton
WOODVIEW HOUSE
Enniscoe, Castlehill,
Crossmolina, Co Mayo

Crossmolina
Tel: 096 31125
Email: noranaughton@eircom.net
Web: www.welcome.to/woodviewhouse

Country home, beside Lough Conn. Family Research Centre. Ceide Fields close by. Fishing arranged. Boats/Ghille - Hire. Tea/Coffee facilities. 3km Pontoon/Castlebar Rd. Ground floor bedrooms.

B&B	4	Ensuite	€25.50/€25.50	Dinner	-
B&B	2	Standard	€23/€23	Partial Board	-
Single Rate			€36 /€38.50	Child reduction	25%

Crossmolina 3km

Open: 1st April-31st October

Harry Feeney
THE FOXFORD LODGE
Pontoon Road,
Foxford, Co Mayo

Foxford
Tel: 094 57777 Fax: 094 57778
Email: sales@thefoxfordlodge.ie
Web: www.thefoxfordlodge.ie

The Foxford Lodge is famous for its trademarks of hospitality and friendliness. A luxurious special interest home for those who like quality with style.

B&B	3	Ensuite	€30/€30	Dinner	€20
B&B	1	Standard	€30/€30	Partial Board	-
Single Rate			€36/€36	Child reduction	50%

In Foxford

Open: 1st January-30th November

Killala 3km

Mrs Mary O'Hara
BEACH VIEW HOUSE
Ross, Killala, Co Mayo

Killala
Tel: **096 32023**

Bungalow on peninsula surrounded by award winning Beaches. Fishing, Walking, Historical interests. On route to Ceide Fields. 2km off R314 Northbound of Killala.

B&B	3	Ensuite	€25.50	Dinner	-
B&B	1	Standard	€23	Partial Board	-
Single Rate			€36	Child reduction	33.3%

Open: 1st January-20th December

In Kiltimagh

Mrs Mary Carney
HILLCREST
Kilkelly Rd, Kiltimagh, Co Mayo

Kiltimagh
Tel: **094 81112**
Email: **carneyandrea@eircom.net**

Comfortable family home on spacious landscaped grounds. Ideal touring base for West of Ireland. 5 min drive Knock Shrine and Connaught Regional Airport.

B&B	6	Ensuite	€25.50	Dinner	-
B&B	-	Standard	-	Partial Board	-
Single Rate			€38.50	Child reduction	25%

Open: All Year Except Christmas

Knock 1km

Maureen Carney & Family
BURREN
Kiltimagh Road, Knock, Co Mayo

Knock
Tel: **094 88362**　　Fax: **094 88362**
Email: **carneymaureenc@eircom.net**

On R323, west off N17, 1km from roundabout. All ground floor rooms. Hairdryers, electric blankets, TV's. Lounge with tea/coffee making facilities. Private parking.

B&B	4	Ensuite	€25.50	Dinner	-
B&B	-	Standard	-	Partial Board	-
Single Rate			€38.50	Child reduction	33.3%

Open: 1st June-30th September

In Knock

Mrs Kathleen Carty
CARRAMORE HOUSE
Airport Road, Knock, Co Mayo

Knock
Tel: **094 88149**　　Fax: **094 88154**

Family home 500 metres from Shrine. Electric blankets, TV, Hairdryers, Complimentary Tea/Coffee. Routes planned. Guidance on Genealogy Tracing. Convenient to bus stop. Own parking lot.

B&B	6	Ensuite	€25.50/€25.50	Dinner	-
B&B	-	Standard	-	Partial Board	-
Single Rate			€38.50/€38.50	Child reduction	33.3%

Open: 17th March-31st October

In Knock

Ms Mary Coyne
AISHLING HOUSE
Ballyhaunis Road, Knock, Co Mayo

Knock
Tel: **094 88558**

Spacious, warm & welcoming off N17. Tea/Coffee, Private parking. Ideal touring West, historical places, lakes, golf, horse riding. Beside Shrine. Near Airport.

B&B	5	Ensuite	€25.50	Dinner	-
B&B	1	Standard	€23	Partial Board	-
Single Rate			€38.50	Child reduction	33.3%

Open: All Year

In Knock

Taffe Family
ESKERVILLE
Claremorris Rd,
Knock, Co Mayo

Knock
TEL: **094 88413**

Beige Dormer Bungalow situated on Claremorris/Galway Road. In Knock N17. Private Parking. Mature Gardens. Credit cards. Children welcome.

B&B	4	Ensuite	€25.50	Dinner	€17
B&B	1	Standard	€23	Partial Board	€264
Single Rate			€36	Child reduction	33.3%

Open: All Year

In Louisburgh

Mrs Claire Kenny
SPRINGFIELD HOUSE
Westport Rd, Louisburgh,
Co Mayo

Louisburgh
TEL: **098 66289**

On main Louisburgh/Westport Road (R335). Safe sandy Beaches, Sea & River Fishing. Ideal area for Walking, Mountain Climbing & Cycling.

B&B	3	Ensuite	€25.50	Dinner	-
B&B	1	Standard	€23	Partial Board	-
Single Rate			€36	Child reduction	25%

Open: January-November

In Louisburgh

Mrs Ann McNamara
WHITETHORNS
Bunowen Road, Louisburgh,
Co Mayo

Louisburgh
TEL: **098 66062**

Bungalow in scenic location on Bunowen road off R335 at Roman Catholic Church, 5 minutes walk to Louisburgh. Safe sandy Beaches, Walking, Cycling, Fishing.

B&B	4	Ensuite	€26	Dinner	-
B&B	-	Standard	-	Partial Board	-
Single Rate			€38.50	Child reduction	25%

Open: 15th April-30th September

Louisburgh 3km

Mrs Mary Sammin
THE THREE ARCHES
Askelane, Louisburgh,
Co Mayo

Louisburgh
TEL: **098 66484**
EMAIL: **3arches@gofree.indigo.ie**
WEB: **http://gofree.indigo.ie/~3arches**

Modern bungalow with panoramic view. Ideal touring centre for Clare Island. Croagh Patrick. Safe Sandy Beaches. Scenic Walks. Home Cooking.

B&B	2	Ensuite	€26	Dinner	€20
B&B	2	Standard	€23	Partial Board	-
Single Rate			-	Child reduction	50%

Open: 1st May-30th September

Mulranny 1km

Mrs Catherine Reilly
BREEZEMOUNT B&B
Mulranny, Co Mayo

Mulranny
TEL: **098 36145**   FAX: **098 36145**
EMAIL: **kayjim@gofree.indigo.ie**

Modern bungalow with panoramic view, opposite Croagh Patrick on Clew Bay, adjoining Golf Links. Ideal location for touring Achill Island.

B&B	4	Ensuite	€25.50	Dinner	€17
B&B	2	Standard	€24	Partial Board	-
Single Rate			€36	Child reduction	25%

Open: 1st January-23rd December

Mrs Maureen McGovern
ANCHOR HOUSE
The Quay, Newport,
Co Mayo

Newport
TEL: **098 41178**   FAX: **098 41178**
EMAIL:**mcgovernmotors@tinet.ie**

Quiet residential area on the Waterfront. Convenient to Town, Restaurants, Pubs. Ideal base for Touring, Golf, Fishing and Walking. TA Vouchers accepted. B&B from €25.40 to €44.45.

B&B	4	Ensuite	€25.50/€32	Dinner	-
B&B	1	Standard	€25.40	Partial Board	-
Single Rate			€36 /€44.45	Child reduction	25%

In Newport

Open: 1st March-31st October

Maria & Stephen Breen
LINDEN HALL
Altamount Street,
Westport, Co Mayo

Westport
TEL: **098 27005**   FAX: **098 27650**
EMAIL: **lindenhall@iol.ie**
WEB: **www.iol.ie/~lindenhall**

Excellent location in Westport Town. Spacious period townhouse, large rooms, TV & armchairs. Breakfast menu. Walk to hotels, bars & restaurants.

B&B	4	Ensuite	€26/€32	Dinner	-
B&B	1	Standard	€23/€26	Partial Board	-
Single Rate			€36/€38	Child reduction	50%

In Westport

Open: All Year Except Christmas

John & Mary Cafferkey
HAZELBROOK
Deerpark East, Newport Road,
Westport, Co Mayo

Westport
TEL: **098 26865**
EMAIL: **hazelbrookhouse@eircom.net**

Modern home in a quiet residential area. 4 mins walk to Town Centre. Ideally situated for touring the West Coast. Reflexology and Massage available. Car park.

B&B	6	Ensuite	€26/€26	Dinner	-
B&B	-	Standard		Partial Board	-
Single Rate			€39/€39	Child reduction	25%

In Westport

Open: All Year

Ann Cusack
ARD BAWN
Leenane Road, Westport,
Co Mayo

Westport
TEL: **098 26135**

Spacious tastefully decorated bungalow close to Westport on Leenane/Clifden road (N59). 8 minutes walk to Town. Many recommendations, nice views.

B&B	3	Ensuite	€25.50	Dinner	-
B&B	-	Standard	-	Partial Board	-
Single Rate				Child reduction	50%

In Westport

Open: 1st March-31st October

Mary & John Doherty
LUI-NA-GREINE
Castlebar Road, Westport,
Co Mayo

Westport
TEL: **098 25536**

Bungalow on N5 scenic area within walking distance of Town. Spacious gardens. Car park. Recommended "Guide to Ireland", "En Irlande"

B&B	4	Ensuite	€26/€28	Dinner	-
B&B	2	Standard	€23	Partial Board	-
Single Rate			€36/€38.50	Child reduction	50%

Westport 1km

Open: 29th March-29th October

Westport 1km

Brian & Michelle Durcan
INDIAN WELLS
19 Knockranny Village,
Castlebar Road N5,
Westport, Co Mayo

Westport
Tel: **098 28418**

Modern, spacious, colonial style house. 1km from Town Centre. In quiet, exclusive residential area, 400m off N5. All rooms ensuite.

B&B	4	Ensuite	€26/€30	Dinner	-
B&B	-	Standard		Partial Board	-
Single Rate			€38.50/€44	Child reduction	-

Open: 7th January-20th December

Westport 1km

Mrs Vera English
HILLSIDE LODGE
Castlebar Road, Westport,
Co Mayo

Westport
Tel: **098 25668**   Fax: **098 25668**
Email: **veraandjohn@unison.ie**
Web: **www.homepage.eircom.net/~hillsidelodge**

Warm welcoming family home just a short distance from Town. Ideal touring base for Achill, Connemara and Knock. Take N5 from Westport past Shell Garage on left.

B&B	2	Ensuite	€25.50	Dinner	-
B&B	1	Standard	€23	Partial Board	-
Single Rate			€38.50	Child reduction	25%

Open: 1st February-15th December

In Westport

Maureen & Peter Flynn
CEDAR LODGE
Kings Hill, Newport Rd N59,
Westport, Co Mayo

Westport
Tel: **098 25417**   Fax: **098 25417**
Email: **mflynn@esatclear.ie**
Web: **homepage.eircom.net/~cedarlodgewestport**

Welcoming peaceful bungalow, landscaped gardens (Award 1997). Irish hospitality. Great breakfast menu, 6 min walk Town, near Golf. Frommer, Routard, Rough Guide, Best B&B's Recommended.

B&B	4	Ensuite	€26/€28	Dinner	-
B&B	-	Standard	-	Partial Board	-
Single Rate			€39/€43	Child reduction	-

Open: 1st February-20th December

Westport 1km

Mrs Angela Gavin
CARRABAUN HOUSE
Carrabaun, Leenane Road,
Westport, Co Mayo

Westport
Tel: **098 26196**   Fax: **098 28466**
Email: **carrabaun@anu.ie**
Web: **www.anu.ie/carrabaunhouse**

New spacious period house. Panoramic views. Hairdryer, TV, Trouser Press, Tea/Coffee, Electric Blanket, Breakfast menu. Near Golfing, Pubs, Restaurants, N59. AA ◆◆◆◆.

B&B	6	Ensuite	€27/€29	Dinner	-
B&B	-	Standard	-	Partial Board	-
Single Rate			€40/€40	Child reduction	25%

Open: 1st January-21st December

Westport 7km

Mrs Maureen Geraghty
ST BRENDANS
Kilmeena, Westport,
Co Mayo

Westport
Tel: **098 41209**

Dormer type house, 3 guest rooms upstairs and 3 family rooms downstairs. Close to all amenities, Fishing. Ideal touring base. 18 hole and 9 hole golf courses nearby.

B&B	3	Ensuite	€25.50	Dinner	-
B&B	-	Standard	-	Partial Board	-
Single Rate			€38.50	Child reduction	50%

Open: 15th April-30th September

In Westport

Mrs Bridget Gibbons
BROADLANDS
**Quay Road, Westport,
Co Mayo**

Tel: **098 27377**

Large bungalow, situated on the coast road to Louisburgh. Close to Town Centre, Westport Quay, Pubs & Restaurants.

B&B	5	Ensuite	€26.50/€28	Dinner	-
B&B	-	Standard		Partial Board	-
Single Rate			€38.50/€39	Child reduction	-

Open: All Year

Westport 12km

Mrs Beatrice Gill
SEA BREEZE
**Kilsallagh, Westport,
Co Mayo**

Tel: **098 66548**
Email: **seabreeze@eircom.net**
Web: **http://homepage.eircom.net/~beatricegill/**

Comfortable, friendly home, breathtaking views. From Westport take R335 to avail of hospitality and delicious food. Close to Pubs, Restaurants, Croagh Patrick, Beach.

B&B	3	Ensuite	€26/€27	Dinner	€20
B&B	-	Standard		Partial Board	-
Single Rate			€38.50/€38.50	Child reduction	50%

Open: All Year

In Westport

Joseph Higgins
AISLINGS TOWNHOUSE
**Castlebar Street, Westport,
Co Mayo**

Tel: **098 29230**

Newly constructed townhouse. Family run. Built on historical site. Guaranteed comfort, hospitality, and all the comforts of a modern home. Opposite Castlecourt.

B&B	4	Ensuite	€25.50/€31.74	Dinner	-
B&B	-	Standard		Partial Board	-
Single Rate			€38.50	Child reduction	-

Open: 15th March-31st October

Westport 2km

Mary Hughes
ROCKVILLE
**Moyhastin, Westport,
Co Mayo**

Tel: **098 28949**   Fax: **098 28949**
Email: **marhugh@gofree.indigo.ie**
Web: **www.rockvilleguesthouse.com**

Majestic peaceful setting. Award winning gardens. View of Lake, Croagh Patrick and Clew Bay. Guest lounge, breakfast menu, electric blankets. Golf, Walking, Cycling.

B&B	4	Ensuite	€25.50/€27	Dinner	-
B&B	-	Standard		Partial Board	-
Single Rate			€38.50/€38.50	Child reduction	50%

Open: 1st March-31st October

Mary Jordan
ROSMO HOUSE
**Rosbeg, Westport,
Co. Mayo**

Tel: **098 25925**
Email: **rosmohouse@unison.ie**

Purpose built house. Quiet location on T39/R335 Coast Road. Short distance Croagh Patrick, Harbour, Pubs, Restaurants. Satellite TV, Video, Power Showers, Tea/Coffee facilities. Car Park.

B&B	4	Ensuite	€25.50/€28	Dinner	-
B&B	-	Standard	-	Partial Board	-
Single Rate				Child reduction	25%

Westport 1.5km

Open: 1st May-31st October

Mary Kelly
BIRCHSIDE
Streamstown, Belclare,
Westport, Co Mayo

Westport

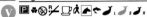

TEL: **098 25406**
EMAIL: **edkelly@eircom.net**

New spacious house on T39/R335 Coast Road. Close to Beaches, Pubs, Restaurants. Panoramic views Croagh Patrick, Clew Bay. Private parking. Tea/Coffee facilities. 2 km Quay.

B&B	2	Ensuite	€26/€28	Dinner	-
B&B	1	Standard	€25/€25	Partial Board	-
Single Rate			€36/€38	Child reduction	50%

Westport 4.5km

Open: May-September

Robert & Sheila Kilkelly
ST ANTHONY'S
Distillery Rd, Westport,
Co Mayo

Westport

TEL: **098 28887**   FAX: **098 25172**
EMAIL: **robert@st-anthonys.com**
WEB: **www.st-anthonys.com**

Enjoy a little luxury in an 1820 Built Town House. Private parking on one acre of grounds. Riverside. Tea/Coffee facilities. Two ensuites with Jacuzzi.

B&B	5	Ensuite	€30/€35	Dinner	-
B&B	-	Standard	-	Partial Board	-
Single Rate			-	Child reduction	-

In Westport

Open: All Year

Ronan & Eithne Larkin
AODHNAIT
Rosbeg, Westport,
Co Mayo

Westport

TEL: **098 25784**   FAX: **098 26258**
EMAIL: **aodhnait@eircom.net**
WEB: **www.aodhnait.ie**

Quiet country home on the shores of Clew Bay. Ideal base for Mayo/Connemara. Walking distance of Harbour. Home baking, Breakfast menu. AA ◆◆◆◆. On coast road.

B&B	4	Ensuite	€26/€30	Dinner	-
B&B	-	Standard	-	Partial Board	-
Single Rate			€38.50/€40	Child reduction	25%

Westport 3km

Open: 6th January-18th December

Mrs Angela McDonagh
DOVEDALE
Rampart Wood,
Golf Course Rd,
Westport, Co Mayo

Westport

TEL: **098 25154**   FAX: **098 25154**
EMAIL: **dovedale@ireland.com**

Modern home set in woodland surroundings. Mature gardens. Private parking. 10 mins walk to Town Centre. Golf, Horse riding, Sailing. Route N59, Newport road 1km.

B&B	4	Ensuite	€25.50/€28	Dinner	-
B&B	1	Standard	€24/€25.50	Partial Board	-
Single Rate			€36/€40	Child reduction	-

Westport 1km

Open: 1st April-31st October

Mrs Margaret Madigan
ADARE HOUSE
Quay Road, Westport,
Co Mayo

Westport

TEL: **098 26102**   FAX: **098 26202**
EMAIL: **adarehouse@eircom.net**
WEB: **homepage.eircom.net/~adarehouse/**

New house T39/R335. 7 minutes walk Town, Pubs, Restaurants. Panoramic views. Orthopaedic beds. Guest Lounge. Tea/Coffee facilities. Breakfast menu.

B&B	5	Ensuite	€26/€28	Dinner	-
B&B	1	Standard	€23/€25	Partial Board	-
Single Rate			€36/€36	Child reduction	50%

In Westport

Open: 1st January-20th December

Mrs Mary Mitchell
CILLCOMAN LODGE
Rosbeg, Westport, Co Mayo

Westport
TEL: **098 26379**
EMAIL: **cillcomanlodge@eircom.net**
WEB: **cillcomanlodge.com**

Situated on Coast Road. Quiet location with parking facilities and garden. Guest TV lounge. Adjacent to Harbour, Pubs & Restaurants.

B&B	6	Ensuite	€25.50/€28	Dinner	-
B&B	-	Standard		Partial Board	-
Single Rate			€38.50/€38.50	Child reduction	33.3%

Westport 1.5km

Open: 1st April-30th October

Mrs Ann O'Flaherty
GLENDERAN
Rosbeg, Westport,
Co Mayo

Westport
TEL: **098 26585**   FAX: **098 27352**
EMAIL: **glenderan@anu.ie**
WEB: **www.anu.ie/glenderan/index.html**

New house, quiet location beside Harbour. Walking distance Pubs/Restaurants. Satellite TV, Coffee/Tea, Hairdryers bedrooms. Car Park. T39/R335. Past Quays Pub, 200 mtrs turn left.

B&B	4	Ensuite	€27/€28	Dinner	-
B&B	2	Standard	€25/€26	Partial Board	-
Single Rate			€36/€40	Child reduction	50%

Westport 1.5km

Open: 1st March-31st October

Mrs Kay O'Malley
RIVERBANK HOUSE
Rosbeg, Westport Harbour,
Co Mayo

Westport
TEL: **098 25719**

Country peacefulness, on T39/R335. Walking distance Pubs/Restaurants, Home baking, Car Park, Tea/Coffee facilities. Recommended 300 best B&B Guide, AA ◆◆◆.

B&B	8	Ensuite	€27/€28	Dinner	-
B&B	-	Standard	-	Partial Board	-
Single Rate			€38.50	Child reduction	33.3%

Westport 2km

Open: 15th March-31st October

Mrs Marian O'Malley
MOHER HOUSE
Liscarney, Westport,
Co Mayo

Westport
TEL: **098 21360**
EMAIL: **moherbandb@eircom.net**
WEB: **homepage.eircom.net/~moherhouse**

Country home on N59. Award winning garden '99. Breakfast, Dinner, Veg Menu. Home cooking. Afternoon Tea on arrival. Peat fire in lounge. Off Western Way. Walkers Best B&B. Pub transport.

B&B	3	Ensuite	€26 /€27	Dinner	€18
B&B	1	Standard	€23/€26	Partial Board	-
Single Rate			€36/€39	Child reduction	33.3%

Westport 8km

Open: 1st March-31st October

Vincent & Catherine O'Reilly
EMANIA
Castlebar Road, Sheeaune,
Westport, Co Mayo

Westport
TEL: **098 26459/28751**
EMAIL: **vinnieoreilly@hotmail.com**

Country dwelling, own grounds. Private parking. Located on N5 Road between Westport and Castlebar. Friendly, hospitable atmosphere. Tea/Coffee on arrival.

B&B	2	Ensuite	€25.50/€25.50	Dinner	€18
B&B	2	Standard	€23/€23	Partial Board	-
Single Rate			€36/€38.50	Child reduction	50%

Westport 1.3km

Open: June-September

Westport 9km

Mrs Catherine Owens
SEACREST HOUSE
**Claggan, Kilmeena,
Westport, Co Mayo**

Westport
TEL: **098 41631**

Mountain/sea views, breakfast menu, home baking, dinner on request. Beside Golf course. Excellent Fishing/Walking area. Signposted on N59.

B&B	4	Ensuite	€26	Dinner	€18
B&B	2	Standard	€23/€23	Partial Board	€264
Single Rate			€36/€39	Child reduction	-

Open: 15th April-31st September

Westport 1km

Mrs Noreen Reddington
BROOKLODGE
**Deerpark East, Newport Rd,
Westport, Co Mayo**

Westport
TEL: **098 26654**
EMAIL: **brooklodgebandb@eircom.net**
WEB: **homepage.eircom.net/~brooklodgebandb**

Modern home, quiet residential area. 5 minutes walk Town. Warm welcome, with Tea/Coffee on arrival. Recommended 400 Best B&B's Ireland.

B&B	4	Ensuite	€26/€28	Dinner	-
B&B	-	Standard	-	Partial Board	-
Single Rate			€38.50/€38.50	Child reduction	50%

Open: 1st March-31st October

In Westport

Julie & Aiden Redmond
HARMONY HEIGHTS
**Kings Hill, Newport Road,
Westport, Co Mayo**

Westport
TEL: **098 25491**

Original family home-traditional Irish hospitality. Elevated bungalow with veranda, flowers/shrubs. Route 59. Third turn left from Newport Road Bridge.

B&B	2	Ensuite	€25.50	Dinner	-
B&B	1	Standard	€23	Partial Board	-
Single Rate			€36/€36	Child reduction	25%

Open: All Year Except Christmas

In Westport

Mrs Michelle Reidy
WOODVILLE LODGE
**Knockranny, Westport,
Co Mayo**

Westport
TEL: **098 27822**   FAX: **098 27822**
EMAIL: **mra@anu.ie**
WEB: **www.yeilding.com/woodville_lodge.htm**

Woodville Lodge is very close to many fine Pubs and excellent Restaurants. An ideal location for touring Connemara and Achill Island. Breathtaking scenery.

B&B	4	Ensuite	€25.50/€30	Dinner	-
B&B	-	Standard	-	Partial Board	-
Single Rate			€38.50/€45	Child reduction	25%

Open: 1st January-20th December

Westport

A Ruane
ANNA LODGE
**6 Distillery Court, Westport,
Co Mayo**

Westport
TEL: **098 28219**
EMAIL: **ruane@ireland.com**

Welcoming new Town house set in a cul-de-sac surrounded by the magnificent original Eighteenth Century Distillery walls.

B&B	3	Ensuite	€25.50/€27	Dinner	-
B&B	-	Standard	-	Partial Board	-
Single Rate			€40/€40	Child reduction	-

Open: 1st January-20th December

Mrs Marie Ruane
WOODVIEW HOUSE
**Buckwaria, Castlebar Rd N5,
Westport, Co Mayo**

Tel: **098 27879**
Email: **truane@iol.ie**
Web: **www.woodviewhouse.com**

New home, quiet location on own ground. Peaceful wooded area. Private parking. Award winning Gardens and House. 0.5km off N5. Walking distance of Town. Breakfast Menu.

B&B	6	Ensuite	€26/€29	Dinner	-
B&B	-	Standard		Partial Board	-
Single Rate			€40/€44	Child reduction	25%

Westport 1km

Open: 1st February-30th November

Mrs Valerie Sammon
AILLMORE
**Knockranny Village,
Castlebar Rd N5,
Westport, Co Mayo**

Tel: **098 27818**
Email: **vsammon@eircom.net**
Web: **www.westport.mayo-ireland.ie/Aillmore.htm**

Cosy, modern home in peaceful location. Just 15 mins walk to Town. Extensive Local/Irish history Library available. 500m off N5. Warm welcome assured.

B&B	4	Ensuite	€25.50/€30	Dinner	-
B&B	-	Standard		Partial Board	-
Single Rate			€40/€45	Child reduction	50%

Westport 1km

Open: All Year Except Christmas

Christine Scahill
LURGAN HOUSE
**Carnalurgan, Westport,
Co Mayo**

Tel: **098 27126**   Fax: **098 27126**
Email: **lurganhouse@eircom.net**

Georgian house N59/R335. Spacious bedrooms. Central to suggested driving tours. Close to Pubs/Restaurants/Sandy Beaches/Golf/Fishing/Croagh Patrick.

B&B	3	Ensuite	€25.50/€25.50	Dinner	-
B&B	1	Standard	€23	Partial Board	-
Single Rate			€36/€38.09	Child reduction	50%

Westport 1km

Open: 31st January-25th November

Mrs Rita Sheridan
ALTAMONT HOUSE
**Ballinrobe Road,Westport,
Co Mayo**

Tel: **098 25226**

Pre-famine (1848). Tastefully modernised home, 5 minutes walk from Town Centre. Interesting Garden for guests use. Recommended "300 Best B&B's Ireland"

B&B	5	Ensuite	€27	Dinner	-
B&B	3	Standard	€25	Partial Board	-
Single Rate			-	Child reduction	25%

In Westport

Open: 15th March-1st November

Peter Last & Ingeborg Vogt
TIGHBEAG
**Glaspatrick, Murrisk,
Westport, Co Mayo**

Tel: **098 64988**   Fax: **098 64988**
Email: **tighbeag@anu.ie**
Web: **www.anu.ie/tighbeag**

Beautifully situated overlooking Clew Bay & Bertra Strand guarded by Croagh Patrick. Tighbeag is the ideal place for a walking, relaxing or golf holiday.

B&B	4	Ensuite	€25.50	Dinner	€17
B&B	-	Standard	-	Partial Board	€264
Single Rate			€38.50	Child reduction	50%

Westport 8km

Open: All Year

In Westport

Bredgeen & Andy Walsh
CALHAME HOUSE
3 Knockranny Village,
Knockranny, Westport,
Co Mayo

Westport
TEL: 098 28138   FAX: 098 28138

Experience the comforts of our spacious ensuite rooms with breakfast menu, TV, Hairdryer, Tea/Coffee in all rooms. Private carpark. 10 mins walk to town 400m of N5.

B&B	4	Ensuite	€25.50/€28	Dinner	-
B&B	-	Standard	-	Partial Board	-
Single Rate			€38.50/€44.50	Child reduction	25%

Open: 1st January-22nd December

Westport 5km

Aidan & Mary Walsh
EAGLE BROOK
Knockrooskey, Westport,
Co Mayo

Westport
TEL: **098 35347**
EMAIL: **eaglebrook@eircom.net**
WEB: **homepage.eircom.net/~eaglebrook**

Modern country home. Main Galway/Westport Road (R330). Adjacent to Ballintubber Abbey. Easy access to Croagh Patrick. Award winning garden with panoramic views.

B&B	2	Ensuite	€25.50/€25.50	Dinner	-
B&B	2	Standard	€23/€23	Partial Board	-
Single Rate			€36/€38.50	Child reduction	-

Open: 1st June-10th September

Clew Bay, Co. Mayo

The county that gave Ireland its last High King and modern Ireland its first President.
Rich in wonderful landscape containing Rivers, Lakes, Mountains, Moorlands, Archaeological Features and Forest Park.
A fisherman's paradise, also numerous Golf Courses and other leisure activities.

Mrs Noreen Fayne
FAIRWAYS
Hodson Bay, Athlone,
Co Roscommon

Athlone
TEL: 0902 94492

Dormer bungalow on N61 - 6km Athlone. 1km from Golf Club, Hodson Bay Hotel and Lough Ree - Mature Gardens - Extensive Parking.

B&B	3	Ensuite	€25.50	Dinner	-
B&B	-	Standard	-	Partial Board	-
Single Rate			-	Child reduction	-

Athlone 6km

Open: 1st March-30th November

Mrs Catherine Harney
REESIDE
Barrymore, Athlone,
Co Roscommon

Athlone
TEL: 0902 92051
EMAIL: reeside@oceanfree.net
WEB: www.reeside.com

Country Home on four acres. Road N61, beside Lough Ree & River Shannon. Close to Hodson Bay Hotel, Athlone Golf Club. Luxury cruiser available for trips on Lough Ree.

B&B	4	Ensuite	€26/€26	Dinner	-
B&B	-	Standard	-	Partial Board	-
Single Rate			€38.50/€38.50	Child reduction	50%

Athlone 5km

Open: 1st January-21st December

Mrs Teresa Hegarty
CASTLESIDE HOUSE
Kiltoom, Athlone,
Co Roscommon

Athlone
TEL: 0902 89195   FAX: 0902 89195
EMAIL: castlesidehouse@eircom.net

Quiet Country home adjacent Moyvannion Castle. Convenient to Lough Ree, Fishing, Boating, Water Sports, Golf, Hodson Bay Hotel, Horse Riding.

B&B	4	Ensuite	€25.50/€30	Dinner	€17
B&B	1	Standard	-	Partial Board	€264
Single Rate			€38.50/€40	Child reduction	50%

Athlone 7km

Open: 1st March-30th November

Gerald & Eleanor Kelly
LOUGHREE LODGE
Kiltoom, Athlone,
Co Roscommon

Athlone
TEL: 0902 89214   FAX: 0902 89349
EMAIL: eleanorcousinskelly@hotmail.com

Spacious residence situated on beautiful landscaped gardens overlooking Lough Ree. On N61, 7km from Athlone. Relaxed friendly atmosphere.

B&B	4	Ensuite	€25.50	Dinner	-
B&B	-	Standard	-	Partial Board	-
Single Rate			€38.50	Child reduction	25%

Athlone 7km

Open: 1st March-31st October

Nora Ward
CARRICK VIEW
**Curraghboy, Athlone,
Co Roscommon**

Athlone
TEL: **0902 88294**

Dormer bungalow in peaceful country surroundings 6km off N61. TV Lounge, Private parking. Ideal base for Touring, Golfing, Fishing. Hodson Bay 8km.

			Dinner	-
B&B	4	Ensuite	€25.50	
B&B	-	Standard		Partial Board	-
Single Rate			€38.50	Child reduction	50%

Athlone 12km

Open: 1st March-31st October

Mary Cooney
CESH CORRAN
**Abbey Tce, Sligo Rd,
Boyle, Co Roscommon**

Boyle
TEL: **079 62265**   FAX: **079 62265**
EMAIL: **cooneym@iol.ie**
WEB: **www.marycooney.com**

Beautifully restored Edwardian town house on old Dublin/Sligo road, overlooking Boyle Abbey and River. Private parking. Near King House Forrest Park, Lakes.

				Dinner	-
B&B	3	Ensuite	€30/€40	Partial Board	-
B&B	-	Standard			
Single Rate			€40/€45	Child reduction	25%

In Boyle

Open: 1st January-23rd December

Carmel & Martin Dolan
AVONLEA
**Carrick Road, Boyle,
Co Roscommon**

Boyle
TEL: **079 62538**

Family run modern house on Carrick road R294, off N4 Dublin/Sligo road. Close to Forest Park Hotel, Boyle Abbey, King House, Walking route and Forest Park.

				Dinner	-
B&B	2	Ensuite	€25.50/€27.50	Partial Board	-
B&B	1	Standard	€23/€25		
Single Rate			€36/€36	Child reduction	25%

Boyle 1km

Open: All Year

Brenda McCormack
ROSDARRIG
**Dublin Road, Boyle,
Co Roscommon**

Boyle
TEL: **079 62040**
EMAIL: **rosdarrig@yahoo.co.uk**

Modern home on edge of Town. Irish hospitality. Walk to Pubs/Restaurants. Views Curlieu mountains/surrounding farmland. Close to Boyle Abbey/Forest Park Hotel/ Lakes/Forest Park.

				Dinner	-
B&B	5	Ensuite	€25.50	Partial Board	-
B&B	-	Standard	-		
Single Rate			€38.50	Child reduction	25%

Boyle 1km

Open: 1st March-31st October

Christina & Martin Mitchell
ABBEY HOUSE
Boyle, Co Roscommon

Boyle
TEL: **079 62385**   FAX: **079 62385**

Victorian house nestled between Boyle River and Abbey. Within walking distance of Town Centre and Forest Park. Large mature gardens.

				Dinner	-
B&B	5	Ensuite	€28/€28	Partial Board	-
B&B	1	Standard	€25.50/€25.50		
Single Rate			€36/€36	Child reduction	25%

Boyle 1km

Open: 1st March-31st October

Castlerea 1km

Mrs Rita Morgan
ARMCASHEL B&B
Knock Rd, Castlerea,
Co Roscommon

Castlerea
TEL: **0907 20117**
EMAIL: **morgan_rita@hotmail.com**

Modern spacious dormer bungalow on N60. Peaceful surroundings overlooking Clonalis Estate. Base for touring. Daily train to and from Dublin. Knock 25 mins. Galway 60 mins.

B&B	6	Ensuite	€25.50/€27	Dinner	-
B&B	-	Standard	-	Partial Board	-
Single Rate			€38.50	Child reduction	33.3%

Open: 7th January-21st December

In Rooskey Village

Mrs Carmel Davis
AVONDALE HOUSE
Rooskey, Carrick-on-Shannon,
Co Roscommon

Rooskey
TEL: **078 38095**
EMAIL: **avondalerooskey@eircom.net**

Luxury two storey house family run. Highly recommended. Peaceful surroundings. Situated near river Shannon, Famine Museum 12km. Fishing nearby. Midway Dublin/Donegal.

B&B	4	Ensuite	€25.50/€25.50	Dinner	-
B&B	-	Standard	-	Partial Board	-
Single Rate			€38.50/€38.50	Child reduction	33.3%

Open: 1st January-30th November

Roscommon

Catherine Campbell
WESTWAY
Galway Road, Roscommon,
Co Roscommon

Roscommon
TEL: **0903 26927**

Easy to find on N63 within walking distance of Roscommon Town. Spacious bedrooms. Relax in our conservatory with complimentary tea and coffee.

B&B	4	Ensuite	€25.50/€25.50	Dinner	-
B&B	-	Standard	-	Partial Board	-
Single Rate			-	Child reduction	50%

Open: All Year Except Christmas

Roscommon 2km

Mrs Kathleen Carthy
HILLCREST HOUSE
Racecourse Road,
Roscommon,
Co Roscommon

Roscommon
TEL: **0903 25201**

Warm hospitality in a modern country house in scenic location. Ideal base for touring West and Midlands. Situated on the N60 beside Roscommon Racecourse.

B&B	4	Ensuite	€25.50/€25.50	Dinner	-
B&B	-	Standard	-	Partial Board	-
Single Rate			€38.50/€38.50	Child reduction	50%

Open: All Year

In Roscommon

Noelle Hynes
RIVERSIDE HOUSE
Riverside Avenue,
Circular Road, Roscommon,
Co Roscommon

Roscommon
TEL: **0903 26897**

Modern dormer bungalow set in mature grounds in Roscommon Town within walking distance of Golf course, Castle and Museum.

B&B	2	Ensuite	€25.50	Dinner	-
B&B	2	Standard	€23	Partial Board	-
Single Rate			€38.50	Child reduction	50%

Open: All Year

Strokestown

Mrs Ans Clyne
LAKESHORE LODGE
Kilglass Lake, Clooneen,
Strokestown, Co Roscommon

TEL: **078 33966**   FAX: **078 33966**
EMAIL: **lakeshorelodgeireland@eircom.net**
WEB: **www.lakeshorelodgeireland.com**

Modern home with gardens to Kilglass Lake. Jetty, Angling boats. 7km Strokestown Park House-Famine museum. Dutch, French, German spoken. Ideal fishing base.

B&B	4	Ensuite	€26/€30	Dinner	€18
B&B	-	Standard	-	Partial Board	-
Single Rate			€39/€41	Child reduction	-

Strokestown 7km

Open: 1st April-30th September

Public Holidays for 2002

New Years Day	-	Tuesday 1st January	(R.of Ire. & N. Ire.)
Bank Holiday	-	Monday 19th March	(R.of Ire. & N. Ire.)
Good Friday	-	Friday 29th March	(R.of Ire. & N. Ire.)
Easter Monday	-	Monday 1st April	(R.of Ire. & N. Ire.)
May Day Holiday	-	Monday 6th May	(R.of Ire. & N. Ire.)
Bank Holiday	-	Monday 27th May	(N.Ire.)
June Holiday	-	Monday 3rd June	(R.of Ire)
Orangeman's Day	-	Friday 12th July	(N.Ire.)
August Holiday	-	Monday 5th August	(R.of Ire)
Bank Holiday	-	Monday 26th August	(N.Ire.)
October Holiday	-	Monday 28th October	(R.of Ire)
Christmas Day	-	Wednesday 25th December	(R.of Ire. & N. Ire.)
St Stephen's Day	-	Thurday 26th December	(R.of Ire. & N. Ire.)

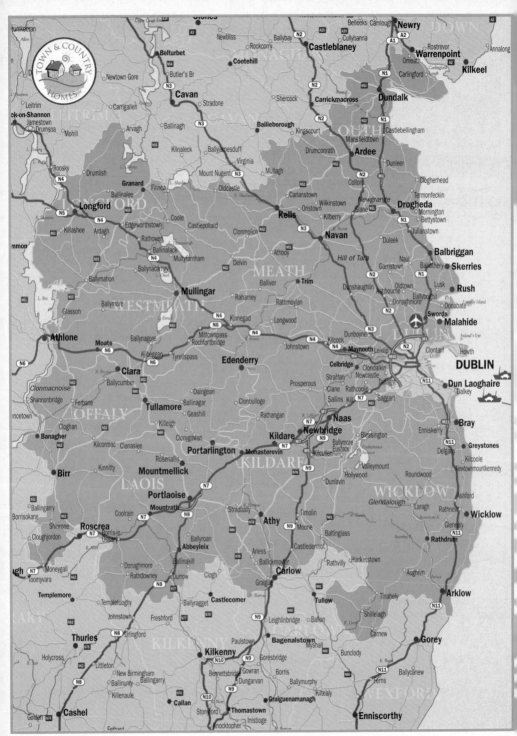

Midlands East

Where Dreams Come True......

The East Coast & Midlands Region of Ireland stretches from the golden beaches of the East Coast to the mountains of Wicklow, the Cooley Peninsula and the Slieve Blooms, to the majestic Shannon in the Midlands, this the most varied of Ireland's holiday regions. In this part of Ireland there is something for everyone - all types of activity holidays, including some of the finest parkland and links courses in the world; outstanding angling, both freshwater and sea; superb equestrian facilities, including the Irish Racing Classics; spectacular walking terrain, relaxing cruises and exciting adventure breaks.

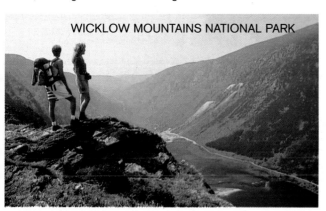

WICKLOW MOUNTAINS NATIONAL PARK

The range of visitor attractions, ancient monuments including Newgrange, heritage sites such as Clonmacnoise and Glendalough, great houses and gardens, quality restaurants and interesting comfortable affordable accommodation make the East Coast and Midlands the ideal location for that well earned holiday break.

Area Representatives

KILDARE
Mrs Agnes Donoghue, Woodcourte House, Moone, Athy, Co Kildare
Tel: 0507 24167 Fax: 0507 24326
LAOIS
Mrs Lily Saunders, Rosedene, Limerick Road, Portlaoise, Co Laois
Tel: 0502 22345 Fax: 0502 22345
LOUTH
Mrs Marian Witherow, Krakow, 190 Ard Easmuinn, Dundalk, Co Louth
Tel: 042 9337535
MEATH
Ann Marie Russell, Sycamores, Dublin Rd, Navan, Co. Meath
Tel: 046 23719 Fax: 046 21261
Mrs Anne Finnegan, Woodtown House, Athboy, Co Meath
Tel: 046 35022 Fax: 046 35022
OFFALY
Ms Marguerite Kirwan, Treascon Lodge, Portarlington, Co Offaly
Tel: 0502 43183 Fax: 0502 43183
WESTMEATH
Mr Jim Denby, Shelmalier House, Cartrontroy, Athlone, Co Westmeath
Tel: 0902 72245/72145 Fax: 0902 73190
WICKLOW
Mrs Fiona Byrne, Glen na Smole, Ashtown Lane, Marlton Road, Wicklow, Co Wicklow   Tel: 0404 67945 Fax: 0404 68155
Mrs Ann Griffin, Lettermore, Corballis, Rathdrum, Co Wicklow
Tel: 0404 46506   Fax: 0404 43183

ℹ️ Tourist Information Offices
**OPEN ALL YEAR
EXCEPT LONGFORD TOWN**

Mullingar
Market House
Tel: 044 48650

Dundalk
Jocelyn Street
Tel: 042 9335484

Wicklow
Rialto House
Fitzwilliam Square
Tel: 0404 69117

Portlaoise
James Fintan Lalor Ave
0502 21178

Trim
Mill Street
046 37111

Longford Town
Longford UDC
Market Square
Tel: 043 46566

Website: **www.ecoast-midlands.travel.ie**

On Dublin's doorstep. Renowned for Horse-racing, The Curragh, Naas, Punchestown and the National Stud. Rich in history, abounding in great houses, Japanese and Arcadian gardens and Forest Park. Excellent golf clubs and Peatland Interpretative Centre, Canals, Angling and Cruising - a visitors paradise.

Agnes & Tony Donoghue
WOODCOURTE HOUSE
Moone, Athy, Co Kildare

Athy

TEL: **0507 24167**   FAX: **0507 24326**
EMAIL: **woodcourthouse@hotmail.com**

Country home with extensive gardens. In woodland setting. On N9. 35 miles Dublin, hourly bus service. Taxi available. Close to Golf courses, Race tracks, Fishing, Lovely Walks locally.

B&B	3	Ensuite	€30/€32	Dinner	€20
B&B	1	Standard	€27.74/€28	Partial Board	€270
Single Rate			€36/€38	Child reduction	25%

Athy 5km

Open: All Year

Mr Myles Doyle
BALLINAGAPPA
COUNTRY HOUSE
Clane, Co Kildare

Clane

TEL: **045 892087**   FAX: **045 892087**
EMAIL: **ballinagappahouse@eircom.net**
WEB: **www.ballinagappa.com**

1862 period Georgian country house. Kept in original Georgian style. High class country cooking a warm welcome on our doorstep. RAC ◆◆◆◆◆, Sparkling Diamond.

B&B	2	Ensuite	€44.50/€44.50	Dinner	-
B&B	1	Standard		Partial Board	-
Single Rate			€44.50/€51	Child reduction	-

Clane 3km

Open: All Year

Ms Una Healy
STRAFFAN B&B
Dublin Rd, Straffan,
Co Kildare

Clane/Straffan

TEL: **01 6272386**
EMAIL: **judj@gofree.indigo.ie**
BUS NO: **123, 120**

Spacious gardens, Power showers. Barberstown Castle and Kclub 2mins. Golf, Fishing, Mondello, Goffs nearby. Dublin 17 miles. Airport 45 mins. Exit M4 at Maynooth, Exit N7 at Kill.

B&B	3	Ensuite	€30/€40	Dinner	-
B&B	-	Standard		Partial Board	-
Single Rate			€38.50/€45	Child reduction	25%

Clane 4.8km

Open: 1st January-22nd December

Mr Brian Lynch
KERRY'S
Dublin Road,
Clane, Co Kildare

Clane

TEL: **045 892601**
EMAIL: **kerrysbb@hotmail.com**
BUS NO: **120, 123**

Peaceful home on Dublins doorstep. Dublin 30 min, Airport/Ferries 40 mins, Pubs/Restaurants 1 min. Curragh/Naas/Punchestown race courses, Mondello nearby. Car park.

B&B	4	Ensuite	€25.50/€30	Dinner	-
B&B	-	Standard		Partial Board	-
Single Rate			€38.50/€50	Child reduction	50%

In Clane Village

Open: 2nd January-22nd December

"The Laurels"

In Clane

Mrs Mary Lynch
THE LAURELS
**Dublin Road, Clane,
Co Kildare**

Clane
TEL: **045 868274**

Dublin 30 mins drive. Bus to and from City Centre. Convenient to Airport/Ferries.

B&B	3	Ensuite	€27	Dinner	-
B&B	-	Standard	-	Partial Board	-
Single Rate			€38.50	Child reduction	50%

Open: 1st May-30th September

Clane 4.5km

Ms Maura Timoney
SHRIFF LODGE
**Painstown on R407,
Clane, Co Kildare**

Clane
TEL: **045 869282**　FAX: **045 869982**
EMAIL: **shrifflodge@eircom.net**
WEB: **homepage.eircom.net/~shrifflodge**

On R407, Dublin 20 miles, M4 6 miles. Convenient Airport/Ferries, Curragh, Naas, Punchestown Races. Donadea Forest Park, Golf K Club, Knockanally, Pinetrees.

B&B	3	Ensuite	€26/€30	Dinner	-
B&B	-	Standard	-	Partial Board	-
Single Rate			€35/€41	Child reduction	-

Open: April-October

Kilcock 4km

Mrs Kathleen Farrell
BREEZY HEIGHTS
**Cappagh, Kilcock,
Co Kildare**

Kilcock
TEL: **0405 41183**

2 mins off Dublin/Galway N4 road. Dublin 30 mins. Convenient to Airport/Ferries. Quiet & peaceful. Golf, Fishing nearby.

B&B	2	Ensuite	€25.50 /€25.50	Dinner	-
B&B	1	Standard	€23/€23	Partial Board	-
Single Rate			€36/€36	Child reduction	25%

Open: 31st March-30th November

The Foran Family
HEATHERVILLE B&B
**Shaughlins Glen, Confey,
Leixlip, Co Kildare**

Leixlip
TEL: **01 6245156/6060923**
EMAIL: **forans@iol.ie**
BUS NO: **66**

Leixlip 3km

Rural setting. 2 miles Leixlip, 12 miles Dublin, 30 mins Airport/Ferry. Secure parking. Exit M4/N4 into Leixlip Town. Right at traffic lights to T junction, left 1.2miles.

B&B	3	Ensuite	€28/€32	Dinner	-
B&B	-	Standard	-	Partial Board	-
Single Rate			€38.50	Child reduction	50%

Open: 1st January-22nd December

Maynooth 2km

Mrs Maureen Downes
AARONBEG
**Moyglare, Maynooth,
Co Kildare**

Maynooth
TEL: **01 6292074**
EMAIL: **aaronbeg@eircom.net**
WEB: **www.aaronbeg.bigstep.com**

New two storey purpose built bed & breakfast situated in rural area. Beside Moyglare Stud Farm.

B&B	4	Ensuite	€30/€30	Dinner	-
B&B	-	Standard	-	Partial Board	-
Single Rate			€38.50/€38.50	Child reduction	50%

Open: 15th January-15th December

Monasterevin 1km

Annette Cullen
THE GABLES
Coole, Monasterevin,
Co Kildare

Monasterevin

TEL: **045 525564**   FAX: **045 525564**
EMAIL: **thegables@eircom.net**

Enjoy excellent accomodation in "The Venice of Ireland". Our home is just a short picturesque walk across the aqueduct from the town. Dublin 50 minutes.

B&B	2	Ensuite	€25.50/€30	Dinner	-
B&B	1	Standard	€23/€26	Partial Board	-
Single Rate			€36/€40	Child reduction	50%

Open: 31st March- 31st October

Naas 4km

Mrs Bridie Doherty
TWO MILE HOUSE
Naas, Co Kildare

Naas

TEL: **045 879824**

Peaceful location - 200 yds off N9 Dublin/Waterford Road. Dublin 30 mins drive. Convenient to Airport and Ferries.

B&B	3	Ensuite	€27/€30	Dinner	-
B&B	-	Standard		Partial Board	-
Single Rate			€40/€40	Child reduction	50%

Open: 2nd February-2nd November

Mrs Olive Hennessy
DUN AONGHUS
Beggars End, Naas,
Co Kildare

Naas

TEL: **045 875126**   FAX: **045 898069**
EMAIL: **dunaonghus@hotmail.com**

Tranquil location near town. Just off R410. 4 mins N7. Ideal for visiting Kildare, Dublin, Wicklow. Golf, Equestrian horseracing. 1 hour Airport and Ferryports.

B&B	4	Ensuite	€28/€33	Dinner	-
B&B	2	Standard	€25/€30	Partial Board	-
Single Rate			€32/€42	Child reduction	25%

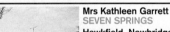

Naas 2km

Open: 2nd January-20th December

Newbridge 3km

Mrs Kathleen Garrett
SEVEN SPRINGS
Hawkfield, Newbridge,
Co Kildare

Newbridge

TEL: **045 431677**

Bungalow, beside Newbridge and N7. Convenient to National Stud, Japanese Gardens, Curragh, Naas. Punchestown Race Course, Boat, Airport, Dog-racing & Mondello nearby.

B&B	3	Ensuite	€27.94/€33	Dinner	€18
B&B	-	Standard	-	Partial Board	-
Single Rate			€38.50/€38.50	Child reduction	50%

Open: 1st May-31st October

In Newbridge

Mrs Breda Kelly
BELLA VISTA
105 Moorefield Park,
Newbridge, Co Kildare

Newbridge

TEL: **045 431047**   FAX: **045 438259**
EMAIL: **belavista@eircom.net**
WEB: **www.bellavistaireland.com**

Long established residence in quiet residential area. Convenient to Curragh, Punchestown, Japanese Gardens. Rooms en-suite, TV, Video, Hairdryers, Tea-making facilities.

B&B	4	Ensuite	€27/€38	Dinner	€18
B&B	-	Standard	-	Partial Board	-
Single Rate			€38.50/€44	Child reduction	25%

Open: All Year

Mary O'Shea
KERRYHILL
Morristown, Biller,
Newbridge, Co Kildare

Newbridge
TEL: **045 432433**

Spacious bungalow, Private Car Park, Easy Access, Japanese Gardens, National Stud, Airport, Ferries, Horse, Dog, Motor Racing.

B&B	2	Ensuite	€28/€35	Dinner	-
B&B	1	Standard	€26/€30	Partial Board	-
Single Rate			€40/€40	Child reduction	**25%**

Newbridge 1km

Open: 1st March-31st October

Ireland
Car Hire Operators 2002

Approved by the Car Rental Council of Ireland in Association with Bord Failte

www.carrentalcouncil.ie

Laois is a picturesque inland county. Rich in historical houses and garden's, heritage sites, Museums, Golfing, Angling, Bogs, canals and rivers. Discover the Slieve Bloom mountains, their waterfalls and nature trails. The visitors relax and enjoy peace and tranquillity.

Maureen Lalor
COIS NA TINE
Portlaoise Road,
Abbeyleix , Co Laois

Abbeyleix
Tel: **0502 31976**

Charming bungalow. On main Dublin Cork route, 1km from Abbeyleix Heritage Town. Adjacent to Golf, Pony/Riding, Fishing Pubs/Restaurants.

B&B	3	Ensuite	€25.50	Dinner	-
B&B	-	Standard		Partial Board	-
Single Rate			€38.50	Child reduction	**25%**

Abbeyleix 1km

Open: 7th January-20th December

Mrs Janet Dooley
LANLEY B&B
Mountsalem, Coolrain,
Portlaoise, Co Laois

Coolrain/Portlaoise
Tel: **0502 35013**

Warm welcoming home at the foot of the Slieve Bloom Mountains. Situated off main Dublin Limerick Road (N7), 20km from Portlaoise, just 8km from Mountrath. Ideal touring base.

B&B	3	Ensuite	€25.50/€25.50	Dinner	-
B&B	1	Standard	€23/€25.50	Partial Board	-
Single Rate			€36/€36	Child reduction	**33.3%**

Portlaoise 20km

Open: 1st January-23rd December

Abigail McEvoy
GAROON HOUSE
Birr Road, Mountmellick,
Co Laois

Mountmellick
Tel: **0502 24641**   Fax: **0502 44514**
Email: **abigailm@oceanfree.net**
Web: **http://islandireland.com/garoonhouse**

Spacious, tastefully decorated home on large manicured grounds. Central location for touring any part of Ireland. Personally supervised breakfast menu.

B&B	5	Ensuite	€30	Dinner	-
B&B	-	Standard		Partial Board	-
Single Rate			€40	Child reduction	**25%**

Mountmellick 1km

Open: 31st March-20th October

Noreen Murphy Ui Laighin
CONLAN HOUSE
Killanure, Mountrath,
Co Laois

Mountrath
Tel: **0502 32727**   Fax: **0502 32727**
Email: **conlanhouse@oceanfree.net**
Web: **homepage.eircom.net/~conlanhouse**

Spacious friendly home. Tea/Coffee/Homebaking on arrival. Personal attention assured. Extensive breakfast menu. Central for touring. Maps/Books. 1 1/2 hours Dublin and Shannon Airports.

B&B	3	Ensuite	€30/€40	Dinner	€23
B&B	-	Standard	-	Partial Board	€300
Single Rate			€38.50/€40	Child reduction	**50%**

Mountrath 7km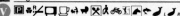

Open: All Year

Mrs Vera Hade
RENARD
Limerick Road, Portlaoise,
Co Laois

Tel: **0502 21735**   Fax: **0502 21735**

Warm welcoming home on N7 West (R445). Relaxed atmosphere. Tea/Scones on arrival. Close to all amenities. 1hour to Dublin.

B&B	1	Ensuite	€26	Dinner	-
B&B	2	Standard	€24	Partial Board	-
Single Rate			€36/€38.50	Child reduction	25%

Portlaoise 1km   **Open:** 1st January-23rd December

Maurice & Mary Murphy
OAKVILLE
Mountrath Road, Portlaoise,
Co Laois

Tel: **0502 61970**   Fax: **0502 61970**
Email: **oakvillebandb@eircom.net**

Situated on R445 N7 west. Crossroads of Ireland. Shops, Restaurants, Pubs, Theatre nearby. Family run. Tour guide on premises. Italian spoken. Private carpark.

B&B	3	Ensuite	€25.50/€28	Dinner	-
B&B	1	Standard	€23/€25.50	Partial Board	-
Single Rate			€36/€38.50	Child reduction	25%

Portlaoise   **Open:** 7th January-14th December

Mr Dermot O'Sullivan
8 Kellyville Park,
Portlaoise,
Co Laois

Tel: **0502 22774**

Charming well preserved old house beside town car park. Centrally located to all amenities. Town house. 50 metres from Tourist Office.

B&B	5	Ensuite	€31.74/€31.74	Dinner	-
B&B	-	Standard	-	Partial Board	-
Single Rate			€44.44/€44.44	Child reduction	10%

In Portlaoise   **Open:** 2nd January-20th December

Mrs Lily Saunders
ROSEDENE
Limerick Road, Portlaoise,
Co Laois

Tel: **0502 22345**   Fax: **0502 22345**
Email: **rosedenebb@eircom.net**

Peaceful, relaxing home. Personal attention. Bedrooms have multichannel TV, Tea/Coffee, Hairdryers. Walking distance Pubs, Restaurants. On N7 R445 West. Central location. Dublin 80km.

B&B	2	Ensuite	€25.50	Dinner	-
B&B	1	Standard	€23	Partial Board	-
Single Rate			€36/€39	Child reduction	25%

Portlaoise 1km   **Open:** 7th January-22nd December

Carole England
BALLAGHMORE HOUSE
Ballaghmore, Borris-In-Ossary,
Co Laois

Tel: **0505 21366**
Email: **ballaghmorehse@eircom.net**

Spacious country house, situated on N7 Dublin-Limerick road, halfway between Borris-In-Ossory and Roscrea. Dublin 1.5 hrs, Limerick 1.25 hrs. Highly recommended.

B&B	4	Ensuite	€27/€30	Dinner	€25
B&B	-	Standard	-	Partial Board	-
Single Rate			€38.50/€38.50	Child reduction	25%

Roscrea 5km   **Open:** 2nd January-21st December

Longford - this inland county is approximately 80 miles from Dublin. The county is rich in literary associations. The wonderful landscape is a blend of bogland, lakeland, pastureland and Wetland. Anglers can take advantage of the excellent facilities here.

Longford Town 10km

Miss Bridie Kenny
ARDKEN
Ardagh,
Co Longford

Ardagh
TEL: **043 75029**   FAX: **043 75029**
EMAIL:ardken@iol.ie

Beautiful house in unique estate village. Winner of National Tidy Towns award. Identified as Heritage Village just off N4, N55.

B&B	3	Ensuite	€25.50 /€25.50	Dinner	€23
B&B	-	Standard	-	Partial Board	€264
Single Rate			€38.50/€38.50	Child reduction	**50%**

Open: All Year

Longford

Mandy Etherton
OLDE SCHOOLHOUSE
Garrowhill, Newtownforbes,
Co Longford

Longford
TEL: **043 24854**
EMAIL: **mandy1@eircom.net**
WEB: **www.inet-sec.com/mandy.htm**

Unique old world charm, spacious, in countryside. Fishing, Golf, Pitch & Putt, Trekking nearby. From Longford bypass (N4) take R198 towards Drumlish for 3 miles. Crossroads turn right.

B&B	3	Ensuite	€25.50/€25.50	Dinner	€17
B&B	-	Standard	-	Partial Board	€264
Single Rate			€38.50/€38.50	Child reduction	**50%**

Open: 20th January-20th December

Longford 4km

Mrs Eileen Prunty
EDEN HOUSE
Newtownforbes, Longford,
Co Longford

Longford
TEL: **043 41160**

Peaceful home in picturesque village off Newtownforbes on N4. All facilities closeby. Refreshments on arrival. Orthopaedic beds, Electric blankets, TV.

B&B	4	Ensuite	€28	Dinner	-
B&B	1	Standard	€26	Partial Board	-
Single Rate			€36	Child reduction	-

Open: All Year Except Christmas

RESERVATIONS

- Confirm phone bookings in writing without delay with agreed deposit.
- To avoid misunderstandings later, check rate on booking and clarify any additional changes which may apply to your booking.
- Give details of any special requirements.
- State clearly day, date of arrival and departure date.

The diversity of scenery, historical/archeological sites, sporting and shopping attractions within easy access from Dublin and Belfast ports/airports.

The tranquillity of the Boyne Valley and Newgrange, to the splendour and panoramic views of Carlingford Lough at the base of the Mourne Mountains makes Louth the ideal base for all tourists.

Mrs Sheila Magennis
CARRAIG MOR
Blakestown, Ardee,
Co Louth

Ardee

TEL: **041 6853513**   FAX: **041 6853513**
EMAIL: **info@carraigmor.com**
WEB: **www.carraigmor.com**

Spacious comfortable home N2 (Dublin/Derry) 2 km south Ardee. Restaurants, Golf, Fishing nearby. Central to Monasterboice, Mellifont, Newgrange. Dublin Airport 45mins.

B&B	4	Ensuite	€25.50	Dinner	-
B&B	-	Standard		Partial Board	-
Single Rate			€38.50/€38.50	Child reduction	50%

Ardee 2km

Open: All Year

Mrs Lyn Grills
MOURNEVIEW
Belmont, Carlingford,
Co Louth

Carlingford

TEL: **042 9373551**   FAX: **042 9373551**
EMAIL: **mourneview@iolfree.ie**

Enjoy home comforts in family run B&B. Tranquil. Views of Mourne and Cooley Mountains. Spacious rooms. Sign for Carlingford. Off Dublin/Belfast road (N1).

B&B	6	Ensuite	€25.50/€26.66	Dinner	-
B&B	-	Standard		Partial Board	-
Single Rate			€38.50/€38.50	Child reduction	50%

Carlingford 2km

Open: All Year

Mrs Wendy Hanratty
GROVE HOUSE
Grove Road, Carlingford,
Co Louth

Carlingford

TEL: **042 9373494**
EMAIL: **hanrattj@gofree.indigo.ie**

Purpose built B&B situated in the medieval town of Carlingford. TV and tea making facilities, electric blankets. Breakfast menu. Private parking. Large family rooms available.

B&B	4	Ensuite	€28/€32	Dinner	-
B&B	-	Standard	-	Partial Board	-
Single Rate			€38.50/€51	Child reduction	50%

In Carlingford

Open: All Year

Marie McCarthy
THE HIGHLANDS
Irish Grange, Carlingford,
Co Louth

Carlingford

TEL: **042 9376104**
EMAIL: **thehighlands@eircom.net**
WEB: **www.thehighlandscarlingford.com**

Family run B&B, with luxury rooms. Scenic relaxed environment overlooking Carlingford Lough. Spacious landscaped gardens. Private parking. Signposted on R173.

B&B	3	Ensuite	€26/€27	Dinner	-
B&B	-	Standard	-	Partial Board	-
Single Rate			€40	Child reduction	50%

Carlingford 3km

Open: 1st February-31st October

Carlingford

Mrs Jackie Woods
SHALOM
Ghan Road,
Carlingford, Co Louth

TEL: **042 9373151**
EMAIL: **kevinwoods@eircom.net**
WEB: **www.jackiewoods.com**

Situated beside the Sea in the Medieval town of Carlingford. Overlooked by the Mourne Mountains on one side and the Cooley Mountains on the other.

B&B	5	Ensuite	€26/€26	Dinner	-
B&B	-	Standard	-	Partial Board	-
Single Rate			€38.50/€38.50	Child reduction	50%

Carlingford   **Open:** All Year

Mrs Mary Dolores McEvoy
THE CROSS GARDEN
Ganderstown, Clogherhead,
Drogheda, Route 166,
Co Louth

Clogherhead

TEL: **041 9822675**

Overlooking Irish Sea, Modern dormer bungalow, on elevated site. Clogherhead one mile on Termonfeckin Road. All rooms private facilities. Warm welcome.

B&B	2	Ensuite	€25.50/€25.50	Dinner	-
B&B	1	Standard	€25.50/€25.50	Partial Board	-
Single Rate			€36/€36	Child reduction	25%

Drogheda 5km   **Open:** All Year

Mrs Christine Dunne
LINKS VIEW
Golf Links Road, Bettystown,
Drogheda, Co Louth

Drogheda

TEL: **041 9827222**
EMAIL: **fergus_dunne@hotmail.com**

Peaceful home beside Golf course & Beach. 30 mins Airport. Convenient to Newgrange, Facing North in Bettystown, take 3rd turn left after Golf club.

B&B	1	Ensuite	€28/€30	Dinner	-
B&B	2	Standard	€28/€30	Partial Board	-
Single Rate			€36/€36	Child reduction	-

Drogheda 4km   **Open:** 1st January-15th December

Mrs Mona Dunne
SALLYWELL HOUSE B&B
Hill-of-Rath, Tullyallen,
Drogheda, Co Louth

Drogheda

TEL: **041 9834816**   FAX: **041 9834436**
EMAIL: **dunnemckeever@iegateway.net**
WEB: **www.dreamwater.com/sallywell**

Country Bungalow. Fish Pond, Patio/Conservatory. Large Gardens. 8km to Newgrange. 3km Monasterboice Tower and Celtic Cross. 28km from Dublin Airport. 2km Town Centre.

B&B	4	Ensuite	€28/€31	Dinner	€17
B&B	-	Standard	-	Partial Board	-
Single Rate			€38.50/€38.50	Child reduction	25%

Drogheda 2km   **Open:** 3rd January-23rd December

Rhona Hill
DRUMADOON
Waterunder, Collon Rd,
Drogheda, Co Louth

Drogheda

TEL: **041 9838495**

Peaceful country home ideally located on Drogheda/Collon Rd. R168 to tour Boyne Valley. Golf, Fishing, Beaches nearby. Warm welcome. Garden for guests.

B&B	2	Ensuite	€30/€33	Dinner	-
B&B	1	Standard	€28/€28	Partial Board	-
Single Rate			€38/€38	Child reduction	-

Drogheda 2km   **Open:** 1st April-31st October

Mrs Angela Kerrigan
KILLOWEN HOUSE
Woodgrange, Dublin Rd,
Drogheda, Co Louth

Drogheda

Tel: **041 9833547**　　Fax: **041 9833547**
Email: **killowenhouse@unison.ie**
Web: **http://homepage.eircom.net/~killowenhouse**

Luxury home 50m off N1, near Hotels, 25 mins Airport, 40 mins City Centre. Good base touring Boyne Valley, near Newgrange, Monasterboice, Beach, Golf. Spacious rooms. All facilities.

B&B	3	Ensuite	€28.50/€32	Dinner	-
B&B	2	Standard	€28.50/€28.50	Partial Board	-
Single Rate			€36/€44.50	Child reduction	25%

Drogheda 3km

Open: All Year Except Christmas

Mrs Mary McCabe
SHERDARA
Beaulieu Cross,
Termonfeckin Road,
Drogheda, Co Louth

Drogheda

Tel: **041 9836159**

A warm welcome awaits you at our modern bungalow on Drogheda - Termonfeckin road. Conservatory Diningroom. Breakfast menu. Convenient Newgrange, Golf & Airport.

B&B	3	Ensuite	€27	Dinner	-
B&B	1	Standard	€25	Partial Board	-
Single Rate			€36	Child reduction	25%

Drogheda 5km

Open: 1st May-30th September

Cepta & Eobhain McDonnell
TULLYESKER COUNTRY HOUSE
Dundalk Road (N1)
Monasterboice, Drogheda,
Co Louth

Drogheda

Tel: **041 9830430/9832624** Fax: **041 9832624**
Email: **mcdonnellfamily@ireland.com**
Web: **www.tullyeskerhouse.com**

Offical highest grade ◆◆◆◆◆ family home, 3 acre garden, panoramic view. Orthopaedic bed's, Tea and Coffee, Multi TV, Gourmet breakfast menu. Parking, Airport 25 miles.

B&B	5	Ensuite	€28/€33	Dinner	-
B&B	-	Standard	-	Partial Board	-
Single Rate			-	Child reduction	-

Drogheda 4km

Open: 1st February-30th November

Tara McDonnell
BOYNE HAVEN HOUSE
Dublin Road, Drogheda,
Co Louth

Drogheda

Tel: **041 9836700**　　Fax: **041 9836700**
Email: **taramcd@ireland.com**
Web: **www.boynehaven.com**

Truly magnificent, not to be missed. Award winning AA ◆◆◆◆. Drogheda South on N1, Airport 20 mins. Luxurious en-suite rooms, TV, Breakfast menu. Opposite Europa Hotel.

B&B	4	Ensuite	€30/€38	Dinner	-
B&B	-	Standard	-	Partial Board	-
Single Rate			€44.50/€50	Child reduction	-

Drogheda 2km

Open: All Year

Mrs Betty Nallen
ELEVENTH TEE HOUSE
Golf Links Road, Bettystown,
Drogheda, Co Louth

Drogheda

Tel: **041 9827613**　　Fax: **041 9827613**
Email: **bettynallen@hotmail.com**

Situated in beautiful gardens adjoining Golf Course. Large Beach 0.5km. Bettystown 1.5km. Convenient Newgrange, Mosney. Airport 30 mins. 4km off N1, Road no R150.

B&B	3	Ensuite	€28/€32	Dinner	-
B&B	1	Standard	-	Partial Board	-
Single Rate			€36/€44	Child reduction	25%

Drogheda 5km

Open: 1st January-30th November

In Drogheda

Peter & Mary Phillips
ORLEY HOUSE
Bryanstown, Dublin Road,
Drogheda, Co Louth

Drogheda

Tel: **041 9836019**   Fax: **041 9836019**
Email: **orleyhouse@eircom.net**
Web: **homepage.eircom.net/~orleyhouse**

Luxurious Town home off N1. Conservatory Dining Room. Airport 20 mins, near Bus/Rail /Ferries/3 Golf Courses/Newgrange/Boynevalley/Hotels/Shops and Restaurants.

B&B	4	Ensuite	€29.20/€33	Dinner	€20.32
B&B	-	Standard	-	Partial Board	-
Single Rate			€38.50/€44.44	Child reduction	-

Open: All Year

Drogheda 4km

Anne Walsh
CASTLEGADDERY
Tullyallen, Drogheda,
Co Louth

Drogheda

Tel: **041 9839299**   Fax: **041 9847901**
Email: **annesbandb@hotmail.com**
Web: **www.castlegadderybandb.com**

Luxurious B&B 4km north west of Drogheda on R168 - Collon Rd. 45mins-Dublin Airport. Close to Mellifont Abbey, Williams Glen, Bru-na, Boinne, Monasterboice.

B&B	2	Ensuite	€26/€32	Dinner	-
B&B	2	Standard	€25/€31	Partial Board	-
Single Rate			€36/€39	Child reduction	-

Open: All Year

Dundalk 4km

Mrs Evelyn Carolan
LYNOLAN
Haynestown, Dundalk,
Co Louth

Dundalk

Tel: **042 9336553**   Fax: **042 9336553**
Email: **lynolan@indigo.ie**
Web: **www.indigo.ie/~lynolan/**

Luxury Home in peaceful rural setting situated off new motorway, 700m from roundabout. Convenient to Fairways Hotel, Restaurants, DKIT. Signposted off N1/N52.

B&B	5	Ensuite	€26/€28	Dinner	€18
B&B	1	Standard	€24/€26	Partial Board	-
Single Rate			€36/€36	Child reduction	50%

Open: 15th January-15th December

Dundalk 3km

Mrs Patricia Murphy
PINEWOODS
Dublin Road, Dundalk,
Co Louth

Dundalk

Tel: **042 9321295**
Email: **olmurphy@eircom.net**
:

Traditional Irish welcome in home just off Dublin/Belfast motorway beside Fairways Hotel. Going north, turn right at traffic lights on N1, for Castlebellingham going south, turn left.

B&B	5	Ensuite	€26/€33	Dinner	-
B&B	-	Standard	-	Partial Board	-
Single Rate			€40/€44	Child reduction	25%

Open: All Year

Dundalk 5km

Brenda Rogers
BLACKROCK HOUSE
Main Street, Blackrock
Village, Dundalk,
Co Louth

Dundalk

Tel: **042 9321829/9322909** Fax: **042 9322909**
Email: **blackrockhsedundalk@eircom.net**

Home by shore. Lounge has panoramic view Dundalk Bay. First class Bars and Restaurants. Dundalk Golf Club, Fairways Htl, Bird Sanctuary nearby. 50 mins Dublin Airport/Belfast.

B&B	6	Ensuite	€26/€30	Dinner	-
B&B	-	Standard	-	Partial Board	-
Single Rate			€38.50/€38.50	Child reduction	-

Open: 1st January-15th December

In Dundalk

Mrs Marian Witherow
KRAKOW
190 Ard Easmuinn,
Dundalk, Co Louth

Dundalk

TEL: **042 9337535**
EMAIL: **krakow@eircom.net**

Modern bungalow covenient to Railway Station and Derryhale Hotel. Walking distance to Town Centre. First turn right after Railway Stn. 2 directional signs- KRAKOW B&B.

B&B	6	Ensuite	€27/€27	Dinner €19
B&B	-	Standard	-	Partial Board -
Single Rate			€39/€39	Child reduction 25%

Open: All Year

Omeath 1km

Mrs Eileen McGeown
DELAMARE HOUSE
Ballyoonan, Omeath,
Co Louth

Omeath

TEL: **042 9375101**
EMAIL: **eileenmcgeown@eircom.net**

In peaceful rural area, overlooking Carlingford Lough and Mourne Mountains. On Carlingford/ Omeath road opposite Calvary Shrine. Carlingford 3 miles.

B&B	2	Ensuite	€25.50/€25.50	Dinner -
B&B	1	Standard	€23/€23	Partial Board -
Single Rate			€36/€38.50	Child reduction 50%

Open: 15th March-15th November

BOOKINGS

We recommend your first and last night is pre-booked. Your hosts will make a booking for you at your next selected home for the cost of the phone call. When travelling in high season (June, July, August), it is essential to pre-book your accommodation – preferably the evening before, or the following morning to avoid disappointment.

WHEN TRAVELLING OFF-SEASON IT IS ADVISABLE TO CALL AHEAD AND GIVE A TIME OF ARRIVAL TO ENSURE YOUR HOSTS ARE AT HOME TO GREET YOU.

Visit the stoneage passage tombs of Newgrange/Knowth, Christian sites of Kells and Hill of Tara. Navan - Capital town and Slane picturesque estate village. Trim Castle now open - Europe's largest Anglo Norman Castle. Craft shop and Visitors Centre. Activities: Golf, Equestrian, Fishing, Gardens, Fine Dining and Quaint Pubs.

Ashbourne 2km

Mrs Kathleen Kelly
BALTRASNA LODGE
Baltrasna, Ashbourne, Co Meath

Ashbourne

TEL: **01 8350446**
EMAIL: **baltrasnalodge@eircom.net**
BUS No: **103**

Luxury home on large grounds. Dublin City/Airport 20 mins. 3rd house R125 off N2. 1 single, 1 double, 2 family(2 double beds per room). Private guest entrance.

				Dinner	-
B&B	4	Ensuite	€31/€45	Dinner	-
B&B	-	Standard	-	Partial Board	-
Single Rate			€38/€50	Child reduction	-

Open: 4th January-20th December

Athboy 7km

Colin & Anne Finnegan
WOODTOWN HOUSE
Athboy, Co Meath

Athboy

TEL: **046 35022**   FAX: **046 35022**
EMAIL: **woodtown@iol.ie**
WEB: **www.iol.ie/~woodtown**

"Staying here is like experiencing a fairytale". Fishing, golf, garden visits arranged. Signposted N51 Delvin/Athboy Rd.

B&B	2	Ensuite	€32/€35	Dinner	€17
B&B	1	Standard	€26/€28	Partial Board	-
Single Rate			€36/€40	Child reduction	25%

Open: 1st April-30th September

Drogheda 6km

Jean A.M. Strong
WOODVIEW HOUSE
Bettystown Cross, Bettystown, Co Meath

Bettystown

TEL: **041 9827911**

Set in a scenic woodland area. Very close to beach, golf, tennis & equestrian centre. 25 mins Dublin Airport & 20 mins Newgrange & Boyne Valley region. Close to Baltray Seapoint golf club.

B&B	4	Ensuite	€32	Dinner	-
B&B	-	Standard	-	Partial Board	-
Single Rate			€38.50	Child reduction	50%

Open: 2nd January-18th December

Dunboyne 4km

Mrs Anne Mannion
GORTKERRIN B&B
Piercetown, Dunboyne, Co Meath

Dunboyne

TEL: **01 8252096**   FAX: **01 8252096**
BUS No: **70**

Large dormer bungalow on 4 acres. Located on the Dublin/Navan road N3. Airport 15 mins. 20 mins from Dublin City. Tattersalls and Fairyhouse 3km.

B&B	3	Ensuite	€25.50/€25.50	Dinner	-
B&B	-	Standard	-	Partial Board	-
Single Rate			€38.50	Child reduction	-

Open: 1st April-31st October

Dunshaughlin 5km

Jo Morris
KILLEENTIERNA HOUSE
Powderlough, Dunshaughlin,
Co Meath

TEL: **01 8259722**   FAX: **01 8250673**
EMAIL: **imorris@clubi.ie**
WEB: **www.killeentierna.bizhosting.com**

Welcoming residence. Direct dial, TV, Gardens, Parking. Quality Lounge Bar and Restaurant adjacent to N3. 5km south of Dunshaughlin, 25 mins from Dublin Airport and City Centre.

B&B	5	Ensuite	€27/€30	Dinner	-
B&B	-	Standard		Partial Board	-
Single Rate			€40	Child reduction	25%

Open: 1st January-20th December

Drogheda 5km

Mrs Deirdre Cluskey
KEENOGUE HOUSE
Julianstown, Co Meath

TEL: **041 9829118**   FAX: **041 9829980**

Modern bungalow on working farm just off the N1 road. Convenient to Newgrange Boyne Valley. 20 mins Dublin Airport, 30 mins Dublin City.

B&B	4	Ensuite	€28/€32	Dinner	-
B&B	-	Standard		Partial Board	-
Single Rate			€40/€50	Child reduction	33.3%

Open: 2nd January-20th December

Drogheda 5km

Una Garvey
SMITHSTOWN LODGE
Dublin Road, Drogheda,
Co Meath

TEL: **041 9829777/9829020**
EMAIL: **unagarvey@eircom.net**

Luxurious home 3 miles south of Drogheda on N1. 20 mins Dublin Airport, 5 mins to Beach and Golf, 20 mins Newgrange and Boyne Valley. Breakfast menu. Routard recommended.

B&B	6	Ensuite	€25.50/€32	Dinner	-
B&B	-	Standard		Partial Board	-
Single Rate			€38.50/€38.50	Child reduction	50%

Open: All Year

Mrs Maureen Kington
BARDEN LODGE
Whitecross, Julianstown,
Co Meath

TEL: **041 9829369/9829910** FAX: **0419829369**
EMAIL: **kington@eircom.net**
WEB: **www.dirl.com/meath/barden-lodge.htm**
BUS NO: **100**

A warm welcome awaits in this quiet country house, off main N1 road north of Dublin. Close to all amenities, Newgrange, Boyne Valley. 20 mins Dublin Airport, 30 mins Dublin City.

B&B	2	Ensuite	€26/€32	Dinner	-
B&B	2	Standard	€25/€32	Partial Board	-
Single Rate			€36/€45	Child reduction	33.3%

Drogheda 5km

Open: All Year Except Christmas

Kells 1.5km

Tom & Marie Clarke
BIRCHWOOD
Balrath, Kells,
Co Meath

TEL: **046 40688**   FAX: **046 40688**
EMAIL: **clarket@iol.ie**

Modern Country Farmhouse. Panoramic view, N52, Kells-Mullingar. Airport 1 hr. Good local restaurants. Convenient Newgrange, Loughcrew Cairns, Kells Cross, Golf Clubs.

B&B	4	Ensuite	€26/€27.50	Dinner	-
B&B	-	Standard		Partial Board	-
Single Rate			€40/€40	Child reduction	25%

Open: 1st January-23rd December

In Kells

Rosemary Murray
WOODVIEW
**Athboy Road, Kells,
Co Meath**

Kells

TEL: **046 40200**
EMAIL: **rosemurray@eircom.net**

Quiet area, Kells Town. Tea/Coffee, TV in bedrooms. Walking distance Pubs, Restaurants. Golf, Fishing, Horseriding nearby. Convenient to Newgrange etc. 1hour Dublin Airport on R164.

B&B	2	Ensuite	€26/€27	Dinner	-
B&B	1	Standard	€23/€24	Partial Board	-
Single Rate			€36	Child reduction	50%

Open: All Year

Kells 3km

Peggy O'Reilly
TEACH CUAILGNE
**Carlanstown, Kells,
Co Meath**

Kells

TEL: **046 46621**   FAX: **046 46046**
EMAIL: **pegreilly@eircom.net**

Luxury home. Bedrooms on ground floor. Carlanstown Village N52. 3km from Kells, Headfort Golf Club. Convenient to Airport, Newgrange, Lough Crew. Breakfast choice, Orthapaedic beds.

B&B	2	Ensuite	€26/€27	Dinner	-
B&B	2	Standard	€24/€25	Partial Board	-
Single Rate			€38/€40	Child reduction	50%

Open: 1st January-20th December

In Navan Town

Mrs Pauline Boylan
ATHLUMNEY MANOR
**Athlumney, Duleek Road,
Navan, Co Meath**

Navan

TEL: **046 71388**
EMAIL: **stay@athlumneymanor.com**
WEB: **www.athlumneymanor.com**

Luxurious home overlooking Athlumney Castle. Rooms en-suite with TV, Coffee facilities, Phone. Minutes walk to Town Centre. Secure parking. Hourly bus to Dublin. On R153.

B&B	6	Ensuite	€26/€30	Dinner	-
B&B	-	Standard		Partial Board	-
Single Rate			€38.50/€38.50	Child reduction	25%

Open: All Year

Teresa & Gerard Brennan
VILLAGE B&B
**Kilmessan Village, Navan,
Co Meath**

Navan

TEL: **046 25250**
EMAIL: **villagebnb@eircom.net**

Scenic village off N3, beside Pubs/Hotel/Restaurant. Ideal base Hill of Tara (4km), Newgrange, Trim/Dunsany Castles, Boyne Drive. Dublin Airport/City 30 mins.

B&B	5	Ensuite	€26/€32	Dinner	-
B&B	1	Standard	€26/€32	Partial Board	-
Single Rate			€38/€38	Child reduction	50%

Navan 10km

Open: All Year

Navan 2km

Mrs Louie Burke
RAHEEN
**Trim Road, Navan,
Co Meath**

Navan

TEL: **046 23791**

Luxury bungalow Navan/Trim road (R161), Navan 2Km. Airport 30Km. Mature gardens. TV in rooms. Newgrange, Tara, Trim Castle nearby. Refreshments on arrival.

B&B	2	Ensuite	€26/€30	Dinner	-
B&B	2	Standard	€23/€26	Partial Board	-
Single Rate			€39	Child reduction	25%

Open: 1st January-23rd December

Mrs Mary Callanan
LIOS NA GREINE
Athlumney, Duleek Road,
(R153) Navan,
Co Meath

Navan

TEL: **046 28092**   FAX: **046 28092**
EMAIL: **call@hotmail.com**

Luxury home 1km off N3 on Duleek/Ashbourne/Airport (R153). Rooms Ensuite with TV, Tea/Coffee facilities. 30 mins Dublin Airport. Nearby Newgrange, Trim Castle, Tara.

B&B	2	Ensuite	€26/€30	Dinner	-
B&B	1	Standard	€23/€26	Partial Board	-
Single Rate			€39/€39	Child reduction	33.3%

Navan 1km

Open: All Year

Mrs Paula Casserly
BOYNE DALE
Donaghmore, Slane Road,
Navan, Co Meath

Navan

TEL: **046 28015**   FAX: **046 28015**
EMAIL: **boynedale@iolfree.ie**

Exclusive B&B on Navan-Slane road. Groundfloor bedrooms. Extensive breakfast menu. Easy accessability to Dublin, with the advantages of being in the country.

B&B	3	Ensuite	€26/€30	Dinner	-
B&B	2	Standard	€23/€26	Partial Board	-
Single Rate			€39	Child reduction	25%

Navan 2km

Open: 1st March-31st October

Margaret Dunne
DUNLAIR HOUSE
Old Road, Athlumney,
Navan, Co Meath

Navan

TEL: **046 72551**
EMAIL: **dunlair@hotmail.com**
WEB: **homepage.eircom.net/~dunlair**

Luxury house, quiet location just off R153, 1km Navan Town, Ensuite rooms with TV/Tea/Coffee facilities, convenient to Airport.

B&B	4	Ensuite	€26/€30	Dinner	-
B&B	-	Standard	-	Partial Board	-
Single Rate			€39	Child reduction	33.3%

Navan 1km

Open: All Year

Kathleen Keogan
HILLCREST
Slane Rd (N51), Navan,
Co Meath

Navan

TEL: **046 23125**
EMAIL: **keogank@eircom.net**

A warm friendly home on Slane Road N51. Convenient to Newgrange, Tara and other Historical sites. Close to Dublin Airport. Tea and Coffee on arrival.

B&B	3	Ensuite	€26/€30	Dinner	-
B&B	1	Standard	€23/€26	Partial Board	-
Single Rate			€39/€39	Child reduction	33.3%

Navan 1.5km

Open: 16th January-16th December

Mrs Nora Loughran
MEADOW VIEW
Slane Road (N51), Navan,
Co Meath

Navan

TEL: **046 23994/73131** FAX: **046 73131**
EMAIL: **meadowview@eircom.net**

Luxurious home minutes from Town Centre with award winning gardens. Rooms Ensuite with multi channel TV, Tea facilities. Convenient to Newgrange/Airport.

B&B	2	Ensuite	€26/€30	Dinner	-
B&B	1	Standard	€23 /€26	Partial Board	-
Single Rate			€39	Child reduction	33%

In Navan

Open: 3rd January-20th December

Packie & Caroline McDonnell
OCTAVE HOUSE
Somerville Road, Kentstown,
Navan, Co Meath

Navan/Slane

TEL: **041 9825592**
EMAIL: **carolinemon@eircom.net**
WEB: **www.octavehouse.com**

Superb spacious home in tranquil village. Ideally situated off N2 (R153). Newgrange 10km, Airport 25min. Local pub closeby. Warm friendly welcome awaits you.

B&B	3	Ensuite	€26/€30	Dinner	-
B&B	-	Standard	-	Partial Board	-
Single Rate			€39/€42	Child reduction	25%

Navan/Slane 6km

Open: All Year

Ann Marie Russell
SYCAMORES
Dublin Road, Navan,
Co Meath

Navan

TEL: **046 23719** FAX: **046 21261**

Luxurious bungalow on N3 south of Navan. Private parking. Overlooking the river Boyne. Antique furnishings, Books, Paintings, Silver. Homecooking, good Restaurants.

B&B	3	Ensuite	€26/€30	Dinner	-
B&B	1	Standard	€26/€30	Partial Board	-
Single Rate			€39/€39	Child reduction	-

In Navan

Open: 6th January-20th December

Mrs Betty Gough
MATTOCK HOUSE
Newgrange, Slane,
Co Meath

Newgrange

Tel: **041 9824592**   Fax: **041 9824592**

Bungalow situated off N51 East of Slane. Half price vouchers and tours arranged to Newgrange, Knowth and Visitors Centre. Convenient to Airport and Ferries.

B&B	2	Ensuite	€26/€29	Dinner	-
B&B	1	Standard	€26	Partial Board	-
Single Rate			€36/€39	Child reduction	50%

Drogheda 7km

Open: All Year

Mrs Lily Bagnall
HILLVIEW HOUSE
Gernonstown, Slane,
Co Meath

Slane

Tel: **041 9824327**
Email: **hillviewhouse@dol.ie**

Luxurious family home, situated on own grounds, beautiful landscaped gardens. Convenient to historic monuments and Towns. Tea and coffee facilities.

B&B	3	Ensuite	€26/€29	Dinner	-
B&B	-	Standard		Partial Board	-
Single Rate			€39/€39	Child reduction	25%

Slane 2km

Open: 30th January-30th November

Roly Bond
BONDIQUE HOUSE
Cullen, Beauparc,
Slane, Co Meath

Slane

Tel: **041 9824823**   Fax: **041 9824823**
Email: **bondique@iol.ie**

Situated on N2, 4km south of Slane. Bru na Boinne/Newgrange 8km. Navan/Drogheda 10 mins. Dublin Airport/ City 30 mins.

B&B	2	Ensuite	€27/€29	Dinner	-
B&B	2	Standard	€25/€27	Partial Board	-
Single Rate			€36/€38.50	Child reduction	25%

Slane 4km

Open: All Year

Mrs Ann Curtis
WOODVIEW
Flemington, Balrath,
Co Meath

Slane

Tel: **041 9825694**
Email: **info@meathtourism.ie**
Web: **www.meathtourism.ie**

Luxury bungalow 6km south of Slane, 100 metres off N2 Dublin/Derry Rd. Convenient to Newgrange Visitor Centre. Dublin Airport 30 mins. Ferries 45 mins.

B&B	2	Ensuite	€26/€29	Dinner	-
B&B	1	Standard	€26/€29	Partial Board	-
Single Rate			€38/€38	Child reduction	25%

Slane 6km

Open: 1st March-15th October

Mrs Mary Hevey
BOYNE VIEW
Slane, Co Meath

Slane

Tel: **041 9824121**
Email: **info@meathtourism.ie**
Web: **www.meathtourism.ie**

Georgian period house overlooking scenic Boyne Valley, close to all historical monuments. N2 Dublin Road Slane Village. Dublin Airport 45 minutes.

B&B	3	Ensuite	€26/€29	Dinner	-
B&B	-	Standard	-	Partial Board	-
Single Rate			€38.50/€38.50	Child reduction	25%

In Slane Village

Open: 10th January-20th December

97

Olive Owens
SAN GIOVANNI HOUSE
**Dublin Road, Slane,
Co Meath**

TEL: **041 9824147**

Large modern house on N2 in picturesque Boyne Valley, breathtaking view from house. 7km from Newgrange. 30 mins from Dublin Airport.

B&B	3	Ensuite	€26/€29	Dinner	-
B&B	-	Standard		Partial Board	-
Single Rate			€38.50/€39	Child reduction	**33.3%**

Slane 2km

Open: All Year Except Christmas

Mrs Marie Warren
CASTLE VIEW HOUSE
Slane, Co Meath

TEL: **041 9824510**   FAX: **041 9824510**
EMAIL: **castleview@oceanfree.net**

Modern bungalow on N51 overlooking Slane Castle Demesne. Close to historical sites, friendly atmosphere. Ideal touring base. Dublin Airport 45 mins.

B&B	4	Ensuite	€26/€29	Dinner	-
B&B	1	Standard	€26/€26	Partial Board	-
Single Rate			€36/€39	Child reduction	-

In Slane

Open: 14th January-22nd December

Ms Joan Maguire
SEAMROG
**Hill of Tara, Tara,
Co Meath**

TEL: **046 25296**

Homely B&B located on the Hill of Tara with beautiful views, experience the awe of Tara and then relax with us in our home. 10km from Navan off the N3.

B&B	2	Ensuite	€25.50/€25.50	Dinner	-
B&B	1	Standard	€23/€23	Partial Board	-
Single Rate			€36/€36	Child reduction	-

Navan 10km

Open: 1st May-1st October

Bernadette Gibbons
BOYNE LODGE B&B
**Rathnally, Trim,
Co Meath**

TEL: **046 81058**   FAX: **046 81059**
EMAIL: **boynelodge@eircom.net**
WEB: **homepage.eircom.net/~boynelodge**

Modern spacious country home, secludedly set on the Boyne. Trim 2km, 1km off the R161. 35 mins from Dublin Airport. Ideal for touring Boyne Valley.

B&B	2	Ensuite	€25.50	Dinner	-
B&B	1	Standard	€23	Partial Board	-
Single Rate			€36	Child reduction	-

Trim 3km

Open: 1st May-1st October

Marie Keane
TIGH CATHAIN
**Longwood Road,
Trim, Co Meath**

TEL: **046 31996**   FAX: **046 31996**
EMAIL: **mariekeane@esatclear.ie**

Tudor style country house on 1 acre mature gardens on R160. Large luxury ensuite rooms with Tea/Coffee, TV, Private park, Trim Castle 1km, Airport 40 mins.

B&B	3	Ensuite	€28/€32	Dinner	-
B&B	-	Standard		Partial Board	-
Single Rate			€39/€42	Child reduction	**33.3%**

Trim 1km

Open: 1st February-30th November

In Trim

Mrs Eliz. (Libby) O'Loughlin
WHITE LODGE B&B
New Road (Navan Road),
Trim, Co Meath

Tel: **046 36549/37697** Fax: **046 36549**
Email: **whitelodgetrim@eircom.net**
Web: **www.whitelodgetrim.com**

Town house, large ground floor bedrooms with TV/Tea in rooms. Restaurants closeby. 700m Town Centre/Trim Castle. Airport 40 mins. Frommer/Dumont recommended.

B&B	5	Ensuite	€28/€32	Dinner	-
B&B	1	Standard	€25/€30	Partial Board	-
Single Rate			€38/€42	Child reduction	-

Open: 1st February-30th November

Trim 1.5km

Anne O'Regan
CRANNMOR HOUSE
Dunderry Rd, Trim,
Co Meath

Tel: **046 31635** Fax: **046 38087**
Email: **cranmor@eircom.net**
Web: **www.crannmor.com**

Georgian country house with gardens on the outskirts of Trim "Heritage" town. Convenient to Golf, Fishing and Boyne Valley. 35 mins Airport.

B&B	4	Ensuite	€25.50/€31.74	Dinner	-
B&B	-	Standard	-	Partial Board	-
Single Rate			€38.50/€44.44	Child reduction	25%

Open: All Year Except Christmas

Trim Castle, Trim, Co. Meath

backdrop to "Braveheart" and largest Anglo Norman Castle in Europe.

A county of Ancient Kingdoms, Rolling Mountains, The mighty river Shannon and the most precious Irish Jewel "Clonmacnoise". Tour Castles, visit Peatlands, cruise the river Shannon and Grand canal. Play Golf and Fish and always feel welcome in the "Faithful County".

Mrs Carmel Horan
LAKYLE
Shannon Harbour,
Cross, Banagher,
Co Offaly

Banagher
TEL: **0509 51566**
EMAIL: **carmelhoran@hotmail.com**

Georgian style house, 3km off N62, convenient Bog-Rail Tours, Bird Watching (Corncrake), Fishing, Golf, Horse-Riding, Boating, Canoeing, Pitch-Putt. Clonmacnois.

B&B	3	Ensuite	€25.50/€25.50	Dinner	-
B&B	-	Standard	-	Partial Board	-
Single Rate			-	Child reduction	25%

Banagher 2km

Open: May-October

Carmel Finneran
THE GABLES B&B
Castle Street, Cloghan,
Co Offaly

Cloghan
TEL: **0902 57355**
EMAIL: **cfinneran@eircom.net**

House in Village of Cloghan, 4 bedroom's ensuite. Bog tour 16km, Clonmacnoise 18km, Slieve Bloom mountains 18km. Boora Parklands 10km. Birr Castle 16km. N62 R357.

B&B	4	Ensuite	€25.50	Dinner	€17
B&B	-	Standard	-	Partial Board	-
Single Rate			€38.50	Child reduction	25%

Birr 16km

Open: 1st January-20th Decembe

Mrs Catherine Harte
KAJON HOUSE
Creevagh, Clonmacnoise,
Co Offaly

Clonmacnoise
TEL: **0905 74191**   FAX: **0905 74191**
EMAIL: **kajonhouse@eircom.net**
WEB: **kajonhouse.cjb.net**

Home on elevated site overlooking River Shannon. Tea/Coffee & homemade scones. Le Guide du Routard, Let's go Ireland, Lonely Planet, Trotters recommended.

B&B	5	Ensuite	€25.50	Dinner	€17.78
B&B	2	Standard	€23	Partial Board	-
Single Rate			-	Child reduction	25%

Shannonbridge 5km

Open: 1st February-30th Octobe

Catherine & Dermot Byrne
AUBURN LODGE
Colonel Perry Street,
Edenderry, Co Offaly

Edenderry
TEL: **0405 31319**
EMAIL: **auburnlodge@eircom.net**

Townhouse Tea/Coffee, TV bedrooms. Gardens, Car park. Off N4 en route to the West. Airport, Ferryports 60 mins. Great Fishing, Golf. Central base for touring.

B&B	5	Ensuite	€25.50	Dinner	€17
B&B	1	Standard	€23	Partial Board	-
Single Rate			€36	Child reduction	50%

In Town

Open: All Yea

Kinnitty

In Kinnitty

Christina Byrne
ARDMORE HOUSE
**The Walk, Kinnitty,
Co Offaly**

Tel: **0509 37009**
Email: **ardmorehouse@eircom.net**
Web: **www.kinnitty.net**

Victorian House, Slieve Bloom Mountains. 2 hours Airport, Ferryports. Brass beds, turf fire, home baking. Walking, Equestrian, Irish music, Birr Castle Gardens/Telescope. Clonmacnoise.

B&B	4	Ensuite	€27/€32	Dinner	-
B&B	1	Standard	€25.50/€27	Partial Board	-
Single Rate			€38/€44.50	Child reduction	-

Open: All Year

Portarlington

Portarlington 4km

Liam & Marguerite Kirwan
TREASCON LODGE
Portarlington, Co Offaly

Tel: **0502 43183**   Fax: **0502 43183**
Email: **treasconlodgeportarlington@eircom.net**

Country home on two acres. Tennis Court, Playground in quiet setting. All rooms ensuite. Golf 5 mins. Wheelchair access.

B&B	2	Ensuite	€26/€26	Dinner	-
B&B	1	Standard	€23/€23	Partial Board	-
Single Rate			€36/€36	Child reduction	33.3%

Open: All Year Except Christmas

Shannonbridge

Ballinasloe 10km

Mrs Patricia Corbett
RACHRA HOUSE
(SHANNON VIEW)
**Shannonbridge,
via Athlone, Co Offaly**

Tel: **0905 74249**
Email: **rachrahouse@eircom.net**
Web: **www.rachrahouse.shannonbridge.net**

Modern house in picturesque village overlooking rivers Shannon and Suck. Clonmacnoise 6km. Bog Railtours 3km. Fishing, Golf, Horse-Riding, Tennis.

B&B	2	Ensuite	€25.50	Dinner	-
B&B	2	Standard	€23	Partial Board	-
Single Rate			€36	Child reduction	25%

Open: April-October

Shannonbridge

In Shannonbridge Village

Mrs Celine Grennan
THE BUNGALOW
**River View, Shannonbridge,
Athlone, Co Offaly**

Tel: **0905 74180**   Fax: **0905 74180**
Email: **shannonbungalow@eircom.net**
Web: **www.infowing.ie/fishing/ac/bung.htm**

In picturesque village with panoramic view of Shannon. Clonmacnoise 6km, Bog tours, Pubs, Fishing, Golf, Swimming, Tennis, Horseriding.

B&B	5	Ensuite	€25.50	Dinner	€17
B&B	1	Standard	€23	Partial Board	€264
Single Rate			€36	Child reduction	33.3%

Open: April-October

Tullamore

Tullamore 10km

Mrs Bernadette Keyes
CANAL VIEW
COUNTRY HOUSE
**Killina, Rahan,
Tullamore, Co Offaly**

Tel: **0506 55868/55522** Fax: **0506 55034**
Email: **canalview@eircom.net**

10km from Tullamore overlooking canal. Sauna, Steamroom, Massage, Reiki, Beauty crystal treatments available. Pedal and row boating.

B&B	4	Ensuite	€26	Dinner	-
B&B	-	Standard		Partial Board	-
Single Rate			€38.50	Child reduction	33.3%

Open: 1st April-30th October

Mrs Anne O'Brien
GORMAGH
**Durrow, Tullamore,
Co Offaly**

Tullamore
TEL: **0506 51468**

Secluded Home, 5 mins drive North of Tullamore on N52. Use of natural materials throughout the house is in harmony with wildflower gardens.

B&B	4	Ensuite	€26	Dinner
B&B	1	Standard	€23	Partial Board
Single Rate			€38.50	Child reduction

Tullamore 4km

Open: 1st February-15th December

A warm welcome awaits you in Westmeath, Ireland's undiscovered lakelands. Situated in the heart of Ireland with magnificent lakes, an anglers paradise, also Golfing, Horse-riding and Water-sports. Travel the Belvedere Fore, or Lough Ree Trails or explore the heritage sites/visitor attractions.

Pat & Teresa Byrne
BENOWN HOUSE
Glasson, Athlone,
Co Westmeath

Athlone
TEL: **0902 85406**   FAX: **0902 85776**
EMAIL: **benownhouse@glasson.com**
WEB: **www.glasson.com**

Relaxing residence in picturesque village 100m off N55 to Glasson Golf. Choice Restaurants, Pubs, Fishing, Sailing. Good food. Tea/Coffee , TV, Hairdryer in rooms.

B&B	5	Ensuite	€25.50/€31.50	Dinner	-
B&B	1	Standard	€23/€29	Partial Board	-
Single Rate			€36/€40	Child reduction	25%

Athlone 8km   **Open:** All Year

Mrs Joan Collins
DUN MHUIRE HOUSE
Bonavalley, Dublin Road
(Town Route), Athlone,
Co Westmeath

Athlone
TEL: **0902 75360**

N6 Town route. Close to town and Athlone Institute of Technology. All rooms with multi channel TV, Tea/Coffee making facilities. Vouchers accepted.

B&B	2	Ensuite	€25.50	Dinner	-
B&B	2	Standard	€23	Partial Board	-
Single Rate			€36/€36	Child reduction	50%

In Athlone   **Open:** All Year

Sean & Carmel Corbett
RIVERVIEW HOUSE
Summerhill, Galway Road (N6),
Athlone, Co Westmeath

Athlone
TEL: **0902 94532**   FAX: 0902 94532
EMAIL: **riverviewhouse@hotmail.com**
WEB: **www.riverviewhousebandb.com**

Two storey red brick on N6 Galway Road. Five minutes drive from town centre. Private car park. Credit cards accepted. AA ◆◆◆◆.

B&B	4	Ensuite	€25.50/€26	Dinner	-
B&B	-	Standard		Partial Board	-
Single Rate			€38.50/€38.50	Child reduction	25%

Athlone 2km   **Open:** 1st March-15th December

Jim & Nancy Denby
SHELMALIER HOUSE
Cartrontroy, Athlone,
Co Westmeath

Athlone
TEL: **0902 72245/72145** FAX: **0902 73190**
EMAIL: **shelmal@iol.ie**

Beautiful house and gardens in quiet location. Signposted off R446 and N55. All in room services. AA ◆◆◆◆. Award winning breakfast menu. Private Parking.

B&B	7	Ensuite	€26	Dinner	-
B&B	-	Standard		Partial Board	-
Single Rate			€39	Child reduction	33.3%

Athlone 2km   **Open:** 1st February-20th December

Mrs Maura Duggan
VILLA ST JOHN
Roscommon Road,
Athlone, Co Westmeath

Athlone

TEL: **0902 92490**   FAX: **0902 92490**
EMAIL: **villastjohn@eircom.net**

Ideally situated on N61 off N6. Convenient to Bars, Restaurants, Lough Ree, Clonmacnoise, 2 Golf courses. TV, Coffee, Hairdryers in bedrooms. Private secure parking at rear of house.

B&B	5	Ensuite	€26	Dinner	-
B&B	3	Standard	€23	Partial Board	-
Single Rate			€36/€39	Child reduction	**50%**

Athlone 2km

Open: 3rd January-20th December

Mrs Catherine Fox
DE PORRES
Cornamaddy, Ballykeeran,
Athlone, Co Westmeath

Athlone

TEL: **0902 75759**
EMAIL: **deporres@iol.ie**

Signposted off Cavan Rd N55. Quiet location, private carpark, beautiful gardens. Clonmacnoise, Restaurants, Lakes, Golf nearby. TV, Tea/Coffee rooms. Customer Service Award winner.

B&B	3	Ensuite	€25.50/€25.50	Dinner	-
B&B	1	Standard	€23/€23	Partial Board	-
Single Rate			€38.50/€38.50	Child reduction	**33.3%**

Athlone 2km

Open: 1st April-31st October

Roy & Rose Gandy
HEATHER VIEW
Auburn, Dublin Road,
Athlone, Co Westmeath

Athlone

TEL: **0902 72710**
EMAIL: **heather.view@unison.ie**

Large bungalow 1 acre garden, quiet cul-de-sac off Dublin road, beside Institute of Technology. Large car park. TV, Tea/Coffee, Electric Blanket, Trouser Press, Hairdryer.

B&B	4	Ensuite	€28	Dinner	-
B&B	-	Standard	-	Partial Board	-
Single Rate			€39	Child reduction	-

In Athlone

Open: All Year

Jim & Eucharia King
BUSHFIELD HOUSE
Cornamaddy, Blyry,
Athlone, Co Westmeath

Athlone

TEL: **0902 75979**
EMAIL: **euchariaking@ireland.com**
WEB: **http://www.dragnet-systems.ie/dira/bushfield**

Signposted N6/N55. Exit Blyry off bypass. TV's, Phones, Tea/Coffee. Pub nearby. Restaurants 2Km. Clonmacnoise 20 mins. Conservatory. Customer Service Award winner.

B&B	5	Ensuite	€25.50	Dinner	-
B&B	1	Standard		Partial Board	-
Single Rate			€38.50	Child reduction	**50%**

Athlone 2km

Open: 6th January-20th December

Mrs Mary Linnane
BURREN LODGE
Creggan, Dublin Road,
Athlone, Co Westmeath

Athlone

TEL: **0902 75157**
EMAIL: **burrenlodge@ireland.com**
WEB: **www.burrenlodge.com**

Close to roundabout at Texaco Filling Station/Centra. Adjacent Creggan Court Hotel on N6. 15 mins to Clonmacnoise. Regular daily bus service to Dublin from door. TV, Tea/Coffee.

B&B	3	Ensuite	€25.50	Dinner	-
B&B	1	Standard	€23	Partial Board	-
Single Rate			€36/€38.50	Child reduction	**33.3%**

Athlone 2km

Open: All Year

Ann Meade
HARBOUR HOUSE
Ballykeeran, Athlone,
Co Westmeath

TEL: **0902 85063**   FAX: **0902 85933**
EMAIL: **ameade@indigo.ie**

Luxurious quiet home on Lough Ree, 1.5km off N55 in Ballykeeran, Fishing, Golf, Restaurants locally. Tea/Coffee/TV, hairdryer facilities.

B&B	6	Ensuite	€25.50/€25.50	Dinner -
B&B	-	Standard	-	Partial Board -
Single Rate			€38.50/€38.50	Child reduction **25%**

Athlone 5km

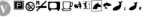

Open: 1st March-31st October

Mrs Joanne Mulligan
MOUNT ALVERNA HOUSE
Monksland, Athlone,
Co Westmeath

TEL: **0902 94016**

Spacious bungalow. All rooms en-suite. Private grounds off N6 on R362. Near Clonmacnoise, Golf, Fishing, Open Farm, Pub and Restaurants.

B&B	4	Ensuite	€26	Dinner -
B&B	-	Standard	-	Partial Board -
Single Rate			€38.50	Child reduction **33.3%**

Athlone 3km

Open: April-October

Mrs Audrey O'Brien
BOGGANFIN HOUSE
Roscommon Road, Athlone,
Co Westmeath

TEL: **0902 94255**   FAX: **0902 94255**

Tudor style res, off N6, on N61, near roundabout opposite Renault Garage. Guide to Ireland recom, Customer Service Award. Adjacent to Town Lakes, Leisure Centre, Pubs.

B&B	5	Ensuite	€25.50/€25.50	Dinner -
B&B	1	Standard	€23/€23	Partial Board -
Single Rate			€36/€36	Child reduction **25%**

Athlone 1.5km

Open: 20th January-20th December

Carmel & Oliver O'Neill
A GLASSON STONE LODGE
Glasson, Athlone,
Co Westmeath

TEL: **0902 85004**
EMAIL: **glassonstonelodge@eircom.net**
WEB: **www.glassonstonelodge.com**

Beautiful house and garden in quaint village in centre of Ireland, on N55. Good breakfast. TV, Tea/Coffee in room's. Near Clonmacnoise. Excellent Restaurants, Pubs 2 min walk. Golf, Fishing.

B&B	6	Ensuite	€25.50/€32	Dinner -
B&B	-	Standard	-	Partial Board -
Single Rate			€38.50/€55	Child reduction -

Athlone 4km

Open: 1st March-30th November

Des & Mary O'Neill
AVONREE HOUSE
Coosan, Athlone,
Co Westmeath

TEL: **0902 75485**

House, Gardens. Close N6 (Exit Coosan No.3 Junction) and N55. Italian spoken. Two Golf Clubs-10mins. Non-smoking. Clonmacnoise 20 mins, Dublin 1hr 20 mins.

B&B	5	Ensuite	€25.50	Dinner -
B&B	-	Standard	-	Partial Board -
Single Rate			€38.50	Child reduction -

Athlone 1km

Open: 1st March-31st October

Jimmy & Eileen Whelehan
THE VILLAGE B&B
Killucan, Co Westmeath

Kinnegad

Tel: **044 74760**   Fax: **044 74973**
Email: **thevillageinn@oceanfree.net**

Follow B&B sign on route N4 North, West of Kinnegad. Royal Canal Fishing 2 km. Golf courses 14km on route Trim, Newgrange.

B&B	2	Ensuite	€25.50/€25.50	Dinner	
B&B	1	Standard	€23/€23	Partial Board	
Single Rate			€36/€36	Child reduction	25%

In Village

Open: All Ye

Mrs May Glynn
RAILWAY LODGE
**Cartronkeel, Ballymore Rd,
Moate, Co Westmeath**

Moate

Tel: **0902 81596**
Email: **james.glynn@mkg.com**

Bungalow situated in peaceful area with landscaped Gardens, private car parking, home cooking, rooms ensuite. Knowledge of German and French.

B&B	2	Ensuite	€25.50/€28	Dinner	
B&B	1	Standard	€23/€25	Partial Board	
Single Rate			€36/€36	Child reduction	25%

In Moate

Open: All Year Except Christma

Mrs Ethna Kelly
COOLEEN COUNTRY HOME
**Ballymore Rd, Moate,
Co Westmeath**

Moate

Tel: **0902 81044**

Picturesque bungalow set in private gardens. 2km off N6. Close to Golf, Pitch and Putt, Clonmacnoise, Heritage Centre. Home cooking, Turf fires.

B&B	3	Ensuite	€25.50	Dinner	
B&B	-	Standard	-	Partial Board	
Single Rate			€38.50	Child reduction	50%

Moate 2km

Open: 15th January-15th Decembe

Tony & Mary Barry
WOODSIDE
**Dublin Road, Mullingar,
Co Westmeath**

Mullingar

Tel: **044 41636**

Attractive family home set in peaceful location. 10 mins walking distance from Town Centre. All rooms en-suite. Residents lounge.

B&B	4	Ensuite	€30/€31.50	Dinner	
B&B	-	Standard	-	Partial Board	-
Single Rate			€38.50/€38.50	Child reduction	33.3%

In Mullingar

Open: 1st January-20th Decembe

Catherine Bennet
TURNPIKE LODGE
**Dublin Road, Petits Wood,
Mullingar, Co Westmeath**

Mullingar

Tel: **044 44913**   Fax: **044 44913**

Friendly family home. Two large family rooms, Residents lounge, relaxing atmosphere. 2 minutes drive off N4.

B&B	5	Ensuite	€30/€31.50	Dinner	
B&B	-	Standard	-	Partial Board	
Single Rate			€38.50/€50	Child reduction	

Mullingar 1.5km

Open: All Yea

Sean & Dympna Casey
HILLTOP
Delvin Road (N52 off N4),
Rathconnell, Mullingar,
Co Westmeath

TEL: **044 48958** FAX: **044 48013**
EMAIL: **hilltopcountryhouse@eircom.net**
WEB: **www.hilltopcountryhouse.com**

Unique modern Country home, Award winning garden/breakfast. One hour from Dublin. AA selected ◆◆◆◆, Recommended Frommer, Dillard/Cousin, Sullivan guides.

B&B	5	Ensuite	€28/€30	Dinner	-
B&B	-	Standard		Partial Board	-
Single Rate			€40/€40	Child reduction	-

Mullingar 3km

Open: 1st February-30th November

Rita Fahey
BALLINAFID LAKE HOUSE
Ballinafid, Longford Road,
Mullingar, Co Westmeath

TEL: **044 71162**
EMAIL: **rfahey@ireland.com**

Spacious bungalow on the N4 Longford Rd. 8km from Mullingar beside the Covert Pub opposite Ballinafid Lake. Guest sitting room. Laundry facilities, Gardens.

B&B	4	Ensuite	€25.50	Dinner	-
B&B	-	Standard		Partial Board	-
Single Rate			€38.50	Child reduction	-

Mullingar 8km

Open: 1st April-31st October

Josephine Garvey
GREENHILLS
Castletown Geog,
Mullingar, Co Westmeath

TEL: **044 26353** FAX: **044 26353**
EMAIL: **josgarvey@eircom.net**

Old restored spacious country house in the heart of the Lake District. Very warm welcome assured. Pets welcome. Tea/Coffee on arrival.

B&B	3	Ensuite	€25.50	Dinner	€17
B&B	-	Standard	-	Partial Board	
Single Rate			€38.50	Child reduction	33.3%

Castletown Geog 3km

Open: All Year

Mrs Regina Healy
GLENMORE HOUSE
Dublin Road, Mullingar,
Co Westmeath

TEL: **044 48905**
EMAIL: **reghealy@eircom.net**

Georgian house set in four acres of secluded Woodlands and Lawns. Tranquil peaceful and restful. Fishing, Golf, Tennis and Horseriding nearby.

B&B	2	Ensuite	€30/€31.50	Dinner	-
B&B	2	Standard	€25/€25	Partial Board	-
Single Rate			€36/€38	Child reduction	25%

Mullingar

Open: 10th January-16th December

Mrs May McCarthy
MOORLAND
Marlinstown, Curraghmore,
(Off N4) Mullingar,
Co Westmeath

TEL: **044 40905**

House off main Dublin Road. Six rooms with private facilities. Turf Fires, Electric Blankets. Warm welcome.

B&B	6	Ensuite	€28	Dinner	-
B&B	-	Standard	-	Partial Board	-
Single Rate			€38.50	Child reduction	-

Mullingar 2.5km

Open: All Year

Mrs Margaret McCormack
MC CORMACKS B&B
Old Dublin Road, Mullingar,
Co Westmeath

Mullingar
TEL: **044 41483**

On Old Dublin Road, 100 metres from Mullingar Bypass, adjacent to Roundabout. Tennis court and Pool table on grounds. Open access to farmyard and picnic area.

B&B	2	Ensuite	€25.50	Dinner	-
B&B	2	Standard	€23	Partial Board	-
Single Rate			€36/€37	Child reduction	33.3%

Mullingar 2km   **Open:** 1st March-31st October

Dolores & Anthony Quinn
MARLINSTOWN COURT
Dublin Road, Mullingar,
Co Westmeath

Mullingar
TEL: **044 40053**

Situated in a beautiful setting on own grounds. 1 mile Town Centre. All rooms ensuite, Residents lounge. Secluded parking. 2 mins off N4, 1 hour from Dublin.

B&B	5	Ensuite	€30/€32	Dinner	-
B&B	-	Standard		Partial Board	-
Single Rate			€38.50/€50	Child reduction	33.3%

Mullingar 1.5km   **Open:** 1st January-20th December

APPROVED ACCOMMODATION SIGNS

Approved Accommodation Signs
This sign will be displayed at most premises which are approved to Irish Tourist Board Standards.

Panneaux d'homologation des établissements
Ces panneaux sont affichés dans la plupart des établissements homologués selon les normes de l'Office du tourisme irlandais.

Plakette für Geprüfte Unterkunft
Diese Plaketten werden an den meisten Häusern angezeigt, die von auf die Einhaltung der Normen der irischen Fremdenverkehrsbehörde überprüft und zugelassen wurden.

Borden voor goedgekeurde accommodatie
Deze borden vindt u bij de meeste huizen die zijn goedgekeurd door voor de normen van de Ierse Toeristenbond.

Simbolo di sistemazione approvata
Questi simboli saranno esposti nella maggior parte delle case approvate (associazione dei Bed & Breakfast approvati per qualità), rispondenti agli standard dell'Ente del Turismo Irlandese.

Símbolo de alojamiento aprobado
Estos símbolos se muestran en los establecimientos que han sido aprobados por bajos los estandars de la Oficina de Turismo Irlandesa.

Skyltar för Godkänd logi
Dessa skyltar finns vid de flesta gästhus som har godkänts (Föreningen för kvalitetsgodkända gästhus AB), enligt irländska turisföreningens normer.

Wicklow, the "Garden of Ireland", bounded on the east by sandy beaches and the west by lakes and mountains. Monastic site at Glendalough. Excellent facilities for Golf, Angling, Watersports and Walking. Convenient Dublin/Rosslare with easy access along N11 and N81.

Deirdre Bishop-Power
VALENTIA
Coolgreany Rd, Arklow,
Co Wicklow

TEL: **0402 39200**   FAX: **0402 39200**
EMAIL: **valentiahouse@esatclear.ie**
WEB: **www.geocities.com/valentiahouse**

Comfortable family home. Lovely conservatory dining room. Ideal touring base for Garden of Ireland. Good beaches. 1hr to Dublin and Wexford. Easy walk to Town.

B&B	4	Ensuite	€27.50/€37.50	Dinner		-
B&B	-	Standard		Partial Board		-
Single Rate			€39/€45	Child reduction		25%

In Arklow   **Open:** All Year

Mrs Margaret Connors
GLENDALE HOUSE
Wexford Road, Arklow,
Co Wicklow

TEL: **0402 32816**

Modern friendly home, prize winning garden. Base for Dublin, Wexford, Waterford. Ballykissangel 10 mins. Sea, Golf, Leisure Centres. Excellent Pubs, Hotels nearby.

B&B	3	Ensuite	€25.50/€28	Dinner		-
B&B	-	Standard		Partial Board		-
Single Rate			€38.50/€38.50	Child reduction		33.3%

Arklow 1km   **Open:** All Year

Mrs Lourdes Crotty
VALE VIEW
Coolgreaney Rd, Arklow,
Co Wicklow

TEL: **0402 32622**   FAX: **0402 32622**
EMAIL: **pat.crotty@ifi.ie**

Edwardian hse with period furnishings on landscaped gardens. Panoramic views. Rooftop Sun Lounge. 200m off roundabout on R772 Main St. Ideal touring base.

B&B	4	Ensuite	€27/€30	Dinner		-
B&B	-	Standard		Partial Board		-
Single Rate			€38.50/€40	Child reduction		25%

In Arklow   **Open:** 1st March-1st November

Ms Catherine Dunne
DOBAN
Carrig Mor, Dublin Rd,
Arklow, Co Wicklow

TEL: **0402 32580**
EMAIL: **doban@tinet.ie**

Purpose built spacious home in quiet cul-de-sac. Award winning garden. Private parking. Convenient to all local amenities. Ideal tourist base.

B&B	2	Ensuite	€27/€29.50	Dinner		-
B&B	1	Standard	€27/€29.50	Partial Board		-
Single Rate			€36/€36	Child reduction		-

Arklow 1km   **Open:** 1st January-30th November

Audrey & Joe Good
INVER DEA
52 Ferrybank, Arklow,
Co Wicklow

TEL: 0402 33987

Red Brick House at pedestrian lights on main road entering Arklow from Dublin. 5 mins. walk town Centre or Beach.

B&B	4	Ensuite	€25.50/€29	Dinner	-
B&B	-	Standard	-	Partial Board	-
Single Rate			€38.50/€42	Child reduction	25%

In Arklow

Open: 14th February-30th November

Mrs Kathleen Hendley
SWANLAKE
Sea Road, Arklow,
Co Wicklow

TEL: 0402 32377

Modern bungalow on coast road close to Arklow Bay Hotel and caravan park. Overlooking sea and beach. Close to Town Centre.

B&B	3	Ensuite	€25.50/€27	Dinner	-
B&B	-	Standard	-	Partial Board	-
Single Rate			-	Child reduction	25%

Arklow 1.5km

Open: 17th March-31st October

Mrs Rita Kelly
FAIRY LAWN
Wexford Road, Arklow,
Co Wicklow

TEL: 0402 32790

1km from Arklow on the Wexford/Gorey Road. Tea/Coffee facilities in bedrooms. Recommended in the 300 Best B&B Guide. Credit Cards accepted.

B&B	3	Ensuite	€27	Dinner	-
B&B	1	Standard	€25	Partial Board	-
Single Rate			€36/€38.50	Child reduction	50%

Arklow 1km

Open: 1st January-20th December

Imelda Kennedy
HILL BREEZE B&B
Barniskey, Arklow,
Co Wicklow

TEL: 0402 33743
EMAIL: hillbreeze@hotmail.com

Comfortable family home, ideal place to relax with panoramic views. 2km off N11, take Redcross Road off Roundabout.

B&B	2	Ensuite	€25.50/€25.50	Dinner	-
B&B	1	Standard	€25.39/€25.39	Partial Board	-
Single Rate			€36/€36	Child reduction	25%

Arklow 4km

Open: 1st March-1st October

Mrs Geraldine Nicholson
PINEBROOK B&B
5 Ticknock Close,
Briggs Lane, Arklow,
Co Wicklow

TEL: 0402 31527   FAX: 0402 31527
EMAIL: pinebrook@eircom.net
WEB: www.pinebrook.net

Modern detached townhouse within walking distance of Town Centre. Very quiet area with secure parking. Close to all amenities including beach and swimming pool.

B&B	3	Ensuite	€27.50/€27.50	Dinner	-
B&B	-	Standard	-	Partial Board	-
Single Rate			€38/€38	Child reduction	50%

Open: All Year

Maeve O'Connor
THE GABLES
Ballygriffin, Arklow,
Co Wicklow

Arklow

Tel: **0402 33402**
Email: **maeve.oconnor@oceanfree.net**
Web: **www.gables-arklow.com**

Spacious country home. Landscaped gardens, Tea facilites. Electric blankets. Breakfast menu. Tennis court. Dublin/Rosslare one hour. Signposted roundabout Arklow.

B&B	4	Ensuite	€26/€28	Dinner	-
B&B	-	Standard	-	Partial Board	-
Single Rate			€38.50	Child reduction	50%

Arklow 3km

Open: 1st March-1st November

Jean O'Shea Conlon
MOUNT USHER VIEW
Ashford, Co Wicklow

Ashford

Tel: **0404 40543**

Dormer bungalow, mature gardens, bordering Mount Usher gardens, ten minutes to Druids Glen Golf Course, 5 mins drive to swimming pool with gym.

B&B	4	Ensuite	€25.50	Dinner	-
B&B	-	Standard	-	Partial Board	-
Single Rate			-	Child reduction	50%

In Ashford

Open: All Year

Mrs Nancy Joynt
CARRIG LODGE
Ballylusk, Ashford,
Co Wicklow

Ashford

Tel: **0404 40278**   Fax: **0404 40278**
Email: **carriglodge@oceanfree.net**

Spacious country home. Ideal touring base. Close to Pubs, Restaurants and world famous Mount Usher Gardens. Dublin/Rosslare 1hr. Dun Laoghaire 30 mins.

B&B	3	Ensuite	€27/€30	Dinner	-
B&B	1	Standard	€23	Partial Board	-
Single Rate			€36/€38	Child reduction	-

Ashford 2km

Open: 1st April-31st October

Mrs Phyl Long
BARTRAGH
Dublin Road, Ashford,
Co Wicklow

Ashford

Tel: **0404 40442**   Fax: **0404 49012**
Email: **info@bartragh.com**
Web: **www.bartragh.com**

300 metres from Ashford village on Dublin Road (N11). Walking distance to Pubs/Restaurants. 30 minutes Dun Laoghaire Ferryport. Rural setting.

B&B	4	Ensuite	€25.50/€25.50	Dinner	-
B&B	-	Standard	-	Partial Board	-
Single Rate			-	Child reduction	-

In Ashford

Open: 1st March-31st October

Mrs Aine Shannon
CARRIGLEN
Ballinahinch, Ashford,
Co Wicklow

Ashford

Tel: **0404 40627**
Email: **carriglen@eircom.net**

500 metres Ashford Village/off Main road/on Devils Glen Glendalough road. 5 min walk Pubs/Restaurants. Mount Usher Gardens. Dublin 45 min, Dunlaoghaire 35 min.

B&B	3	Ensuite	€25.50/€27.50	Dinner	-
B&B	-	Standard	-	Partial Board	-
Single Rate			€38.50/€38.50	Child reduction	25%

Ashford 1km

Open: All Year

Wicklow 4km

Aileen Synnott
ROSSANA
Ashford, Co Wicklow

Ashford
TEL: **0404 40163**
EMAIL: **rossana@eircom.net**

150 metres off N11, 50 mins Dublin, 30 mins Dun Laoghaire. Excellent Pubs, Restaurants. Close to Mount Usher gardens, Powercourt, Glendalough, Avoca (Ballykissangel).

B&B	3	Ensuite	€27/€30	Dinner	-
B&B	-	Standard		Partial Board	-
Single Rate			€39	Child reduction	-

Open: All Year

Avoca 2km

Mrs Doreen Burns
GREENHILLS
**Knockanree Lower,
Avoca, Co Wicklow**

Avoca
TEL: **0402 35197**   FAX: **0402 35197**

Bungalow in scenic peaceful surroundings near Avoca - The location of "Ballykissangel". Ideal touring area. Convenient to Handweavers, Glendalough, Dublin, Rosslare.

B&B	3	Ensuite	€28/€28	Dinner	-
B&B	-	Standard		Partial Board	-
Single Rate			€38.50/€38.50	Child reduction	-

Open: May-September

Avoca 2km

Mervyn & Jackie Burns
ASHDENE
**Knockanree Lower,
Avoca, Co Wicklow**

Avoca
TEL: **0402 35327**   FAX: **0402 35327**
EMAIL: **ashdene@eircom.net**
WEB: **homepage.eircom.net/~ashdene**

Award winning home near Handweavers and Ballykissangel. Tennis Court, Lounge with refreshments. Ideal touring base. Dublin/Rosslare 1 1/2 hrs. See homepage.

B&B	4	Ensuite	€28/€28	Dinner	-
B&B	1	Standard	€25/€25	Partial Board	-
Single Rate			€36/€38.50	Child reduction	25%

Open: 1st April-20th October

Avoca 5km

Mrs Rose Gilroy
KOLIBA
**Beech Road, Avoca,
Co Wicklow**

Avoca
TEL: **0402 32737**   FAX: **0402 32737**
EMAIL: **koliba@eircom.net**
WEB: **www.koliba.com**

Highly recommended country home. Panoramic views of Arklow Bay. Avoca location of Ballykissangel. Dublin, Rosslare 1 hour. In Avoca, turn right facing "Fitzgeralds".

B&B	3	Ensuite	€27.50	Dinner	-
B&B	-	Standard		Partial Board	-
Single Rate			-	Child reduction	25%

Open: 31st March-31st October

In Avoca

Mrs Bernie Ivers
CHERRYBROOK
COUNTRY HOME
Avoca, Co Wicklow

Avoca
TEL: **0402 35179**   FAX: **0402 35765**
EMAIL: **cherrybandb@eircom.net**
WEB: **www.cherrybrookhouse.com**

Highly recommended home in Avoca. Home of Avoca Handweavers. Minutes walk from Fitzgeralds bar of Ballykissangel. Ideal location for Golf, Walking and Touring the Garden County. AA ◆◆◆.

B&B	4	Ensuite	€28/€28	Dinner	€20
B&B	-	Standard		Partial Board	€275
Single Rate			€43.50/€43.50	Child reduction	33.3%

Open: All Year

Avoca 5km

Mrs Aine McGovern
ROCKVIEW
Beech Rd, Avoca,
Co Wicklow

Avoca
TEL: **0402 39011**   FAX: **0402 39011**
EMAIL: **rockview@oceanfree.net**

Quiet countryside with panoramic views of Arklow Bay. All rooms ground floor. Dublin/Rosslare 1.5hrs.Take R772 off N11 facing Fitzgeralds pub, turn right.

B&B	4	Ensuite	€28/€28	Dinner	-
B&B	-	Standard		Partial Board	-
Single Rate			€43.50/€43.50	Child reduction	33.3%

cc P ⊗ ⅋ ⌁ ▭ ⬚ ⅛ ⬗ ⬅ J s J ᴿ   **Open:** 4th March-31st October

---

In Avoca

Mrs Margaret McGraynor
GLENDALE HOUSE
Avoca, Co Wicklow

Avoca
TEL: **0402 35780**   FAX: **0402 35780**
EMAIL: **glendhouse@eircom.net**
WEB: **homepage.eircom.net/~glendale**

New purpose built bungalow in Avoca. 5 min walk to Fitzgeralds Pub of Ballykissangel fame. Orthopaedic beds, Hairdryers. Breakfast menu. R77 off N11 facing Fitzgeralds Pub turn right.

B&B	4	Ensuite	€26/€27.50	Dinner	-
B&B	-	Standard		Partial Board	-
Single Rate			-	Child reduction	25%

cc P ⅋ ⌁ ▭ ⬚ ⬗ ⅛ ⬅ J s J ᴿ   **Open:** 1st January-4th November

---

Blessington 6km

Mrs Andrea Begg
AVELIN
Poulaphouca, Ballymore
Eustace, Near Blessington,
Co Wicklow

Blessington
TEL: **045 864524**   FAX: **045 864823**
EMAIL: **begg@iol.ie**
WEB: **www.celticretreat.com**
BUS NO: **65**

Comfortable welcoming home by lakes and mountains. Transport to Golf, Hill walking, ancient sites and gardens etc; also Celtic holiday retreats-see website.

B&B	4	Ensuite	€29/€33	Dinner	-
B&B	-	Standard		Partial Board	-
Single Rate			€39.50/€45	Child reduction	25%

cc P ⊗ ⅋ ⌁ ▭ ⬚ ✕ ⬗ ⅛ ⬅ J ʟ J ᴿ   **Open:** 8th January-15th December

---

Blessington 6km

Mrs Mary Curley
THE HEATHERS
Poulaphouca,
Ballymore-Eustace,
Co Wicklow

Blessington
TEL: **045 864554**
EMAIL: **theheathers@eircom.net**
BUS NO: **65**

Bungalow beside Poulaphouca Lakes. 6km Blessington, 3km Russborough House. 25 min Glendalough, near National Stud, Japanese Gardens, Golf, Angling, Punchestown.

B&B	2	Ensuite	€29/€34	Dinner	€23
B&B	2	Standard	€25.50/€32	Partial Board	-
Single Rate			€38/€40	Child reduction	25%

cc P ⅋ ⌁ ▭ ⬚ ↩ ✕ ⅛ ⬅ J ʟ J ᴿ   **Open:** All Year Except Christmas

---

In Blessington

Mrs Patricia Gyves
HAYLANDS HOUSE
Dublin Road, Blessington,
Co Wicklow

Blessington
TEL: **045 865183**
EMAIL: **hayland@eircom.net**
BUS NO: **65**

AIB hospitality award winner. Spacious bungalow in quiet surroundings on N81 in scenic area. Dublin Airport and Ferries 55 mins. Ideal location for touring.

B&B	5	Ensuite	€25.50/€25.50	Dinner	-
B&B	1	Standard	€23/€23	Partial Board	-
Single Rate			€36/€38.50	Child reduction	25%

P ⊗ ⅋ ⌁ ↩ ⬗ ⬅ J ʟ   **Open:** 1st February-31st October

Dublin 35km

Adrienne McCann
BEECHWOOD HOUSE
Manor Kilbride, Blessington,
Co Wicklow

TEL: **01 4582802**   FAX: **01 4582802**
EMAIL: **amccann@beechwoodhouse.ie**
WEB: **www.beechwoodhouse.ie**
BUS NO: **65**

Beautiful country house set in 2 acres. Mature gardens. 24 miles south of Dublin City lying between Blessington Lakes and the Wicklow Mountains.

B&B	6	Ensuite	€32/€64	Dinner		€23
B&B	-	Standard		Partial Board		
Single Rate			€44.50/€64	Child reduction		50%

Open: 2nd January-23rd December

Bray 1.5km

Mrs Kay Kelly
OLD RECTORY
Herbert Road, Bray,
Co Wicklow

TEL: **01 2867515**   FAX: **01 2867515**

Gothic Victorian Rectory, picturesque setting near Bray, Bus, Ferry, Golf, Mountains, Sea. 20km Dublin (N11). Bus No. 145 to Rapid Rail.

B&B	3	Ensuite	€26.66/€30.47	Dinner	-
B&B	-	Standard	-	Partial Board	-
Single Rate			€35.55/€44.44	Child reduction	25%

Open: 1st January-22nd December

In Bray

Mrs Peggy Kelly
ROSSLYN HOUSE
Killarney Road, Bray,
Co Wicklow

TEL: **01 2860993**   FAX: **01 2862419**
BUS NO: **45, 45A, 84**

Elegant Victorian residence beside Bray Town Hall. Close to Rapid Rail, Bus, Car Ferry, Mountains, Sea. 20km Dublin N11 route.

B&B	4	Ensuite	€30/€35	Dinner	-
B&B	-	Standard	-	Partial Board	-
Single Rate			-	Child reduction	-

Open: March-October

In Bray

Mrs Kathleen Roseingrave
IVERAGH
44 Meath Road, Bray,
Co Wicklow

TEL: **01 2863877**
EMAIL: **iveragh@hotmail.com**
BUS NO: **84, 45**

Detached period residence beside sea. Close to Rapid Rail, Bus, Car Ferry, Sporting Amenities. Dun Laoghaire 6 mls, Dublin 12 mls.

B&B	5	Ensuite	€27/€32	Dinner	-
B&B	1	Standard	€25.50/€25.50	Partial Board	-
Single Rate			-	Child reduction	-

Open: 17th March-30th October

Mrs Eilish Cummins
CORNER HOUSE
Enniskerry, Co Wicklow

TEL: **01 2860149**   FAX: **01 2860149**
BUS NO: **44**

Old world house situated in Enniskerry Village. Close to Powerscourt Gardens and Waterfall. Convenient Car Ferries and Airport. Dublin 20km on N11. All bedrooms have own showers.

B&B	-	Ensuite	-	Dinner	-
B&B	3	Standard	€25.39/€28	Partial Board	-
Single Rate			€35.55/€35.55	Child reduction	-

Open: 4th January-22nd December

In Enniskerry

Mrs Kay Lynch
CHERBURY
Monastery, Enniskerry,
Co Wicklow

Enniskerry
Tel: **01 2828679**
Bus No: **44**

Large Bungalow, Landscaped gardens. Ideal base for touring Wicklow. Convenient Powerscourt, Glendalough, Golf, Car Ferry, Airport, Dublin 20km.

B&B	3	Ensuite	€30/€35	Dinner	-
B&B	-	Standard	-	Partial Board	-
Single Rate			-	Child reduction	-

Enniskerry 1km

Open: All Year

Kay O'Connor
OAKLAWN
Glaskenny, Enniskerry,
Co Wicklow

Enniskerry
Tel: **01 2860493**
Email: **johnb@indigo.ie**
Web: **www.oaklawn.20m.com**
Bus No: **185**

Delightful house. Just off Glencree Road, idyllic country setting. Beside Powerscourt and Wicklow Way. Convenient Car Ferries, Airport, Dublin 25km.

B&B	2	Ensuite	€27.50/€32.50	Dinner	-
B&B	2	Standard	€25.50/€27.50	Partial Board	-
Single Rate			€38	Child reduction	50%

Enniskerry 4km

Open: 1st March-31st October

Barry & Bernie Smyth
COILLTE
4 Enniskerry Demesne,
Enniskerry, Co Wicklow

Enniskerry
Tel: **01 2766614**   Fax: **01 2766618**
Email: **smyt@eircom.net**
Web: **homepage.eircom.net/~barcoillte**
Bus No: **44, DART**

Coillte in award winning Enniskerry Demesne opposite Powerscourt and next to Summerhill Hotel, five minutes stroll from Enniskerry Village.

B&B	3	Ensuite	€42/€42	Dinner	-
B&B	-	Standard	-	Partial Board	-
Single Rate			-	Child reduction	-

In Enniskerry

Open: 1st January-21st December

Mrs Carmel Hawkins
CARMEL'S
Glendalough, Annamoe,
Co Wicklow

Glendalough
Tel: **0404 45297**   Fax: **0404 45297**
Email: **carmelsbandb@eircom.net**
Web: **homepage.eircom.net/~carmels**

When touring Wicklow have a break at this hospitable well established country home. Set in the heart of the Wicklow Mountains. 5 mins drive Glendalough near to Airport & Ferries R755.

B&B	4	Ensuite	€27.50/€30	Dinner	-
B&B	-	Standard	-	Partial Board	-
Single Rate			-	Child reduction	25%

In Annamoe

Open: 1st March-15th November

Mrs Valerie Merrigan
GLENDALE
Glendalough,
Co Wicklow

Glendalough
Tel: **0404 45410**   Fax: **0404 45410**
Email: **merrigan@eircom.net**

Country Home set in scenic Wicklow Mountains, situated 1.5km Glendalough. On Laragh to Annamoe Road, 0.5km from Shops, Restaurants and Pub.

B&B	4	Ensuite	€26/€26	Dinner	-
B&B	-	Standard	-	Partial Board	-
Single Rate			€38.50/€46	Child reduction	25%

In Laragh

Open: 1st January-23rd December

Martha O'Neill
GLENDALOUGH
RIVER HOUSE
Derrybawn, Glendalough,
Co Wicklow

TEL: **0404 45577**   FAX: **0404 45577**
EMAIL: **glendaloughriverhouse@hotmail.com**

200 year old stone restored house. All bedrooms have beautiful river views. Located on walking trail to Glendalough. Excellent breakfast menu.

B&B	4	Ensuite	€36/€50	Dinner	-
B&B	-	Standard	-	Partial Board	-
Single Rate			€50/€63.50	Child reduction	25%

Laragh 1km

Open: 3rd January-15th November

Margaret Berkery
CULLAUN
Sea Road, Kilcoole,
Co Wicklow

TEL: **01 2875998**
BUS NO: **84, 84A**

Dormer bungalow, private car parking, only 5 km from Greystones and 30 mins drive from Car Ferry (via N11). Adjacent Glenroe/Druids Glen.

B&B	3	Ensuite	€26/€28	Dinner	-
B&B	-	Standard	-	Partial Board	-
Single Rate			€38.50/€40	Child reduction	25%

Greystones 5km

Open: 1st May-31st October

Ms Mary Doyle
LA CASA
Kilpedder Grove, Kilpedder,
Greystones, Co Wicklow

TEL: **01 2819703**
EMAIL: **lacasabb@yahoo.com**
BUS NO: **184**

Situated in Kilpedder village N11 route. 10 mins Greystones, Airport 1 hour, Ferries 30 mins. 184 bus Greystones/Bray, DART every 20 mins, Glendalough. 30 min drive, Powercourt 15 min.

B&B	2	Ensuite	€25.50/€31.75	Dinner	-
B&B	1	Standard	€24.13/€30.48	Partial Board	-
Single Rate			€36/€38.10	Child reduction	-

Greystones 5km

Open: 1st February-30th November

Malcolm & Penny Hall
GLANDORE
St Vincent Rd,
Burnaby Estate,
Greystones, Co Wicklow

TEL: **01 2874364**   FAX: **01 2874364**
BUS NO: **84**

House of great charm, set in mature gardens in beautiful old world estate. Five minutes from all amenities.

B&B	4	Ensuite	€28/€32	Dinner	-
B&B	-	Standard	-	Partial Board	-
Single Rate			€39	Child reduction	33.3%

In Greystones

Open: All Year

Mary & Michael Hogan
THORNVALE
Kilpedder, Greystones,
Co Wicklow

TEL: **01 2810410**
EMAIL: **hoganwicklow@eircom.net**
BUS NO: **184**

Modern family home on 1.5 acre gardens. Exit N11 for Kilquade at Kilpedder, immediate right. Ideal for touring Wicklow & Dublin. DART at Greystones/Bray.

B&B	4	Ensuite	€26/€28	Dinner	-
B&B	-	Standard	-	Partial Board	-
Single Rate			€38.50/€40	Child reduction	-

Greystones 6km

Open: All Year

Mrs Kathleen Nunan
SILLAN LODGE
Church Lane, Greystones,
Co Wicklow

Greystones
TEL: **01 2875535**
EMAIL: **sillanlodge@ireland.com**
BUS NO: **84, 84X**

Sillan Lodge is situated off a peaceful tree lined avenue, with extensive grounds, mountain and sea views. Close to City, Car Ferry and Rapid Rail service (DART). Scenic drives nearby.

B&B	2	Ensuite	€28/€32	Dinner	-
B&B	1	Standard	€28/€28	Partial Board	-
Single Rate			€39/€39	Child reduction	-

In Greystones

Open: March-October

Joe & Patricia Treacy
CASTANEA
Rathdown Road, Greystones,
Co Wicklow

Greystones
TEL: **01 2876373**   FAX: **01 2878025**
EMAIL: **castanea@ireland.com**
BUS NO: **84, 84X, 184**

Secluded home N11 to R761/2. Lovely gardens, Patio. Safe Parking. Close to best Restaurants, Sea, Dart. Ideal base for Dublin, Golf, Heritage gardens, Mountains.

B&B	4	Ensuite	€26/€28	Dinner	-
B&B	-	Standard	-	Partial Board	-
Single Rate			€35/€40	Child reduction	33.3%

In Greystones

Open: 15th March-31st October

Mrs Kathleen Healy
HOLLYWOOD LODGE
Glendalough Road,
Hollywood,
Co Wicklow

Hollywood
TEL: **045 864230**
BUS NO: **65**

Cosy mountain home R756 near Lakes, Glendalough, National Stud, Japanese Gardens. Racing, Golf, Walking. Le Routard, Le Petit Fute Guide, Bleue Vasion recommended. Truly Irish home.

B&B	4	Ensuite	€26/€26	Dinner	-
B&B	-	Standard	-	Partial Board	-
Single Rate			€38.50/€38.50	Child reduction	25%

Blessington 12km

Open: March-October

TP & Frances MacDermott
AN T'AOIBHNEAS
Sliabhcorragh, Hollywood,
Co Wicklow

Hollywood
TEL: **045 864577**

Pleasant tasteful home in a natural environment with exquisite mountain views. Located 3km off N81 on R756 Hollywood/Glendalough Road. Good Restaurants.

B&B	3	Ensuite	€25.50/€28	Dinner	-
B&B	-	Standard	-	Partial Board	-
Single Rate			€38.50/€40	Child reduction	50%

Hollywood 3km

Open: 31st January-10th December

Agnes Reilly
CHESTNUT HOUSE
Hollywood Lower, Hollywood,
Co Wicklow

Hollywood/Blessington
TEL: **045 864661**   FAX: **045 864661**

On N81 in the scenic Hollywood Glen. Convenient for visiting Russborough House, Glendalough, Powerscourt, National Stud & Japanese Gardens. Airport 45 mins.

B&B	4	Ensuite	€28.57/€28.57	Dinner	-
B&B	-	Standard	-	Partial Board	-
Single Rate			€38.50/€44.44	Child reduction	25%

Blessington 6km

Open: 1st January-23rd December

In Newtownmountkennedy

Catherine Tierney
DRUIDS HOUSE
Kilmacullagh,
Newtownmountkennedy,
Co Wicklow

TEL: **01 2819477**

Ideal base Glendalough, Powerscourt, Mount Usher Gardens. Walking distance Druids Glen Golf Course. Bray 10 mins, Dublin 40 minutes. Breakfast menu. Tea/Coffee/TV all rooms.

B&B	3	Ensuite	€25.50	Dinner	-
B&B	-	Standard		Partial Board	-
Single Rate			€38.50	Child reduction	50%

Open: All Year

Rathdrum 2km

Mr Gerry Fulham
ABHAINN MOR HOUSE
Corballis, Rathdrum,
Co Wicklow

TEL: **0404 46330**   FAX: **0404 43150**
EMAIL: **abhainnmor@eircom.net**
WEB: **homepage.eircom.net/~wicklowbandb/**

Enjoy good food in a comfortable home with spacious gardens. Family rooms. Close to Glendalough and Avoca. 2km south of Rathdrum R752.

B&B	6	Ensuite	€28/€30	Dinner	€18
B&B	-	Standard	-	Partial Board	€280
Single Rate			€40/€40	Child reduction	33.3%

Open: 1st January-20th December

Mrs Ann Griffin
LETTERMORE
Corballis, Rathdrum,
Co Wicklow

TEL: **0404 46506**   FAX: **0404 43183**
EMAIL: **lettermore@eircom.net**
WEB: **homepage.eircom.net/~lettermore**

Country home 2km south of Rathdrum, Avoca Road (R752). Close Avondale, Meetings of Waters, Avoca, Glendalough. From Airport M50 to Blessington, Hollywood, Wicklow Gap, Laragh, Rathdrum.

B&B	4	Ensuite	€25.50/€28	Dinner	€19
B&B	1	Standard	€25.50/€25.50	Partial Board	€267
Single Rate			€38/€38	Child reduction	33.3%

Rathdrum 2km

Open: 1st March-31st October

Marina Long & Sean Lyons
BEECHLAWN
Corballis, Rathdrum,
Co Wicklow

TEL: **0404 46474**   FAX: **0404 43389**
EMAIL: **caj@tinet.ie**

Modern bungalow in large garden on Avoca road. Close to Avondale, Glendalough, Town, Bus and Train. Private parking.

B&B	3	Ensuite	€27	Dinner	€20
B&B	1	Standard	€25	Partial Board	€280
Single Rate			€38.50	Child reduction	25%

Rathdrum 1km

Open: 1st February-30th November

Rathdrum 2km

Mrs Maeve Scott
ST BRIDGET'S
Corballis, Rathdrum,
Co Wicklow

TEL: **0404 46477**
EMAIL: **stbridgets@eircom.net**

Quiet countryside location. 2km south of Rathdrum town R753. Just 50 yds off Avoca road R752. All bedrooms on ground floor. Adjacent to Avondale, Avoca, Glendalough, Wicklow Mountains.

B&B	3	Ensuite	€27.50 /€30	Dinner	-
B&B	-	Standard	-	Partial Board	-
Single Rate			€40/€40	Child reduction	25%

Open: 1st January-20th December

Mrs Eileen Sheehan
THE HAWTHORNS
Corballis, Rathdrum,
Co Wicklow

Rathdrum

Tel: **0404 46683/46217**   Fax: **0404 46217**
Email: **thehawthorns1@eircom.net**
Web: **homepage.eircom.net/~thehawthorns**

Modern bungalow in award winning garden. 1/2 km from Rathdrum and railway station. Ideal centre for Golf, Fishing, Walking. 1hr to Airport and Ferries. Lonely Planet Recommended.

B&B	1	Ensuite	€28	Dinner	-
B&B	2	Standard	€25	Partial Board	-
Single Rate			€38	Child reduction	33.3%

In Rathdrum

Open: 6th January-18th December

Mrs Fiona Byrne
GLEN NA SMOLE
Ashtown Lane, Marlton Road,
Wicklow, Co Wicklow

Wicklow

Tel: **0404 67945**   Fax: **0404 68155**
Email: **byrneglen@eircom.net**
Web: **homepage.eircom.net/~byrneglen**

Comfortable family home. Award winning breakfasts. 2km Grand Hotel/Beehive Pub off Wicklow/Wexford Road. Golf, Fishing arranged. Low season discounts.

B&B	4	Ensuite	€25.50/€28	Dinner	€17
B&B	-	Standard	-	Partial Board	€264
Single Rate			€30/€35	Child reduction	50%

Wicklow 2km

Open: March-November

Mrs Rita Byrne
ROSITA
Dunbur Park, Wicklow Town,
Co Wicklow

Wicklow

Tel: **0404 67059**

Luxurious spacious home overlooking Wicklow Bay. Take coast road, turn into Dunbur Park at pedestrian crossing. 5 minutes walk to Town.

B&B	4	Ensuite	€28/€30	Dinner	-
B&B	-	Standard	-	Partial Board	-
Single Rate			€40.63/€42	Child reduction	-

In Wicklow

Open: 1st March-31st October

Catherine Doyle
DROM ARD
Ballynerrin Lr, Wicklow Town,
Co Wicklow

Wicklow

Tel: **0404 66056**   Fax: **0404 66056**
Email: **dromardwicklow@excite.com**

Modern spilt-level home with splendid views of Mountains, Sea, Countryside. Within easy reach of Glendalough. Ideal base for touring South-East, Dublin-Rosslare.

B&B	3	Ensuite	€26/€28	Dinner	-
B&B	1	Standard	€24/€26	Partial Board	-
Single Rate			€36/€36	Child reduction	33.3%

Wicklow 2km

Open: 1st March-31st October

Mrs Lyla Doyle
SILVER SANDS
Dunbur Road, Wicklow,
Co Wicklow

Wicklow

Tel: **0404 68243**
Email: **lyladoyle@eircom.net**

Overlooking Wicklow Bay. Drive straight through Wicklow Town, take coast road. Recommended by Frommer/O'Sullivan and Elsie Dillards "300 Best B&Bs".

B&B	4	Ensuite	€28/€30	Dinner	-
B&B	1	Standard	€28/€28	Partial Board	-
Single Rate			€36.50/€43.50	Child reduction	25%

In Wicklow

Open: 1st March-30th November

Mrs Sylvia Doyle
SWALLOW'S REST
Ballynerrin, Wicklow Town, Co Wicklow

Wicklow
TEL: **0404 68718**
EMAIL: **pdmd@indigo.ie**

Modern house with spectacular lake, sea and country view. Large spacious rooms, homely but with all modern facilities. Private grounds for guests use.

B&B	5	Ensuite	€28/€28	Dinner	-
B&B	-	Standard	-	Partial Board	-
Single Rate			€38.50/€40	Child reduction	33.3%

Wicklow 1.5km

Open: 1st March-1st October

Mrs Helen Gorman
THOMOND HOUSE
St Patricks Road Upr, Wicklow, Co Wicklow

Wicklow
TEL: **0404 67940**   FAX: **0404 67940**
EMAIL: **thomondhouse@eircom.net**

House with balcony. Wonderful views Sea, Mountains. 1km past RC Church. Frommer, Lets Go, Lonely Planet, Rough Guide recommended. Golf arranged. Warm welcome.

B&B	2	Ensuite	€25.50/€28	Dinner	-
B&B	3	Standard	€23/€25.50	Partial Board	-
Single Rate			€36/€36	Child reduction	-

Wicklow 1km

Open: 1st April-31st October

Mrs Hilary McGowan
ARCH HOUSE
Ballynerrin, Wicklow Town, Co Wicklow

Wicklow
TEL: **0404 68176**
EMAIL: **hilarymcgowan@eircom.net**
WEB: **www.angelfire.com**

A dormer bungalow with a panoramic view of Wicklow Bay and Mountains. Golf, Fishing, Horseriding nearby. A friendly welcome awaits you.

B&B	3	Ensuite	€25.50/€28	Dinner	-
B&B	1	Standard	€24/€27	Partial Board	-
Single Rate			€36/€38.50	Child reduction	50%

Wicklow 1.5km

Open: 1st March-31st October

Mrs Ann Mitchell
OLANDA
Dunbur Park, Wicklow, Co Wicklow

Wicklow
TEL: **0404 67579**

Comfortable welcoming home bungalow in peaceful quiet location. 5 minutes walk to Town. Take Coast Road, turn right at pedestrian crossing into Dunbur Park.

B&B	2	Ensuite	€28	Dinner	-
B&B	2	Standard	€25.50	Partial Board	-
Single Rate			€36	Child reduction	50%

In Wicklow

Open: 1st January-1st December

SYMBOL

**LOOK OUT FOR THIS SYMBOL WHICH
ALL MEMBERS OF TOWN & COUNTRY HOMES
DISPLAY**

Ireland's Tourist Information Network

Tourist Information

WELCOME TO IRELAND and to the services provided by our Tourist Information Network. In addition to tourist information and room reservations, many of our offices provide a wide range of services, all designed to aid you in your holiday planning and help you to enjoy to the full, all that Ireland has to offer.

OUR SERVICES AT A GLANCE

- Accommodation Booking Service
- Bureau de Change Facilities
- Computer-speeded Gulliver Reservation Service
- Guide Books For Sale
- Itinerary and Route Planning
- Local and National Information
- Local Craft Displays
- Map Sales
- Multi-lingual facilities
- Souvenirs
- Stamps and Postcards
- What's on in the Area and Nationally

* Some Tourist Information Offices may not provide all of the services or facilities listed here.

Follow the Shamrock

LOOK FOR THE SHAMROCK SIGN on accommodation. It is your guarantee that premises on which it is displayed provide accommodation which is inspected and whose standards are approved and regulated by agencies supervised by Bord Fáilte, the Irish Tourist Board.

Of course all accommodation booked on your behalf through Tourist Information Offices is fully approved and regulated in this manner.

Ask for our free guide to the locations of all 123 Tourist Information Offices throughout the country - your guide to better service and a happier holiday.

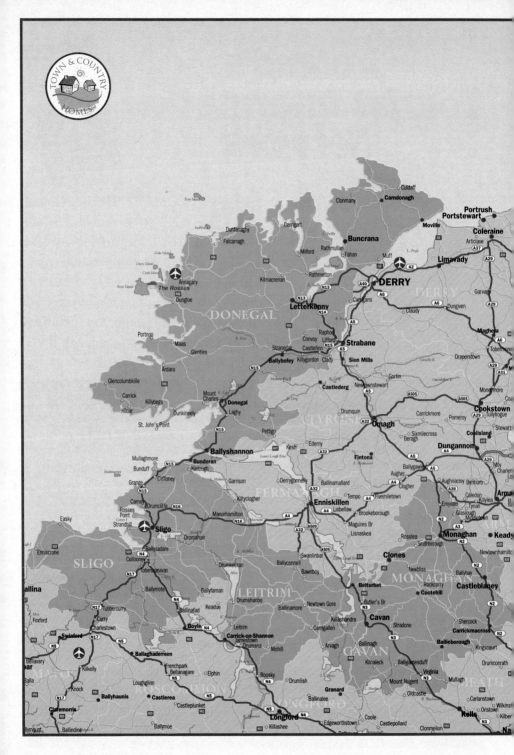

Discover the North West and discover the best of Ireland! This is truly the greenest part of Europe's Green Island...unspoilt, uncrowded and undiscovered.

In the counties of Cavan, Donegal, Leitrim, Monaghan and Sligo there is a wealth of scenery, heritage and hospitality. With geography that ranges from wild Atlantic coast through gentle meandering rivers to sylvan lakeland, and a history that dates from Neolithic archaeology through to modern Irish writing, every interest can be met.

Glenveagh National Park

For the active there are classic links and parkland golf courses; superb equestrian centres; hill walking and mountain climbing; summer schools of every variety; wide open beaches, some with world class surfing; and at the end of every day Irish hospitality at its best in bars and restaurants.

Area Representatives

CAVAN
Mrs Susan McCauley, Rockwood House, Cloverhill, Belturbet, Co Cavan
Tel: 047 55351 Fax: 047 55373
DONEGAL
Mrs Breid Kelly, Ardglas, Lurgybrack, Sligo Road, Letterkenny,
Co Donegal Tel: 074 22516/25140 Fax: 074 22516
Mr John Hughes, Randwick, Bundoran Road, Ballyshannon,
Co Donegal Tel: 072 52545 Fax: 072 52545
Mrs Ann McClean, Credo House, Benroe, Killybegs, Co Donegal
Tel: 073 31364 Fax: 073 31364
LEITRIM
Mrs Valerie Cahill, Attyrory Lodge, Dublin Rd, Carrick-on-Shannon,
Co Leitrim Tel: 078 20955 Fax: 078 20955
SLIGO
Mrs Tess Haughey, Rathnashee, Teesan, Donegal Road N15, Sligo, Co Sligo
Tel: 071 43376 Fax: 071 42283
Mrs Noreen Donoghue, Rossli House, Doocastle, Tubbercurry,
Co SligoTel: 071 85099 Fax: 071 85099

Tourist Information Offices
OPEN ALL YEAR

Sligo Town
Temple Street
Tel: 071 61201

Donegal Town
The Quay
Tel: 073 21148

Carrick-on-Shannon
The Old Barrel
Store
Tel: 078 20170

Letterkenny
Derry Road
Tel: 074 21160

Cavan Town
Farnham Street
Tel: 049 4331942

Monaghan Town
Market House
Tel: 047 81122

Website: : **www.irelandnorthwest.ie**

Cavan, a county rich in history and culture is also a haven for the lover of the quiet outdoors. The Angler, Golfer, Horse-rider and Hill-walker are all catered for. Swimming, Tennis, River Cruising and many other activities will make your visit an unforgettable one.

Ballyconnell 1.5km

Patrick & Ann Duignan
HILLCREST HOUSE
Slievebricken,
Ballyconnell, Co Cavan

Ballyconnell
TEL: **049 9526475**

1.5km from Ballyconnell on the Killeshandra Rd. Relax with Golfing at Slieve Russell Hotel and Country Club or cruise the Shannon, Erne waterway. all within 3km.

B&B	3	Ensuite	€32	Dinner	-
B&B	-	Standard	-	Partial Board	-
Single Rate			€38.50	Child reduction	25%

Open: All Year

Bawnboy 3km

Catherine & Joseph O'Reilly
LAKE AVENUE HOUSE
Port, Bawnboy,
Co Cavan

Bawnboy
TEL: **049 9523298**   FAX: **049 9523298**
EMAIL: **lakeave@eircom.net**

Beautiful new home, quiet scenic rural setting. Ideal base for Fishing, Touring, Walking, Cycling and Golf. 3km from Bawnboy on N3. Belturbet/Swanlinbar Rd.

B&B	4	Ensuite	€25.50/€28	Dinner	€17
B&B	-	Standard	-	Partial Board	-
Single Rate			€38.50/€38.50	Child reduction	50%

Open: 8th January-16th December

Belturbet 6km

James & Susan McCauley
ROCKWOOD HOUSE
Cloverhill, Belturbet,
Co Cavan

Belturbet
TEL: **047 55351**   FAX: **047 55373**
EMAIL: **jbmac@eircom.net**

Lovely country house situated in secluded peaceful woodlands and surrounded by lawns and gardens on the N54, 2 miles from Butlersbridge, 6 miles Cavan.

B&B	4	Ensuite	€28	Dinner	-
B&B	-	Standard	-	Partial Board	-
Single Rate			€38.50	Child reduction	25%

Open: All Year Except Christmas

In Cavan

Ms Eileen Flynn
GLENDOWN
33 Cathedral Road, Cavan,
Co Cavan

Cavan
TEL: **049 4332257**
EMAIL: **glendown@eircom.net**

Warm friendly comfortable home, residential area. Convenient to Equestrian centre/ Golf course/Sports Complex. Good Fishing and Genealogy Research centre.

B&B	4	Ensuite	€27/€27	Dinner	-
B&B	-	Standard	-	Partial Board	-
Single Rate			€38.50/€38.50	Child reduction	25%

Open: 20th February-20th December

In Cavan

Ann & Paddy Gaffney
OAKDENE
29 Cathedral Rd., Cavan,
Co Cavan

Cavan
Tel: 049 4331698

Spacious comfortable home. Residential area. 10 minutes walking from Town Centre. Convenient to Equestrian Centre, Sports Complex, Golf Club, Fishing. Close to N3, Cavan by-pass.

			Dinner	-
B&B	4	Ensuite €27/€27		
B&B	-	Standard	Partial Board	-
Single Rate		€38.50/€38.50	Child reduction	25%

Open: 1st January-21st December

Cavan 2km

Ben & Teresa Gaffney
ROCKVILLA
Moynehall, Cavan,
Co Cavan

Cavan
Tel: 049 4361885   Fax: 049 4361885
Web: rockvilla@eircom.net

Situated just off the N55 approaching from N3. Left at "Shell" gas station. Help with Genealogical research in Cavan. Ideal Dublin-Donegal stopover. Parking.

			Dinner	-
B&B	4	Ensuite €27		
B&B	-	Standard	Partial Board	-
Single Rate		€38.50	Child reduction	25%

Open: 1st January-21st December

Cavan 2.5km

Mrs Alacoque O'Brien
BALLYCLOONE HOUSE
Golf Links Road, Cavan,
Co Cavan

Cavan
Tel: 049 4362310
Email: michaelobrien53@eircom.net

Luxurious friendly accommodation, quiet road. Convenient to Town Centre, Golf Club, Equestrian Centre, Sports Complex.

			Dinner	-
B&B	2	Ensuite €28		
B&B	1	Standard €28	Partial Board	-
Single Rate		€38.50	Child reduction	25%

Open: 1st January-20th December

Cootehill

Mrs Vera Greenan
THE BEECHES
Station Road, Cootehill,
Co Cavan

Cootehill
Tel: 049 5552307

Modern dormer bungalow, situated in cul-de-sac off Shercock Road. Prime fishing area, home cooking and warm welcome to all visitors.

			Dinner	€17
B&B	2	Ensuite €25.50/€25.50		
B&B	1	Standard €23/€23	Partial Board	-
Single Rate		-	Child reduction	25%

Open: 1st February-31st October

Killeshandra 2km

Mrs Maura O'Reilly
CLOONEEN HOUSE
Belturbet Rd., T52/R201
Killeshandra, Co Cavan

Killeshandra
Tel: 049 4334342   Fax: 049 4334342
Email: clooneen_house@esatclear.ie

Turn right facing Ulster Bank. Dormer bungalow situated T52/R201. Ideal stopover between Dublin/Donegal. Help with Ancestral tracing. Killykeen Park, Walks, Fishing, Pony Trekking.

			Dinner	-
B&B	2	Ensuite €25.50		
B&B	2	Standard €23	Partial Board	-
Single Rate		€36/€38.50	Child reduction	25%

Open: April-October

Mrs Julie Mulvany Fox
LISDUFF HOUSE B&B
Lisduff, Virginia,
Co Cavan

Virginia
Tel: **046 45054**   Fax: **046 45054**
Web: **www.lisduffhse.ie**

Renovated 18th century Farmhouse, N3, overlooking Lough Crew, Hill of Four, Lough Ramor, Blackwater River, St Killian's Heritage Centre, Mullagh.

B&B	5	Ensuite	€26/€28	Dinner	-
B&B	-	Standard	-	Partial Board	-
Single Rate			€38.50	Child reduction	25%

Virginia 3km   **Open:** All Year

Mrs Emily McHugo
THE WHITE HOUSE
Oldcastle Road, Virginia,
Co Cavan

Virginia
Tel: **049 8547515**   Fax: **049 8547515**
Email: **mchugo@esatclear.ie**

Warm welcome, breakfast menu. Tea/Coffee bedrooms. Forest walks. Fish at Lough Ramor. Horseriding, Watersports. Visit Loughcrew, Newgrange, Fore Abbey.

B&B	4	Ensuite	€25.50/€31.75	Dinner	-
B&B	-	Standard	-	Partial Board	-
Single Rate			-	Child reduction	50%

Virginia 1km   **Open:** 1st April-31st October

Mrs Bernie O'Reilly
ST KYRAN'S
Dublin Road, Virginia,
Co Cavan

Virginia
Tel: **049 8547087**

Luxurious, ranch-type bungalow on Lough Ramor's shore. Panoramic view, mature gardens, excellent breakfast menu, electric blankets, tea making facilities.

B&B	2	Ensuite	€28	Dinner	-
B&B	2	Standard	€25	Partial Board	-
Single Rate			€36/€36	Child reduction	25%

Virginia 1km   **Open:** 1st April-29th September

BOOKINGS

We recommend your first and last night is pre-booked. Your hosts will make a booking for you at your next selected home for the cost of the phone call. When travelling in high season (June, July, August), it is essential to pre-book your accommodation – preferably the evening before, or the following morning to avoid disappointment.

WHEN TRAVELLING OFF-SEASON IT IS ADVISABLE TO CALL AHEAD AND GIVE A TIME OF ARRIVAL TO ENSURE YOUR HOSTS ARE AT HOME TO GREET YOU.

Donegal is undoubtedly one of Ireland's most beautiful and rugged counties, with its spectacular scenery, rambling hills, magnificent mountains, lakes and its many blue-flag beaches, so too, has its heritage and culture. Noted for its hospitality and friendliness. Famous for it's tweed, hand knits and traditional music. Catering for all leisure and sporting activities.

Jackie Bonner Sharkey
BAYVIEW HOUSE
Annagry(R259) (Anagaire)
The Rosses, Co Donegal

Annagry The Rosses
TEL: **075 48175**
EMAIL: **jns@eircom.net**

Quiet relaxing residence in Gaeltacht. Scenic views, Beaches, Hillclimbing nearby. Errigal-Dunlewey 15km. Glenveagh Park 25km. Daniel O'Donnell Hotel 8km.

B&B	3	Ensuite	€25.50	Dinner	-
B&B	1	Standard	€23	Partial Board	-
Single Rate			€36/€38.50	Child reduction	25%

In Annagry

Open: 1st April-31st October

Bennett Family
BAY VIEW COUNTRY HOUSE
Portnoo Road, Ardara,
Co Donegal

Ardara
TEL: **075 41145**   FAX: **075 41145**
EMAIL: **chbennett@eircom.net**

Spacious, overlooking sea. Large gardens. Breakfast award 1994. Recommended: Frommers, AA, Real Guide, Fodors. Tea/coffee facilities. Turf fire. Credit Cards.

B&B	6	Ensuite	€25.50/€25.50	Dinner	-
B&B	-	Standard		Partial Board	-
Single Rate			€38.50/€38.50	Child reduction	25%

Ardara 1km

Open: 1st February-15th December

Mrs Eva Friel
THALASSA COUNTRY HOME
Narin, Portnoo,
Co Donegal

Ardara Portnoo
TEL: **075 45151**

Magnificent coastal region overlooking Ocean, Lake, Beaches, 18-hole Golf Course, Scenic Walks. Ancient Historic Monuments. Warm welcoming home. Recommended Guide de Routard.

B&B	4	Ensuite	€25.50/€28	Dinner	€17
B&B	-	Standard	-	Partial Board	€285
Single Rate		-		Child reduction	25%

Ardara 5km

Open: 1st March-21st November

Vincent & Susan McConnell
ROSEWOOD COUNTRY HOUSE
Killybegs Road, Ardara,
Co Donegal

Ardara
TEL: **075 41168**   FAX: **075 41818**
EMAIL: **jmccon@gofree.indigo.ie**

Recommended by Le Guide de Routard, Ireland's best 300 B&B's. Fresh baked muffins and home-made jam served for breakfast. Tea/Coffee served in Guest lounge on arrival. Credit cards.

B&B	6	Ensuite	€25.50	Dinner	-
B&B	-	Standard	-	Partial Board	-
Single Rate		-		Child reduction	25%

Ardara 1km

Open: 1st Feburary-30th November

Mrs Evelyn Campbell
STRANORLAR HOUSE
Stranorlar, Co Donegal

TEL: **074 30225**   FAX: **074 30225**

Beautifully restored Victorian home run by Paddy and Evelyn Campbell as a Bed and Breakfast. The perfect base from which to explore the spectacular beauty of Donegal.

B&B	4	Ensuite	€43.18/€43.18	Dinner	-
B&B	-	Standard		Partial Board	-
Single Rate			€38.50/€38.50	Child reduction	33.3%

Stranorlar 1km

Open: 31st January-30th November

Judy McDermott
HILL TOP
Letterkenny Road, Stranorlar, Co Donegal

Ballybofey Stranorlar

TEL: **074 31185**
EMAIL: **admiran@unison.ie**

Comfortable home set among the rolling hills of Donegal. Good touring base. Golf and Fishing facilities available locally. Lake fishing with small boat available.

B&B	3	Ensuite	€25.50	Dinner	-
B&B	-	Standard		Partial Board	-
Single Rate			€38.50	Child reduction	25%

Ballybofey Stranorlar 1km

Open: 1st April-30th September

Mrs Mary McGranaghan
TEEVICKMOY HOUSE
Letterkenny Road, Ballybofey, Co Donegal

Ballybofey Stranorlar

TEL: **074 31866**   FAX: **074 31866**
EMAIL: **mmcgranaghan@eircom.ie**

Quiet rural location overlooking Steeple Woodlands, 0.5KM up from N13. Ideal Touring, Heritage base for NW. Sporting/Fishing/Beltony Stone Circle.

B&B	4	Ensuite	€25.50/€25.50	Dinner	-
B&B	-	Standard		Partial Board	-
Single Rate			€30/€30	Child reduction	50%

Ballybofey 3km

Open: 1st April-4th November

Mrs Gertrude Patton
FINN VIEW HOUSE
Lifford Road, Ballybofey/Stranorlar, Co Donegal

Ballybofey Stranorlar

TEL: **074 31351**

Modern dormer bungalow. Ideal touring centre for Glenveagh National Park and Giants Causeway. Salmon Fishing, 18 hole Golf Course.

B&B	2	Ensuite	€25.50	Dinner	-
B&B	1	Standard	€23	Partial Board	-
Single Rate			€36/€38.50	Child reduction	25%

Ballybofey Stranorlar 1km

Open: 1st April-30th September

Mrs Mary Conlon
TEEVOGUE
Bundoran Road, Ballyshannon, Co Donegal

Ballyshannon

TEL: **072 51386**   FAX: **072 51386**
EMAIL: **teevogue@iol.ie**

Bungalow overlooking Bay on N15, Spectacular view. Convenient to Donegal & Belleek China, Celtic Weave, Beaches, Horse Riding, Golf, Fishing. Rooms ensuite, TV, Hairdryer, Homebaking.

B&B	4	Ensuite	€25.50/€25.50	Dinner	€17
B&B	-	Standard		Partial Board	-
Single Rate			€38.50/€38.50	Child reduction	33.3%

Ballyshannon 1km

Open: May-October

John & Clare Hughes
RANDWICK
Bundoran Road, Ballyshannon,
Co Donegal

Ballyshannon

Tel: **072 52545**   Fax: **072 52545**
Email: **randwick9@eircom.net**

House on N15, magnificent views overlooking Erne Estuary. Le Guide du Routard. On parle francais. AIB Accommodation and Services Award 1998.

B&B	4	Ensuite	€25.50	Dinner	€17
B&B	1	Standard	€23	Partial Board	-
Single Rate			€36/€36	Child reduction	50%

Ballyshannon 1km   **Open:** 1st March-31st December

Mrs Deirdre Kelly
ASHBROOK HOUSE
Ashbrook Drive,
Rossnowlagh Rd,
Ballyshannon, Co Donegal

Ballyshannon

Tel: **072 51171**
Email: **ashbrook_house@hotmail.com**
Web: **ashbrookhouse.tripod.com**

Newly built luxury home on scenic Rossnowlagh coast road(R231). Short walk to Town. All rooms TV, Tea/Coffee, Power Showers, Hairdryers-Smoke Free home.

B&B	3	Ensuite	€26	Dinner	-
B&B	-	Standard	-	Partial Board	-
Single Rate			€38.50	Child reduction	-

Ballyshannon 1km   **Open:** 1st April-31st October

Siobain & George Luke
ASPEN
Parkhill, Ballyshannon,
Co Donegal

Ballyshannon

Tel: **072 52065**   Fax: **072 52065**
Email: **gluke@eircom.net**
Web: **homepage.eircom.net/~aspen**

Bungalow on N15 in scenic location. Non-smoking house, power showers, email facilities. Ballyshannon 1 mile, Belleek Pottery 4 miles, Donegal Castle 10 miles.

B&B	3	Ensuite	€25.50/€25.50	Dinner	€17
B&B	-	Standard	-	Partial Board	-
Single Rate			€38.50/€38.50	Child reduction	50%

Ballyshannon 2km   **Open:** 1st March-31st October

Mrs Agnes McCaffrey
CAVANGARDEN HOUSE
Donegal Road, Ballyshannon,
Co Donegal

Ballyshannon

Tel: **072 51365**
Email: **cghouse@iol.ie**

Georgian house 1750, Donegal Road (route N15) on 380-acres, 0.5KM Driveway, Antique Furniture, Beach, Golf Course, Fishing, Belleek. Frommer recommended.

B&B	6	Ensuite	€30/€35	Dinner	€19
B&B	-	Standard	-	Partial Board	-
Single Rate			€38.50/€40	Child reduction	33.3%

Ballyshannon 3km   **Open:** All Year Except Christmas

Mrs B McCaffrey
ROCKVILLE HOUSE
Belleek Road, Ballyshannon,
Co Donegal

Ballyshannon

Tel: **072 51106**
Email: **rockvillehouse@eircom.net**

Late 17th century, overlooking River Erne. Convenient to Bundoran, Belleek Pottery, Rossnowlagh Beaches. Experience peace & beauty of old refurbished house.

B&B	4	Ensuite	€26.02/€26.02	Dinner	-
B&B	2	Standard	€23.49/€23.49	Partial Board	-
Single Rate			€36/€36	Child reduction	25%

In Ballyshannon   **Open:** All Year Except Christmas

Mrs Rose McCaffrey
ARDPATTON HOUSE
Cavangarden, Ballyshannon, Co Donegal

Ballyshannon
TEL: **072 51546**

Ardpatton House is a warm comfortable family home on a large working farm on route N15. Close to Donegal Town, Belleek, with Golf, Fishing, Beaches.

B&B	6	Ensuite	€26/€26	Dinner	€19
B&B	-	Standard	-	Partial Board	
Single Rate			€38.50/€38.50	Child reduction	50%

Ballyshannon 5km

Open: 1st April-31st October

Karen McGee
ELM BROOK
East Port, Ballyshannon, Co Donegal

Ballyshannon
TEL:**072 52615**
EMAIL: **elmbrookbandb@eircom.net**

Spacious, modern home in peaceful location, yet convenient to all amenities. 3 mins walk Town Centre. Ideal touring base.

B&B	3	Ensuite	€25.50	Dinner	-
B&B	-	Standard	-	Partial Board	-
Single Rate			€38.50	Child reduction	33.3%

In Ballyshannon

Open: 1st March-31st October

Florence & Pat McMenamin
AVAREST
Tullyhorkey, Donegal Road, Ballyshannon, Co Donegal

Ballyshannon
TEL: **072 51059**
EMAIL: **avarest@iol.ie**

Modern bungalow on N15. Quiet location. Smoke free home. Ideal base for touring Donegal. Belleek China nearby.

B&B	3	Ensuite	€25.50	Dinner	-
B&B	-	Standard	-	Partial Board	-
Single Rate			€38.50	Child reduction	25%

Ballyshannon 2km

Open: 1st May-30th September

Mrs Marie Vaughan
CALDRA
Lisnakelly, Buncrana, Co Donegal

Buncrana
TEL: **077 63703**

Modern spacious family run home overlooking Lough Swilly and Town. Convenient to beaches, golf, fishing, parks, restaurants & pubs. Friendly warm atmosphere.

B&B	4	Ensuite	€27.50/€27.50	Dinner	-
B&B	-	Standard	-	Partial Board	-
Single Rate			€38.50/€38.50	Child reduction	50%

Buncrana 1.5km

Open: All Year Except Christmas

Bernie Dillon
GILLAROO LODGE
West End, Bundoran, Co Donegal

Bundoran
TEL: **072 42357**　　FAX: **072 42172**
EMAIL: **gillaroo@iol.ie**
WEB: **www.gillaroo.net**

Superbly located B&B on main road. Close to Beaches, Waterworld, Golf, Hillwalking. Angling Centre with angling guides, Tackle and Boat hire. Drying and Tackle room.

B&B	4	Ensuite	€25.50/€27.50	Dinner	-
B&B	1	Standard	€23/€23	Partial Board	-
Single Rate			€36/€38	Child reduction	25%

In Bundoran

Open: 1st January-30th November

Derry City 8km

Mrs J Martin
MOUNT ROYD
COUNTRY HOME
Carrigans, Co Donegal

Carrigans Near Derry
TEL: **074 40163**   FAX: **074 40400**
EMAIL: jmartin@mountroyd.com
WEB: www.mountroyd.com

Giants Causeway 1 hour. Grianan Aileach nearby. Old style home. Ground floor bedroom. Breakfast winner. Frommer Guide de Routard. AA & RAC◆◆◆◆. Finalist AA landlady year 2000.

B&B	4	Ensuite	€25.50/€25.50	Dinner	-
B&B	-	Standard	-	Partial Board	-
Single Rate			€38.50/€38.50	Child reduction	-

Open: All Year

In Carrigart

Fidelma Cullen
MEVAGH HOUSE
Milford Road, Carrigart,
Letterkenny, Co Donegal

Carrigart
TEL: **074 55693**   FAX: **074 55512**
EMAIL:mevaghhousebedbreakfast@hotmail.com

Family run B&B overlooking Mulroy Bay. 1/2km from Carraigart at entrance to Rosguill Peninsula and Atlantic Drive. Tea/coffee on arrival. Guest lounge.

B&B	4	Ensuite	€25.50	Dinner	-
B&B	-	Standard	-	Partial Board	-
Single Rate			€38.50	Child reduction	33.3%

Open: All Year

Carrigart 5km

Ann & Myles Gallagher
SONAS
Upper Carrick, Carrigart,
Letterkenny, Co Donegal

Carrigart
TEL: **074 55401**   FAX: **074 55195**
EMAIL: sonas1@indigo.ie

"Sonas" Modern Dormer Bungalow overlooking Bay combining modern facilities with old style hospitality. Ideal touring base. Home baking. Power showers.

B&B	5	Ensuite	€25.50	Dinner	€19
B&B	-	Standard	-	Partial Board	-
Single Rate			€38.50	Child reduction	50%

Open: 1st January 20th December

Clonmany 5km

Fidelma McLaughlin
FOUR ARCHES
Urris, Clonmany,
Inishowen, Co Donegal

Clonmany Inishowen
TEL: **077 76561**

Modern bungalow surrounded by Sea and Mountains. Ideal for touring Inishowen Peninsula. Near Mamore Gap. 20km from Malin Head. 20km from Buncrana Town.

B&B	5	Ensuite	€25.50/€25.50	Dinner	-
B&B	-	Standard	-	Partial Board	-
Single Rate			€38.50/€38.50	Child reduction	50%

Open: All Year Except Christmas

Malin 6km

Mrs Anne Lynch
CEECLIFF HOUSE
Culdaff, Inishowen,
Co Donegal

Culdaff
TEL: **077 79159**   FAX: **077 79159**

Family run home. Excellent views of Beach, River & Mountains. Close to all amenities.

B&B	3	Ensuite	€25.50/€25.50	Dinner	-
B&B	-	Standard	-	Partial Board	-
Single Rate			€38.50/€38.50	Child reduction	25%

Open: 1st January-23rd December

Sile Callaghan
THE GAP LODGE
Barnesmore Gap,
Donegal Town, Co Donegal

Donegal Town

TEL: **073 21956**
EMAIL: **gaplodge@eircom.net**
WEB: **www.gaplodge.com**

10 minutes drive from Donegal Town. Our spacious family run home is on the Letterkenny & Derry road, left side. Credit Cards accepted.

B&B	5	Ensuite	€25.50/€25.50	Dinner	-
B&B	-	Standard	-	Partial Board	-
Single Rate			€36/€36	Child reduction	25%

Donegal Town 8km

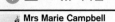

Open: All Year

Mrs Marie Campbell
LYNDALE
Doonan, Donegal Town,
Co Donegal

Donegal Town

TEL: **073 21873**
EMAIL: **lyndale@inet-sec.com**
WEB: **www.inet-sec.com/lyndale.htm**

Luxurious home 200 metres off Coast Rd.(N56) next to Mill Park Hotel & Leisure Centre, Breakfast menu, Homebaking, TV, Electric Blankets,Hairdryers, Tea/Coffee all rooms. Donegal Town 5min.

B&B	5	Ensuite	€25.50	Dinner	-
B&B	-	Standard	-	Partial Board	-
Single Rate			€38.50	Child reduction	25%

Donegal Town

Open: 1st January-30th November

Mrs Christina Doherty
RIVERBANK HOUSE
Tullygallen, Donegal P.O,
Co Donegal

Donegal Town

TEL: **073 23199**
EMAIL: **riverbank_house@hotmail.com**

Modern comfortable home, spacious bedrooms with relaxed family atmosphere. Situated 3km south of Donegal Town.

B&B	3	Ensuite	€26.50/€26.50	Dinner	-
B&B	-	Standard	-	Partial Board	-
Single Rate			€38.50/€38.50	Child reduction	25%

Donegal Town 3km

Open: 1st March-31st October

Bernadette Dowds
ISLAND VIEW HOUSE
Tullaghcullion, Donegal Town,
Co Donegal

Donegal Town

TEL: **073 22411**
EMAIL: **dowdsb@indigo.ie**
WEB: **www.eirbyte.com/islandview**

New two storey Georgian style house overlooking Donegal Bay. 10 minute walk to Town Centre. Ideal base for touring North West Donegal.

B&B	4	Ensuite	€25.50/€28	Dinner	-
B&B	-	Standard	-	Partial Board	-
Single Rate			€40.63	Child reduction	25%

Donegal Town 1km

Open: All Year Except Christmas

Mrs Kathleen Durcan
CRANAFORD
Ardeskin, Donegal Town,
Co Donegal

Donegal Town

TEL: **073 21455**
EMAIL: **cranaford@ireland.com**

Modern family bungalow in peaceful residential area. Walking distance to town. Ideal touring base. Rooms with TV and Tea/Coffee facilities.

B&B	2	Ensuite	€25.50	Dinner	-
B&B	1	Standard	€23	Partial Board	-
Single Rate			€36/€38.50	Child reduction	25%

Donegal 1km

Open: 1st April-31st October

Donegal Town 4km

Mrs Sheila Gatins
HILLCREST COUNTRY HOME
Ballyshannon Road, Laghey,
Donegal, Co Donegal

Donegal Town
TEL: **073 21837**   FAX: **073 21674**
EMAIL: **sheilagatins@unison.ie**

Quiet location in small village off N15. Donegal Golf course and blue flag Beach closeby. Recommended Best 300 B&B. Tea/Coffee making facilities.

B&B	2	Ensuite	€25.50	Dinner	-
B&B	1	Standard	€23	Partial Board	-
Single Rate			€36	Child reduction	25%

Open: 1st May-1st October

Donegal 1km

Mrs Margaret Geary
KNOCKNAGOW
Ballydevitt, Donegal,
Co Donegal

Donegal Town
TEL: **073 21052**

Modern bungalow situated in quiet countryside. Close to all amenities. Ideal touring base, excellent Shops, Crafts, Restaurants nearby.

B&B	1	Ensuite	€25.50	Dinner	-
B&B	2	Standard	€23	Partial Board	-
Single Rate			€36	Child reduction	50%

Open: 31st March-30th September

Donegal 6km

Mrs Mary J Harvey
CLYBAWN
Station Road, Mountcharles,
Co Donegal

Donegal Mountcharles
TEL: **073 35076**

Modern bungalow in scenic location overlooking Donegal Bay. Lake, River and Sea Fishing nearby. Donegal Town 6km, Murvagh Golf Course 15km. Private car park.

B&B	3	Ensuite	€25.50/€25.50	Dinner	€17
B&B	1	Standard	€23/€23	Partial Board	-
Single Rate			€36/€38.50	Child reduction	33.3%

Open: 1st April-30th September

Donegal 2.5km

Liam & Joan McCrea
THE COVE LODGE
Drumgowan, Donegal Town,
Co Donegal

Donegal Town
TEL: **073 22302**
EMAIL: **thecovelodge@ireland.com**
WEB: **www.donegalnet.com/thecovelodge**

Charming country residence overlooking Donegal Bay, just off N15 on R267. Golf Course, Beaches. Craft village. Comfort and relaxation assured.

B&B	4	Ensuite	€27/€33	Dinner	-
B&B	-	Standard	-	Partial Board	-
Single Rate			€40/€46	Child reduction	25%

Open: 1st March-31st October

Donegal Town 4km

Bried McGinty
MEADOW LANE B&B
Birchill, Donegal Town,
Co Donegal

Donegal Town
TEL: **073 23300**

Luxurious Country House on N15. 4km North of Donegal Town. Magnificient views of Bluestack Mountain. Ideal touring base. Peaceful and quiet.

B&B	6	Ensuite	€27.50/€32.50	Dinner	-
B&B	-	Standard	-	Partial Board	-
Single Rate			€38.50/€40	Child reduction	25%

Open: 1st January-15th December

Donegal 8km

Mrs Mary McGinty
ARDEEVIN
Lough Eske, Barnesmore,
Donegal, Co Donegal

Donegal Town Lough Eske
Tel: **073 21790**   Fax: **073 21790**
Email: **seanmcginty@eircom.net**
Web: **members.tripod.com/~Ardeevin**

Charming country residence, magnificent view Lough Eske, Bluestack Mountains. Guide de Routard, Frommer recommended. AA ◆◆◆◆. RAC ◆◆◆◆, RAC Sparkling Diamond Award.

B&B	6	Ensuite	€27.50/€32.50	Dinner	-
B&B	-	Standard	-	Partial Board	-
Single Rate			€38.50/€40	Child reduction	25%

Open: 18th March-30th November

Donegal Town 8km

Mrs Noreen McGinty
THE ARCHES
COUNTRY HOUSE
Lough Eske, Barnesmore,
Co Donegal

Donegal Town Lough Eske
Tel: **073 22029**   Fax: **073 22029 (man)**
Email: **archescountryhse@eircom.net**
Web: **www.archescountryhse.com**

Luxurious residence, all rooms having panoramic views of Lough Eske/Bluestacks. Guide de Routard, Lonely Planet, Birrbauns, McQuillans Ireland recommended.

B&B	6	Ensuite	€27.50/€32.50	Dinner	-
B&B	-	Standard	-	Partial Board	-
Single Rate			€38.50/€40	Child reduction	-

Open: All Year

In Donegal

Marie McGowan
THE WATERS EDGE
Glebe, Donegal Town,
Co Donegal

Donegal Town
Tel: **073 21523**
Email: **thewatersedgebb2000@hotmail.com**

Sligo road R267, opposite school, turn into cul-de-sac at Ballinderg House, 5th House down. Overlooking Bay/15th Century Abbey Ruins.

B&B	4	Ensuite	€25/€30	Dinner	-
B&B	-	Standard	-	Partial Board	-
Single Rate			-	Child reduction	-

Open: 15th January-15th December

In Donegal

Mrs Bridget McGuinness
BAY VIEW
Golf Course Road,
Donegal Town, Co Donegal

Donegal Town
Tel: **073 23018**

Quiet location overlooking Donegal Bay. Excellent Golfing, Fishing, sand Beaches, Walking trails nearby. Ten minutes walk Town Centre. R267 off N15.

B&B	4	Ensuite	€25.50/€25.50	Dinner	-
B&B	-	Standard	-	Partial Board	-
Single Rate			-	Child reduction	-

Open: 1st Feburary-30th November

Donegal Town 5km

Mrs Shona McNeice
LAKELAND B&B
Birchill, Lough Eske,
Donegal Town, Co Donegal

Donegal Town Lough Eske
Tel: **073 22481**   Fax: **073 22481**
Email:**mcneice@gofree.indigo.ie**

Modern country residence with superb panoramic view of Lough Eske and Blue Stack Mountains. 3 miles from Donegal Town just off N15 Ballybofey road. Ideal touring base.

B&B	4	Ensuite	€27.50/€32.50	Dinner	-
B&B	-	Standard	-	Partial Board	-
Single Rate			€38.50/€40	Child reduction	25%

Open: 15th January-15th December

Mrs Mary T Martin
BAYSIDE
Mullinasole, Laghey,
Co Donegal

Donegal Town
TEL: **073 22768**   FAX: **073 22768**

Coastal residence off N15 overlooking inlet of Donegal Bay. Golf Course and Beach 1km. Central touring location. Tea/coffee facilities.

B&B	5	Ensuite	€25.50/€25.50	Dinner	-
B&B	1	Standard		Partial Board	-
Single Rate			€36/€36	Child reduction	25%

Donegal Town 6km

Open: 16th March-31st October

Mrs Georgina Morrow
HIGHFIELD
The Haugh, Lough Eske Road,
Donegal Town, Co Donegal

Donegal Town
TEL: **073 22393**
EMAIL: **georginamorrow@tinet.ie**

Quiet elevated home with lovely view, close to Harvey's Point Country Hotel. Leave Donegal via N56, first turn right, signposted Lough Eske road for 2km.

B&B	3	Ensuite	€25.50/€32	Dinner	-
B&B	-	Standard		Partial Board	-
Single Rate			-	Child reduction	-

Donegal 2km

Open: 1st February-30th November

Mrs Bernie Mulhern
MILLTOWN HOUSE
Ardlenagh, Sligo Road,
Donegal Town, Co Donegal

Donegal Town
TEL: **073 21985**   FAX: **073 21985**
EMAIL: **milltown@oceanfree.net**

Spacious home on R267 (off N15). Ideal touring base. Convenient Beaches, Golf, Fishing, Craft Village. Opposite Park Golf Driving Range.

B&B	4	Ensuite	€25.50/€30	Dinner	-
B&B	-	Standard		Partial Board	-
Single Rate			€38.50/€40	Child reduction	33.3%

Donegal 2km

Open: 1st March-30th November

Breege & Martin Mulhern
ROSEARL
The Glebe, Donegal Town,
Co Donegal

Donegal Town
TEL: **073 21462**
EMAIL: **rosearl@eircom.net**

Modern spacious home in quiet residential area. 5 mins walk Town Centre. Golf, Beaches, Crafts nearby. Ideal touring base.

B&B	4	Ensuite	€25.50/€30	Dinner	-
B&B	1	Standard	€25.50/€30	Partial Board	-
Single Rate			€40/€45	Child reduction	33.3%

In Donegal

Open: All Year

Mrs Eileen Mulhern
ARDLENAGH VIEW
Ardlenagh, Sligo Road
(R267 off N15), Donegal PO,
Co Donegal

Donegal Town
TEL: **073 21646**

Spacious, elevated home, with view of Donegal Hills and Bay, 3 mins drive from Donegal Town on R267 off N15. Quiet location. Ideal touring base.

B&B	6	Ensuite	€25.50/€30	Dinner	-
B&B	-	Standard		Partial Board	-
Single Rate			€38.50/€40	Child reduction	50%

Donegal 2km

Open: All Year Except Christmas

In Donegal

Ms Caroline Needham
INCHBURGH B&B
Coast Road, Doonan,
Donegal Town, Co Donegal

Donegal Town
TEL: **073 21273**
EMAIL: **cneedham@eircom.net**

Bungalow on N56 situated 3/4km from Donegal Town. Peaceful location off main road. TV's, Tea/Coffee facilities in rooms.

B&B	3	Ensuite	€25.50	Dinner	-
B&B	1	Standard	€23	Partial Board	-
Single Rate			€38.50	Child reduction	25%

Open: 1st April-31st October

Donegal 5km

Martin & Edel Walsh
DRUMGOWAN HOUSE
Drumgowan, Donegal Town,
Co Donegal

Donegal Town
TEL: **073 22557**
EMAIL: **drumgowanhouse@eircom.net**

New modern dormer bungalow situated just off Donegal Towns by-pass (N15). 5 mins drive from Town Centre. Secure parking. Scenic peaceful location.

B&B	2	Ensuite	€25.50	Dinner	-
B&B	1	Standard	€23	Partial Board	-
Single Rate			€36/€36	Child reduction	25%

Open: All Year Except Christmas

In Dunfanaghy

Mrs Roisin McHugh
ROSMAN HOUSE
Dunfanaghy,
Co Donegal

Dunfanaghy
TEL: **074 36273/36393** FAX: **074 36273**
EMAIL: **rossman@eircom.net**
WEB: **come.to/rosmanhouse**

Luxurious modern bungalow with spectacular views. 300 Best B&B's recommended. Breakfast menu, Electric blankets, Hairdryers, Radio Alarms.

B&B	5	Ensuite	€25.50/€30	Dinner	-
B&B	-	Standard	-	Partial Board	-
Single Rate			€38.50/€40	Child reduction	25%

Open: All Year

In Dunfanaghy

Mrs Anne Marie Moore
THE WHINS
Dunfanaghy, Letterkenny,
Co Donegal

Dunfanaghy
TEL: **074 36481** FAX: **074 36481**
EMAIL: **whins@hotmail.com**
WEB: **whins.ibusinessdot.com**

Award winning home, with unique character. Recommended for comfort hospitality and "Fine Breakfasts" - New York Times. Opposite beach, Golf course.

B&B	4	Ensuite	€27/€29	Dinner	-
B&B	-	Standard	-	Partial Board	-
Single Rate			€38.50/€40	Child reduction	25%

Open: February-November

In Dunfanaghy

Bridget Moore
CARRIGAN HOUSE
Kill, Dunfanaghy,
Co Donegal

Dunfanaghy
TEL: **074 36276** FAX: **074 36276**
EMAIL: **carriganhouse@oceanfree.net**

Luxurious modern home 5 min walk from village. Ideal touring base. Glenveagh National Park, Dunlewey Lakeside. Tea/Coffee facilities. Breakfast menu.

B&B	4	Ensuite	€27/€29	Dinner	-
B&B	-	Standard	-	Partial Board	-
Single Rate			€38.50/€40	Child reduction	25%

Open: March-November

Mrs Noreen Greene
SEA VIEW
Mill Road, Dungloe,
Co Donegal

Dungloe
TEL: 075 21353

Spacious house overlooking Dungloe Bay and Mountains. Convenient to Beaches and Golf Course. Ideal for fishing enthusiasts. 5 min walk Town Centre.

B&B	6	Ensuite	€25.50	Dinner	-
B&B	-	Standard		Partial Board	-
Single Rate			€38.50	Child reduction	50%

In Dungloe

Open: March-November

Mrs B McLaughlin
MARTELLO HOUSE
Meenmore, Dungloe,
Co Donegal

Dungloe
TEL: 075 21669
EMAIL: martellos@tinet.ie

Family run Bungalow, peaceful setting. Breathtaking sea view. Ideal for Fishing, Golf, Beaches, Touring Arranmore Island, Glenveagh. Clock, Radios, Hairdryers.

B&B	4	Ensuite	€25.50/€25.50	Dinner	-
B&B	-	Standard		Partial Board	-
Single Rate			€38.50/€38.50	Child reduction	-

Dungloe 2km

Open: 1st March-1st November

Christina Cannon
CUAN-NA-MARA
Ballyness, Falcarragh,
Co Donegal

Falcarragh
TEL: 074 35327

Dormer bungalow overlooking Ballyness Bay & Tory Island. Glenveagh National Park 16km. Golf, Fishing, miles of Beach locally. Electric blankets. Guide du Routard recommended.

B&B	2	Ensuite	€25.50	Dinner	-
B&B	2	Standard	€23	Partial Board	-
Single Rate			€36/€36	Child reduction	-

Falcarragh 1km

Open: 1st June-30th September

Ms Margaret Murphy
FERNDALE
Falcarragh, Co Donegal

Falcarragh
TEL: 074 65506

Bungalow on scenic route N.W. 200m from Falcarragh. Beaches, Mountains, Fishing, Golfing nearby. Within easy reach of Glenveagh National Park & Tory Island.

B&B	1	Ensuite	€25.50	Dinner	-
B&B	3	Standard	€23	Partial Board	-
Single Rate			€36	Child reduction	50%

In Falcarragh

Open: 1st May-30th September

Mrs J P Byrne
CORNER HOUSE
Cashel, Glencolumbkille,
Co Donegal

Glencolumkille
TEL: 073 30021

Situated in peaceful valley of Glencolumbkille, Ardara road, five minutes from Folk Museum, Sandy Beaches. Hill climbing & good fishing.

B&B	4	Ensuite	€25.50/€25.50	Dinner	-
B&B	-	Standard		Partial Board	-
Single Rate			€38.50	Child reduction	33.3%

Killybegs 28km

Open: April-30th September

Mary Ita Boyle
AVALON
**Glen Road, Glenties,
Co Donegal**

Glenties

Tel: **075 51292**   Fax: **075 51292**
Email: **miboyle@eircom.net**

Family run home, in a scenic location. Setting for Brian Friels play "Dancing at Lughnasa". Ideal place when touring the county. Coeliacs catered for.

B&B	3	Ensuite	€25.50	Dinner	€17
B&B	1	Standard	€23	Partial Board	€264
Single Rate			€36/€38.50	Child reduction	33.3%

Glenties 1km

Open: January-November

**Rosaleen Campbell &
Conal Gallagher**
LISDANAR HOUSE
**Mill Road, Glenties,
Co Donegal**

Glenties

Tel: **075 51800**
Email: **lisdanar@eircom.net**
Web: **http://homepage.eircom.net/~lisdanar**

Luxurious spacious home. Country setting yet only 2 mins walk to the village on N56. Half way between Glenveagh National Park and Slieve League. Many extras.

B&B	4	Ensuite	€27/€30	Dinner	-
B&B	-	Standard		Partial Board	-
Single Rate			€38.50/€38.50	Child reduction	-

In Glenties

Open: 1st April-1st November

Mrs Margaret McCafferty
CLARADON COUNTRY
HOUSE
**Glen Road, Glenties,
Co Donegal**

Glenties

Tel: **075 51113**   Fax: **075 51113**
Email: **mccafferty@eircom.net**

Scenic mountain views/walks. Local Heritage/Museum/Beach/Golf 12km. Advice/Central for touring county. Fishing. 5 Tidy Towns wins. Genealogy help. On R253.

B&B	4	Ensuite	€25.50	Dinner	€17
B&B	-	Standard		Partial Board	€264
Single Rate			€38.50	Child reduction	33.3%

Glenties 1km

Open: 1st January-16th December

Mrs Marguerite McLoone
MARGUERITE'S
**Lr Main Street, Glenties,
Co Donegal**

Glenties

Tel: **075 51699**

Modern new house located in Town. Ideal base for touring. Beach/Golf 8 miles, local Museum, Scenic Walks, Fishing.

B&B	4	Ensuite	€25.50	Dinner	-
B&B	-	Standard		Partial Board	-
Single Rate			€38.50	Child reduction	33.3%

In Glenties

Open: All Year

Mrs Mary Regan
ARDLANN
**Mill Rd, Glenties,
Co Donegal**

Glenties

Tel: **075 51271**
Email: **ardlann@eircom.net**

On N56. Spacious house with panoramic views from all rooms. Beside Museum, Hotel & Church. Touring base for "Highlands & Islands of Donegal". Golf/Beach 10km.

B&B	3	Ensuite	€25.50/€26.50	Dinner	-
B&B	1	Standard	€23/€24	Partial Board	-
Single Rate			€36/€36	Child reduction	50%

In Glenties

Open: March-November

Ms Grainne Cafferty
ROOM WITH A VIEW
Coast Road, Kilcar,
Co Donegal

Kilcar
TEL: **073 38018**   FAX: **073 31976**
EMAIL: **grainne@donegalrefrigeration.ie**

200 year old refurbished house on scenic road to Kilcar. Overlooking Donegal Bay/Sligo Mountains. Ideal for Sliabh League. Walking distance to Beaches/Restaurants. All rooms with sea view.

B&B	2	Ensuite	€25.50/€30	Dinner	-
B&B	1	Standard	€23.50/€25	Partial Board	-
Single Rate			€36/€38.50	Child reduction	-

Killybegs 7km   **Open:** 1st June-30th October

Ms Mary Anderson
CORNTON HOUSE
Old Fintra Road, Killybegs,
Co Donegal

Killybegs
TEL: **073 31588**
EMAIL: **manderson@tinet.ie**
WEB: **homepage.tinet.ie/~manderson**

Modern family home set in quiet scenic location. Beautiful gardens, superb views. 1km west of Killybegs(10 mins walk). Ideal touring base. Angling, Pony trekking, Beach, Restaurants nearby.

B&B	4	Ensuite	€25.50/€29.84	Dinner	-
B&B	-	Standard		Partial Board	-
Single Rate			€38.50	Child reduction	33.3%

Killybegs 1km   **Open:** March-November

The Cahill Family
LISMOLIN COUNTRY HOME
Fintra Road, Killybegs,
Co Donegal

Killybegs
TEL: **073 31035/32310**   FAX: **073 32310**
EMAIL: **lismolincountryhome@hotmail.com**

Frommer, Guide de Routard recommended. Quiet location 1km west of Killybegs. Mountain view, Scenic walks. Rooms have TV, Hairdryer, Tea/Coffee.

B&B	5	Ensuite	€25.50/€27.50	Dinner	-
B&B	-	Standard		Partial Board	-
Single Rate			€38.50/€40	Child reduction	33.3%

Killybegs 1km   **Open:** 1st June 30th-September

Mrs Helena Cunningham
OCEAN VIEW
Largy, Killybegs,
Co Donegal

Killybegs
TEL: **073 31576**   FAX: **073 31576**
EMAIL: **helenaoceanview@eircom.net**

Luxurious home on elevated site 5km west of Killybegs. Spectacular views of Atlantic Ocean, Sligo Mountains. Beaches, Restaurants nearby. Slieve League 14km.

B&B	6	Ensuite	€25.50/€31.75	Dinner	-
B&B	-	Standard		Partial Board	-
Single Rate			€38.50/€44.45	Child reduction	25%

Killybegs 5km   **Open:** May-September

Mrs Margaret Doogan
LUPRA LODGE
Fintra Road, Killybegs,
Co Donegal

Killybegs
TEL: **073 32135**   FAX: **073 32135**

Comfortable octagonal shaped home in quiet location, 100 metres off the main Killbegs to Glencolumcille road. Good restaurants nearby. Slieve League 14km.

B&B	3	Ensuite	€25.50/€28	Dinner	-
B&B	-	Standard		Partial Board	-
Single Rate			€38.50/€38.50	Child reduction	25%

Killybegs 1km   **Open:** 1st April-30th September

Mrs Pauline Doogan
FINTRAGH HOUSE
Fintra Road, Killybegs,
Co Donegal

Killybegs
TEL: **073 31324**   FAX: **073 31324**
EMAIL: **fintrahouse@eircom.net**

Its your destination, warm cheerful home, in the largest fishing port in Ireland. Near Blue Flag beach. Ideal touring base for scenic route, on Kilcar road.

				Dinner	-
B&B	3	Ensuite	€25.50/€28	Dinner	-
B&B	-	Standard		Partial Board	-
Single Rate			€38.50	Child reduction	33.3%

Killybegs 1km

Open: All Year Except Christmas

Mrs Ann Keeney
HOLLYCREST LODGE
Donegal Road, Killybegs,
Co Donegal

Killybegs
TEL: **073 31470**
EMAIL: **hollycrest@hotmail.com**

Recommended 300 Best B&B's. On main Donegal/Killybegs road, situated on right. Guests TV lounge. Bedrooms Tea/coffee facilities, Hairdryers.

				Dinner	-
B&B	3	Ensuite	€25.50/€28	Dinner	-
B&B	1	Standard	€23/€25	Partial Board	-
Single Rate			€36/€38.50	Child reduction	25%

Killybegs 1km

Open: 1st February-30th November

Frankie & Ann McClean
CREDO HOUSE
Benroe, Killybegs,
Co Donegal

Killybegs
TEL: **073 31364**   FAX: **073 31364**
EMAIL: **credohouse@eircom.net**

Luxurious secluded accommodation at edge of Atlantic, magnificent sea & mountain views. Delicious cooking, friendly atmosphere (off R263). Highly recommended.

				Dinner	€25
B&B	5	Ensuite	€25.50/€35	Dinner	€25
B&B	-	Standard	-	Partial Board	€350
Single Rate			€38.50/€48	Child reduction	25%

Killybegs 3km

Open: April-October

Phyllis Melly
BANNAGH HOUSE
Fintra Road, Killybegs,
Co Donegal

Killybegs
TEL: **073 31108**
EMAIL: **bannaghhouse@eircom.net**

Modern bungalow on elevated site overlooking Killybegs Harbour and Fishing Fleet. Rooms ensuite. Private car park. Frommer recommended, 300 best B&B's.

				Dinner	-
B&B	4	Ensuite	€25.50/€26.50	Dinner	-
B&B	-	Standard	-	Partial Board	-
Single Rate			-	Child reduction	-

In Killybegs

Open: 1st April-31st October

Mrs Ellen O'Keeney
GLENLEE HOUSE
Fintra Road, Killybegs,
Co Donegal

Killybegs
TEL: **073 31026**   FAX: **073 31026**

Modern bungalow on main Killybegs - Glencolmcille Road, situated on right - hand side with fountain in garden. Beautiful Fintra Beach 1km.

				Dinner	-
B&B	5	Ensuite	€25.50/€30	Dinner	-
B&B	-	Standard		Partial Board	-
Single Rate			€38.50	Child reduction	33.3%

Killybegs 1km

Open: 1st April-30th September

Tully Family
TULLYCULLION HOUSE
Tullaghacullion, Killybegs,
Co Donegal

Killybegs
TEL: **073 31842**   FAX: **073 31842**
EMAIL: **tullys@gofree.indigo.ie**
WEB: **www.infowing.ie/fishing/ac/tu2.htm**

New luxurious country home. Conservatory. Secluded, elevated 2 acre site. Panoramic view overlooking Killybegs Port/Hills/Farmland/Donkeys. Boat shaped signs (N56).

B&B	5	Ensuite	€26/€30	Dinner	-
B&B	-	Standard	-	Partial Board	-
Single Rate			€35/€38	Child reduction	25%

Killybegs 2km   **Open:** March-November

Catherine A Walsh
OILEAN ROE HOUSE
Fintra Rd, Killybegs,
Co Donegal

Killybegs
TEL: **073 31192**
EMAIL: **walsh01@eircom.net**

Spacious 2 storey home, near Beach & Restaurants. Convenient to Slieve League, Glencolumbkille & Killybegs Harbour. TV & Tea in lounge.

B&B	4	Ensuite	€25.50/€25.50	Dinner	-
B&B	-	Standard	-	Partial Board	-
Single Rate			€38.50/€38.50	Child reduction	50%

Killybegs 1km   **Open:** 12th March-30th September

Daniel & Genevieve McElwee
FERN HOUSE
Lower Main Street,
Kilmacrennan, Letterkenny,
Co Donegal

Kilmacrennan
TEL: **074 39218**

Bright spacious two storey town house in village on N56 to Dunfanaghy. Glenveagh National Park 16K. Bars/Restaurants walking distance.

B&B	4	Ensuite	€25.50	Dinner	-
B&B	-	Standard	-	Partial Board	-
Single Rate			€38.50	Child reduction	-

Letterkenny 9km   **Open:** January-November

Mrs Sophia Boyle
BRIDGEBURN HOUSE
Trentagh, Letterkenny,
Co Donegal

Letterkenny
TEL: **074 37167**
EMAIL: **sophia@bridgeburnhouse.com**
WEB: **www.bridgeburnhouse.com**

15 mins drive from Letterkenny N56 to village of Kilmacrennan, turn left at signpost for Churchill - 5km. Ideal for Glenveagh Park, Flaxmill, Glebe Gallery.

B&B	3	Ensuite	€25.50/€27.50	Dinner	€17
B&B	1	Standard	€23/€25	Partial Board	€264
Single Rate			€36/€38.50	Child reduction	50%

Letterkenny 9km   **Open:** All Year

Mrs Jennie Bradley
RADHARC NA GIUISE
Kilmacrennan Road,
Letterkenny, Co Donegal

Letterkenny
TEL: **074 22090/25139**   FAX: **074 25139**
EMAIL: **bradleybb21@hotmail.com**

Spacious home overlooking town on N56 to Glenveagh National Park and West Donegal. 0.5km above Hospital. TV, Tea/Coffee and Hairdryer in bedrooms.

B&B	6	Ensuite	€25.50	Dinner	-
B&B	-	Standard	-	Partial Board	-
Single Rate			€38.50	Child reduction	33.3%

Letterkenny 1km   **Open:** 8th January-20th December

Mrs Elizabeth Cullen
ARDLEE
Gortlee, Letterkenny,
Co Donegal

TEL: 074 21943   FAX: 074 21943
EMAIL: lizcullen@eircom.net

Modern house close to town Bus Station, Theatre, Hotels. TV, Tea tray in rooms. Turn left off Ramelton road opposite Aldi store, up Gortlee road, next left at top.

B&B	5	Ensuite	€25.50/€27	Dinner	-
B&B	1	Standard	€23/€25	Partial Board	-
Single Rate			€38.50/€38.50	Child reduction	33.3%

Letterkenny 1km

Open: All Year

Nuala Duddy
PENNSYLVANIA HOUSE B&B
Curraghleas Mountain Top,
Letterkenny, Co Donegal

TEL: 074 26808   FAX: 074 28905
EMAIL: pennsylvania.house@indigo.ie
WEB: indigo.ie/~pennbb

Spacious rooms. Superb views. Central for touring Glenveigh National Park, Giants Causeway. Peaceful. Off N56. Laundry facilities. Electric blankets. Home baking.

B&B	4	Ensuite	€38.10/€44.45	Dinner	-
B&B	-	Standard		Partial Board	-
Single Rate			€44.45	Child reduction	-

Letterkenny 2km

Open: All Year Except Christmas

Danny & May Herrity
TOWN VIEW
Leck Road, Letterkenny,
Co Donegal

TEL: 074 21570/25138
EMAIL: townview@eircom.net

Frommer & Guide du Routard listing. Food awards. 3 downstairs rooms. Teamaking, Hairdryers, Electric blankets. Cross bridge at Dunnes Stores, keep left for 1km.

B&B	6	Ensuite	€25.50	Dinner	-
B&B	-	Standard	-	Partial Board	-
Single Rate			€38.50	Child reduction	-

Letterkenny 1km

Open: All Year

Breid & Paddy Kelly
ARDGLAS
Lurgybrack, Sligo Road,
Letterkenny, Co Donegal

TEL: 074 22516/25140 FAX: 074 22516
EMAIL: ardglas@yahoo.co.uk
WEB: www.ardglas.com

Spacious home panoramic views. 1km from Dryarch roundabout and Holiday Inn on N13 to Sligo. Ideal tour and golf base. TV, Hairdryer, Tea Facilities, Frommer.

B&B	6	Ensuite	€25.50	Dinner	-
B&B	-	Standard	-	Partial Board	-
Single Rate			€38.50	Child reduction	33.3%

Letterkenny 3km

Open: 1st April-30th September

Majella Leonard
OAKLANDS B&B
8 Oakland Park, Gortlee Road,
Letterkenny, Co Donegal

TEL: 074 25529   FAX: 074 25205
EMAIL: oakland@unison.ie
WEB: www.bandbdonegal.net

Family run B&B in quiet cul-de-sac opposite Aldi. 5 mins walk from Bars, Clubs, Restaurants. Ideal base for touring NW Region.

B&B	4	Ensuite	€25.50/€25.50	Dinner	-
B&B	-	Standard	-	Partial Board	-
Single Rate			-	Child reduction	50%

Letterkenny 1km

Open: All Year

Mrs Mary McBride
RINNEEN
Woodland, Ramelton Road,
Letterkenny, Co Donegal

Letterkenny
TEL: 074 24591

Modern home situated in peaceful countryside. Warm welcome. Convenient to local amenities. Ideal base for touring the North West of Ireland and Northern Ireland.

B&B	1	Ensuite	€25.50	Dinner	-
B&B	2	Standard	€23	Partial Board	-
Single Rate			€36/€38.50	Child reduction	33.3%

Letterkenny 6km

Open: 1st March-30th November

Mrs Maureen McCleary
GLENCAIRN HOUSE
Ramelton Road, Letterkenny,
Co Donegal

Letterkenny
TEL: 074 24393/25242
EMAIL: glencairnbb@hotmail.com

Panoramic view from patio. On R245, near Mount Errigal Hotel/Silver Tassie and Golf. Central for touring. Guide du Routard recommended. All ground floor bedrooms, TV/Tea/Coffee/Hairdryer.

B&B	5	Ensuite	€25.50	Dinner	-
B&B	1	Standard	€23	Partial Board	-
Single Rate			€36/€38.50	Child reduction	33.3%

Letterkenny 2km

Open: 1st January-20th December

Leonie McCloskey
BLACKWOOD HOUSE
Ramelton Road, Letterkenny,
Co Donegal

Letterkenny
TEL: 074 26364
EMAIL: blackwoodbb@eircom.net

Warm hospitality offered in this tastefully decorated home. Well situated on main Ramelton road R245. Home baking and breakfast menu available.

B&B	4	Ensuite	€25.50/€25.50	Dinner	-
B&B	-	Standard	-	Partial Board	-
Single Rate			€38.50	Child reduction	50%

Letterkenny 2km

Open: All Year Except Christmas

Philomena McDaid
LARKFIELD B&B
Drumnahoe, Letterkenny,
Co Donegal

Letterkenny
TEL: 074 21478

Quiet comfortable house. Secure private parking. Great view. First left past Holiday Inn on N13 towards Letterkenny. Tea on arrival. Ideal for touring Giants Causeway, Glenveagh National Park.

B&B	2	Ensuite	€25.50/€25.50	Dinner	-
B&B	1	Standard	€23/€23	Partial Board	-
Single Rate			€36/€36	Child reduction	25%

Letterkenny 2km

Open: 6th January-23rd December

Mrs Sara Maguire
PARK HOUSE
Doobalagh, Sligo Road,
Letterkenny, Co Donegal

Letterkenny
TEL: 074 24492

Frommer recommended. Panoramic view, 2 miles from Dry/Arch roundabout, on N13 to Sligo. Ideal base for touring North-West. TV, Hairdryers, Tea/Coffee.

B&B	4	Ensuite	€25.50/€25.50	Dinner	-
B&B	-	Standard	-	Partial Board	-
Single Rate			€38.50/€38.50	Child reduction	33.3%

Letterkenny 3km

Open: All Year Except Christmas

Ms M A Murray
PINE TREES
Gortlee, Letterkenny,
Co Donegal

Letterkenny
TEL: **074 24111**

Quiet location off N56 to National Park. 10 mins Town, Golf, Horseriding. All rooms ground floor and garden view. TV, Hairdryer, Tea/Coffee facilities. Near all Hotels.

B&B	2	Ensuite	€25.50	Dinner	-
B&B	1	Standard	€24.13	Partial Board	-
Single Rate			€36/€38.09	Child reduction	33.3%

Letterkenny 1km

Open: April-October

Eugene & Ann O'Donnell
WHITE PARK B&B
Ballyraine, Letterkenny,
Co Donegal

Letterkenny
TEL: **074 24067**   FAX: **074 67597**

On R245 to Ramelton. Large comfortable home. Spacious groundfloor rooms. Superb location for touring. 30 mins Glenveagh National Park & beach. 5 mins walk Mount Errigal Hotel, Pitch & Putt.

B&B	6	Ensuite	€25.50/€28	Dinner	-
B&B	-	Standard	-	Partial Board	-
Single Rate			€38.50/€38.50	Child reduction	33.3%

Letterkenny 1km

Open: 7th January-20th December

Eileen Burke
ROANINISH
Narin, Portnoo,
Co Donegal

Narin-Portnoo
TEL: **075 45207**   FAX: **075 45207**

Elevated home with magnificent view of sea. Beside Blue Flag beach, golf course, historical interests, fishing, walks. Rooms TV, tea making. Ardara, Portnoo.

B&B	4	Ensuite	€26/€28	Dinner	-
B&B	-	Standard	-	Partial Board	-
Single Rate			€38.50/€40	Child reduction	-

In Town

Open: 1st June-30th September

Mrs Ena Corry
CRAMMOND HOUSE
Market Square, Ramelton,
Co Donegal

Ramelton
TEL: **074 51055**

Warm hospitality offered in 18th century home. Convenient to Restaurants etc. Family & triple rooms available. Le Guide du Routard recommended.

B&B	2	Ensuite	€25.50/€25.50	Dinner	-
B&B	2	Standard	€23/€23	Partial Board	-
Single Rate			€36/€38.50	Child reduction	50%

In Ramelton

Open: 1st April-31st October

Mrs Shirley Chambers
Strabane Road
Raphoe, Co Donegal

Raphoe
TEL: **074 45410**

Modern house in peaceful location. 3 minutes walk from Raphoe, Beltony Stone Circle 4km. Tea making facilities. Ideal touring base Giants Causeway, Grianan Aileach.

B&B	4	Ensuite	€25.50	Dinner	-
B&B	-	Standard	-	Partial Board	-
Single Rate			€38.50	Child reduction	33.3%

In Raphoe

Open: 1st April-31st October

Co Leitrim with it's beautiful Lakelands, it's deep valleys and unspoiled terrain is famous for it's international coarse angling cruising and overseas tourists enjoy numerous festivals and attractions. Horse-riding, Golfing, Cycling, Hill-walking and other outdoor activities.

Mrs Eileen Breen	Ballinamore
SUI MHUIRE	TEL: **078 44189**
Cleendargen, Ballinamore, Co Leitrim	EMAIL: **eileen_breen16@hotmail.com**

Situated 2.5 acres, scenic surroundings, Excellent fishing, golf, own boats. Entry/Exit drives. Situated route N202 Swanlinbar/Enniskillen Road. Highly recommended.

B&B	6	Ensuite	€25.50/€25.50	Dinner	€17
B&B	-	Standard	-	Partial Board	€264
Single Rate			€38.50/€38.50	Child reduction	-

Ballinamore 2km

Open: 1st April-October

Mrs Julie Curran	Ballinamore
THE OLD RECTORY	TEL: **078 44089**
Fenagh, Glebe, Ballinamore, Co Leitrim	EMAIL: **theoldrectoryleitrim@eircom.net** WEB: **www.theoldrectoryireland.com**

The Old Rectory is an atmospheric 19th century Georgian Home on 50 acres of woodland overlooking Fenagh Lake and located beside Fenagh's historic Abbey's.

B&B	2	Ensuite	€30/€32	Dinner	€17
B&B	2	Standard	€25/€27	Partial Board	€264
Single Rate			€36/€38.50	Child reduction	25%

Ballinamore 4.5km

Open: 10th January-1st December

Mrs Valerie Cahill	Carrick-on-Shannon
ATTYRORY LODGE	TEL: **078 20955** FAX: **078 20955**
Dublin Road, Carrick-on-Shannon, Co Leitrim	EMAIL: **attyrorylodge@eircom.net**

Roots dating 100 years in Leitrim. Complimentary interior capturing warmth and history in style. Rough Guide recommended. Located on N4 Dublin/Sligo/Donegal route.

B&B	5	Ensuite	€25.50	Dinner	€17
B&B	-	Standard	-	Partial Board	€264
Single Rate			€38.50	Child reduction	25%

Carrick-on-Shannon 1km

Open: 1st January-23rd December

Gerard & Jeanette Conefrey	Carrick-on-Shannon
CANAL VIEW HOUSE	TEL: **078 42056** FAX: **078 42261**
Keshcarrigan, Carrick-on-Shannon, Co Leitrim	EMAIL: **canalviewcountryhome@eircom.net**

Delightful country home and Restaurant with breathtaking view of Cruisers passing. All rooms with pleasant outlook. Quiet walks and cycle routes. Fishing on doorstep. Music in Pubs.

B&B	6	Ensuite	€32/€32	Dinner	-
B&B	-	Standard	-	Partial Board	-
Single Rate			€39/€39	Child reduction	-

In Keshcarrigan

Open: All Year

In Carrick-on-Shannon

Mrs Breedge Nolan
VILLA FLORA
Station Road,
Carrick-on-Shannon,
Co Leitrim

Carrick-on-Shannon
TEL: **078 20338**

Modernised Georgian House, walking distance to Town Centre and Railway Station. Adjacent N4. Fishing and Boating Facilities, Pub Entertainment.

B&B	3	Ensuite	€30/€40	Dinner	-
B&B	1	Standard	€25/€35	Partial Board	-
Single Rate			€35/€45	Child reduction	25%

Open: 1st April–30th October

Carrick-on-Shannnon 10km

Mr Michael O'Sullivan
LAKELANDS
Acuintass, Aghamore,
Carrick-on-Shannon,
Co Leitrim

Carrick-on-Shannon
TEL: **078 25952**
EMAIL: **lakelandsbandb@eircom.net**

Spacious two storey house on 1 acre with views of lovely Leitrim and the River Shannon located on N4, 6 miles from Carrick-on-Shannon.

B&B	4	Ensuite	€28/€32	Dinner	-
B&B	-	Standard	-	Partial Board	-
Single Rate			€38.50/€38.50	Child reduction	50%

Open: 1st March–31st October

Carrick-on-Shannon 1km

Eleanor & Seamus Shortt
MOYRANE HOUSE
Dublin Road,
Carrick-on-Shannon,
Co Leitrim

Carrick-on-Shannon
TEL: **078 20325**
EMAIL: **eleanorshortt@eircom.net**
WEB: **homepage.eircom.net/~eleanorshortt**

Highly recommended. Real Irish home. Peacefully set back from N4 Dublin/Sligo/Donegal route. Breakfast choices, French spoken. Credit cards. Near lively riverside town and quiet countryside.

B&B	3	Ensuite	€25.50	Dinner	-
B&B	1	Standard	€23	Partial Board	-
Single Rate			€38.50	Child reduction	25%

Open: 1st April–31st October

Drumshanbo 1km

Mrs Mairin Heron
FRAOCH BAN
Corlough, Drumshanbo,
Co Leitrim

Drumshanbo
TEL: **078 41260**
EMAIL: **fraochban@eircom.net**

Highly recommended home on R207, overlooking Lough Allen. Views of lake & mountains. Pamper yourself with Reflexology, Aromatherapy, Beauty Therapy or relax in Sauna.

B&B	4	Ensuite	€26	Dinner	€18
B&B	-	Standard	-	Partial Board	€264
Single Rate			€38.50	Child reduction	25%

Open: 1st April–31st October

TELEPHONE

- Operator assisted calls within Ireland   Dial 10
- International telephone operator   Dial 11818
- Directory Enquiries   Dial 11811

FOR TROUBLE-FREE TELEPHONE CALLS FROM PUBLIC PAY PHONES IT IS ADVISABLE TO PURCHASE A TELE-PHONE CALLCARD AVAILABLE IN POST OFFICES AND WHEREVER YOU SEE A CALLCARD SIGN.

TO DIAL IRELAND FROM ABROAD: Country Access Code + 353 + Area Code (omit first zero) + Local Number

'County of the Little Hills'. The constant presence of the attractive lakes - Muckno, Gasslough, Erny and Darty has a special appeal to the sportsman. The intriguing roads winding around the hills serve to portray the dignified charm of pastoral landscape.

Margaret Flanagan
SHANMULLAGH HOUSE
Killanny Rd (off Dundalk Rd)
Carrickmacross,
Co Monaghan

Carrickmacross
TEL: **042 9663038**   FAX: **042 9661915**
EMAIL: **flanagan@esatclear.ie**

Modern artistically decorated house in rural surroundings. Convenient to Nuremore Hotel & Country Club. Golf, Fishing, Horse Riding locally.

B&B	5	Ensuite	€25.50/€25.50	Dinner	-
B&B	-	Standard		Partial Board	-
Single Rate			€38.50	Child reduction	50%

Carrickmacross 3km

Open: February-1st December

Mrs Eilish McConnell
BRAEVIEW HOUSE
Toneyellida, Donaghmoyne,
Carrickmacross,
Co Monaghan

Carrickmacross
TEL: **042 9663465**

Modern bungalow overlooking N2 Dublin/Derry road. Private parking. Tea/Coffee/TV/Hairdryer facilities. Close by Golf, Fishing, Equestrian. Kavanagh Country.

B&B	3	Ensuite	€25.50/€28	Dinner	-
B&B	-	Standard	-	Partial Board	-
Single Rate			€38.50	Child reduction	33.3%

Carrickmacross 4km

Open: 8th January-18th December

The Russell Family
NUREBEG HOUSE
Ardee Road, Carrickmacross,
Co Monaghan

Carrickmacross
TEL: **042 9661044**

Situated N2 Dublin/Derry Road. Beside Nuremore Hotel, 2 miles Carrickmacross. Fishing, Horse Riding, Golf locally. Central Touring, Newgrange, Carlingford

B&B	5	Ensuite	€25.50	Dinner	-
B&B	1	Standard	€25.40	Partial Board	-
Single Rate			€36	Child reduction	25%

Carrickmacross 3km

Open: All Year

Pat & Vera Conlon
BLITTOGUE HOUSE B&B
Dublin Road, Castleblaney,
Co Monaghan

Castleblaney
TEL: **042 9740476**
EMAIL: **blittogue.house@ireland.com**

New luxury family run home, near scenic Lough Muckno. Walking, Fishing, Golf, Horse Riding, Bowling, Boating, Skiing. On N2. Restaurants, pubs. Warm welcome.

B&B	3	Ensuite	€25.50	Dinner	-
B&B	2	Standard	€23	Partial Board	-
Single Rate			€36/€38.50	Child reduction	25%

Castleblaney 1km

Open: All Year

Mrs Anne Rooney
CLONKEEN COTTAGE
Clonkeencole, Clones,
Co Monaghan

Clones

TEL: **047 51268**
EMAIL: **clonkeencottage@hotmail.com**

Situated in the heart of Drumlin region, relax and enjoy warm and friendly hospitality. Ideal base for touring North, Midlands

B&B	3	Ensuite	€26		Dinner	€17
B&B	-	Standard	-		Partial Board	-
Single Rate			€38.50		Child reduction	**50%**

Clones 1.5km

ⓥ cc 🅿 ⤴❌ ...   **Open:** 7th January-21st December

Anna & Fergus Murray
AN TEACH BAN
Main Street, Emyvale,
Co Monaghan

Emyvale

TEL: **047 87198**   FAX: **047 87198**
EMAIL: **anteachban@eircom.net**
WEB: **www.anteachban.com**

Modern spacious family residence situated in the picturesque village of Emyvale, 11km north of Monaghan Town.

B&B	4	Ensuite	€26		Dinner	-
B&B	-	Standard	-		Partial Board	-
Single Rate			€38.50/€38.50		Child reduction	**33.3%**

In Emyvale Village

ⓥ cc ...   **Open:** 2nd January-20th December

APPROVED ACCOMMODATION SIGNS

Approved Accommodation Signs
This sign will be displayed at most premises which are approved to Irish Tourist Board Standards.

Panneaux d'homologation des établissements
Ces panneaux sont affichés dans la plupart des établissements homologués selon les normes de l'Office du tourisme irlandais.

Plakette fúr Geprúfte Unterkunft
Diese Plaketten werden an den meisten Häusern angezeigt, die von auf die Einhaltung der Normen der irischen Fremdenverkehrsbehörde über-prüft und zugelassen wurden.

Borden voor goedgekeurde accommodatie
Deze borden vindt u bij de meeste huizen die zijn goedgekeurd door voor de nor-men van de Ierse Toeristenbond.

Simbolo di sistemazione approvata
Questi simboli saranno esposti nella maggior parte delle case approvate (associazione dei Bed & Breakfast approvati per qual- ità), rispondenti agli standard dell'Ente del Turismo Irlandese.

Símbolo de alojamiento aprobado
Estos símbolos se muestran en los establecimientos que han sido aprobados por bajos los estandars de la Oficina de Turismo Irlandesa.

Skyltar för Godkänd logi
Dessa skyltar finns vid de flesta gästhus som har godkänts (Föreningen för kvalitetsgodkän-da gästhus AB), enligt irländska turisföreningens normer.

Sligo has surprising contrasting landscapes, spectacular scenery, dream for painters, writers, historians, and archaeologists.
Sligo has the second largest megalithic cemetery in Europe.
Sandy beaches - Golf - Fishing - Theatre - Equestrian - Water Sports - Traditional music, good restaurants and a warm welcome for visitors.

Mrs Ann Campbell
SEASHORE
Off Ballina Road (N59),
Lisduff, Ballisodare,
Co Sligo

Ballisodare
TEL: **071 67827**   FAX: **071 67827**
EMAIL: **seashore@oceanfree.net**
WEB: **www.seashoreguests.com**

Country home with Conservatory/Dining room overlooking Knocknarea, Ox Mountains, Ballisodare Bay. Tennis Court, Jacuzzi. AA ♦♦♦ listed. Seashore walks, birdwatching facility.

B&B	4	Ensuite	€30/€32	Dinner	-
B&B	1	Standard	-	Partial Board	-
Single Rate			€32/€38	Child reduction	25%

Ballisodare 4.5km   **Open:** All Year

Mrs Noreen Mullin
MILLHOUSE
Keenaghan, Ballymote,
Co Sligo

Ballymote
TEL: **071 83449**

AIB "Best Overall" and Galtee breakfast award winning superb family home, peaceful location. Private tennis court. TV, Hairdryers. Megalithic tomb, Castle.

B&B	5	Ensuite	€26/€28	Dinner	-
B&B	-	Standard	-	Partial Board	-
Single Rate			€36/€38.50	Child reduction	33.3%

In Ballymote   **Open:** 10th January-18th December

Freda Monaghan
GLEBE HOUSE
Rathcormac, Drumcliffe,
Co Sligo

Drumcliffe
TEL: **071 45074**
EMAIL: **fredamonaghan@sligoweb.zzn.com**

Situated in the heart of Yeats Country in the picturesque village of Rathcormac. 3 miles from Sligo N15 with Church, Shop, Pubs and Restaurant within walking.

B&B	2	Ensuite	€25.50/€25.50	Dinner	€17
B&B	1	Standard	€23/€23	Partial Board	€264
Single Rate			€36/€38.50	Child reduction	25%

Sligo 5km   **Open:** All Year

Mrs Masie Rooney
CASTLETOWN HOUSE
Drumcliffe, Co Sligo

Drumcliffe
TEL: **071 63204**
EMAIL: **f_rooney_ie@yahoo.co.uk**

Situated beneath the bliss of Benbulben Mountains. Peaceful location. Hospitality, nearby W. B. Yeats grave. Glencar Waterfalls. Restaurants, Lisadell Hse.

B&B	3	Ensuite	€26/€26	Dinner	-
B&B	1	Standard	-	Partial Board	€264
Single Rate			€36/€36	Child reduction	25%

Sligo 9km   **Open:** April-October

Grange 2km

Mrs Una Brennan
ARMADA LODGE
Donegal Road N15,
Grange North, Co Sligo

Grange
TEL: **071 63250**   FAX: **071 63250**
EMAIL: **armadalodge@eircom.net**
WEB: **www.armadalodge.com**

Peaceful tranquility. Ride on Beach. Climb Benbulben. Walk or Bike, Sea Angling & Diving, Golf, Archaeology. Wonderful rooms & breakfasts, Laundry. Seaweed Baths.

B&B	6	Ensuite	€26/€28	Dinner	-
B&B	-	Standard	-	Partial Board	-
Single Rate			€38.50/€38.50	Child reduction	33.3%

Open: 1st May-30th September

Grange 1km

Mattie & Patricia Hoey
ROWANVÍLLE LODGE
Grange, Co Sligo

Grange
TEL: **071 63958**
EMAIL: **rowanville@hotmail.com**

Luxury home, scenic setting by mountains/sea, on N15. Home cooking, Breakfast conservatory/menu. RAC AA ◆◆◆. Horseriding, sandy beaches. Private gardens.

B&B	3	Ensuite	€25.50/€28	Dinner	€20
B&B	-	Standard	-	Partial Board	-
Single Rate			€38.50/€38.50	Child reduction	25%

Open: 15th March-October

Grange 2km

Mrs Maureen McGowan
MOUNT EDWARD LODGE
Off N15, Ballinfull, Grange,
Co Sligo

Grange
TEL: **071 63263**   FAX: **071 63263**
EMAIL: **mountedwardlodge@eircom.net**

Panoramic peaceful setting off N15. Views Sea, Mountains. Midway Sligo/Donegal. Breakfast conservatory, Breakfast menu. TV, Tea/Coffee, Electric blankets. Golf, Horseriding. Credit cards.

B&B	3	Ensuite	€26	Dinner	-
B&B	2	Standard	€23	Partial Board	-
Single Rate			€36/€38	Child reduction	25%

Open: 7th January-15th December

In Grange

Mrs Kathleen Neary
ROSSWICK
Grange, Co Sligo

Grange
TEL: **071 63516**
EMAIL: **rosswick@eircom.net**

Family home, Personal attention. Panoramic view of Benbulben, Benwisken. Beaches, Horse riding, Hillwalking. Yeats Country closeby. TV, Hairdryer, Clock Radio all rooms. Breakfast menu.

B&B	2	Ensuite	€26/€28	Dinner	-
B&B	2	Standard	€23/€23	Partial Board	-
Single Rate			€36/€36	Child reduction	25%

Open: 1st April-31st October

Rosses Point 5km

Mrs Mary Conefrey
BAYVIEW
Doonierin, Cregg,
Rosses Point, Co Sligo

Rosses Point
TEL: **071 62148**

In quiet scenic countryside overlooking Drumcliffe Bay and majestic view of Benbulben. Golf, Restaurants nearby. Ideal base for touring.

B&B	3	Ensuite	€26/€28	Dinner	-
B&B	-	Standard	-	Partial Board	-
Single Rate			€40/€42	Child reduction	25%

Open: 1st April-31st October

Mrs Ita Connolly
IORRAS
Ballincar, Rosses Point Road,
Sligo, Co Sligo

Rosses Point
TEL: **071 44911**

Modern spacious home situated 2kms on Sligo to Rosses Point Road. TV, Tea/coffee in bedrooms. Golf, Sailing, Beach nearby. Breakfast menu.

B&B	4	Ensuite	€26/€30	Dinner	-
B&B	-	Standard	-	Partial Board	-
Single Rate			€38.50/€38.50	Child reduction	**50%**

Sligo 4km

Open: 1st April-19th October

Mrs I Fullerton
SEA PARK HOUSE
Rosses Point Road, Sligo,
Co Sligo

Rosses Point
TEL: **071 45556**   FAX: **071 45556**
EMAIL: **seaparkhouse@eircom.net**

3.5km from Sligo on R291 Rosses Point rd. 3km Beach, Sailing, Golf. Extensive b'fast menu. TV, Tea/Coffee, Hairdryers in bedrooms. Orthopaedic beds. Many recommendations.

B&B	4	Ensuite	€26/€30	Dinner	-
B&B	2	Standard	€23/€27	Partial Board	-
Single Rate			€36/€38.50	Child reduction	**33.3%**

Sligo 3.5km

Open: 7th January-22nd December

Mrs Cait Gill
KILVARNET HOUSE
Rosses Point, Co Sligo

Rosses Point
TEL: **071 77202**
EMAIL: **kilvarnethouse@eircom.net**
WEB: **homepage.eircom.net/~kilvarnet**

Modern comforts, traditional hospitality. In heart of Yeats Country, within walking distance of championship Golf Course, Yacht Club, Beaches, Restaurants.

B&B	4	Ensuite	€26/€30	Dinner	-
B&B	-	Standard	-	Partial Board	-
Single Rate			€38.50	Child reduction	-

Sligo Town 8km

Open: 1st April-31st October

Kelly Family
SERENITY
Doonierin, Kintogher,
Rosses Point, Co Sligo

Rosses Point
TEL: **071 43351**

Award winner for hospitality. High quality food and accomodation. Superb Bay and Mountain views, cul-de-sac. Seaside location. You wont find a nicer place.

B&B	3	Ensuite	€27/€32	Dinner	-
B&B	1	Standard	€24/€27	Partial Board	-
Single Rate			€39/€45	Child reduction	-

Rosses Point 5km

Open: 1st April-31st October

Mrs Marian Nealon
SANIUD
Ballincar, Rosses Point,
Co Sligo

Rosses Point
TEL: **071 42773**

Welcoming family home. Quiet location beside Ballincar House Hotel. Convenient to Beaches, Golf, Sailing, Tennis in heart of Yeats Country.

B&B	3	Ensuite	€26/€30	Dinner	-
B&B	-	Standard	-	Partial Board	-
Single Rate			€38.50/€38.50	Child reduction	-

Sligo 4km

Open: 1st April-30th September

Mrs Mary Scanlon
PHILMAR HOUSE
**Ballincar, Rosses Point Rd,
Sligo, Co Sligo**

TEL: **071 45014**

Old style with modern comforts in quiet, scenic location. Large gardens for guests. Minutes from Golf course, Beaches, Sailing, Tennis.

B&B	2	Ensuite	€26/€30	Dinner	-
B&B	2	Standard	€24/€26	Partial Board	-
Single Rate			€37/€40	Child reduction	25%

Sligo 4km

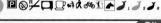

Open: 1st March-1st November

Mrs Renagh Burns
OCHILLMORE HOUSE
**Scarden-Beg Strandhill Road,
Co Sligo**

TEL: **071 68032**

Dormer Bungalow on Strandhill/Airport Road. TV, Hairdryers, Electric Blankets, Tea making facilities. Close Beach, Airport, Golf, Megalithic Tombs, Mountains.

B&B	4	Ensuite	€22/€23	Dinner	-
B&B	-	Standard	-	Partial Board	-
Single Rate			€28/€28	Child reduction	50%

Sligo 4km

Open: All Year

Mary Cadden
LISSADELL
**Mailcoach Road (N15/N16),
Sligo, Co Sligo**

TEL: **071 61937**

5 minute walk Town Centre. On N15/16. 200 yards off N4. TV, Hairdryers. Tea/Coffee facilities all rooms. Non-smoking.

B&B	3	Ensuite	€28/€29.50	Dinner	-
B&B	-	Standard	€38.50/€38.50	Partial Board	-
Single Rate				Child reduction	-

In Sligo

Open: 8th January-15th December

Mary & Tommy Carroll
ARD CUILINN LODGE
**Drumiskabole (R284),
Sligo, Co Sligo**

TEL: **071 62925**
EMAIL: **ardcuiln@esatclear.ie**

Luxury accommodation, tranquil scenic surroundings. Home cooking. Guide du Routard, Petit Fute recommended. Near Lough Gill, 1km off N4(Carrowroe roundabout) R284. Warm welcome.

B&B	2	Ensuite	€26/€27	Dinner	-
B&B	2	Standard	€23/€24	Partial Board	-
Single Rate			-	Child reduction	-

Sligo 5km

Open: 1st March-31st October

Mrs Mary Conway
STONECROFT
**off Donegal Road (N15),
Kintogher, Sligo, Co Sligo**

TEL: **071 45667**   FAX: **071 44200**
EMAIL: **stonecroft_sligo@yahoo.com**

Cosy home in Yeats country 300m off N15 Donegal Road. Near Drumcliffe Church. Superb views. Credit Cards, TV, Tea facilities.

B&B	5	Ensuite	€28/€28	Dinner	-
B&B	-	Standard	-	Partial Board	-
Single Rate			€39/€39	Child reduction	25%

Sligo 4km

Open: 1st April-31st October

Sligo 3km

Peter & Martha Davey
CARBURY HOUSE
Teesan, Sligo,
Co Sligo

Sligo

TEL: **071 43378**   FAX: **071 47433**
EMAIL: **carbury@indigo.ie**
WEB: **www.carburyhouse.com**

Luxurious spacious home on N15. Warm welcome. All rooms ensuite, Orthopaedic beds, Clocks, TV, Power Showers. 3 kms from Sligo. Touring base Sligo/Donegal.

B&B	6	Ensuite	€26/€29	Dinner	€17
B&B	-	Standard	-	Partial Board	-
Single Rate			€38.50/€38.50	Child reduction	50%

Open: 4th January-24th December

Des & Nan Faul
AISLING
Cairns Hill, Sligo,
Co Sligo

Sligo Town

TEL: **071 60704**   FAX: **071 60704**
EMAIL: **aislingsligo@eircom.net**

Overlooking garden and sea. All rooms ground floor. Signposted 300m Sligo Park Hotel off N4. AA ◆◆◆, cosy. Listed in many Guides. Electric Blankets, TV's, Hairdryers.

B&B	3	Ensuite	€26.50/€29	Dinner	-
B&B	1	Standard	€24/€26.50	Partial Board	-
Single Rate			€37/€39.50	Child reduction	-

Open: 1st January-22nd December

Sligo 1km

Geraldine Gorman
GLENVALE
Cornageeha Upper,
Pearse Road, Sligo, Co Sligo

Sligo Town

TEL: **071 61706**
EMAIL: **geraldinegorman@eircom.net**

Friendly family home on N4. 100 metres after Sligo Park Hotel. Private Parking. Close to Races, Sports Complex. Tea/Coffee, H/Dryer, TV, AA ◆◆◆ Award.

B&B	4	Ensuite	€26/€30	Dinner	-
B&B	-	Standard	-	Partial Board	-
Single Rate			€38.50/€38.50	Child reduction	50%

Open: All Year

Sligo 3km

Tess Haughey
RATHNASHEE
Teesan, Donegal Road N15,
Sligo, Co Sligo

Sligo

TEL: **071 43376**   FAX: **071 42283**

Welcome to an Irish home. Scenic Area. Midway Sligo/Drumcliff en route Donegal. Homebaking. Many recommendations. Frommer, Guide du Routard. Lounge with extensive library. Old books.

B&B	2	Ensuite	€25.50/€25.50	Dinner	€17
B&B	1	Standard	€23/€25	Partial Board	€264
Single Rate			€36/€38.50	Child reduction	-

Open: 30th March-30th September

Sligo 1.5km

Mary Hennessy
DAINGEAN
Hazelwood Rd, Ballinode,
Co Sligo

Sligo

TEL: **071 45706**
EMAIL: **daingeanhennessy@eircom.net**

Friendly family home, situated 1.5 km from Town Centre. Close to all amenities. Spacious garden. Hazelwood Park, Lough Gill, Parkes Castle nearby.

B&B	3	Ensuite	€26/€30	Dinner	-
B&B	-	Standard	-	Partial Board	-
Single Rate			€38.50	Child reduction	25%

Open: 1st March-30th November

Mrs Christina Jones
CHESTNUT LAWN
**Cummeen, Strandhill Road,
Sligo, Co Sligo**

Sligo
TEL: **071 62781**   FAX: **071 62781**

Modern spacious dormer bungalow situated 3km from Sligo Town on main Strandhill/Airport road. Close to Megalithic Tombs. T.V, Hairdryers.

B&B	2	Ensuite	€26	Dinner	-
B&B	1	Standard	€24	Partial Board	-
Single Rate			€38	Child reduction	25%

Sligo 3km

Open: 21st January-21st December

Mrs Veronica Kane
GLENVIEW
**Cummeen, Strandhill Road,
Sligo, Co Sligo**

Sligo
TEL: **071 70401/62457**   FAX: **071 62457**

Modern bungalow Strandhill Road, Megalithic Tombs. Golf, Beaches, Airport, Colour TV, Hairdryers, Electric Blankets, Tea making facilities, Lets Go recommended.

B&B	4	Ensuite	€25.50/€25.50	Dinner	-
B&B	-	Standard	-	Partial Board	-
Single Rate			€38.50/€38.50	Child reduction	50%

Sligo 2km

Open: January-November

Mrs Marie Kelly
ST JUDE'S
**Rathonoragh, Strandhill Road,
Sligo, Co Sligo**

Sligo
TEL: **071 60858**   FAX: **071 60858**
EMAIL: **saintjudes@eircom.net**

Close Airport, Bus, Railway station. Surfing, Swimming, Seaweed baths nearby. Climb Knocknarea Mountain, Megalithic Tombs, Heritage & Genealogy society. Electric blankets, Tea facilities.

B&B	2	Ensuite	€25.50	Dinner	-
B&B	1	Standard	€23	Partial Board	-
Single Rate			€36	Child reduction	25%

Sligo 3km

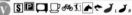

Open: 31st March-31st October

Mrs Shirley Kilfeather
LAR-EASA
**12 Kestrel Drive, Kevinsfort,
Strandhill Road, Co Sligo**

Sligo
TEL: **071 69313**   FAX: **071 69313**
EMAIL: **lareasa@iolfree.ie**

Situated within the parklands of Kevinsfort House. Ideally located for touring Yeats Country and Carrowmore tombs. Complimentary Fishing. Ballisodare River (on selected dates).

B&B	3	Ensuite	€28/€29.50	Dinner	-
B&B	-	Standard	-	Partial Board	-
Single Rate			€38.50/€38.50	Child reduction	25%

Sligo 1km

Open: 1st January-30th November

Mrs Ursula Leyden
RENATE HOUSE
**Upper John Street, Sligo,
Co Sligo**

Sligo
TEL: **071 62014/69093** FAX: **071 69093**

Frommer listed. Beside Bus/Train station. All amenities, Restaurants, Pubs, Tourist Office, Theatre, Hospitals, Churches. TV, Tea/Coffee, Hairdryer, Radio.

B&B	4	Ensuite	€26/€29	Dinner	-
B&B	2	Standard	€23/€25	Partial Board	-
Single Rate			€36/€36	Child reduction	25%

In Sligo

Open: 6th January-20th December

In Sligo

Ronan & Doreen MacEvilly
TREE TOPS
Cleveragh Road
(off Pearse Rd N4),
Sligo Town, Co Sligo

Sligo Town
TEL: **071 60160**   FAX: **071 62301**
EMAIL: **treetops@iol.ie**
WEB: **www.sligobandb.com**

5 minutes walk Town Centre. T.V, Hairdryers, Direct Dial Telephones, Tea Facilities all rooms. Non smoking. Frommer, Guide du Routard recommended.

B&B	5	Ensuite	€28/€29.50	Dinner	-
B&B	-	Standard	-	Partial Board	-
Single Rate			€38.50/€38.50	Child reduction	-

Open: 8th January-15th December

Sligo 4km

Mary McGoldrick
ST MARTIN DE PORRES
Drumshanbo Rd, Carraroe,
Sligo, Co Sligo

Sligo
TEL: **071 62793**
EMAIL: **stmdeporres@eircom.net**

Peaceful rural setting, 1km off N4 at Carraroe roundabout on R284. Convenient to Lough Gill, Megalithic Tombs, Forest Walks. Secure parking. TV, Electric blankets.

B&B	4	Ensuite	€26/€27	Dinner	-
B&B	-	Standard	-	Partial Board	-
Single Rate			€38.50/€39	Child reduction	50%

Open: 6th January-20th December

Sligo 2km

Evelyn & Declan McPartland
TEACH EAMAINN
off N16 Hazelwood,
Old Manorhamilton Rd,
Co Sligo

Sligo
TEL: **071 43393**   FAX: **071 43393**
EMAIL: **info@teacheamonn.com**

Situated on two acres off R286. Tea room, over looking Knocknarea, Benbulben, Ox Mountains, Sligo Bay. T.V and Hairdryers. Parties special rate.

B&B	6	Ensuite	€25.50	Dinner	-
B&B	-	Standard	-	Partial Board	-
Single Rate			€38.50	Child reduction	-

Open: 1st April-30th November

Sligo 1.5km

Mel & Kathleen Noonan
STRADBROOK
Cornageeha, Pearse Road,
Sligo, Co Sligo

Sligo Town
TEL: **071 69674/50663** FAX: **071 69933**
EMAIL: **stradbrook@eircom.net**
WEB: **www.stradbrook.com**

Welcoming family home on N4. Sligo Park Hotel 100 metres. All facilities. Guide du Routard/AA recommended. Beaches, Golf, Fishing nearby. Ideal base for touring Yeats Country/Donegal.

B&B	4	Ensuite	€25.50/€28	Dinner	-
B&B	-	Standard	-	Partial Board	-
Single Rate			€38.50/€38.50	Child reduction	25%

Open: All Year

Sligo 1.5km

Mrs Bernie O'Connor
ALVERNO
Cairns Hill Rd off N4,
Sligo Town, Co Sligo

Sligo Town
TEL: **071 62893**

2 storey Georgian house. Modern facilities.

B&B	2	Ensuite	€26	Dinner	-
B&B	1	Standard	€24	Partial Board	-
Single Rate			€36	Child reduction	-

Open: 2nd April-30th September

In Sligo

Elma O'Halloran
ROSSCAHILL
19 Marymount, Pearse Road,
Sligo, Co Sligo

Tel: **071 61744**

Entering Sligo, N4, turn left into Marymount opposite ESSO station before second set of traffic lights. Located in quiet Cul-de-Sac.

B&B	3	Ensuite	€27/€29.50	Dinner	-
B&B		Standard	-	Partial Board	-
Single Rate			€38.50/€38.50	Child reduction	-

Open: April-October

Sligo 2km

Olivia Quigley
BENWISKIN LODGE
Shannon Eighter,
Off Donegal Road N15,
Sligo, Co Sligo

Tel: **071 41088**   Fax: **071 41088**
Email: **pquigley@iol.ie**
Web: **www.benwiskin.com**

Welcoming home, country setting. 2km Sligo, 50m off N15 behind "The Red Cottage". All facilities. Yeats Grave, Beach, Golf closeby.

B&B	5	Ensuite	€26/€29	Dinner	-
B&B	1	Standard	-	Partial Board	-
Single Rate			€38.50/€38.50	Child reduction	-

Open: 2nd January-22nd December

Sligo 8km

Mrs Carmel Connolly
KNOCKNAREA HOUSE
Shore Road, Strandhill,
Co Sligo

Tel: **071 68313/68810**
Email: **connollyma@eircom.net**

Large family home beside Beach, Seaweed Baths, Golf, Surfing, Horse Riding, Airport. Ideal for peaceful scenic walks. TV and Tea/Coffee in all rooms.

B&B	4	Ensuite	€25.50	Dinner	-
B&B		Standard	-	Partial Board	-
Single Rate			€38.50	Child reduction	50%

Open: March-October

Tubbercurry 1km

Mrs Mary Brennan
EDEN VILLA
Ballina Road,
Tubbercurry, Co Sligo

Tel: **071 85106**   Fax: **071 85106**
Email: **edenvilla@ireland.com**
Web: **www.sligotourism.com**

A warm welcome awaits you at our luxurious family home. Tea/Coffee, Homebaking on arrival. Guest TV lounge with peat fire, breakfast menu. Ideal touring base. 250mtrs off N17.

B&B	2	Ensuite	€26/€29	Dinner	-
B&B	1	Standard	€25/€27	Partial Board	-
Single Rate			€36/€38.50	Child reduction	33.3%

Open: 10th January-10th December

Mrs Monica Brennan
ROCKVILLE
Charlestown Road,
Tubbercurry, Co Sligo

Tel: **071 85270**
Email: **rockville_monica@yahoo.com**
Web: **www.sligotourism.com**

Quiet, friendly Irish home on N17. Tea/Coffee, Home baking on arrival, Hairdryers, Electric blankets, Clock radios. Breakfast menu. Knock Airport 10 miles.

B&B	3	Ensuite	€26/€29	Dinner	-
B&B	1	Standard	€25/€27	Partial Board	-
Single Rate			€36/€38.50	Child reduction	33.3%

In Tubbercurry

Open: 10th January-10th December

Mrs Joan Brett
ST ENDA'S
Charlestown Rd, Tubbercurry,
Co Sligo

Tubbercurry
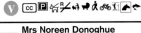
TEL: **071 85100**
EMAIL: **st_endas@ireland.com**
WEB: **www.sligotourism.com**

Friendly family home on N17. Scenic area. Home baking, Electric blankets. Gardens, Fishing and Golf nearby. Knock Airport 10 miles, Knock Shrine 22 miles.

B&B	4	Ensuite	€26/€29	Dinner	-
B&B	-	Standard	-	Partial Board	-
Single Rate			€38.50	Child reduction	**33.3%**

Tubbercurry 1km

Open: 8th January-15th December

Mrs Noreen Donoghue
ROSSLI HOUSE
Doocastle, Tubbercurry,
Co Sligo

Tubbercurry
TEL: **071 85099**   FAX: **071 85099**
EMAIL: **rossli@esatclear.ie**
WEB: **tubbercurrybandb.com**

Rural setting. Tea/Coffee. Hairdryers, Electric blankets. Laundry facilities. Conservatory. Frommer Guide, Le Guide du Routard, Interconnections listed. Travel 6km on Ballymote road.

B&B	4	Ensuite	€25.50/€25.50	Dinner	€19
B&B	-	Standard	-	Partial Board	-
Single Rate			€38.50/€38.50	Child reduction	**33.3%**

Tubbercurry 6km

Open: All Year

Mrs Teresa Kelly
PINEGROVE
Ballina Road, Tubbercurry,
Co Sligo

Tubbercurry
TEL: **071 85235**
EMAIL: **pinegrove@ireland.com**
WEB: **www.sligotourism.com**

Friendly atmosphere, home-baking, evening meals, electric blankets. Gardens, Fishing, Shooting & Golf. Knock Shrine. 300 metres off N17.

B&B	5	Ensuite	€26/€29	Dinner	-
B&B	-	Standard	-	Partial Board	-
Single Rate			€38.50	Child reduction	**33.3%**

Tubbercurry

Open: All Year

Mrs Teresa O'Gorman
ANNALEA HOUSE
Tubbercurry,
Co Sligo

Tubbercurry
TEL: **071 85141**

Bungalow located on N17 with Award winning gardens, viewed from conservatory. Individual attention a priority. Fishing, Golf available locally.

B&B	2	Ensuite	€25.50	Dinner	-
B&B	1	Standard	€23	Partial Board	-
Single Rate			€36	Child reduction	**33.3%**

In Tubbercurry

Open: 10th January-10th December

Mrs Maeve Walsh
CRUCKAWN HOUSE
Ballymote/Boyle Rd,
Tubbercurry, Co Sligo

Tubbercurry
TEL: **071 85188**   FAX: **071 85188**
EMAIL: **cruckawn@esatclear.ie**
WEB: **www.sligotourism.com**

Award winning family home in peaceful suburb, overlooking Golf Course. AIB "Best Hospitality". Many recommendations, Guide de Routard. AA ◆◆◆. Sunlounge, Laundry. Off N17 on R294 road.

B&B	5	Ensuite	€26/€29	Dinner	-
B&B	-	Standard	-	Partial Board	-
Single Rate			€39	Child reduction	**33.3%**

In Tubbercurry

Open: 17th March-4th November

Northern Ireland

Welcome to Northern Ireland! Gloriously green countryside, spectacular coast and mountains - an ancient land with a rich historical and cultural tradition and some of the friendliest people anywhere.

Visit our capital city of Belfast, famous for its industrial heritage and birthplace of the Titanic, where you can experience a unique combination of award winning restaurants, traditional pubs, history and culture. Also well worth a visit is the city of Derry, one of the finest examples of a walled city in Europe and Armagh, the ecclesiastical capital of Ireland.

Northern Ireland is perfect for a host of outdoor pursuits. A day's walking amid spectacular scenery, an exhilarating horseback gallop along a quiet beach or a relaxing game of golf on one of our many famous courses. Alternatively you might consider a breathtaking bike ride on one of our new cycle routes, a peaceful afternoon boating or fishing or a leisurely stroll through the National Trust gardens of Mount Stewart.

The Majestic mountains of Mourne, the uncongested waterways of Lough Erne, the breathtaking Antrim coast with its world heritage site at the Giant's Causeway. The list is endless but whatever your preference - seaside, town, city or countryside, there is a special place for you to stay.

Carrick-a-rede

Area Representative

NORTHERN IRELAND

CO ANTRIM
Mrs Valerie McFall, Valley View Country House, 6A Ballyclough Road, Bushmills, Co Antrim BT57 8TU
Tel: 028 20741608/41319 Fax: 028 20742739

CO DOWN
Mrs Liz McMorris, Swan Lodge, 30 St Patricks Road, Saul, Downpatrick, Co Down BT30 7JQ
Tel: 028 44615542 Fax: 087 07052501

CO LONDONDERRY
Mrs Averil Campbell, Killennan House, 40 Killennan Road, Drumahoe, Co Londonderry BT47 3NG
Tel: 028 71301710 Fax: 028 71301710

Tourist Information Offices

Armagh
Old Bank Building
40 English St.,
BT61 7BA
Tel: 028 37521800

Belfast
Belfast Welcome
Centre
47 Donegall Place
BT1 5AD
Tel: 028 90246609

Derry
44 Foyle Street,
BT48 6AT
Tel: 028 7126 7284

Dungannon
Killymaddy TIC
190 Ballygawley Road
BT70 1TF
Tel: 028 8776 7259

Enniskillen
Wellington Road,
BT74 7EF
Tel: 028 6632 3110

Giant's Causeway
44 Causeway Road
BT57 8SU
Tel: 028 2073 1855

Larne
Narrow Gauge Road,
BT40 1XB
Tel: 028 2826 0088

Newcastle Centre
10-14 Central
Promenade
BT33 0AA
Tel: 028 4372 2222

www.**discovernorthernireland.com**

159

Last year, Northern Ireland Farm and Country Holidays Association members were included in this publication for the first time. This year we are delighted to announce that membership has not only grown but now includes members of the Bed and Breakfast Association - NI.

This increased choice of comfortable, welcoming homes will offer you, the visitor a greater opportunity to experience our unique hospitality and sample the quality and range of our home cooking.

Nestling in the shadow of a mountain or glen, or situated in sight of a lake or beach, our properties are dotted all over this glorious region and offer a "home-from-home" atmosphere to both the holidaymaker and business person alike.

All of our establishments are rigorously inspected and certified on an annual basis by the Northern Ireland Tourist Board and are open all year round unless otherwise stated.

We are delighted that our members are included in this publication. They look forward to greeting you and making your stay in Northern Ireland a truly memorable experience.

Louie Reid
NIFCHA

Jim Milliken
AAANI

Valerie Brown
GLENMORE HOUSE
White Park Road, Ballycastle,
Co Antrim

Ballycastle

Tel: **028 20763584**   Fax: **028 20762378**
Email: **glenmorehouse@lineone.net**

New building with panoramic sea view on the B15 and set on 90 acres for walks with fishing lake. Central for Causeway and Glens. TV and Tea making facilities in room. Tea on arrival.

B&B	6	Ensuite	Stg£17/£20	Dinner	-
B&B	-	Standard	-	Partial Board	-
Single Rate			Stg£28.50	Child reduction	50%

Ballycastle 3km

Open: All Year

Megan Donnelly
PORTCAMPLEY
8 Harbour Rd, Ballintoy
Ballycastle, BT54 6NA
Co Antrim

Ballycastle

Tel: **028 207 68200**   Fax: **028 207 68200**
Email: **m.donnelly@btclick.com**
Web: **www.portcampley.8k.com**

Spacious modern bungalow. Panoramic views of Rathlin Island and Scottish Coastline. Central to Causeway Coast and Glens. Home cooking and friendly atmosphere assured.

B&B	5	Ensuite	Stg£16/£19.50	Dinner	Stg£12
B&B	1	Standard	-	Partial Board	-
Single Rate			Stg£20/£26	Child reduction	50%

Ballycastle 6km

Open: All Year

Margaret & Andrew Neely
NEELSGROVE FARM
51 Carnearney Rd, Ahoghill,
Ballymena, BT42 2PL
Co Antrim

Ballymena

Tel: **028 2587 1225**   Fax: **028 2587 8704**
Email: **msneely@btinternet.com**
Web: **www.neelsgrove.freeserve.co.uk**

Farmhouse set in 1 acre garden in a rural location. Excellent base for touring to North Coast, Glens of Antrim, Giants Causeway. Convenient to Galgorm Manor & Tullyglass Hotels.

B&B	2	Ensuite	Stg£18.50	Dinner	Stg£10
B&B	1	Standard	Stg£16	Partial Board	-
Single Rate				Child reduction	-

Ballymena 9km

Open: 1st January-30th November

Olive & Roger Nicholson
RAVENHILL GUEST HOUSE
690 Ravenhill Road,
Belfast BT6 0BZ, Co Antrim

Belfast

Tel: **028 90207444**   Fax: **028 90282590**
Email: **roger@ravenhillguesthouse.com**
Web: **www.ravenhillguesthouse.com**
Bus No: **83, 84, 85, 86, 78, 79**

Warm welcoming Victorian home in South Belfast. Comfortable well equipped rooms. Delicious breakfast. Easy access to airports, ferries and motorways.

B&B	5	Ensuite	Stg£25/£27.50	Dinner	Stg£18
B&B	-	Standard	-	Partial Board	-
Single Rate			Stg£37.50/£40	Child reduction	-

Belfast 2km

Open: All Year

Mrs J Brown
BROWNS COUNTRY HOUSE
174 Ballybogey Road,
Bushmills BT52 2LP,
Co Antrim

Bushmills

Tel: **028 20732777**   Fax: **028 20731627**
Email: **brownscountryhouse@hotmail.com**
Web: **www.brownscountryhouse.co.uk**

Family run home near Giants Causeway. Reputation for superb food & friendly atmosphere. Near to beaches & Golf links. Good touring base B62. Off B17 to Coleraine.

B&B	8	Ensuite	Stg£20/£22	Dinner	-
B&B	-	Standard	-	Partial Board	-
Single Rate			Stg£25/£25	Child reduction	33.3%

Bushmills 4.5km

Open: 3rd January-19th December

Mrs Valerie McFall
VALLEY VIEW
COUNTRY HOUSE
6A Ballyclough Road,
Bushmills, BT57 8TU Co Antrim

Bushmills

TEL: **028 20741608/41319** FAX: **028 20742739**
EMAIL: **valerie.mcfall@btinternet.com**
WEB: **www.nifcha.com/valleyview**

Attractive country house. Beautiful views. Friendly atmosphere, Tea on arrival. Close to Giants Causeway, Rope Bridge and Distillery. Off B17 to Coleraine.

B&B	7	Ensuite	Stg£18/20	Dinner	-
B&B	-	Standard		Partial Board	-
Single Rate			Stg£23/£25	Child reduction	50%

Bushmills 6km **Open:** All Year Except Christmas

Mr & Mrs C Kelly
KEEF HALLA
COUNTRY HOUSE
20 Tully Road, Nutts Corner,
BT29 4SW Co Antrim

Crumlin

TEL: **028 90825491** FAX: **028 90825940**
EMAIL: **info@keefhalla.com**
WEB: **www.keefhalla.com**

Nearest 4 star guesthouse to Belfast International Airport. All rooms are ensuite with STV, Direct Dial Telephone, Tea/Coffee. A great base for touring Northern Ireland. Free e-mail service available.

B&B	7	Ensuite	Stg£25	Dinner	Stg£15
B&B	-	Standard		Partial Board	Stg£200
Single Rate			Stg£35/40	Child reduction	50%

Crumlin 4km **Open:** All Year

Anne McKavanagh
CALDHAME LODGE
102 Moira Rd, Nutts Corner,
Crumlin BT29 4HG, Co Antrim

Crumlin

TEL: **028 94423099** FAX: **028 94423099**
EMAIL: **info@caldhamelodge.co.uk**
WEB: **www.caldhamelodge.co.uk**

Award winning hse, mins from Belfast Int. Airport. Luxurious home, digital TV, Tea/Coffee. Bridal suite/jacuzzi/4 poster bed. Restaurants & Pubs. 25 mins Belfast.

B&B	6	Ensuite	Stg£20/£25	Dinner	Stg£15
B&B	-	Standard		Partial Board	-
Single Rate			Stg£30/£35	Child reduction	25%

Crumlin 1.9km **Open:** All Year

Mrs Olive McAuley
CULLENTRA HOUSE
16 Cloughs Road,
Cushendall, BT44 0SP
Co Antrim

Cushendall

TEL: **028 21771762** FAX: **028 21771762**
EMAIL: **cullentra@hotmail.com**
BUS NO: **150**

Award winning B&B nestled amidst panoramic views of Antrim Coast and Glens. Close to Giants Causeway, Rope Bridge etc. Last B&B on Cloughs road.

B&B	3	Ensuite	Stg£18/£18	Dinner	Stg£12.50
B&B	-	Standard		Partial Board	-
Single Rate				Child reduction	33.3%

Cushendall 2km **Open:** All Year

James & Ann McHenry
DIESKIRT FARM
104 Glen Road, Glenariff,
BT44 0RG
Co Antrim

Glenariff

TEL: **028 21771308** FAX: **028 21771185**
EMAIL: **dieskirt@hotmail.com**
WEB: **www.dieskirt.8k.com**

A working farm with its own private scenic walks just off Antrim Coast Road A2. 5 mins walk from Glenariffe Forest Park/Restaurant. Listed in Le Guide du Routard Irelande.

B&B	2	Ensuite	Stg£17/£17	Dinner	-
B&B	1	Standard	Stg£14/£14	Partial Board	-
Single Rate			Stg£22/£22	Child reduction	25%

Cushendall 8km **Open:** 15th May-December

Waterfoot 2km

Mrs Rose Ward
LURIG VIEW B&B
38 Glen Rd, Glenariff,
Ballymena BT44 0RF,
Co Antrim

Glenariff
TEL: **028 217 71618**
EMAIL: **rose_ward@amserve.net**
BUS NO: **150**

Immaculate home, overlooking Glen of Glenariffe. Ground floor accommodation, close to Moyle Way, Forest Park, Giants Causeway. Coastal route A2, Inland route A43.

B&B	2	Ensuite	Stg£18	Dinner	-
B&B	-	Standard		Partial Board	-
Single Rate			Stg£22	Child reduction	33.3%

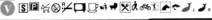

Open: All Year

In Armagh

J Kee
BALLINAHINCH HOUSE
47 Ballygroobany Rd, Richhill,
BT61 9NA, Co Armagh

Armagh
TEL: **028 388 70081**   FAX: **028 388 70081**
EMAIL: **ballinahinchhouse@bigfoot.com**
WEB: **www.ballinahinchhouse.com**

Victorian residence with picturesque setting in the countryside. Ideal base for touring Northern Ireland. Visit our website for more details. Keen prices.

B&B	2	Ensuite	Stg£20	Dinner	-
B&B	1	Standard		Partial Board	-
Single Rate			Stg£25	Child reduction	-

Open: All Year

Armagh 1km

Alice McBride
HILLVIEW LODGE
33 Newtownhamilton Rd,
Armagh BT60 2PL
Co Armagh

Armagh
TEL: **028 3752 2000**   FAX: **028 3752 8276**
EMAIL: **alice@hillviewlodge.com**
WEB: **www.hillviewlodge.com**

This family run accommodation offers high standard facilities with sky tv, floodlit golf driving range on premises. Disabled facilities available.

B&B	6	Ensuite	Stg£25	Dinner	-
B&B	-	Standard	-	Partial Board	-
Single Rate			Stg£30	Child reduction	50%

Open: All Year

Banbridge 5km

Norman & Esther Kerr
MOURNEVIEW
32 Drumnascamph Road,
Laurencetown, Gilford,
BT63 6DU Co Down

Banbridge
TEL: **028 40626270/24251** FAX: **028 40624251**
EMAIL: **mourneview@dial.pipex.com**

Situated on A50 between Banbridge and Gilford. Ideal base to see Co Down Coast/Mourne Mountains/Linen homelands. 30 mins to Airports/Belfast. Excellent Restaurants nearby.

B&B	4	Ensuite	Stg£18/£18	Dinner	-
B&B	-	Standard	-	Partial Board	-
Single Rate			Stg£22/£22	Child reduction	33.3%

Open: All Year Except Christmas

Downpatrick 4.8km

Mrs Patricia Forsythe
ROSEBANK COUNTRY HOUSE
108 Ballyduggan Road,
Downpatrick, BT30 8HF
Co Down

Downpatrick
TEL: **028 44617021**   FAX: **028 44619521**
EMAIL: **jbforsy@yahoo.co.uk**

Luxurious accommodation, warm welcome. Good food. Spacious ensuite bedrooms. TV, Tea/Coffee, guest lounge. On main A25, scenic route to Mournes Historic Downpatrick.

B&B	3	Ensuite	Stg£20	Dinner	Stg£12.50
B&B	-	Standard	-	Partial Board	-
Single Rate			Stg£25/£30	Child reduction	50%

Open: All Year Except Christmas

Downpatrick 4km (V)

John & Liz McMorris
SWAN LODGE
30 St Patricks Road, Saul,
Downpatrick BT30 7JQ,
Co Down

Downpatrick
TEL: **028 44615542** FAX: **087 07052501**
EMAIL: **breaks@swanldg.force9.co.uk**
WEB: **www.swanldg.force9.co.uk**

Superbly situated overlooking Strangford Lough, St Patricks Heritage area. Ideal touring base. Luxury family home in scenic surroundings. Excellent cuisine.

B&B	3	Ensuite	Stg£22/£22	Dinner	Stg£15
B&B	-	Standard		Partial Board	-
Single Rate			Stg£31/£31	Child reduction	33.3%

Open: 2nd January-15th December

Kilkeel 4km (V)

Trainor Family
HILL VIEW HOUSE
18 Bog Rd, Attical, Kilkeel,
BT34 4HT Co Down

Kilkeel
TEL: **028 417 64269** FAX: **028 417 64269**

Luxury farmhouse in Mourne Mountains offering hospitality since 1903. TV, Tea/Coffee. Near licenced restaurant. Sign for Hillview and Attical Village on A2 & B27.

B&B	2	Ensuite	Stg£18/£20	Dinner	-
B&B	1	Standard		Partial Board	-
Single Rate			Stg£20/£22	Child reduction	-

Open: 7th January-20th December

Newcastle 1.25km (V)

Mrs Jan Joyce and Mrs Pam Horrox
OAKLEIGH HOUSE
30 Middle Tollymore Rd,
Newcastle BT33 0JJ, Co Down

Newcastle
TEL: **028 43723353/43726816** FAX: **028 43723353**
EMAIL: **jan.joyce@which.net**
WEB: **www.travel-ireland.com/oakleigh**

A family run bungalow at the foot of the Mourne Mountains and close to Tollymore Forest Park close to Royal Co. Down golf course. Warm welcome assured.

B&B	3	Ensuite	Stg£20/£25	Dinner	-
B&B	-	Standard		Partial Board	-
Single Rate			Stg£25/£25	Child reduction	-

Open: 2nd January-15th December

Newtownards 5.5km (V)

Mrs Geraldine Bailie
BALLYNESTER HOUSE
1a Cardy Rd (off Mountstewart Rd) Newtownards
BT22 2LS Co Down

Newtownards
TEL: **028 42788386** FAX: **028 42788986**
EMAIL: **geraldine.bailie@virgin.net**
WEB: **www.ballynesterhouse.com**

AA ◆◆◆◆◆, hospitality at its best! Relax in tranquil surroundings. Superb location, Lough views, in the heart of the Ards Peninsula beside Mount Stewart N.T.

B&B	2	Ensuite	Stg£25/£25	Dinner	-
B&B	1	Standard	-	Partial Board	-
Single Rate			Stg£30/£30	Child reduction	50%

Open: All Year Except Christmas

In Coleraine (V)

Mrs Dorothy Chandler
COOLBEG
2E Grange Road, Coleraine,
BT52 ING, Co Londonderry

Coleraine
TEL: **028 7034 4961** FAX: **028 7034 3278**
EMAIL: **dorothy@coolbeg.totalserve.co.uk**
WEB: **www.coolbeg.totalserve.co.uk**

Modern bungalow on edge of town. Fully accessible to wheelchair users. On entering town from A26/A29 at Lodge road roundabout take turn for town - then 1st turn left.

B&B	4	Ensuite	Stg£20/£22	Dinner	-
B&B	1	Standard	-	Partial Board	-
Single Rate			Stg£18	Child reduction	33.3%

Open: All Year Except Christmas

Mrs Ann Millar
GLENLEARY FARMHOUSE
12 Glenleary Rd, Coleraine
BT51 3QY, Co Londonderry

Coleraine

TEL: **028 70342919**   FAX: **028 70352130**
EMAIL: **glenleary.farm@virgin.net**
WEB: **glenlearyfarm.co.uk**
BUS NO: **116**

A warm welcome 5 minutes south of Coleraine just off A29. For a scenic peaceful view near all area tourist attractions with 2 restaurants nearby.

B&B	1	Ensuite	Stg£18/£22	Dinner	Stg£10
B&B	2	Standard	Stg£16/£20	Partial Board	Stg£184
Single Rate			Stg£16/£20	Child reduction	25%

Coleraine 1.4km

Open: All Year Except Christmas

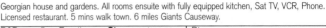

Winston Wallace
BREEZEMOUNT
26 Castlerock Rd, Coleraine
BT51 3HP, Co Londonderry

Coleraine

TEL: **028 703 44615**   FAX: **028 703 28478**
EMAIL: **breezemounthouse@csi.com**
WEB: **www.breezemount.co.uk**

Georgian house and gardens. All rooms ensuite with fully equipped kitchen, Sat TV, VCR, Phone. Licensed restaurant. 5 mins walk town. 6 miles Giants Causeway.

B&B	5	Ensuite	Stg£16.50/£16.50	Dinner	-
B&B	-	Standard		Partial Board	-
Single Rate			Stg£23.50/£23.50	Child reduction	50%

In Coleraine

Open: All Year

Mrs Elizabeth Buchanan
ELAGH HALL
Buncrana Road, Derry,
BT48 8LU
Co Londonderry

Derry

TEL: **028 71263116**
EMAIL: **lizelagh@yahoo.com**

Listed historic house, spacious gardens, own spring water. Views of Grianan Castle & Donegal Hills. From City take A2 Buncrana road for 2 miles, right Elagh road

B&B	2	Ensuite	Stg£20	Dinner	-
B&B	1	Standard	Stg£18	Partial Board	-
Single Rate			-	Child reduction	50%

Derry 3km

Open: April-October

Mrs Averil Campbell
KILLENNAN HOUSE
40 Killennan Road, Drumahoe,
BT47 3NG
Co Londonderry

Derry

TEL: **028 71301710**   FAX: **028 71301710**
EMAIL: **averil@killennan.co.uk**
WEB: **www.killennan.co.uk**

Warm welcome, 19th century country house, beautiful gardens. 10 mins from Derry, Airport. Ideal touring base. Off A6 to Belfast, take B118 Eglinton.

B&B	3	Ensuite	Stg£18/£20	Dinner	-
B&B	-	Standard	-	Partial Board	-
Single Rate			Stg£23/£25	Child reduction	50%

Derry 8km

Open: All Year Except Christmas

TELEPHONING BETWEEN NORTHERN IRELAND AND REPUBLIC OF IRELAND

DIALLING FROM THE REPUBLIC OF IRELAND INTO NORTHERN IRELAND
Callers in the Republic of Ireland can dial either 048 followed by the eight digit number or 00 44 28 followed by the eight digit number.

DIALLING FROM NORTHERN IRELAND INTO THE REPUBLIC OF IRELAND
Callers in Northern Ireland should dial 00 353 followed by premises number (whilst always taking care to drop the zero prefix of the area code).

Dungiven 5km

Mrs Florence Sloan
DRUMCOVITT HOUSE
704 Feeny Road, Feeny,
Derry, BT47 4SU
Co Londonderry

Feeny
TEL: **028 77781224**   FAX: **028 77781224**
EMAIL: **drumcovitt.feeny@btinternet.com**
WEB: **www.drumcovitt.com**

Georgian farm house 103 hectares. Log fires, oil heating, gracious rooms. Walks, Birds, Selfcater, Visit Sperrin, Causeway, Donegal, Derry 14km. A6/B74 1km east Feeny.

B&B	-	Ensuite	-	Dinner	Stg£16
B&B	3	Standard	Stg£20/£24	Partial Board	-
Single Rate			Stg£20/£24	Child reduction	33.3%

Open: All Year

Limavady 5km

Mrs Rosemary Kane
BALLYHENRY HOUSE
172 Seacoast Rd, Limavady,
BT49 9EF, Co Londonderry

Limavady
TEL: **028 7772 2657**

Attractive award winning farmhouse on 350 acres. Farm situated in the lovely River Roe Valley nestling near the mountains, blue flag beach. Convenient to Giants Causeway.

B&B	1	Ensuite	Stg£20/£20	Dinner	Stg£12.50
B&B	2	Standard	Stg£18/£20	Partial Board	-
Single Rate			Stg£22/£25	Child reduction	33.3%

Open: All Year

Giants Causeway

Mrs Helen McCracken
THE POPLARS
352 Seacoast Rd, Bellarena,
Limavady, BT49 0LA
Co Londonderry

Limavady

Tel: **028 777 50360**   Fax: **028 777 50360**

Attractive farm bungalow in mature gardens. Picturesque views of Binevenagh Mountains and Donegal Hills. Warm welcome. On A2, 6.5 miles north of Limavady.

B&B	3	Ensuite	Stg£20/£21	Dinner	-
B&B	3	Standard	Stg£17/£18	Partial Board	-
Single Rate			Stg£22/£23	Child reduction	50%

Limavady 4km

  cc   P   🏠 📺 🍴 ☕   ✗ ♿ 🚲 👜 ⬆ s 🎣 R

Open: All Year

Mrs Maureen McKean
BRAEHEAD HOUSE
22 Brae Head Rd,
Londonderry BT48 9XE,
Londonderry

Londonderry

Tel: **028 712 63195**   Fax: **028 712 63195**

Georgian farmhouse on mixed farm overlooking River Foyle and Golf Course, panoramic views. TV, tea/coffee in rooms. Kennels available.

B&B	2	Ensuite	Stg£18/£20	Dinner	-
B&B	1	Standard	Stg£17/£19	Partial Board	-
Single Rate			Stg£20	Child reduction	25%

Derry 3km

🏠 📺 ☕ ⬆ 🎣

Open: All Year Except Christmas

Rosemary Armstrong
ARCH TULLYHONA HOUSE
59 Marble Arch Road,
Florencecourt, Enniskillen,
BT92 1DE Co Fermanagh

Enniskillen

Tel: **028 66348452**
Email: tullyguest60@hotmail.com
Web: **www.archhouse.com**

◆◆◆◆. Winner-15 awards. Restaurant seats 50+. Near Marble Arch Caves/Florencecourt Hse/ Belleek Pottery. Children welcome. Follow signs for caves Enniskillen Rd, left Swanlinbar road. R.O.I. 048.

B&B	6	Ensuite	Stg£21/£22	Dinner	Stg£12
B&B	-	Standard		Partial Board	-
Single Rate			Stg£26/£27	Child reduction	50%

Enniskillen 11km

 cc S P 🏠 📺 🍴 ✗ ♿ 🚲 👜 ⬅ 🎣 R

Open: All Year

Omagh 1.5km

Mrs Mary Montgomery
CLANABOGAN HOUSE
85 Clanabogan Road,
Omagh, BT78 1SL
Co Tyrone

Omagh
TEL: **028 82241171**   FAX: **028 82241171**
EMAIL: **r&m@clanaboganhouse.freeserve.co.uk**
WEB: **www.clanaboganhouse.freeserve.co.uk**

A restored period residence set in 5 acres of woodland and gardens. Bar, Golf, Driving range and Pony stables on site. Spacious rooms. Friendly relaxed atmosphere.

B&B	6	Ensuite	Stg£25	Dinner	-
B&B	2	Standard	Stg£22.50	Partial Board	-
Single Rate	-		Stg£25	Child reduction	25%

Open: All Year

Omagh 12km

Louie Reid
GREENMOUNT LODGE
58 Greenmount Road,
Gortaclare, Omagh,
BT79 0YE Co Tyrone

Omagh
TEL: **028 82841325**   FAX: **028 82840019**
EMAIL: **greenmountlodge@lineone.net**
WEB: **www.greenmountlodge.com**

Luxury ◆◆◆◆ guesthouse set in mature woodlands. Guest laundry facilities. Off A5 south of Omagh, turn right after Carrickkeel Pub. 1 mile on left.

B&B	8	Ensuite	Stg£20	Dinner	Stg£12.50
B&B	-	Standard		Partial Board	-
Single Rate			Stg£25	Child reduction	50%

Open: All Year

Mrs Joan Davison
FORTVIEW
36 Tullyboy Rd, Cookstown,
BT45 7YE Co Tyrone

Cookstown
TEL: **028 867 62640**   FAX: **028 867 64230**
EMAIL: **b-bfortview@talk21.com**
WEB: **www.smoothhound.co.uk/hotels/**

Warm hospitality in cosy dairy farm, home 5km north of Cookstown, signposted on A29 Cookstown - Moneymore carriageway. Newly re-decorated, well equipped rooms, one on ground floor.

B&B	1	Ensuite	Stg£18	Dinner	-
B&B	1	Standard	Stg£17	Partial Board	-
Single Rate			Stg£18	Child reduction	33.3%

Cookstown 5km

Open: April-October

Newcastle, Co Down

enjoy a bigger kind of welcome...

Holiday in the land of giants.

Next time you're planning your holiday, try Northern Ireland for size. The massive, mysterious Giant's Causeway will take your breath away.

There's so much to see and do in this fascinating country. Don't miss Belfast, with its classic Victorian architecture, vibrant festivals and traditional musical sessions in the city pubs. Take in a round or two of golf on our world class courses. Come horse riding in the beautiful Mountains of Mourne or cycling in the nine glens of Antrim. Enjoy a walking tour or relax with a cruise on Lough Erne in County Fermanagh.

We can offer almost any kind of holiday - and this is only a glimpse of what's available. For an even bigger picture, give us a call.

It's easy to find out more. Call

Republic of Ireland
01 679 1851/679 1977

Great Britain
00 44 171 766 9920

United States
00 1 212-922 0101

Germany
00 49 69-234 504

Canada
00 1 416-925 6368

 Northern Ireland Tourist Board

16 Nassau St, Dublin 2.

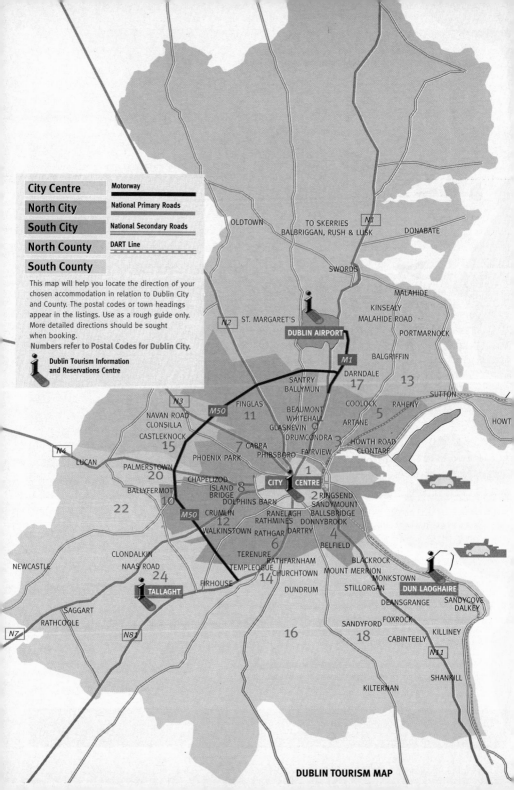

City Centre
North City
South City
North County
South County

Motorway
National Primary Roads
National Secondary Roads
DART Line

This map will help you locate the direction of your
chosen accommodation in relation to Dublin City
and County. The postal codes or town headings
appear in the listings. Use as a rough guide only.
More detailed directions should be sought
when booking.
Numbers refer to Postal Codes for Dublin City.

Dublin Tourism Information
and Reservations Centre

OLDTOWN
TO SKERRIES
BALBRIGGAN, RUSH & LUSK
N1
DONABATE

SWORDS

MALAHIDE

KINSEALY
MALAHIDE ROAD
PORTMARNOCK

N2   ST. MARGARET'S

DUBLIN AIRPORT

M1
BALGRIFFIN

DARNDALE
17   13

SANTRY
BALLYMUN
SUTTON

N3

M50

NAVAN ROAD
CLONSILLA
CASTLEKNOCK

FINGLAS
11

BEAUMONT
WHITEHALL
GLASNEVIN
9
DRUMCONDRA
3

COOLOCK   RAHENY
5
ARTANE

HOWTH

15

N4

LUCAN

CABRA
7
PHOENIX PARK
PHIBSBORO

FAIRVIEW
HOWTH ROAD
CLONTARF

PALMERSTOWN
20

BALLYFERMOT
10

CHAPELIZOD
ISLAND
BRIDGE
8
DOLPHINS BARN

CITY   CENTRE
1

RINGSEND
2
SANDYMOUNT

22

M50
12
CRUMLIN

WALKINSTOWN

RANELAGH
RATHMINES
RATHGAR   DARTRY
6

BALLSBRIDGE
DONNYBROOK
4

BELFIELD

CLONDALKIN
NAAS ROAD
24

TERENURE
RATHFARNHAM
TEMPLEOGUE
CHURCHTOWN
14

FIRHOUSE

TALLAGHT

DUNDRUM

BLACKROCK

MOUNT MERRION
MONKSTOWN
STILLORGAN

DUN LAOGHAIRE

NEWCASTLE

SAGGART
RATHCOOLE

N7

N81

DEANSGRANGE
SANDYCOVE
DALKEY

SANDYFORD   FOXROCK
18   CABINTEELY   KILLINEY

16

N11

KILTERNAN

SHANKILL

DUBLIN TOURISM MAP

Dublin

Dublin, Ireland's capital, steeped in history and buzzing with youthful energy. From its gracious Georgian Squares and terraces, mountain walks and sandy beaches to the intimacy of its pub and cafe life, Dublin is a thriving centre for culture. It is home to a great literary tradition where the cosmopolitan and charming converge in an atmosphere of delightful diversity.

Fine museums and art galleries chronicle its long and colourful past while the pubs and cafes buzz with traditional entertainment. Dublin's attractions are many from castles, museums and art galleries to the lively spirit of Temple Bar within a half hour of the city centre there are mountain walks, stately homes and gardens, sandy beaches and quaint fishing villages.

During your stay with us you will sample some of the charm of Dublin and particularly the warmth and wit of its people that has never ceased to win the heart of the visitor.

Area Representatives

DUBLIN
Mrs Rita Kenny, Seaview, 166 Bettyglen, Raheny, Dublin 5
Tel: 01 831 5335

Mrs Noreen McBride, 3 Rossmore Grove, Off Wellington Lane, Templeogue, Dublin 6W Tel: 01 490 2939 Fax: 01 492 9416

Tourist Information Offices

Dublin

Dublin Tourism Centre
Suffolk St.,
Dublin 2
Tel: 1850 230 330
O'Connell St.,
Dublin 1
Internet:
http://www.visitdublin.com
Email: information@dublin-tourism.ie

Arrivals Hall
Dublin Airport

Dun Laoghaire Harbour
Ferry Terminal Building
Dun Laoghaire
Co Dublin

Baggot Street Bridge
Dublin 2

The Square Towncentre
Tallaght, Dublin 24

City Centre 2km

Carmel Chambers
25 Anglesea Road,
Ballsbridge, Dublin 4

Ballsbridge

TEL: **01 6687346**   FAX: **01 6687346**
BUS NO: **7A, 7, 8, 45, 84, 63**

Edwardian home. Located in popular Ballsbridge, close to Bus, Rail (Dart), Embassies, Art Galleries, Trinity College, Point Theatre & RDS.

B&B	1	Ensuite	€40/€40	Dinner	-
B&B	3	Standard	€35/€35	Partial Board	-
Single Rate			€35/€60	Child reduction	-

Open: 5th January-20th December

Dublin 2km

Mrs Therese Clifford Sanderson
CAMELOT
37 Pembroke Park,
Ballsbridge, Dublin 4

Ballsbridge

TEL: **01 6680331**   FAX: **01 6671916**
BUS NO: **10, 46A**

Victorian home, friendly atmosphere. Close to City Centre, RDS, American Embassy, Museums, Art Galleries, Universities. Fine Restaurants within walking distance.

B&B	3	Ensuite	€42	Dinner	-
B&B	-	Standard		Partial Board	-
Single Rate			€55	Child reduction	-

Open: 1st January-15th December

Colm Dunne
AARON HOUSE
152 Merrion Road,
Ballsbridge, Dublin 4

Ballsbridge

TEL: **01 2601644**   FAX: **01 2601651**
EMAIL: **aaronhouse@indigo.ie**
WEB: **www.aaronhouse.com**
BUS NO: **5, 7, 8, 45**

In Ballsbridge

Luxurious accommodation. All rooms en-suite. Convenient to Point Theatre, RDS, Golf Clubs, all Embassies, Restaurants. Direct-dial telephones.

B&B	6	Ensuite	€35/€57	Dinner	-
B&B	-	Standard		Partial Board	-
Single Rate			€45/€100	Child reduction	25%

Open: All Year

In Ballsbridge

Ms Catherine Foy
20 Pembroke Park
Ballsbridge,
Dublin 4

Ballsbridge

TEL: **01 6683075**
EMAIL: **catherinefoy@eircom.net**

Victorian house just minutes walk from City Centre. Warm, friendly atmosphere. Close to RDS, Universities, Embassies, RTE, Lansdowne Stadium. Serviced by Aircoach.

B&B	3	Ensuite	€36/€42	Dinner	-
B&B	-	Standard	-	Partial Board	-
Single Rate			€57/€57	Child reduction	-

Open: All Year

In Ballsbridge

Leslie Griffin
AARON COURT
144 Merrion Road,
Ballsbridge, Dublin 4

Ballsbridge

TEL: **01 2602631**
EMAIL: **aaroncourt@yahoo.com**
BUS NO: **5, 7, 8, 45, DART**

Elegant family residence in the heart of Ballsbridge. All rooms en-suite, direct dial phones, TV. RDS, Point, Restaurant, Embassies.

B&B	6	Ensuite	€35/€65	Dinner	-
B&B	-	Standard	-	Partial Board	-
Single Rate			€45/€115	Child reduction	25%

Open: All Year

City Centre 1.5km

Teresa Muldoon
OAK LODGE
4 Pembroke Park,
Off Clyde Rd, Ballsbridge,
Dublin 4

Ballsbridge

TEL: **01 6606096/6681721** FAX: **01 6681721**
EMAIL: **oaklodgebandb@hotmail.com**
WEB: **www.fullfry.ie/oaklodgebandb.htm**
BUS No: **10, 46A**

Victorian residence close to RDS, Universities, Embassies, Dart. Breakfast menu. Direct Air Coach from Airport. Nearest stop Jury's Hotel.

B&B	3	Ensuite	€30/€40	Dinner	-
B&B	1	Standard	-	Partial Board	-
Single Rate			€30/€60	Child reduction	50%

Open: 2nd January-17th December

Dublin 3km

Joan Donnellan
HAZELHURST
166 Stillorgan Rd,
Donnybrook, Dublin 4

Donnybrook

TEL: **01 2838509** FAX: **01 2600346**
EMAIL: **hazelhurst@iolfree.ie**
BUS No: **10, 46A, 46B**

Luxurious spacious residence situated on N11. Adjacent Embassies, UCD, Montrose Hotel, RTE, RDS, main route to Ferry. Private car park. AA ♦♦♦♦.

B&B	6	Ensuite	€40/€50	Dinner	-
B&B	-	Standard	-	Partial Board	-
Single Rate			€65/€65	Child reduction	25%

Open: 1st March-15th December

Donnybrook 1.5km

Helen Martin
MONTROSE LODGE
164 Stillorgan Road,
Donnybrook, Dublin 4

Donnybrook

TEL: **01 2691590** FAX: **01 2691590**
EMAIL: **montroselodge1@eircom.net**
BUS No: **3, 10, 46, 46A, 46B, 746**

Spacious home situated on N11. Adjacent to UCD, RTE, Montrose Hotel, RDS and on main route to ferry. Ideally located for business & leisure. Secure parking.

B&B	3	Ensuite	€35/€45	Dinner	-
B&B	-	Standard	-	Partial Board	-
Single Rate			€48/€57	Child reduction	50%

Open: All Year Except Christmas

Dublin 2.2km

Mrs Mai Bird
ST DUNSTANS
25A Oakley Rd, Ranelagh,
Dublin 6

Ranelagh

TEL: **01 4972286**
BUS No: **11, 11A, 11B, 13B, 44, 48**

Edwardian townhouse. Frommer recommended. Convenient City Centre, RDS, Ferry, Jurys, Universities. Launderette, Restaurants, Banks and Post Office in immediate vicinity.

B&B	-	Ensuite	-	Dinner	-
B&B	3	Standard	€26/€29	Partial Board	-
Single Rate			€35/€35	Child reduction	-

Open: All Year Except Christmas

Dublin 6km

Mrs Beatrice O'Connor
CRANOG
15 Butterfield Avenue,
Rathfarnham, Dublin 14

Rathfarnham

TEL: **01 4943660**
EMAIL: **beatriceoconnor@oceanfree.net**
BUS No: **15B, 75, 15**

Family home. 15B bus stop outside house to City Centre. Tea/Coffee maker. Near N81 M50 motorway. Restaurants, Shop, Pub, Bank nearby.

B&B	2	Ensuite	€30/€33	Dinner	-
B&B	1	Standard	€28/€30	Partial Board	-
Single Rate			€35/€40	Child reduction	-

Open: 1st February-30th November

Mrs Aida Boyle
ST JUDES
6 Fortfield Tce,
Upper Rathmines, Dublin 6

Rathmines
TEL: **01 4972517**
Bus No: **14A, 13**

Beautiful Victorian home, well maintained, quiet locality. Spacious bedrooms. 7 min Shops, Restaurants, Banks, Pubs, Churches, Parks, Walks, RDS, Dart, Point Theatre.

B&B	2	Ensuite	€25.50/€30	Dinner	-
B&B	3	Standard	€23/€23	Partial Board	-
Single Rate			-	Child reduction	-

Dublin 3km

Open: All Year

Nola Martini
PINEHILL
Sandyford Village,
Dublin 18

Sandyford Village
TEL: **01 2952061**   FAX: **01 2958291**
EMAIL: **martini@indigo.ie**
WEB: **www.martini.pair.com**
Bus No: **44, 114, DART**

Charming Cottage style home with modern amenities. Close to Leopardstown Race Course (Stillorgan), Dun Laoghaire Ferry Port.

B&B	2	Ensuite	€38/€44.50	Dinner	-
B&B	2	Standard	€35/€38	Partial Board	-
Single Rate			€44.50/€50	Child reduction	-

Dublin City 8km

Open: 4th January-20th December

Mrs Dolores Abbott Murphy
14 Sandymount Castle Park,
off Gilford Road,
Sandymount, Dublin 4

Sandymount
TEL: **01 2698413**
Bus No: **3**

Quiet safe location beside Village, Sea, Bus, Rail (DART), Embassies, Museums, Art Galleries, Point Theatre, RDS, UCD, Trinity, St Vincents Hospital.

B&B	1	Ensuite	€32/€32	Dinner	-
B&B	2	Standard	€28/€28	Partial Board	-
Single Rate			€39/€39	Child reduction	-

Dublin 2km

Open: 1st May-30th September

Mrs Kathleen Lee
ARDAGH HOUSE
6 St Annes Road Sth,
South Circular Road,
Dublin 8

South Circular Road
TEL: **01 4536615**
Bus No: **19, 121, 122**

Home overlooking Grand Canal. Convenient to all places of interest. Bus 19, 121, 122. Road opposite John Player and Sons. 2.5km to City Centre. Easy access to N1, N4, N7, N11, M50.

B&B	3	Ensuite	€29.50/€32	Dinner	-
B&B	1	Standard	€29.50/€29.50	Partial Board	-
Single Rate			€40/€40	Child reduction	-

Dublin City 2.5km

Open: 30th January-30th November

Mrs Noreen Devine
CLARENDON B&B
293 Orwell Park Grove,
Templeogue, Dublin 6W

Templeogue
TEL: **01 4500007**   FAX: **01 4565725**
Bus No: **150, 54A, 15A**

Located off N81, exit at Spawell roundabout onto Wellington Lane, straight through next round-about, see B&B sign on right.

B&B	4	Ensuite	€25.50/€63.50	Dinner	-
B&B	-	Standard	-	Partial Board	-
Single Rate			€38.50/€38.50	Child reduction	25%

Dublin 6km

Open: All Year Except Christmas

Dublin 6km

Ms Maura Leahy
ABBEY COURT
7 Glendown Court,
Off Templeville Rd,
Templeogue, Dublin 6W

Templeogue
Tel: **01 4562338**

Comfortable, friendly, smoke-free home in quiet cul-de-sac. Near M50, N4, N7 and Car Ferry.
Leisure facilities locally.

B&B	2	Ensuite	€28/€30.50	Dinner	-
B&B	1	Standard	-	Partial Board	-
Single Rate			€36	Child reduction	-

Open: All Year

Dublin 6km

Mrs Noreen McBride
3 Rossmore Grove,
Off Wellington Lane,
Templeogue, Dublin 6W

Templeogue
Tel: **01 4902939**   Fax: **01 4929416**
Email: **denismb@iol.ie**
Bus No: **150, 54A**

Frommer, AA recommended. 20 mins City & Airport. Bus every 10 mins to City. Near Restaurant &
M50. Located off N81 at Spawell roundabout first right Rossmore Rd.

B&B	2	Ensuite	€30/€33	Dinner	-
B&B	2	Standard	€28/€30	Partial Board	-
Single Rate			€38.50/€40	Child reduction	-

Open: 15th January-15th December

Dublin City 6km

Mrs Mary McGreal
SEEFIN
28 Rossmore Grove,
Templeogue, Dublin 6W

Templeogue
Tel: **01 4907286**   Fax: **01 4907286**
Email: **mcgreal_28@yahoo.co.uk**
Bus No: **150, 54A**

Modern home in cul-de-sac off Wellington Lane. 1/2km from Spawell roundabout on N81. On
Ferry and Bus Routes. 5mins M50 motorway. Restaurants, Pubs, Sporting facilities locally.

B&B	2	Ensuite	€30/€33	Dinner	-
B&B	1	Standard	€28/€30	Partial Board	-
Single Rate			€38.50/€40	Child reduction	-

Open: 15th January-15th December

Dublin City 4km

Mrs Ellie Kiernan
LOUGHKIERN
65 Rockfield Ave, Terenure,
Dublin 12

Terenure
Tel: **01 4551509**
Bus No: **15A, 150**

Comfortable modern family home. 15 mins to City. Convenient to Restaurants, Sports Centre,
Bus, Park, Links Road and Ferry Terminal.

B&B	1	Ensuite	€27.94/€31.76	Dinner	-
B&B	2	Standard	€25.40/€29.22	Partial Board	-
Single Rate			€36/€36	Child reduction	25%

Open: All Year Except Christmas

RESERVATIONS

- Confirm phone bookings in writing without delay with agreed deposit.
- To avoid misunderstandings later, check rate on booking and
  clarify any additional changes which may apply to your booking.
- Give details of any special requirements.
- State clearly day, date of arrival and departure date.

Monica & Michael Leydon
AARONA
150 Clonkeen Rd,
Deansgrange, Blackrock,
Co Dublin

Blackrock

TEL: **01 2893972**
EMAIL: **aarona.bandb.ireland@gmx.net**
BUS NO: **45**

Exquisitely situated beside all amenities. Bus to City Centre. Dun Laoghaire, Ferry Port 5 mins.
Highest standards maintained in friendly family atmosphere.

B&B	3	Ensuite	€32/€32	Dinner	-
B&B	-	Standard	-	Partial Board	-
Single Rate			€44.50/€44.50	Child reduction	-

Dun Laoghaire 2km

Open: All Year Except Christmas

Mrs Mary Corbett Monaghan
46 Windsor Park,
Off Stradbrook Road,
Blackrock, Co Dublin

Blackrock

TEL: **01 2843711** FAX: **01 2802737**
EMAIL: **monaghanwindsor@eircom.net**
BUS NO: **46A, 7, 8**

Bright comfortable family home, convenient to Ferry, Restaurants, Bus and Salthill DART Station.
Secure car parking. Ideal touring base.

B&B	2	Ensuite	€30/€30	Dinner	-
B&B	2	Standard	€26/€26	Partial Board	-
Single Rate			€36/€45	Child reduction	-

Dun Laoghaire 2km

Open: 1st April-31st October

Steve & Maria Gavin
LYNDEN
2 Mulgrave Tce,
Dun Laoghaire, Co Dublin

Dun Laoghaire

TEL: **01 2806404** FAX: **01 2302258**
EMAIL: **lynden@iol.ie**
BUS NO: **7, 7A, 8, 45A, 46A, 59, 111, DART**

Georgian house. Quiet location. Adjacent Buses, Train, Shops. Car Ferry 5 mins walk. Early breakfasts. parking, TV & tea making facilities.

B&B	2	Ensuite	€28	Dinner	-
B&B	2	Standard	€24.50	Partial Board	-
Single Rate			€37/€40	Child reduction	50%

In Dun Laoghaire

Open: All Year

Mrs Ann Harkin
7 Claremont Villas
(Off Adelaide Road),
Glenageary, Dun Laoghaire,
Co Dublin

Dun Laoghaire

TEL: **01 2805346** FAX: **01 2805346**
EMAIL: **harkinann@hotmail.com**
WEB: **www.claremonthouse.net**
BUS NO: **8, 59, DART**

Victorian home built 1876. 2 mins walk to train (DART) near ferry, bus, own restaurant "Daniels".
Quiet cul-de-sac. Ample parking on St. Early breakfast.

B&B	4	Ensuite	€28/€32	Dinner	-
B&B	1	Standard	€26	Partial Board	-
Single Rate			€34/€40	Child reduction	50%

Dun Laoghaire 1km

Open: All Year Except Christmas

Mrs Mary Kane
SEAVIEW HOUSE
2 Granite Hall,
Rosmeen Gardens,
Dun Laoghaire, Co Dublin

Dun Laoghaire

TEL: **01 2809105** FAX: **01 2809105**
EMAIL: **seaviewbedandbreakfast@hotmail.com**
BUS NO: **7, 7A, 8**

Comfortable detached family home in quiet cul-de-sac within walking distance Dart, Sea Front and
all amenities. Parking.

B&B	3	Ensuite	€32/€35	Dinner	-
B&B	-	Standard	-	Partial Board	-
Single Rate			-	Child reduction	-

Dun Laoghaire

Open: 1st January-15th December

In Dun Laoghaire

Mary O'Farrell

Dun Laoghaire

WINDSOR LODGE
3 Islington Ave, Sandycove,
Dun Laoghaire, Co Dublin

Tel: **01 2846952**   Fax: **01 2846952**
Email: **winlodge@eircom.net**
Bus No: **7, 8, DART**

Victorian Home beside Dublin Bay. Close to all amenities. 5 minutes Stena Ferry. Beside Bus/Dart. 20 minutes City Centre.

B&B	4	Ensuite	€25.50/€35	Dinner	-
B&B	-	Standard	-	Partial Board	-
Single Rate			€38/€57	Child reduction	50%

Open: 1st January-23rd December

Dalkey 2km

Mrs Bridie O'Leary

Dun Laoghaire

ROSEMONT
51 Bellevue Road, Glenageary,
Dun Laoghaire, Co Dublin

Tel: **01 2851021**   Fax: **01 2851021**
Email: **rosemont51@eircom.net**
Bus No: **59, 7, 7A**

Bright comfortable home. Quiet location, convenient to Bus, Train and Ferry. Close to Fitzpatrick Castle, Killiney. Early breakfast. Private parking.

B&B	3	Ensuite	€28/€32	Dinner	-
B&B	1	Standard	-	Partial Board	-
Single Rate			€38/€43	Child reduction	25%

Open: 1st February-30th November

Mrs Connie O'Sullivan

Dun Laoghaire

DUNCREE
16 Northumberland Avenue,
Dun Laoghaire, Co Dublin

Tel: **01 2806118**
Bus No: **7, 7A, 46A**

Comfortable Georgian house, quiet location. Adjacent to Buses, Trains & Shops. Car Ferry 5 mins walk.

B&B	2	Ensuite	€29	Dinner	-
B&B	2	Standard	€25	Partial Board	-
Single Rate			€32	Child reduction	25%

Open: 1st January-22nd December

In Dun Laoghaire

Des & Marie Power

Dun Laoghaire

ARIEMOND
47 Mulgrave Street,
Dun Laoghaire, Co Dublin

Tel: **01 2801664**   Fax: **01 2801664**
Email: **ariemond@hotmail.com**
Bus No: **8, 7, 46A, 45A, DART**

Georgian house Town Centre. Ferry five minutes walk. Beside Buses and Train. Dublin City centre 15 minutes. Golf and Rock climbing nearby.

B&B	3	Ensuite	€29	Dinner	-
B&B	2	Standard	€25	Partial Board	-
Single Rate			€50/€58	Child reduction	-

Open: 1st January-20th December

Dun Laoghaire 2km

Ms Betty MacAnaney

Killiney

70 Avondale Rd,
Killiney, Co Dublin

Tel: **01 2859952**   Fax: **01 2859952**
Email: **mcananey@hotmail.com**
Web: **www.macananey.com**
Bus No: **59**

Quiet area, 4 minute drive to Car Ferry. 12-minute walk to Glenageary Dart Station. Dalkey close by. Easy reach City Centre & Co. Wicklow. Private Parking.

B&B	3	Ensuite	€30/€33	Dinner	-
B&B	1	Standard	€30/€30	Partial Board	-
Single Rate			€38/€45	Child reduction	25%

Open: February-November

In Lucan

Colette Egan
MOAT LODGE
Newcastle Road, Lucan,
Co Dublin

Lucan

TEL: **01 6241584**   FAX: **01 6281356**
BUS NO: **66A,67,67A,25,25A,66**

Exclusive 17th Century House convenient to Shops, Bus, City Centre. Ideal base for Golf & Fishing. Off N4. Near N7, N3, M50.

B&B	4	Ensuite	€30/€30	Dinner	-
B&B	-	Standard	-	Partial Board	-
Single Rate			€44/€44	Child reduction	-

Open: All Year

Lucan 1km

Seamus & Patricia McCormack
BEAUMONT
Newcastle Road, Lucan,
Co Dublin

Lucan

TEL: **01 6281956**
BUS NO: **25, 25A, 66, 67**

Modern bungalow just off N4, convenient to City, Airport and Car Ferry. Private car park. Bedrooms non-smoking.

B&B	4	Ensuite	€25.50/€28	Dinner	-
B&B	-	Standard	-	Partial Board	-
Single Rate			€38.50/€40	Child reduction	25%

Open: 5th January-20th December

In Rathcoole

Mrs Ann Eagers
BANNER HOUSE
Main St, Rathcoole,
Co Dublin

Rathcoole

TEL: **01 4589337**   FAX: **01 4589337**
BUS NO: **69**

Modern family home, 100 yds off N7. Convenient to Pub/Restaurant, beside bus stop. Conservatory for guests use. Golf & Horseriding nearby. Airport, City Centre, 30 mins.

B&B	5	Ensuite	€25/€28	Dinner	-
B&B	-	Standard	-	Partial Board	-
Single Rate			€38	Child reduction	-

Open: All Year Except Christmas

Rathcoole 2km

Elizabeth Freeland
HILLBROOK
Redgap, Rathcoole,
Co Dublin

Rathcoole

TEL: **01 4580060**
EMAIL: **lizfreeland@hotmail.com**
BUS NO: **69**

Welcoming home in scenic countryside, adjacent to Golf, Horseriding, Pitch & Putt. Dublin City, Airport 30 minutes. Close to N7. Convenient to all main routes.

B&B	2	Ensuite	€25.50/€29	Dinner	-
B&B	2	Standard	-	Partial Board	-
Single Rate			€36/€38	Child reduction	25%

Open: All Year Except Christmas

Rathcoole 1.5km

Elizabeth Keogh
BEARNA RUA LODGE
Redgap, Rathcoole,
Co Dublin

Rathcoole

TEL: **01 4589920/4587880**   FAX: **01 4587880**
EMAIL: **bearnarualodge@hotmail.com**
BUS NO: **69**

Panoramic view, peaceful rural setting yet only 30 mins from Airport/Dublin City. Adjacent to Forest walks, Horseriding, Golf. Off N7. 1.5km from Village.

B&B	4	Ensuite	€28/€32	Dinner	-
B&B	-	Standard	-	Partial Board	-
Single Rate			€39/€44	Child reduction	-

Open: 9th January-17th December

Rathcoole 3km

Mrs Mary Spillane
GREENACRES
Kilteel Road, Rathcoole,
Co Dublin

Rathcoole
Tel: **01 4580732**   Fax: **01 4580732**
Bus No: **69**

Bungalow 2 miles from Rathcoole on Kilteel Rd, opposite Beech Park Golf Club. Riding Stables locally.

B&B	4	Ensuite	€30/€33	Dinner	-
B&B	1	Standard	€28/€30	Partial Board	-
Single Rate			€38.50/€40	Child reduction	-

Open: 1st January-20th December

Bray 3km

Mrs Eileen McNamee
CORGLASS
15 Shanganagh Grove,
Quinns Road, Shankill,
Co Dublin

Shankill
Tel: **01 2820370**
Bus No: **45, 45A, 84, DART**

Comfortable house, South Dublin. Quiet cul-de-sac beside Sea, Golf, Dun Laoghaire Ferry and scenic Wicklow. Off N11.

B&B	2	Ensuite	€27/€32	Dinner	-
B&B	1	Standard	€25.50/€25.50	Partial Board	-
Single Rate			-	Child reduction	-

Open: 1st February-30th November

Botanic Gardens, Dublin 9.

Mrs Mary O'Reilly
RATHLEEK
13 Brookwood Rd, Artane,
Dublin 5

Artane

Tel: 01 8310555
Bus No: 42, 42B, 42C, 27

10 mins Beaumont Hospital, City Centre, Irish Ferries, Car Ferry, Connolly Station, Central Bus Station. Dart. Sea Front. Tea, TV, Radio, Hairdryer all rooms.

B&B	-	Ensuite	-	Dinner	-
B&B	3	Standard	€27	Partial Board	-
Single Rate			€36	Child reduction	-

Dublin 4km

Open: 1st March-31st October

Kevin & Anne Rogers
BLAITHIN B&B
18 St Brendans Avenue,
Artane, Dublin 5

Artane

Tel: 01 8483817   Fax: 01 8674029
Email: blaithin@oceanfree.net
Bus No: 27, 42

Luxurious family home. Excellent rooms with Tea/Coffee, TV. Close to Seafront, Golf. City 10 min. Buses at door. Airport 15 min, Ferry 10 min. Safe Parking.

B&B	3	Ensuite	€30/€33	Dinner	-
B&B	2	Standard	€25/€30	Partial Board	-
Single Rate			€42/€50	Child reduction	-

Dublin 5km

Open: 10th January-15th December

Mrs Marie O'Reilly
67 The Pines, Auburn Ave,
Castleknock, Dublin 15

Castleknock

Tel: 01 8215560   Fax: 01 8215560
Bus No: 37,39, 38

Select area, close Phoenix Park. Adjacent M50 Motorway linking with routes North, South, West. City 15 mins. Airport 15 mins.

B&B	1	Ensuite	€30.50 /€30.50	Dinner	-
B&B	2	Standard	€28/€28	Partial Board	-
Single Rate			€40/€40	Child reduction	-

Dublin 6km

Open: March-September

Caroline & Paul Connolly
KINCORA LODGE
54 Kincora Court, Clontarf,
Dublin 3

Clontarf

Tel: 01 8330220   Fax: 01 8330007
Email: kincoralodge@eircom.net
Bus No: 130

Modern home quiet area. Parking. 15 mins Airport, City Centre, Ferrypoint. Theatre, Golf Courses, Beach, Park within walking distance. TV, Tea/Coffee facilities, Hairdryers all rooms.

B&B	3	Ensuite	€35/€42	Dinner	-
B&B	-	Standard	-	Partial Board	-
Single Rate			€50/€64	Child reduction	25%

Dublin 4km

Open: 5th January-20th December

Mrs Eileen Cummiskey Kelly
GARRYBAWN
18 Copeland Avenue,
Clontarf, Dublin 3

Clontarf

Tel: 01 8333760
Bus No: 20, 20B, 42, 31

Near Point Theatre, Airport, Ferryport, City Centre. 2km Croke Park, 1km Buses to Centre no.'s 20, 20B, 42, 31.

B&B	2	Ensuite	€28.50	Dinner	-
B&B	1	Standard	€25.50	Partial Board	-
Single Rate			€36	Child reduction	25%

Dublin 3km

Open: All Year Except Christmas

Mrs Susan Delahunty
GLENBROOK
34 Howth Road, Clontarf,
Dublin 3

Clontarf
Tel: 01 8331117/8532265
Email: delahunty@dol.ie
Bus No: 29A, 31, 31A, 31B, 32, 32A, 32B

Victorian town house, close to City, Ferryport, Airport, Bus and Rail Terminals. Beach and Golf courses nearby.

B&B	2	Ensuite	€32 /€38	Dinner	-
B&B	1	Standard	-	Partial Board	-
Single Rate			€38/€51	Child reduction	25%

Dublin City 3km

Open: 1st March-31st October

Miss M Dereymont
18 Seacourt,
St Gabriel's Road,
Clontarf, Dublin 3

Clontarf
Tel: 01 8333313
Bus No: 130

Georgian residence, convenient to City, Airport, Ferry, Restaurants, Point Theatre. Non smoking. Adults only. Closes 1am (opposite St. Gabriel's Church). Shops nearby.

B&B	1	Ensuite	€36.19/€40.63	Dinner	-
B&B	2	Standard	€34.91/€38.09	Partial Board	-
Single Rate			€63.49/€69.82	Child reduction	-

Dublin 5km

Open: 1st April-31st October

John & Delia Devlin
ANNAGH HOUSE
301 Clontarf Road, Clontarf,
Dublin 3

Clontarf
Tel: 01 8338841   Fax: 01 8338841
Bus No: 130

Charming Victorian house, convenient to City, Airport, Ferryport, Restaurants, Pubs, Theatres, Golf, Beach. Superb location to explore culture of Dublin. Bus route.

B&B	3	Ensuite	€31.74/€34.29	Dinner	-
B&B	-	Standard	-	Partial Board	-
Single Rate			-	Child reduction	-

Dublin 5km

Open: 1st January-22nd December

Jackie Egan
VALENTIA HOUSE
37 Kincora Court, Clontarf,
Dublin 3

Clontarf
Tel: 01 8338060   Fax: 01 8339990
Email: jackieegan@esatclear.ie
Web: www.valentiahousebandb.com
Bus No: 130

Family run home, convenient City/Airport/Ferry/Point Theatre/Beach/Golf Clubs/Restaurants. 130 Bus from Abbey St. to Clontarf road Bus Depot. Left here, right at crossroads, first right & first right.

B&B	4	Ensuite	€29.50/€37.50	Dinner	-
B&B	-	Standard	-	Partial Board	-
Single Rate			€50/€70	Child reduction	25%

Dublin City 4km

Open: 3rd January-20th December

Mrs Moira Kavanagh
SPRINGVALE
69 Kincora Drive,
Off Kincora Grove, Clontarf,
Dublin 3

Clontarf
Tel: 01 8333413
Email: moira_kav@hotmail.com
Web: www.springvaledublin.com
Bus No: 29A, 31, 32, 130, DART

Modern house, quiet residential area. 15 mins Airport, Car Ferry, City, Point Theatre. Frommer Recommended. Tea/coffee facilities. 4 rooms with shower only.

B&B	-	Ensuite	-	Dinner	-
B&B	4	Standard	€27	Partial Board	-
Single Rate			€36	Child reduction	-

Dublin 4km

Open: 1st January-22nd December

Mrs Eileen P Kelly
TORC HOUSE
17 Seacourt, St Gabriels Rd,
(off Seafield Rd) Clontarf,
Dublin 3

Clontarf
TEL: 01 8332547
BUS NO: 130

Detached Georgian house, residential area. Convenient City, Airport, Ferry Port, Beach, Golf, Rose Gardens, Point. Frommer/RAC/Sullivan Guide recommended.

B&B	2	Ensuite	€32/€32	Dinner	-
B&B	1	Standard	€28/€28	Partial Board	-
Single Rate			€50/€50	Child reduction	-

Dublin City 5km

Open: 15th May-31st October

Joseph & Mary Mooney
WILLOWBROOK
14 Strandville Ave East,
Clontarf, Dublin 3

Clontarf
TEL: 01 8333115
EMAIL: willowbrook@ireland.com
WEB: www.willowbrookbandb.com
BUS NO: 130, DART

Gracious detached home on quiet street. Close to City, Ferry port, Airport, Beach, Golf Courses, Bus & Rail services. First left off Clontarf Rd coming from City.

B&B	3	Ensuite	€32/€38	Dinner	-
B&B	-	Standard	-	Partial Board	-
Single Rate			€55/€55	Child reduction	-

Dublin 3km

Open: All Year Except Christmas

Mrs Mary Wright
LAWRENCE HOUSE
26 St Lawrence Rd, Clontarf,
Dublin 3

Clontarf
TEL: 01 8332539   FAX: 01 8332539
EMAIL: info@lawrence-house.com
WEB: www.lawrence-house.com
BUS NO: 130, 31, 32, 29A, 31A, 32B

Lovely Victorian house. 10 minutes to City, DART, Car Ferry, Airport and Point Theatre. Private car parking. Buses 130, 31, 31A, 32, 32B, 29A to St Lawrence Rd.

B&B	5	Ensuite	€32/€38	Dinner	-
B&B	-	Standard	-	Partial Board	-
Single Rate			€55/€55	Child reduction	-

Dublin 2.5km

Open: All Year Except Christmas

Mrs Roma Gibbons
JOYVILLE
24 St Alphonsus Road,
Drumcondra, Dublin 9

Drumcondra
TEL: 01 8303221
BUS NO: 3, 11, 11A, 16, 16A, 41

Victorian town house off main Airport road. Convenient to Car Ferry, Botanic Gardens, City Centre.

B&B	-	Ensuite	-	Dinner	-
B&B	4	Standard	€25	Partial Board	-
Single Rate			€31	Child reduction	-

Dublin City 1km

Open: 7th January-20th December

Mrs Hilda Gibson
THE GABLES
50 Iona Crescent
off Hollybank Road,
Drumcondra, Dublin 9

Drumcondra
TEL: 01 8300538
BUS NO: 3, 11, 16, 33, 36, 41, 51A

Comfortable family home off main Airport Road (N1), 10 minutes Airport, Car Ferry, City Centre, Point Theatre, Private Car Park.

B&B	3	Ensuite	€31	Dinner	-
B&B	1	Standard	-	Partial Board	-
Single Rate			€32/€37	Child reduction	-

Dublin 2km

Open: All Year

Mrs Ann Griffin
MUCKROSS HOUSE
Claude Road off Whitworth Rd,
Drumcondra, Dublin 9

Drumcondra
TEL: **01 8304888**
EMAIL: **muckrosshouse01@eircom.net**
WEB: **www.muckrosshousedublin.com**
BUS NO: **13, 40, 40A, 40B**

Situated off main Airport road (N1). Convenient to City Centre, Airport, Car Ferry & Point Depot. Private enclosed car parking.

B&B	5	Ensuite	€32/€35	Dinner	-
B&B	-	Standard	-	Partial Board	-
Single Rate			€40	Child reduction	-

Dublin 1km

Open: 2nd January-20th December

Mrs Cait Cunningham Murray
30 Walnut Ave,
Courtlands Estate,
off Griffith Ave, Drumcondra,
Dublin 9

Drumcondra
TEL: **01 8379327**
BUS NO: **3, 16, 16A, 41, 41A, 13A**

Modern home, off Griffith Ave overlooking park. Off N1 convenient to Airport, City Centre and B&I Ferry. Very quiet location. Smoke free home.

B&B	2	Ensuite	€28/€28	Dinner	-
B&B	1	Standard	€25/€25	Partial Board	-
Single Rate			-	Child reduction	-

Dublin City 4km

Open: 1st April-30th September

Mrs Gemma Rafferty
GREEN-VIEW
36 Walnut Avenue,
Courtlands, Off Griffith Ave,
Drumcondra, Dublin 9

Drumcondra
TEL: **01 8376217**
BUS NO: **3, 13A, 16, 16A ,41A, 41B**

Peaceful location opposite Park off N1. 10 mins City Centre, Airport, Car Ferry, Golf Courses.

B&B	2	Ensuite	€28	Dinner	-
B&B	1	Standard	€25	Partial Board	-
Single Rate			-	Child reduction	-

Dublin City 4km

Open: 15th March-15th December

Irene Coyle Ryan
BLANFORD HOUSE
37 Lambay Road,
off Griffith Ave, Drumcondra,
Dublin 9

Drumcondra
TEL: **01 8378036**
BUS NO: **11, 11A, 13A**

Town house near Airport, Ferry Port, Botanic Gardens. Forbairt, Point Theatre. Dublin City University. Bonsecours Hospital. Mater Hospital.

B&B	1	Ensuite	€28.50/€28.50	Dinner	-
B&B	3	Standard	€25.50/€25.50	Partial Board	-
Single Rate			€36/€36	Child reduction	-

Dublin City 3km

Open: All Year Except Christmas

Mrs Teresa Ryan
PARKNASILLA
15 Iona Drive,
Drumcondra,
Dublin 9

Drumcondra
TEL: **01 8305724**
BUS NO: **11, 16, 16A, 41, 13, 19, 19A, 3.**

Edwardian detached residence, off main Airport Road N1, 10 minutes to City Centre, Airport, Car Ferry, Bus & Rail Terminals.

B&B	2	Ensuite	€29/€29	Dinner	-
B&B	2	Standard	€25/€25	Partial Board	-
Single Rate			€32/€32	Child reduction	-

Dublin 1.5km

Open: 1st January-21st December

Mrs Margaret McLoughlin-O'Connell
LOYOLA
18 Charleville Road,
Phibsboro, Dublin 7

Phibsboro
TEL: 01 8389973
BUS No: 10, 38, 120, 121, 122

Victorian house convenient to Rail, Bus, Airport, Car Ferry Terminals. Zoo, Public Parks, Mater Hospital, Link Roads.

B&B	2	Ensuite	€29	Dinner	-
B&B	2	Standard	€26	Partial Board	-
Single Rate			€36/€38	Child reduction	20%

Dublin City 1km

Open: 1st January-15th December

Mrs Maureen Flynn
FOUR SEASONS
15 Grange Park Green,
Raheny, Dublin 5

Raheny
TEL: 01 8486612
BUS No: 29A, 31, 32

Convenient to City Centre, Car Ferry, Airport, DART and Bus. Private parking. Restaurants in Village. TV lounge with Tea/Coffee, Hairdryers in rooms.

B&B	4	Ensuite	€29/€30	Dinner	-
B&B	-	Standard	-	Partial Board	-
Single Rate			-	Child reduction	-

Dublin City 7km

Open: 6th January-20th December

Mrs Eileen Keane
BREIFNE
23 Bettyglen, Raheny,
Dublin 5

Raheny
TEL: 01 8313976
BUS No: 31, 31A, 32

Large detached house overlooking sea. Private parking. 10km Dublin Airport, 6km B&I Car Ferry, 4km City Centre, Guest Lounge.

B&B	3	Ensuite	€28/€29	Dinner	-
B&B	1	Standard	€26/€27	Partial Board	-
Single Rate			€36/€36	Child reduction	33.3%

In Raheny

Open: 1st January-20th December

Mrs Rita Kenny
SEAVIEW
166 Bettyglen, Raheny,
Dublin 5

Raheny
TEL: 01 8315335
EMAIL: rita.kenny@ireland.com
BUS No: 31, 31A, 32, 32B

Large semi detached house overlooking Sea. Private parking. Convenient to Airport, Car Ferry, DART, Buses, Golf Courses. Orthopaedic beds, Tea in rooms. Room rate.

B&B	2	Ensuite	€30	Dinner	-
B&B	1	Standard	€26	Partial Board	-
Single Rate			-	Child reduction	25%

Dublin City 5km

Open: 1st January-23rd December

SYMBOL

LOOK OUT FOR THIS SYMBOL WHICH
ALL MEMBERS OF
TOWN & COUNTRY HOMES
DISPLAY

Balbriggan 4km

Jacqueline Clarke
KNIGHTSWOOD B&B
6 Knightswood, Balrothery
Balbriggan, Co Dublin

Balbriggan

TEL: **01 8411621**
EMAIL: **clarketom@eircom.net**

Comfortable residence. Airport 20 minutes, Golf Course & Hostelry nearby. Take N1 north from Airport, 1st exit for Balbriggan (R132) 3km.

B&B	2	Ensuite	€29/€30.50	Dinner	-
B&B	1	Standard	€25.50/€29	Partial Board	-
Single Rate			€36/€38	Child reduction	25%

Open: 17th May-30th September

Howth 1.5km

Mrs Rosaleen Hobbs
HAZELWOOD
2 Thormanby Woods,
Thormanby Road, Howth,
Dublin 13

Howth

TEL: **01 8391391**   FAX: **01 8391391**
EMAIL: **101706.3526@compuserve.com**
WEB: **www.hazelwood.net**
BUS NO: **31B, DART**

Modern dormer bungalow in own grounds. Ample car parking. Convenient Golf, Beach, Restaurants, Scenic Cliff Walks & Fishing Village. City centre 25mins.

B&B	6	Ensuite	€32	Dinner	-
B&B	-	Standard	-	Partial Board	-
Single Rate			-	Child reduction	50%

Open: 3rd January-20th December

Swords 4km

Ms Patricia Butterly
BROOKFIELD LODGE B&B
Blakes Cross, Belfast Road,
Lusk, Co Dublin

Lusk

TEL: **01 8430043**   FAX: **01 8430177**
EMAIL: **trishb@indigo.ie**
BUS NO: **100**

Modern country home, 10 minutes north Dublin Airport N1. Ignore sign for Lusk, continue past Esso garage for 400 metres. Located on junction N1/R129.

B&B	4	Ensuite	€25/€38	Dinner	-
B&B	-	Standard	-	Partial Board	-
Single Rate			€38/€58	Child reduction	-

Open: 10th January-30th November

Swords 9km

Freda Rigney
IVY BUNGALOW
Ballough, Lusk,
Co Dublin

Lusk

TEL: **01 8437031**
EMAIL: **ivybungalowlusk@yahoo.com**

Quaint country home off Belfast Dublin road. 10 mins North of Dublin Airport. City Centre 30 mins. Peaceful surroundings. Ground floor accommodation. Pub 300 yards.

B&B	3	Ensuite	€28/€35	Dinner	-
B&B	1	Standard	€25/€25	Partial Board	-
Single Rate			€38/€51	Child reduction	33.3%

Open: 3rd January-23rd December

Malahide 3km

Mrs Monica Fitzsimons
PEBBLE MILL
Kinsealy, Malahide,
Co Dublin

Malahide

TEL: **01 8461792**
EMAIL: **pat.fitzsimons@esatlink.com**
BUS NO: **42, 43**

Country home on 4 Acres. Golf, Horseriding, Yachting, Castle closeby. Airport 7mins, B&I 20 mins. Room rates. TV, Hairdryers, Tea/Coffee all rooms.

B&B	3	Ensuite	€28/€30	Dinner	-
B&B	-	Standard	-	Partial Board	-
Single Rate			-	Child reduction	50%

Open: 1st March-31st October

Maura & Jim Halpin
HEATHER VIEW
Malahide Road, Kinsealy,
Co Dublin

Malahide

Tel: **01 8453483** Fax: **01 8453818**
Email: **hview@eircom.net**
Bus No: **42, 43, Airport 230**

Luxury country home on R107, Airport 6km. Castle 1km, M50 3km. Parking. All rooms TV, Clockradio, Hairdryer, Tea/Coffee. Breakfast menu.

B&B	5	Ensuite	€32/€35	Dinner	-
B&B	-	Standard	-	Partial Board	-
Single Rate			-	Child reduction	-

Malahide 3km

Open: All Year Except Christmas

Mrs Noreen Handley
AISHLING
59 Biscayne (off Coast Rd)
Malahide, Co Dublin

Malahide

Tel: **01 8452292** Fax: **01 8452292**
Bus No: **32A, 42, 102, 230 Airport**

Pass Grand Hotel, 2nd turn right after Islandview Hotel. Excellent accommodation, overlooking Beach. Adjacent Golf, Yachting, Castle, Restaurants,15 mins Airport.

B&B	2	Ensuite	€29/€29	Dinner	-
B&B	1	Standard	€29/€29	Partial Board	-
Single Rate			-	Child reduction	-

Malahide 1.5km

Open: April-September

Olive Hopkins
EVERGREEN
Kinsealy Lane, Malahide,
Co Dublin

Malahide

Tel: **01 8460185**
Email: **evergreendub@eircom.net**
Bus No: **42**

Luxury home on 1 acre. Private parking. Malahide/Restaurants 1 mile. TV, Hairdryers all rooms. Turn right before main entrance to Malahide Castle/Park. Airport 10 mins. Ferry/City 20 mins.

B&B	4	Ensuite	€28/€29	Dinner	-
B&B	1	Standard	€26/€27	Partial Board	-
Single Rate			€36/€38	Child reduction	33.3%

Malahide 2km

Open: 1st Feburary-30th November

Mrs Jane F Kiernan
LISCARA
Malahide Road, Kinsealy,
Dublin 17

Malahide

Tel: **01 8483751** Fax: **01 8483751**
Bus No: **42, 43**

Private parking. Airport 10 mins, City/Ferry 20 mins. Convenient Golf, Cinemas, Malahide Castle & Town, Swimming Pools. M50 1 Mile. On R107. Michelin recommended.

B&B	6	Ensuite	€32/€32	Dinner	-
B&B	-	Standard	-	Partial Board	-
Single Rate			€45/€45	Child reduction	-

Malahide 4.5km

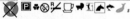

Open: 1st March-31st October

Mrs Cathy McConnell
SAN JUAN
Baskin Lane,
Kinsealy, Dublin 17

Malahide

Tel: **01 8460424** Fax: **01 8460910**
Bus No: **42, 43**

Country style residence on one acre. 5 mins to Airport, close to Malahide Castle/Village, 20 mins to City Centre.

B&B	3	Ensuite	€32	Dinner	-
B&B	1	Standard	€28	Partial Board	-
Single Rate			€44	Child reduction	-

Malahide 2km

Open: 1st February-30th November

Mrs Elizabeth O'Brien
PEGASUS
56 Biscayne Coast Rd,
Malahide, Co Dublin

Malahide

TEL: **01 8451506**   FAX: **01 8451506**
BUS NO: **42, 32A, 102, 230**

Excellent accommodation beside Beach, Golf, Castle & Restaurants. Airport 15 mins. Pass Grand Hotel & Island View Hotel, second turn right, keep left, left again.

B&B	2	Ensuite	€32	Dinner	-
B&B	1	Standard	€28	Partial Board	-
Single Rate			€30	Child reduction	-

Malahide 1.5km

Open: 1st February-30th November

Mrs Sile O'Donovan
CASTLELAKE
15 St Andrew's Grove,
Malahide, Co Dublin

Malahide

TEL: **01 8455042**   FAX: **01 8455042**
EMAIL: **sileod@iol.ie**
BUS NO: **42**

Quiet location in Malahide off Church road. Grand Hotel nearby. Off street parking. Public transport to Dublin. Airport 4 miles. Large family suite (with 2 bathrooms).

B&B	4	Ensuite	€32/€35	Dinner	-
B&B	-	Standard	-	Partial Board	-
Single Rate			€40/€45	Child reduction	25%

In Malahide

Open: 1st April-31st October

Mrs Mary Sweeney
SOMERTON
The Mall, Malahide Village,
Co Dublin

Malahide

TEL: **01 8454090**
EMAIL: **somerton@iol.ie**
WEB: **32A, 42, 102, 230, DART**

In heart of Malahide village. All social amenities within short walking distance. City Centre within easy reach by bus or train. True Irish welcome assured. Home from home comforts.

B&B	4	Ensuite	€40	Dinner	-
B&B	-	Standard	-	Partial Board	-
Single Rate			-	Child reduction	25%

In Malahide Village

Open: 1st January-15th December

Mrs Anne Askew
HOWTH VIEW
9 Beach Park
on Blackberry Lane,
Portmarnock, Co Dublin

Portmarnock

TEL: **01 8460665**   FAX: **01 8169895**
EMAIL: **howthview@oceanfree.net**
WEB: **www.howthview.com**
BUS NO: **32, 32A, 102, 230, DART.**

First right after Portmarnock Hotel. Fourth house on the right. Modern detached house. Convenient to several Golf courses, Airport, Ferryport and Beach.

B&B	4	Ensuite	€28/€30	Dinner	-
B&B	-	Standard	-	Partial Board	-
Single Rate			€40/€45	Child reduction	25%

Malahide 3km

Open: All Year

Mrs Margaret Creane
ROBINIA
452 Strand Rd, Portmarnock,
Co Dublin

Portmarnock

TEL: **01 8462987**
BUS NO: **32, 32A, 102, 230**

Modern home overlooking Beach. Convenient to Golf, City, Malahide Castle. On Airport and City Bus route.

B&B	2	Ensuite	€30/€32	Dinner	-
B&B	1	Standard	€30/€30	Partial Board	-
Single Rate			-	Child reduction	-

Malahide 3km

Open: 7th January-20th December

Marie D'Emidio

SOUTHDALE
143 Heather Walk,
Portmarnock, Co Dublin

Portmarnock

TEL: **01 8463760**   FAX: **01 8463760**
BUS NO: **32, 32A, 32B, 102, 230**

A pleasant friendly family home. Beach and Golf within walking distance. Airport 15 mins, City 30 min. Bus and Rail service.

B&B	4	Ensuite	€29/€31	Dinner	-
B&B	-	Standard	-	Partial Board	-
Single Rate			€39/€42	Child reduction	-

Malahide 1.5km

Open: 1st January-23rd December

Ms Marie Doran

ROSMAY
468B Strand Road,
Portmarnock, Co Dublin

Portmarnock

TEL: **01 8463175**
BUS NO: **32, 32B, 32A, 102, 230, DART**

Modern house overlooking Beach. Golf courses nearby. Convenient to City, Airport and Ferry. Bus route to City, Airport and Malahide Castle.

B&B	3	Ensuite	€28.55/€31.70	Dinner	-
B&B	-	Standard	-	Partial Board	-
Single Rate			€44.45/€50.75	Child reduction	25%

Malahide 2km

Open: May-October

Mr Sean Keane

GREENSIDE
47 Beach Park, Portmarnock,
Co Dublin

Portmarnock

TEL: **01 8462360**   FAX: **01 8462360**
EMAIL: **greenside@eircom.net**
WEB: **homepage.eircom.net/~greenside**
BUS NO: **32, 230** (AIRPORT)

Large town house, Airport 7 miles, Bus 230. City 9 miles, Bus and Rail. Beach and Golf 200 yards. Guest lounge with patio access.

B&B	4	Ensuite	€28.57/€31.74	Dinner	-
B&B	-	Standard	-	Partial Board	-
Single Rate			€35.55/€38.09	Child reduction	33.3%

Portmarnock 1km

Open: 4th January-20th December

Mrs Mary Lee

TARA
14 Portmarnock Crescent,
Portmarnock, Co Dublin

Portmarnock

TEL: **01 8462996**
BUS NO: **32, 32A, DART, 102, 230**

First turn right after Sands Hotel then sharp left. Near Beach, City Bus Route, convenient to Golf Club, Airport, Ferryport.

B&B	1	Ensuite	€27.93/€30.47	Dinner	-
B&B	2	Standard	€25.39/€27.93	Partial Board	-
Single Rate			€44.44	Child reduction	-

Malahide 2km

Open: 1st March-31st October

Aileen Lynch

OAKLEIGH
30 Dewberry Park,
Portmarnock, Co Dublin

Portmarnock

TEL: **01 8461628**
EMAIL: **aileenlynch@eircom.net**
BUS NO: **32, 32A, 102, DART**(AIRPORT 230)

Past Sands Hotel, 1st right, Wendell Ave, Then 2nd right. Beach, Restaurants, Golf. Airport 15 mins, City 30 mins. Malahide Castle 2 miles.

B&B	3	Ensuite	€30	Dinner	-
B&B	-	Standard	-	Partial Board	-
Single Rate			€45	Child reduction	-

Portmarnock 1km

Open: 1st January-20th December

Mrs Kathleen O'Brien
CLARA
22 Beach Park,
Portmarnock, Co Dublin

Portmarnock

Tel: **01 8461936**
Bus No: **32,32A,102,230**

Comfortable family home. Second turn right after the Portmarnock Hotel and Golf links "Blackberry Lane". Next right into Beachpark and right again.

B&B	2	Ensuite	€26/€28	Dinner	-
B&B	1	Standard	€26	Partial Board	-
Single Rate			-	Child reduction	-

Open: 1st March-31st October

Malahide 3km

Mrs Margaret Treanor
SEAGLADE HOUSE
off Coast Road,
At Round Tower, Portmarnock,
Co Dublin

Portmarnock

Tel: **01 8462458/8462232** Fax: **01 8460179**
Bus No: **32,32A,102,230**

Spacious home in secluded grounds of 3 acres, directly overlooking Irish Sea. Dublin Airport 15 mins, City Centre 30 mins.

B&B	6	Ensuite	€32/€34	Dinner	-
B&B	-	Standard	-	Partial Board	-
Single Rate			€50/€50	Child reduction	-

Open: 1st January-21st December

Malahide 2km

Mrs Bridget Whelan
SAN MARINO
40 Carrickhill Road,
Portmarnock, Co Dublin

Portmarnock

Tel: **01 8169883/8463220**
Email: **sanmarino@eircom.net**
Bus No: **32, 32A, 102, DART, 230** Airport

Pass Portmarnock Golf Hotel, to traffic lights then turn right up Carrickhill Road 500 metres. Golf courses, Airport 9km. City 10km. Ferry10km. M50 6km. Beach 500m.

B&B	2	Ensuite	€32/€32	Dinner	-
B&B	1	Standard	-	Partial Board	-
Single Rate			€45/€45	Child reduction	-

Open: 1st January-10th December

Portmarnock 1km

Mrs Violet Clinton
THE REEFS
Balbriggan Coast Road,
Skerries, Co Dublin

Skerries

Tel: **01 8491574**
Bus No: **33**

Spacious comfortable home overlooking the Sea. Golf nearby. "Ireland Guide" recommended. Convenient to Dublin City and Newgrange. Airport 20 kms.

B&B	4	Ensuite	€28.57/€31.74	Dinner	-
B&B	-	Standard	-	Partial Board	-
Single Rate			-	Child reduction	25%

Open: 1st April-30th September

Skerries 1km

Mary Halpin
GREENVALE
Holmpatrick, Skerries,
Co Dublin

Skerries

Tel: **01 8490413**
Email: **halpinm@indigo.ie**
Bus No: **33**

Large Victorian House overlooking Sea and Islands in quiet location close to Town Centre. Dublin 30 kms, Airport 20 kms.

B&B	4	Ensuite	€32	Dinner	-
B&B	-	Standard	-	Partial Board	-
Single Rate			€45	Child reduction	25%

Open: 31st March-31st October

In Skerries

In Skerries

Margaret Swan
HILL HOUSE
**Milverton, Skerries,
Co Dublin**

Skerries

TEL: **01 8491873**
BUS No: **33**

Luxury bungalow in quiet scenic area. Beaches, Golf, Sailing, Horse Riding, archaelogical and historic interests nearby. Dublin 25 mins. Airport 15 mins.

B&B	1	Ensuite	€27/€30	Dinner	-
B&B	2	Standard	€23.50/€26	Partial Board	-
Single Rate			€32/€40	Child reduction	**25%**

Open: 1st March-30th September

Howth 2km

Mrs Geraldine Conlan
THE MEADOWS
**257 Sutton Park,
Sutton, Dublin 13**

Sutton

TEL: **01 8390257/2835741**
BUS No: **31, 32, DART**

Highly rated Bed & Breakfast. 15 mins from Dublin City by Dart Train. 15 mins from Airport.

B&B	-	Ensuite	-	Dinner	-
B&B	3	Standard	€28	Partial Board	-
Single Rate			€36	Child reduction	**50%**

Open: 1st January-15th December

Dublin 10km

Ms Colette Gillett
**55 Glencarraig,
Sutton, Dublin 13**

Sutton

TEL: **01 8325553**
EMAIL: **cgillett@esatclear.ie**
BUS No: **31, DART**

Family house in the heart of Sutton. Howth/Dart/Bus-5 minutes. City Airport/Ferry 15 minutes.

B&B	2	Ensuite	€30	Dinner	-
B&B	1	Standard	€26	Partial Board	-
Single Rate			€37	Child reduction	-

Open: 1st February-31st October

Dublin City 10km

Eileen Hobbs
HILLVIEW
**39 Sutton Park, Dublin Road,
Sutton, Dublin 13**

Sutton

TEL: **01 8324584**
EMAIL: **hillviewhouse@ireland.com**
BUS No: **31, 32**

Friendly comfortable home, peaceful surroundings. 5 minutes walk to Dart/Bus. Convenient to Point Theatre, City centre, Ferry. 10 minutes to Howth. 15 minutes to Airport.

B&B	3	Ensuite	€27/€29	Dinner	-
B&B	1	Standard	€25/€26	Partial Board	-
Single Rate			€38/€46	Child reduction	**50%**

Open: 10th January-10th December

Dublin 10km

Mrs Mary McDonnell
DUN AOIBHINN
**30 Sutton Park, Sutton,
Dublin 13**

Sutton

TEL: **01 8325456**   FAX: **01 8325213**
EMAIL: **mary_mcdonnell@ireland.com**
BUS No: **31, 31A, 31B, 32, 32A, DART**

Luxurious detached home in quiet residential area facing amenity park. Adjacent coast road. City Centre 10km, Airport 12km. Howth 3km. Dart/Bus 3 mins walk.

B&B	3	Ensuite	€28/€32	Dinner	-
B&B	-	Standard	-	Partial Board	-
Single Rate			€45/€50	Child reduction	-

Open: 7th January-16th December

Mrs Eileen Staunton
APPLEWOOD
20 Offington Drive, Sutton,
Dublin 13

Sutton

TEL: **01 8324442**   FAX: **01 8324442**
EMAIL: **spotta@iol.ie**
BUS NO: **31, 31A, 31B**

Friendly family home in quiet area on Howth Peninsula. One mile before Howth. Restaurants, walking nearby. Close to Bus, DART. 20 mins to City, Airport & Ferry.

B&B	2	Ensuite	€25.50	Dinner	-
B&B	1	Standard	€24	Partial Board	-
Single Rate			€36	Child reduction	-

Howth Village 3km

Open: 15th January-23rd December

Mrs Eileen Sutton
SUTTONS B&B
154 Sutton Park, Sutton,
Dublin 13

Sutton

TEL: **01 8325167**   FAX: **01 8395516**
EMAIL: **suttonsbandb@iol.ie**
BUS NO: **DART, 31/32, AERDART**

Excellent accommodation close to Seafront & Dart Station. 15 mins Airport, Point Theatre, City Centre, Ferry, Golfing, Fishing, Restaurants, Amenities nearby

B&B	2	Ensuite	€30/€33	Dinner	-
B&B	1	Standard	-	Partial Board	-
Single Rate			€36	Child reduction	-

Dublin 10km

Open: 6th January-16th Decenber

Mrs Rosemarie Barrett O'Neill
BLACKBRIDGE AIRPORT
LODGE
Lissenhall, Swords,
Co Dublin

Swords/Airport

TEL: **01 8407276**
EMAIL: **blackbridge.lodge@indigo.ie**
BUS NO: **41,41B,41C,33**

Situated just off Belfast/Dublin Road. 3.5km Airport, 12km City. Room rates, reliable transport arranged, private car park.

B&B	5	Ensuite	€22/€32	Dinner	-
B&B	-	Standard	-	Partial Board	-
Single Rate			€32 /€57	Child reduction	33.3%

Swords 1km

Open: 14th January-14th December

Mrs Sarah Byrne
ASHMORE
Chapel Lane, Rolestown,
Swords, Co Dublin

Swords

TEL: **01 8404391**
EMAIL: **ashmorehouse@hotmail.com**
BUS NO: **41B**

Quiet country home 15 mins Dublin Airport. From Airport take N1 North, left at next roundabout R108 to the Naul and follow signs for Ashmore B&B.

B&B	3	Ensuite	€30/€35	Dinner	-
B&B	-	Standard	-	Partial Board	-
Single Rate			€40/€45	Child reduction	25%

Swords 7km

Open: 1st February-30th November

Mrs Sara Daniels
DAWN HOUSE
Balheary, Swords/Airport,
Co Dublin

Swords/Airport

TEL: **01 8403111**   FAX: **01 8403111**
EMAIL: **sara.daniels@oceanfree.net**
BUS NO: **41,41B,33,33B,41C**

Quiet area, off Dublin/Belfast rd, 8 mins Airport, 20 mins City. Private car park. From Airport N1 bypass Swords, through "Estuary roundabout", 300 mts on turn left.

B&B	5	Ensuite	€30/€30	Dinner	-
B&B	-	Standard	-	Partial Board	-
Single Rate			€38.50/€38.50	Child reduction	25%

Swords 1km

Open: 1st March-31st October

Margaret Farrell
HOLLYWOOD B&B
Hollywood, Ballyboghil,
Co Dublin

Swords/Ballyboghil

TEL: **01 8433359**   FAX: **01 8433359**
EMAIL: **hwood@indigo.ie**

Country home 15 minutes Airport, 25 minutes City. From Airport take N1 North, 2 miles past Swords turn next left after Esso Garage onto R129, follow signs for Hollywood Lakes Golf Club.

B&B	4	Ensuite	€26 /€29	Dinner	-
B&B	-	Standard		Partial Board	-
Single Rate			€39/€42	Child reduction	-

Ballyboghil 3km

Open: All Year

Betty Keane
HALF ACRE
Hynestown, Naul,
Co Dublin

Swords/Balbriggan

TEL: **01 8413306**

Country home. Touring base. Airport 20 mins, City 45 mins, Coast 10 mins. Private car park. N1 exit after 8 miles at first bridge left to R108.

B&B	3	Ensuite	€26.66/€26.66	Dinner	-
B&B	-	Standard		Partial Board	-
Single Rate			€38.50/€38.50	Child reduction	-

Balbriggan 8km

Open: 1st January-23rd December

Kathleen Kenegan
CEDAR HOUSE
Jugback Lane, Swords,
Co Dublin

Swords

TEL: **01 8402757**   FAX: **01 8402041**
BUS NO: **41, 33, 41B**

Situated 5 mins walk from Swords main st. Modern town house, 5 mins drive from Airport. 30 mins from City Centre. Carpark. Home from home.

B&B	4	Ensuite	€29.20/€31.75	Dinner	-
B&B	-	Standard		Partial Board	-
Single Rate			€38.10/€41.90	Child reduction	33.3%

In Swords

Open: 1st January-18th December

Gabrielle Mary Leonard
STELLAMARIS
22 Watery Lane, Swords,
Co Dublin

Swords

TEL: **01 8403976**
BUS NO: **41, 41B, 33, 33B**

Town house, 5 minutes walk from Swords main street. 5 minutes drive from Airport. 30 mins from Dublin City Centre. Frequent buses. Good taxi service.

B&B	3	Ensuite	€32/€32	Dinner	-
B&B	-	Standard	-	Partial Board	-
Single Rate				Child reduction	-

In Swords

Open: 1st January-30th November

TELEPHONE

- Operator assisted calls within Ireland — Dial 10
- International telephone operator — Dial 11818
- Directory Enquiries — Dial 11811

FOR TROUBLE-FREE TELEPHONE CALLS FROM PUBLIC PAY PHONES IT IS ADVISABLE TO PURCHASE A TELE-PHONE CALLCARD AVAILABLE IN POST OFFICES AND WHEREVER YOU SEE A CALLCARD SIGN.

TO DIAL IRELAND FROM ABROAD: Country Access Code + 353 + Area Code (omit first zero) + Local Number

Dublin Viking Adventure

Malahide Castle

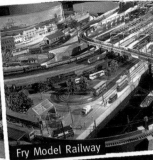
Fry Model Railway

Something to write home about

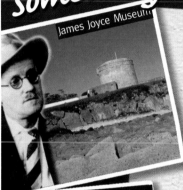
James Joyce Museum

Shaw Birthplace

Dublin Writers Museum

Dear Sarah

We're having an amazing time, Dublin is even more than we expected. Our first stop was Malahide Castle - a magnificent place with splendid rooms and antique furnishings. In the grounds we found the Fry Model Railway, it's like a small boy's wildest dream and your father couldn't get enough of it. Back in town we went to Dublin's Viking Adventure. We didn't just meet live vikings, we smelt them as well ! It was just like being in Dublin a thousand years ago.

The history here is something else, it's certainly the land of scholars (though we're not sure about the saints yet). We started our literary round-up at the Shaw Birthplace (where 'GBS' was born) - a real Victorian experience. Our next stop was the Dublin Writers Museum, in a gorgeous old Georgian house all gilt and plasterwork, full of literary memorabilia. It's astonishing how many great writers were Irish, and all with such fascinating lives ! Of course the best of the lot has the James Joyce Museum all to himself in a great spot by the sea in Sandycove. I was so thrilled to be there where Ulysses begins that I made your father promise to read it - tonight !

We had planned to come home at the weekend but we're having such a great time we might just stay another week.

Bye for now,
Lots of love -
Mum & Dad

For further information please contact:
Tel:+353 1 846 2184 Fax:+353 1 846 2537
enterprises@dublintourism.ie
www.visitdublin.com

Dublin
Tourism
Enterprises

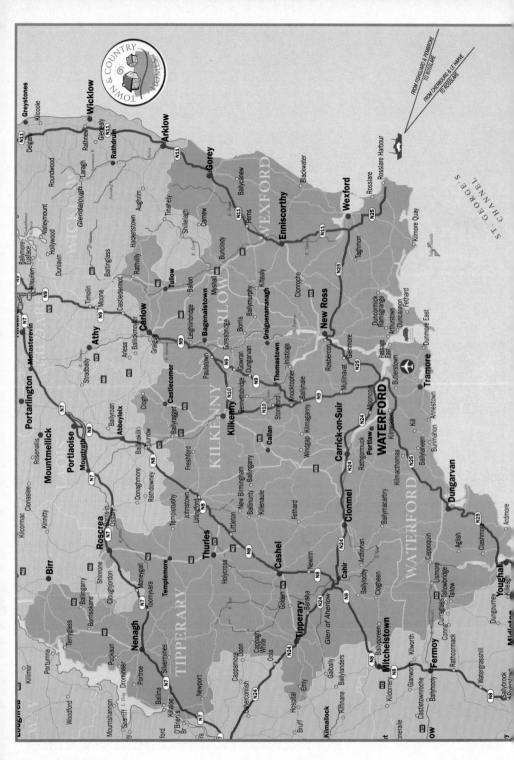

South East

The well-known term "Sunny South East" derives equally from the mildness of the climate and the warmth of the people in this lovely corner of Ireland.

There are five counties in the region - Carlow, Kilkenny, South Tipperary, Waterford and Wexford, and five major river systems - the Barrow, Blackwater, Nore, Slaney, and the Suir. Their undulating valleys criss-cross the region as they meander peacefully through the fertile landscape which is dotted with more heritage sites than virtually any other tourism region in Ireland.

Cahir Castle

The South East is a mix of seaside and activity - the coastal resorts from Courtown to Ardmore backed by a mix of opportunities to golf, fish, horse-ride, walk and cycle. For the more leisurely, there are gardens in abundance and riverside villages where time still stands still!

Area Representatives

CARLOW
Mrs Mary Dwyer-Pender, Barrow Lodge, The Quay, Carlow Town, Co Carlow
Tel: 0503 41173
KILKENNY
Mr Pat Banahan, Church View, Cuffesgrange, Callan Road, Kilkenny, Co Kilkenny Tel: 056 29170 Fax: 056 29170
Mr John Cahill, Launard House, Maiden Hill, Kells Road, Kilkenny, Co Kilkenny Tel: 056 51889 Fax: 056 71017
TIPPERARY
Ms Joan Brett Moloney, Tir Na Nog, Dualla, Cashel, Co Tipperary
Tel: 062 61350 Fax: 062 62411
Mrs Teresa Russell, Bansha Castle, Bansha, Co Tipperary
Tel: 062 54187 Fax: 062 54294
WATERFORD
Mrs Phyllis McGovern, Ashleigh, Holy Cross, Cork Road, Waterford, Co Waterford Tel: 051 375 171 Fax: 051 375 171
Mrs Margo Sleator, Rosebank House, Clonea Road (R675), Dungarvan, Co Waterford Tel: 058 41561
Maureen Wall, Suncrest, Slieverue, Ferrybank, Via Waterford, Co Waterford
Tel: 051 832732 Fax: 051 851861
WEXFORD
Mrs Ann Sunderland, Hillside House, Tubberduff, Gorey, Co Wexford
Tel: 055 21726/22036 Fax: 055 22567

ℹ️ Tourist Information Offices
OPEN ALL YEAR EXCEPT ROSSLARE

Waterford
The Granary
The Quay
Tel: 051 875823

Carlow
College St
Tel: 0503 31554

Clonmel
Sarsfield Street
Tel: 052 22960

Dungarvan Town
Centre
The Square
Tel: 058 41741

Gorey
Main Street
Tel: 055 21248

Kilkenny
Shee Alms House
Rose Inn Street
Tel: 056 51500

Rosslare
Kilcrane
Tel: 053 33232

Wexford
Crescent Quay
Tel: 053 23111

Website: **www.ireland.southeast.travel.ie**

Situated in the great river valley of the Barrow and Slaney, famous for salmon and trout. This extensive waterways is renowned for cruising. Visit the Brown Hill Dolmen; Magnificent golf courses. Enjoy Cycling, Walking, Horse-riding or explore the countryside.

Mairead Heffernan
ORCHARD GROVE
N9 Wells, Bagenalstown,
Co Carlow

Bagenalstown
TEL: **0503 22140**
EMAIL: **orchardgrove@eircom.net**
WEB: **www.carlowtourism.com/orchard.html**

Warm welcoming family home. Superb accommodation. Midway Carlow/Kilkenny. On N9. Breakfast Menu. Ideal base touring South East. Golf, Fishing, Walking. Childrens play area. AA ♦♦♦♦.

B&B	3	Ensuite	€28/€30	Dinner	€19
B&B	1	Standard	€25/€27	Partial Board	€300
Single Rate			€36/€36	Child reduction	50%

Bagenalstown 2km

Open: 1st January-30th November

Mrs Kathleen Tallon
KNOCKRIGG HOUSE
Wells, Royal Oak,
Bagenalstown, Co Carlow

Bagenalstown
TEL: **0503 22555**   FAX: **0503 22555**
EMAIL: **knockrigghse@eircom.net**
WEB: **www.knockrigghouse.com**

Luxurious family run B&B. TV, Hairdryer all rooms. Guest lounge. Midway Carlow/Kilkenny on N9. Near Bus/Rail route. Beside River Barrow. Dublin/Rosslare 1hr 15mins.

B&B	4	Ensuite	€27/€32	Dinner	€17
B&B	-	Standard		Partial Board	€280
Single Rate			€38.50/€38.50	Child reduction	50%

Bagenalstown 2km

Open: 1st January-15th December

Pat & Noeleen Dunne
GREENLANE HOUSE
Dublin Road, Carlow Town,
Co Carlow

Carlow
TEL: **0503 42670**   FAX: **0503 30903**
EMAIL: **greenlanehse@hotmail.com**

Luxury town house situated N9. Ideal place to relax or use as base for exploring Historical and Archictectural gems of East and South East Ireland. 1 hour from Dublin/Rosslare. Private car park.

B&B	7	Ensuite	€29.20/€33	Dinner	-
B&B	-	Standard		Partial Board	-
Single Rate			€38.50/€38.50	Child reduction	-

In Carlow

Open: All Year Except Christmas

Mrs Mary Dwyer-Pender
BARROW LODGE
The Quay, Carlow Town,
Co Carlow

Carlow Town
TEL: **0503 41173**
EMAIL: **georgepender@eircom.net**

Always a popular choice with visitors due to our central riverside location. A short stroll from Carlow's excellent Restaurants, Clubs and Pubs.

B&B	5	Ensuite	€28/€31	Dinner	-
B&B	-	Standard		Partial Board	-
Single Rate			€38.50/€38.50	Child reduction	-

In Carlow

Open: February-November

In Carlow

Carmel & James O'Toole
BORLUM HOUSE
Kilkenny Road, Carlow,
Co Carlow

Tel: **0503 41747**

Built as a Coaching Inn in the early 1800's, Borlum House is set in secluded gardens where guests can enjoy Georgian charm & the comforts expected by discerning guests.

B&B	4	Ensuite	€30/€35	Dinner	-
B&B	-	Standard	-	Partial Board	-
Single Rate			€38.50/€38.50	Child reduction	25%

Open: 1st March-30th November

Tullow 1km

Anne & Edward Byrne
LABURNUM LODGE
Bunclody Road, Tullow,
Co Carlow

Tel: **0503 51718**
Email: **lablodge@indigo.ie**

Elegant Georgian house. Downstairs accommodation. Overlooking Mount Wolseley golf course. Altamount garden. Midway Dublin/Rosslare. Orthopaedic beds, Electric blankets, Hairdryers.

B&B	6	Ensuite	€28/€30	Dinner	-
B&B	-	Standard	-	Partial Board	-
Single Rate			€38.50/€38.50	Child reduction	25%

Open: 1st January-15th December

BROWNE'S DOLMEN
CO. CARLOW

Kilkenny - Medieval Capital of Ireland, its splendid castle as its centre-piece is home to Ireland's best known craft centre. County Kilkenny offers visitors an ideal base for touring the South East, a couple of days here will reward the discerning visitor.

In Bennettsbridge

Mrs Sheila Cole
NORELY THEYR
Barronsland, Bennettsbridge, Co Kilkenny

Bennettsbridge
TEL: **056 27496**
EMAIL: **norelytheyr@eircom.net**

Luxurious, spacious bungalow, Rosslare/Kilkenny Road. Quiet, restful, friendly accommodation. Tea/coffee room facilities. Breakfast selection.

B&B	2	Ensuite	€25.50 /€30	Dinner	€17
B&B	2	Standard	€23/€25.50	Partial Board	€264
Single Rate			€36/€42.50	Child reduction	25%

Open: All Year

In Bennettsbridge

Margaret Cullen
THE LOFT
Bennettsbridge, Co Kilkenny

Bennettsbridge
TEL: **056 27147**   FAX: **056 27147**

Large rooms. Buffet & Full Irish Breakfast. Walking distance Pubs, Restaurants, Mosse Jackson Pottery's. Close: Golf, Fishing, Pet Farm. Touring Base.

B&B	3	Ensuite	€29	Dinner	-
B&B	2	Standard	€26	Partial Board	-
Single Rate			€36	Child reduction	25%

Open: All Year

Callan 6km

Mrs Mary Butler
HARTFORD HOUSE
Graigue, Kilmanagh, Co Kilkenny

Callan
TEL: **056 69215**
EMAIL: **marypbutler@eircom.net**

Comfortable home in tranquil location. Home baking. Traditional music. Close to woodland walk, Nature reserve and Ballykeeffe Amphitheatre on R695 Kilmanagh.

B&B	3	Ensuite	€26/€32	Dinner	-
B&B	-	Standard		Partial Board	-
Single Rate			€38.50/€44.45	Child reduction	25%

Open: 1st Febuary-30th November

In Freshford
198

Mrs Priscilla Flanagan
POMADORA HOUSE
Clinstown Road, Freshford, Co Kilkenny

Freshford
TEL: **056 32256**

Home on Hunter Stud on R693 to Cashel. Gardens, Fishing, Horseriding, Hunting in Winter. Stabling for Horses, Dog Kennels, meals.

B&B	3	Ensuite	€30	Dinner	€20
B&B	-	Standard	-	Partial Board	-
Single Rate			€40	Child reduction	25%

Open: All Year

Mrs Bridget Nolan
CASTLE VIEW
**Balleen, Freshford,
Co Kilkenny**

TEL: **056 32181**
EMAIL:**bridgetnolan@eircom.net**

Bungalow, peaceful location, panoramic view of country side. Orthopaedic beds. 15 mins drive to Kilkenny City on route to Rock of Cashel.

B&B	2	Ensuite	€25.50/€25.50	Dinner	-
B&B	1	Standard	€23/€23	Partial Board	-
Single Rate			€36/€36	Child reduction	50%

Freshford 3km

Open: All Year

Pat & Monica Banahan
CHURCH VIEW
**Cuffesgrange, Callan Road,
Kilkenny, Co Kilkenny**

TEL: **056 29170** FAX: **056 29170**
EMAIL: **churchview@eircom.net**
WEB: **www.churchviewkilkenny.com/**

Warm comfortable luxurious home on the main Clonmel/Cork/Killarney route, N76. Only 4 minutes drive from the medieval city of Kilkenny. Peaceful location. A warm welcome assured.

B&B	4	Ensuite	€26/€27	Dinner	-
B&B	2	Standard	€24/€25	Partial Board	-
Single Rate			€41/€44	Child reduction	25%

Kilkenny City 4km

Open: All Year

Ms Miriam Banville
BANVILLE'S B&B
**49 Walkin Street, Kilkenny,
Co Kilkenny**

TEL: **056 70182**
EMAIL: **mbanville@eircom.net**

Warm comfortable home near City Centre. Private parking. Rooms Ensuite, Multichannel TV, Hairdryers, Alarm Clocks.

B&B	4	Ensuite	€26	Dinner	-
B&B	-	Standard	-	Partial Board	-
Single Rate			€36	Child reduction	-

In Kilkenny

Open: All Year

Mrs Nuala Brennan
MELROSE HOUSE
**Circular Road, Kilkenny,
Co Kilkenny**

TEL: **056 65289** FAX: **056 65289**
EMAIL: **brennanpn@eircom.net**

Modern family run B&B. N76 opposite Hotel Kilkenny. 8 mins walk to City Centre. Private parking. Guest garden, quiet location. Multi channel TV, Hairdryers, Radio in rooms.

B&B	3	Ensuite	€26/€32	Dinner	-
B&B	1	Standard	€25/€28	Partial Board	-
Single Rate			€36/€40	Child reduction	-

In Kilkenny City

Open: 4th January-20th December

Ms Angela Byrne
CELTIC HOUSE
**18 Michael Street,
Kilkenny City,
Co Kilkenny**

TEL: **056 62249**

Excellent location, walk everywhere. In the heart of Kilkenny City. Built 1998. Private lock-up. Parking. 4 min walk Bus and Train Station. Excellent standards. TV, Tea/Coffee facilities.

B&B	4	Ensuite	€25.50/€25.50	Dinner	-
B&B	-	Standard	-	Partial Board	-
Single Rate			€38.50/€38.50	Child reduction	33.3%

In Kilkenny

Open: January-18th December

Mrs Rita Byrne
MAJELLA
**Waterford Road, Kilkenny,
Co Kilkenny**

Kilkenny
TEL: **056 21129**

Modern comfortable bungalow on main Kilkenny/Waterford Road. Convenient to City and all amenities. TV lounge with Tea/Coffee. Breakfast choice.

B&B	4	Ensuite	€28/€30	Dinner -
B&B	-	Standard		Partial Board -
Single Rate			€40/€40	Child reduction -

Kilkenny 1km   **Open:** 1st May-31st October

John & Sandra Cahill
LAUNARD HOUSE
**Maiden Hill, Kells Road,
Kilkenny, Co Kilkenny**

Kilkenny
TEL: **056 51889**   FAX: **056 71017**
EMAIL: **launardhouse@email.com**
WEB: **www.launardhouse.com**

Luxurious purpose built home. "Irish Experts" and Hidden Places Guides recommended. "A Touch of Class". Some superior rooms with king beds (supp).

B&B	5	Ensuite	€26/€36	Dinner -
B&B	-	Standard	-	Partial Board -
Single Rate			-	Child reduction -

Kilkenny 1km   **Open:** 1st February-31st October

Mary Cahill
BREAGAGH VIEW
**1 Maiden Hill, Kells Road,
Kilkenny, Co Kilkenny**

Kilkenny
TEL: **056 61353**

Luxurious home & gardens. Purpose built B&B. Extra spacious bedrooms. TV/Hairdryers/Electric Blankets, close to Hotel, overlooking ring road.

B&B	4	Ensuite	€25.50/€31.74	Dinner -
B&B	-	Standard	-	Partial Board -
Single Rate			-	Child reduction -

Kilkenny 1km   **Open:** 1st February-1st December

Mrs Marie Callan
LICHFIELD HOUSE
**Bennettsbridge Rd, Kilkenny,
Co Kilkenny**

Kilkenny
TEL: **056 65232**   FAX: **056 70614**
EMAIL: **lichfieldhouse@eircom.net**
WEB: **www.lichfieldhouse.com**

Georgian Country Home on 1acre. Quiet location 5 min drive from Kilkenny City on R700. Recommended Le Routard~Edmonton Journal~West Australian.

B&B	3	Ensuite	€26/€31	Dinner -
B&B	-	Standard		Partial Board -
Single Rate			€40/€44	Child reduction 33.3%

Kilkenny 2km   **Open:** 4th January-10th December

Mrs Joan Cody
OAKLAWN B&B
**8 Oakwood, Kilfera,
Bennettsbridge Road,
Kilkenny, Co Kilkenny**

Kilkenny
TEL: **056 61208**

Modern detached bungalow on the R700 main New Ross/Rosslare Road. Quiet area. Tastefully decorated. Set in mature lawns.

B&B	2	Ensuite	€25.50/€30	Dinner -
B&B	1	Standard		Partial Board -
Single Rate			€38/€38	Child reduction 50%

Kilkenny 4km   **Open:** March-October

Mrs Mary Cody
OLINDA
Castle Road, Kilkenny,
Co Kilkenny

Kilkenny
TEL: **056 62964**

Comfortable house, quiet location. Large garden area for guests. Tea/Coffee facilities. Walking distance to Pubs and Restaurants. Private parking. Hairdryers, Alarm clocks.

B&B	2	Ensuite	€25.50	Dinner	-
B&B	1	Standard	€23	Partial Board	-
Single Rate			-	Child reduction	25%

In Kilkenny

Open: 1st March-31st October

Mrs Vicky Comerford
PARK VILLA
Castlecomer Road, Kilkenny,
Co Kilkenny

Kilkenny
TEL: **056 61337**
EMAIL: vicpat@eircom.net
WEB: www.kilkennybedandbreakfast.com

Failte!! Modern family run home. Opposite Newpark Hotel. Prize gardens. Kettle always boiling. Warm welcome guaranteed. Rooms ensuite TV/Hairdryers. Convenient to Bus, Rail, Pubs, Golf etc.

B&B	5	Ensuite	€26/€32	Dinner	-
B&B	-	Standard		Partial Board	-
Single Rate			€38.50/€38.50	Child reduction	25%

In Kilkenny

Open: 1st January-20th December

Ms Breda Dore
AVILA B&B
Freshford Road, Kilkenny,
Co Kilkenny

Kilkenny
TEL: **056 51072**   FAX: **056 51072**
EMAIL: doreb@indigo.ie
WEB: www.avilakilkenny.com

Family run B&B within 15 minutes walk of City Centre. Located in quiet area. Warm welcome and best Irish breakfast guaranteed. Beside St. Lukes and Auteven Hospital R693.

B&B	3	Ensuite	€26/€32	Dinner	-
B&B	1	Standard	€24/€26	Partial Board	-
Single Rate			-	Child reduction	25%

Kilkenny City 1km

Open: 6th January-16th December

Mrs Margaret Drennan
HILLGROVE
Warrington,
Bennettsbridge Road,
Kilkenny, Co Kilkenny

Kilkenny
TEL: **056 51453/22890** FAX: **056 51453**
EMAIL: hillgrove@esatclear.ie
WEB: http://homepage.eircom.net/~hillgrove

National Breakfast Award-Winning Country Home, furnished with antiques, on R700. Orthopaedic beds, Electric blankets. Recommended Frommer, Dillard/Causin, Denver Post.

B&B	5	Ensuite	€28/€28	Dinner	-
B&B	-	Standard		Partial Board	-
Single Rate			€38.50/€38.50	Child reduction	50%

Kilkenny 2km

Open: 1st Febuary-30th November

Mrs Helen Dunning
DUNBOY
10 Parkview Drive,
off Freshford Road,
Kilkenny City, Co Kilkenny

Kilkenny
TEL: **056 61460**   FAX: **056 61460**
EMAIL: dunboy@eircom.net
WEB: www.dunboy.com

Welcoming home in quiet cul-de-sac. Le Routard Recommended. Close to City Centre. Take Freshford road R693, turn left at second roundabout, then right.

B&B	4	Ensuite	€26/€32	Dinner	-
B&B	-	Standard	-	Partial Board	-
Single Rate				Child reduction	-

Kilkenny 1km

Open: 8th March-1st November

Mrs Ella Dunphy
AUBURN LODGE
Warrington,
Bennettsbridge Road,
Kilkenny, Co Kilkenny

Kilkenny
TEL: **056 65119**   FAX: **056 70008**
EMAIL: **patdunphy@eircom.net**

AA Recommended. Country home beside Riding School. Orthopaedic beds, electric blankets, TV, Hairdryers. Quiet area on R700. Car parking. Tennis Court.

B&B	3	Ensuite	€28.50/€30	Dinner	-
B&B	2	Standard	€25.75	Partial Board	-
Single Rate			€36	Child reduction	**25%**

Kilkenny 2km

Open: 20th January-20th December

Mrs Bernadette Egan
KNOCKAVON HOUSE
Dublin/Carlow Road,
Kilkenny, Co Kilkenny

Kilkenny
TEL: **056 64294**

Luxurious town house accommodation. Beside city centre. 3 Minutes to Bus Station, Pubs, Restaurants, Theatre and Golf Club.

B&B	5	Ensuite	€25.50/€28.57	Dinner	-
B&B	-	Standard	-	Partial Board	-
Single Rate			€38.50/€38.50	Child reduction	-

In Kilkenny City

Open: All Year

Mrs Oonagh Egan Twomey
CARRAIG RUA
Dublin Rd, Kilkenny City,
Co Kilkenny

Kilkenny City
TEL: **056 22929**

Elegant two storey city house on N10. 4 mins walk to bus and rail station. Close to City Centre, Kilkenny Castle, Langtons, Hotels and Restaurants.

B&B	5	Ensuite	€26/€32	Dinner	-
B&B	1	Standard	€24/€26	Partial Board	-
Single Rate			€45	Child reduction	**25%**

In Kilkenny City

Open: 5th January-15th December

Agnes & Frank Fennelly
SAN JOSE
Baun, Castlecomer Rd,
Kilkenny, Co Kilkenny

Kilkenny
TEL: **056 21198**

Elegant villa style residence, antique furnished. Large mature Gardens. 2km north of Newpark Hotel on N77. Breakfast menu. Tea/Coffee, Hairdryers, Orthopaedic beds, Electric blankets.

B&B	2	Ensuite	€26/€30	Dinner	-
B&B	1	Standard	€24/€27	Partial Board	-
Single Rate			€36/€40	Child reduction	**25%**

Kilkenny 2km

Open: 1st February-30th November

Mrs Marie Finnegan
ARDEE HOUSE
Springmount, Waterford Road,
Kilkenny, Co Kilkenny

Kilkenny
TEL: **056 62699**   FAX: **056 62699**
EMAIL: **ptf@indigo.ie**
WEB: **www.ardeehouse.com**

Town house N10 beside Springhill Court Hotel. Breakfast menu. Guests Lounge. Bedrooms TV, Hairdryers, Radio/Alarm Clocks. Reduction low season.

B&B	5	Ensuite	€27/€30	Dinner	-
B&B	1	Standard	€27/€30	Partial Board	-
Single Rate			-	Child reduction	-

Kilkenny 2km

Open: All Year Except Christmas

Mrs Joan Flanagan
BURWOOD
Waterford Road, Kilkenny,
Co Kilkenny

Kilkenny
Tel: **056 62266**

Modern bungalow on Kilkenny/Waterford Road. Enclosed car-park. "300 Best B & B's" Recommended. Convenient to City Centre.

B&B	3	Ensuite	€28/€30	Dinner	-
B&B	1	Standard	€26/€28	Partial Board	-
Single Rate			€40	Child reduction	25%

Kilkenny 1km

Open: 1st May-30th September

Pauline Flannery
ASHLEIGH
Waterford Rd, Kilkenny,
Co Kilkenny

Kilkenny
Tel: **056 22809**

Bungalow main Waterford Rd (R910 off N10). Convenient Hotels, Castle & City. Breakfast menu. Tea/Coffee available. Reduction low season. Frommer Guide, Berkeley Europe recommended.

B&B	2	Ensuite	€28/€30	Dinner	-
B&B	1	Standard	€28/€28	Partial Board	-
Single Rate			€36	Child reduction	25%

Kilkenny 1km

Open: January-November

Mrs Breda Hennessy
SILVER SPRINGS
Waterford Road, Kilkenny,
Co Kilkenny

Kilkenny
Tel: **056 62513**
Email: **silverspringsbandb@eircom.net**

Beautiful dormer bungalow on main Kilkenny/Waterford road (N10). Convenient to Hotels, Castle, City, Golf. Breakfast menu, Tea/Coffee making facilities.

B&B	4	Ensuite	€28 /€31	Dinner	-
B&B	1	Standard	€26/€31	Partial Board	-
Single Rate			-	Child reduction	33.3%

Kilkenny City 1km

Open: January-10th December

Michael Hennessy
SHILLOGER HOUSE
Callan Road (N76), Kilkenny,
Co Kilkenny

Kilkenny
Tel: **056 63249**   Fax: **056 64865**
Email: **shillogherhouse@tinet.ie**
Web: **www.shillogherhouse.com**

Luxurious home. All bedrooms Tea/Coffee makers, TV, Internet Station, Phones. Garden Conservatory. Susan Causin recommended. RAC AA ◆◆◆◆. Breakfast menu. Ideal touring base.

B&B	6	Ensuite	€25.50/€40	Dinner	-
B&B	-	Standard	-	Partial Board	-
Single Rate			-	Child reduction	25%

Kilkenny

Open: All Year

Mrs Teresa Holden
AUBURNDALE
Springmount, Waterford Rd,
Kilkenny, Co Kilkenny

Kilkenny
Tel: **056 62716**   Fax: **056 71238**
Email: **auburndale@eircom.net**
Web: **homepage.eircom.net/~auburndale/**

On N10 adjacent Springhill Hotel. Bedrooms incl. Hairdryers, TV. Tea/Coffee in the reading lounge. Ideal touring base for the South East. Hard to leave, easy to find.

B&B	5	Ensuite	€30/€35	Dinner	-
B&B	-	Standard	-	Partial Board	-
Single Rate			-	Child reduction	-

Kilkenny 1km

Open: 1st February-5th November

Liam & Brigid Holohan
ALCANTRA
Maidenhill, Kells Road,
Kilkenny, Co Kilkenny

Kilkenny
Tel: **056 61058**   Fax: **056 61058**
Email: **alcantra@tinet.ie**
Web: **homepage.eircom.net/~alcantra**

Spacious comfortable home with guest lounge and conservatory, located on R697. Exactly 1km from City Centre. Numerous recommendations. AA ◆◆◆◆.

B&B	4	Ensuite	€26/€32	Dinner	-
B&B	-	Standard	-	Partial Board	-
Single Rate		-		Child reduction	-

Kilkenny 1km

Open: 1st January-20th December

Mrs Mary Lawlor
RODINI
Waterford Road,
(R910 off N10) Kilkenny,
Co Kilkenny

Kilkenny City
Tel: **056 21822/70836**
Email: **rodini@eircom.net**

Comfortable home. Convenient Hotels, City Centre, Castle and other amenities. Family room. Electric blankets, Hairdryers available. Ideal base to tour the beautiful historic South East.

B&B	5	Ensuite	€25.50/€31	Dinner	-
B&B	-	Standard	-	Partial Board	-
Single Rate			€38.50/€40	Child reduction	50%

Kilkenny 1km

Open: All Year

Bill & Helen McEvoy
BREFFNI
Waterford Road, Kilkenny,
Co Kilkenny

Kilkenny
Tel: **056 63344**

Detached Dormer Bungalow. Easy access to Hotels, Castle, Golf Clubs, Fishing, Shops. Tea/Coffee available. Reduction low season. In Kilkenny.

B&B	3	Ensuite	€26/€28	Dinner	-
B&B	-	Standard	-	Partial Board	-
Single Rate			-	Child reduction	50%

In Kilkenny

Open: 1st February-20th December

Ms Katherine Molloy
MENA HOUSE
Castlecomer Road (N78),
Kilkenny, Co Kilkenny

Kilkenny
Tel: **056 65362**

Antique furnished luxurious home. Prize gardens. TV all rooms. Tea making facilities. Breakfast choice, homemade preserves. Adjacent New Park Hotel, Golf, Swimming, Horse-riding.

B&B	7	Ensuite	€26/€32	Dinner	-
B&B	2	Standard	€23/€30	Partial Board	-
Single Rate			€36/€38.50	Child reduction	50%

In Kilkenny City

Open: All Year Except Christmas

RESERVATIONS

- Confirm phone bookings in writing without delay with agreed deposit.
- To avoid misunderstandings later, check rate on booking and clarify any additional changes which may apply to your booking.
- Give details of any special requirements.
- State clearly day, date of arrival and departure date.

Mrs Maud Morrissey
BEECH LODGE B&B
Bennettsbridge Road,
Kilkenny, Co Kilkenny

Kilkenny
Tel: **056 64083**

Warm friendly home, quiet location on main New Ross/Rosslare road. Picturesque garden. Spacious rooms. Orthopaedic beds, Electric blankets. Conservatory for guests.

B&B	4	Ensuite	€25.50/€29.50	Dinner	-
B&B	-	Standard	-	Partial Board	-
Single Rate			€38.50	Child reduction	25%

Kilkenny City 2km   cc P ⊗ ⅃ ⌐ ♨ ℡ ▲ ↩ ♪ ℛ   **Open:** 1st January-30th November

Ms Carmel Nolan
THE RISE
Dunmore, Kilkenny,
Co Kilkenny

Kilkenny
Tel: **056 64534**
Email: **carmeljn@gofree.indigo.ie**

A warm welcome awaits our guests at our newly renovated 19th Century family farm home. Tea/Coffee on arrival. Stroll through our fields at your leisure etc.

B&B	2	Ensuite	€26/€26	Dinner	-
B&B	2	Standard	€23/€26	Partial Board	-
Single Rate			€36/€36	Child reduction	33.3%

Kilkenny 2km   S P ⅃ ⌐ ♨ ♪ ℡ ▲ ↩ ♪ ℛ   **Open:** All Year

Mrs Nora O'Connor
SUNDOWN
Freshford Rd, Kilkenny,
Co Kilkenny

Kilkenny City
Tel: **056 21816**
Email: **sundownbandb@eircom.net**

Welcoming friendly home situated on Freshford road R693. Walking distance City Centre. Large car park. TV, Radio, Hairdryers all rooms. New Greyhound Stadium and Hospital nearby.

B&B	4	Ensuite	€26/€32	Dinner	-
B&B	1	Standard	€26/€32	Partial Board	-
Single Rate			€36/€36	Child reduction	25%

Kilkenny City 1km   cc P ⅃ ⌐ ♨ ℡ ▲ ↩   **Open:** March-November

Mrs Teresa O'Neill
HILLCREST
College Gardens, Callan Rd,
Kilkenny, Co Kilkenny

Kilkenny
Tel: **056 65560**
Email: **teresaoneill@ireland.com**

Family home in quiet cul-de-sac off Callan/Cork Rd N76. Hotel Kilkenny 300m. Walking distance of City. Orthopaedic beds, Electric blankets, Hairdryers.

B&B	2	Ensuite	€26/€30	Dinner	-
B&B	2	Standard	€23/€25	Partial Board	-
Single Rate			€37/€40	Child reduction	25%

Kilkenny 1km   cc P ⅃ ♨ ℡ ▲   **Open:** April-November

Josephine O'Reilly
CARRIGLEA
Archers Avenue, Castle Road,
Kilkenny, Co Kilkenny

Kilkenny City
Tel: **056 61629**
Email: **archers@iol.ie**

Spacious elegant home. Five minutes walk to City Centre, Pubs, Restaurants etc. Situated in quiet residential cul-de-sac. 3 minutes walk past Castle on right.

B&B	2	Ensuite	€26/€28	Dinner	-
B&B	1	Standard	€24/€25	Partial Board	-
Single Rate			-	Child reduction	33.3%

In Kilkenny   cc P ⊗ ⅃ ♨ ℡ ▲ ♪ ℛ   **Open:** 1st Febuary-30th November

Mrs V Rothwell
DUNROMIN
Dublin Rd, Kilkenny,
Co Kilkenny

Kilkenny
Tel: **056 61387**   Fax: **056 70736**
Email: **valtom@oceanfree.net**

A warm welcome to our 19th Century family home (on Dublin road N10). Walking distance Medieval City Centre. Golf, Horse Riding nearby. Kettle always boiling.

B&B	5	Ensuite	€28/€32	Dinner	-
B&B	-	Standard	-	Partial Board	-
Single Rate			-	Child reduction	-

In Kilkenny City

Open: 1st March-14th December

Kathleen Ryan
THE MEADOWS
6 Greenfields Road, Bishops
Meadows, Kilkenny City,
Co Kilkenny

Kilkenny
Tel: **056 21649**   Fax: **056 21649**
Email: **kryan@indigo.ie**
Web: **www.themeadows.bizland.com**

Quiet area off R693. Home baking. Menu. Walking distance City. Orthopaedic beds, Electric blankets, Hairdryer, Ironing facilities in room. Itinerary planned.

B&B	2	Ensuite	€28/€32	Dinner	-
B&B	1	Standard	-	Partial Board	-
Single Rate			€36/€38.50	Child reduction	25%

Kilkenny City 1km

Open: 1st January-12th December

Mrs Helen Sheehan
CNOC MHUIRE
Castle Road, Kilkenny,
Co Kilkenny

Kilkenny
Tel: **056 62161**   Fax: **056 62161**
Email: **cnocmhuire@eircom.net**
Web: **www.cnocmhuire.com**

Warm comfortable home off Rosslare Road (R700). Quiet location. Orthopaedic beds, electric blankets. Hairdryers. Parking. 10 minute walk to centre and Castle.

B&B	4	Ensuite	€28/€32	Dinner	-
B&B	-	Standard	-	Partial Board	-
Single Rate			€38.50	Child reduction	25%

Kilkenny City 1km

Open: 15th January-21st December

Ms Ruby Sherwood
ASHBURY LODGE
Castlecomer Road, Kilkenny,
Co Kilkenny

Kilkenny City
Tel: **056 21572**   Fax: **056 22892**
Email: **rubys@esatclear.ie**

Secluded home on elevated site surrounded by mature gardens. Warm friendly atmosphere near Newpark Hotel on N77. Car park. Spacious rooms, TV, Hairdryer, Visa.

B&B	3	Ensuite	€28	Dinner	-
B&B	1	Standard	€27	Partial Board	-
Single Rate			€38	Child reduction	50%

Kilkenny 2km

Open: All Year Except Christmas

Jim & Joan Spratt
CHAPLINS
Castlecomer Road, Kilkenny,
Co Kilkenny

Kilkenny
Tel: **056 52236**
Email: **chaplins@eircom.net**

Spacious Town house N77. All rooms equipped with Multi-Channel TV. Hairdryers, Tea/Coffee. RAC selected AA ◆◆◆.

B&B	6	Ensuite	€27/€35	Dinner	-
B&B	-	Standard	-	Partial Board	-
Single Rate			-	Child reduction	25%

In Kilkenny City

Open: 1st January-23rd December

Kilkenny 3km

Mrs Marie Trait
ARD ALAINN
Keatingstown, Kilkenny,
Co Kilkenny

Kilkenny
TEL: **056 67680**

Nice country home on outskirts of Kilkenny. Central heating, lovely view of country side. Peaceful and quiet location.

B&B	4	Ensuite	€26/€32	Dinner	-
B&B	-	Standard		Partial Board	-
Single Rate			€38.50/€38.50	Child reduction	-

Open: 1st January-20th December

In Kilkenny City

Mary & Eamonn Wogan
TIR NA NOG
Greenhill (off
Castlecomer Rd), Kilkenny,
Co Kilkenny

Kilkenny City
TEL: **056 65250/62345** FAX: **056 63491**
EMAIL: **emw@iol.ie**
WEB: **homepages.iol.ie/~emw**

Luxurious ensuite rooms, incl. TV/Radio, Trouserpress/Iron, Hairdryer, Breakfast menu. Convenient to Bus/Rail Station and City Centre.

B&B	5	Ensuite	€26/€31	Dinner	-
B&B	-	Standard	€26/€31	Partial Board	-
Single Rate			€38.50/€38.50	Child reduction	-

Open: All Year

Thomastown

Mrs Helen Blanchfield
ABBEY HOUSE
Jerpoint Abbey, Thomastown,
Co Kilkenny

Thomastown
TEL: **056 24166** FAX: **056 24192**

House (1750). Opposite Jerpoint Abbey. Between Waterford & Kilkenny on N9. Rosslare 1hr. Mount Juliet 5 mins. Dublin 2 hrs. Private parties speciality. AA ◆◆◆◆.

B&B	7	Ensuite	€28.57/€44.44	Dinner	-
B&B	-	Standard	-	Partial Board	-
Single Rate			€31.74/€50.79	Child reduction	25%

Open: 1st January-23rd December

Thomastown 3km

Mrs Julie Doyle
CARRICKMOURNE HOUSE
New Ross Road, Thomastown,
Co Kilkenny

Thomastown
TEL: **056 24124** FAX: **056 24124**

Elevated site, surrounded by scenic views peaceful country setting. Convenient Jerpoint Abbey, Mount Juliet Golf, Fishing, Restaurants. AA ◆◆◆. 2km off New Ross Rd.

B&B	5	Ensuite	€25.50/€38	Dinner	-
B&B	-	Standard	-	Partial Board	-
Single Rate			€38.50/€50	Child reduction	25%

Open: 15th January-15th December

TELEPHONE

- Operator assisted calls within Ireland   Dial 10
- International telephone operator   Dial 11818
- Directory Enquiries   Dial 11811

FOR TROUBLE-FREE TELEPHONE CALLS FROM PUBLIC PAY PHONES IT IS ADVISABLE TO PURCHASE A TELE-PHONE CALLCARD AVAILABLE IN POST OFFICES AND WHEREVER YOU SEE A CALLCARD SIGN.
TO DIAL IRELAND FROM ABROAD: Country Access Code + 353 + Area Code (omit first zero) + Local Number

The loveliest and most scenic inland county in Ireland. Known as the Golden Vale county, lends itself to a longer stopover with its rolling plains and mountains. The River Suir transverses its entire length. Visit - Abbeys, Castles, and historic moats. Pony Trekking, Golf, Fishing, Greyhound and Horse racing. Hill Walking, Birdwatching. Many walking tours available.

Borrisokane 1.9km

Carmen & Wolfgang Rodder
DANCER COTTAGE
Curraghmore, Borrisokane,
Co Tipperary

Borrisokane

TEL: **067 27414**   FAX: **067 27414**
EMAIL: **dcr@eircom.net**
WEB: **dancercottage.cjb.net**

Comfortable house, quiet rural location. Large garden for guests. Fresh seasonal home cooking/baking, children welcome, Bicycles. Golf, Lough Derg nearby.

B&B	4	Ensuite	€25.50/€28	Dinner	€21.50
B&B	-	Standard		Partial Board	-
Single Rate			€38.50	Child reduction	33.3%

Open: 1st February-1st November

Cahir 1km

Butler Family
CARRIGEEN CASTLE
Cahir, Co Tipperary

Cahir

TEL: **052 41370**   FAX: **052 41370**
EMAIL: **carrigeencastle@yahoo.co.uk**
WEB: **www.tipp.ie/butlerca.htm**

Manor of Cahir. Historic (prison) home. Warm, comfortable, spacious, overlooking Town. Walled garden. Walking distance Bus/Train. Ideal touring base.

B&B	3	Ensuite	€30/€30	Dinner	-
B&B	4	Standard	€25/€25	Partial Board	-
Single Rate			€40/€40	Child reduction	-

Open: 2nd January-15th December

Cahir 1km

Ms Kay Byrne
ARBUTUS
Tipperary Road, Cahir,
Co Tipperary

Cahir

TEL: **052 41617**

Comfortable family home. Spacious en-suite rooms, TV, Hairdryers. Tea/Coffee. View the Galtee mountains on N24 off N8 roundabout. Walking distance town centre.

B&B	2	Ensuite	€25.50/€25.50	Dinner	-
B&B	1	Standard	€23/€23	Partial Board	-
Single Rate			€36/€38.50	Child reduction	25%

Open: 1st May-1st November

Cahir 1km

Mrs Patricia Devereaux
SCARAGH HOUSE
Grangemore, Cahir,
Co Tipperary

Cahir

TEL: **052 42105**   FAX: **052 42105**
EMAIL: **wildev@eircom.net**

Luxurious olde world home in picturesque setting, opposite entrance to famous Swiss Cottage/Park/Riverside walk. Forest/Galtee mountain views. Peaceful location.

B&B	3	Ensuite	€25.50/€28	Dinner	-
B&B	-	Standard	-	Partial Board	-
Single Rate			€38.50/€38.50	Child reduction	25%

Open: All Year

Mrs Jo Doyle
KILLAUN
Clonmel Road, Cahir,
Co Tipperary

Cahir
TEL: 052 41780
EMAIL: killaunbandb@eircom.net

Bungalow, bedrooms overlooking spacious gardens, 5 mins walk from town, Bus and Train Station. Golf, Fishing and Horseriding closeby. On N24

B&B	3	Ensuite	€25.50/€25.50	Dinner	-
B&B	-	Standard	-	Partial Board	-
Single Rate			€38.50/€38.50	Child reduction	25%

In Cahir

Open: All Year Except Christmas

Mrs Marian Duffy
THE HOMESTEAD
Mitchelstown Road, Cahir,
Co Tipperary

Cahir
TEL: 052 42043

Spacious modern bungalow near Town Centre, TV bedrooms; Large private car park; Families welcome; Ideal Touring Base; Tea/Coffee on arrival.

B&B	4	Ensuite	€25.50	Dinner	-
B&B	-	Standard	-	Partial Board	-
Single Rate			€38.50	Child reduction	25%

In Cahir

Open: 2nd January-30th November

Mrs Mary English
BROOKFIELD HOUSE
Old Cashel Road, Cahir,
Co Tipperary

Cahir
TEL: 052 41936

Comfortable homely residence. All rooms have TV., Hairdryers, Tea/Coffee making facilities. Private parking. Conservatory and Guest Lounge.

B&B	2	Ensuite	€25.50	Dinner	-
B&B	1	Standard	€23	Partial Board	-
Single Rate			€36/€38.50	Child reduction	25%

Cahir 1km

Open: 1st April-30th September

Mrs Breda Fitzgerald
ASHLING
Cashel Road, Cahir,
Co Tipperary

Cahir
TEL: 052 41601

Ground level family home, smoke free. Antique furnishing. Prize winning gardens, electric blankets, Tea/Coffee making facilities. Country Inns recommended.

B&B	3	Ensuite	€25.50/€25.50	Dinner	-
B&B	-	Standard	-	Partial Board	-
Single Rate			€38.50/€38.50	Child reduction	-

Cahir 1km

Open: 1st January-23rd December

Margaret Neville
HOLLYMOUNT HOUSE
Upper Cahir Abbey, Cahir,
Co Tipperary

Cahir
TEL: 052 42888

Get away from it all! wind your way to the top of the mountain road, for peace and tranquillity. Only 5 minutes drive from town. Spectacular view. Quiet.

B&B	2	Ensuite	€25.50	Dinner	-
B&B	2	Standard	€23	Partial Board	-
Single Rate			€36/€38.50	Child reduction	25%

Cahir 2km

Open: All Year

Mrs Hannah-Mai O'Connor
SILVER ACRE
Clonmel Road, Cahir,
Co Tipperary

Cahir

TEL: 052 41737
EMAIL: hoconnor315@eircom.net

Modern bungalow, Tourism award winner, in quiet cul-de-sac. Private parking. Bus, Train, Fishing, Golf nearby. Tea and Coffee facilities.

B&B	3	Ensuite	€25.50/€25.50	Dinner	-
B&B	-	Standard	-	Partial Board	-
Single Rate			€38.50/€38.50	Child reduction	25%

In Cahir

Open: 1st February-30th November

Liam and Patricia Roche
TINSLEY HOUSE
The Square, Cahir,
Co Tipperary

Cahir

TEL: 052 41947   FAX: 052 41947

19th Century Town House. Former antique shop with bedrooms upstairs. Separate sitting room for guests with Tea/Coffee making facilities. Period decor and Roof Garden accessible to guests.

B&B	3	Ensuite	€25.50	Dinner	-
B&B	-	Standard	-	Partial Board	-
Single Rate			€36/€38.50	Child reduction	-

In Cahir

Open: 1st February-10th December

The Coady Family
THE GRAND INN
Nine-Mile-House,
Carrick-On-Suir,
Co Tipperary

Carrick-On-Suir

TEL: 051 647035   FAX: 051 647035
EMAIL: thegrandinn9@eircom.net

Former 17th century Bianconi Inn Family Home. In scenic Valley of Slievenamon. Spacious gardens. Antique furnishings. On Clonmel/Kilkenny Road N76.

B&B	3	Ensuite	€25.50	Dinner	-
B&B	2	Standard	€23	Partial Board	-
Single Rate			€36/€38.50	Child reduction	33.3%

Carrick-on-Suir 11km

Open: All Year

Anna & Patrick Hayes
ROCKVILLE HOUSE
Cashel,
Co Tipperary

Cashel

TEL: 062 61760

Located between 12th Century Abbey and the famous Royal Historic Castle. Recommended family home, relaxing garden. Local amenities. Secure car park.

B&B	6	Ensuite	€25.50/€25.50	Dinner	-
B&B	-	Standard	-	Partial Board	-
Single Rate			€38.50/€38.50	Child reduction	25%

In Cashel Town

Open: All Year

Mrs Mary Hickey
GORT-NA-CLOC
Ardmayle, Cashel,
Co Tipperary

Cashel

TEL: 0504 42362   FAX: 0504 42002
EMAIL: gortnaclocbandb@hotmail.com

Comfortable home in peaceful countryside, North West of Cashel on Gooldscross Road. Fishing, Golf, Walks. Private parking. Orthopaedic beds. Internet access.

B&B	3	Ensuite	€26	Dinner	-
B&B	2	Standard	€23	Partial Board	-
Single Rate			€36	Child reduction	50%

Cashel 7km

Open: 1st March-31st October

Mrs Mary A Kennedy
THORNBROOK HOUSE
Dualla/Kilkenny Rd (R691),
Cashel, Co Tipperary

Cashel

TEL: 062 62388   FAX: 062 61480
EMAIL: thornbrookhouse@eircom.net

Elegant country home. Antique furnishing, Landscaped gardens. Orthopaedic beds, Hairdryers, Tea/coffee, TV in all bedrooms. Internationally acclaimed.

B&B	3	Ensuite	€29/€32	Dinner	-
B&B	2	Standard	€25/€28	Partial Board	-
Single Rate			€38/€45	Child reduction	25%

Cashel 1km

Open: 1st April-31st October

Carmel & Pat Lawrence
MARYVILLE
Bank Place, Cashel,
Co Tipperary

Cashel

TEL: 062 61098   FAX: 062 61098
EMAIL: maryvill@iol.ie

Family welcome. Town Centre. Panoramic views of "Rock". 13th Century Abbey adjoining garden. Photographers delight. Private Parking. Home of World Champion Irish Dancer.

B&B	6	Ensuite	€26/€29	Dinner	€17
B&B	-	Standard	-	Partial Board	-
Single Rate			€40	Child reduction	25%

In Cashel

Open: All Year

Mrs Evelyn Moloney
ROS-GUILL HOUSE
Kilkenny/Dualla Road,
Cashel, Co Tipperary

Cashel

TEL: 062 62699   FAX: 062 61507

Elegant country home, overlooking Rock of Cashel. Superbly appointed. Breakfast Award Winner. Hairdryers, Tea/Coffee in bedrooms. Recommended Internationally. Credit Cards.

B&B	4	Ensuite	€30/€32	Dinner	-
B&B	1	Standard	€28/€30	Partial Board	-
Single Rate			€44.50/€44.50	Child reduction	25%

Cashel 1km

Open: April-October

Joan Brett Moloney
TIR NA NOG
Dualla, Cashel,
Co Tipperary

Cashel

TEL: 062 61350   FAX: 062 62411
EMAIL: tnanog@indigo.ie
WEB: www.tirnanogbandb.com

Award winning - friendly country home. Landscaped gardens. Peaceful surroundings. Home Baking, Peat Fires, Orthopaedic Beds. R691 Cashel/Kilkenny Road. Dinner/Breakfast Menu.

B&B	5	Ensuite	€25.50/€32	Dinner	€19.50
B&B	1	Standard	€23/€29	Partial Board	-
Single Rate			€36/€44.50	Child reduction	25%

Cashel 5km

Open: All Year

Mrs Sarah Murphy
INDAVILLE
Cashel, Co Tipperary

Cashel

TEL: 062 62075
EMAIL: indaville@eircom.net

Charming period home. Superb view of Rock of Cashel. Built in 1729 on 4 acres of Beechwood. Centrally located on N8, south of Main Street. Large comfortable rooms.

B&B	4	Ensuite	€28/€30	Dinner	-
B&B	-	Standard	-	Partial Board	-
Single Rate			€38.50/€40	Child reduction	50%

In Cashel

Open: 1st March-30th November

Mrs Breda O'Grady
ROCKVIEW HOUSE
**Bohermore, Cashel,
Co Tipperary**

Tᴇʟ: **062 62187**

Modern bungalow situated in the Town of Cashel. Panoramic view of the Rock of Cashel. Tea & Coffee in Bedrooms. Breakfast Menu. Friendly hospitality.

B&B	3	Ensuite	€25.50	Dinner	-
B&B		Standard	-	Partial Board	-
Single Rate			-	Child reduction	25%

Open: 17th March-31st October

Ellen Ryan & Paul Lawrence
ABBEY HOUSE
**1 Dominic Street, Cashel,
Co Tipperary**

Tᴇʟ: **062 61104**   Fᴀx: **062 61104**
Eᴍᴀɪʟ: **teachnamainstreach@eircom.net**

Town House, opposite Dominic's Abbey. 150 metres Rock of Cashel. Television/Tea/Coffee all bedrooms. Parking. Town Centre 50 metres.

In Cashel

B&B	4	Ensuite	€26/€29	Dinner	€17
B&B	1	Standard	€23	Partial Board	-
Single Rate			€36/€38	Child reduction	25%

Open: 1st February-31st November

Mrs Dorothy Mason
GEORGESLAND
**Dualla/Kilkenny Road,
Cashel, Co Tipperary**

Tᴇʟ: **062 62788**   Fᴀx: **062 62788**
Eᴍᴀɪʟ: **georgesland@hotmail.com**

Modern Country Home, situated R691 Dualla/Kilkenny Road. Set in peaceful landscaped gardens, surrounded by scenic countryside. Secure parking. Orthopaedic beds.

Cashel 1km

B&B	4	Ensuite	€28/€28	Dinner	-
B&B	-	Standard	-	Partial Board	-
Single Rate			€38.50/€38.50	Child reduction	33.3%

Open: All Year Except Christmas

Michael & Laura Ryan
ASHMORE HOUSE
**John Street, Cashel,
Co Tipperary**

Tᴇʟ: **062 61286**   Fᴀx: **062 62789**
Eᴍᴀɪʟ: **ashmorehouse@eircom.net**
Wᴇʙ: **www.ashmorehouse.com**

Georgian Family Home, heart of Cashel, Warm Welcome, Spacious Gardens, Private Parking, Residents Lounge, Touring Base, all amenities nearby. AA ♦♦♦.

In Cashel

B&B	5	Ensuite	€32/€38	Dinner	€25.39
B&B		Standard	-	Partial Board	-
Single Rate			€44.50/€44.50	Child reduction	50%

Open: All Year

Mary & Matt Stapleton
PALM GROVE HOUSE
**Dualla/Kilkenny Road,
Cashel, Co Tipperary**

Tᴇʟ: **062 61739**
Eᴍᴀɪʟ: **sstapleton@eircom.net**

Highly recommended family home. Scenic view in quiet location. Take R688 from Cashel, turn left after Church on R691 and "Palm Grove" 1km on right.

Cashel 1km

B&B	3	Ensuite	€25.50	Dinner	-
B&B	2	Standard	€23	Partial Board	-
Single Rate			€36/€38.50	Child reduction	25%

Open: 1st May-25th October

Mrs Sheila Cox
EDERMINE HOUSE
Rathronan, Fethard Rd,
Clonmel, Co Tipperary

Clonmel
TEL: **052 23048**   FAX: **052 23048**
EMAIL: **spike1@esatclear.ie**

Spacious dormer bungalow overlooking farm beside modern Equestrian Centre. Secure private parking. Golf, Fishing nearby.

B&B	2	Ensuite	€25.50/€25.50	Dinner	-
B&B	2	Standard	€23/€23	Partial Board	-
Single Rate			€36/€38.50	Child reduction	25%

Clonmel 2km   **Open:** 7th January-19th December

Mrs Lily Deely
BEENTEE
Ballingarrane, Cahir Road N24
Clonmel, Co Tipperary

Clonmel
TEL: **052 21313**
EMAIL: **deely@ireland.com**

Comfortable family bungalow, quiet cul-de-sac on main Limerick, Rosslare, Cork, Waterford road N24. Private parking.

B&B	3	Ensuite	€25.50/€25.50	Dinner	-
B&B	1	Standard	€23/€23	Partial Board	-
Single Rate			€36/€36	Child reduction	33.3%

Clonmel 1km   **Open:** All Year

Denis & Kay Fahey
FARRENWICK COUNTRY
HOUSE
Poulmucka, Curranstown,
Clonmel, Co Tipperary

Clonmel
TEL: **052 35130**   FAX: **052 35377**
EMAIL: **kayden@ciubi.ie**
WEB: **www.farrenwick.com**

AA ♦♦♦ accommodation R687, 3km, NW off N24 and 6.5km, SE off N8. Family Rooms. Credit Cards. Tour Guide Service.

B&B	3	Ensuite	€25.50/€35	Dinner	-
B&B	1	Standard	€23/€33	Partial Board	-
Single Rate			€36/€45	Child reduction	33.3%

Clonmel 9km   **Open:** 7th January-15th December

Mrs Nuala Healy
OAK HILL LODGE
Kilcash, Clonmel,
Co Tipperary

Clonmel
TEL: **052 33503**   FAX: **052 33503**
EMAIL: **healy@eircom.net**
WEB: **www.iol.ie/tipp/oakhill-lodge.htm**

Country Lodge 20 acres. Under Slievenamon & Kilcash Castle on N76. Kilkenny 29kms, Clonmel 10kms. Woodlands & Gardens. Tea & Scones on arrival. Email facilities.

B&B	3	Ensuite	€26/€26	Dinner	-
B&B	-	Standard	-	Partial Board	-
Single Rate			€38.50/€38.50	Child reduction	25%

Ballypatrick 2km   **Open:** All Year

Ms Agnes McDonnell
CLUAIN FHIA
25 Ballingarrane, Clonmel,
Co Tipperary

Clonmel
TEL: **052 21431**

Family home, quiet cul de sac. Main Limerick, Cork, Waterford, Rosslare Rd N24. Private parking.

B&B	2	Ensuite	€25.50/€32	Dinner	-
B&B	2	Standard	€23	Partial Board	-
Single Rate			€38.50	Child reduction	33.3%

Clonmel 1km   **Open:** All Year

Mr Michael J Moran
LISSARDA
Old Spa Road, Clonmel,
Co Tipperary

Clonmel
TEL: 052 22593/22294

Spacious purpose built residence within walking distance of Town Centre. Landscaped gardens. Power showers, TV, Tea/Coffee, Hairdryers. Breakfast menu.

B&B	4	Ensuite	€26/€30	Dinner	-
B&B	-	Standard	-	Partial Board	-
Single Rate			€38.50/€38.50	Child reduction	33.3%

In Clonmel

Open: 1st January-20th December

Mrs Rita Morrissey
HILLCOURT
Marlfield, Clonmel,
Co Tipperary

Clonmel
TEL: 052 21029/29711
EMAIL:ejmorrissey@hotmail.com

Bungalow in peaceful surroundings 300 metres off main Cork/Limerick Rd (N24). Golf, Fishing within 2 miles. TV.

B&B	5	Ensuite	€25.50/€25.50	Dinner	-
B&B	-	Standard	-	Partial Board	-
Single Rate			€38.50	Child reduction	50%

Clonmel 1.5km

Open: All Year

Ms Breda O'Shea
ASHBOURNE
Coleville Road, Clonmel,
Co Tipperary

Clonmel
TEL: 052 22307   FAX: 052 22307
EMAIL: ashbourn@iol.ie

Period spacious home overlooking River, a few minutes walk from Town Centre, Shops, Pubs and Clubs. TV, hairdryers and tea/coffee facilities, all rooms. Private parking.

B&B	3	Ensuite	€26/€30	Dinner	-
B&B	-	Standard	-	Partial Board	-
Single Rate			€38.50€38.50	Child reduction	33.3%

In Clonmel

Open: 2nd January-18th December

David & Jacinta Stott
KILMOLASH
Kilmolash Upper
Springmount, Clonmel,
Co Tipperary

Clonmel
TEL: 052 35152
EMAIL: kilmolash@eircom.net
WEB: www.dirl.com/tipperary/kilmolash.htm

Friendly country house in peaceful scenic surroundings overlooking the Suir Valley. Situated 2km off main Clonmel/Cahir road (N24) & only 16km from Cashel.

B&B	2	Ensuite	€27	Dinner	-
B&B	1	Standard	€25	Partial Board	-
Single Rate			€39	Child reduction	25%

Clonmel 7km

Open: All Year

Mrs Margaret Whelan
AMBERVILLE
Glenconnor Rd,
(off Western Rd) Clonmel,
Co Tipperary

Clonmel
TEL: 052 21470
EMAIL: amberville@eircom.net

Spacious bungalow off Western road near Hospitals. Ideal base for touring, Hillwalking, Golf, Fishing. Guests TV lounge with Tea/Coffee facilities. Visa Cards.

B&B	3	Ensuite	€25.50	Dinner	-
B&B	2	Standard	€23	Partial Board	-
Single Rate			€36	Child reduction	33.3%

In Clonmel

Open: 1st January-1st November

Mrs Mary Lynch
SHANNONVALE HOUSE
Dromineer, Nenagh,
Co Tipperary

Dromineer
Tel: **067 24102**   Fax: **067 24102**

Modern two storey house, close to Lough Derg. Quiet location in an idyllic setting. All the comforts of home.

B&B	3	Ensuite	€25.50	Dinner	€17
B&B	-	Standard	-	Partial Board	-
Single Rate			€38.50	Child reduction	50%

Nenagh 9km

Open: 17th March-30th September

The Stanley Family
BALLINACOURTY HOUSE
Glen of Aherlow,
Co Tipperary

Glen of Aherlow
Tel: **062 56000**   Fax: **062 56230**
Email: **info@ballinacourtyhse.com**
Web: **ballinacourtyhse.com**

Situated in a beautiful valley. Our 18th Century modernised home was once a stable courtyard. Restaurant with resident Chef. Tennis, Forest walks start at gate.

B&B	4	Ensuite	€25.50	Dinner	€25
B&B	1	Standard	€23	Partial Board	€320
Single Rate			€36	Child reduction	50%

Tipperary 13km

Open: 1st February-30th November

Brian & Mary Devine
WILLIAMSFERRY HOUSE
Fintan Lalor Street,
Nenagh, Co Tipperary

Nenagh
Tel: **067 31118**   Fax: **067 31256**
Email: **williamsferry@eircom.net**

AA ◆◆◆. Elegant townhouse 1830. Private parking. Guest lounge. TV, Hairdryer, Tea/Coffee facilities in rooms. Central to Town. Very comfortable. Warm welcome.

B&B	6	Ensuite	€26/€29	Dinner	-
B&B	-	Standard	-	Partial Board	-
Single Rate			€38.50/€38.50	Child reduction	33.3%

In Nenagh

Open: 1st January-22nd December

Mary & William Hayes
MARYVILLE
Ballycommon,
Near Dromineer,
Nenagh, Co Tipperary

Nenagh
Tel: **067 32531**
Email: **maryvilleguest@eircom.net**

Comfortable home in quiet location in Ballycommon Village. On R495 to Dromineer Bay on Lough Derg, off N7 adjacent to renowned Bar/Restaurant. Home cooking.

B&B	2	Ensuite	€25.50/€26	Dinner	-
B&B	1	Standard	€23/€25	Partial Board	-
Single Rate			€38.50/€40	Child reduction	33.3%

Nenagh 4km

Open: All Year

Mrs Kathleen Healy
RATHNALEEN HOUSE
Golf Club Road, Old Birr Road,
Nenagh, Co Tipperary

Nenagh
Tel: **067 32508**

Neo-Georgian house, antique furniture in all rooms. Quiet location. Spacious grounds, Golf, Fishing, Horse Riding Arena nearby. Good touring base.

B&B	2	Ensuite	€25.50	Dinner	-
B&B	3	Standard	€23	Partial Board	-
Single Rate			€36/€38.09	Child reduction	25%

Nenagh 2km

Open: All Year Except Christmas

Mrs Joan Kennedy
THE COUNTRY HOUSE
Thurles Road, Kilkeary,
Nenagh, Co Tipperary

Nenagh
TEL: **067 31193**

Luxurious residence recommended Frommer Guide. Large parking. Rooms Tea/coffee facilities. Breakfast menu. Orthopaedic beds. Fishing, Golf, Horse riding nearby.

B&B	3	Ensuite	€25.50	Dinner	-
B&B	2	Standard	€23	Partial Board	-
Single Rate			€36	Child reduction	33.3%

Nenagh 6km

Open: All Year

Mrs Gay McAuliffe
AVONDALE
Tyone, Nenagh,
Co Tipperary

Nenagh
TEL: **067 31084**
EMAIL: **gay.mcauliffe@oceanfree.net**

Comfortable, detached residence across from Hospital. Quiet location. Tea/Coffee facilities, Orthopaedic beds. Ideal for touring Midlands. Golf, Fishing, Tennis.

B&B	3	Ensuite	€26/€29	Dinner	-
B&B	1	Standard	€23/€26	Partial Board	-
Single Rate			€36/€36	Child reduction	25%

Nenagh 1km

Open: All Year Except Christmas

Mary McGeeney
COOLANGATTA
Brocka, Ballinderry,
Nenagh, Co Tipperary

Nenagh/Lough Derg
TEL: **067 22164**
EMAIL: **lmcgeene@ie.packardbell.org**

Spectacular views of Lough Derg and surrounding Countryside. Breakfast menu, Tea/Coffee, Lounge with TV/Video. Use of landscaped garden. Folk dancing classes.

B&B	3	Ensuite	€25.50/€25.50	Dinner	-
B&B	-	Standard		Partial Board	€265
Single Rate			€38.50/€38.50	Child reduction	50%

Nenagh 20km

Open: 1st March-31st October

Tom & Patricia McKeogh
WILLOWBROOK
Belleen (Portroe Rd),
Nenagh, Co Tipperary

Nenagh
TEL: **067 31558**   FAX: **067 41222**
EMAIL: **willowbrook@oceanfree.net**

Relax in a peaceful atmosphere amid landscaped surroundings. Ideal base for touring/business. Itinerary planned, Breakfast menu. R494 Nenagh/Portroe road.

B&B	6	Ensuite	€26/€29	Dinner	-
B&B	-	Standard		Partial Board	-
Single Rate			€38.50	Child reduction	50%

Nenagh 2km

Open: All Year

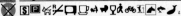

Margaret & PJ Mounsey
ASHLEY PARK HOUSE
Ashley Park, Nenagh,
Co Tipperary

Nenagh Lough Derg
TEL: **067 38223**   FAX: **067 38013**
EMAIL: **margaret@ashleypark.com**
WEB: **www.ashleypark.com**

17th Century house stands on the shores of Lough Orna. Centrally located, ideal for those who love tranquillity. Golfing, private Lake with boat for fishing. Woodlands for private walks.

B&B	5	Ensuite	€31.74/€44.44	Dinner	€31.74
B&B	1	Standard	€31.74/€38.09	Partial Board	-
Single Rate			€38.09/€44.44	Child reduction	33.3%

Nenagh

Open: All Year

In Terryglass

Sheila & Oliver Darcy
LAKE LAND LODGE
Terryglass, Nenagh,
Co Tipperary

Terryglass
TEL: **067 22069**   FAX: **067 22069**
EMAIL: **lakelandlodge@eircom.net**

Luxurious accommodation in beautiful scenic area. "A home away from home" Close to all Lake amenities eg. Fishing, Water Sports, Traditional Music, Golf etc.

B&B	2	Ensuite	€26	Dinner	-
B&B	1	Standard	€26	Partial Board	-
Single Rate			€36	Child reduction	33.3%

Open: 1st January-23rd December

In Thurles

Mrs Ellen Cavanagh
CUILIN HOUSE
Templemore Road N62,
Thurles, Co Tipperary

Thurles
TEL: **0504 23237**   FAX: **0504 26075**
EMAIL: **thurlesbandb@eircom.net**
WEB: **homepage.eircom.net/~thurlesbandb/bord.htm**

Luxurious accommodation spacious decorative bedrooms, TV, Tea/Coffee, homebaking, breakfast menu, worldwide guest recommendations, itineraries planned, geneology tracing assistance.

B&B	3	Ensuite	€28	Dinner	-
B&B	-	Standard		Partial Board	-
Single Rate			€38.50	Child reduction	50%

Open: March-November

Thurles 3km

Ms Noreen O'Mahony
HAWTHORN VIEW
Knockroe, Horse & Jockey/
Cashel Rd N62, Thurles,
Co Tipperary

Thurles
TEL: **0504 21710**

Luxurious bungalow on own private grounds, secluded gardens. On N62 route. Ideal touring base Holycross Abbey, Rock of Cashel, 2 mins Thurles Golf club. TV, Tea/Coffee, Homebaking.

B&B	3	Ensuite	€26/€29	Dinner	-
B&B	-	Standard		Partial Board	-
Single Rate			€38.50/€38.50	Child reduction	50%

Open: 1st March-30th November

Thurles 6km

Anna Stakelum
BOHERNA LODGE
Clohane, Tipperary Road,
Holycross, Thurles,
Co Tipperary

Thurles
TEL: **0504 43121**
EMAIL: **boherna@oceanfree.net**
WEB: **www.dirlcom/tipperary/boherna-lodge.htm**

Spacious country home, peaceful surrounding. Warm professional welcome. Ideal base for touring Holycross Abbey, Rock of Cashel. Golf, Fishing, Riding nearby.

B&B	3	Ensuite	€25.50/€25.50	Dinner	€17
B&B	1	Standard	€23/€23	Partial Board	-
Single Rate			€36/€36	Child reduction	33.3%

Open: 1st January-20th December

Tipperary 1.5km

Mrs Noreen Collins
PURT HOUSE
Bohercrowe, Emly Road,
Tipperary Town, Co Tipperary

Tipperary
TEL: **062 51938**
EMAIL: **purthouse@eircom.net**

Warm welcome R515 to Killarney, Tea/Coffee, TV, Hairdryers in bedrooms, hot scones, Credit cards, laundry facilities, Irish Night arranged.

B&B	5	Ensuite	€27/€30	Dinner	€17
B&B	1	Standard	€26/€29	Partial Board	-
Single Rate			€36/€38	Child reduction	33.3%

Open: 1st March-31st October

Mrs Kay Crowe
RIVERSIDE HOUSE
Galbally Road,
Tipperary Town,
Co Tipperary

Tipperary
TEL: **062 51219/51245** FAX: **062 51219**
EMAIL: **riversidehouse@hotmail.com**

Superbly situated home, main Cork route (R662). 5 mins walk Town Centre. All facilities in bedrooms. Guests Lounge, Sports Complex, Swimming Pool, Tennis & Cinema nearby, available to guests.

B&B	2	Ensuite	€28	Dinner	-
B&B	1	Standard	€25	Partial Board	-
Single Rate			€36	Child reduction	33.3%

In Tipperary

Open: 1st March-31st October

Douglas & Angela Edinborough
BALLYKISTEEN LODGE
Monard, Co Tipperary

Tipperary
TEL: **062 33403** FAX: **062 33711**
EMAIL: **ballykisteenlodge@oceanfree.net**
WEB: **www.tipp.ie/ballykis.htm**

Luxurious residence. Adjacent to Ballykisteen Golf & Country Club, Tipperary Racecourse. 10 minutes to Tipperary. Breakfast menu. TV, Tea/Coffee facilities. TV lounge.

B&B	4	Ensuite	€25.50/€29	Dinner	-
B&B	-	Standard	-	Partial Board	-
Single Rate			€38.50/€38.50	Child reduction	25%

Tipperary Town 3km

Open: 1st April-30th November

Mrs Margaret Merrigan
TEACH GOBNATHAN
Glen of Aherlow,
Golf Links Road, Brookville,
Tipperary, Co Tipperary

Tipperary
TEL: **062 51645**

Suburban home in scenic location beside Golf Club. Close to all amenities. Turn down at traffic lights, centre of Tipperary town, right at roundabout, two bends past Golf Club. Failte.

B&B	3	Ensuite	€25.50/€25.50	Dinner	€17
B&B	1	Standard	€23/€23	Partial Board	-
Single Rate			€36/€36	Child reduction	25%

Tipperary 1.5km

Open: 1st March-31st October

Mrs Mary O'Neill
VILLA MARIA
Limerick Road,
Tipperary Town, Co Tipperary

Tipperary
TEL: **062 51557**

Modern bungalow N24 Waterford/Limerick Road. Footpath to Tipperary. Limerick-Junction Station, Ballykisteen Golf, Tipperary Racecourse 1.5KM. Tea/coffee served.

B&B	2	Ensuite	€25.50/€26.50	Dinner	-
B&B	1	Standard	€23.50/€23.50	Partial Board	-
Single Rate			€36/€38.50	Child reduction	25%

Tipperary 2km

Open: May-September

Mrs Mary Quinn
CLONMORE HOUSE
Cork/Galbally Rd,
Tipperary Town, Co Tipperary

Tipperary
TEL: **062 51637**
EMAIL: **clonmorehouse@eircom.net**

Bungalow 5 mins walk town, scenic surroundings, overlooking Galtee Mountains, Frommer, Birnbaun, Best B&B Guides recommended. Ground floor bedrooms, Electric blankets.

B&B	5	Ensuite	€27/€27	Dinner	-
B&B	-	Standard	-	Partial Board	-
Single Rate			€38.50	Child reduction	-

In Tipperary

Open: 1st March-31st October

Mrs Marian Quirke
AISLING
Glen of Aherlow Road,
Tipperary, Co Tipperary

Tipperary
TEL: **062 33307** FAX: **062 82955**
EMAIL: **ladygreg@oceanfree.net**

Relaxed country location beside Golf Club. Family run homely atmosphere. Take route R664 from traffic lights Tipperary Town. Base for touring Tipperary Triangle. Near Castles ruins etc.

B&B	4	Ensuite	€25.50/€25.50	Dinner	€17
B&B	-	Standard	-	Partial Board	
Single Rate			€38.50/€38.50	Child reduction	50%

Tipperary 1.5km

Open: All Year

Mrs Teresa Russell
BANSHA CASTLE
Bansha,
Co Tipperary

Tipperary
TEL: **062 54187** FAX: **062 54294**
EMAIL: **johnrus@iol.ie**
WEB: **www.iol.ie/tipp/bansha-castle.htm**

Historic country house. Private gardens, Mature trees. Snooker room. Superb cooking. Walking/cycling. Pre booking recommended. 10 mins south Tipperary N24.

B&B	5	Ensuite	€32/€32	Dinner	€23
B&B	1	Standard	€32/€32	Partial Board	-
Single Rate			€38/€38	Child reduction	50%

Tipperary 8km

Open: 1st January-20th December

Cahir Castle

Waterford, The Crystal County boasts of splendid scenery, mountain passes, miles of spectacular coastline with safe and sandy beaches. The city of Waterford is a bustling maritime city, with 1,000 years of History, Museums and Heritage centres to see and explore.

Mrs Mary Byron Casey
BYRON LODGE
Ardmore, Co Waterford

Ardmore
TEL: **024 94157**

Home of Nora Roberts Irish Triology books. Monastic settlement. Georgian house. Superbly situated, 150 years old. Private parking. Historic Village of Artists and Writers. Cliff Walks.

B&B	4	Ensuite	€25.50/€28	Dinner	-
B&B	2	Standard	€23/€25	Partial Board	-
Single Rate			€36	Child reduction	-

In Youghal

Open: 1st April-30th October

Ms Theresa Troy
CUSH
Duffcarrick, Ardmore,
Co Waterford

Ardmore
TEL: **024 94474**

Situated adjacent picturesque Ardmore, off N25, with views of Bay, historic Ancient sites and surrounding countryside. Warm personal welcome assured.

B&B	1	Ensuite	€26/€28	Dinner	-
B&B	2	Standard	€24/€26	Partial Board	-
Single Rate			-	Child reduction	-

Ardmore 2km

Open: 1st April-30th September

Richard & Nora Harte
CNOC-NA-RI
Nire Valley, Ballymacarby Via
Clonmel, Co Waterford

Ballymacarbry Nire Valley
TEL: **052 36239**
EMAIL: **nharte@ireland.com**
WEB: **homepage.eircom.net/~cnocnari/**

Luxurious home highly recommended. Exhilerating views. TV, Hairdryers, Electric Blankets. Excellent breakfast. Walking, Golfing, fishing, horse riding, touring.

B&B	3	Ensuite	€32/€32	Dinner	-
B&B		Standard	-	Partial Board	-
Single Rate			€40/€40	Child reduction	25%

Clonmel 14km

Open: 1st February-1st November

Mrs Catherine Mary Scanlan
COOLHILLA
Ballyhane, Cappoquin,
Co Waterford

Cappoquin
TEL: **058 54054** FAX: **058 54054**
EMAIL: **coolhilla@eircom.net**

'Ambassador of Tourism' winner. Home Cooking, Tea/Coffee facilities. All rooms en-suite/TV. Ideal location. Walking, Fishing, Golfing. Excellent food & Irish music. Main N72. Credit cards accepted.

B&B	3	Ensuite	€27.50 /€27.50	Dinner	€22
B&B	-	Standard	-	Partial Board	€292
Single Rate			€38.50/€38.50	Child reduction	50%

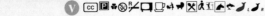

Cappoquin 5km

Open: All Year Except Christmas

Mrs Onra Fennell
MAPLE LEAF
Windgap (Cork Rd),
Dungarvan, Co Waterford

Dungarvan
Tel: **058 41921**
Email: **onra@esatclear.ie**

Second left junction after last roundabout, West of Dungarvan, 200mts off N25. Panoramic view of Dungarvan Bay and mountains. Landscaped gardens.

B&B	3	Ensuite	€25.50/€28	Dinner	€19
B&B	-	Standard	-	Partial Board	-
Single Rate			€38.50	Child reduction	50%

Dungarvan 6km   **Open:** 1st January-20th December

Sheila Lane
BALLINAMORE HOUSE
Ballyduff, Dungarvan,
Co Waterford

Dungarvan
Tel: **058 42146**

Just off R672, 3km west Dungarvan. Superior ground floor accommodation homely atmosphere in idyllic setting. Near Town, Fishing, Golf, Horseriding and Walking. Patio, garden for guests.

B&B	3	Ensuite	€25.50	Dinner	-
B&B	-	Standard	-	Partial Board	-
Single Rate			€38.50	Child reduction	50%

Dungarvan 3km   **Open:** All Year Except Christmas

Bridget Maher
HELVICK VIEW
Ring, Dungarvan,
Co Waterford

Dungarvan
Tel: **058 46297**

Seaside bungalow overlooking Dungarvan Bay and Helvick Head and a view of Comeragh Mountains. Rose garden for visitors.

B&B	4	Ensuite	€25.50/€25.50	Dinner	-
B&B	-	Standard	-	Partial Board	-
Single Rate			-	Child reduction	-

Dungarvan 8km   **Open:** 20th April-30th September

Mrs Patricia McCarthy
BRICKEY VALLEY
Coolnagour, Dungarvan,
Co Waterford

Dungarvan
Tel: **058 45056**
Email: **brickeyvalleyb.b@oceanfree.net**
Web: **www.waterford-accommodation.com/brickey.htm**

Spacious bedrooms, power showers, Breakfast menu. Situated in peaceful location, sign posted at The Spring Roundabout.

B&B	3	Ensuite	€25.50/€25.50	Dinner	-
B&B	-	Standard	-	Partial Board	-
Single Rate			€38.50/€38.50	Child reduction	50%

Dungarvan 3km   **Open:** 1st March-31st October

Teresa McGrath
TARA HILLS
Ballyguiry, Dungarvan,
Co Waterford

Dungarvan
Tel: **058 45166**   Fax: **058 45166**
Email: **tarahills@holidayhound.com**
Web: **www.tarahillsbandb.net**

Modern bungalow, friendly atmosphere. Panoramic views. Close to mountains and beaches. Overlooking West Waterford Golf Course.

B&B	2	Ensuite	€25.50/€25.50	Dinner	-
B&B	1	Standard	€24/€24	Partial Board	-
Single Rate			-	Child reduction	50%

Dungarvan 8km   **Open:** 16th March-30th September

Ann & Jim Mulligan
AN BOHREEN
Killineen West, Dungarvan, Co Waterford

Dungarvan

Tel: **051 291010**   Fax: **051 291011**
Email: **mulligans@anbohreen.com**
Web: **www.anbohreen.com**

Quiet, intimate. 400 meters off N25. Mountain, sea views. Waterford Crystal 20 min. Walking at your door. Excellent food served including 4 course dinner.

B&B	4	Ensuite	€32/€32	Dinner	€30
B&B	-	Standard	-	Partial Board	-
Single Rate			€50/€50	Child reduction	-

Dungarvan 6km

Open: 15th March-30th October

Sheila Norris
BAYSIDE
Gold Coast Road, Dungarvan, Co Waterford

Dungarvan

Tel: **058 44318**
Email: **pnorris@gofree.indigo.ie**
Web: **www.bayside.s5.com**

Seafront dormer bungalow in a rural setting, overlooking Dungarvan Bay. Private car park.

B&B	4	Ensuite	€25.50/€28	Dinner	-
B&B	-	Standard	-	Partial Board	-
Single Rate			€38.50/€38.50	Child reduction	-

Dungarvan 5km

Open: 4th January-22nd December

Helen O'Connell
HILLCREST
Waterford Road, Tarr's Bridge, Dungarvan, Co Waterford

Dungarvan

Tel: **058 42262**

Bungalow on Waterford/Cork road(N25). Adjacent 18 hole Golf Course. Rosslare 1.5 hours. Electric blankets. Safe Parking. Ideal touring centre. Early breakfasts served.

B&B	2	Ensuite	€25.50/€25.50	Dinner	-
B&B	1	Standard	€23/€23	Partial Board	-
Single Rate			€36/€36	Child reduction	50%

Dungarvan 3km

Open: 1st April-31st October

Mrs R Prendergast
THE OLD RECTORY
Waterford Rd, Dungarvan, Co Waterford

Dungarvan

Tel: **058 41394**   Fax: **058 41394**
Email: **theoldrectory@cablesurf.com**
Web: **homepage.eircom.net/~1108**

Waterford side of town on N25, Offstreet Parking. Walking distance of Town Centre. TV, Tea/Coffee facilities in bedrooms. 3x18 Hole Golf Courses nearby.

B&B	4	Ensuite	€26/€30	Dinner	-
B&B	-	Standard	-	Partial Board	-
Single Rate			€38.50/€38.50	Child reduction	50%

In Dungarvan

Open: All Year

Mrs Alice Shanley
TOURNORE HOUSE
Abbeyside, Dungarvan, Co Waterford

Dungarvan

Tel: **058 44370**
Email: **tournore.house@oceanfree.net**

Magnificent 18th Century country house located just off N25 and close to Town Centre/Golf/Beaches etc. Private parking. Tennis Court. Warm welcome assured.

B&B	3	Ensuite	€28.57/€31.75	Dinner	-
B&B	1	Standard	€25.39/€28.57	Partial Board	-
Single Rate			€38.10	Child reduction	-

Dungarvan 1km

Open: 1st January-21st December

Mrs Margo Sleator
ROSEBANK HOUSE
Clonea Road (R675),
Dungarvan, Co Waterford

Dungarvan
TEL: **058 41561**
EMAIL: **msleator@eircom.net**
WEB: **www.rosebankhouse.com**

Take R675 from Dungarvan, following signposting for Clonea Strand, own signposting en-route, Tea/Coffee in lounge. Highly recommended. Varied Breakfast menu.

B&B	3	Ensuite	€25.50/€28	Dinner	€19
B&B	1	Standard	€23/€25.50	Partial Board	-
Single Rate			€36/€38.50	Child reduction	-

Dungarvan 3km   Ⓥ ⒸⒸ 🅿 ... **Open:** 1st March-22 December

Winnie & Tony Brooke
SPRINGFIELD
Dunmore East,
Co Waterford

Dunmore East
TEL: **051 383448**
EMAIL: **springfieldbb@esatclear.ie**
WEB: **www.springfield-dunmore.com**

Luxurious home in beautiful peaceful surroundings only 200 metres from Beach, Restaurants and Bars. Breakfast menu. Secure Parking.

B&B	6	Ensuite	€26/€29	Dinner	-
B&B	-	Standard	-	Partial Board	-
Single Rate		-		Child reduction	25%

In Dunmore East   Ⓥ ⒸⒸ 🅿 ... **Open:** 1st March-31st October

---

Elizabeth Hayes
COPPER BEECH
Harbour Road, Dunmore East,
Co Waterford

Dunmore East
TEL: **051 383187/385957**
EMAIL: **copperbeech@ireland.com**

Delightful family home, Village Centre overlooking Harbour. Beside Beaches, Tennis, Sailing, Golf. Excellent Restaurants. Private parking. Frommer recommended.

B&B	4	Ensuite	€26/€29	Dinner	-
B&B	-	Standard	-	Partial Board	-
Single Rate		-		Child reduction	-

In Dunmore East   Ⓥ ⒸⒸ 🅿 ... **Open:** March-October

Phyllis & Ed Lannon
CHURCH VILLA
Dunmore East, Co Waterford

Dunmore East
TEL: **051 383390**   FAX: **051 383023**
EMAIL: **churchvilla@eircom.net**
WEB: **homepage.eircom.net/~churchvilla**

Victorian Town House, centre Village. Idyllic surrounds. Excellent Restaurants, Pubs walking distance. Five Golf courses nearby. Swim, Sail, Cliff walk. Email access.

B&B	6	Ensuite	€26/€29	Dinner	-
B&B	-	Standard	-	Partial Board	-
Single Rate			€38.50/€38.50	Child reduction	25%

In Dunmore East   Ⓥ ⒸⒸ Ⓢ ... **Open:** All Year Except Christmas

---

Mrs Kathleen Martin
CREADEN VIEW
Harbour Road, Dunmore East,
Co Waterford

Dunmore East
TEL: **051 383339**   FAX: **051 383339**

Highly Recommended charming friendly home centre of Village. Walking distance Restaurants, Bars, Beaches, Golf club 2km. Recommended Frommer/Lonely Planet. Breakfast menu.

B&B	6	Ensuite	€26/€29	Dinner	-
B&B	-	Standard	-	Partial Board	-
Single Rate			€38.50/€38.50	Child reduction	25%

In Dunmore East   Ⓥ ⒸⒸ Ⓢ ... **Open:** 1st March-31st October

Mrs Carmel McAllister
MC ALLISTERS
4 Wellington Terrace,
Dunmore East,
Co Waterford

Dunmore East
TEL: **051 383035**
EMAIL: **mcallisterbb@hotmail.com**

Period luxurious townhouse combining old world charm & all modern comforts. Overlooking Beach & Harbour. Peaceful location yet central.

B&B	3	Ensuite	€25.50/€28	Dinner	-
B&B	-	Standard	-	Partial Board	-
Single Rate				Child reduction	50%

In Dunmore East

Open: 1st April-30th September

Thelma Mee
BROSNA LODGE
1 The Blaskets, Ballymabin,
Dunmore East, Co Waterford

Dunmore East
TEL: **051 383983**   FAX: **051 383983**
EMAIL: **brosnalodge@eircom.net**

Relaxing garden. Near sea. Visit Waterford Crystal. Gourmet restaurants. Special offers. Golf, fishing, cycling. Private parking. Children welcome.

B&B	3	Ensuite	€26/€28	Dinner	-
B&B	-	Standard	-	Partial Board	-
Single Rate			€38.50/€38.50	Child reduction	25%

In Dunmore East

Open: 1st March-31st October

The Sutton Family
GLOR NA MARA
Kilmacleague, Dunmore East,
Co Waterford

Dunmore East
TEL: **051 383361**   FAX: **051 383361**
EMAIL: **tsutton@gofree.indigo.ie**

Country home, peaceful scenic surroundings. Golf, Fishing, Scenic Walks. Good food locally. All rooms ensuite with TV, Tea/Coffee facilities. Dunmore East 5km.

B&B	3	Ensuite	€25.50	Dinner	-
B&B	-	Standard	-	Partial Board	-
Single Rate			€38.50	Child reduction	50%

Dunmore East 5km

Open: 1st March-30th September

Ronan & Moira Power
CAPELLA
Texaco Station, Lemybrien,
Dungarvan, Co Waterford

Lemybrien/Dungarvan
TEL: **051 291535**   FAX: **051 291968**
EMAIL: **capella@eircom.net**

Situated at foot of Comeragh Mountains on N25 between Waterford & Dungarvan. Close to amenities. Adjacent to Crotty's Pub, Lemybrien, Waterford Crystal 25 mins drive.

B&B	3	Ensuite	€25.50/€26.66	Dinner	€17
B&B	1	Standard	€23/€24.12	Partial Board	-
Single Rate			€29.20/€29.20	Child reduction	50%

Dungarvan 7km

Open: 1st January-30th November

Mrs June Power
BEECHCROFT
Deerpark Road, Lismore,
Co Waterford

Lismore
TEL: **058 54273**   FAX: **058 54273**

A warm welcome awaits you in our home. TV, Hairdryers, Electric blankets all bedrooms. Tea/Coffee facilities. Drying room. Mature Garden. Leave N72 at Lismore. Located opposite Infants School.

B&B	2	Ensuite	€26.50/€27.50	Dinner	-
B&B	1	Standard	€25/€25	Partial Board	-
Single Rate			€36/€36	Child reduction	25%

In Lismore

Open: All Year Except Christmas

In Lismore

Shaun & Daphne Power
PINE TREE HOUSE
Ballyanchor, Lismore,
Co Waterford

Lismore
Tel: **058 53282**
Email: **pinetreehouse@oceanfree.net**

Comfortable family home on outskirts of heritage town of Lismore. Walking distance to Lismore Castle & gardens. Very peaceful pleasant surroundings. Large private gardens. N72.

B&B	3	Ensuite	€25.50/€28	Dinner	-
B&B	-	Standard	-	Partial Board	-
Single Rate			€38.50/€38.50	Child reduction	25%

Open: January-November

Tramore 1km

Mrs Sheila Brennan
CLUAIN RINN
Pickardstown,
Tramore, Co Waterford

Tramore
Tel: **051 381560**
Email: **sheilabrennan@oceanfree.net**

Spacious friendly home. Large bedrooms. Quiet location. Waterford side of Tramore. Off R675. Generous breakfast menu. TV lounge. Tea/Coffee.

B&B	2	Ensuite	€25.50/€28	Dinner	-
B&B	1	Standard	€23	Partial Board	-
Single Rate			€36	Child reduction	50%

Open: 1st May-30th September

In Tramore

Mrs Maria Byrne
KILLERIG HOUSE
Lower Branch Rd, Tramore,
Co Waterford

Tramore
Tel: **051 381075**

200 year old town house in Tramore opposite Splashworld Amusement park and Beach. Beside Majestic Hotel and Bus stop. 10km from Waterford Crystal & City.

B&B	6	Ensuite	€30/€32	Dinner	-
B&B	-	Standard	-	Partial Board	-
Single Rate			€40/€50	Child reduction	25%

Open: All Year

In Tramore

Mrs Lillian Delaney
WESTCLIFFE
5 Newtown, Tramore,
Co Waterford

Tramore
Tel: **051 381365**
Email: **westclif@indigo.ie**

Modern two storey house overlooking Tramore. 2 mins from 18 hole Golf Course. Guest sitting room.

B&B	4	Ensuite	€27.50/€33	Dinner	-
B&B	1	Standard	€25/€30	Partial Board	-
Single Rate			€40/€50	Child reduction	50%

Open: 1st January-1st December

SYMBOL

**LOOK OUT FOR THIS SYMBOL WHICH
ALL MEMBERS OF
TOWN & COUNTRY HOMES DISPLAY**

In Tramore

Frank & Majella Heraughty
GLENART HOUSE
Tivoli Rd, Tramore,
Co Waterford

Tramore
TEL: **051 381236**   FAX: **051 391236**
EMAIL: **tourismse@eircom.net**

Elegant restored 1920's detached residence. Convenient Racecourse, Splashworld, Beach & Golf. Friendly atmosphere. Breakfast menu. Tea/coffee facilities. Ideal touring base.

B&B	4	Ensuite	€28/€35	Dinner	-
B&B	-	Standard	-	Partial Board	-
Single Rate			€40	Child reduction	**50%**

Open: 1st March-1st December

In Tramore

Anne Lawlor
FERN HILL
Newtown, Tramore,
Co Waterford

Tramore
TEL: **051 390829**   FAX: **051 390829**
EMAIL: **fernhill@tramore.net**

Warm and luxurious house opposite Tramore Golf Club and 1km from Beach. Beautiful views of Tramore Bay. All facilities within the area.

B&B	4	Ensuite	€25.50/€31	Dinner	-
B&B	1	Standard	€23/€28	Partial Board	-
Single Rate			€36/€39	Child reduction	**33.3%**

Open: 1st March-30th October

In Tramore

Mrs Anne McCarthy
SEAMIST
Newtown, Tramore,
Co Waterford

Tramore
TEL: **051 381533**   FAX: **051 381533**
EMAIL: **annflor@iol.ie**
WEB: **www.tramore.net/seamist/**

Luxurious spacious home. Renowned generous breakfast. On site parking at rear. On coastal historical walk. 250 metres from Tramore Golf Club, signposted on R675.

B&B	3	Ensuite	€25.50/€28	Dinner	-
B&B	-	Standard	-	Partial Board	-
Single Rate			€38.50/€38.50	Child reduction	**25%**

Open: 1st March-31st October

In Tramore

Mrs Olive McCarthy
OBAN
1 Eastlands Pond Road,
Tramore, Co Waterford

Tramore
TEL: **051 381537**

"Breakfast over the Bay" in central comfortable home. Walking distance to Racecourse, Beach, Pubs, Restaurants etc. Extensive Breakfast menu. Ideal touring base.

B&B	3	Ensuite	€25.50/€27	Dinner	-
B&B	1	Standard	€23/€25	Partial Board	-
Single Rate			€36/€38.50	Child reduction	**50%**

Open: 8th January-16th December

In Tramore

Mrs Rosaleen McGrath
ARD MOR HOUSE
Doneraile Drive, Tramore,
Co Waterford

Tramore
TEL: **051 381716**

Family home centrally located in quiet area overlooking the Bay. Bedrooms with sea view. Walking distance Restaurants, Pubs, Beaches, Splashworld, Golf. Lonely Planet, Lets Go Guides.

B&B	3	Ensuite	€26/€32	Dinner	-
B&B	-	Standard	-	Partial Board	-
Single Rate			€40	Child reduction	**33.3%**

Open: April-October

In Tramore

Oliver McSherry
THE ANNER
33 Newtown Hill, Tramore,
Co Waterford

Tramore
TEL: 051 381628
EMAIL: theanner33@hotmail.com

Luxury welcoming home. AA ◆◆◆◆ selected. Quiet cul-de-sac. Full breakfast menu, home baking. Private parking. Turn off R675, opposite Tramore Golf Club.

B&B	3	Ensuite	€25.50/€29	Dinner	-
B&B	-	Standard	-	Partial Board	-
Single Rate			€38.50/€38.50	Child reduction	25%

Open: 1st January-22nd December

Thomas & Elizabeth Moran
SEA COURT
Tivoli Road, Tramore,
Co Waterford

Tramore
TEL: 051 386244
EMAIL: sea-court@tramore.net
WEB: www.tramore.net/tramore/seacourt.htm

Friendly home in the heart of Tramore. All rooms with multi-channel TV, Tea/Coffee facilities. Guest lounge. Secure parking. Extensive Breakfast menu.

B&B	6	Ensuite	€29	Dinner	-
B&B	-	Standard	€29	Partial Board	-
Single Rate			€38.50	Child reduction	50%

Open: 1st March-October

In Tramore

Mrs Marie Murphy
GLENORNEY BY THE SEA
Newtown, Tramore,
Co Waterford

Tramore
TEL: 051 381056   FAX: 051 381103
EMAIL: glenoney@iol.ie
WEB: www.glenorney.com

Award winning luxurious spacious home panoramic view Tramore Bay. RAC & AA ◆◆◆◆'s selected with Sparkling Diamond award. 2 family suites. Extensive menu.

B&B	6	Ensuite	€27.50/€35	Dinner	-
B&B	-	Standard	-	Partial Board	-
Single Rate			€40/€50	Child reduction	20%

Open: All Year

In Tramore

Niall & Penny Nordell
NORLANDS
Glen Road, Tramore,
Co Waterford

Tramore
TEL: 051 391132
EMAIL: nordell@eircom.net
WEB: www.tramore.net/tramore/norlands.

Luxurious family home beside Racecourse - 10 min drive to Waterford Crystal. Tranquil surroundings. 8 magnificent Golf courses - 30 min drive. Golfers welcome.

B&B	3	Ensuite	€30/€30	Dinner	-
B&B	-	Standard	-	Partial Board	-
Single Rate			€40/€40	Child reduction	33.3%

Open: 6th January-20th December

In Tramore

Mrs Anne O'Connor
ARDVIEW HOUSE
Lower Branch Road, Tramore,
Co Waterford

Tramore
TEL: 051 381687   FAX: 051 381687
EMAIL: john041@gofree.indigo.ie

Georgian house - panoramic view of bay. Satellite TV all rooms. Tea/Coffee all rooms. Breakfast menu. Credit cards, Very central. Warm welcome assured.

B&B	4	Ensuite	€25.50/€29.50	Dinner	-
B&B	2	Standard	€23/€25.50	Partial Board	-
Single Rate			€36/€38	Child reduction	33.3%

Open: All Year

Ann & John O'Meara

Tramore 2km

KNOCKVILLE
Moonvoy, Tramore,
Co Waterford

TEL: **051 381084**
EMAIL: **knockville@iolfree.ie**

Country home in rural area on R682, 7km from N25. Owner chef. Breakfast/Dinner menu. Bring your own wine. Tea/Coffee facilities. Private parking. Credit cards.

B&B	3	Ensuite	€25.50/€25.50	Dinner	€17
B&B	2	Standard	€23/€23	Partial Board	€264
Single Rate			€36/€38.50	Child reduction	50%

Open: 1st March-1st November

Pat & Hilary O'Sullivan

In Tramore

CLIFF HOUSE
Cliff Road, Tramore,
Co Waterford

TEL: **051 381497/391296**   FAX: **051 381497**
EMAIL: **hilary@cliffhouse.ie**
WEB: **www.cliffhouse.ie**

"Simply the Best" luxurious. AA ◆◆◆◆. Panoramic view Tramore Bay. Family suites. Extensive menu. Recommended Le Routard, Dillard/Causin Fran/Frank Sullivan Guides.

B&B	6	Ensuite	€30/€32	Dinner	-
B&B	-	Standard		Partial Board	-
Single Rate			€40/€50	Child reduction	25%

Open: February-December

Mrs Teresa O'Sullivan

In Tramore

TIVOLI HOUSE
Waterford Road, Tramore,
Co Waterford

TEL: **051 390208**   FAX: **051 390208**
EMAIL: **tivoli@iolfree.ie**
WEB: **www.dirl.com/waterford/tivoli-house.htm**

Spacious friendly home overlooking Tramore Bay. Beside Splashworld, Golf, Racecourse, Beach, Surfing, Waterford Crystal. 1 hour Rosslare, 300M from roundabout. Breakfast menu.

B&B	4	Ensuite	€25.50/€30	Dinner	-
B&B	-	Standard		Partial Board	-
Single Rate			€38.50/€38.50	Child reduction	33.3%

Open: 1st January-20th December

Neil & Maria Skedd

In Tramore

CLONEEN
Love Lane, Tramore,
Co Waterford

TEL: **051 381264**   FAX: **051 381264**
EMAIL: **cloneen@iol.ie**
WEB: **www.cloneen.net**

Family run bungalow set in landscaped gardens. Sun Lounge and Patio for guests. Quiet location with private parking. Beach, Golf and Splashworld nearby.

B&B	4	Ensuite	€30/€30	Dinner	€18
B&B	-	Standard		Partial Board	€264
Single Rate			€40	Child reduction	50%

Open: 1st March-31st October

Mrs Jo St John

In Tramore

VENEZIA HOUSE
Church Road Grove,
Tramore, Co Waterford

TEL: **051 381412**
EMAIL: **veneziahouse@ireland.com**
WEB: **www.come.to/veneziahouse**

Spacious bungalow quiet cul de sac, landscaped gardens, secure parking. 3 mins beach & amenities. Lonely Planet, Lets Go, Dillard/Causin Guides acclaimed. Breakfast menu.

B&B	3	Ensuite	€27/€30	Dinner	-
B&B	-	Standard	-	Partial Board	-
Single Rate				Child reduction	33.3%

Open: April-October

Frank & Margaret Walsh
SUMMERHILL LODGE
Ballycarnane, Tramore,
Co Waterford

Tramore
TEL: **051 381938**   FAX: **051 391333**

Quality welcoming home with private parking and gardens. 10 mins walk Beach. Approach via Main Street and Summerhill 200 yards past Credit Union and Catholic Church.

B&B	6	Ensuite	€29/€32	Dinner	-
B&B	-	Standard	-	Partial Board	-
Single Rate			€38.50/€44	Child reduction	-

In Tramore

Open: 1st February-30th November

Aine & Joe Whelan
TURRET HOUSE
2 Church Road, Town Centre,
Tramore, Co Waterford

Tramore
TEL: **051 386342**
EMAIL: **turrethouse@hotmail.com**

"Tramore at it's Best". Quiet home in the heart of Tramore with superb views. All facilities. Family suite. Private parking.

B&B	4	Ensuite	€26/€31	Dinner	-
B&B	-	Standard	-	Partial Board	-
Single Rate			€38.50/€45	Child reduction	50%

In Tramore

Open: 1st March-31st October

Susan Bailey-Daunt
SAMUELS HERITAGE
Ballymaclode Halfway House,
Dunmore Rd, Waterford,
Co Waterford

Waterford
TEL: **051 875094**   FAX: **051 304013**
EMAIL: **samuelsheritage@eircom.net**

Family home, panoramic views, quiet and peaceful country surroundings, close proximity to Beaches, Golf, Angling, Walking, Horseriding and wide choice of Restaurants.

B&B	3	Ensuite	€27/€28	Dinner	-
B&B	-	Standard	-	Partial Board	-
Single Rate			€39/€40	Child reduction	25%

Waterford 5km

Open: 1st January-19th December

Mrs Eithne Brennan
HILLVIEW LODGE
Kilmeaden, Co Waterford

Waterford
TEL: **051 384230**
EMAIL: **hillviewlodgebandb@eircom.net**
WEB: **homepage.eircom.net/~hillviewlodge**

Two storey house with large mature garden on N25. Horse Riding and Golf, Driving Range nearby. Convenient to Waterford Crystal.

B&B	4	Ensuite	€26	Dinner	-
B&B	1	Standard	€23	Partial Board	-
Single Rate			€39	Child reduction	25%

Waterford 7km

Open: 1st March-31st October

Annette Comiskey
OLD PAROCHIAL HOUSE
Priest Lane, Robinstown,
Glenmore (via Waterford),
Co Waterford

Waterford
TEL: **051 880550**   FAX: **051 880550**
EMAIL: **anastasiacomiskey@hotmail.com**

Built in 1870 this former Parochial House is set in beautiful gardens with fountain, gazebo & orchards. Modern facilities with old world charm. 50m off N25.

B&B	2	Ensuite	€25.50/€25.50	Dinner	-
B&B	2	Standard	€23/€23	Partial Board	-
Single Rate			€36/€38.50	Child reduction	50%

New Ross/Waterford 12km

Open: 2nd January-23rd December

Miriam Corcoran
CLADDAGH
Lr Newrath, Ferrybank,
Waterford, Co Waterford

Waterford
Tel: **051 854797**
Email: **mashacorcoran@yahoo.com**

Modern home, quiet area, situated off N9/N24. Adjacent to 18 hole Golf Course. Private Car Park, Tea/Coffee in Bedrooms.

B&B	5	Ensuite	€26/€28	Dinner	-
B&B	-	Standard	-	Partial Board	-
Single Rate			€38.50/€40	Child reduction	25%

Waterford 2.5km

Open: 1st March-31st October

Patrick & Noreen Dullaghan
LOUGHDAN
Newrath, Dublin Rd,
Waterford, Co Waterford

Waterford
Tel: **051 876021**
Email: **info@loughdan.net**
Web: **www.loughdan.net**

Modern house Dublin/Limerick Rd. N9/N24. Convenient Golf, Bus/Train Station. Tea/Coffee facilities, TV, Hairdryers in bedrooms. Breakfast menu.

B&B	5	Ensuite	€26/€28	Dinner	-
B&B	1	Standard	€25/€25	Partial Board	-
Single Rate			€38/€40	Child reduction	25%

Waterford 1km

Open: 1st February-30th November

Mrs Catherine Evans
ROSEWOOD
Slieverue Via Waterford,
Co Waterford

Waterford
Tel: **051 832233**   Fax: **051 358389**
Email: **cevans@rosewood-waterford.com**
Web: **www.rosewood-waterford.com**

Family run purpose built B&B, beautiful gardens. Located in the small country village of Slieverue on the N25, 3km from Waterford City. Convenient to Waterford Crystal and Golf.

B&B	4	Ensuite	€26/€26	Dinner	-
B&B	-	Standard	-	Partial Board	-
Single Rate			€38.50/€38.50	Child reduction	25%

Waterford City 3km

Open: 1st February-30th October

Mrs Ann Fitzgerald
DAWN B&B
Kildarmody, Kilmeaden,
Co Waterford

Waterford
Tel: **051 384465**
Email: **dawnb.and.b@esatclear.ie**

Modern bungalow in peaceful quiet area. 1/2km off N25. 12 km Waterford Crystal. Restaurants and Pub in walking distance. Private Car park, garden for guests.

B&B	3	Ensuite	€25.50	Dinner	-
B&B	-	Standard	-	Partial Board	-
Single Rate			€38.50	Child reduction	33.3%

Waterford City 12km

Open: All Year

Margaret C Fitzmaurice
BLENHEIM HOUSE
Blenheim Heights,
Waterford, Co Waterford

Waterford
Tel: **051 874115**
Email: **blenheim@eircom.net**
Web: **homepage.eircom.net/~blenheim/**

Georgian residence C1763. Furnished throughout with Antiques & object d'art. Surrounded by lawns and private Deer Park. Convenient to Waterford Castle and Faithlegg Golf clubs.

B&B	6	Ensuite	€30/€30	Dinner	-
B&B	-	Standard	-	Partial Board	-
Single Rate			€32/€32	Child reduction	

Waterford 3.5km

Open: All Year

Phil Harrington
BROOKDALE HOUSE
Carrigrue, Ballinaneeshagh,
Waterford, Co Waterford

Waterford

TEL: **051 375618**

Quiet location, landscaped gardens, car park, 400m off Cork/Waterford Road (N25). Joint award of excellence 1998, 1999 & 2000. 1km Waterford Crystal.

B&B	3	Ensuite	€26	Dinner	-
B&B	-	Standard	-	Partial Board	-
Single Rate			€39	Child reduction	25%

Waterford 3km

Open: 1st April-31st October

Mrs Margaret Hayes
ARRIVISTE
Holycross, Cork Road,
Butlerstown, Co Waterford

Waterford

TEL: **051 354080**   FAX: **051 354080**
EMAIL: **arriviste_bb@hotmail.com**

Country house, central heated. Private car park. Lounge, TV rooms, Tea/Coffee facilities. Large relaxing Conservatory. Landscaped gardens. Situated on N25. 2km from Waterford Crystal.

B&B	5	Ensuite	€26/€26	Dinner	€17
B&B	-	Standard	-	Partial Board	-
Single Rate			€39/€39	Child reduction	25%

Waterford 4.5km

Open: 15th January-15th December

Bernadette Kiely
ASHFIELD B&B
Belmount Road, Ferrybank,
Waterford, Co Waterford

Waterford

TEL: **051 832266**
EMAIL: **ashfieldwfd@eircom.net**

Comfortable family home on N25. Rosslare 55 mins. Close to Golf, Shops, Crystal Factory and Beaches. Ideal for touring Southeast. TV Lounge with Tea/Coffee Facilities.

B&B	3	Ensuite	€26/€28	Dinner	-
B&B	1	Standard	-	Partial Board	-
Single Rate			€36/€36	Child reduction	25%

Waterford 2km

Open: 1st March-31st October

Mrs Eileen Landy
BELMONT HOUSE
Belmont Road, Rosslare Road,
Ferrybank, Waterford,
Co Waterford

Waterford

TEL: **051 832174**
EMAIL: **belmonthouse@eircom.net**

Easy to find on Waterford/Rosslare Rd N25. Spacious Modern house. No smoking. Private parking. AA & RAC listed. Tea/Coffee facilities. Convenient to Crystal Factory, Golf, Train & Bus City 2km.

B&B	4	Ensuite	€26/€29	Dinner	-
B&B	2	Standard	€23/€25	Partial Board	-
Single Rate			€42/€45	Child reduction	-

Waterford City 2km

Open: 1st May-31st October

Phyllis McGovern
ASHLEIGH
Holy Cross, Cork Road,
Waterford, Co Waterford

Waterford

TEL: **051 375171**   FAX: **051 375171**
EMAIL: **ashleighhouse@eircom.net**
WEB: **www.ashleigh-house.com**

Award of Excellence winner. Spacious home, gardens, carpark. On N25 close to Waterford Crystal, Pub & Restaurant. TV, Tea/Coffee in rooms. Breakfast menu.

B&B	6	Ensuite	€26/€28	Dinner	-
B&B	-	Standard	-	Partial Board	-
Single Rate			€39/€41	Child reduction	25%

Waterford 4km

Open: 6th January-20th December

John & Ann Morrissey
WOODSIDE HOUSE
Whitfield, Cork Rd,
Waterford, Co Waterford

Waterford
TEL: **051 384381**   FAX: **051 384547**
EMAIL: **woodsidehouse@eircom.net**
WEB: **www.woodsidehouse.com**

Spacious country house, 5 mins drive Waterford Crystal, Main Cork road (N25). Ideal touring, Golfing base. Best Homestay Award winner. Highly recommended.

B&B	6	Ensuite	€27/€27	Dinner	€19
B&B	-	Standard	-	Partial Board	
Single Rate			€38.50/€39	Child reduction	25%

Kilmeaden 1.5km

Open: 21st January-21st December

Mrs Mary Naughton
UTOPIA B&B
Butlerstown,
Co Waterford

Waterford
TEL: **051 384157**   FAX: **051 384157**

Bungalow with large mature landscaped gardens, on N25. Waterford Crystal 3km. Exclusive entrance to guests. Parking. Breakfast menu. Tea/Coffee Facilities.

B&B	3	Ensuite	€26/€26	Dinner	-
B&B	-	Standard	-	Partial Board	-
Single Rate			€38.50/€38.50	Child reduction	33.3%

Waterford 3km

Open: 31st March-31st October

Mrs Marian O'Keeffe
ST ANTHONY'S
Ballinaneesagh, Cork Road,
Waterford, Co Waterford

Waterford
TEL: **051 375887**   FAX: **051 353063**

Spacious bungalow with landscaped garden on N25 near Waterford Crystal. Breakfast menu. Colour TV, Tea/Coffee facilities, Hairdryers, Electric Blankets. Frommer reader recommended.

B&B	6	Ensuite	€26/€26	Dinner	-
B&B	-	Standard	-	Partial Board	-
Single Rate			€38.50/€38.50	Child reduction	25%

Waterford 2km

Open: All Year Except Christmas

Terence & Anne O'Neill
ST. JOSEPH'S
Ballinaneeshagh, Cork Road,
Waterford, Co Waterford

Waterford
TEL: **051 376893**
EMAIL: **oneillanneie@yahoo.co.uk**

Spacious friendly home. Waterford/Cork N25 2 mins. Crystal Factory. Cable TV, Tea/Coffee facilities in bedrooms. City Bus service. Breakfast menu.

B&B	3	Ensuite	€26/€26	Dinner	-
B&B	-	Standard	-	Partial Board	-
Single Rate			€38.50/€40	Child reduction	25%

Waterford 1.5km

Open: January-31st November

Mrs Phyllis O'Reilly
ANNVILL HOUSE
1 The Orchard, Kingsmeadow,
Waterford, Co Waterford

Waterford
TEL: **051 373617**   FAX: **051 373617**

From City turn right at N25 roundabout, at lights turn left. 2 mins from Crystal factory. Winner of CIE Int'l Awards of Excellence. Frommer Recommended. Tea/Coffee, Hairdryers. City Bus.

B&B	4	Ensuite	€26	Dinner	-
B&B	1	Standard	€23	Partial Board	-
Single Rate			€39	Child reduction	-

Waterford City 1km

Open: 1st January-21st December

Mrs Alice O'Sullivan-Jackman — Waterford
THE PINES
Knockboy, Dunmore Road,
Waterford, Co Waterford

TEL: 051 874452 FAX: 051 841566
EMAIL: bjackman@eircom.net
WEB: http://homepage.eircom.net/~pines/

Picturesque rural bungalow, near Hospital, Airport. Breakfast menu. Fishing, Golf, Beaches, Pubs, Seafood Restaurants locally. http://homepage.eircom.net/~pines/

B&B	5	Ensuite	€29/€30	Dinner	-
B&B	-	Standard	-	Partial Board	-
Single Rate			€38.50	Child reduction	-

Waterford City 3km

Open: 1st January-30th November

Paul & Breda Power — Waterford
DUNROVEN B&B
Ballinaneesagh, Cork Rd, N25
Waterford City,
Co Waterford

TEL: 051 374743 FAX: 051 377050
EMAIL: dunroven@iol.ie
WEB: www.dunroven-ireland.com

Modern home. Cork/Waterford road N25. 2 minutes Crystal Factory, W.I.T. College. Cable TV, Tea/Coffee, Hairdryers. Breakfast menu. City bus IMP. No Smoking house.

B&B	6	Ensuite	€26	Dinner	-
B&B	-	Standard	-	Partial Board	-
Single Rate			€38.50	Child reduction	-

Waterford City 1.5km

Open: All Year Except Christmas

Mrs Rena Power — Waterford
GLENCREE
The Sweep, Kilmeaden,
Co Waterford

TEL: 051 384240

Country home off Cork/Waterford (N25). Crystal Factory, Horse Riding, Pubs, Restaurants locally. Ideal for Coastal, Mountain or Heritage tours.

B&B	3	Ensuite	€26	Dinner	-
B&B	2	Standard	€23	Partial Board	-
Single Rate			€36/€38.50	Child reduction	25%

Waterford 9km

Open: 1st March-31st October

Mrs Marie Prendergast — Waterford
TORY VIEW
Mullinavat,
Co Waterford

TEL: 051 885513 FAX: 051 885513

Modern house on N9 Dublin/Kilkenny Road. Tea/Coffee Facilities, TV, Hairdryers in Bedrooms. Convenient Golf & Waterford Crystal.

B&B	4	Ensuite	€25.50	Dinner	-
B&B	1	Standard	€23	Partial Board	-
Single Rate			€36/€38.50	Child reduction	25%

Waterford 8km

Open: 1st March-31st October

Helen Quinn — Waterford
WHITE WEBBS
Ballinaneeshagh, Waterford,
Co Waterford

TEL: 051 370696

Joint Award of excellence 1998, 1999 & 2000. Quiet location, landscaped gardens, car park. 1km Waterford Crystal. 400m off Cork/Waterford Road (N25).

B&B	3	Ensuite	€26	Dinner	-
B&B	1	Standard	-	Partial Board	-
Single Rate			€39	Child reduction	25%

Waterford 3km

Open: 1st April-31st October

Maureen Wall
SUNCREST
Slieverue, Ferrybank, Via
Waterford, Co Waterford

Waterford
TEL: **051 832732**   FAX: **051 851861**
EMAIL: **suncrest@inet-sec.com**
WEB: **www.inet-sec.com/suncrest.htm**

Split level bungalow in quiet rural location 600 metres off N25 Waterford/Rosslare road. In Slieverue village, Waterford City 3kms, Rosslare 50 mins. Ideal base for touring South East.

B&B	5	Ensuite	€26	Dinner	-
B&B	-	Standard	-	Partial Board	-
Single Rate			€38.50	Child reduction	25%

Waterford 3km

Open: 1st February-30th November

Mrs Patricia Wall
SAN-MARTINO
Ballinaneeshagh, Cork Rd,
Waterford, Co Waterford

Waterford
TEL: **051 374949**

Modern bungalow on main Waterford/Cork road. 3 mins from Waterford Crystal Factory. Tea/Coffee facilities. Winner of Award of Excellence for 1998 and 1999.

B&B	5	Ensuite	€26	Dinner	-
B&B	-	Standard	-	Partial Board	-
Single Rate			€38.50	Child reduction	-

Waterford City 2km

Open: 1st February-30th November

Siobhan Walsh
KINARD
Kilmeaden,
Co Waterford

Waterford
TEL: **051 384505**   FAX: **051 384505**
EMAIL: **kinard@eircom.net**
WEB: **homepage.eircom.net/~kinard**

Bungalow set in mature gardens on N25. Crystal Factory, Beaches, Restaurants, Mountains near-by. TV, Tea/Coffee in all rooms.

B&B	2	Ensuite	€26	Dinner	-
B&B	1	Standard	€23	Partial Board	-
Single Rate			€38.50	Child reduction	25%

Waterford 9km

Open: 1st April-30th September

Mrs Stella White
BALLYCANAVAN LODGE
Faithlegg, Half Way House,
Waterford, Co Waterford

Waterford
TEL: **051 873928**   FAX: **051 873928**
EMAIL: **ballycanavanlodge@ireland.com**

Country house set in mature gardens. Adjacent to Golf Courses, Restaurants. Passage East Car Ferry 4km. Ideal location for activity holiday.

B&B	2	Ensuite	€28/€28	Dinner	-
B&B	1	Standard	€26/€26	Partial Board	-
Single Rate			€36/€39	Child reduction	25%

Waterford 6km

Open: 14th March-31st October

RESERVATIONS

- Confirm phone bookings in writing without delay with agreed deposit.
- To avoid misunderstandings later, check rate on booking and clarify any additional changes which may apply to your booking.
- Give details of any special requirements.
- State clearly day, date of arrival and departure date.

A region rich in history, landscaped with ancient Castles, Abbeys and Museums. Savor the dramatic scenery of Hook peninsula or leisurely enjoy the sunny South East's golden beaches. Gateway to Britain and Europe - Wexford is famous for its Opera Festival.

Mrs Ann Crosbie
GLENDINE COUNTRY HOUSE
Arthurstown, Co Wexford

Arthurstown

TEL: **051 389258** FAX: **051 389677**
EMAIL: **glendinehouse@eircom.net**
WEB: **www.glendinehouse.com**

We invite you to our charming 1830 Georgian home. We offer superb accommodation, bedrooms enjoy sweeping views of the Estuary. From N25, take R733. AA♦♦♦♦.

B&B	4	Ensuite	€32/€40	Dinner	-
B&B	-	Standard		Partial Board	-
Single Rate			€44/€50	Child reduction	25%

Waterford 7km

Open: All Year Except Christmas

Ms Phil Kinsella
MEADOW SIDE B&B
Ryland Street, Bunclody,
Co Wexford

Bunclody

TEL: **054 76226/77459** FAX: **054 76226**

Elegant stone Georgian Town House ideally situated. Tea/Coffee on arrival, TV Lounge, spacious rooms ensuite. Private Car Park.

B&B	3	Ensuite	€25.50/€31.74	Dinner	-
B&B	1	Standard	€25.39/€31.74	Partial Board	-
Single Rate			€36/€38.09	Child reduction	-

In Bunclody

Open: All Year Except Christmas

Mrs Liz O'Connell-Jones
WESTON HOUSE
Church Rd, Bunclody,
Co Wexford

Bunclody

TEL: **054 76435**
EMAIL: **econnell-jones@esatclear.ie**

18th Century town house in grounds of 2.5 acres. All rooms en-suite. Tea/Coffee making facilities. Private car park. TV lounge. 3 mins walk to town.

B&B	3	Ensuite	€25.50/€30	Dinner	-
B&B	-	Standard		Partial Board	-
Single Rate			€38.50/€45	Child reduction	25%

In Bunclody

Open: All Year

Mary Parle
ARAS-MUILLINN
Ambrosetown, Duncormick,
Co Wexford

Duncormick

TEL: **051 563145** FAX: **051 563245**

New refurbished modern house. Comfortable surroundings and homely atmosphere. 20 mins from Ferry Port. Early Breakfast.

B&B	2	Ensuite	€25.50	Dinner	-
B&B	1	Standard	€23	Partial Board	-
Single Rate			€36	Child reduction	-

Wexford 22.4km

Open: January-20th December

Mrs A Delany
ST JUDES
Munfin, Tomnalossitt,
Enniscorthy, Co Wexford

Enniscorthy
TEL: **054 33011**　　FAX: **054 37831**
EMAIL: **anndelany@eircom.net**

Home located 2km off the N30 on Bree Rd. Scenic countryside. Nearest B&B to Enniscorthy Golf club. Early Breakfast. Rosslare Ferryport 38km. Bedrooms ground floor.

B&B	4	Ensuite	€25.50/€25.50	Dinner	€17
B&B	1	Standard	€23/€23	Partial Board	
Single Rate			€36/€38.50	Child reduction	50%

Enniscorthy 4km　　**Open:** 1st January-1st December

Helen Kenny
MOYHILL
Bellefield, Enniscorthy,
Co Wexford

Enniscorthy
TEL: **054 34739**
EMAIL: **helenkenny@ireland.com**

50 metres off Enniscorthy/Kiltealy/Kilkenny rd (R702). Signposted on N30. From N11, follow signpost for Kilteely at roundabout. Rosslare 40km, Dublin 120km.

B&B	2	Ensuite	€25.50/€26	Dinner	-
B&B	1	Standard	€23	Partial Board	-
Single Rate			€38.50	Child reduction	-

Enniscorthy 1km　　**Open:** 1st May-30th September

Mrs Noreen Byrne
PERRYMOUNT COUNTRY HOME
Inch, Gorey,
Co Wexford

Gorey
TEL: **0402 37418**
EMAIL: **perrymount@eircom.net**

Situated 50 metres off Dublin/Rosslare Road (N11) at Inch North of Gorey. TV, Tea/Coffee facilities in rooms. Breakfast menu. Pub, Restaurant 50 metres.

B&B	3	Ensuite	€25.50/€28	Dinner	€19
B&B	-	Standard	-	Partial Board	€300
Single Rate			€38.50/€40	Child reduction	50%

Gorey 8km　　**Open:** 1st January-20th December

Mrs Martina Redmond
CARRAIG VIEW
Ballycale, Gorey,
Co Wexford

Gorey
TEL: **055 21323**　　FAX: **055 21323**
EMAIL: **carraigview@eircom.net**

Select accommodation, rooms ensuite with TV, Hairdryer, Tea/Coffee facilities. Breakfast menu. Situated on the R741 or turn off N11 at Clough Beach nearby.

B&B	2	Ensuite	€25.50/€28	Dinner	-
B&B	1	Standard	€23/€25.50	Partial Board	-
Single Rate			€36/€38.50	Child reduction	33.3%

Gorey 2km　　**Open:** 1st January-20th December

Mrs Ann Sunderland
HILLSIDE HOUSE
Tubberduff, Gorey,
Co Wexford

Gorey
TEL: **055 21726/22036** FAX: **055 22567**
EMAIL: **hillsidehouse@eircom.net**
WEB: **hillside.virtualave.net**

Spacious modern hse, ideal for touring South East. 3 km off N11, North of Gorey. All rooms Tea/Coffee, TV, Hairdryers, Electric blankets. Guest lounge with open fire. AA ◆◆◆◆.

B&B	6	Ensuite	€28/€32	Dinner	€20.50
B&B	-	Standard	-	Partial Board	€300
Single Rate			€38.50/€38.50	Child reduction	50%

Gorey 5km　　**Open:** 1st January-20th December

Mary Cousins
GROVESIDE
Ballyharty, Kilmore,
Co Wexford

Kilmore Quay

TEL: **053 35305**   FAX: **053 35305**
EMAIL: **grovesidefarmb-b@iolfree.ie**
WEB: **www.iolfree.ie/grovesidefarmb_b**

On quiet country rd, Arable farm. TV, Hairdryer all rooms. Home baking, Restaurants. 20 mins Rosslare, Wexford, Sandy Beaches, Saltee Islands, Kilmore Quay Marina.

B&B	3	Ensuite	€25.50/€25.50	Dinner	-
B&B	-	Standard	-	Partial Board	-
Single Rate			€38.50/€38.50	Child reduction	25%

Kilmore Quay 5km

Open: 15th April-30th September

Mr Colin Campbell
WOODLANDS HOUSE
Carrigbyrne,
Co Wexford

New Ross

TEL: **051 428287**   FAX: **051 428287**
EMAIL: **woodwex@eircom.net**

Beautifully situated between Wexford and Waterford (N25). 30 Minutes to Rosslare. Tastefully refurbished. Guest lounge. Country walks. Early Breakfast. AA RAC.

B&B	4	Ensuite	€27.50/€27.50	Dinner	€19
B&B	-	Standard	-	Partial Board	-
Single Rate			€38.50/€38.50	Child reduction	-

New Ross 14km

Open: 15th March-October

Mrs Noreen Fallon
S.R.N, S.C.M.
KILLARNEY HOUSE
The Maudlins, New Ross,
Co Wexford

New Ross

TEL: **051 421062**
EMAIL: **noreenfallon@eircom.net**

Frommer recommended. Rooms ground floor. Breakfast menu. Peaceful. Electric blankets. Reduction for more than 1 night. Complimentary Tea/Coffee, Breakfast anytime. Rosslare Ferry 45 mins.

B&B	2	Ensuite	€25.50/€25.50	Dinner	-
B&B	1	Standard	€23/€23	Partial Board	-
Single Rate			€36/€38.50	Child reduction	33.3%

New Ross 2km

Open: April-September

Mrs Ann Foley
RIVERSDALE HOUSE
Lr William Street, New Ross,
Co Wexford

New Ross

TEL: **051 422515**   FAX: **051 422800**
EMAIL: **riversdalehouse@eircom.net**
WEB: **www.riversdalehouse.com**

Spacious ensuite bedrooms (one triple) with TV, Tea/Coffee, Electric blankets, Hairdryers. Parking. Sun Lounge. Gardens. Non smoking home. 5 mins walk to Town Centre.

B&B	4	Ensuite	€26/€27	Dinner	-
B&B	-	Standard	-	Partial Board	-
Single Rate			€38.50/€38.50	Child reduction	-

In New Ross

Open: 1st March-1st December

Mrs Philomena Gallagher
ROSVILLE HOUSE
Knockmullen, New Ross,
Co Wexford

New Ross

TEL: **051 421798**
EMAIL: **rosvillehouse@oceanfree.net**
WEB: **members.tripod.com/~rosvillehouse**

Modern home in peaceful surroundings. Guaranteed hospitality/comfort. Overlooking River Barrow. Rosslare Ferries 40mins. Early breakfast. Private Parking.

B&B	4	Ensuite	€25.50/€25.50	Dinner	-
B&B	1	Standard	€23/€23	Partial Board	-
Single Rate			€36/€36	Child reduction	-

New Ross 1km

Open: March-November

Susan & John Halpin
OAKWOOD HOUSE
Ring Road (N30),
Mountgarrett, New Ross,
Co Wexford

New Ross

Tel: **051 425494**   Fax: **051 425494**
Email: **susan@oakwoodhouse.net**
Web: **www.oakwoodhouse.net**

Luxury purpose built non-smoking home, with a view. Spacious bedrooms with TV, tea/coffee facilities. Irish pubs closeby. RAC ◆◆◆◆ and Sparkling Diamond award. Early breakfast.

B&B	4	Ensuite	€30/€32	Dinner	-
B&B	-	Standard	-	Partial Board	-
Single Rate			€40/€45	Child reduction	25%

New Ross 1km

Open: 1st April-31st October

Annette Kinsella
GREENPARK
Creakan Lower, New Ross,
Co Wexford

New Ross

Tel: **051 421028**   Fax: **051 421028**

Greenpark is an Olde Worlde country house. Just off the R733, 4km from New Ross. 45 mins drive from Rosslare. Peaceful rural setting. No weddings.

B&B	2	Ensuite	€28/€28	Dinner	-
B&B	1	Standard	€25/€25	Partial Board	-
Single Rate			€38/€45	Child reduction	25%

New Ross 4km

Open: 1st Febuary-30th November

Mrs Ann Kelly
DECCA HOUSE
Rosslare,
Co Wexford

Rosslare

Tel: **053 32410**
Email: **deccahouse@eircom.net**

Early breakfast. Location R740 (1km off main N25). Quiet area. Convenient Ferries. Access/Visa. Private parking.

B&B	3	Ensuite	€25.50	Dinner	-
B&B	2	Standard	€23	Partial Board	-
Single Rate			-	Child reduction	-

Rosslare 3km

Open: February-November

Sue & Neil Carty
MARIANELLA
Kilrane, Rosslare Harbour,
Co Wexford

Rosslare Harbour

Tel: **053 33139**

Comfortable bungalow on N25. 1km Ferry Port. All rooms on ground floor with TV & Tea/Coffee facilities. Guest lounge. Early breakfast. Restaurants nearby.

B&B	4	Ensuite	€25.50/€25.50	Dinner	-
B&B	2	Standard	€23/€23	Partial Board	-
Single Rate			€36/€38.50	Child reduction	33.3%

Rosslare Harbour 1km

Open: All Year Except Christmas

Kay Crean
OLD ORCHARD LODGE
Kilrane, Rosslare Harbour,
Co Wexford

Rosslare Harbour

Tel: **053 33468**
Email: **oldorchardlodge@eircom.net**
Web: **homepage.eircom.net/~oldorchardlodge/**

1km Ferry. Early breakfast available. Private Parking. All rooms ensuite, Tea/Coffee & TV. Beside good Restaurants & Pubs. On quiet country road opposite Pubs in Kilrane village.

B&B	5	Ensuite	€25.50/€25.50	Dinner	-
B&B	-	Standard	-	Partial Board	-
Single Rate			€38.50/€38.50	Child reduction	-

Rosslare Harbour 1km

Open: 1st January-23rd December

Rosslare Harbour 5km

Mrs Margaret Day
ASHLEY LODGE B&B
Ballycowan, Tagoat,
Rosslare Harbour,
Co Wexford

Rosslare Harbour
Tel: **053 31991**
Email: **ashleylodgetagoat@hotmail.com**

The house is 400 metres off the N25 to Rosslare Harbour. Turn on to R736 at Tagoat Village, Ashley Lodge is on the Right, 400 metres off N25.

B&B	4	Ensuite	€25.50/€27	Dinner	-
B&B		Standard	-	Partial Board	-
Single Rate			€38.50/€38.50	Child reduction	25%

Open: All Year Except Christmas

Wexford

Ms Helen Farrell
PADUA
Kilscoran, Tagoat,
Rosslare Harbour,
Co Wexford

Rosslare Harbour
Tel: **053 31373**

Modern family home, 1km from Rosslare Harbour on main road. Early Breakfast. Private Parking. Near to all facilities. Hairdryers in rooms. Biker's welcome.

B&B	3	Ensuite	€25.50	Dinner	-
B&B		Standard	-	Partial Board	-
Single Rate			€38.50	Child reduction	25%

Open: All Year

Rosslare Harbour 1.5km

Anne Gleeson
WAYSIDE HOUSE
Ballygeary, Kilrane,
Rosslare Harbour, Co Wexford

Rosslare Harbour
Tel: **053 33475**

Country house on quiet road off N25. 1km Rosslare Port. Rooms with shower/toilet, TV, Tea/Coffee. Private Parking. Early breakfast.

B&B	3	Ensuite	€25.50	Dinner	-
B&B		Standard	-	Partial Board	-
Single Rate			€38.50	Child reduction	50%

Open: 31st March-31st October

Rosslare Harbour

Dorothy Healy
LORANDA LODGE
Ballygillane,
Rosslare Harbour, Co Wexford

Rosslare Harbour
Tel: **053 33804**   Fax: **053 33804**
Email: **loranda@esatclear.ie**

Peaceful location 5 mins from Ferry. Early breakfast. Turn up village at Church, Supermarket on left, Railway club on right, next turn on right, house on left.

B&B	3	Ensuite	€25.50	Dinner	-
B&B		Standard	-	Partial Board	-
Single Rate			€38.50	Child reduction	50%

Open: 1st March-31st October

In Rosslare Harbour

Mr Stephen Hession
ASGARD B&B
1 The Moorings,
Rosslare Harbour,
Co Wexford

Rosslare Harbour
Tel: **053 33602**   Fax: **053 33602**
Email: **asgardbb@ireland.com**
Web: **www.asgardbb.com**

Friendly Irish Home located 500m from the Ferry Port, Bus and Train Terminals. Close to Pubs, Hotels, Restaurants and Bank. Early Breakfast. TV, rooms en-suite.

B&B	3	Ensuite	€25.50	Dinner	-
B&B		Standard	-	Partial Board	-
Single Rate			€38.50	Child reduction	33.3%

Open: 1st March-30th November

Rosslare Harbour Village 1km

Mrs Kathleen Lawlor
CARRAGH LODGE
Station Road,
Rosslare Harbour,
Co Wexford

Rosslare Harbour
Tel: 053 33492

Modern bungalow on quiet side road off N25. 3 minutes drive from Ferryport. TV, Tea & Coffee facilities.

B&B	3	Ensuite	€25.50	Dinner	-
B&B	1	Standard	€23	Partial Board	-
Single Rate			€36/€38.50	Child reduction	-

Open: 1st March-30th November

Rosslare Harbour 2km

Mrs Carmel Lonergan
CLOVER LAWN
Kilrane, Rosslare Harbour,
Co Wexford

Rosslare Harbour
Tel: 053 33413
Email: cloverlawn@eircom.net
Web: homepage.eircom.net/~cloverlawn

Highly recommended comfortable home. 1km from Ferry Port. In Kilrane Village turn left between pubs 3rd house on right. Early Breakfast. Golf, Beaches, Restaurants, Bus and Rail nearby.

B&B	2	Ensuite	€25.50/€25.50	Dinner	-
B&B	2	Standard	€23/€23	Partial Board	-
Single Rate			€36/€38.50	Child reduction	33.3%

Open: 1st March-1st November

Rosslare Harbour

Mary McDonald
OLDCOURT HOUSE
Rosslare Harbour,
Co Wexford

Rosslare Harbour
Tel: 053 33895
Email: oldcrt@gofree.indigo.ie
Web: gofree.indigo.ie/~oldcrt

Modern house overlooking Rosslare Bay. Close to Hotels & Ferryport. Early Breakfast. Golf, Beaches nearby. AA ◆◆◆◆ selected.

B&B	6	Ensuite	€25/€30	Dinner	-
B&B	-	Standard	-	Partial Board	-
Single Rate			€35/€35	Child reduction	33.3%

Open: 1st February-1st December

Rosslare Harbour 5km

Catherine McHugh
BALLYCOWAN LODGE
Tagoat, Co Wexford

Rosslare Harbour
Tel: 053 31596   Fax: 053 31596

Secluded peaceful location only 150m off N25. 5 mins to Ferry. Early Breakfast. All rooms TV & Tea/Coffee making facilities.

B&B	4	Ensuite	€25.50/€25.50	Dinner	-
B&B	-	Standard	-	Partial Board	-
Single Rate			€38.50/€38.50	Child reduction	50%

Open: All Year Except Christmas

In Rosslare Harbour

Brigid Murphy
ABRAE HOUSE
Kilrane, Rosslare Harbour,
Co Wexford

Rosslare Harbour
Tel: 053 33283   Fax: 053 33283

Luxury home on main N25. Restaurants and Tourist Amenities within walking distance. 2 mins to Ferry. Early Breakfast.

B&B	4	Ensuite	€25.50/€28.50	Dinner	-
B&B	-	Standard	-	Partial Board	-
Single Rate			-	Child reduction	-

Open: 2nd January-23rd December

Rosslare Harbour 1km

Mrs Dorothy O'Brien
BORO LODGE
Kilrane, Rosslare Harbour,
Co Wexford

Rosslare Harbour
Tel: **053 33610**

Modern bungalow 200ms off main N25 at Kilrane. 3mins drive from Ferry & Rail. Convenient to Golf, Beach, Bus, Restaurant. Early breakfast. Private parking.

B&B	2	Ensuite	€25.50/€25.50	Dinner -
B&B	2	Standard	€23/€23	Partial Board -
Single Rate			-	Child reduction -

Open: 1st February-31st October

In Rosslare Harbour

Mr & Mrs D O'Donoghue
LAUREL LODGE
Rosslare Harbour,
Co Wexford

Rosslare Harbour
Tel: **053 33291**

Comfortable home on quiet road off Rosslare Harbour Village. 1km from Ferry. Within walking distance of 3 Hotels.

B&B	4	Ensuite	€25.50/€25.50	Dinner -
B&B	-	Standard		Partial Board -
Single Rate			€38.50/€38.50	Child reduction -

Open: 1st March-31st October

In Rosslare Harbour

Ann O'Dwyer
AILESBURY
5 The Moorings,
Rosslare Harbour, Co Wexford

Rosslare Harbour
Tel: **053 33185**   Fax: **053 33185**
Email: **ailesb@eircom.net**

Comfortable home. Closest B&B on N25 to Ferryport, Rail/Bus terminals. Restaurants nearby. AA listed, Orthopaedic beds, Hairdryers. Early breakfast. Secure garage for motorcycles/bicycles.

B&B	3	Ensuite	€25.50/€29	Dinner -
B&B	1	Standard		Partial Board -
Single Rate			€36/€42	Child reduction -

Open: 1st March-15th November

In Rosslare

Ms Una Stack
DUNGARA B&B
Kilrane, Rosslare Harbour,
Co Wexford

Rosslare Harbour
Tel: **053 33391**   Fax: **053 33391**
Email: **unastack@eircom.net**

Comfortable home with friendly atmosphere on N25. 1km to Ferry. TV, Electric Blankets, Tea/Coffee in rooms. Early Breakfast. Shops and Restaurants nearby.

B&B	5	Ensuite	€25.50/€25.50	Dinner -
B&B	1	Standard	€23	Partial Board -
Single Rate			€38	Child reduction 50%

Open: 1st January-23rd December

Rosslare Harbour 2km

Ms Siobhan Whitehead
KILRANE HOUSE
Kilrane, Rosslare Harbour,
Co Wexford

Rosslare Harbour
Tel: **053 33135**   Fax: **053 33739**
Email: **florrieo@eircom.net**

Period house. Many original features, superb ornate. Guest lounge. Opposite Pub, Restaurants. 3 mins drive from Ferry. Recommended by many guides.

B&B	6	Ensuite	€25.50/€28	Dinner -
B&B	-	Standard	-	Partial Board -
Single Rate			€38.50/€45	Child reduction 33.3%

Open: 1st January-23rd December

James F Cahill
ARD RUADH MANOR
Spawell Road, Wexford,
Co Wexford

Wexford
Tel: **053 23194**   Fax: **053 23194**
Email: **ardruadh@hotmail.com**
Web: **ardruadh-manor.com**

Luxurious Victorian house (1893). One acre private gardens. Beside all amenities. AA ◆◆◆◆ selected. Ferry 15mins. 3 mins walk to Town Centre. Sea views.

B&B	6	Ensuite	€26/€40	Dinner	-
B&B	-	Standard	-	Partial Board	-
Single Rate			€38.50/€52	Child reduction	-

Wexford

Open: All Year

Peter & Mary Caulfield
NEWTOWN HOUSE
Newtown Road, Wexford,
Co Wexford

Wexford
Tel: **053 43253**

Luxurious family home on elevated site. Scenic view, convenient to Beaches, Golf, Fishing and Horseriding. Ideal tourists base for Wexford.

B&B	3	Ensuite	€25.50/€27	Dinner	-
B&B	1	Standard	€23/€27	Partial Board	-
Single Rate			€36/€38.09	Child reduction	25%

Wexford 2.5km

Open: 1st January-22nd December

Ms Grainne Cullen
GRANVILLE HOUSE
Clonard Road, Wexford,
Co Wexford

Wexford
Tel: **053 22648**
Email: **emmetcullen@eircom.net**
Web: **www.accomodationireland.net**

Luxury accomodation in warm friendly family home surrounded by award winning gardens. Interior designed to the highest standards. Close to N11 and N25.

B&B	6	Ensuite	€26/€32	Dinner	-
B&B	-	Standard	-	Partial Board	-
Single Rate			€32/€38	Child reduction	-

Wexford 1.5km

Open: February-December

Mrs Angela Doocey
TOWNPARKS HOUSE
Coolcotts, Wexford,
Co Wexford

Wexford
Tel: **053 45191**

Purpose-built Georgian house off R769. 10mins walk Town Centre. 20mins Rosslare Ferries. Tea/Coffee facilities, Clock Radios, Hairdryers. Early Breakfast.

B&B	4	Ensuite	€27/€28	Dinner	-
B&B	1	Standard	€27/€28	Partial Board	-
Single Rate			€38/€40	Child reduction	33.3%

In Wexford

Open: All Year Except Christmas

Mrs Jackie Dooley
THE BROMLEY
Country House,
Coolcotts Lane, Wexford,
Co Wexford

Wexford
Tel: **053 46222**   Fax: **053 46222**
Email: **thebromley@eircom.net**

Magnificent country house, spacious bedrooms tastefully decorated. Peaceful scenic surroundings. 2 mins Wexford Town, 15 mins Rosslare Harbour/Beach.

B&B	3	Ensuite	€26/€32	Dinner	-
B&B	-	Standard	-	Partial Board	-
Single Rate			€38.50/€44	Child reduction	50%

Open: 3rd January-20th December

Mrs Maureen Gurhy
LITTLE ASH
Glenville Road, Clonard,
Co Wexford

Wexford
Tel: **053 41475**

Warm friendly home surrounded by 1 acre of beautiful gardens. Family rooms, Electric blankets, Hairdryers. Ferry 15 mins. Early Breakfasts. N25/N11 roundabout (R769).

B&B	3	Ensuite	€25.50/€30	Dinner	-
B&B	1	Standard		Partial Board	-
Single Rate			€36/€40	Child reduction	**50%**

Wexford 2km

Open: 1st January-23rd December

Mrs Maureen Keogh
ELMLEIGH
Coolcots, Wexford Town,
Co Wexford

Wexford
Tel: **053 44174**
Email: **maureen.keogh@oceanfree.net**

Modern home in peaceful residential area. Secure parking. Guests garden. Family rooms. 1 minute from N11/N25. 10 mins walk to Town Centre. 20 mins to Ferry, Rosslare.

B&B	3	Ensuite	€25.50/€25.50	Dinner	-
B&B	1	Standard	€23/€23	Partial Board	-
Single Rate			€36/€36	Child reduction	**33.3%**

Wexford Town

Open: 6th January-20th December

Ms Sarah I Lee
ROCKCLIFFE
Coolballo, Wexford,
Co Wexford

Wexford
Tel: **053 43130**
Email: **sarahlee@ireland.com**

Lovely landscaped garden on 1 acre. Scenic views. Frommer Recommended. N25 from Rosslare Harbour through roundabout towards Wexford. R730 Junction left after "Farmers Kitchen".

B&B	3	Ensuite	€25.40/€25.40	Dinner	-
B&B	1	Standard	€22.86/€22.86	Partial Board	-
Single Rate			€31.87/€31.87	Child reduction	-

Wexford 3km

Open: 1st April-31st October

Ms Mary D Moore
ROCKVILLE
Rocklands,
Wexford Town, Co Wexford

Wexford
Tel: **053 22147**   Fax: **053 22147**
Email: **marydm@indigo.ie**

Comfortable home, quiet location. Southern fringe Wexford town (R730). Private parking, secluded gardens. Walking distance Town Centre. Ferry 15 minutes.

B&B	3	Ensuite	€25.50/€25.50	Dinner	-
B&B	1	Standard	€23/€23	Partial Board	-
Single Rate			€38.50/€38.50	Child reduction	**25%**

In Wexford

Open: 1st January-20th December

Mrs Fionnuala Murphy
THE GALLOPS B&B
Bettyville, Newtown Road,
Wexford, Co Wexford

Wexford
Tel: **053 44035**   Fax: **053 44950**

Beautiful home architecturally designed, excellent accommodation. Tea/Coffee, TV's, Hairdryers. Overlooking garden. Scenic views. Early breakfast. 1mile Town centre. Private Car park.

B&B	4	Ensuite	€32/€35	Dinner	-
B&B	-	Standard		Partial Board	-
Single Rate			€38.50/€44	Child reduction	**50%**

Wexford 2km

Open: 2nd January-20th December

Wexford 4km

Nicholas & Kathleen Murphy
GLENHILL
**Ballygoman, Barntown,
Co Wexford**

Wexford
Tel: **053 20015**

Modern home peaceful surroundings. Guaranteed hospitality. On N25 15 mins Rosslare Ferries. Early breakfast. Private car park. Ferrycarrig 2km. Wexford 4km.

B&B	3	Ensuite	€25.50 /€26	Dinner	-
B&B	-	Standard	-	Partial Board	-
Single Rate			-	Child reduction	25%

Open: 1st January-20th December

Mrs Kathleen Nolan
DARRAL HOUSE
**Spawell Road, Wexford,
Co Wexford**

Wexford
Tel: **053 24264**   Fax: **053 24284**

Beautiful period house (1803). Luxury accommodation. AA ◆◆◆◆. Wexford Town centre 3 mins walk, Car Ferry 15 mins. Private car park.

B&B	4	Ensuite	€26/€38	Dinner	-
B&B	-	Standard	-	Partial Board	-
Single Rate			€32/€45	Child reduction	-

Open: 1st January-20th December

In Wexford

David & Mary O'Brien
AUBURN HOUSE
**2 Auburn Tce, Redmond Road,
Wexford, Co Wexford**

Wexford
Tel: **053 23605**   Fax: **053 42725**
Email: **mary@obriensauburnhouse.com**
Web: **www.obriensauburnhouse.com**

Built in 1891, our elegantly restored townhouse offers excellent accommodation. Rooms are charming and spacious, many enjoying a view of the River Slaney.

B&B	4	Ensuite	€32.50/€32.50	Dinner	-
B&B	1	Standard	€30/€32.50	Partial Board	-
Single Rate			€38/€40	Child reduction	-

Open: 2nd January-18th December

In Wexford

Mrs Ellen O'Connor
BROMPTON
**Newtown Road,
Wexford, Co Wexford**

Wexford
Tel: **053 40863**   Fax: **053 40863**

Luxury home, rooms ensuite tea/coffee. Private parking. Sitting room & garden. 10 mins walk Town Centre, 15mins car ferry, close to race course & heritage centre.

B&B	3	Ensuite	€25.50/€28	Dinner	-
B&B	1	Standard	€23/€25.50	Partial Board	-
Single Rate			€36/€38	Child reduction	-

Open: All Year

In Wexford

Mrs Breda O'Grady
VILLA MARIA
**Ivy Lane, Coolcots,
Wexford, Co Wexford**

Wexford
Tel: **053 45143**

Modern bungalow in private cul-de-sac. Convenient Heritage Park, Golf, Rosslare Ferry. Tea/Coffee facilities & TV in bedrooms, early Breakfast.

B&B	3	Ensuite	€25.50/€28	Dinner	-
B&B	1	Standard	€23/€25.50	Partial Board	-
Single Rate			-	Child reduction	33.3%

Open: 7th January-22nd December

Ms Margaret Redmond
FERRYCARRIG LODGE
Park, Ferrycarrig Road,
Wexford

Wexford

Tel: **053 42605** Fax: **053 42606**
Email: **ferrycarrig@wexford-accommodation.com**
Web: **www.wexford-accommodation.com**

Charming, relaxing residence, nestled on riverbank. Individually designed rooms, 10 min walk Heritage Park, Hotel, Quality Restaurants, Ferries 15 mins.

B&B	4	Ensuite	€32/€38	Dinner	-
B&B	-	Standard	-	Partial Board	-
Single Rate			€38.50/€45	Child reduction	50%

Wexford 2km

Open: All Year

Mrs Catherine Saunderson
FARRANSEER HOUSE
Coolcots, Wexford,
Co Wexford

Wexford

Tel: **053 44042**

Spacious home in Wexford Town. Landscaped grounds. Convenient to local amenities. TV bedrooms and lounge. Tea/Coffee facilities. Early Breakfast.

B&B	2	Ensuite	€27/€28	Dinner	-
B&B	2	Standard	€25.39/€25.39	Partial Board	-
Single Rate			€38/€40	Child reduction	-

In Wexford

Open: All Year

Ms Imelda Scallan
THE BLUE DOOR B&B
18 Lower George Street,
Wexford, Co Wexford

Wexford

Tel: **053 21047**
Email: **bluedoor@indigo.ie**
Web: **www.thebluedoorwexford.com**

Luxury accommodation in Georgian Townhouse. Views of Westgate Castle. Beside traditional Irish music Pubs, Restaurants, Shops. Bus/Rail 2 mins walk. Opposite Whites Hotel.

B&B	4	Ensuite	€30/€35	Dinner	-
B&B	-	Standard	-	Partial Board	-
Single Rate			€35/€40	Child reduction	50%

In Wexford

Open: All Year

Eamonn & Margaret Sreenan
MAPLE LODGE
Ballycrane, Castlebridge,
Co Wexford

Wexford

Tel: **053 59195** Fax: **053 59195**
Email: **sreenan@tinet.ie**
Web: **gofree.indigo.ie/~mapleldg**

Tea & Scones await you in our home on R741. 4km Wexford, 6km Curracloe Beach, 20 mins Rosslare Port. Breakfast menu. Home baking. AA ♦♦♦♦. Award winning gardens. Golf arranged.

B&B	4	Ensuite	€28/€32	Dinner	-
B&B	-	Standard	-	Partial Board	-
Single Rate			€39/€45	Child reduction	25%

Wexford 4km

Open: 1st March-1st November

Mrs Christina Toomey
BEDFORD HOUSE
Ballymorris, Clonard,
Wexford, Co Wexford

Wexford

Tel: **053 45643**
Email: **bedford@eircom.net**

Situated on Duncannon New Line Road (R733) 0.5 kms off N25. 15 mins Rosslare Ferry. Early breakfast. Large family room.

B&B	4	Ensuite	€25.50/€28.50	Dinner	-
B&B	-	Standard	-	Partial Board	-
Single Rate			€38.50/€38.50	Child reduction	50%

Wexford 3km

Open: All Year Except Christmas

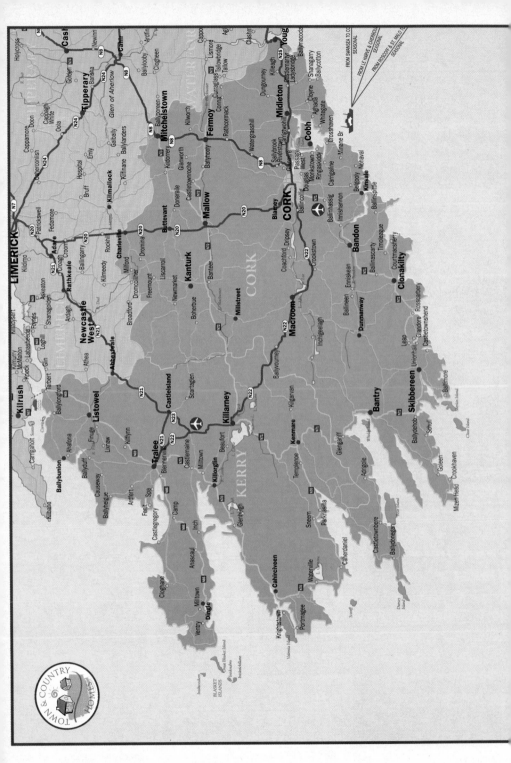

Cork / Kerry

Located in the south-west corner of Ireland, the Cork and South Kerry region offers its visitors a great diversity of scenery, culture and leisure activities. The region claims some of the most varied and spectacular scenery in the country. Here you will find the full range of holiday options to ensure a memorable, refreshing and very different holiday.

The South Western coastline, sculptured by the ice-age and influenced by the warm waters of the Gulf Stream, is steeped in ancient history and folklore from the East and West Cork coasts, The Beara and Dingle Peninsulas, and from the Ring of Kerry to the Lakes of Killarney and the Bandon, Lee and Blackwater Valleys.

Ross Castle, Killarney

Some of Ireland's best international festivals are hosted in the region and attractions for all the family, guarantees a fun filled holiday.

Area Representatives

CORK
Mrs Georgina Coughlan, Glebe House, Tay Road, Cobh, Co Cork
Tel: 021 4811373 Fax: 021 4811373
Ms Peggie Downing, Bru na Pairce, 7 Slip Park, Bantry, Co Cork
Tel: 027 51603
Ms Patricia Blanchfield, Blanchfield House, Rigsdale (Cork/Bandon N71)
Halfway, Ballinahassig, Co Cork
Tel: 021 4885167 Fax: 021 4885805
KERRY
Mrs Noreen Dineen, Manor House, 18 Whitebridge Manor,
Ballycasheen, Killarney, Co Kerry
Tel: 064 32716 Fax: 064 32716
Mrs Margaret Ryle, Crana-Li, Greenlawn, Blennerville,
Tralee, Co Kerry Tel: 066 7124467
Mrs Margaret Brown, Old Cable House, Cable Station, Waterville, Co Kerry
Tel: 066 9474233 Fax: 066 9474869

Tourist Information Offices
OPEN ALL YEAR
Cork
Aras Failte, Grand Parade
Tel: 021 4273251

Blarney
Tel: 021 4381624

Killarney
Beech Road
Tel: 064 31633

Skibbereen
Town Hall
Tel: 028 21766

Refer to page 121 for information

Cork, the southern capital, Ireland's largest county. West Cork warmed by the Gulf stream with spectacular scenic beauty. Experience the tranquillity of East Cork with its sandy beaches. Get lost in nature in North Cork through rolling hills and valleys.

In Ballincollig

Mrs Rose Cotter
WESTFIELD HOUSE
West Village, Ballincollig,
Co Cork

Ballincollig
TEL: **021 4871824**   FAX: **021 4877415**
EMAIL: **rosecotter@tinet.ie**

Welcoming Tea/Coffee on arrival. Modern house, adjacent Ballincollig main Cork/Killarney N22. On bus route, convenient Blarney, Airport, Ferry, Dogtrack.

B&B	2	Ensuite	€26/€28	Dinner	-
B&B	1	Standard	€23/€25	Partial Board	-
Single Rate			€36/€38	Child reduction	25%

Open: 1st January-23rd December

Ballincollig 2km

Mrs Maureen Cronin
THE MILESTONE
Ovens, Ballincollig,
Co Cork

Ballincollig
TEL: **021 4872562**   FAX: **021 4872562**
EMAIL: **milestone@eircom.net**

AA ◆◆◆ Award. On N22 road, Ballincollig 2km. Tea/Coffee/Hairdryer in large rooms. Warm welcome. Highly commended. Central, Airport-Ferry-Cork-Blarney-Kinsale-Cobh.

B&B	5	Ensuite	€26/€28	Dinner	-
B&B	-	Standard		Partial Board	-
Single Rate			€38.50/€38.50	Child reduction	25%

Open: 8th January-20th December

Ballincollig 11.5km

John & Elizabeth Plaice
MUSKERRY HOUSE
Farnanes, Co Cork

Ballincollig
TEL: **021 7336469**   FAX: **021 7336469**

Cork/Killarney road N22. Entry from N22/R619 intersection. Ballincollig 11.5km. Spacious rooms, full bathrooms. Central - Airport, Ferry, Blarney, West Cork and Kerry. Restaurant 5 min.

B&B	6	Ensuite	€28/€28	Dinner	-
B&B	-	Standard	-	Partial Board	-
Single Rate			€39/€39	Child reduction	25%

Open: 16th January-20th December

Kinsale 14km

Ms Patricia Blanchfield
BLANCHFIELD HOUSE
Rigsdale (Cork/Bandon N71),
Halfway, Ballinahassig,
Co Cork

Ballinhassig Kinsale
TEL: **021 4885167**   FAX: **021 4885805**
EMAIL: **blanchfield@eircom.net**

Period country home on N71, near City Airport, Ferry Port, Kinsale. Good tour base West Cork/Kerry. Private Salmon, Trout Fishing. AA ◆◆. Breakfast/Dinner menus.

B&B	2	Ensuite	€25.50/€35	Dinner	€25
B&B	4	Standard	€23/€30	Partial Board	€329
Single Rate			€36/€45	Child reduction	25%

Open: 1st January-8th December

248

Mrs Anna Casey
SUNVILLE HOUSE
Sunville, Ballycotton,
Co Cork

Ballycotton
TEL: 021 4646271

Sea and shore angling. Salmon rivers. Bird sanctuary. 5 min from beach. Tranquil setting near Ballycotton. Lovely cliff walks. Sun lounge. Home baking. A warm welcome.

B&B	3	Ensuite	€25.50/€31.74	Dinner	-
B&B	-	Standard		Partial Board	-
Single Rate			€38.50/€38.50	Child reduction	33.3%

Ballycotton 3km

Open: All Year

Mrs Margaret Harrington
CHANNEL VIEW
Baltimore, Co Cork

Baltimore
TEL: 028 20440
EMAIL: channelview@eircom.net

Spacious Dormer Bungalow, private car park, spectacular views overlooking the Bay. Sailing, Fishing, Island Trips, Diving, Scenic Walks, Golf, Tea/Coffee facilities.

B&B	5	Ensuite	€26/€30	Dinner	-
B&B	-	Standard		Partial Board	-
Single Rate			€40/€50	Child reduction	33.3%

In Baltimore

Open: March-October

Marguerite O'Driscoll
RATHMORE HOUSE
Baltimore, Co Cork

Baltimore
TEL: 028 20362   FAX: 028 20362
EMAIL: rathmorehouse@eircom.net

Rathmore house, overlooking harbour and islands, is the perfect place to relax and unwind. An area of understated beauty. A warm welcome awaits you.

B&B	6	Ensuite	€26	Dinner	€17
B&B	-	Standard		Partial Board	€270
Single Rate			€35	Child reduction	50%

Baltimore 2km

Open: All Year

Mrs Anne Buckley
ST ANNE'S
Clonakilty Road, Bandon,
Co Cork

Bandon
TEL: 023 44239   FAX: 023 44239
EMAIL: stannesbandon@eircom.net

Georgian house. Walled gardens. Near Town Centre. Convenient to Golf, Beaches, Fishing and Walking. Teamaking facilities. Airport 16 miles.

B&B	6	Ensuite	€27/€28	Dinner	-
B&B	-	Standard		Partial Board	-
Single Rate			€38.50/€38.50	Child reduction	33.3%

Bandon 1km

Open: All Year Except Christmas

Mrs Carmel Nash
RIVERVIEW
7 Riverview Estate, Bandon,
Co Cork

Bandon
TEL: 023 41080   FAX: 023 41607
EMAIL: nashf@indigo.ie

Friendly relaxed home edge of town. Scenic views. 30 mins to Airport, Ferry. Convenient Golf, Beaches and Kinsale. Ideal touring West Cork, Kerry.

B&B	4	Ensuite	€27/€28	Dinner	-
B&B	-	Standard		Partial Board	-
Single Rate			€38.50	Child reduction	-

In Bandon

Open: All Year

249

Bandon 1km

Mrs Theresa O'Connor
ASHGROVE HOUSE
Castle Road, Bandon,
Co Cork

Bandon
TEL: 023 41033

Patio back and front, 5 minutes from Town Centre. House on Golf Club road. Beach 6km from House. Kinsale 20km.

			Dinner	-
B&B	4	Ensuite	€26.66/€31.74	Partial Board	-
B&B	-	Standard	-	Child reduction	-
Single Rate			€38.50/€38.50		

Open: All Year

In Bandon

Kathleen O'Donovan
AR NEAMH
Knockbrogan, Bandon,
Co Cork

Bandon
TEL: 023 41129
EMAIL: arneamh@yahoo.com

New dormer style house built on private site with landscaped garden.

				Dinner	-
B&B	4	Ensuite	€31.74	Partial Board	-
B&B	-	Standard	-	Child reduction	-
Single Rate			€38.50		

Open: 1st January-23rd December

In Bandon

Ms Mary Rose O'Donovan
FLORAVILLE
Mill Place, Bandon,
Co Cork

Bandon
TEL: 023 42232

Georgian town house, beautiful gardens, centre of Bandon. Antique furnishings. Power showers, some with jacuzzi bath. Guest lounge. Car park.

				Dinner	-
B&B	2	Ensuite	€32/€39	Partial Board	-
B&B	-	Standard	-	Child reduction	33.3%
Single Rate			€39/€50		

Open: 1st January-20th December

In Bantry

Mrs Eileen Andrews
FERNDEENE
4 Slip Lawn, Bantry,
Co Cork

Bantry
TEL: 027 50146   FAX: 027 50146
BUS NO: 8

Warm hospitality in comfortable home off N71. Menu. Private car park. Bicycle garage. Tea/Coffee, TV in bedrooms. Credit Cards. Ideal touring West Cork/Kerry.

				Dinner	-
B&B	3	Ensuite	€26	Partial Board	-
B&B	-	Standard	-	Child reduction	25%
Single Rate			€38.50		

Open: 1st March-31st October

Bantry 3km

Mrs Genny Dooley
ATLANTIC VIEW
Gurteenroe, Bantry,
Co Cork

Bantry
TEL: 027 51221

Superb Sea and Mountain views, secluded and peaceful location with attractive gardens. Beside Golf club. Bantry/Glengarriff road N71. Private car parking.

				Dinner	-
B&B	3	Ensuite	€26/€26	Partial Board	-
B&B	-	Standard	-	Child reduction	25%
Single Rate			€39/€39		

Open: March-October

Ms Peggie Downing
BRU NA PAIRCE
7 Slip Park, Bantry,
Co Cork

Bantry
TEL: **027 51603**

Modern home quiet locality, overlooking Caha mountains. 5 minutes walk from Town. Centre of West Cork and South Kerry.

B&B	2	Ensuite	€26/€26	Dinner	-
B&B	1	Standard	-	Partial Board	-
Single Rate			€36/€36	Child reduction	25%

Open: 1st January-23rd December

Maggie Doyle
ATLANTIC SHORE
Newtown, Bantry,
Co Cork

Bantry
TEL: **027 51310**   FAX: **027 52175**
EMAIL: **divebantry@aol.com**

A spacious purpose built bungalow with a panoramic view of Bantry Bay. 50 metres past 30mph speed sign off Bantry/Glengarriff road N71.

B&B	5	Ensuite	€26	Dinner	-
B&B	1	Standard	€23	Partial Board	-
Single Rate			€36	Child reduction	25%

Bantry 1km

Open: 1st March-30th November

Mrs Phyllis Foley
ARD NA GREINE
Newtown, Bantry,
Co Cork

Bantry
TEL: **027 51169**   FAX: **027 51169**
WEB: **www.dirl.com/cork/ard-na-greine.htm**

Country home, peaceful scenic setting overlooking nature gardens & countryside. One mile Bantry. Off N71 off Glengarriff/Killarney Rd. House signs on main N71 Rd.

B&B	4	Ensuite	€27/€28	Dinner	-
B&B	-	Standard		Partial Board	-
Single Rate			€40/€46	Child reduction	25%

Bantry 1km

Open: 1st March-30th November

Mrs Brenda Harrington
LEYTON
23 Slip Lawn, Bantry,
Co Cork

Bantry
TEL: **027 50665**
EMAIL: **leyton@iolfree.ie**

Friendly relaxing home, quiet area. Breakfast menu. Car park. Bicycle garage. Off N71. Signposted at junction Glengarriff Rd end of Bantry Town. 5 mins to Town Centre.

B&B	3	Ensuite	€25.50	Dinner	-
B&B	1	Standard	€23	Partial Board	-
Single Rate			€37.50	Child reduction	25%

In Bantry

Open: April-October

Mrs Sheila Harrington
ELMWOOD HOUSE
6 Slip Lawn, Bantry,
Co Cork

Bantry
TEL: **027 50087**

Warm friendly home off main road. Tea/Cakes on arrival, Town 5 minutes. Turf fire, Bicycle garage. Archivist. Off N71. Signposted end of Town near Peace Park.

B&B	2	Ensuite	€25.50	Dinner	-
B&B	2	Standard	€23	Partial Board	-
Single Rate			-	Child reduction	50%

In Bantry

Open: All Year

Ms Tosca Kramer
THE MILL
Newtown, Bantry,
Co Cork

Tel: **027 50278**   Fax: **027 50278**
Email: **bbthemill@eircom.net**
Bus No: **8**

Well established accommodation, (N71) Bantry (1km), AA◆◆◆, RAC, highly recommended. Own art on display. All rooms with TV. Laundry service.

B&B	6	Ensuite	€25/€30	Dinner	-
B&B	-	Standard	-	Partial Board	-
Single Rate			€45/€50	Child reduction	25%

Bantry 1km

Open: 1st April-31st October

Kathleen Lynch
AVOCA HOUSE
Durrus, Bantry, Co Cork

Tel: **027 61511**   Fax: **027 61511**
Email: **avoca@emara.com**

Situated in Durrus village. Avoca House offers a warm welcome and a good breakfast menu. Ideally situated for touring Sheeps Head & Mizen Head Penninsula's.

B&B	4	Ensuite	€25.50/€25.50	Dinner	€17
B&B	-	Standard	-	Partial Board	-
Single Rate			€38.50/€38.50	Child reduction	25%

Bantry 10km

Open: 1st January-20th December

Siobhan Lynch
LA MIRAGE
Droumdaniel, Ballylickey,
Bantry, Co Cork

Tel: **027 50688**
Email: **lamirage@eircom.net**

Elevated spacious country home, overlooking Bantry Bay. Peaceful location, friendly atmosphere, Tea/Coffee, home baking on arrival, off N71.

B&B	2	Ensuite	€25.50/€28	Dinner	-
B&B	2	Standard	€23/€25	Partial Board	-
Single Rate			€36/€42	Child reduction	25%

Bantry 4km

Open: April-September

Ms Mary C McCarthy
TIROROA
Gurteenroe, Near Ballylickey,
Bantry, Co Cork

Tel: **027 50287**
Bus No: **8**

On Bantry/Glengarriff road (N71). Panoramic view Lake, Sea, Mountains. Ideal for touring Ring of Beara and Mizen Head. Tea/Coffee, TV in rooms. Credit cards.

B&B	3	Ensuite	€26	Dinner	-
B&B	-	Standard	-	Partial Board	-
Single Rate			€38.50	Child reduction	25%

Bantry 4km

Open: 9th March-31st October

Mrs Cait Murray
ROCKLANDS
Gurteenroe, Bantry,
Co Cork

Tel: **027 50212**
Bus No: **8**

Modern Bungalow on Bantry/Glengarriff Rd. N71. Magnificent views Bantry Bay, Lake, Sea, Mountains. Tea/Coffee, home baking on arrival. Private parking. Close to all tourist amenities.

B&B	3	Ensuite	€25.50/€28	Dinner	-
B&B	-	Standard	-	Partial Board	-
Single Rate			€36/€42	Child reduction	25%

Bantry 4km

Open: March-September

Mrs Kathleen O'Donovan
ASHLING
Cahir, Bantry,
Co Cork

Bantry
Tel: **027 50616**

Bungalow with panoramic views of Bantry Bay and Caha Mountains. Ideally situated for touring or relaxing. Private parking. Close to 18 hole Golf course.

B&B	3	Ensuite	€26	Dinner	-
B&B	1	Standard	€23	Partial Board	-
Single Rate			€39	Child reduction	25%

Bantry 3km

Open: 1st May-30th September

Mrs Breda O'Regan
SUNVILLE
Newtown, Bantry,
Co Cork

Bantry
Tel: **027 50175**

Bungalow situated in select area, 5 minutes walk to Town and Sea. Family run. Close to all tourist amenities.

B&B	3	Ensuite	€26/€26	Dinner	-
B&B	1	Standard	€23/€23	Partial Board	-
Single Rate			-	Child reduction	33.3%

In Bantry

Open: May-October

Mrs Margaret O'Sullivan
PARK VIEW
Newtown, Bantry,
Co Cork

Bantry
Tel: **027 51174**   Fax: **027 51174**
Bus No: **8**

Modern home, ideal touring centre. On main Bantry Glengarriff (N71). Beaches, Golf, Fishing, Horse Riding convenient. Scenic drives. Choice of breakfast.

B&B	2	Ensuite	€25.50/€25.50	Dinner	-
B&B	2	Standard	€23/€23	Partial Board	-
Single Rate			€36	Child reduction	25%

Bantry 1km

Open: All Year

Vincent & Margaret O'Sullivan
SONAMAR
Dromleigh South, Bantry,
Co Cork

Bantry
Tel: **027 50502**
Email: **sonamar@iol.ie**

Distinctive bungalow with extensive gardens, overlooking town, unsurpassed view of Bantry Bay. Scenic walks, quiet location. Signposted from the square.

B&B	3	Ensuite	€26/€26	Dinner	-
B&B	2	Standard	€23/€23	Partial Board	-
Single Rate			€36/€39	Child reduction	-

Bantry 2km

Open: 1st May-30th September

Ursula Schiesser
SHANGRI-LA
Glengarriff Road,
Newtown/Bantry,
Co Cork

Bantry
Tel: **027 50244**   Fax: **027 50244**
Email: **schiesserbb@eircom.net**

Bungalow with spectacular views of Bantry Bay. Spacious garden. Tea/Coffee making facilities. Credit Cards welcome, Golf nearby. German/French spoken.

B&B	6	Ensuite	€28/€28	Dinner	€18
B&B	-	Standard		Partial Board	-
Single Rate			€38.50/€38.50	Child reduction	25%

In Bantry

Open: 15th February-15th November

Mrs Joan Sweeney
HIGHFIELD
Newtown, Bantry, Co Cork

Bantry
TEL: **027 50791**
EMAIL: **highfieldbantry@eircom.net**
BUS NO: **7**

Situated on main Bantry/Glengarriff Road. Overlooking Bantry Bay. Electric blankets, hairdryers available. Garage for bicycles. Close to all amenities.

B&B	4	Ensuite	€25.50	Dinner	-
B&B	-	Standard	-	Partial Board	-
Single Rate			€38.50	Child reduction	50%

Bantry 1km

Open: 28th March-30th October

Helen Allcorn
ALLCORN'S COUNTRY HOME
Shournagh Road, Blarney,
Co Cork

Blarney
TEL: **021 4385577** FAX: **021 4382828**
EMAIL: **info@allcorns.com**
WEB: **www.allcorns.com**

Really spacious country home/gardens beside Shournagh river. Surrounded by mature woods and meadows. Just off R617 Blarney/Killarney Road.

B&B	3	Ensuite	€27/€30	Dinner	-
B&B	1	Standard	-	Partial Board	-
Single Rate			€36/€38	Child reduction	25%

Blarney 2km

Open: April-October

Mrs Veronica Annis-Sisk
YVORY HOUSE
Killowen, Blarney,
Co Cork

Blarney
TEL: **021 4381128**
EMAIL: **yvoryhouse@hotmail.com**

Modern luxury bungalow in scenic farming location. Horseriding, Golf, Music locally, TV in bedrooms, Tea/Coffee facilities. 1km off Blarney/Killarney Rd. (R617)

B&B	2	Ensuite	€26/€28	Dinner	-
B&B	1	Standard	€24/€24	Partial Board	-
Single Rate			€36/€41	Child reduction	25%

Blarney 1km

Open: April-November

Mrs Mary Buckley
LAURISTON
Coolowen, Blarney,
Co Cork

Blarney
TEL: **021 4381007**

Luxury bungalow in landscaped gardens. Located on second crossroad, on Station road. All rooms with TV, Hairdryers, Tea/Coffee. Cork City 10 mins, Blarney 5 mins. Private parking.

B&B	2	Ensuite	€25.50/€29.20	Dinner	-
B&B	1	Standard	€23/€25.50	Partial Board	-
Single Rate			€36	Child reduction	25%

Blarney 2km

Open: 1st March-30th November

Mrs Philomena Bugler
LYNVARA
Killard, Blarney, Co Cork

Blarney
TEL: **021 4385429**

Modern home, bedrooms on ground floor. Private parking. Heating, Tea/Coffee, Hairdryers. Breakfast menu. Cork 5 miles, Airport 9 miles. Walking distance to Blarney.

B&B	2	Ensuite	€26/€28	Dinner	-
B&B	1	Standard	€24/€25	Partial Board	-
Single Rate			€38/€38	Child reduction	25%

Blarney 1km

Open: 1st April-14th November

Pat & Regina Coughlan
THE WHITE HOUSE
Shean Lower,
Blarney, Co Cork

Blarney
TEL: **021 4385338**
EMAIL: **info@thewhitehouseblarney.com**
WEB: **www.thewhitehouseblarney.com**

Well heated luxurious home, overlooking Castle. All rooms with Satellite TV, Tea/coffee facilities, hairdryers. AA ◆◆◆◆ selected. Breakfast menu.

B&B	6	Ensuite	€28/€31	Dinner	-
B&B	-	Standard	-	Partial Board	-
Single Rate			€40/€50	Child reduction	25%

In Blarney

Open: 7th January-20th December

Mrs Anne Cremin
ASHCROFT
Stoneview, Blarney,
Co Cork

Blarney
TEL: **021 4385224**
EMAIL: **ashcroft@iol.ie**
WEB: **www.iol.ie/~ashcroft**

Ashcroft offers magnificent views of Blarney Castle and Golf course. Rooms with TV, Tea/Coffee, Hairdryers and Power Showers. Breakfast menu. Follow signs for Blarney Golf course.

B&B	4	Ensuite	€25.50/€30	Dinner	-
B&B	-	Standard	-	Partial Board	-
Single Rate			€38.50/€40.63	Child reduction	25%

Blarney 1.5km

Open: 1st February-30th November

Fran & Tony Cronin
HILLVIEW HOUSE
Killard, Blarney, Co Cork

Blarney
TEL: **021 4385161**
EMAIL: **hillview_blarney@yahoo.co.uk**
WEB: **www.blarneyaccommodation.com**

Beautiful view. Ground floor rooms. Car park. Sun Lounge. Pressurised showers, Cable TV, Hairdryers. Extensive Breakfast Menu. Walking distance to Blarney.

B&B	4	Ensuite	€26/€28	Dinner	-
B&B	-	Standard	-	Partial Board	-
Single Rate			€38.50/€41	Child reduction	25%

Blarney 1km

Open: 7th January-15th December

Mrs Mary Falvey
CUANAN HOUSE
12 Castle Close Road,
Blarney, Co Cork

Blarney
TEL: **021 4385329**
EMAIL: **cuanan@iname.com**

Family run comfortable home. Refreshments on arrival. Find us 400m east of Blarney Square. Walking distance to Castle, Restaurants, Shops, Music and Bus.

B&B	-	Ensuite	-	Dinner	-
B&B	3	Standard	€23	Partial Board	-
Single Rate			€36	Child reduction	-

In Blarney

Open: 1st February-15th November

Neil & Noreen Finnegan
THAR AN UISCE
Magoola, Dripsey,
Co Cork

Blarney
TEL: **021 7334788**
EMAIL: **tharanuisce@eircom.net**

Lakeside setting on Blarney/Killarney route R618. All rooms ensuite with TV, Tea/Coffee, Hairdryers. Fishing, Waterskiing, Riverside walk all alongside.

B&B	3	Ensuite	€25.50	Dinner	-
B&B	-	Standard	-	Partial Board	-
Single Rate			€38.50	Child reduction	50%

Blarney 9km

Open: 1st May-31st October

Eucharia Hannon
WESTWOOD COUNTRY HOUSE
Dromin, Blarney,
Co Cork

Blarney
TEL: 021 4385404
EMAIL: westwood.country.house@oceanfree.net

Luxurious home. Elegantly furnished. TV's, Hairdryers. Tea, scones on arrival. Convenient to Blarney Castle, Shops, Pubs, Restaurants. Superb base for touring Killarney, Kinsale, Cobh.

B&B	3	Ensuite	€28/€30	Dinner	-
B&B	-	Standard	-	Partial Board	-
Single Rate			€38.50/€44	Child reduction	-

Blarney 5km

Open: 1st February-20th December

Mrs Bridget Harrington
CURRAC BUI
30 Castle Close Drive,
Blarney, Co Cork

Blarney
TEL: 021 4385424/021 2390038
EMAIL: curracbui@tinet.ie
WEB: www.curracbui.com

Personally run modern home. 5 min walk Blarney Castle/Local amenities/Cork Bus route. Bedrooms with TV, Hairdryers, Tea/Coffee. Home baking, Breakfast choice.

B&B	3	Ensuite	€26/€28	Dinner	-
B&B	1	Standard	€24/€25	Partial Board	-
Single Rate			€36/€38.50	Child reduction	33.3%

In Blarney

Open: 1st April-31st October

Mrs Eileen Hempel
EDELWEISS HOUSE
Leemount, Carrigrohane,
Co Cork

Blarney
TEL: 021 4871888   FAX: 021 4871888
EMAIL: edelweisshouse@eircom.net
WEB: www.homepage.eircom.net/~edelweisshouse/

Swiss style home overlooking river Lee. TV in rooms, Hairdryers. Credit cards accepted. 4.5 miles Blarney, Cork City 2 miles on N22. Killarney road signposted.

B&B	3	Ensuite	€26/€28	Dinner	-
B&B	3	Standard	€23/€24	Partial Board	-
Single Rate			€36/€38	Child reduction	25%

Cork City 6km

Open: March-December

Mrs Anne Hennessy
BLARNEY VALE HOUSE
Cork Road (R617),
Blarney, Co Cork

Blarney
TEL: 021 4381511
EMAIL: info@blarneyvale.com
WEB: www.blarneyvale.com

Luxurious home on private grounds overlooking village. AA ◆◆◆◆ selected, friendly atmosphere. Bedrooms with TV, Hairdryers, Tea/Coffee facilities. Breakfast menu. Cork City 8 mins.

B&B	4	Ensuite	€28/€31	Dinner	-
B&B	-	Standard	-	Partial Board	-
Single Rate			€40/€50	Child reduction	25%

In Blarney

Open: February-November

Mrs Margaret Kearney
SUNVILLE
1 Castle Close Lawn,
Blarney, Co Cork

Blarney
TEL: 021 4381325

Modern comfortable home 5 mins walk to Castle, Restaurants, Shops, Entertainment. Adjacent to bus route and beautiful country walk. Tea/Coffee facilities.

B&B	2	Ensuite	€26/€28	Dinner	-
B&B	1	Standard	-	Partial Board	-
Single Rate			€36/€38	Child reduction	50%

In Blarney

Open: 1st April-1st December

Susan & Brian Kenna
LANESVILLE B&B
Killard, Blarney, Co Cork

Blarney
TEL: **021 4381813**
EMAIL: **kennab@indigo.ie**
WEB: **www.lanesvillebandb.com**

Newly opened family run home. Walking distance to Blarney Castle and Shops. Rooms with TV, Tea/Coffee making facilities. Full breakfast menu. Private parking.

B&B	4	Ensuite	€26/€28	Dinner	-
B&B	-	Standard	-	Partial Board	-
Single Rate			€38.50/€40	Child reduction	25%

Blarney 1km

Open: 2nd January-20th December

Mrs Cecilia Kiely
CLARAGH
Waterloo Road, Blarney,
Co Cork

Blarney
TEL: **021 4886308**   FAX: **021 4886308**
EMAIL: **claraghbandb@eircom.net**
WEB: **www.claragh.com**

All bedrooms with TV, Tea/Coffee, Electric Blankets, Hairdryers. Breakfast menu includes French Toast. Recommended McQuillan/Sullivan Guides. Private Parking.

B&B	4	Ensuite	€26/€28	Dinner	-
B&B	-	Standard	-	Partial Board	-
Single Rate			€38.50/€39.50	Child reduction	-

Blarney 5km

Open: 1st April-31st October

Maura Lane
BELLEVUE HOUSE
Station Road, Blarney,
Co Cork

Blarney
TEL: **021 4381686**

Enjoy the best of Irish hospitality in friendly modern home. Close to Castle, restaurants, shops, golf and all other amenities.

B&B	2	Ensuite	€25.50/€30	Dinner	-
B&B	1	Standard	€23.50	Partial Board	-
Single Rate			€36/€40.63	Child reduction	25%

Blarney 1km

Open: 1st April-2nd November

Mrs Anne Lynch
THE GABLES
Stoneview, Blarney,
Co Cork

Blarney
TEL: **021 4385330**
EMAIL: **anne@gablesblarney.com**

Former Victorian Rectory on two acres, overlooking Blarney Castle. Golf course - Bar & Restaurant alongside. Home baking. Private parking. Itineraries arranged.

B&B	3	Ensuite	€27.50	Dinner	-
B&B	-	Standard	-	Partial Board	-
Single Rate			€40	Child reduction	-

Blarney 2km

Open: 1st March-30th November

Mrs Caroline Morgan
KILLARNEY HOUSE
Station Road, Blarney,
Co Cork

Blarney
TEL: **021 4381841**   FAX: **021 4381841**
EMAIL: **killarneyhouseblarney@eircom.net**

Purpose built luxury accommodation on 1 acre of landscaped gardens. Adjacent to Castle, Restaurants, Shops & Entertainment. Private Car park.

B&B	6	Ensuite	€28/€31	Dinner	-
B&B	-	Standard	-	Partial Board	-
Single Rate			€40/€50	Child reduction	25%

Blarney 1km

Open: All Year

Mrs Janet Murphy-Hallissey

Blarney

PINE FOREST HOUSE
Elmcourt, Blarney,
Co Cork

TEL: **021 4385979**   FAX: **021 4382917**
EMAIL: **info@pineforestbb.com**
WEB: **www.pineforestbb.com**

Spacious bungalow situated in peaceful wooded area with large landscaped garden. 1km on Blarney/Killarney Road (617). Tea and Coffee on arrival. Private parking.

B&B	4	Ensuite	€26/€28	Dinner	-
B&B	-	Standard		Partial Board	-
Single Rate			€38.50/€41	Child reduction	25%

Blarney 1km

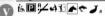

Open: All Year Except Christmas

Mrs Marian Nugent

Blarney

COOLIM
Coolflugh Tower, Blarney,
Co Cork

TEL: **021 4382848**
EMAIL: **nugent.coolim@oceanfree.net**
WEB: **www.coolimbb.com**

Spacious, luxurious, family home with large garden. Private parking. Refreshments on arrival. Home baking. Blarney Castle 4km (on R617). Muskerry Golf club 1km.

B&B	3	Ensuite	€28/€30	Dinner	-
B&B	-	Standard		Partial Board	-
Single Rate			€38.50	Child reduction	33.3%

Blarney 4km

Open: 2nd January-23rd December

Mrs Mary O'Brien

Blarney

FIRGROVE
1 Castle Close Villas,
Blarney, Co Cork

TEL: **021 4381403**

Well recommended quiet comfortable home. Friendly atmosphere. Mins walk Bus, Castle, Shops, Restaurants, Golf. Ideal touring base. From village square, 2nd turn left on Castle Close road.

B&B	2	Ensuite	€26.66/€28	Dinner	-
B&B	1	Standard	€24.20/€25.50	Partial Board	-
Single Rate			€36/€40.65	Child reduction	-

In Blarney

Open: 1st March-30th November

Mrs Ita O'Donovan

Blarney

KNOCKAWN WOOD
Curraleigh, Inniscarra,
Co Cork

TEL: **021 4870284**   FAX: **021 4870284**
EMAIL: **odknkwd@iol.ie**
WEB: **homepages.iol.ie/~odknkwd/**

Picturesque, restful. Tea & scones. Electric blankets. Meal without notice. Cork, Ferry, Airport 30 mins, N22/R618, Blarney/Killarney Rd R618. Inniscarra fishing.

B&B	3	Ensuite	€26/€28	Dinner	€17
B&B	1	Standard	€23/€25	Partial Board	-
Single Rate			€36/€38	Child reduction	50%

Blarney 6km

Open: All Year

Mrs Gertie O'Shea

Blarney

TRAVELLERS JOY
Tower, Blarney,
Co Cork

TEL: **021 4385541**
EMAIL: **travellersjoy@iolfree.ie**

Blarney/Killarney R617. Causin/Dillard recommended. Private parking. Prizewinning gardens. Tea/Coffee in bedrooms. Quality breakfasts. Close to all amenities.

B&B	3	Ensuite	€27/€31	Dinner	-
B&B	-	Standard		Partial Board	-
Single Rate			€40/€45	Child reduction	50%

Blarney 4km

Open: 1st February-15th December

Mrs Rose O'Sullivan
AVONDALE LODGE
Killowen, Blarney,
Co Cork

Blarney
TEL: **021 4381736**
EMAIL: **avondalelodge@eircom.net**

Warm friendly home with superb views. Walking distance to village/castle. Golf, horseriding, music locally. Tea/coffee, hairdryers and TV in rooms. Breakfast menu. Private garden/parking.

B&B	4	Ensuite	€26/€28	Dinner	-
B&B	-	Standard	-	Partial Board	-
Single Rate			€38.50/€41	Child reduction	25%

Blarney 1km

Open: 2nd January-23rd December

Chef Billie & Catherine Phelan
PHELAN'S WOODVIEW HOUSE
Tweedmount, Blarney,
Co Cork

Blarney
TEL: **021 4385197**   FAX: **021 4385197**

Enjoy Gourmet Cooking at Phelans, Seafood a speciality. TV in bedrooms. Tea/coffee facilities, Credit Cards. Frommer & Eye Witness Guides recommended.

B&B	7	Ensuite	€28/€31	Dinner	€23
B&B	1	Standard	€22/€25	Partial Board	-
Single Rate			€40/€50	Child reduction	25%

Blarney 3km

Open: 1st March-1st November

Mrs Olwen Venn
MARANATHA COUNTRY HOUSE
Tower, Blarney,
Co Cork

Blarney
TEL: **021 4385102**   FAX: **021 4382978**
EMAIL: **douglasvenn@eircom.net**
WEB: **www.maranathacountryhouse.com**

Stroll through the beautiful private gardens and woodlands surrounding this lovely Victorian mansion. Spacious romantic bedrooms. Beautiful historic antiques throughout.

B&B	4	Ensuite	€26.50/€45	Dinner	-
B&B	1	Standard	-	Partial Board	-
Single Rate			€35/€65	Child reduction	50%

Blarney 2km

Open: 15th March-30th November

Gretta O'Grady
CHESTNUT LODGE
Carrigaline, Co Cork

Carrigaline Cork Airport Ferryport
TEL: **021 4371382**   FAX: **021 4372818**
EMAIL: **chestnutlodge@eircom.net**

Luxurious home, peaceful surroundings, Golf, Angling, Horseriding, Cinema, Restaurants, Beaches. Sun-lounge, patio. Ferryport 5km, Airport 10km. Cork City 10km.

B&B	4	Ensuite	€28/€40	Dinner	€21
B&B	-	Standard	-	Partial Board	-
Single Rate			€38.50/€51	Child reduction	25%

Carrigaline 1km

Open: 6th January-18th December

Mrs Ann O'Leary
THE WILLOWS
Ballea Road, Carrigaline,
Co Cork

Carrigaline Cork Ferryport Airport
TEL: **021 4372669**   FAX: **021 4372669**

Split level house with gardens front and rear. Fishing, Golfing, Horse Riding, and Beaches 3km. Cork Airport 6km. Ringaskiddy Ferry 5km.

B&B	3	Ensuite	€28/€30	Dinner	-
B&B	2	Standard	€24/€26	Partial Board	-
Single Rate			€36/€40	Child reduction	-

Carrigaline 1km

Open: 2nd January-20th December

In Carrigtwohill

Miss Margot Seymour
DUN-VREEDA HOUSE
Carrigtwohill, Co Cork

Carrigtwohill
TEL: **021 4883169**

Off N25 Cork, Waterford/Rosslare road at Carrigtwohill. Near Fota Wildlife, Cobh, and Jameson Heritage Centre. Golf, Fishing, Riding nearby. Bus route. Church in area. Snacks, light meals.

B&B	2	Ensuite	€25.50	Dinner	-
B&B	2	Standard	€23	Partial Board	-
Single Rate			€38.50	Child reduction	50%

Open: All Year

Castletownbere 1km

Mrs Mary Donegan
REALT-NA-MARA
Castletownbere, Co Cork

Castletownbere
TEL: **027 70101**

Friendly home big garden, overlooks sea on Glengarriff Castletownbere road. Near Beara Way walking route. Near Town, Golf, Fishing. Tea/Coffee facilities on request.

B&B	4	Ensuite	€25.50	Dinner	-
B&B	1	Standard	€23	Partial Board	-
Single Rate			€36/€38.50	Child reduction	25%

Open: All Year

Castletownbere 1.5km

Mrs Noralene McGurn
SEA BREEZE
Derrymihan, Castletownbere, Beara Peninsula, Co Cork

Castletownbere
TEL: **027 70508** FAX: **027 70508**
EMAIL: **mcgurna@gofree.indigo.ie**

Warm friendly home. Situated on seafront overlooking Bere Island. Near Beara Way walking route. Ideal base for touring. Beara a peaceful spot.

B&B	3	Ensuite	€26/€30	Dinner	-
B&B	-	Standard	-	Partial Board	-
Single Rate			€38.50/€38.50	Child reduction	50%

Open: 1st May-20th December

Ardgroom Village 5km

Mary & John Gerard O'Sullivan
SEA VILLA
Castletownberehaven Cst Rd, Ardgroom Inward, Beara Peninsula, Co Cork

Castletownberehaven Ardgroom
TEL: **027 74369** FAX: **027 74369**
EMAIL: **seavilla1@eircom.net**

New luxurious home, tranquil scenic location on Coast Rd/Beara way, surrounded by Sea, Mountains and unspoiled rugged landscape. TV, trouser press, clock radio & hairdryer in all rooms.

B&B	3	Ensuite	€25.50/€25.50	Dinner	-
B&B	-	Standard	-	Partial Board	-
Single Rate			€38.50/€38.50	Child reduction	25%

Open: 1st April-31st October

Clonakilty 1km

Sean & Eileen Clancy
SEA BREEZE
Carhue, Clonakilty, Co Cork

Clonakilty
TEL: **023 34427**
EMAIL: **seabreezeclan@eircom.net**

Tranquility and total relaxation in this idyllic home, just off N71, less than 1km from town. Close to all amenities. A warm welcome assured.

B&B	4	Ensuite	€28/€30	Dinner	-
B&B	-	Standard	-	Partial Board	-
Single Rate			€38.50/€38.50	Child reduction	25%

Open: All Year

Tony & Noreen Driscoll
BAY VIEW HOUSE
Old Timoleague Road,
Clonakilty, Co Cork

Clonakilty
TEL: **023 33539**
EMAIL: **bayviewhouse@eircom.net**
WEB: **www.bayviewclonakilty.com**

Luxurious home, in delightful garden setting. Extensive breakfast menu. Peaceful scenic location, off N71 at roundabout on Cork/Kinsale approach. Town 3 mins walk.

B&B	5	Ensuite	€26/€30	Dinner	-
B&B	1	Standard		Partial Board	-
Single Rate			€36/€45	Child reduction	**33.3%**

In Clonakilty

Open: 1st March-31st October

Ms Maeve O'Grady Williams
MACLIAM LODGE
Western Road, Clonakilty,
Co Cork

Clonakilty
TEL: **023 35195**
EMAIL: **macliamlodge@eircom.net**
WEB: **www.westcorkbandb.com**

Newly refurbished home. All rooms TV, Tea/Coffee, Power showers, Hairdryers. Ideal touring base. On the N71, from Cork drive through town to West side. Welcome assured.

B&B	6	Ensuite	€28/€32	Dinner	-
B&B	-	Standard		Partial Board	-
Single Rate			€38.50/€40	Child reduction	**50%**

In Clonakilty

Open: All Year

Mrs Marie Hanly
GLENDINE
Tawnies Upper, Clonakilty,
Co Cork

Clonakilty
TEL: **023 34824**
EMAIL: **glendine@eircom.net**
WEB: **www.glendine.com**

Panoramic views of surrounding countryside, overlooking town. Country hillside setting, 10 mins. walk from town. Signposted from Church. Breakfast menu.

B&B	3	Ensuite	€25.50/€30	Dinner	-
B&B	-	Standard	-	Partial Board	-
Single Rate			-	Child reduction	-

In Clonakilty

Open: 1st February-30th November

Mrs Clare Hayes
WYTCHWOOD
Emmet Square, Clonakilty,
Co Cork

Clonakilty
TEL: **023 33525**   FAX: **023 35673**
EMAIL: **wytchost@iol.ie**

Georgian house with walled garden in a peaceful and tranquil setting. Breakfast choice. Le Guide du Routard and Lonely Planet recommended.

B&B	6	Ensuite	€28/€32	Dinner	-
B&B	-	Standard	-	Partial Board	-
Single Rate			€38.50/€45	Child reduction	-

In Clonakilty

Open: 7th January-20th December

Mrs Ann Lehane
BALARD HOUSE
Ballymacowen, Clonakilty,
Co Cork

Clonakilty
TEL: **023 33865**   FAX: **023 33865**

Modern home in peaceful location on Kinsale/Clonakilty road R600. Restaurants, Beaches, Sailing, Golf & Horseriding within easy reach.

B&B	3	Ensuite	€25.50	Dinner	-
B&B	-	Standard		Partial Board	-
Single Rate			€38.50	Child reduction	**50%**

Clonakilty 4km

Open: 1st May-31st September

Noreen & David McMahon
NORDAV
off Western Road
(Fernhill Rd), Clonakilty,
Co Cork

Clonakilty
TEL: **023 33655**   FAX: **023 33655**

Very private, 300 mts Church & Town Centre. Award winning gardens. 1 Family suite (includes 2 bedrooms & lounge). 1 suite with verandah, €35 p.p.s. Studio apartment.

B&B	4	Ensuite	€26/€30	Dinner	-
B&B	-	Standard	-	Partial Board	-
Single Rate			€38.50/€42	Child reduction	-

In Clonakilty   **Open:** April-September

Mrs Breda Moore
SHALOM
Ballyduvane, Clonakilty,
Co Cork

Clonakilty
TEL: **023 33473**

Modern bungalow in rural setting on main Clonakilty - Skibbereen Road (N71). 2km Clonakilty Town, 6km beautiful sandy Inchydoney Beach.

B&B	2	Ensuite	€25.50	Dinner	-
B&B	1	Standard	€23	Partial Board	-
Single Rate			-	Child reduction	**50%**

Clonakilty 2km   **Open:** March-October

Mrs Chris O'Brien
MELROSE
The Miles, Clonakilty,
Co Cork

Clonakilty
TEL: **023 33956/33961** FAX: **023 33961**
EMAIL: **melroseclon@eircom.net**
WEB: **www.melrosewestcork.com**

Warm welcoming home 400mtrs off N71, large garden. Power showers. Tranquil location, ideal for touring Cork and Kerry. Restaurants, beaches, all amenities nearby.

B&B	4	Ensuite	€28/€30	Dinner	-
B&B	1	Standard	€28/€30	Partial Board	-
Single Rate			€38	Child reduction	**50%**

In Clonakilty   **Open:** 1st January-30th November

Angela O'Driscoll
AISLING HEIGHTS
Clogheen Meadows,
Clogheen, Clonakilty,
West Cork, Co Cork

Clonakilty
TEL: **023 33491**

Beautifully decorated newly built house in nice area close to all amenities and within walking distance of town.

B&B	4	Ensuite	€27/€30	Dinner	-
B&B	-	Standard	-	Partial Board	-
Single Rate			€38.50/€40	Child reduction	-

In Clonakilty   **Open:** 1st February-31st October

Mrs Nora O'Regan
ASSUMPTION HOUSE
Ballinascarthy, Clonakilty,
Co Cork

Clonakilty
TEL: **023 39268**

Situated on N71, in Ballinascarthy. Warm welcoming home. Freshly prepared wholesome food. Home baking a speciality. Ideal location to beaches & day tours.

B&B	2	Ensuite	€28/€30	Dinner	-
B&B	1	Standard	€25/€28	Partial Board	-
Single Rate			€38/€40	Child reduction	**33.3%**

Clonakilty 3km   **Open:** 12th March-31st October

Mrs Georgina Coughlan
GLEBE HOUSE
Tay Road, Cobh,
Co Cork

Cobh
TEL: **021 4811373**   FAX: **021 4811373**
EMAIL: **glebehouse@eircom.net**
WEB: **glebehousecobh.com**

Warm spacious friendly home. Convenient Fota, Golf, Ferryport, Airport. Over bridge at Fota, turn left 2 miles to Crossroads, turn left. Breakfast menu. French spoken.

B&B	4	Ensuite	€28/€32	Dinner	-
B&B	-	Standard	-	Partial Board	-
Single Rate			€38.50/€45	Child reduction	25%

Cobh 2km   Ⓥ cc ⓅR⤫◻➡️⚓🛶↩️🚶 s   **Open:** April-October

Mrs Phyllis Fortune
ARDEEN B&B
3 Harbour Hill, Cobh
Co Cork

Cobh
TEL: **021 4811803**

Period house, central location. Adjacent to St. Colmans Cathedral. Offers maginificent sea views. The Town Heritage Centre and Railway Station within a walk.

B&B	4	Ensuite	€28	Dinner	-
B&B	-	Standard	-	Partial Board	-
Single Rate			€38.50	Child reduction	50%

In Cobh   Ⓥ S◻➡️🚶🚴🛶↩️🚶 s   **Open:** 1st January-21st December

---

Mrs Noreen Hickey
MOUNT VIEW
Beechmount, Cobh,
Co Cork

Cobh
TEL: **021 4814260**   FAX: **021 4814260**
EMAIL: **mountview8@eircom.net**
WEB: **www.irelandmadeeasy.com**

Town house spectacular view of Cathedral and harbour. Close to International and local ferries and Queenstown Story. Private car park. Signposted at Cathedral.

B&B	4	Ensuite	€25.50/€32	Dinner	-
B&B	-	Standard	-	Partial Board	-
Single Rate			€38.50/€45	Child reduction	33.3%

In Cobh   Ⓥ cc S ⓅR⤫◻ ☕🚴🛶↩️🚶 s 🚶R   **Open:** All Year Except Christmas

---

Pat & Martha Hurley
HIGHLAND
Ballywilliam, Cobh,
Co Cork

Cobh
TEL: **021 4813873**   FAX: **021 4813873**
EMAIL: **highlandcobh@eircom.net**

Modern home with panoramic views, close to Local and International Ferries. Fota Golf, Wildlife Park, Queenstown Story. Ground floor rooms on request.

B&B	5	Ensuite	€26/€32	Dinner	-
B&B	-	Standard	-	Partial Board	-
Single Rate			€40/€45	Child reduction	25%

Cobh 1.4km   Ⓥ cc S Ⓟ⊗R⤫◻ ☕🛶↩️🚶 s   **Open:** 1st March-31st October

---

Mrs Bernadette de Maddox
TEARMANN
Ballynoe, Cobh,
Co Cork

Cobh
TEL: **021 4813182**   FAX: **021 4814011**

19th Century Traditional House. Lovely garden. Car park. Close Heritage Centres, FOTA, Golf etc. Airport and Port 25 mins. Follow R624, pass by cross river ferry, 1st left up road on left.

B&B	2	Ensuite	€26/€26	Dinner	€18
B&B	1	Standard	€23/€23	Partial Board	-
Single Rate			€38/€38	Child reduction	-

Cobh 2km   Ⓥ Ⓟ🌿◻🛶↩️🚶 s 🚶R   **Open:** 1st March-31st October

Tallow 2km

Kevin Ryan
THE GRANGE
**Curraglass, Conna,
Near Tallow, Co Cork**

Conna
TEL: **058 56247**   FAX: **058 56247**

Large three storey Georgian house dating back to 1840. Set on 8 acres of mature gardens & wood
lands. Ideally based. Fishing on the Blackwater 5 mile. Nine excellent Golf courses within 12 miles.

B&B	3	Ensuite	€32	Dinner	-
B&B	-	Standard	-	Partial Board	-
Single Rate			€38.50	Child reduction	25%

Open: 15th February-15th November

Cork City 5km

Mrs Mary Bayer
WHITE LODGE
**Airport Cross, Kinsale Road,
Cork, Co Cork**

Cork City Airport Kinsale Road
TEL: **021 4961267**

Take Airport road to roundabout at Airport gates, take Cork exit off roundabout, 100m on, turn left
down side road. We are first B&B on left. City 6km.

B&B	3	Ensuite	€25.50	Dinner	€19
B&B	1	Standard	€23.86	Partial Board	-
Single Rate			€36	Child reduction	50%

Open: 10th January-20th December

Cork 5km

Mrs Helena Higgins
HELENA
**Kinsale Road, Ballygarvan,
Co Cork**

Cork City Airport Kinsale Road
TEL: **021 4888126**

Modern bungalow overlooking picturesque countryside on the main Cork Airport/Kinsale road.
From Cork N27=R600, 5 mins drive to Airport, Ferryport 8km.

B&B	2	Ensuite	€25.50/€25.50	Dinner	-
B&B	1	Standard	€24/€24	Partial Board	-
Single Rate			€36/€36	Child reduction	25%

Open: 1st April-31st October

Kinsale 8km

Mrs Brid O'Connor
BEECHWOOD
**Curra, Riverstick,
Co Cork**

Cork City Airport Kinsale Road
TEL: **021 4771456**

Country home set in scenic and tranquil surroundings, off R600 (Airport/Kinsale Road). Convenient
to Airport, Ferry Port and Kinsale.

B&B	4	Ensuite	€25.50	Dinner	-
B&B	-	Standard	-	Partial Board	-
Single Rate			€38.50	Child reduction	25%

Open: 1st May-30th September

Cork City 6km

Mrs Breeda Savage
GREEN ISLE
**Ballygarvan Village,
Off Airport/Kinsale Road,
Co Cork**

Cork City Airport Kinsale Road
TEL: **021 4888171**

Country Home in scenic valley off Cork/Kinsale road. Airport 2km. Near Kinsale. Ferryport 8km.
Tea/Coffee, Hairdryer in rooms. Visa.

B&B	2	Ensuite	€25.50/€25.50	Dinner	-
B&B	1	Standard	€24/€24	Partial Board	-
Single Rate			€36/€36	Child reduction	25%

Open: 6th January-20th December

Mrs Ilona Kiely
ARBORETUM HOUSE
Ardarostig, Bishopstown,
Cork City, Co Cork

Cork City Bishopstown
TEL: **021 4342056**   FAX: **021 4342056**
EMAIL: **arboretumhouse@eircom.net**
WEB: http://homepage.eircom.net/~arboretumhouse
BUS NO: **8**

Elegant country residence set in spacious gardens, just 1km off N25 on N71. Convenient to Cork Greyhound Track, Airport, Ferry, CIT and University Hospital.

B&B	3	Ensuite	€27/€32	Dinner	-
B&B	-	Standard		Partial Board	-
Single Rate			€38.50/€44.50	Child reduction	25%

Cork City 8km

Open: 1st March-31st October

Mrs Kay O'Donovan
DUNDERG
38 Westgate Road,
Bishopstown, Cork City,
Co Cork

Cork City Bishopstown University
TEL: **021 4543078**   FAX: **021 4543078**
EMAIL: **dunderg@eircom.net**
WEB: **homepage.eircom.net/~dunderg**
BUS NO: **5 & 8**

Quiet location 400m off N71 Bishopstown Bar. Convenient to Greyhound Stadium, Leisure centre, University Hospital, UCC, FAS, West Cork, Killarney, Ferry, Airport.

B&B	4	Ensuite	€30/€32	Dinner	-
B&B	-	Standard	-	Partial Board	-
Single Rate			-	Child reduction	25%

Cork City 2km

Open: 1st February-30th November

Mrs Barbara Ahern
BRANDON
Hillgrove Lawn,
South Douglas Road,
Cork City, Co Cork

Cork City Douglas Area
TEL: **021 4893859**
BUS NO: **6**

Detached house in quiet cul-de-sac. Convenient to Airport, Ferry, Bus, Shopping, Restaurant, Bars, Golf. Parking. TV in bedrooms. 4km to City. Near O'Sullivan's Pharmacy.

B&B	3	Ensuite	€25.50/€28.57	Dinner	-
B&B	1	Standard	€23/€23	Partial Board	-
Single Rate			€36/€38.10	Child reduction	-

Cork City 2.5km

Open: 1st January-20th December

Mrs Catherine Edwards
RIVER VIEW
Douglas East, Cork,
Co Cork

Cork City Douglas Area
TEL: **021 4893762**
EMAIL: **edwardsc@eircom.net**
BUS NO: **7**

Victorian 1890 home in Douglas Village, near Barrys Pub. Convenient Restaurants Shopping Centres, Churches, Airport, Ferry. Cable TV all bedrooms. Access via tunnel to Douglas Village.

B&B	3	Ensuite	€25.50/€32.50	Dinner	-
B&B	-	Standard	-	Partial Board	-
Single Rate			€38.50/€45	Child reduction	25%

Cork 3km

Open: January-18th December

Mrs Elizabeth O'Shea & Family
FATIMA HOUSE
Grange Road, Douglas,
Cork City, Co Cork

Cork City Douglas Area
TEL: **021 4362536**   FAX: **021 4362536**
EMAIL: **fatimabandb@eircom.net**
BUS NO: **6 & 7**

South ring = N25. Kinsale road roundabout. Airport exit = N27 immediate left Little Chef/Touchdown Tavern. 2km. Parking. City buses. Taxi. Menu. Room rates. Visa.

B&B	4	Ensuite	€25.50/€32.50	Dinner	-
B&B	-	Standard	-	Partial Board	-
Single Rate			€38.50/€45	Child reduction	-

Cork City 4km

Open: 1st January-15th December

Cork City 1km

Mrs Evelyn O'Sullivan
COOLFADDA HOUSE
**Douglas Road, Cork City,
Co Cork**

Cork City Douglas Area
TEL: **021 4363489**
BUS NO: **7, 7A, 6, 10**

Spacious home in garden setting. Accessed from Douglas road up short driveway. Walking distance City Center. Bus, Train & Airport close by. Near St. Finbars Hospital and Briar Rose Pub.

B&B	2	Ensuite	€27/€32	Dinner	-
B&B	3	Standard	€24.50/€27	Partial Board	-
Single Rate			€38/€45	Child reduction	33.3%

Open: 15th March-31st October

Cork 3km

Mrs Ann Ryan
HILLCREST HOUSE
**South Douglas Road,
Cork, Co Cork**

Cork City Douglas Area
TEL: **021 4891178**
BUS NO: **6**

Detached family home. Bedrooms overlooking large garden. Walking distance City Centre, Golf, Swimming, Shops nearby. Airport, Ferry, TV all bedrooms.

B&B	2	Ensuite	€28/€32	Dinner	-
B&B	1	Standard	€25/€26	Partial Board	-
Single Rate			€36/€40	Child reduction	25%

Open: 1st April-31st October

In Cork City

Mr Kevin Flynn
AARAN HOUSE B&B
**49 Lower Glanmire Road,
Cork City, Co Cork**

Cork City Lower Glanmire Road
TEL: **021 4551501**   FAX: **021 4551501**
EMAIL: **aarankev@hotmail.com**

Town House, adjacent to Train Station. Easy walking distance to Bus Station and City Centre 5 mins. Early Breakfast.

B&B	6	Ensuite	€26/€28	Dinner	-
B&B	-	Standard	-	Partial Board	-
Single Rate			€38.50/€38.50	Child reduction	25%

Open: All Year

In Cork City

Mrs Marjorie Flynn
KENT HOUSE
**47 Lower Glanmire Road,
Cork City, Co Cork**

Cork City Lower Glanmire Road
TEL: **021 4504260**

Family run home adjacent to Railway Station and Bus Station. City Centre 5 mins walk.

B&B	4	Ensuite	€26/€28	Dinner	-
B&B	2	Standard	€23/€26	Partial Board	-
Single Rate			€36/€38	Child reduction	-

Open: All Year

In Cork

Ellen Murray
OAKLAND B&B
**51 Lower Glanmire Road,
Cork, Co Cork**

Cork City Lower Glanmire Road
TEL: **021 4500578**
BUS NO: **11**

Our house was built in the 18th Century. It is a terraced house within 5 mins walk of the Bus Station, City Centre and adjacent to the Railway Station.

B&B	5	Ensuite	€26/€28	Dinner	-
B&B	-	Standard	-	Partial Board	-
Single Rate			€38.50/€39	Child reduction	-

Open: 1st January-23rd December

In Cork

Jerry Spillane
NUMBER FORTY EIGHT
48 Lr. Glanmire Rd,
Cork, Co Cork

Cork City Lower Glanmire Road
TEL: 021 4505790   FAX: 021 4505790

Victorian town house on Cork/Dublin road (N8). Adjacent to Railway Station. Walking distance to City Centre/Bus Station. Home baking.

B&B	6	Ensuite	€28/€36	Dinner	-
B&B	-	Standard		Partial Board	-
Single Rate			€38.50/€38.50	Child reduction	-

Open: All Year

Cork City 2km

Mrs Pauline Hickey
BERKLEY LODGE B&B
Model Farm Road (R608),
Cork, Co Cork

Cork City Dennehy's Cross Wilton Area
TEL: 021 4341755   FAX: 021 4347522
EMAIL: peak@esatclear.ie
WEB: www.esatclear.ie/~berkleylodgebb
BUS NO: 5 & 8

Comfortable family home on R608 (City End). Western suburbs off Wilton Rd N71-N22 at Dennehys Cross near University Hospital, FAS, RTC, UCC, Airport. West Cork/Killarney roads, City 5 mins.

B&B	4	Ensuite	€30/€32	Dinner	-
B&B	-	Standard		Partial Board	-
Single Rate			€38.50/€45	Child reduction	50%

Open: 1st January-21st December

Cork City 2km

Mrs Rita O'Herlihy
55 Wilton Gardens,
off Wilton Road, Cork City,
Co Cork

Cork City Wilton University
TEL: 021 4541705
BUS NO: 8 & 5

Situated quiet park, off Wilton Road, convenient to West Cork, Killarney roads, Airport, University, Hospital, College. Frommer recommended.

B&B	2	Ensuite	€27/€28	Dinner	-
B&B	1	Standard	€24/€25	Partial Board	-
Single Rate			€36/€38.50	Child reduction	-

Open: February-November

Cork City 2km

Michael & Patricia Flavin
ALBATROSS
Clogheen,
Blarney Road, Cork,
Co Cork

Cork City
TEL: 021 4392315
EMAIL: albatross@eircom.net
BUS NO: 2

Situated in peaceful area. 2km City Centre, 3km Blarney. Convenient Cork City, Gaol, Tennis, Golf. Horseriding locally. An Irish welcome. Near Clogheen Church.

B&B	3	Ensuite	€28.57	Dinner	-
B&B	-	Standard	-	Partial Board	-
Single Rate			-	Child reduction	-

Open: March-October

Cork City 1km

Barry & Goretti Guilfoyle
MARIAVILLE HOUSE
Coolgarten Park,
Off Magazine Road,
Cork, Co Cork

Cork City
TEL: 021 4316508   FAX: 021 4632067
EMAIL: barguilfoyle@eircom.net
BUS NO: 10

Family run home, quiet location. Private secure parking. Convenient to Airport, University College Cork, University Hospital. Close to Restaurants, Pubs, main Bus Routes. City Centre 15 mins walk.

B&B	4	Ensuite	€25.50/€28	Dinner	-
B&B	-	Standard		Partial Board	-
Single Rate			€38.50/€38.50	Child reduction	-

Open: 1st June-30th September

Cork City 1km

Mrs Breeda Higgins
7 Ferncliff
Bellevue Park, St Lukes,
Cork City, Co Cork

Cork City

TEL: **021 4508963**   FAX: **021 4508963 (man)**
BUS No: **7 & 8**

Victorian home, quiet cul-de-sac. Bus/Train Stations/City Centre 1km. Take left at T after Ambassador Hotel, then straight ahead, and on right.

B&B	2	Ensuite	€25.50/€25.50	Dinner	-
B&B	2	Standard	€23/€23	Partial Board	-
Single Rate			€36/€38.50	Child reduction	33.3%

Open: March-November

Cork 2km

Anne & David Lynch
ST ANTHONY'S
Clogheen, Blarney Road,
Cork, Co Cork

Cork

TEL: **021 4392547**
BUS No: **2**

Comfortable bungalow close to Cork City and Blarney Castle. Golf/Fishing nearby. Home baking, breakfast menu, nice garden & patio.

B&B	2	Ensuite	€25.50/€25.50	Dinner	-
B&B	1	Standard	€23/€23	Partial Board	-
Single Rate			-	Child reduction	33.3%

Open: 1st March-1st November

In Crookhaven

Maureen & James Newman
GALLEY COVE HOUSE
Crookhaven, West Cork,
Co Cork

Crookhaven Mizen Head

TEL: **028 35137**   FAX: **028 35137**
EMAIL: **galleycove@eircom.net**
WEB: **www.galleycovehse.com**

Friendly comfortable accommodation in peaceful scenic location. Overlooking Atlantic Ocean and Fastnet lighthouse. Near Mizen head and Barleycove. Child Reduction.

B&B	3	Ensuite	€30/€35	Dinner	-
B&B	1	Standard	€27/€30	Partial Board	-
Single Rate			€40/€45	Child reduction	-

Open: 1st March-30th November

Drimoleague 2km

Mrs Marian Collins
ROSELAWN HOUSE
Derrygrea, Drimoleague,
Co Cork

Drimoleague Skibbereen

TEL: **028 31369**
EMAIL: **roselawnhouse@eircom.net**

Elegant country house on Cork/Bantry R586 route. Local amenities. Skibbereen 12km. Bantry 20km. Homely atmosphere. Maps of walking routes of Drimoleague available.

B&B	2	Ensuite	€25.50/€25.50	Dinner	€17
B&B	1	Standard	€23/€23	Partial Board	€264
Single Rate			€36/€38.50	Child reduction	50%

Open: 1st March-1st November

Fermoy 1km

Mrs Patricia O'Leary
PALM RISE
Barrys Boreen,
Duntahane Road,
Fermoy, Co Cork

Fermoy

TEL: **025 31386**

Friendly modern home in peaceful scenic surroundings. Close to fishing, horse riding, Leisure Centre and scenic walks. 1km from N8-main Dublin/Cork road.

B&B	3	Ensuite	€30/€33	Dinner	-
B&B	1	Standard	€30/€33	Partial Board	-
Single Rate			€36/€40	Child reduction	-

Open: 6th January-19th December

In Glengarriff

Mrs Rita Barry-Murphy
COIS COILLE
Glengarriff, Co Cork

Glengarriff
Tel: **027 63202**

Warm hospitality in comfortable home overlooking Glengarriff harbour. Award winning garden in quiet woodland setting. Extensive breakfast menu, home baking.

B&B	6	Ensuite	€27	Dinner	-
B&B	-	Standard		Partial Board	-
Single Rate			€38	Child reduction	25%

Open: 1st May-30th September

Glengarriff 3km

Mrs Kathleen Connolly
CARRAIG DUBH HOUSE
Droumgarriff, Glengarriff, Co Cork

Glengarriff
Tel: **027 63146**
Email: **carraigdubhhouse@hotmail.com**

Lovely family home in quiet peaceful location. 150m off main road overlooking Harbour and Golf club. Nice walking area. Tea/Coffee and Hairdryer in bedrooms. Lovely breakfast menu.

B&B	3	Ensuite	€25.50/€25.50	Dinner	-
B&B	-	Standard		Partial Board	-
Single Rate			€38.50	Child reduction	25%

Open: 15th March-31st October

In Glengarriff

Mrs Maureen MacCarthy
MAUREENS
Glengarriff Village Home, Glengarriff, Co Cork

Glengarriff
Tel: **027 63201**

Two storey house adjacent/picturesque village. Beside ancient Oak Forest, Sea, Mountains, Lakes and Rivers. Opposite entrance to Garinish island.

B&B	4	Ensuite	€25.50/€25.50	Dinner	-
B&B	2	Standard	€23	Partial Board	-
Single Rate			€36/€36	Child reduction	-

Open: All Year

In Glengarriff

Eileen O'Sullivan & Imelda Lyne
ISLAND VIEW HOUSE
Glengarriff, Co Cork

Glengariff
Tel: **027 63081** Fax: **027 63600**
Email: **islandview@ireland.com**

Comfortable family home in peaceful scenic area. 10 minutes walk to town - 150 metres off main road. Ideal touring centre. Breakfast menu. Hairdryers all rooms.

B&B	6	Ensuite	€25.50/€28	Dinner	-
B&B	-	Standard		Partial Board	-
Single Rate			€38.50/€40	Child reduction	25%

Open: 22nd March-1st November

In Goleen

Ms Sue Hill
THE HERON'S COVE
The Harbour, Goleen, West Cork, Co Cork

Goleen
Tel: **028 35225** Fax: **028 35422**
Email: **suehill@eircom.net**
Web: **www.heronscove.com**

Comfortable rooms, good food, wine. Near Barleycove, Mizen Head. Hairdryers, Electric blankets. Restaurant. Fresh fish/local produce. AA ◆◆◆◆. A la carte. On harbour.

B&B	5	Ensuite	€35/€35	Dinner	-
B&B	-	Standard	-	Partial Board	-
Single Rate			-	Child reduction	-

Open: All Year Except Christmas

Mrs Kathleen Cummins
ELLAMORE
Ballymountain, Innishannon,
Co Cork

Innishannon near Kinsale
TEL: **021 4775807**
EMAIL: **ellamore@oceanfree.net**
WEB: **www.ellamore.com**

Country residence, convenient to Airport, Ferryport. Follow signpost for Ballymountain House off N71 at Innishannon Bridge. Next house on left.

B&B	3	Ensuite	€26/€31	Dinner	-
B&B	-	Standard	-	Partial Board	-
Single Rate			€38	Child reduction	25%

Innishannon 3km

Open: 1st May-30th September

Mrs Phyl Grace
HILLSIDE
Millview Road, Kanturk,
Co Cork

Kanturk
TEL: **029 50241**

A mature rambling garden welcomes you to this restful house, with pictures, old furnishings & books. Local Golf & Fishing.

B&B	3	Ensuite	€28/€28	Dinner	-
B&B	2	Standard	€25/€25	Partial Board	-
Single Rate			€36/€40	Child reduction	-

In Kanturk

Open: 29th April-30th September

John & Eleanor Bateman
ROCKLANDS HOUSE
Compass Hill, Kinsale,
Co Cork

Kinsale
TEL: **021 4772609**   FAX: **021 4702149**
EMAIL: **rocklandshouse@eircom.net**
WEB: **www.kinsaletown.com**

Set in 3 acres of woodland on a scenic walking trail, 3 minutes drive from Town Centre. Rooms with Balconies overlooking the inner Harbour. Guest Lounge.

B&B	6	Ensuite	€30/€45	Dinner	-
B&B	-	Standard	-	Partial Board	-
Single Rate			€50/€75	Child reduction	-

Kinsale 1km

Open: 14th February-15th November

Mrs Ita Carey
ORCHARD COTTAGE
Farrangalway, Kinsale,
Co Cork

Kinsale
TEL: **021 4772693**
EMAIL: **orchardcottage@eircom.net**

Quiet Country Home adjacent to Kinsale's 18-hole Golf course. All rooms TV, Clock Radios, Hairdryers, Tea/Coffee, AA ◆◆◆. Airport Ferry 20 km. 500 mts off R607.

B&B	4	Ensuite	€30	Dinner	-
B&B	-	Standard	-	Partial Board	-
Single Rate			€40	Child reduction	25%

Kinsale 3km

Open: 7th January-20th December

Mrs Joan Collins
WATERLANDS
Cork Road, Kinsale,
Co Cork

Kinsale
TEL: **021 4772318**   FAX: **021 4774873**
EMAIL: **info@collinsbb.com**
WEB: **www.collinsbb.com**

Luxury accommodation, Breakfast Conservatory, Electric Blankets, Tea/Coffee, Extensive breakfast menu. Highly recommended, AA ◆◆◆◆, Ideal touring base. Golf nearby. Airport 20 mins.

B&B	4	Ensuite	€27/€32	Dinner	-
B&B	-	Standard	-	Partial Board	-
Single Rate			€45/€45	Child reduction	25%

Kinsale 1km

Open: 1st March-1st November

Phyllis & PJ Crowe
WATERSIDE HOUSE
Dromderrig, Kinsale,
Co Cork

Kinsale

Tel: **021 774196**   Fax: **021 774196**

Picturesque setting in spacious seaside garden. View of inner Harbour. Kinsale is a pleasant 1km waterside walk. Golf courses, Beaches nearby. R600 from Kinsale, right by Big Bridge.

B&B	4	Ensuite	€28/€35	Dinner	-
B&B	-	Standard	-	Partial Board	-
Single Rate			€38/€50	Child reduction	-

Kinsale 1km

Open: 15th February-1st December

Mrs Kathleen Cummins
BAY VIEW
Clasheen, Kinsale,
Co Cork

Kinsale

Tel: **021 4774054**
Email: **bayviewbb@indigo.ie**
Web: **www.cork-guide.ie/kinsale/bayview/welcome.html**

Comfortable modern spacious home. Panoramic views overlooking Bay and countryside from dining room. Breakfast menu. "Le guide du Routard" recommended.

B&B	3	Ensuite	€26/€28	Dinner	-
B&B	-	Standard	-	Partial Board	-
Single Rate			-	Child reduction	-

Kinsale 1km

Open: 1st April-30th September

Peggy & Eamonn Foley
FERNVILLE
Lower Cove, Kinsale,
Co Cork

Kinsale

Tel: **021 4774874**   Fax: **021 4774874**
Email: **fernville@oceanfree.net**
Web: **www.dirl.com/cork/fernville.htm**

Luxury B&B with Sea views on Kinsales outer Harbour. 1 min to Beach/Fishing. 10 mins drive to Kinsale, signs from Charles Fort. Airport/Ferry 30 mins.

B&B	3	Ensuite	€26/€32	Dinner	-
B&B	-	Standard	-	Partial Board	-
Single Rate			€40/€50	Child reduction	25%

Kinsale 4km

Open: 15th March-28th October

Ms Gillian Good
GLEBE COUNTRY HOUSE
Ballinadee, Nr Kinsale,
Bandon, Co Cork

Kinsale

Tel: **021 4778294**   Fax: **021 4778456**
Email: **glebehse@indigo.ie**
Web: **http://indigo.ie/~glebehse/**

Charming family run Georgian Rectory close to Beaches, Bandon & Kinsale. Take N71 to Innishannon Bridge, follow signs for Ballinadee. AA ◆◆◆◆.

B&B	4	Ensuite	€32/€45	Dinner	€30
B&B	-	Standard	-	Partial Board	-
Single Rate			€45/€57	Child reduction	50%

Kinsale 10km

Open: 4th January-21st December

Mrs Teresa Gray
ROCKVILLE
The Rock, Kinsale,
Co Cork

Kinsale

Tel: **021 4772791**

Modern well appointed split level home overlooking Kinsale Town and Harbour and within five minutes walk of Town Centre.

B&B	3	Ensuite	€26/€30	Dinner	-
B&B	-	Standard	-	Partial Board	-
Single Rate			€38.50/€40	Child reduction	-

In Kinsale

Open: March-November

271

Mrs M Griffin
HILLSIDE HOUSE
Camp Hill, Kinsale,
Co Cork

Kinsale
TEL: 021 4772315   FAX: 021 4772315
EMAIL: hillside@oceanfree.net :

Beautiful spacious home. Award winning gardens. On 1601 battle site, overlooks Town. Frommer recommended. Car park. Guests conservatory. 10-15 mins walk Town. Menu.

B&B	6	Ensuite	€26/€32	Dinner	-
B&B	-	Standard	-	Partial Board	-
Single Rate			-	Child reduction	25%

Kinsale 1km

Open: 7th January-20th December

Orla Griffin
GRIFFIN'S RIVERSIDE HOUSE
Kippagh, Kinsale,
Co Cork

Kinsale
TEL: 021 4774917
EMAIL: riversidehouse@esatclear.ie

Panoramic ocean view. Luxury accommodation. TVs, Hairdryers, Tea/coffee, private gardens. Car park. All amenities. Walking distance, Golf/Fishing arranged. Power showers.

B&B	6	Ensuite	€27/€32	Dinner	-
B&B	-	Standard	-	Partial Board	-
Single Rate			€44.45/€44.45	Child reduction	25%

Kinsale 1km

Open: All Year Except Christmas

Brian & Valerie Hosford
WOODLANDS HOUSE
Cappagh, Kinsale,
Co Cork

Kinsale
TEL: 021 4772633   FAX: 021 4772649
EMAIL: info@woodlandskinsale.com
WEB: www.woodlandskinsale.com

Modern luxurious accommodation. Beautiful views of Kinsale Town and Harbour. 7 mins walk to Town Centre. En suite. Private parking. TV, DD Telephone, breakfast menu.

B&B	3	Ensuite	€32/€45	Dinner	-
B&B	-	Standard	-	Partial Board	-
Single Rate			€32/€50	Child reduction	25%

In Kinsale

Open: 1st March-12th November

Mrs Joan Hurley
FOYLE
Acres, Kinsale,
Co Cork

Kinsale
TEL: 021 4772363
EMAIL: foylebandb@eircom.net

Modern bungalow in rural setting with conservatory/patio for guests use. On R600 Coast road. Old Head Golf course, Beaches nearby. Airport/Ferryport 20km.

B&B	4	Ensuite	€27.50/€32	Dinner	-
B&B	-	Standard	-	Partial Board	-
Single Rate			€45/€55	Child reduction	25%

Kinsale 3km

Open: 1st March-31st October

Mrs Mary Hurley
SCEILIG HOUSE
Ard Brack, Scilly,
Kinsale, Co Cork

Kinsale
TEL: 021 4772832   FAX: 021 4772832
EMAIL: hurleyfamily@eircom.net

Town house set in layered gardens overlooking Kinsale Harbour. Seaview from bedrooms with private patio/balcony. Frommer and "La Guide" recommended. Follow Scilly sign on entry to Town.

B&B	3	Ensuite	€25/€35	Dinner	-
B&B	-	Standard	-	Partial Board	-
Single Rate			€50/€70	Child reduction	33.3%

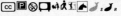

In Kinsale

Open: All Year

In Kinsale

Mrs Teresa Hurley
CEPHAS HOUSE
**Compass Hill, Kinsale,
Co Cork**

Kinsale

TEL: **021 4772689**   FAX: **021 4772689**
EMAIL:**thurley@boinet.ie**

Town house, beautiful private garden. Magnificent seaviews from bedrooms with balcony. Scenic walk to town. Guide du Routard recommended.

			Dinner	-
B&B	3	Ensuite	€25/€35	
B&B	-	Standard	-	Partial Board	-
Single Rate			€50/€70	Child reduction	-

Open: 1st March-31st October

Kinsale 2km

Mrs Nora Kelly
VALLEY-VIEW
**Hospital Road, Coolvalanane,
Kinsale, Co Cork**

Kinsale

TEL: **021 4772842**
EMAIL: **valleyview@iol.ie**

Spacious bungalow in scenic farming area. Overlooking open countryside, close to Beaches, Golf and Fishing. Airport, Ferry, half hour drive.

			Dinner	-
B&B	2	Ensuite	€25.50/€27.50	
B&B	2	Standard	€23/€25	Partial Board	-
Single Rate			€36/€38	Child reduction	50%

Open: All Year

Kinsale 3.5km

Mrs Myrtle Levis
WALYUNGA
**Sandycove, Kinsale,
Co Cork**

Kinsale

TEL: **021 4774126**   FAX: **021 4774126**
EMAIL: **info@walyunga.com**
WEB: **www.walyunga.com**

Bright spacious modern bungalow. Unique design, landscaped gardens, outstanding ocean & valley views, Sandy Beaches, Scenic Coastal walks.Internationally acclaimed.

			Dinner	-
B&B	4	Ensuite	€29/€38	
B&B	1	Standard	€25/€29	Partial Board	-
Single Rate			-	Child reduction	25%

Open: 1st March-28th October

In Kinsale

Anthony & Fiona McCarthy
SEA BREEZE
**Featherbed Lane, Kinsale,
Co Cork**

Kinsale

TEL: **021 4774854**

Dormer Bungalow with view of Harbour from some bedrooms. 3 mins walk Town Centre, private carpark, sailing, fishing and beaches nearby.

			Dinner	-
B&B	4	Ensuite	€28/€34	
B&B	-	Standard	-	Partial Board	-
Single Rate			€44/€51	Child reduction	25%

Open: All Year Except Christmas

In Kinsale

Brian & Ann McCarthy
ROCK VIEW
**The Glen, Kinsale,
Co Cork**

Kinsale

TEL: **021 4773162**
WEB: **www.dragnet-system's.ie/dira/rockview.htm**

Award winning attractive comfortable home located in the heart of Kinsale Town Centre. Car park and bicycle lockup behind house. Adjacent Church, Shop, Pubs.

			Dinner	-
B&B	4	Ensuite	€28/€35	
B&B	-	Standard	-	Partial Board	-
Single Rate			€44/€51	Child reduction	25%

Open: All Year

Mr & Mrs Michael McCarthy
HILL TOP B&B
Sleaveen Heights, Kinsale,
Co Cork

Kinsale
Tel: **021 4772612**

Modern spacious bungalow, conservatory overlooking Kinsale Harbour and James's Fort. Close Museum, Beaches, Golf, Yachting, Marina, Fishing. 3 mins walk Town.

B&B	6	Ensuite	€28/€34	Dinner	-
B&B	-	Standard		Partial Board	-
Single Rate			€44/€51	Child reduction	25%

In Kinsale

Open: All Year

Martina Murphy
FOUR WINDS
Watersland, Kinsale,
Co Cork

Kinsale
Tel: **021 4774822**

Luxury new accomodation set in peaceful area on 1 acre of beautiful garden. Kinsale 1km/Airport 20 mins/Ferry 30 mins.

B&B	3	Ensuite	€25.50/€30	Dinner	-
B&B	1	Standard	€23/€26	Partial Board	-
Single Rate			€36/€45	Child reduction	25%

Kinsale 1km

Open: 1st April-1st November

Mrs Theresa Murphy
TESBEN HOUSE
Old Head/Golf Links Road,
Barrells Cross, Kinsale,
Co Cork

Kinsale
Tel: **021 4778354**   Fax: **021 4778354**
Email: **tesbenhouse@eircom.net**
Web: **homepage.eircom.net/~tesbenhouse**

Tranquil surroundings unrivalled. Picturesque view R600 West Cork/Kerry. "Old Head" Golf Links 4km. "Le Guide du Routard" recommended. Ferryport 20km.

B&B	2	Ensuite	€28/€31	Dinner	-
B&B	2	Standard	€24/€27	Partial Board	-
Single Rate			€40/€45	Child reduction	25%

Kinsale 5km

Open: 1st March-25th November

Mrs Eileen O'Connell
DOONEEN
Ardcarrig, Bandon Road,
Kinsale, Co Cork

Kinsale
Tel: **021 4772024**
Email: **dooneenbandb@esatclear.ie**
Web: **www.ireland-discover.com/dooneen.htm**

Modern house in peaceful setting with views of inner and outer Harbour, TV lounge, private parking, garage for cycles, secluded gardens. Town area.

B&B	3	Ensuite	€25.50/€35	Dinner	-
B&B	1	Standard	€25/€25	Partial Board	-
Single Rate			€38	Child reduction	-

In Kinsale

Open: All Year Except Christmas

Mrs Phil O'Donovan
ROSSBRIN
Harbour Heights, Cappagh,
Kinsale, Co Cork

Kinsale
Tel: **021 4772112**

Luxury bungalow, quiet residential park. Panoramic views, gardens. Convenient all amenities. Breakfast menu. Rooms TV, Tea/Coffee. From St Multose Church on Bandon Road, go 630m, turn left as signposted

B&B	3	Ensuite	€26/€28	Dinner	-
B&B	1	Standard	-	Partial Board	-
Single Rate			-	Child reduction	25%

In Kinsale

Open: March-November

In Kinsale

Betty & Pat O'Farrell
15 Main Street
Kinsale, Co Cork

Kinsale

Tel: **021 4774169**   Fax: **021 4774169**
Email: **bettyofarrell@eircom.net**
Web: **homepage.eircom.net/~patofarrell/**

Town centre historical building, comfortable family home. French/German spoken. Convenient Sailing, Golfing, Fishing, Beaches, Restaurants, Historical sites, Bicycle lock-up.

B&B	3	Ensuite	€25.50/€32.50	Dinner	-
B&B	1	Standard	€23/€25.50	Partial Board	-
Single Rate		-		Child reduction	-

Open: All Year Except Christmas

In Kinsale

Mrs Mary O'Neill
SEA GULL HOUSE
Cork Street, Kinsale,
Co Cork

Kinsale

Tel: **021 4772240**
Email: **marytap@iol.ie**
Web: **seagullhouse.com**

Next door to "Desmond Castle", wine museum built 1500. Near Beach, Fishing & Golf. Kinsale Gourmet Town. Groups welcome.

B&B	5	Ensuite	€30/€32	Dinner	-
B&B	1	Standard	-	Partial Board	-
Single Rate			€40	Child reduction	-

Open: March-October

Kinsale 4km

Mrs Claire O'Sullivan
RIVERMOUNT HOUSE
Barrells Cross, Old Head Rd,
Kinsale, Co Cork

Kinsale

Tel: **021 4778033**   Fax: **021 4778225**
Email: **rivermnt@iol.ie**
Web: **www.rivermount.com**

Award winning luxurious home overlooking the river. AA & RAC ◆◆◆◆ with Sparkling Diamond Award. Extensive Breakfast menu. Recommended by many guides. Just off R600.

B&B	6	Ensuite	€27.50/€33	Dinner	-
B&B	-	Standard	-	Partial Board	-
Single Rate			€40/€55	Child reduction	25%

Open: 1st February-1st November

Mrs Phil Price
DANABEL
Sleaveen, Kinsale,
Co Cork

Kinsale

Tel: **021 4774087**
Email: **info@danabel.com**
Web: **www.danabel.com**

Modern house, quiet area. Town 3 mins walk. Orthopaedic beds. Hairdryers, Teamaking. Airport/Ferry 20 mins. Harbour view some bedrooms. Frommer recommended/Star Rating.

B&B	5	Ensuite	€26/€35	Dinner	-
B&B	-	Standard	-	Partial Board	-
Single Rate			€44/€64	Child reduction	25%

Open: All Year

Mrs Bernie Ryan Godkin
GOLDEN GARDEN
Cappagh, Kinsale,
Co Cork

Kinsale

Tel: **021 4772490**

Luxury accommodation with old world charm, in secluded garden overlooking Harbour. Tastefully decorated, antique furniture. Victorian style sittingroom. Power showers.

B&B	4	Ensuite	€28/€45	Dinner	-
B&B	-	Standard	-	Partial Board	-
Single Rate			€32/€45	Child reduction	-

Open: 1st March-31st October

Mrs Ann Salter
CROSSWAYS
Ardbrack, Kinsale,
Co Cork

Kinsale
TEL: 021 4772460 FAX: 021 4772460

Modern spacious home overlooking inner Harbour. Adjacent to Scenic Walks, Fishing, Golfing, Pub Entertainment & Gourmet Restaurants.

B&B	5	Ensuite	€28/€38	Dinner	-
B&B	-	Standard	-	Partial Board	-
Single Rate			-	Child reduction	-

In Kinsale

Open: All Year Except Christmas

Margo Searls
LANDFALL HOUSE
Cappagh, Kinsale,
Co Cork

Kinsale
TEL: 021 4772575 FAX: 021 4772575
EMAIL: landfallhouse@eircom.net

Luxury spacious home and gardens. Panoramic views over River, Harbour and Town. Ideal touring base. Private parking. Breakfast menu. Minutes to Town. Power showers, Hairdryers etc.

B&B	4	Ensuite	€27/€32	Dinner	-
B&B	-	Standard	-	Partial Board	-
Single Rate			€38.50/€50	Child reduction	25%

In Kinsale

Open: 1st February-30th November

June & Jack Sheehan
VILLA MARIA
Cork Road, Kinsale,
Co Cork

Kinsale
TEL: 021 4772627

Comfortable Villa, Scenic views, Conservatory, Garden. Cork-Kinsale Bus route. Quiet 3 mins walk Town. On R600 near Music, Pubs, Restaurants, Golf, Beaches, Airport, Ferryport.

B&B	6	Ensuite	€27/€32	Dinner	-
B&B	-	Standard	-	Partial Board	-
Single Rate			-	Child reduction	50%

In Town

Open: March-November

Ms Nora Lucey
NORVILLE HOUSE
Balymakeera, Macroom,
Co Cork

Macroom
TEL: 026 45486 FAX: 026 45486

Luxury house with a beautiful view. 2 min off N22 situated on the Cork to Killarney road. 50 min from Cork/Blarney, 20 min from Killarney and Kenmare. Gardens with Crazy Golf & Picnic area.

B&B	5	Ensuite	€25.50/€25.50	Dinner	-
B&B	1	Standard	€23/€23	Partial Board	-
Single Rate			€38.50/€38.50	Child reduction	50%

Macroom 7km

Open: All Year

Mrs Geraldine Manning
RICHALDINE HOUSE
Gurteenroe, Macroom,
Co Cork

Macroom
TEL: 026 41966 FAX: 026 41966

Two storey town house with garden. Family run. 0.5km from Town Centre. On N22 Killarney direction opposite Esso petrol station.

B&B	3	Ensuite	€25.50	Dinner	-
B&B	-	Standard	-	Partial Board	-
Single Rate			€38.50	Child reduction	50%

In Macroom

Open: 7th January-20th December

Macroom 9km

Sean & Margaret Moynihan
AN CUASAN
Coolavokig, Macroom,
Co Cork

Macroom
Tel: **026 40018**
Email: **cuasan@eircom.net**
Web: **www.welcome.to/cuasan**

Tranquil setting on N22, Blarney/Killarney. Dilliard/Causin recommended. Landscaped gardens, Walking, Golf, Traditional music family. Downstairs rooms. Bicycle shed.

B&B	5	Ensuite	€28	Dinner	-
B&B	1	Standard	€26	Partial Board	-
Single Rate			€37/€39	Child reduction	50%

Open: April-October

Macroom 5km

Kathleen & Brendan Mulcahy
FOUNTAIN HOUSE
Cork Road, Macroom,
Co Cork

Macroom
Tel: **026 43813**   Fax: **026 41425**

Lakeside N22 landscaped gardens. Ground floor rooms. Private parking. Warm hospitality. Breakfast menu, Home baking. Touring base Blarney, Killarney, Bantry.

B&B	6	Ensuite	€28/€28	Dinner	-
B&B	-	Standard	-	Partial Board	-
Single Rate			€39/€39	Child reduction	50%

Open: 1st March-30th November

Mrs Peggy Twomey
WESTON HEIGHTS
The Mills, Ballyvourney,
Macroom, Co Cork

Macroom
Tel: **026 45097/45936** Fax: **026 45097**

Charming family run 18th Century Georgian house on N22. Cead Mile Failte. Prize winning gardens. Close to all local amenities, Golf, Fishing, Walking, Horse Riding, Pubs and Restaurants.

B&B	5	Ensuite	€28	Dinner	€19
B&B	-	Standard	-	Partial Board	€264
Single Rate			€38.50	Child reduction	50%

Open: All Year

In Mallow

Mrs Sheila Clifford
ARD-NA-LAOI
Opp Convent of Mercy,
Bathview, Mallow, Co Cork

Mallow
Tel: **022 22317**   Fax: **022 22317**

Period residence, opposite Convent of Mercy. Mature gardens in centre of Town. Very private. Ideally situated for Fishing, Golfing, Swimming.

B&B	4	Ensuite	€25.50/€25.50	Dinner	-
B&B	-	Standard	-	Partial Board	-
Single Rate			€38.50/€38.50	Child reduction	50%

Open: 1st March-31st October

Mallow 2km

Mrs B Courtney
RATHMORE HOUSE
Fermoy Road, Mallow,
Co Cork

Mallow
Tel: **022 21688**

Peaceful setting beside Fermoy/Waterford Mitchelstown/Dublin Road. Rosslare Ferryport route. Spacious grounds, parking. Home baking. Tea/coffee in rooms.

B&B	3	Ensuite	€25.50	Dinner	-
B&B	2	Standard	€23	Partial Board	-
Single Rate			-	Child reduction	-

Open: 1st June-1st November

In Mallow

Anne Doolan
RIVERVALE LODGE
Bearforest, Mallow,
Co Cork

Mallow
Tel: **022 22218**
Email: **river.vale@indigo.ie**

In tranquil setting with panoramic views overlooking River Blackwater, Castle and Deerpark. Access to riverside walks. 4 minutes walk to Town Centre.

B&B	3	Ensuite	€25.50	Dinner	-
B&B		Standard		Partial Board	-
Single Rate			€38.50	Child reduction	33.3%

Open: 2nd January-23rd December

In Mallow

Mrs Mary Kiely
HILL TOP VIEW
Navigation Road, Mallow,
Co Cork

Mallow
Tel: **022 21491**   Fax: **022 21491**
Email: **mkhilltopview@eircom.net**

Country residence adjacent Racecourse/Fishing, Golf, Horseriding nearby. Touring centre. TV, Tea/Coffee facilities, Hairdryers, Breakfast menu, Conservatory, Secluded gardens.

B&B	6	Ensuite	€26	Dinner	-
B&B	-	Standard	-	Partial Board	-
Single Rate			€38.50	Child reduction	25%

Open: 1st March-31st October

Mallow 15km

Mrs Eva Lane
PARK SOUTH
Doneraile, Mallow,
Co Cork

Mallow
Tel: **022 25296**
Email: **parksouth@eircom.net**
Web: **parksouth.foundmark.com**

Situated 1km off N73. Dublin, Killarney, Cork, Ringaskiddy, Rosslare, Ferry. Fishing, Golf, Racecourse, Parks, Gardens (Ann's Grove). Bicycle shed. Qualified Cert cook. Hot scones on arrival.

B&B	3	Ensuite	€26/€26	Dinner	€20
B&B	1	Standard	€23/€23	Partial Board	€270
Single Rate			€36/€40	Child reduction	25%

Open: All Year

In Mallow

Mrs Winifred O'Donovan
OAKLANDS
Springwood,
Off Killarney Road,
Mallow, Co Cork

Mallow
Tel: **022 21127**   Fax: **022 21127**
Email: **oaklands@eircom.net**

AA ◆◆◆, Le Guide du Routard recommended. Quiet location, Breakfast conservatory. Short walk to town, train, races. N20/N72 Roundabout (150 yds) signposted.

B&B	4	Ensuite	€25.50	Dinner	-
B&B		Standard	-	Partial Board	-
Single Rate			€38.50	Child reduction	33.3%

Open: 1st April-31st October

In Mallow

Sean & Margaret O'Shea
ANNABELLA LODGE
Mallow,
Co Cork

Mallow
Tel: **022 43991**
Email: **moshea@esatclear.ie**
Web: **http://www.annabella-lodge.com**

Purpose built luxury accommodation. Hairdryers, Electric Blankets. Ideally situated 5 mins walk Town Centre, Railway Station. Adjacent Race Course, Golf. On N72.

B&B	6	Ensuite	€28/€32	Dinner	-
B&B	-	Standard	-	Partial Board	-
Single Rate			€39/€41	Child reduction	25%

Open: All Year

Mrs M Walsh
RIVERSIDE HOUSE
Navigation Road, Mallow,
Co Cork

Mallow
TEL: **022 42761**

Country house set in scenic area overlooking river Blackwater on N72. Ideal base for touring. Convenient Town Centre, Racecourse, Railway Station.

B&B	6	Ensuite	€26	Dinner	-
B&B	-	Standard	-	Partial Board	-
Single Rate			€38.50	Child reduction	25%

In Mallow   **Open:** All Year

Mrs Eileen Dowling
AMANDA
Cahermone, Midleton,
Co Cork

Midleton
TEL: **021 4631135**   FAX: **021 4631135**

Situated on the (N25). Waterford side of Midleton Town, near Jameson and Cobh Heritage Centre, Ballymaloe House, Fishing and Golf nearby.

B&B	4	Ensuite	€25.50	Dinner	-
B&B	-	Standard	-	Partial Board	-
Single Rate			€38.50	Child reduction	50%

Midleton 1km   **Open:** 1st April-1st November

Mrs Margaret Harty
SWAN LAKE
Loughaderra, Castlemartyr,
Midleton, Co Cork

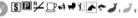
Midleton
TEL: **021 4667261**

Overlooking Loughaderra Lake, 400m off N25, between Midleton and Castlemartyr. Convenient Midleton & Cobh, Heritage Centre, Ballymaloe Hse, Fota Wildlife.

B&B	2	Ensuite	€25.50/€25.50	Dinner	-
B&B	1	Standard	€23/€23	Partial Board	-
Single Rate			€36/€38.50	Child reduction	50%

Midleton 4km   **Open:** 17th March-31st October

Mrs Mary Quinlan
SUNDOWN HOUSE
Kilmountain, Castlemartyr,
Midleton, Co Cork

Midleton
TEL: **021 4667375**

0.5km off Midleton to Waterford N 25, near Jameson Heritage Centre. Ballymaloe House, Blarney Castle, Deep Sea Angling/Lake Fishing, Golf nearby.

B&B	3	Ensuite	€25.50	Dinner	-
B&B	2	Standard	€23	Partial Board	-
Single Rate			€36/€36	Child reduction	50%

Midleton 5km   **Open:** 1st April-1st November

Mrs Margaret Tobin
DECIES B&B
Castleredmond, Midleton,
Co Cork

Midleton
TEL: **021 4632645**   FAX: **021 4634665**

Family home off N25, 15 minutes walk to Midleton Town & Jameson Heritage Centre. Restaurants, Traditional music. Convenient to Blarney Castle, Fota, Cobh, Golf Courses, Fishing, Ballycotton.

B&B	3	Ensuite	€25.50/€31.74	Dinner	-
B&B	1	Standard	€25.39/€31.74	Partial Board	-
Single Rate			€36	Child reduction	-

In Midleton   **Open:** April-November

Mrs Margaret Kiely
COOLACUNNA
Fermoy Road, Mitchelstown, Co Cork

Mitchelstown
TEL: **025 24170**

Modern bungalow on own grounds on main Cork/Dublin Road, overlooking Galtee Mountains. Mitchelstown Caves nearby. 3 mins walk from Town.

B&B	2	Ensuite	€25.50/€25.50	Dinner	-
B&B	1	Standard	€23/€23	Partial Board	-
Single Rate			€36/€36	Child reduction	33.3%

In Mitchelstown

Open: 1st April-31st October

Mrs Betty Luddy
RIVERSDALE
Limerick Road R513, Mitchelstown, Co Cork

Mitchelstown
TEL: **025 24717**   FAX: **025 24717**
EMAIL: **bettyluddy@eircom.net**

Situated just off N8 (Dublin/Cork Rd.) Golf Course at rear. Fishing rivers. Parks/Gardens. Convenient to Mitchelstown Caves.

B&B	2	Ensuite	€25.50/€25.50	Dinner	-
B&B	1	Standard	€23/€23	Partial Board	-
Single Rate			€36/€38.50	Child reduction	33.3%

Mitchelstown 1km

Open: All Year

Mrs Mary O'Connell
PALM LODGE
Limerick Road R513, Mitchelstown,Co Cork

Mitchelstown
TEL: **025 24687**   FAX: **025 85599**
EMAIL: **palmlodgebb@hotmail.com**
WEB: **www.dirl.com/cork/palm-lodge.htm**

Peaceful scenic home and gardens overlooking Golf Course/Mountains/Fishing. At centre of South via Dublin-Kerry-Rosslare. TV lounge. Restaurants nearby.

B&B	2	Ensuite	€25.50	Dinner	€17
B&B	1	Standard	€23	Partial Board	€302.25
Single Rate			€36/€38.50	Child reduction	33.3%

Mitchelstown 1km

Open: 1st March-1st November

Ms Anne O'Rahilly
ASHDALE HOUSE
Lower Shanbally, Ringaskiddy, Co Cork

Ringaskiddy
TEL: **021 4378681**   FAX: **021 4378681**
EMAIL: **ashdalebandb@eircom.net**
WEB: **http://ashdalehousecork.com**

Spacious welcoming family home, on Cork/Ringaskiddy route N28. Ferryport (3mins). Surrounded by Golf courses, Angling. An ideal touring base for West Cork.

B&B	5	Ensuite	€28/€30	Dinner	-
B&B	-	Standard	-	Partial Board	-
Single Rate			€36/€40	Child reduction	-

Carrigaline 5km

Open: 2nd January-20th December

Mrs Cathy Gill
SUNNYSIDE
42 Mardyke Street, Skibbereen, Co Cork

Skibbereen Town
TEL: **028 21365**   FAX: **028 21365**
EMAIL: **sunnysideskibb@eircom.net**

Highly recommended, excellent breakfasts hospitality and comfort. Very peaceful, in Town. Orthopaedic beds. Electric blankets. Bicycle storage. Signposted on R595.

B&B	3	Ensuite	€26/€30	Dinner	-
B&B	1	Standard	€23/€26	Partial Board	-
Single Rate			€36/€45	Child reduction	-

In Skibbereen

Open: All Year

Mrs Marguerite McCarthy
MARGUERITES
Baltimore Road, Coronea,
Skibbereen, Co Cork

Skibbereen
Tel: **028 21166**
Email: **marguerites@eircom.net**

Luxury accommodation in landscaped private grounds. Very peaceful, highly recommended. Ideal base for touring West Cork. Signposted on R595.

B&B	2	Ensuite	€26/€28	Dinner	-
B&B	1	Standard	€23/€26	Partial Board	-
Single Rate			€36/€42	Child reduction	-

Skibbereen 1km

Open: All Year

Mrs Hannah Murnane
LAKE VIEW
Shepperton, Skibbereen,
Co Cork

Skibbereen
Tel: **028 33301**

Comfortable home on N71 overlooking beautiful Shepperton Lakes. All amenities locally. Bicycle shed, Electric blankets, Hairdryers, Breakfast menu.

B&B	3	Ensuite	€25.50/€25.50	Dinner	€20
B&B	1	Standard	€23/€23	Partial Board	-
Single Rate			€36/€38.50	Child reduction	50%

Skibbereen 4km

Open: 10th April-1st November

Mrs Hannah O'Cinneide
WOODVIEW
Off Baltimore Road,
Skibbereen, Co Cork

Skibbereen
Tel: **028 21740**

Luxury spacious bungalow, large garden having unique position of rural setting in Skibbereen. Beaches close by. Bicycle storage. Breakfast menu. Golf arranged. Signposted on R595.

B&B	3	Ensuite	€25.50/€32.50	Dinner	-
B&B	1	Standard	€23/€25.39	Partial Board	-
Single Rate			€36/€45	Child reduction	50%

In Skibbereen

Open: 2nd May-30th October

Kathleen O'Donovan
P.K. LODGE
Smorane,
Skibbereen, Co Cork

Skibbereen
Tel: **028 21749**

Warm friendly hospitality in a very spacious luxurious modern home located just off N71. Close to the Town. Peaceful location. Complimentary tea/coffee. Home baking.

B&B	4	Ensuite	€26/€28	Dinner	-
B&B	-	Standard		Partial Board	-
Single Rate			€38.50/€40	Child reduction	33.3%

Skibbereen 1km

Open: All Year

Breda O'Driscoll
SANDYCOVE HOUSE
Castletownend, Skibbereen,
Co Cork

Skibbereen
Tel: **028 36223**
Email:**sandycovehouse@eircom.net**

Seaside location with superb view of Cliffs and Ocean. Beautiful sandy Beach adjacent (100m). Ideal for Rock Fishing, Swimming, Windsurfing, Cliffwalking.

B&B	4	Ensuite	€25/€26	Dinner	-
B&B	-	Standard		Partial Board	-
Single Rate			€38.50/€38.50	Child reduction	25%

Skibbereen 7km

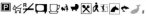

Open: 1st March-31st October

Skibbereen 1.5km

Mrs Eileen O'Driscoll
PALM GROVE
Coolnagurrane, Bantry Road,
Skibbereen, Co Cork

Skibbereen

Tel: **028 21703**   Fax: **028 21703**
Email: **info@palmgrovebb.com**
Web: **www.palmgrovebb.com**

Spacious bungalow overlooking open countryside, 1km off N71 on R593/R594 Bantry/Drimoleague Road, close to Hospital. Frommer recommended.

B&B	2	Ensuite	€26/€30	Dinner		-
B&B	2	Standard	€23/€26	Partial Board		-
Single Rate			€36/€45	Child reduction		25%

Open: 15th February-15th December

Skibbereen 3km

Mrs Carolyn O'Neill
FERN LODGE
Baltimore Road,
Skibbereen, Co Cork

Skibbereen Baltimore

Tel: **028 22327**
Email: **cneill@oceanfree.net**

Comfortable, family run home. Peaceful rural setting Skibbereen/Baltimore road. Lough Ine 2km, Baltimore 7km. All amenities locally.

B&B	6	Ensuite	€25.50	Dinner		-
B&B	-	Standard	-	Partial Board		-
Single Rate			€38.50	Child reduction		50%

Open: 1st March-30th November

In Skibbereen

Mrs K O'Sullivan
WHISPERING TREES
Baltimore Road, Skibbereen,
Co Cork

Skibbereen

Tel: **028 21376**   Fax: **028 21376**
Email: **whistree@gofree.indigo.ie**
Web: **www.cork-guide.ie/**
skibbereen/whisperingtrees/welcome.html

Modern comfortable home set in scenic and tranquil surroundings in suburbs of Town. Tea/Coffee making facilities in Conservatory.

B&B	4	Ensuite	€25.50/€25.50	Dinner		-
B&B	-	Standard	-	Partial Board		-
Single Rate			€38.50/€38.50	Child reduction		-

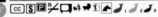

Open: 1st February-31st October

In Skibbereen

Mrs Sheila Poillot
WHITETHORN LODGE
Schull Road, Skibbereen,
Co Cork

Skibbereen

Tel: **028 22372**   Fax: **028 22372**
Email: **whitethornlodge@eircom.net**
Web: **www.cork-guide.ie/**
skibbereen/whitethornlodge/welcome.html

Luxury home & large garden on N71 town suburbs. Extensive breakfast menu, complimentary tea/coffee. Electric blankets in winter. Golf arranged. Warm welcome.

B&B	5	Ensuite	€26/€32	Dinner		-
B&B	-	Standard	-	Partial Board		-
Single Rate			€38.50/€46	Child reduction		-

Open: All Year Except Christmas

Butlerstown 1km

Mrs Mary Holland
ATLANTIC SUNSET
Kilsillagh, Butlerstown,
Bandon, Co Cork

Timoleague

Tel: **023 40115**
Email: **atlanticsunset@hotmail.com**

First class accommodation overlooking Atlantic. Dunworley sandy beaches 1km. Golf, Tennis, Fishing locally. Coastal walks. Leisure Centre 6km.

B&B	2	Ensuite	€28	Dinner		-
B&B	2	Standard	€26	Partial Board		-
Single Rate			€38.50/€38.50	Child reduction		33.3%

Open: 1st January-20th December

Pat & Jo O'Donovan
HARBOUR HEIGHTS
Timoleague, Bandon,
Co Cork

Timoleague
Tel: **023 46232**　　Fax: **023 46232**

Modern bungalow set in tranquil surroundings overlooking Timoleague Abbey & Courtmacsherry Bay. Guest Lounge, Conservatory. Private Car Park. On R600 between Kinsale & Clonakilty.

B&B	3	Ensuite	€27/€30	Dinner	-
B&B	1	Standard	€25/€27	Partial Board	-
Single Rate			€36/€36	Child reduction	33.3%

Clonakilty 8km　　**Open:** 15th March-4th November

Mrs Catherine Ryan
PANORAMA B&B
Chapel Hill, Timoleague,
(Near Kinsale), West Cork,
Co Cork

Timoleague
Tel: **023 46248**　　Fax: **023 46248**
Email: **panoramabb@eircom.net**
Web: **www.dirl.com/cork/panorama.htm**

On R600. Traditional village with unique Pub/Restaurants. Hair salon, Sun lounge - Patio, panoramic view of Abbey and Bay. Unspoilt Nature Reserve, Walks/ Beaches.

B&B	4	Ensuite	€26/€32	Dinner	-
B&B	-	Standard		Partial Board	-
Single Rate			€38.50/€46	Child reduction	33.3%

In Timoleague　　**Open:** All Year Except Christmas

Mrs Carol Kearney
LIS-ARDAGH LODGE B&B
Union Hall, Co Cork

Union Hall
Tel: **028 34951**
Email: **info@lis-ardaghlodge.com**
Web: **www.lis-ardaghlodge.com**

Lis-Ardagh Lodge is a beautiful stone built house enjoying views of the sea and countryside. Situated just 1km from the main N71 Cork to Skibbereen Road.

B&B	3	Ensuite	€25.50/€32	Dinner	-
B&B	-	Standard		Partial Board	-
Single Rate			€38.50	Child reduction	25%

Skibbereen 8km　　**Open:** All Year

Adela A Nugent
SHEARWATER
Keelbeg, Union Hall,
Skibbereen,
Co Cork

Union Hall Glandore
Tel: **028 33178**　　Fax: **028 34020**
Email: **shearwater@esatclear.ie**

"Shearwater" is situated overlooking Glandore Harbour and surrounding countryside. All bedrooms have sea views, the patio area offers outstanding scenery.

B&B	4	Ensuite	€25.50/€30	Dinner	-
B&B	-	Standard	-	Partial Board	-
Single Rate			€38.50/€45	Child reduction	50%

In Union Hall　　**Open:** 1st April-31st October

D & A O'Connell
ARDAGH HOUSE
Union Hall,
West Cork, Co. Cork

Union Hall
Tel: **028 33571**　　Fax: **028 33571**
Email: **info@ardaghhouse**
Web: **www.ardaghhouse.com**

Beautiful 100 yr old authentically restored farmhouse in village. Breakfast menu, hairdryers, TV, electric blankets. Ideal touring base. Fully licenced restaurant.

B&B	4	Ensuite	€25.50/€25.50	Dinner	€17
B&B	-	Standard	-	Partial Board	-
Single Rate			€38.50/€38.50	Child reduction	25%

Skibbereen 8km　　**Open:** 1st January-20th December

283

Mrs Therese Cliffe
THE GABLES
Kinsalebeg,
Youghal, Co Cork

Youghal
TEL: **024 92739**

Two storey building on 1.25 acres site off the N25 with Tennis Court. Close to sandy Beaches, Fishing, Golf, Fota, Jameson Heritage Centre. Ardmore, Youghal, Lismore.

B&B	1	Ensuite	€25.50	Dinner	-
B&B	4	Standard	€23	Partial Board	-
Single Rate			€36	Child reduction	50%

Youghal 8km

Open: 1st March-31st October

Mrs Nuala Connor
LAGILE LODGE
Killeagh, Youghal,
Co Cork

Youghal
TEL: **024 95323**   FAX: **024 95323**
EMAIL: **lagilelodge@eircom.net**
WEB: **homepage.eircom.net/~lagilelodge**

Enjoy farm animals, wildlife on 10 acres, gardens, paddocks, 200m off N25. Nearby pub food, walks. Spacious bedrooms. Breakfast menu, home baking. We enjoy meeting guests.

B&B	4	Ensuite	€25.50/€30	Dinner	-
B&B	-	Standard	-	Partial Board	-
Single Rate			-	Child reduction	25%

Youghal 8km

Open: 1st May-30th September

Maura Coughlan
CARN NA RADHARC
Ardsallagh, Youghal,
Co Cork

Youghal
TEL: **024 92703**
EMAIL: **carnnaradharc@eircom.net**

2km off N25, Youghal Bridge. Magnificent views river, mountains, quiet cul-de-sac. Locally Beaches, Heritage Centres, Fota. Comfortable bedrooms, TV lounge.

B&B	2	Ensuite	€25.50	Dinner	-
B&B	1	Standard	€23	Partial Board	-
Single Rate			€36	Child reduction	50%

Youghal 6km

Open: 1st March-31st October

Angela Cronin
ATTRACTA HOUSE
South Abbey, Youghal,
Co Cork

Youghal
TEL: **024 92062**

Town house overlooking Youghal Bay. Located on the N25 Cork/Rosslare route.

B&B	5	Ensuite	€25.50/€28	Dinner	-
B&B	-	Standard	-	Partial Board	-
Single Rate			€38.50/€38.50	Child reduction	50%

In Youghal

Open: 1st April-31st October

Mrs Eileen Fogarty
BROMLEY HOUSE
Killeagh, Youghal,
Co Cork

Youghal
TEL: **024 95235**

N25 Cork-Rosslare road. Golf, Fishing, Beaches nearby. Convenient Cobh, Midleton Heritage Centres, Blarney. Pub food nearby. Private parking.

B&B	5	Ensuite	€28	Dinner	-
B&B	-	Standard	-	Partial Board	-
Single Rate			€39	Child reduction	-

Youghal 9km

Open: 1st March-30th October

In Youghal

Mrs Phyllis Foley
ROSEVILLE
New Catherine St.,
Youghal, Co Cork

TEL: **024 92571**
EMAIL: **rosevillebandb@eircom.net**

Attractive detached residence situated within the "Olde Town" on the N25 Rosslare/Cork route. Within easy access to all amenities. Extensive breakfast menu. A warm welcome awaits you.

B&B	5	Ensuite	€27.50/€30	Dinner	-
B&B	-	Standard		Partial Board	-
Single Rate			€38.50/€40	Child reduction	**33.3%**

Open: 20th January-20th December

Paddy, Mary & Esther Forde
DEVON VIEW
Pearse Square, Youghal,
Co Cork

TEL: **024 92298**   FAX: **024 90107**
EMAIL: **info@devonview.com**
WEB: **http://www.devonview.com**

Charming well preserved Georgian house with antique furniture and modern house. Centrally located to all amenities. Car park.

B&B	6	Ensuite	€25.50/€25.50	Dinner	-
B&B	-	Standard		Partial Board	-
Single Rate			€38.50	Child reduction	-

Open: All Year Except Christmas

Mrs Eileen Gaine
AVONMORE HOUSE
South Abbey
Youghal, Co Cork

TEL: **024 92617**   FAX: **024 92617**
EMAIL: **avonmoreyoughal@eircom.net**

Elegant 18th Century Georgian House at the entrance to Youghal Harbour within 3 min walk of Youghal's famous clock tower.

B&B	6	Ensuite	€25.50/€32	Dinner	-
B&B	-	Standard		Partial Board	-
Single Rate			€38.50/€38.50	Child reduction	**25%**

Open: 10th January-20th December

In Youghal

Mrs Angela Leahy
LEE HOUSE
29 Friar Street, Youghal,
Co Cork

TEL: **024 92292**
EMAIL:**leahyangela@hotmail.com**

N25 Cork/Rosslare. Comfortable townhouse, central to restaurants, pubs, shops, laundrette, cinema, heritage centre, etc. Beach 5 mins. Private parking. Visa.

B&B	4	Ensuite	€25.50/€28	Dinner	-
B&B	-	Standard	€23/€25.50	Partial Board	-
Single Rate			€38.50/€38.50	Child reduction	**50%**

Open: All Year

Youghal 2km

Mrs Mary Scanlon
GREENLAWN
Summerfield, Youghal,
Co Cork

TEL: **024 93177**

Modern 2 storey home, 2km from Town Centre on the N25. Blue Flag Beach within 5 mins walk. Friendly welcome.

B&B	5	Ensuite	€27.50/€30	Dinner	-
B&B	-	Standard	-	Partial Board	-
Single Rate			€38.50/€40	Child reduction	**25%**

Open: 1st February-31st October

Ms Monica Yeomans
BAYVIEW HOUSE
**Front Strand, Youghal,
Co Cork**

Youghal

TEL: **024 92824**

Beautiful Victorian house, 50 metres from Blue Flag Beach. 1km from Youghal Town. "Guide du Routard" recommended. TV lounge. Warm welcome.

B&B	4	Ensuite	€25.50/€26	Dinner	-
B&B	-	Standard	-	Partial Board	-
Single Rate			€38.50/€38.50	Child reduction	**50%**

Youghal 1km

Open: 1st April-31st October

Discover the magic of Kerry, with its enthralling mountain and coastal scenery and wide diversity of culture and leisure activities. Enjoy the superb hospitality and friendliness of its people in a county that is rich in heritage and history.

Mrs Kathleen O'Connor
FOUR WINDS
Annascaul, Co Kerry

Annascaul (Dingle Peninsula)
Tel: **066 9157168**   Fax: **066 9157174**

Recommended Dillard Causin Guide. Outstanding views, Walks, Mountain Climbing, Beaches, Fishing, Lake/River. Golfing.

B&B	3	Ensuite	€25.50/€26	Dinner	-
B&B	1	Standard	€23/€23	Partial Board	-
Single Rate			€36/€39	Child reduction	25%

In Annascaul

Open: 1st January-22nd December

Katherine Higgins
ARDKEEL HOUSE
Ardfert, Co Kerry

Ardfert
Tel: **066 7134288**   Fax: **066 7134288**
Email: **ardkeelhouse@oceanfree.net**
Web: **www.ardfert.com/ardkeelhouse**

Warm welcoming hospitality. Luxurious home, quiet location off Ardfert/Fenit Road. Walking distance Bars, Restaurants, Tralee Golf Course 4km, Banna Beach 3km.

B&B	3	Ensuite	€25.50/€27	Dinner	€17
B&B	-	Standard	-	Partial Board	€280
Single Rate			€38.50/€38.50	Child reduction	25%

In Ardfert

Open: All Year

Mrs Bridie Sweeney
FAILTE
Tralee Road, Ardfert,
Co Kerry

Ardfert
Tel: **066 7134278**
Email: **bridiesweeney@eircom.net**

Luxurious Bungalow on Tralee/Banna/Ballyheigue road (R551) in historical Ardfert village near Tralee Golf course. Banna beach 3km. Restaurant 2 min walk.

B&B	4	Ensuite	€25.50/€27	Dinner	-
B&B	-	Standard	-	Partial Board	-
Single Rate			€38.50/€40	Child reduction	50%

In Ardfert

Open: 1st March-30th November

Lillian Morgan
RASCALS THE OLD
SCHOOL HOUSE
Barrys Cross, Ballinskelligs,
Co Kerry

Ballinskelligs
Tel: **066 9479340**   Fax: **066 9479340**
Email: **oshmb@iol.ie**
Web: **www.iol.ie/kerry-insight/old-school**

The Old School House, family run home. All home cooked food. Close to Blue Flag Beach. Open turf fire and a song or two each evening. The Kettle is on !!

B&B	4	Ensuite	€25.50/€26	Dinner	€17.14
B&B	-	Standard	-	Partial Board	-
Single Rate			€38.50/€38.50	Child reduction	50%

Waterville 7km

Open: All Year

Mrs Mary Beasley
THE 19TH GREEN
**Golf Links Rd, Ballybunion,
Co Kerry**

Ballybunion

Tel: **068 27592**   Fax: **068 27830**
Email: **the19thgreen@eircom.net**
Web: **www.ballybunions19thgreen.com**

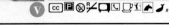

"Golfers Paradise". Directly opposite Golf course. Luxurius purpose built accommodation. Good Seven - Iron to club, Green fee reduction. Early Breakfast. Golf storage and Drying room.

B&B	4	Ensuite	€32/€50	Dinner	-
B&B	-	Standard		Partial Board	-
Single Rate			€45/€63.50	Child reduction	-

Ballybunion 1km

Open: 1st January-20th December

Maurice & Patricia Boyle
THE OLD COURSE
**Golf Links Road,
Ballybunion, Co Kerry**

Ballybunion

Tel: **068 27171**   Fax: **068 27171**
Email: **oldcourse@eircom.net**
Web: **www.oldcoursebb.com**

A warm welcome awaits you in our luxurious, spacious home at Ballybunion's famous Old Course. Green fee reduction. Private car park. Early Breakfasts.

B&B	3	Ensuite	€30/€50	Dinner	-
B&B	-	Standard		Partial Board	-
Single Rate			€45/€60	Child reduction	-

In Ballybunion

Open: 24th March-24th October

Michael & Ann Kissane
SEASHORE
**Doon East, Ballybunion,
Co Kerry**

Ballybunion

Tel: **068 27986**

Modern spacious home with sea views. Car park, early Breakfast, Power Showers. Near Beach and Golf. Tarbert Car Ferry 20 mins drive. Green fee reduction.

B&B	4	Ensuite	€30/€40	Dinner	-
B&B	-	Standard	€23/€30	Partial Board	-
Single Rate			€38.50/€50	Child reduction	**50%**

In Ballybunion

Open: 17th March-1st November

Mrs Anne McCaughey
DOON HOUSE
**Doon Road, Ballybunion,
Co Kerry**

Ballybunion

Tel: **068 27411/27073** Fax: **068 27411**
Email: **doonhouse@eircom.net**

Overlooking Ballybunion and Atlantic Ocean. Beautiful panoramic Sea/Mountain view. (Golfers home away from home). Green fee reductions. Early Breakfasts.

B&B	3	Ensuite	€30/€40	Dinner	-
B&B	-	Standard	-	Partial Board	-
Single Rate			€35/€50	Child reduction	-

In Ballybunion

Open: 1st April-31st October

Nora Quane
KILCONLY HOUSE
**Coast Rd, Ballybunion,
Co Kerry**

Ballybunion

Tel: **068 27633**
Email: **kilconlyhouse@eircom.net**

Peaceful coastal location off R551. North of Town. Breakfast menu, Home baking, Drying room, Patio with sea view. Ideal for touring, Golf, 15 min to Car Ferry.

B&B	3	Ensuite	€30/€40	Dinner	-
B&B	-	Standard		Partial Board	-
Single Rate			€38.50	Child reduction	**50%**

Ballybunion 3km

Open: 1st May-31st October

Sean & Nora Stack
SEANOR HOUSE
Listowel Rd, Ballybunion,
Co Kerry

Ballybunion

Tel: **068 27055**　　Fax: **068 27055**
Email: **bed@eircom.net**

Luxurious welcoming family home 5 mins from Golf & Beach. Early breakfast. Green fee reduction. Tea/Coffee on arrival. Ballybunion/Listowel Rd. (553)

B&B	3	Ensuite	€30/€40	Dinner	-
B&B	-	Standard	-	Partial Board	-
Single Rate			€38.50/€50	Child reduction	50%

Ballybunion 1km　　Open: 1st April-1st November

Mrs Anne Leen
WAVE CREST
Cliff Road, Old Mill,
Ballyheigue, Co Kerry

Ballyheigue

Tel: **066 7133177**

Peaceful country setting. Spectacular scenery. Bedrooms overlooking Bay on edge of Atlantic Ocean with Dingle Mountain range on background.

B&B	2	Ensuite	€25.50	Dinner	-
B&B	1	Standard	€23	Partial Board	-
Single Rate			€36	Child reduction	50%

In Ballyheigue　　Open: 1st May-30th September

Mrs Nuala Sowden
SHANNON VIEW
Ferry Road, Ballyduff,
Tralee, Co Kerry

Ballyduff

Tel: **066 7131324**

Chef owned, evening meals, excellent food. 5 mins to Ballybunion, golf and sandy beaches. Ballyheigue 20 mins. Enroute to Cliffs of Moher, Dingle, Ring of Kerry.

B&B	2	Ensuite	€25.50/€25.50	Dinner	€21.59
B&B	2	Standard	€23.49/€23.49	Partial Board	€266.64
Single Rate			€38.50/€38.50	Child reduction	50%

In Ballyduff　　Open: All Year

Patricia & Garrett Dee
CASTLE VIEW HOUSE
Carrig Island, Ballylongford,
Co Kerry

Ballylongford

Tel: **068 43304**　　Fax: **068 43304**
Email: **castleviewhouse@eircom.net**
Web: **www.castleviewhouse.com**

Relax in peaceful setting on scenic Island (entry by bridge). Facing Carrigafoyle Castle. Tarbert - Killimer Ferry. Ballybunion Golf course nearby. Scenic walks. Good food, Warm welcome.

B&B	6	Ensuite	€25.50/€25.50	Dinner	€17
B&B	-	Standard	-	Partial Board	-
Single Rate			€38.50/€38.50	Child reduction	50%

Ballylongford 2.5km　　Open: 2nd January-20th December

Mrs Noreen Heaphy
GLEBE HOUSE
Rushy Park, Ballylongford,
Co Kerry

Ballylongford

Tel: **068 43555**　　Fax: **068 43229**
Email: **glebeh@iol.ie**
Web: **www.glebehouse.ie**

Period residence, beautifully restored, blending modern convenience with olde world ambiance. Tarbert - Killimer Car Ferry, Ballybunion Golf Course & Beaches nearby.

B&B	4	Ensuite	€25.50/€25.50	Dinner	€17
B&B	-	Standard	-	Partial Board	-
Single Rate			€38.50/€38.50	Child reduction	50%

In Ballylongford　　Open: All Year Except Christmas

289

Mrs Cathy Fitzmaurice
THE OLDE FORGE
Caherdaniel, Ring of Kerry,
Co Kerry

Caherdaniel Ring of Kerry
TEL: **066 9475140**   FAX: **066 9475170**
EMAIL: **oldeforge@eircom.net**
WEB: **www.oldeforge.net**

Family run, overlooking Kenmare Bay. Access to Sea. Breakfast menu. Dillard, Causin Guide. Horseriding, Hill walking, Sea sport, Golf, Fishing, Diving. Kerry Way.

B&B	6	Ensuite	€25.50/€25.50	Dinner	-
B&B	-	Standard	-	Partial Board	-
Single Rate			€38.50/€38.50	Child reduction	50%

Caherdaniel 1km   **Open:** All Year

Donal & Monica Hunt
DERRYNANE BAY HOUSE
Caherdaniel, Co Kerry

Caherdaniel Ring of Kerry
TEL: **066 9475404**   FAX: **066 9475436**
EMAIL: **derrynanebayhouse@eircom.net**
WEB: **www.ringofkerry.net**

Superb accommodation, overlooking Derrynane Bay. Breakfast menu. Golf, Horse-riding, Fishing, Diving, Beaches nearby. Adjacent Kerry Way. AA & Michelin listed.

B&B	5	Ensuite	€26/€28	Dinner	€22
B&B	-	Standard	-	Partial Board	-
Single Rate			€33/€35	Child reduction	25%

Caherdaniel 1km   **Open:** 15th March-23rd December

Mrs Irene Curran
HARBOUR HILL
Knockeens, Cahirciveen,
Co Kerry

Cahirciveen
TEL: **066 9472844**   FAX: **066 9472844**
EMAIL: **harbourhill@eircom.net**
WEB: **www.dirl.com/kerry/harbour-hill.htm**

Luxurious home. Panoramic sea views. Close to all amenities. Skeilig trips. Suitable for allergy sufferers. Single and Family rooms. Special low season rates.

B&B	4	Ensuite	€25.50	Dinner	-
B&B	-	Standard	-	Partial Board	-
Single Rate			€38.50/€38.50	Child reduction	33.3%

Cahirciveen 3km   **Open:** 1st April-30th September

Mrs Eilis Dennehy
SEA BREEZE
Renard Road, Cahirciveen,
Co Kerry

Cahirciveen
TEL: **066 9472609**   FAX: **066 9473275**
EMAIL: **seabreezebandb@eircom.net**
WEB: **homepage.eircom.net/~seabreezebandb**

Friendly atmosphere, spectacular views, Sea, Islands, Castle, Forts. Skellig trips. Recommended Routard, Michelin, Dillard Causin Guides; Breakfast menu. Orthapaedic beds.

B&B	4	Ensuite	€26/€26	Dinner	-
B&B	2	Standard	€23.50/€23.50	Partial Board	-
Single Rate			€36/€38.50	Child reduction	25%

Cahirciveen 1km   **Open:** 1st January-30th November

Mary Guirey
FERRYVIEW
Renard, Cahirciveen,
Co Kerry

Cahirciveen
TEL: **066 9472052**
EMAIL: **info@ferryview-cahersiveen.com**
WEB: **www.ferryview-cahersiveen.com**

Luxury country home. Peaceful setting, spacious rooms. Panoramic sea, Mountain view. Skellig trips. Jacuzzi and Steamroom facility. Tea/Coffee on arrival.

B&B	4	Ensuite	€26.50	Dinner	-
B&B	-	Standard	-	Partial Board	-
Single Rate			€38.50	Child reduction	50%

Cahirciveen 2.5km   **Open:** March-November

Mrs B Landers
Cahirciveen

SAN ANTOINE
Valentia Rd, Cahirciveen,
Co Kerry

TEL: **066 9472521**   FAX: **066 9472521**
EMAIL: **sanantoine@eircom.net**

Set in peaceful landscaped gardens overlooking the Bay. Sea Sports, Golf, Angling, Horse-riding, sandy beaches, scenic walks locally. Breakfast menu.

B&B	6	Ensuite	€26/€26	Dinner	-
B&B	-	Standard	-	Partial Board	-
Single Rate			€38.50	Child reduction	33.3%

In Cahirciveen

Open: 1st April-20th October

Ian & Ann Nugent
Cahirciveen

CUL DRAIOCHTA
Points Cross, Cahirciveen,
Co Kerry

TEL: **066 9473141**   FAX: **066 9473141**
EMAIL: **inugent@esatclear.ie**
WEB: **www.esatclear.ie/~culdraiochta**

Charming family home with panoramic scenery. Excellent location on N70. Highly recommended. Tea/Coffee on arrival. Extensive breakfast menu.

B&B	4	Ensuite	€26	Dinner	€17
B&B	-	Standard	-	Partial Board	-
Single Rate			€38.50	Child reduction	50%

Cahirciveen 1km

Open: All Year

Mrs Claire O'Donoghue
Cahirciveen

OCEAN VIEW
Renard Road, Cahirciveen,
Co Kerry

TEL: **066 9472261**   FAX: **066 9472261**
WEB: **www.oceanview.mainpage.net**

Luxury home overlooking Cahirciveen Bay within walking distance of Town. Rec by Rough Guide, AA ◆◆◆. Excellent location. Skelligs trips arranged.

B&B	6	Ensuite	€25.50	Dinner	-
B&B	-	Standard	-	Partial Board	-
Single Rate			€38.50	Child reduction	25%

Cahirciveen 1km

Open: 3rd January-19th December

Mrs Christina O'Neill
Cahirciveen

IVERAGH HEIGHTS
Carhan Rd, Cahirciveen,
Co Kerry

TEL: **066 9472545**   FAX: **066 9472545**

Luxury spacious rooms overlooking Atlantic Ocean. Trip to Skellig Michael arranged. Ideal for exploring Iveragh Peninsula, Archaeological sites. Recommended Routard, Michelin Guide.

B&B	4	Ensuite	€25.50	Dinner	€17
B&B	-	Standard	€23	Partial Board	-
Single Rate			-	Child reduction	33.3%

In Cahirciveen

Open: All Year

Eileen O'Shea
Cahirciveen

O'SHEAS B&B
Church St, Cahirciveen,
Co Kerry

TEL: **066 9472402**

Friendly family run home. Relax in quiet peaceful location with breathtaking view of Mountain and Sea. Group and Low season reduction. Blue flag Beaches.

B&B	4	Ensuite	€25.50	Dinner	-
B&B	-	Standard	-	Partial Board	-
Single Rate			€38.50	Child reduction	25%

In Cahirciveen

Open: All Year

Camp 4.5km

Mrs Fionnuala Fitzgerald
SUAN NA MARA
Lisnagree, Castlegregory Rd,
Camp, Co Kerry

Camp Castlegregory
TEL: **066 7139258**   FAX: **066 7139258**
EMAIL: **suanmara@eircom.net**
WEB: **www.kerryweb.ie/suanmara**

Peaceful accommodation. Highly recommended Laura Ashley style home. AA ♦♦♦♦. Write up in San Francisco Chronicle. Superb Breakfast menu. Private walk to Golden Beach. Pitch & Putt.

B&B	6	Ensuite	€28/€31	Dinner	-
B&B	-	Standard		Partial Board	-
Single Rate			€40/€60	Child reduction	-

Open: 20th March-31st October

Stradbally 1km

Mrs Mary Ferriter
BEENOSKEE
Cappateige,
Conor Pass Road,
Castlegregory, Co Kerry

Castlegregory Dingle Peninsula
TEL: **066 7139263**   FAX: **066 7139263**
EMAIL: **beenoskee@eircom.net**
WEB: **www.beenoskee.com**

Tastefully decorated rooms overlooking ocean. Spectacular views - Mountains, Islands, Lake. Warm hospitality, Breakfast menu. Homebaking. "Routard" recommended. 1km West Stradbally.

B&B	5	Ensuite	€28/€30	Dinner	€20
B&B	-	Standard		Partial Board	€290
Single Rate			€40	Child reduction	50%

Open: All Year

Castlegregory 2.5km

Mrs Mary Ellen Flynn
BEDROCK
Stradbally, Conor Pass Road,
Castlegregory, Co Kerry

Castlegregory Dingle Peninsula
TEL: **066 7139401**
EMAIL: **bedrockbandb@eircom.net**
WEB: **homepage.eircom.net/~bedrockbandb**

Family run, overlooking Brandon Bay, Maharees Islands, Golf course, Restaurant, Beaches, Fishing, Water Sports, Horse Riding, Mountain Climbing. Breakfast menu.

B&B	4	Ensuite	€28/€30	Dinner	-
B&B	-	Standard		Partial Board	-
Single Rate			€40/€40	Child reduction	50%

Open: All Year

Castlegregory

Ms Mary Kelliher
KELLIHERS
The Station, Castlegregory,
Co Kerry

Castlegregory
TEL: **066 7139295**
EMAIL: **kellihers@hotmail.com**

Luxurious accommodation with spacious ensuite rooms on Dingle Way. Ideal touring base for Dingle Peninsula. Tea/Coffee facilities & TV in bedrooms.

B&B	5	Ensuite	€28/€30	Dinner	-
B&B	-	Standard		Partial Board	-
Single Rate			€40/€40	Child reduction	25%

Open: All Year

Stradbally 3km

Mrs Mary Lynch
STRAND VIEW HOUSE
Kilcummin, Conor Pass Road,
Castlegregory, Co Kerry

Castlegregory Dingle Peninsula
TEL: **066 7138131**   FAX: **066 7138386**
EMAIL: **strandview@eircom.net**
WEB: **www.strandview.com**

Spacious luxury home on sea front overlooking Brandon Bay. AA ♦♦♦♦ Quality Award. Highly recommended in Guides. 3km West of Stradbally.

B&B	4	Ensuite	€28.50/€30	Dinner	-
B&B	-	Standard		Partial Board	-
Single Rate			€38.50/€48	Child reduction	50%

Open: 1st January-15th December

Mrs Catherine Lyons
ORCHARD HOUSE
Castlegregory,
Co Kerry

Castlegregory
TEL: **066 7139164**
EMAIL: **orchardh@gofree.indigo.ie**
WEB: **www.kerryview.com**

Family home in idyllic village - on Dingle Way walk route. Convenient to all cultural, sporting and leisure amenities. Beach 5 minutes walk. Home baking.

B&B	3	Ensuite	€28/€30	Dinner	-
B&B	1	Standard	€28	Partial Board	-
Single Rate			€40	Child reduction	50%

In Castlegregory

CC P ⚌✆✗Ⓐ🕭🛏⛺➔🚶♨♨ₛ♨ᵣ   **Open:** 1st March-31st October

Mrs Maura Moriarty
THE FUCHSIA HOUSE
West Main Street,
Castlegregory, Co Kerry

Castlegregory
TEL: **066 7139508/7139000** FAX: **066 7138386**
EMAIL: **fuchsiahouse@kerryview.com**
WEB: **www.fuchsiahse.com**

New home with old Irish charm. Previous trainee Chef of the year. Home baking, Excellent Breakfast menu. On Dingle Way. Private parking. All amenities nearby.

B&B	4	Ensuite	€28/€30	Dinner	-
B&B	-	Standard		Partial Board	-
Single Rate			€40/€45	Child reduction	50%

In Castlegregory

CC S P ⚌⊗✗▭🕭▭✈✗✗Ⓐ🕭🛏➔♨♨ₛ♨ᵣ   **Open:** All Year

Mrs Annette O'Mahony
THE SHORES COUNTRY HOUSE
Cappatigue, Conor Pass Road, Castlegregory, Co Kerry

Castlegregory Dingle Peninsula
TEL: **066 7139196** FAX: **066 7139196**
EMAIL: **theshores@eircom.net**
WEB: **shores.main-page.com**

Award winning AA ♦♦♦♦♦, luxurious spacious "Laura Ashley" style rooms all panoramic Sea-view. Breakfast/Dinner menu. Highly recommended. 1 mile west Stradbally.

B&B	6	Ensuite	€27.50/€33	Dinner	€23
B&B	-	Standard		Partial Board	€380
Single Rate			€40/€50	Child reduction	33.3%

Dingle 14km

CC S P ⚌⊗✗▭🕭▭✈✗✗Ⓐ🕭🛏➔♨♨ₛ♨ᵣ **Open:** 1st February-30th November

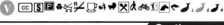

Mrs Agnes Reidy
GOULANE HOUSE
Stradbally, Conor Pass Road, Castlegregory, Co Kerry

Castlegregory Dingle Peninsula
TEL: **066 7139174**
EMAIL: **goulanehouse@eircom.net**

Outstanding Irish hospitality, beautiful views overlooking Brandon Bay/Mountains. 5 min walk Pub/Restaurant. 2 triples, luxury Orthopaedic beds, Tea/Coffee. Numerous recommendations.

B&B	4	Ensuite	€28/€30	Dinner	-
B&B	-	Standard		Partial Board	-
Single Rate			€38.50/€40	Child reduction	50%

In Stradbally

CC S P ⚌⊗✗▭🕭▭✈✗✗Ⓐ🕭🛏➔♨♨ₛ♨ᵣ   **Open:** All Year

Mrs Sheila Rohan
CAISLEAN TI
Castlegregory,
Co Kerry

Castlegregory Dingle Peninsula
TEL: **066 7139183**
EMAIL: **caisleanti@unison.ie**
WEB: **www.caisleanti.com**

Stylish house on Dingle-way. Peaceful surroundings with sea view. Comfort assured. Home Baking. Former Calor Housewife of the year.

B&B	6	Ensuite	€28/€30	Dinner	-
B&B	-	Standard		Partial Board	-
Single Rate			€40/€40	Child reduction	50%

In Castlegregory

CC P ⚌⊗✗▭🕭▭✈Ⓐ🕭🛏➔♨♨ₛ♨ᵣ   **Open:** All Year

Mrs Paula Walsh
SEA-MOUNT HOUSE
Cappatigue,
Conor Pass Road,
Castlegregory, Co Kerry

Castlegregory Dingle Peninsula
Tel: **066 7139229**   Fax: **066 7139229**
Email: **seamount@unison.ie**
Web: **www.kerry-insight.com/sea-mount**

AA ◆◆◆ Quality Award. Highly recommended. This charming home boast outstanding Sea views. Stylishly decorated rooms. Near Restaurant, 1km West Stradbally.

B&B	3	Ensuite	€28/€30	Dinner	-
B&B	-	Standard	-	Partial Board	-
Single Rate			€40/€40	Child reduction	50%

Dingle 14km

Open: 1st April-1st November

Mrs Eileen Cronin
GROTTO VIEW
Currow Village, Killarney,
Co Kerry

Castleisland
Tel: **066 9764646**   Fax: **066 9764646**
Email: **grottoview@eircom.net**

Welcoming modern family home in award winning village off N23. Airport 2km. Ideal for touring Kerry. Spacious ensuite rooms, TV, Tea/Coffee facilities.

B&B	3	Ensuite	€25.50/€25.50	Dinner	€17
B&B	-	Standard	-	Partial Board	€264
Single Rate			€38.50/€38.50	Child reduction	50%

Castleisland 4km

Open: April-October

Lilian Dillon
THE GABLES
Dooneen, Limerick Rd (N21),
Castleisland, Co Kerry

Castleisland
Tel: **066 7141060**   Fax: **066 7141060**
Email: **gablesdillon@eircom.net**
Web: **homepage.eircom.net/~gablesbnb**

Luxurious home overlooking 18 hole golf course (1 min drive) and beautiful landscape. Ideal touring/golfing base. Breakfast menu. Two triple rooms.

B&B	3	Ensuite	€25.50/€28	Dinner	-
B&B	1	Standard	€23/€25.50	Partial Board	-
Single Rate			€36/€38.50	Child reduction	33.3%

Castleisland 3km

Open: All Year Except Christmas

Mrs Eileen O'Connor
GLENBROOK HOUSE
Airport Road, Currow Village,
Castleisland, Killarney,
Co Kerry

Castleisland
Tel: **066 9764488**   Fax: **066 9764488**
Email: **glenbrookhouse@eircom.net**

Highly recommended home. Ideal for touring Kerry. Home cooking a speciality. Signposted off N23. Airport 1km. Visa/Access/Mastercard accepted.

B&B	3	Ensuite	€25.50	Dinner	€17
B&B	1	Standard	€23	Partial Board	-
Single Rate			€36/€38.50	Child reduction	50%

Castleisland 3km

Open: All Year Except Christmas

Breda O'Sullivan
TAILORS LODGE
Killegane, Castleisland,
Co Kerry

Castleisland
Tel: **066 7142170**

Luxurious new purpose built house on the R577 Castleisland/Scartaglen road. Power showers, hairdryers, guest lounge, breakfast menu. Airport 8km. Ideal touring base for Kerry.

B&B	5	Ensuite	€26	Dinner	-
B&B	-	Standard	-	Partial Board	-
Single Rate			€39	Child reduction	25%

In Castleisland

Open: All Year

Mrs Betty Riordan
RONNOCO LODGE
Limerick Rd, Castleisland,
Co Kerry

Castleisland

TEL: **066 7141325**   FAX: **066 7141325**
EMAIL: **bettyriordan@eircom.net**

Experience comfort in family run home. All ground floor bedrooms. TV, Tea/Coffee, radio clock alarms, hairdryers, electric blankets. Family room. Pub transport.

B&B	2	Ensuite	€25.50/€25.50	Dinner	€17
B&B	1	Standard	€25/€25	Partial Board	-
Single Rate			€36/€36	Child reduction	50%

Castleisland 2km

Open: All Year

Mrs Joan Burke
MOUNTAIN VIEW
Ballinamona, Castlemaine,
Co Kerry

Castlemaine

TEL: **066 9767249**

Modern two storey new house with panoramic view. Central for touring Ring of Kerry and Dingle Peninsula. Access/Visa/Euro.

B&B	2	Ensuite	€25.50	Dinner	€17
B&B	1	Standard	€23	Partial Board	-
Single Rate			-	Child reduction	50%

Castlemaine 1km

Open: 1st April-30th October

Mrs Elizabeth O'Sullivan
CAHER HOUSE
Caherfilane, Keel,
Castlemaine, Co Kerry

Castlemaine

TEL: **066 9766126**
EMAIL: **caherf1@eircom.net**

Comfortable residence overlooking Dingle Bay. Central for Dingle, Ring of Kerry, Killarney, Kerry Airport, 15kms, between Castlemaine & Inch, Scenic Walks.

B&B	5	Ensuite	€25.50/€25.50	Dinner	€17
B&B	1	Standard	€23/€23	Partial Board	€264
Single Rate			€36/€38.50	Child reduction	50%

Castlemaine 4km

Open: 1st April-31st October

Mrs Eleanor Begley
CLOOSHMORE HOUSE
Clooshmore, Dingle,
Co Kerry

Dingle

TEL: **066 9151117**

Luxury home on the edge of Dingle Harbour with spectacular views from each bedroom. Featured in many guides American and Japanese.

B&B	3	Ensuite	€26/€30	Dinner	-
B&B	-	Standard	-	Partial Board	-
Single Rate			-	Child reduction	-

Dingle 2km

Open: 1st March-31st October

Mrs Kitty Brosnan
ABHAINN MHOR
Cloghane, Co Kerry

Dingle

TEL: **066 7138211**
EMAIL: **brosnankitty@hotmail.com**
WEB: **www.kerryweb.ie**

Beside village. On Dingle way, foot of Brandon Mountain. Near Dingle, Beaches, Hill walking, Fishing, Archaeology. Coeliacs welcome.

B&B	3	Ensuite	€25.50/€25.50	Dinner	€17
B&B	1	Standard	-	Partial Board	€264
Single Rate			€36/€36	Child reduction	50%

Dingle 10km

Open: March-November

Kerry

Mrs Camilla Browne
BROWNES
Ladies Cross, Dingle,
Co Kerry

Dingle
Tel: **066 9151259**
Email: **jbrownes@iol.ie**
Web: **www.iol/~jbrownes**

Luxurious peaceful country home on Ventry Slea Head Road, overlooking Dingle Bay and Mountains. Tea/Coffee, TV, Hairdryers, Extensive Breakfast menu.

B&B	4	Ensuite	€25.50/€28	Dinner	-
B&B	-	Standard		Partial Board	-
Single Rate			€38.50/€38.50	Child reduction	-

Dingle 1km

Open: 1st April-5th November

Mrs Eileen Carroll
MILESTONE
Milltown, Dingle,
Co Kerry

Dingle
Tel: **066 9151831**
Email: **milstone@iol.ie**
Web: **www.iol.ie/~milstone/index.html**

Quiet home overlooking Dingle Bay, Mount Brandon. All rooms with phone, TV, Clock radio, Hairdryer, Tea/Coffee facilities. Breakfast menu, Private car park.

B&B	6	Ensuite	€25.50/€28	Dinner	-
B&B	-	Standard		Partial Board	-
Single Rate			€38.50/€38.50	Child reduction	25%

Dingle 1km

Open: 15th March-31st October

Mrs Mary Carroll
CEANN TRA HEIGHTS
Ventry, Dingle, Co Kerry

Dingle
Tel: **066 9159866**
Email: **ventry@iol.ie**
Web: **www.dinglewest.com/ventry/bandb/mcarroll/index.html**

Quiet country home in peaceful scenic area overlooking Ventry Harbour/Dingle Bay. Seaview from rooms. In Ventry village. 5 minutes walk to blue flag Beach. Breakfast menu. Tea making facilities.

B&B	4	Ensuite	€25.50/€28	Dinner	-
B&B	-	Standard		Partial Board	-
Single Rate			€38.50/€45	Child reduction	33.3%

Dingle 4km

Open: 14th March-4th November

Eileen Collins
KIRRARY
Avondale, Dingle,
Co Kerry

Dingle
Tel: **066 9151606**
Email: **collinskirrary@eircom.net**

Personal touch. In centre of Town, scenic gardens. Ideal Walkers/Cyclists. Sciuird Archaelogy, Rent - A - Bike. Recommended by Rick Steeves, famous American Tour Guide.

B&B	2	Ensuite	€25.50/€30	Dinner	-
B&B	1	Standard	€25.50/€30	Partial Board	-
Single Rate			€36/€43	Child reduction	-

In Dingle

Open: 1st January-23rd December

Geraldine and Kevin Devane
Goat Street
Dingle, Co Kerry

Dingle
Tel: **066 9151193**
Email: **devanesdingle@eircom.net**
Web: **homepage.eircom.net/~devanesdingle/index.html**

Townhouse, family run, overlooking Dingle Bay. Within walking distance to all amenities. Ideal touring base. TV, clock-radios, hairdryers, Tea/Coffee in bedrooms. Quiet location.

B&B	5	Ensuite	€25.50/€27	Dinner	-
B&B	1	Standard	€24.50/€26	Partial Board	-
Single Rate			-	Child reduction	33.3%

In Dingle

Open: 15th March-31st October

Ballyferriter 3km

Mrs Breda Ferris
COIS CORRAIGH
Emila, Ballyferriter,
Dingle Peninsula,
Co Kerry

Dingle

TEL: 066 9156282 FAX: 066 9156005
EMAIL: coiscorraigh@hotmail.com

Family home convenient to Beaches, Golf Course, Restaurants. Archaeological sites nearby, Gallarus Oratory, Riase, Kilmaoulceadar.

B&B	5	Ensuite	€25.50/€28	Dinner	-
B&B	-	Standard	-	Partial Board	-
Single Rate			€38.50	Child reduction	-

Open: 1st April-30th September

In Dingle

Mrs Bridie Fitzgerald
DINGLE HEIGHTS
Ballinboula, High Road,
Dingle, Co Kerry

Dingle

TEL: 066 9151543 FAX: 066 9152445
EMAIL: dingleheights@hotmail.com

Warm friendly home overlooking Dingle Bay and Harbour. Private parking, Walking distance to Town and all amenities. Quiet location.

B&B	4	Ensuite	€25.50/€28	Dinner	-
B&B	-	Standard	-	Partial Board	-
Single Rate			€38.50/€38.50	Child reduction	25%

Open: March-November

Dingle 4km

Beatrice Flannery
THE PLOUGH
Ventry, Dingle,
Co Kerry

Dingle

TEL: 066 9159727
EMAIL: theplough@iol.ie
WEB: www.ireland-discover.com/plough.htm

Warm friendly home in Ventry Village. Walking distance to all amenities, Panoramic Sea/Mountain views. Breakfast menu. Restaurant nearby. Guest lounge, orthopaedic beds.

B&B	4	Ensuite	€25.50/€28	Dinner	-
B&B	-	Standard	-	Partial Board	-
Single Rate			€38.50	Child reduction	-

Open: All Year Except Christmas

In Dingle

Robbie & Mary Griffin
TOWER VIEW
Farranredmond, Dingle,
Co Kerry

Dingle

TEL: 066 9152990 FAX: 066 9152989
EMAIL: towerviewdingle@eircom.net
WEB: homepage.eircom.net/towerviewdingle/

New home, overlooking Dingle harbour, quiet location. Parking. Mins walk to Town Centre, close to all local amenities. Guest lounge, multi-channel TV, Tea/Coffee. Breakfast menu.

B&B	5	Ensuite	€28/€32	Dinner	-
B&B	-	Standard	-	Partial Board	-
Single Rate			€38.50/€45	Child reduction	33.3%

Open: March-November

In Ballyferriter

Mrs Alice Hannafin
AN SPEICE
Ballyferriter West,
Dingle, Co Kerry

Dingle

TEL: 066 9156254
EMAIL: speice@eircom.net

A warm welcome awaits you at our family run B&B. Tea/Coffee on arrival. Home baking & Breakfast menu. On Slea Head drive. Sea & Mountain views. Close to Village, Golf, Sea & Walks.

B&B	3	Ensuite	€25.50/€25.50	Dinner	-
B&B	-	Standard	€23/€23	Partial Board	-
Single Rate			€36/€36	Child reduction	50%

Open: 1st March-30th October

Kerry

Mary Houlihan
ARD NA GREINE HOUSE
Spa Road, Dingle,
Co Kerry

Dingle
TEL: 066 9151113

AA ♦♦♦♦ Award, RAC, Sparkling Diamond Award. Recommended 300 Best B&B, Ricks Steve'
nationwide. Spacious rooms, Orthopaedic beds, Electric blankets, Fullbaths.

B&B	4	Ensuite	€25.50/€32	Dinner	-
B&B	-	Standard	-	Partial Board	-
Single Rate				Child reduction	-

In Dingle   **Open:** 1st March-1st November

Ms Marguerite Kavanagh
KAVANAGH'S B&B
Garfinny, Dingle, Co Kerry

Dingle
TEL: 066 9151326
EMAIL: mkavan@iol.ie
WEB: www.iol.ie/~mkavan/

Country family run home on main Tralee/Killarney Road. 5 minutes drive to Dingle. Spacious bedrooms, Hairdryers, TV, Tea/Coffee, Electric Blankets in rooms.

B&B	3	Ensuite	€25.50/€30	Dinner	€20
B&B	1	Standard	€23/€27	Partial Board	-
Single Rate			€36/€38.50	Child reduction	33.3%

Dingle 3km   **Open:** 1st April-31st October

James & Hannah Kelliher
BALLYEGAN HOUSE
Upper John Street,
Dingle, Co Kerry

Dingle
TEL: 066 9151702

Luxury home, magnificent views overlooking Dingle Harbour. Car parking. Minutes walk to Town.
Guest lounge. AA recommended. Pass Doyles Restaurant. We are at top of Johns Street on left.

B&B	6	Ensuite	€28/€28.57	Dinner	-
B&B	-	Standard	-	Partial Board	-
Single Rate			€51/€51	Child reduction	25%

In Dingle   **Open:** All Year

Angela Long
TIGH AN DUNA
Fahan, Slea Head, Ventry,
Dingle, Co Kerry

Dingle
TEL: 066 9159822
EMAIL: ventrysleahead@hotmail.com

Peaceful home at Dunbeg Fort, near spectacular Slea Head. Atlantic Ocean. Views from bedrooms/
diningroom. Near Beehives, Blasket Ferry, Restaurants, Beaches. On Dingle Way walk route.

B&B	2	Ensuite	€26/€27	Dinner	-
B&B	1	Standard	€24/€25	Partial Board	-
Single Rate			€36/€38.50	Child reduction	50%

Dingle 8km   **Open:** 1st May-13th October

Mrs Angela McCarthy
CILL BHREAC
Milltown, Dingle, Co Kerry

Dingle
TEL: 066 9151358
EMAIL: cbhreac@iol.ie
WEB: www.iol.ie/~cbhreac/index.htm

Spacious home overlooking Dingle Bay, Mount Brandon. All rooms with radio, hairdryer, electric
blankets. Tea facilities, Satellite TV. Breakfast menu.

B&B	6	Ensuite	€25.50/€28	Dinner	-
B&B	-	Standard	-	Partial Board	-
Single Rate			€38.50/€38.50	Child reduction	33.3%

Dingle 1km   **Open:** 15th February-15th November

Tricia & Jim McCarthy
BALLYBEG HOUSE
Conor Pass Road, Dingle,
Co Kerry

Dingle
Tel: **066 9151569**
Email: **ballybeghse@eircom.net**

Warm peaceful home with breathtaking views. Rooms with Cable TV, Orthopaedic beds, Tea/Coffee, Electric blankets. Extensive Breakfast with view of Harbour.

B&B	4	Ensuite	€26/€29	Dinner	-
B&B	-	Standard	-	Partial Board	-
Single Rate			-	Child reduction	-

Dingle 1 km

Open: April-October

Mrs Ann Murphy
ARD-NA-MARA
COUNTRY HOUSE
Ballymore, Ventry,
Dingle, Co Kerry

Dingle
Tel: **066 9159072**
Email: **annmurphybnb@hotmail.com**

Elevated peaceful country home beside the sea overlooking Ventry Harbour. Rooms en-suite, Breakfast menu. Complimentary Tea/Coffee.

B&B	4	Ensuite	€25.50/€27	Dinner	-
B&B	-	Standard	-	Partial Board	-
Single Rate			€38.50/€38.50	Child reduction	50%

Dingle 4km

Open: 1st March-31st October

Mrs Mary Murphy
THE LIGHTHOUSE
The High Road, Ballinaboula,
Dingle, Co Kerry

Dingle
Tel: **066 9151829**
Email: **lighthousebandb@eircom.net**
Web: homepage.eircom.net/~murphydenis/index.html

Magnificent harbour views. 10 mins walk to town. Recommended "300 Best B&B's". Drive straight up Main St to outskirts of Town, we're third B&B on right.

B&B	6	Ensuite	€25.50/€32	Dinner	-
B&B	-	Standard	-	Partial Board	-
Single Rate			-	Child reduction	50%

In Dingle

Open: 15th February-15th November

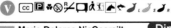

Anne & Pat Neligan
DUININ HOUSE
Conor Pass Road,
Dingle, Co Kerry

Dingle
Tel: **066 9151335**   Fax: **066 9151335**
Email: **pandaneligan@eircom.net**
Web: homepage.tinet.ie/~pandaneligan/

Award winning B&B. Superb location with magnificent views. Recommended by Frommer, Berlitz and 300 Best B&B's. Extensive Breakfast menu. Luxurious Guest conservatory - lounge.

B&B	5	Ensuite	€26/€29	Dinner	-
B&B	-	Standard	-	Partial Board	-
Single Rate			-	Child reduction	-

Dingle 1km

Open: February-November

Marie Dolores NicGearailt
NIC GERAILTS B&B
Bothar Bui, Ballydavid,
Dingle, Co Kerry

Dingle
Tel: **066 9155142**   Fax: **066 9155142**
Email: **mnicgear@indigo.ie**
Web: **www.nicgearailt.com**

Warm friendly home, Gaelic area. Breakfast menu, Home baking. Walkers & hill climbers paradise. Pubs, Restaurants, Beach, Gallarus Oratory, Dingle Way nearby.

B&B	5	Ensuite	€25.50/€28	Dinner	€20
B&B	-	Standard	-	Partial Board	-
Single Rate			€38.50/€38.50	Child reduction	33.3%

Dingle 11km

Open: March-October

Kerry

Mrs Margaret Noonan
CLUAIN MHUIRE HOUSE
**Spa Road, Dingle,
Co Kerry**

Dingle
TEL: **066 9151291**

4 Bedrooms with satellite TV. Tea/Coffee facilities, electric blankets, hairdryer. Private large car park. Credit Cards. House well signposted.

B&B	4	Ensuite	€27/€27	Dinner	-
B&B	-	Standard	-	Partial Board	-
Single Rate			-	Child reduction	-

In Dingle

Open: All Year

Brid & Karl O'Connell
GORT NA GREINE
**Ballymore, Ventry,
Dingle, Co Kerry**

Dingle
TEL: **066 9159783**
EMAIL: **gortnagreine@eircom.net**

Modern home, spectular sea views of Ventry Bay/Skellig Rocks. Guest lounge. Tea/Coffee making facilities. Breakfast choice, home baking.

B&B	4	Ensuite	€25.50/€28	Dinner	-
B&B	-	Standard	-	Partial Board	-
Single Rate			€38.50/€38.50	Child reduction	50%

Dingle 4km

Open: 1st June-31st August

Mrs Kathleen O'Connor
SRAID EOIN HOUSE
**John Street, Dingle,
Co Kerry**

Dingle
TEL: **066 9151409**   FAX: **066 9152156**
EMAIL: **sraideoinhouse@hotmail.com**

Refurbished town house with spacious rooms, quiet location, within walking distance of all Restaurants & Bars. Family atmosphere.

B&B	4	Ensuite	€30/€32	Dinner	-
B&B	-	Standard	-	Partial Board	-
Single Rate			€40/€45	Child reduction	33.3%

In Dingle

Open: 15th March-15th October

Mrs Maureen O'Connor
ANGLERS REST
**Ventry, Dingle Peninsula,
Co Kerry**

Dingle
TEL: **066 9159947**   FAX: **066 9159947**
EMAIL: **avalon@iol.ie**

Family run bungalow on Slea Head drive in Ventry village. Fishing on our own boat. Complimentary Tea/Coffee. Breakfast menu.

B&B	3	Ensuite	€26/€28	Dinner	-
B&B	2	Standard	€24/€25	Partial Board	-
Single Rate			€36/€38	Child reduction	25%

Dingle 4km

Open: 1st March-10th November

Mrs Helen O'Neill
DOONSHEAN VIEW
**High Road,Garfinny,
Dingle, Co Kerry**

Dingle
TEL: **066 9151032**
EMAIL: **doonsheanview@eircom.net**
WEB: **homepage.eircom.net/~doonsheanview**

Tranquil area, sea & mountain views. Off N86 Tralee/Killarney Rd. Ideal for touring Dingle peninsula. Warm welcome. TV lounge, breakfast menu, home baking.

B&B	4	Ensuite	€25.50/€28	Dinner	-
B&B	-	Standard	-	Partial Board	-
Single Rate			€38.50/€40	Child reduction	33.3%

Dingle 2km

Open: March-October

Mrs Mary O'Neill
John Street, Dingle,
Co Kerry

Dingle
Tᴇʟ: **066 9151639**

Purpose built home. Quiet location. 2 minutes walk to Town Centre. Tea/Coffee making facilities, TV, Clock radio, Hairdryer. Guest TV Lounge, choice of Breakfast.

B&B	6	Ensuite	€25.50/€28	Dinner	-
B&B	-	Standard	-	Partial Board	-
Single Rate			€40	Child reduction	25%

In Dingle

Open: 1st March-30th October

Mrs Jacqueline O'Shea
TORANN NA DTONN
Ventry, Dingle,
Co Kerry

Dingle
Tᴇʟ: **066 9159952**
Eᴍᴀɪʟ: **torann@iol.ie**
Wᴇʙ: **www.ireland-discover.com/ventry.htm**

Country Home beside Ventry village, on Slea Head drive. Magnificent Sea view overlooking Bay. 5 mins walk sandy beach. Fishing, Watersports, Scenic walks, Golf, Horse-riding. Breakfast menu.

B&B	5	Ensuite	€25.50/€28	Dinner	-
B&B	-	Standard	-	Partial Board	-
Single Rate			€38.50/€45	Child reduction	25%

Dingle 4km

Open: March-November

Maurice & Therese O'Shea
BALLYMORE HOUSE
Ballymore, Ventry, Dingle,
Co Kerry

Dingle
Tᴇʟ: **066 9159050**
Eᴍᴀɪʟ: **ballyhse@iol.ie**
Wᴇʙ: **www.ballymorehouse.com**

Spacious Country Home with Sea view, tranquil location. Guest TV & reading room. Open coal fire. Extensive Breakfast & Dinner menu. Home cooking our speciality. Numerous recommendations.

B&B	5	Ensuite	€27/€29	Dinner	€21
B&B	1	Standard	€24/€26	Partial Board	€320
Single Rate			€36/€39	Child reduction	-

Dingle 3km

Open: All Year

Eric & Eleanor Prestage
MOUNT EAGLE LODGE
Ventry, Dingle,
Co Kerry

Dingle
Tᴇʟ: **066 9159754**　　Fᴀx: **066 9159754**
Eᴍᴀɪʟ: **lodging@iol.ie**
Wᴇʙ: **www.dinglelodging.com**

Modern home AA ◆◆◆◆. Acclaimed Breakfasts. Spectacular views of Ventry bay from bedrooms, sun lounge, dining room. Local maps and guide books. Spacious, Tranquil.

B&B	4	Ensuite	€30/€40	Dinner	-
B&B	-	Standard	-	Partial Board	-
Single Rate			€38.50/€45	Child reduction	-

Dingle 5km

Open: April-October

Mrs Mary Russell
RUSSELL'S B&B
The Mall, Dingle,
Co Kerry

Dingle
Tᴇʟ: **066 9151747**　　Fᴀx: **066 9152331**
Eᴍᴀɪʟ: **maryr@iol.ie**

Detached house in Town Centre. Private parking, 2 minute walk to bus stop, Restaurants etc. Recommended by Guide du Routard, Reise, Fodors close up.

B&B	6	Ensuite	€25/€30	Dinner	-
B&B	-	Standard	-	Partial Board	-
Single Rate			€32/€43	Child reduction	-

Open: All Year

Kerry

Brid Bowler Sheehy
BALLINVOUNIG HOUSE
Ballinvounig, Dingle,
Co Kerry

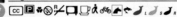

Dingle

Tel: **066 9152104**
Email: **ballinvounighouse@eircom.net**
Web: **homepage.eircom.net/~dbsheehy**

Excellent accommodation in quiet scenic location off main Tralee - Dingle Road. Convenient to all local amenities.

B&B	4	Ensuite	€26/€28	Dinner	-
B&B	-	Standard	-	Partial Board	-
Single Rate			€38.50/€38.50	Child reduction	33.3%

Dingle 1.5km

Open: March-October

Mrs Mary Sheehy
SHEEHY'S
Milltown, Dingle,
Co Kerry

Dingle

Tel: **066 9151453**
Email: **marycsheehy@eircom.net**
Web: **homepage.eircom.net/~sheehysbandb**

Peaceful home on the Cuas - Feoghanach road. Dingle 1km. Close to all amenities. Private parking. Choices of Breakfast. Irish speaking.

B&B	2	Ensuite	€25.50/€28	Dinner	-
B&B	2	Standard	€23/€25	Partial Board	-
Single Rate			€36/€38.50	Child reduction	50%

Dingle 1km

Open: March-November

Mrs Mary B Ui Chiobhain
ARD NA CARRAIGE
Carraig, Ballydavid, Dingle,
Co Kerry

Dingle

Tel: **066 9155295**

Scenic Gaelic area. Close to Beach, Pubs, Restaurants, Dingle Way Walk, Gallarus Oratory, Kilmaolceadar. Tea/Coffee facilities. Breakfast menu.

B&B	4	Ensuite	€25.50/€28.50	Dinner	-
B&B	-	Standard	-	Partial Board	-
Single Rate			€38.50	Child reduction	-

Dingle 10km

Open: 1st May-30th September

Mrs Josephine Walsh
WALSHS TOWNHOUSE B&B
Main Street, Dingle,
Co Kerry

Dingle

Tel: **066 9151147**   Fax: **066 9152975**
Email: **walsthbb@iol.ie**
Web: **www.iol.ie/~walsthbb/**

Luxury Town house in Town centre. Close to Shops, Restaurants & Bus. Ideal location for touring Dingle Peninsula. Breakfast menu. Low season reductions.

B&B	5	Ensuite	€26/€30	Dinner	-
B&B	1	Standard	-	Partial Board	-
Single Rate			€36/€45	Child reduction	-

In Dingle

Open: All Year Except Christmas

Doreen Caulfield
FOREST VIEW
Glenbeigh, Co Kerry

Glenbeigh

Tel: **066 9768140**
Email: **forestviewglenbeigh@eircom.net**

Elegant home in panoramic tranquil setting. Excellent touring location on Ring of Kerry. Adjacent to beach, horseriding, Dooks Golf Club and Kerry Way.

B&B	3	Ensuite	€26	Dinner	-
B&B	1	Standard	-	Partial Board	-
Single Rate			€36	Child reduction	-

Glenbeigh 1.2km

Open: 31st March-31st October

Della Doyle
GLENCURRAH HOUSE
Curraheen, Glenbeigh,
Co Kerry

Glenbeigh
TEL: **066 9768133**   FAX: **066 9768691**
EMAIL: **info@glencurrahhouse.com**
WEB: **www.glencurrahhouse.com**

Delightful country house with picturesque gardens overlooking Dingle Bay on the Ring of Kerry route N70. 1km from Glenbeigh village, Dooks Golf Links nearby.

B&B	5	Ensuite	€27/€32	Dinner	-
B&B	-	Standard	-	Partial Board	-
Single Rate			€38.50/€38.50	Child reduction	-

Glenbeigh 1km

Open: 1st March-31st October

Mrs Bridget McSweeney
HILLCREST HOUSE
Ballycleave, Glenbeigh,
Co Kerry

Glenbeigh
TEL: **066 9769165**   FAX: **066 9769165**

On Glenbeigh Killorglin Road in peaceful scenic area. Close to Lake, Beaches, Dooks Golf, Fishing. Red Fox Restaurant/Bar, Irish music. Bog Museum walking distance. 200m off Main Rd.

B&B	3	Ensuite	€25.50/€25.50	Dinner	-
B&B	1	Standard	€23/€23	Partial Board	-
Single Rate			€36/€38.50	Child reduction	50%

Glenbeigh 4km

Open: 1st April-31st October

Ms Gretta Murphy
BARR VIEW LODGE
Rossbeigh, Glenbeigh,
Co Kerry

Glenbeigh
TEL: **066 9768359**   FAX: **066 9768359**
EMAIL: **barrviewlodge@tinet.ie**

Excellent accommodation in our tastefully decorated home. Magnificent Sea views of Rossbeigh and Dingle Peninsula. Take road to Rossbeigh, go over bridge, two storey house on right.

B&B	3	Ensuite	€25.50	Dinner	-
B&B	-	Standard	-	Partial Board	-
Single Rate			€38.50/€38.50	Child reduction	-

Glenbeigh 2km

Open: All Year Except Christmas

Mrs Anne O'Riordan
MOUNTAIN VIEW
Mountain Stage, Glenbeigh,
Co Kerry

Glenbeigh
TEL: **066 9768541**   FAX: **066 9768541**
EMAIL: **mountainstage@eircom.net**

Quiet peaceful location with breathtaking views. 200 mtrs off Ring of Kerry. Adjacent to Beaches, Fishing - "Kerry Way". Low season reductions.

B&B	4	Ensuite	€25.50/€25.50	Dinner	€17
B&B	-	Standard	-	Partial Board	€264
Single Rate			€38.50/€38.50	Child reduction	50%

Glenbeigh 4.2km

Open: 1st April-31st October

Mrs Noreen O'Toole
OCEAN WAVE
Glenbeigh,
Co Kerry

Glenbeigh Ring of Kerry
TEL: **066 9768249**   FAX: **066 9768412**
EMAIL: **oceanwave@iol.ie**
WEB: **www.kerry-insight.com/oceanwave/**

Enjoy the elegance of an earlier age in Frommer Recommended home overlooking Dingle Bay/Dooks Golf Links. Jacuzzi baths. Extensive breakfast menu. AA ◆◆◆◆.

B&B	6	Ensuite	€29/€32	Dinner	-
B&B	-	Standard	-	Partial Board	-
Single Rate			€40/€40	Child reduction	-

Glenbeigh 1km

Open: 1st March-31st October

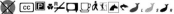

Mrs Bunny Ashe
LOCH EALA
Inch, Annascaul,
Co Kerry

Inch Dingle Peninsula
TEL: **066 9158135**   FAX: **066 9158001**
EMAIL: **locheala@eircom.net**

Luxurious family residence with magnificent Sea and Mountain views from all rooms. Ideal touring base. 2km from Inch Beach. On the main Killarney/Dingle road. Warm welcome assured.

B&B	3	Ensuite	€25.50/€26	Dinner	-
B&B	1	Standard	€23/€23	Partial Board	-
Single Rate			€36/€39	Child reduction	25%

Inch 1km

Open: 1st May-1st October

Mrs Eileen Kennedy
WATERSIDE
Inch, Annascaul,
Co Kerry

Inch Dingle Peninsula
TEL: **066 9158129**
EMAIL: **watersideinch@hotmail.com**

Modern, spacious, friendly, quality accommodation. Adjacent to Beach, Pub, Restaurant. Guest Lounge. Superb, central, scenic seaside setting. Ideal touring base. Private shoreline.

B&B	4	Ensuite	€26/€27	Dinner	-
B&B	-	Standard	-	Partial Board	-
Single Rate			-	Child reduction	25%

In Inch

Open: 1st March-1st November

Mrs Hannah Boland
MUXNAW LODGE
Castletownbere Rd,
Kenmare, Co Kerry

Kenmare
TEL: **064 41252**
EMAIL: **muxnawlodge@eircom.net**

Enchanting house built in 1801. Furnished throughout with antiques. Overlooking Kenmare Bay. All weather Tennis Court. Breakfast menu. Many recommendations.

B&B	5	Ensuite	€28/€32	Dinner	€20.50
B&B	-	Standard	-	Partial Board	-
Single Rate			-	Child reduction	-

Kenmare 1km

Open: All Year

Dan Carraher O'Sullivan
ANNAGRY HOUSE
Sneem Road (N70),
Kenmare, Co Kerry

Kenmare
TEL: **064 41283**
EMAIL: **danscottage@eircom.net**
WEB: **homepage.eircom.net/~inkenmare**

Ideal location on Ring of Kerry road (N70). Kenmare centre 6 mins walk. Peaceful. Spacious ensuite rooms. Bathtubs/Showers. Extensive breakfast menu. Fresh ground coffee. Home baking.

B&B	6	Ensuite	€28/€28	Dinner	-
B&B	-	Standard	-	Partial Board	-
Single Rate			€38.50/€38.50	Child reduction	25%

Kenmare 1km

Open: 15th January-15th December

Mrs Anne Clifford
CHERRY HILL
Killowen,
Kenmare, Co Kerry

Kenmare
TEL: **064 41715**
EMAIL: **cherryhill@eircom.net**

Located on Cork/Kilgarvan road off N22 on R569. Beautiful view of Kenmare river. Near Town, Golf course. Ideal base for touring Ring of Kerry, Beara.

B&B	2	Ensuite	€25.50	Dinner	-
B&B	1	Standard	€23	Partial Board	-
Single Rate			-	Child reduction	50%

Kenmare 1km

Open: 1st May-30th September

Tom Connor
ARDMORE HOUSE
Killarney Road, Kenmare,
Co Kerry

Kenmare
TEL: **064 41406**   FAX: **064 41406**

Spacious home in quiet location adjoining farmlands. RAC acclaimed. Frommer recommended. Town Centre 5 mins walk. Central touring base Ring of Kerry, Beara Peninsula etc.

B&B	5	Ensuite	€28/€28	Dinner	-
B&B	-	Standard	-	Partial Board	-
Single Rate			€38.50/€38.50	Child reduction	50%

In Kenmare

Open: 1st March-31st November

Mrs Edel Dahm
ARD NA MARA
Pier Road, Kenmare,
Co Kerry

Kenmare
TEL: **064 41399**   FAX: **064 41399**

Family home with garden overlooking Kenmare Bay at the front & MacGillycuddy Reeks at the back on the N71 road to Bantry. 5 mins walk into Town. German spoken.

B&B	4	Ensuite	€26/€27	Dinner	-
B&B	-	Standard	-	Partial Board	-
Single Rate			€35/€35	Child reduction	50%

In Kenmare

Open: All Year Except Christmas

Mrs B Dinneen
LEEBROOK HOUSE
Killarney Road, Kenmare,
Co Kerry

Kenmare
TEL: **064 41521**
EMAIL: **leebrookhouse@eircom.net**

Experience genuine hospitality in elegant family home. Located on N71 convenient to Kenmare Town. Ideal touring base Ring of Kerry/Beara.

B&B	4	Ensuite	€26/€28	Dinner	-
B&B	-	Standard	-	Partial Board	-
Single Rate			-	Child reduction	25%

Kenmare 1km

Open: March-November

Mrs Kathleen Downing O'Shea
MELROSE
Gortamullen, Kenmare,
Co Kerry

Kenmare
TEL: **064 41020**
EMAIL: **kathleenmelrose@eircom.net**

Bungalow situated off N71 Killarney road. 5 mins walk to Town Centre. Located in a scenic country area overlooking the Town. Central to all amenities.

B&B	3	Ensuite	€25.50/€30	Dinner	-
B&B	1	Standard	€23/€25	Partial Board	-
Single Rate				Child reduction	-

In Kenmare

Open: 1st April-October

Mrs Marian Dwyer
ROCKCREST HOUSE
Gortamullen, Kenmare,
Co Kerry

Kenmare
TEL: **064 41248**
EMAIL: **dodwy@eircom.net**
WEB: **www.rockcresthouse.com**

Elegant home, spacious rooms, quiet rd. Off N71 Killarney Rd. Scenic location overlooking Druid Circle & Kenmare Town/Mts./Valley, 5 min. walk to Town Centre.

B&B	6	Ensuite	€26/€28	Dinner	-
B&B	-	Standard	-	Partial Board	-
Single Rate			-	Child reduction	33.3%

In Kenmare

Open: All Year

Ian & Sue Eccles
FERN HEIGHT
Lohart, Castletownbere Road,
Kenmare, Co Kerry

Kenmare
Tel: **064 84248**   Fax: **064 84248**
Email: **fernheight@eircom.net**

Situated on R571. Some 15 mins drive towards Castletown Bearhaven. Rural location with views of the Bay, Mountains & Castle. Good food comes as standard.

B&B	3	Ensuite	€26/€29	Dinner	€20
B&B	1	Standard	€25/€27	Partial Board	€300
Single Rate			€37/€40	Child reduction	20%

Kenmare 11km   **Open:** 26th April-4th November

Tony & Sheila Fahy
ROCKVILLA
Templenoe, Kenmare,
Co Kerry

Kenmare
Tel: **064 41331**
Email: **rockvilla@esatclear.ie**
Web: **www.esatclear.ie/~rockvilla**

Rural setting near Templenoe pier. Relaxed friendly atmosphere. Ring of Kerry, Golf club, Coss Strand, Water Sports, Kerryway. Meals by request. Pool Room.

B&B	4	Ensuite	€27/€27	Dinner	-
B&B	1	Standard	€24/€24	Partial Board	-
Single Rate			€36/€36	Child reduction	25%

Kenmare 5km   **Open:** 15th March-31st October

Mrs Mary Fitzgerald
WHISPERING PINES
Glengarriff Road, Kenmare,
Co Kerry

Kenmare
Tel: **064 41194**   Fax: **064 41194**
Email: **wpines@indigo.ie**

Modernised period home. Spacious gardens, 3 minutes walk to Town, Golf course and Kenmare Bay. Recommended Dillard Causin/Sullivan Guide. Breakfast menu.

B&B	4	Ensuite	€26/€30	Dinner	-
B&B	-	Standard	-	Partial Board	-
Single Rate			-	Child reduction	-

In Kenmare   **Open:** 1st February-1st December

Mrs Gretta Gleeson-O'Byrne
WILLOW LODGE
Convent Garden, Kenmare,
Co Kerry

Kenmare
Tel: **064 42301**
Email: **willowlodgekenmare@yahoo.com**

Quietly located, 2 minutes from Town Centre. Ideal base to tour Ring of Kerry & Beara Peninsula. Full facilities and jacuzzi, bath. Good Restaurants, Golf, Walking, Horse Riding & Fishing.

B&B	5	Ensuite	€32/€38	Dinner	-
B&B	-	Standard	-	Partial Board	-
Single Rate			€38/€64	Child reduction	-

In Kenmare   **Open:** All Year

Mrs Bernadette Goldrick
DRUID COTTAGE
Sneem Road, Kenmare,
Co Kerry

Kenmare
Tel: **064 41803**

19th Century Classic stone residence, luxuriously renovated without losing olde world charm. Complimentary tea/coffee. Hill walking enthusiast.

B&B	2	Ensuite	€25.50/€26.50	Dinner	-
B&B	1	Standard	€23/€24	Partial Board	-
Single Rate			€36/€36	Child reduction	33.3%

Kenmare 1km   **Open:** 1st February-30th November

Janet & Aiden McCabe
THE WHITE HOUSE
Cappamore, Killarney Road,
Kenmare, Co Kerry

Kenmare

TEL: **064 42372**   FAX: **064 42372**
EMAIL: **whitehousekenmare@eircom.net**
WEB: **www.kerry-insight.com/white-house**

Idyllic friendly, on Ring. Central Kerry/West Cork/Lakes. Panoramic mountain views. Sky TV, Sunlounge. Relaxing beds.

B&B	2	Ensuite	€25.50/€25.50	Dinner	€17
B&B	1	Standard	€23/€23	Partial Board	€264
Single Rate			€36/€38.50	Child reduction	33.3%

Kenmare 5km   **Open:** All Year

Mrs Maureen McCarthy
HARBOUR VIEW
Castletownbere Haven Road,
Dauros, Kenmare, Co Kerry

Kenmare

TEL: **064 41755**   FAX: **064 42611**
EMAIL: **maureenmccarthy@eircom.net**
WEB: **www.kenmare.com/harbourview**

Award winning luxurious seashore home, panoramic views Kenmare Bay R571. AA ♦♦♦ award. Conservatory Breakfast room. Seafood. Satellite TV/Video, Trouserpress, Iron, Tea/Coffee.

B&B	4	Ensuite	€28/€32	Dinner	-
B&B	2	Standard	€28/€32	Partial Board	-
Single Rate			€40/€45	Child reduction	20%

Kenmare 6km   **Open:** 1st March-31st October

Mrs Rosita McCarthy
ARBUTUS HOUSE
Gortamullen Heights,
Killarney Road, Kenmare,
Co Kerry

Kenmare

TEL: **064 41059**
EMAIL: **arbutushouse@dol.ie**

Peaceful scenic setting overlooking green pastures. Ideal touring base Ring of Kerry/Beara. All rooms TV, Tea/Coffee facilities, Breakfast menu.

B&B	3	Ensuite	€28	Dinner	-
B&B	-	Standard	-	Partial Board	-
Single Rate			-	Child reduction	-

In Kenmare   **Open:** May-September

Ms Helen McGonigle
OLDCHURCH HOUSE
Killowen, Kenmare,
Co Kerry

Kenmare

TEL: **064 42054**
EMAIL: **oldchurchkenmare@hotmail.com**
WEB: **www.kenmare.com/oldchurch**

Luxury house situated on Kenmare-Cork road R569. Ideal place to relax surrounded by mountains, golf course and old church ruin. Excellent Breakfast.

B&B	3	Ensuite	€25/€28	Dinner	-
B&B	-	Standard	-	Partial Board	-
Single Rate			-	Child reduction	33.3%

In Kenmare   **Open:** February-October

Margaret Moore
RIVERVILLE HOUSE
Gortamullen, Kenmare,
Co Kerry

Kenmare

TEL: **064 41775**
EMAIL: **info@rivervillehousekenmare.com**
WEB: **www.rivervillehousekenmare.com**

Comfortable Home, Pine Interior, overlooking Kenmare Town/Mountains. Non smoking. Ring Beara/Kerry touring base.

B&B	3	Ensuite	€28/€32	Dinner	-
B&B	-	Standard	-	Partial Board	-
Single Rate			€45	Child reduction	-

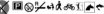

In Kenmare   **Open:** 1st February-30th November

Mrs Maura Murphy
ROSE COTTAGE
The Square, Kenmare,
Co Kerry

Kenmare

TEL: **064 41330**   FAX: **064 41355**

Old World Cottage with private Gardens, having unique position of rural setting in Kenmare Town.

B&B	3	Ensuite	€25/€32	Dinner	-
B&B		Standard	-	Partial Board	-
Single Rate			-	Child reduction	-

In Kenmare   **Open:** All Year Except Christmas

Mrs Lisa O'Brien
THE FORD
Glengarriff Road, Bonane,
Kenmare, Co Kerry

Kenmare

TEL: **064 42431**
EMAIL: **sobrien1@eircom.net**

Nestled in Caha mountains off N71. Bank of Sheen river. Unique family home. Hospitality assured.
Base for Ring of Kerry, Beara Peninsula. Walkers haven.

B&B	3	Ensuite	€25.50/€28.50	Dinner	-
B&B	-	Standard	-	Partial Board	-
Single Rate			€38.50/€40	Child reduction	25%

Kenmare 8km   **Open:** 1st April-31st September

Mrs Julia O'Connor
AN BRUACHAN
Killarney Road, Kenmare,
Co Kerry

Kenmare

TEL: **064 41682**   FAX: **064 41682**
EMAIL: **bruachan@iol.ie**
WEB: **www.kenmare.com**

Friendly home on 1acre of mature gardens on N71, own Riverfront, very quiet. Minutes from Town
Centre. Hill walking enthusiast. Breakfast choice offered.

B&B	4	Ensuite	€26.66/€28.36	Dinner	-
B&B	-	Standard	-	Partial Board	-
Single Rate			€38.50	Child reduction	50%

Kenmare 1km   **Open:** June-September

Anne O'Doherty
BRANDYLOUGHS
Lodge Wood, Kenmare,
Co Kerry

Kenmare

TEL: **064 42147**   FAX: **064 40787**
EMAIL: **brandylochs@eircom.net**
WEB: **www.kenmare.com/brandylochs**

Spacious quality country house overlooking 18 hole Golf club with scenic mountain backdrop - 2
minutes walk to award winning quality Restaurants in town of Kenmare.

B&B	4	Ensuite	€26/€32	Dinner	-
B&B		Standard	-	Partial Board	-
Single Rate			€39/€39	Child reduction	-

In Kenmare   **Open:** 1st March-30th October

Mrs Lynne O'Donnell
O'DONNELLS OF ASHGROVE
Ashgrove, Kenmare,
Co Kerry

Kenmare

TEL: **064 41228**   FAX: **064 41228**

Beautiful home in peaceful setting. Many antiques. Mature garden. Guests welcomed as friends.
German spoken. Angling enthusiast. Recommended Dillard/Causin.

B&B	3	Ensuite	€26/€28	Dinner	-
B&B	1	Standard	-	Partial Board	-
Single Rate			€36/€38.50	Child reduction	-

Kenmare 5km   **Open:** 31st March-31st October

Eilish & Pat O'Shea
THE CAHA'S
Hospital Road, Kenmare,
Co Kerry

Kenmare
TEL: **064 41271**   FAX: **064 41271**
EMAIL: **osheacahas@eircom.net**
WEB: **www.kenmare.com/caha**

Spacious family home in peaceful location with landscaped garden. Extensive Breakfast menu. Just 7 minutes walk from Town past Catholic Church.

B&B	4	Ensuite	€25.50/€30	Dinner	-
B&B	-	Standard	-	Partial Board	-
Single Rate			-	Child reduction	25%

In Kenmare   **Open:** April-November

Mrs Ann O'Sullivan
MOUNTAIN VIEW
Currabeg, Kenmare,
Co Kerry

Kenmare
TEL: **064 42175**   FAX: **064 42175**

On Kerry Way walking route-480 acres of mountain walks. Peaceful, warm, comfortable rooms. Unrivalled view of Kenmare Bay. Signposted off N71 at Riversdale Hotel.

B&B	3	Ensuite	€26/€28	Dinner	€20
B&B	-	Standard	-	Partial Board	€280
Single Rate			€38.50/€38.50	Child reduction	50%

In Kenmare   **Open:** 1st May-30th October

Bernie O'Sullivan
CARRIGMORE HOUSE
Hospital Road, Kenmare,
Co Kerry

Kenmare
TEL: **064 41563**

Comfortable home, spacious rooms. Scenic balcony views. Semi orthopaedic beds, Hairdryers. 5 minutes walk Town Centre. Location haven of rest. Non smoking.

B&B	3	Ensuite	€26/€28	Dinner	-
B&B	-	Standard	-	Partial Board	-
Single Rate			-	Child reduction	33.3%

In Kenmare   **Open:** All Year Except Christmas

Fiona & John O'Sullivan
MYLESTONE HOUSE
Killowen Road, Kenmare,
Co Kerry

Kenmare
TEL: **064 41753**
EMAIL: **mylestonehouse@eircom.net**
WEB: **www.kenmare-insight.com/mylestone**

Excellent spacious accommodation, friendly hospitality. Extensive Breakfast menu. Opposite Golf Course. Ideal Touring base, Ring of Kerry/ Beara Peninsula.

B&B	5	Ensuite	€27/€30	Dinner	-
B&B	-	Standard	-	Partial Board	-
Single Rate			€38.50/€40	Child reduction	25%

In Kenmare   **Open:** 1st March-10th November

Mrs Marian O'Sullivan
OAKFIELD
Castletownberehaven Rd
R571, Dauros, Kenmare,
Co Kerry

Kenmare
TEL: **064 41262**   FAX: **064 42888**
EMAIL: **oakfield@eircom.net**

Luxury country home, spacious warm bedrooms with spectacular views of Kenmare Bay. Breakfast choice. Evening meals, seafood speciality. Home from home.

B&B	4	Ensuite	€28/€28	Dinner	€20
B&B	1	Standard	€28/€28	Partial Board	€280
Single Rate			€40/€40	Child reduction	25%

Kenmare 5km   **Open:** 1st April-1st November

Kenmare 2km

Mrs Eileen M Ryan
RIVER MEADOWS
Sneem Road, Kenmare,
Co Kerry

Kenmare
TEL: **064 41306**   FAX: **064 41306**

Enjoy breakfast in our garden room against a magnificent mountain backdrop. Uniquely rustic area close to Town. Private road leading to seashore. Off N70 Ring of Kerry road.

B&B	4	Ensuite	€25.50/€25.50	Dinner	-
B&B	-	Standard	-	Partial Board	-
Single Rate			€38.50/€38.50	Child reduction	25%

 Open: 1st March-31st November

In Kenmare

Mrs Maureen Sayers
GREENVILLE
The Lodge, Kenmare,
Co Kerry

Kenmare
TEL: **064 41769**

Superb residence overlooking Golf course. Full central heating. Town Centre 1 mins walk. Private parking. Extensive breakfast menu. TV in rooms.

B&B	4	Ensuite	€25/€30	Dinner	-
B&B	-	Standard	€23	Partial Board	-
Single Rate			-	Child reduction	33.3%

 Open: All Year Except Christmas

Kenmare 1km

Mrs Agnes Thornhill
FINNIHY LODGE
Killarney Road, Kenmare,
Co Kerry

Kenmare
TEL: **064 41198**
EMAIL: **finnihylodge@esatclear.ie**

House in scenic woodland setting overlooking Finnihy River, ideally situated for touring West Cork and Kerry. Convenient to Golf & Fishing.

B&B	3	Ensuite	€26/€28	Dinner	-
B&B	1	Standard	-	Partial Board	-
Single Rate			€36/€36	Child reduction	25%

Open: All Year Except Christmas

Kenmare 4km

Mrs Geraldine Topham
GRENANE HEIGHTS
Greenane,
Ring of Kerry Road,
Kenmare, Co Kerry

Kenmare
TEL: **064 41760**   FAX: **064 41760**
EMAIL: **topham@iol.ie**
WEB: **www.grenaneheights.com**

Open-planned, spacious home, pine interior. Spectacular views of Kenmare Bay & Caha Mountains. Ideal base for Ring of Kerry/Beara. Tea/Coffee, Fax/E-mail.

B&B	4	Ensuite	€25.50	Dinner	-
B&B	1	Standard	€23	Partial Board	-
Single Rate			-	Child reduction	25%

 **Open:** 1st May-30th September

---

Kilgarvan 1km

Mrs Mary MacDonnell
BIRCHWOOD
Churchground, Kilgarvan,
Co Kerry

Kilgarvan
TEL: **064 85473**   FAX: **064 85570**
EMAIL: **info@birchwood-kilgarvan.com**
WEB: **www.birchwood-kilgarvan.com**

Home set in 1.5 acre garden in peaceful natural surroundings off R569. AA ◆◆◆◆ Approved. Ideal for touring Ring of Kerry/Beara. Golf, Fishing arranged.

B&B	5	Ensuite	€25.50	Dinner	€18
B&B	-	Standard	-	Partial Board	-
Single Rate			-	Child reduction	33.3%

Open: All Year

Anne Aherne
WINDWAY HOUSE
New Road, Killarney,
Co Kerry

Killarney
TEL: 064 32835   FAX: 064 37887

New Luxurious Bungalow. Ideally located 3 minutes walk from Town Centre. Recommended in all best guides.

B&B	6	Ensuite	€25.50/€30	Dinner	-
B&B	-	Standard	-	Partial Board	-
Single Rate			€38.50/€38.50	Child reduction	-

In Killarney

Open: All Year Except Christmas

Mrs Delia Adams
BRIDGE HOUSE
Coolgarrive, Tralee Road,
Killarney, Co Kerry

Killarney Tralee Road
TEL: 064 31425

200 metres off Killarney-Limerick road. All credit cards accepted and vouchers. Riding Stables and Golf Course nearby. Golfers welcome.

B&B	3	Ensuite	€25.50/€25.50	Dinner	-
B&B	-	Standard	-	Partial Board	-
Single Rate			€38.50/€38.50	Child reduction	-

Killarney 2km

Open: 14th May-14th September

Mrs Margaret Blake
CHARLWOOD TOMIES
Beaufort, Killarney,
Co Kerry

Killarney Beaufort
TEL: 064 44117

Just off Gap of Dunloe Road Lake District- Fishing, Golf, Horse Riding, Scenic woodland and Hill walks. Tours Dingle, Ring of Kerry. Restaurant, Music 2km.

B&B	2	Ensuite	€25.50	Dinner	-
B&B	1	Standard	€23	Partial Board	-
Single Rate			€36	Child reduction	25%

Killarney 8km

Open: 15th March-31st October

Kathy Brosnan
APPLECROFT HOUSE
Woodlawn Road, Killarney,
Co Kerry

Killarney Town
TEL: 064 32782
EMAIL: applecroft@eircom.net
WEB: http://homepage.eircom.net/~applecroft/

Luxury accommodation off N71, peaceful country setting. 12 min walk Killarney Town. Winner of Killarney Looking Good Competition. AA -♦♦♦♦.

B&B	5	Ensuite	€29/€33	Dinner	-
B&B	-	Standard	-	Partial Board	-
Single Rate			€38.50/€50	Child reduction	50%

Killarney 1km

Open: 1st January-12th December

Padraig & Margaret Brosnan
CLOGHROE
14 Scrahan Court,
Killarney, Co Kerry

Killarney
TEL: 064 34818
EMAIL: cloghroe@gofree.indigo.ie

Enjoy warm friendly hospitality in our beautiful home. Quiet location 2 mins walk Town/Bus/Rail. Near Ross Castle/National Park/Lakes/Golf. Tours arranged.

B&B	3	Ensuite	€27/€30	Dinner	-
B&B	-	Standard	-	Partial Board	-
Single Rate			€40/€40	Child reduction	50%

In Killarney

Open: 15th January-15th December

In Killarney

Danny & Bridie Buckley
NABRODA HOUSE
Muckross Road, Killarney,
Co Kerry

Killarney Muckross Road
Tel: **064 31688**

Quality Accommodation. Rooms ensuite, TV and Hairdryers. Multi-channel - Guest lounge. 5 mins walk to Town Centre on main Muckross road. Tea/Coffee facilities.

B&B	5	Ensuite	€28/€28	Dinner	-
B&B	-	Standard	-	Partial Board	-
Single Rate			€38.50/€38.50	Child reduction	25%

Open: April-October

Killarney 5km

Mrs Colleen Burke
BEENOSKEE
Tralee Rd, Killarney,
Co Kerry

Killarney Tralee Road
Tel: **064 32435**   Fax: **064 32435**
Email: **beenoskeebandb@eircom.net**
Web: **www.geocities.com/beenoskeebandb**

Country home on Limerick Rd/N22. Twice National Award of Excellence winner. All rooms TV/Video, Hairdryer, Tea/Coffee. Credit Cards accepted. Landscaped garden. Home Baking.

B&B	4	Ensuite	€25.50/€25.50	Dinner	€17
B&B	-	Standard	-	Partial Board	-
Single Rate			€38.50/€38.50	Child reduction	50%

Open: 1st April-31st October

Killarney 2km

Mrs Veronica Caesar
CAESAR'S
Lissyvigeen, Cork Road,
Killarney, Co Kerry

Killarney Cork Road Area
Tel: **064 31821**

Picturesque residence on N22. Superb location. Chosen and recommended by Irish Times Special Travel Correspondent on South West Ireland.

B&B	4	Ensuite	€25.50/€29.20	Dinner	-
B&B	-	Standard	-	Partial Board	-
Single Rate			€38.50/€38.50	Child reduction	25%

Open: 1st June-30th September

In Killarney

Mrs Eileen Carroll
THE MOUNTAIN DEW
3 Ross Road, Killarney,
Co Kerry

Killarney Town
Tel: **064 33892**   Fax: **064 31332**
Email: **mountain.dew@oceanfree.net**

Modern house in quiet area, 2 mins walk Town, Rail/Bus. Private Car Park. Tours arranged. Breakfast menu. In Killarney. Low season reductions.

B&B	6	Ensuite	€26/€28.50	Dinner	-
B&B	-	Standard	-	Partial Board	-
Single Rate			€38.50/€40	Child reduction	33.3%

Open: All Year

Killarney 3km

Mrs Marie Carroll
CEDAR HOUSE
Loreto Road,
(off Muckross Rd) Killarney,
Co Kerry

Killarney Muckross Road
Tel: **064 32342**   Fax: **064 35156**
Email: **denis@killarneyapartments.com**
Web: **www.killarneyapartments.com**

House adjacent to Lakes, Gleneagle Complex, National Event centre, Ross Golf Club. Spacious bedrooms some with Hairdryers. Tea facilities in rooms. Tours arranged.

B&B	4	Ensuite	€32/€32	Dinner	-
B&B	1	Standard	€30/€30	Partial Board	-
Single Rate			€38/€38	Child reduction	25%

Open: 17th March-31st October

Killarney 5km

Mrs Eileen Casey
CASEYS HOMEDALE
Dunrine, Tralee Road,
Killarney, Co Kerry

Killarney Tralee Road

TEL: **064 33855**   FAX: **064 33855**
EMAIL: **homedale@gofree.indigo.ie**
WEB: **gofree.indigo.ie/~homedale**

Friendly welcome assured, Family run. Ground floor ensuite bedrooms. Panoramic views. Complimentary Tea/Coffee. On N22. Ideal touring base. All tours arranged.

B&B	3	Ensuite	€25.50/€27.50	Dinner	-
B&B	-	Standard		Partial Board	-
Single Rate			€38.50/€38.50	Child reduction	50%

Open: March-November

Killarney 5km

Mrs Mary Casey
DIRREEN HOUSE
Tralee/Limerick Road N22,
Killarney, Co Kerry

Killarney Tralee Road

TEL: **064 31676**   FAX: **064 31676**
EMAIL: **dirreenhouse@eircom.net**
WEB: **homepage.eircom.net/~dirreenhouse**

Comfortable ground floor bedrooms. TV, Tea making facilities. Breakfast menu, Golf/Tours arranged. Coach pick up/drop off from premises. Expanding views of Countryside and Mountains.

B&B	4	Ensuite	€25.50/€27.50	Dinner	€17
B&B	-	Standard		Partial Board	€264
Single Rate			€38.50	Child reduction	33.3%

Open: 15th March-31st October

In Killarney

Liam & Anne Chute
CHUTEHALL
Lower Park Road, Killarney,
Co Kerry

Killarney Town

TEL: **064 37177**   FAX: **064 37178**
EMAIL: **chutehall@eircom.net**
WEB: **www.killarneyaccommodation.net**

New quality accommodation, quiet location. 3 min walk Town Centre, Rail, Bus. Spacious rooms, bath/pressurised shower. Private Car Park. Golf Tours arranged. Lakes nearby.

B&B	5	Ensuite	€26/€38	Dinner	-
B&B	-	Standard	-	Partial Board	-
Single Rate			-	Child reduction	-

Open: 1st March-1st November

Killarney 9km

Mrs Peggy Coffey
HOLLY GROVE
Gap of Dunloe, Beaufort,
Killarney, Co Kerry

Killarney Gap of Dunloe

TEL: **064 44326**   FAX: **064 44326**
EMAIL: **dunloe@eircom.net**
WEB: **www.stayathollygrove.com**

Killorglin N72 road. Spacious bedrooms, 1 with 3 beds. Tea/Coffee facilities, Electric blankets. Pony riding, Golf , Fishing, Climbing, Music nearby. Ideal for touring Kerry Ring/Dingle.

B&B	3	Ensuite	€25.50/€25.50	Dinner	€18
B&B	1	Standard	€23/€23	Partial Board	€300
Single Rate			€36/€38.50	Child reduction	50%

Open: 1st March-31st October

Killarney 3km

Mrs Mary Counihan
VILLA MARIAS HOUSE
Aghadoe, Killarney,
Co Kerry

Killarney Aghadoe

TEL: **064 32307**

Situated in panoramic tranquil setting. Excellent touring area. Golf, Fishing and other amenities close by. Recommended by Dillard Causin guide.

B&B	2	Ensuite	€28/€28	Dinner	-
B&B	1	Standard	€26/€26	Partial Board	-
Single Rate			€36/€36	Child reduction	25%

Open: April-October

Killarney 8km

Mrs Eileen Cremin
MOUNTAIN VIEW
Gap of Dunloe, Beaufort,
Co Kerry

Killarney Gap of Dunloe
TEL: 064 44212

Scenic area. 4km west of Killarney on N72. Turn left for Gap of Dunloe. Continue for 4km more. Golf, Lakes, Hill walking, Horse riding, Restaurant, Music locally.

B&B	2	Ensuite	€25.50	Dinner	-
B&B	1	Standard	€23	Partial Board	-
Single Rate			€36/€38.50	Child reduction	50%

Open: 1st May-30th September

Killarney 5km

Mrs Betty Cronin
DUNROSS HOUSE
Tralee Road, Killarney,
Co Kerry

Killarney Tralee Road
TEL: 064 36322
EMAIL:dunrosshouse@eircom.net

Luxurious home, Killarney 5km (N22). Rooms TV/Tea-making. Adjacent to National Parks, Lakes/Golfing. Excellent location Ring Of Kerry/Dingle.

B&B	4	Ensuite	€25.50/€27.50	Dinner	€17
B&B	-	Standard	-	Partial Board	€264
Single Rate			-	Child reduction	50%

Open:1st March-30th October

Killarney 4km

Mrs Lily Cronin
CRAB TREE COTTAGE
AND GARDENS
Mangerton Road, Muckross,
Killarney, Co Kerry

Killarney Muckross Road
TEL: 064 33169
EMAIL: crabtree@eircom.net

Picturesque cottage in the heart of Killarney, National Park, Lakes. Award winning landscaped gardens. Prime location for hillwalking, mountain climbing. On route of "Kerry Way"

B&B	3	Ensuite	€25.50	Dinner	€20
B&B	1	Standard	€23	Partial Board	-
Single Rate			€38.50	Child reduction	-

Open: 1st April-1st October

Killarney 4km

Paula Cronin
CILL IDE
Muckross Church Rd,
Muckross, Killarney,
Co Kerry

Killarney Muckross Road
TEL: 064 33339
EMAIL: cronin-paula69@hotmail.com

Spacious bungalow, Scenic, Tranquil. Guest sun lounge - TV, Tea/Coffee on arrival. Breakfast menu. Adjacent to Muckross House/Gardens, Lakes.

B&B	2	Ensuite	€25.50	Dinner	-
B&B	2	Standard	€23/€23	Partial Board	-
Single Rate			€36/€36	Child reduction	25%

Open: May-October

Killarney 2km

Mrs Noreen Cudden
THE AMBER LANTERN
Fossa, Killarney,
Co Kerry

Killarney Fossa
TEL: 064 31921
EMAIL: cudden@eircom.net

Well appointed home with balconies, opposite Golf Club, Lakes. Ring of Kerry/Dingle Road. Horse riding, Hill walking. Tours arranged.

B&B	5	Ensuite	€26/€27	Dinner	-
B&B	1	Standard	€24/€24	Partial Board	-
Single Rate			€36/€39	Child reduction	25%

Open: 1st April-31st October

Mrs Agnes Curran
ARBOUR VILLA
Golf Course Road, Fossa,
Killarney, Co Kerry

Killarney Fossa
TEL: **064 44334**
EMAIL: **curran_agnes@hotmail.com**

Ring Kerry/Golf Course road, near Lakes, Gap of Dunloe, Fishing, Horse Riding, Golf 2 km. Ideal Walkers/Climbers. Tours arranged.

B&B	4	Ensuite	€28/€35	Dinner	€25
B&B	-	Standard		Partial Board	-
Single Rate			€38.50/€40	Child reduction	50%

Killarney 5km   (V)   **Open:** 1st June-30th September

Hannah Daly
BROOKFIELD HOUSE
Coolgarrive, Aghadoe,
Killarney, Co Kerry

Killarney Aghadoe
TEL: **064 32077**

Country residence. Signposted 1km Killarney/Tralee/Limerick Road N22. Convenient for touring Ring of Kerry, Dingle, Killarney. Best guides recommended.

B&B	6	Ensuite	€26/€28	Dinner	-
B&B	-	Standard		Partial Board	-
Single Rate			€38.50/€38.50	Child reduction	25%

Killarney 2km   (V)   **Open:** 1st April-30th September

Mrs Deborah Devane
GLENMILL HOUSE
Nunstown, Aghadoe,
Killarney, Co Kerry

Killarney Aghadoe
TEL: **064 34391**
EMAIL: **glenmillhouse@eircom.net**
WEB: **www.kerry-insight.com/glenmill/**

Luxurious home with panoramic views Lakes, Golf Course, McGillicuddy Reeks, National Park. Orthopaedic beds. Airport 15km. Adjacent to Aghadoe Heights Hotel. Tours arranged.

B&B	4	Ensuite	€25.50/€28	Dinner	-
B&B	-	Standard	-	Partial Board	-
Single Rate			€38.50/€38.50	Child reduction	25%

Killarney 3km   (V)   **Open:** 1st March-30th September

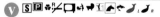

Mrs Mary Devane
REEKS VIEW
Spa, Killarney,
Co Kerry

Killarney Cork Road Area
TEL: **064 33910**   FAX: **064 33910**
EMAIL: **devane@eircom.net**
WEB: **www.kerry-insight.com/reeksview**

Luxurious bungalow off Killarney/Cork road. Signposted at Parkroad roundabout. N22 Cork/Killarney road, take industrial estate exit off roundabout.

B&B	5	Ensuite	€25.50/€25.50	Dinner	€17
B&B	-	Standard		Partial Board	€264
Single Rate			€38.50/€38.50	Child reduction	50%

Killarney 2km   (V)   **Open:** 1st April-1st November

Mrs Noreen Dineen
MANOR HOUSE
18 Whitebridge Manor,
Ballycasheen, Killarney,
Co Kerry

Killarney Cork Road Area
TEL: **064 32716**   FAX: **064 32716**

Modern Georgian Style house in peaceful area. Fishing, Golfing, Swimming. National Park and Lakes, Cabaret and Local Tours arranged.

B&B	4	Ensuite	€25.50/€28	Dinner	-
B&B	-	Standard		Partial Board	-
Single Rate			€38.50/€38.50	Child reduction	-

Killarney 2km   (V)   **Open:** 1st May-30th September

Mrs Aileen Doherty
BEECHWOOD HOUSE
**Cahernane Meadows,
Muckross Road, Killarney,
Co Kerry**

Killarney Muckross Road

Tel: **064 34606**
Email: **jdoh1@gofree.indigo.ie**

Luxurious home. 5 mins walk from Town Centre, Rail, Bus. Adjacent to Muckross House, National Park. Lakes, Mountains, Leisure Centre, Golf. Private Parking. Close to Gleneagle Hotel.

B&B	3	Ensuite	€30	Dinner	-
B&B	-	Standard	-	Partial Board	-
Single Rate			€40	Child reduction	25%

In Killarney

Open: All Year Except Christmas

Mrs Tess Doona
HOLLYBOUGH HOUSE
**Cappagh, Kilgobnet,
Beaufort, Co Kerry**

Killarney Beaufort

Tel: **064 44255**

Quiet scenic location central for Ring of Kerry, near Ireland's highest and most majestic mountains, The McGillycuddy Reeks. Visa accepted.

B&B	3	Ensuite	€25.50/€25.50	Dinner	€19
B&B	1	Standard	€23/€23	Partial Board	-
Single Rate			€36/€36	Child reduction	25%

Killorglin 8km

Open: 31st March-October

Mrs Carmel Dore-O' Brien
TARA
**Gap of Dunloe Road,
Fossa, Killarney, Co Kerry**

Killarney Aghadoe/Fossa

Tel: **064 44355**
Email: **tarabnb@iol.ie**
Web: **www.iol.ie/~tarabnb/tara.htm**

Guide Routard & Hachette. Visa. Quiet & relaxing home off main road. Tea/Coffee, Breakfast menu, Hairdryers. Beautiful gardens N72 West, left Gap Dunloe.

B&B	4	Ensuite	€26/€30	Dinner	-
B&B	1	Standard	€24/€28	Partial Board	-
Single Rate			€36/€40	Child reduction	25%

Killarney 4km

Open: 16th June-30th September

Mrs Noreen Downing
ARDFALLEN HOUSE
**Ross Road,
Killarney, Co Kerry**

Killarney Town

Tel: **064 33632**
Email: **noreendowning@hotmail.com**

Comfortable family home. Quiet scenic location, 4 mins walk to Town, Bus/Rail. Guest lounge. Private Parking. Breakfast choice. Fishing, Golfing, Lakes nearby. Tours arranged.

B&B	3	Ensuite	€27/€28.50	Dinner	-
B&B	-	Standard	-	Partial Board	-
Single Rate			-	Child reduction	-

In Killarney

Open: June-October

Mrs Bridie Doyle
CLONFERT
**Fossa, Killarney,
Co Kerry**

Killarney

Tel: **064 31459**

Spacious family home. Ring of Kerry/Dingle road. Golf, Fishing, Riding 1km. Orthopaedic beds. Golf and tours arranged. Ideal for walkers/cyclists.

B&B	4	Ensuite	€25.50/€30	Dinner	-
B&B	-	Standard	-	Partial Board	-
Single Rate			€38.50/€38.50	Child reduction	25%

Killarney 3km

Open: 15th March-31st October

Mrs Greta Doyle
ALGRET HOUSE
80 Countess Grove,
Off Countess Rd, Killarney,
Co Kerry

Killarney Countess Road Area

Tel: **064 32337** Fax: **064 30936**
Email: **gretad@gofree.indigo.ie**

Friendly home, quiet area. Town 5 min walk. All rooms have multi-channel TV, Tea/Coffee facilities and Hairdryers. Breakfast menu. N71 Muckross road, 1st left, 2nd right.

B&B	6	Ensuite	€26/€30	Dinner	-
B&B	-	Standard	-	Partial Board	-
Single Rate			€40/€50	Child reduction	25%

In Killarney

Open: 1st March-31st October

Mary Theresa & Derry Doyle
ELYOD HOUSE
Ross Road, Killarney,
Co Kerry

Killarney Town

Tel: **064 36544/31510**

Luxurious friendly home situated verge of National Park, Golf, Fishing, Horse-riding nearby. Tours arranged. Breakfast menu. Tea/Coffee facilities available.

B&B	5	Ensuite	€27/€28.50	Dinner	-
B&B	1	Standard	€24€24	Partial Board	-
Single Rate			€38/€38	Child reduction	-

In Killarney

Open: 1st March-1st December

Mrs Sheila Falvey
FALSHEA HOUSE
Tralee Road, Killarney,
Co Kerry

Killarney Tralee Road

Tel: **064 34871**
Email: **falsheahouse@eircom.net**

Purpose built luxury home in scenic peaceful surroundings. All rooms with TV, Tea/Coffee making facilities, Hairdryers. National Award of Excellence Winner. Tours arranged.

B&B	4	Ensuite	€27/€28	Dinner	€21
B&B	-	Standard	-	Partial Board	-
Single Rate			€40/€40	Child reduction	50%

Killarney 4km

Open: 7th January-20th December

Mrs Theresa Ferris
WAYSIDE
Gap of Dunloe, Killarney,
Co Kerry

Killarney Gap of Dunloe

Tel: **064 44284** Fax: **064 44284**
Email: **www.waysideguesthouse@hotmail.com**
Web: **http://www.dirl.com/kerry/wayside.htm**

Peaceful lake/mountain district. Restaurants, Irish music & dancing 1km. Horse riding, Fishing & Golf Courses 1km. Dingle & Ring of Kerry 2km. Breakfast Menu. Off R562.

B&B	1	Ensuite	€27.93	Dinner	-
B&B	3	Standard	€25.39	Partial Board	-
Single Rate			€36/€38.50	Child reduction	50%

Killarney 8km

Open: All Year Except Christmas

Mrs Anne Fleming
GLENDALE HOUSE
Dromadeesirt, Tralee Road,
Killarney, Co Kerry

Killarney Tralee Road

Tel: **064 32152/34952** Fax: **064 32152**
Email: **gdalehse@eircom.net**
Web: **www.kerry-insight.com/glendale**

Luxurious house on Tralee Road (N22). Killarney 6km. Kerry Airport 5 mins drive. All rooms with TV, Tea/Coffee making facilities, Hairdryers. Tours arranged.

B&B	6	Ensuite	€25.50	Dinner	-
B&B	-	Standard	-	Partial Board	-
Single Rate			€38.50	Child reduction	33.3%

Killarney 6km

Open: 1st April-30th September

Killarney Cork Road Area

Mrs Maureen Fleming
SHRAHEEN HOUSE
Ballycasheen (off N22),
Killarney, Co Kerry

Tel: 064 31286/37959 Fax: 064 37959
Email: info@shraheenhouse.com
Web: www.shraheenhouse.com

Luxurious home set in 2.5 acres. Satellite TV, Tea/Coffee, Hairdryer all rooms. Breakfast menu, AA ◆◆◆◆ selected. Tours arranged. Off N22 at Whitebridge sign.

B&B	6	Ensuite	€28/€31	Dinner	-
B&B	-	Standard	-	Partial Board	-
Single Rate			€40/€50	Child reduction	25%

Killarney 2km

Open: 10th January-30th November

Killarney Town

Mrs Philomena Fleming
WHITE OAKS
16 Scrahan Court,
Ross Road, Killarney,
Co Kerry

Tel: 064 31348

Luxurious townhouse in unrivaled locale. 7 min walk from Town, Rail facilities & Bus. TV, Tea making facilities. Tours arranged.

B&B	3	Ensuite	€24.13/€25.39	Dinner	-
B&B	-	Standard	-	Partial Board	-
Single Rate			€35	Child reduction	25%

Killarney 1km

Open: All Year

Killarney Muckross Road

Mr Denis Geaney
PINE CREST
Woodlawn Road, Killarney,
Co Kerry

Tel: 064 31721 Fax: 064 31721

Luxurious bungalow in scenic area, convenient to Lakes, National park, Golf Course, Airport, Ring of Kerry, Dingle, Bus. Taxi from house. 1km from the Gleneagle National Events Centre.

B&B	6	Ensuite	€25.50/€27	Dinner	-
B&B	-	Standard	-	Partial Board	-
Single Rate				Child reduction	-

Killarney 1km

Open: 1st March-30th October

Killarney Tralee Road

Mrs Moira Gorman
GORMAN'S
Tralee Road, Killarney,
Co Kerry

Tel: 064 33149 Fax: 064 33149
Email: mgormans@eircom.net
Web: www.eircom.net/~mgormans

No smoking house, smoking room available. Former B.F. garden prize winners. Low season reductions. Afternoon tea free on arrival. Visa & Vouchers welcome.

B&B	4	Ensuite	€25.50/€27.50	Dinner	€17.50
B&B	-	Standard	-	Partial Board	€264
Single Rate			€38.50/€45.50	Child reduction	33.3%

Killarney 5km

Open: 1st January-23rd December

Killarney Town

Louise Griffin
CHELMSFORD HOUSE
Muckross View,
Countess Grove,
Killarney, Co Kerry

Tel: 064 36402 Fax: 064 33806
Email: info@chelmsfordhouse.com
Web: www.chelmsfordhouse.com

Luxurious friendly home, spacious ensuite rooms, 5 min walk to town. Awaken to magnificent view of Lakes/Mountains. Extensive breakfast menu pancakes etc.! TV Lounge, all tours/shows arranged.

B&B	4	Ensuite	€26/€32	Dinner	-
B&B	-	Standard	-	Partial Board	-
Single Rate				Child reduction	-

In Killarney

Open: 10th January-10th December

Mary Guerin
BELLEVUE
1 Gortroe, Fossa,
Killarney, Co Kerry

Killarney
Tel: **064 34621**

Dormer style, 1.5km West of Killarney, Ring Kerry Rd, Golf, Horseriding, Tours Arranged, Rooms Ensuite, TV, Hairdryers, Private Parking.

B&B	3	Ensuite	€25.50/€25.50	Dinner	-
B&B	-	Standard	-	Partial Board	-
Single Rate			€38.50/€38.50	Child reduction	50%

Killarney 1.5km

Open: April-September

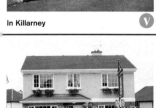

Mrs Mary Howard
COMERAGH HOUSE
Tralee Road, Dunrine,
Killarney, Co Kerry

Killarney Tralee Road
Tel: **064 34435**

Modern home situated on N22. National Award of excellence winner. Convenient base for Ring of Kerry/Dingle. Kerry Airport 10 mins.

B&B	4	Ensuite	€25.50/€25.50	Dinner	-
B&B	-	Standard	-	Partial Board	-
Single Rate			€38.50/€38.50	Child reduction	33.3%

Killarney 5km

Open: 1st April-31st October

Catherine Howe
DUN-A-RI HOUSE
Ross Road, Killarney,
Co Kerry

Killarney Ross Road
Tel: **064 36629**
Email: **dunari@eircom.net**

Located in scenic peaceful area. Opposite Ross Castle Holiday Homes adjacent to Ross Golf Club, National Park. Breakfast Menu, Hairdryers.

B&B	4	Ensuite	€27	Dinner	-
B&B	-	Standard	-	Partial Board	-
Single Rate			€40	Child reduction	-

In Killarney

Open: 1st March-1st November

Mr Tom Kearney
CILLCEARN HOUSE
Ballycasheen Road,
Killarney, Co Kerry

Killarney Cork Road Area
Tel: **064 35670**   Fax: **064 34127**
Email: **info@cillcearn.com**
Web: **www.cillcearn.com**

New luxurious home off N22, set in picturesque surroundings. Forest and river walks. Warm homely atmosphere, cable T.V lounge. Breakfast menu. Golf locally. Tours arranged.

B&B	3	Ensuite	€28/€31	Dinner	-
B&B	1	Standard	€26/€28	Partial Board	-
Single Rate			€36/€38	Child reduction	50%

Killarney 2km

Open: 1st April-31st October

Mrs Nora Kelliher
HAZELWOOD
Park Rd Upper, Ballyspillane,
Killarney, Co Kerry

Killarney Cork Road Area
Tel: **064 34363**   Fax: **064 34363**
Email: **hazel@eircom.net**

Comfortable bungalow, 300m from Park Road roundabout on N22, walking distance from Town. Ideal touring base. Refreshments available. Tours arranged.

B&B	6	Ensuite	€27/€30	Dinner	-
B&B	-	Standard	-	Partial Board	-
Single Rate			€38.50	Child reduction	33.3%

Killarney 1km

Open: 28th March-30th October

319

Mr & Mrs William Kenny
SLIABH LAUCHRA HOUSE
Castlelough, Loretto Road,
Killarney, Co Kerry

Killarney Muckross Road
TEL: 064 32012

Family run house. Landscaped Gardens. 5 mins walk from Lakes, Parklands, Leisure Centre. TV. Guest room, Hairdryers, Tea/Coffee facilities. Award winner AA ♦♦♦.

B&B	6	Ensuite	€25.50/€25.50	Dinner	-
B&B	-	Standard	-	Partial Board	-
Single Rate			€38.50	Child reduction	-

Killarney 1.6km

Open: April-September

Mrs Margaret Lanigan
CARAGH HOUSE
Scrahan Court, Ross Road,
Killarney, Co Kerry

Killarney Town
TEL: 064 34637
EMAIL: caraghhouse@yahoo.com
WEB: www.geocities.com/caraghhouse/ireland.html

Friendly home 2 mins walk Town, Rail, Bus. Ideal touring centre. Beaches, Golf, Fishing, National Park, Pony trekking, Lakes. Tea/Coffee on arrival. Quiet cul de sac.

B&B	3	Ensuite	€26	Dinner	-
B&B	-	Standard	-	Partial Board	-
Single Rate			-	Child reduction	-

In Killarney

Open: May-September

Mrs Josephine Lawlor
NORTHWOOD HOUSE
Muckross View, Killarney,
Co Kerry

Killarney Town
TEL: 064 37181   FAX: 064 37181
EMAIL: info@northwoodhouse.com
WEB: www.northwoodhouse.com

Newly built luxurious town house on quiet residential road with panoramic views of Killarney National Park, Lakes, Mountains, yet only a 5 minute walk to Town. Tours arranged.

B&B	4	Ensuite	€26/€32	Dinner	-
B&B	-	Standard	-	Partial Board	-
Single Rate			-	Child reduction	-

In Killarney

Open: All Year

Mrs Anne Leahy
AVONDALE HOUSE
Tralee Road, Killarney,
Co Kerry

Killarney Tralee Road
TEL: 064 35579   FAX: 064 35197
EMAIL: avondalehouse@eircom.net
WEB: www.kerry-insight.com/avondale

Modern new family run home. Large bedrooms, Scenic views, TV, Tea/Coffee facilities, Hairdryers Electric blankets. Large gardens. Breakfast menu.

B&B	5	Ensuite	€27/€28	Dinner	-
B&B	-	Standard	-	Partial Board	-
Single Rate			€38.50/€44	Child reduction	33.3%

Killarney 3km

Open: 1st February-30th November

Siobhan Leen
LEENS
22 Marian Terrace,
Killarney, Co Kerry

Killarney Town
TEL: 064 32819
EMAIL: siobhanleen@eircom.net
WEB: www.stayatleens.com

Modern house in residential area. At Lewis Rd go straight at roundabout, take 1st left, sign for house on right.

B&B	4	Ensuite	€25.50/€27.93	Dinner	-
B&B	-	Standard	-	Partial Board	-
Single Rate			€38.50/€44.44	Child reduction	25%

In Killarney

Open: All Year

Mrs K Lloyd-Davies
HAVENS REST
Tralee Road N22, Killarney,
Co Kerry

Killarney Tralee Road

Tel: **064 32733**   Fax: **064 32237**
Email: **havensrest@oceanfree.net**
Web: **gofree.indigo.ie/~haverest**

Lake Zurich Travel (USA) recommended - Luxury accommodation with antique furniture. Highly recommended. Real Irish welcome. On N22, 3 mins from Town Centre.

B&B	3	Ensuite	€25.50/€28.50	Dinner	-
B&B	-	Standard	-	Partial Board	-
Single Rate			€38.50/€38.50	Child reduction	25%

Killarney 3km

Open: 1st March-31st October

Mrs Eileen Lucey
MARIAN HOUSE
Woodlawn Road, Killarney,
Co Kerry

Killarney Muckross Road

Tel: **064 31275**   Fax: **064 31275**
Email: **odranlucey@eircom.net**

Adjacent to Lakes, Mountains and National Park. Walking distance from Town, quiet area. Spacious Parking. Beyond Shell Filling Station on Kenmare road take left for Marian House.

B&B	6	Ensuite	€25.50/€27	Dinner	-
B&B	-	Standard	-	Partial Board	-
Single Rate			-	Child reduction	50%

In Killarney

Open: All Year Except Christmas

Ms Pauline Lyne
PARKFIELD HOUSE
Park Road, Killarney,
Co Kerry

Killarney Town

Tel: **064 37022**   Fax: **064 37022**
Email: **paulinelyne@eircom.net**

Luxurious townhouse backing on to farmland within walking distance to Town Centre. Spacious parking. Tours arranged.

B&B	6	Ensuite	€25.50/€31.74	Dinner	-
B&B	-	Standard	-	Partial Board	-
Single Rate			€38.50/€44.44	Child reduction	-

In Killarney

Open: March-November

Mrs Chriss Mannix
FLESK LODGE
Muckross Road, Killarney,
Co Kerry

Killarney Muckross Road

Tel: **064 32135**   Fax: **064 32135**
Email: **fleskldg@gofree.indigo.ie**

Luxury bungalow walking distance from Town. Close to all amenities. Beside Gleneagle Hotel Complex. Landscaped garden.

B&B	6	Ensuite	€28/€30	Dinner	€18
B&B	-	Standard	-	Partial Board	-
Single Rate			€39/€40	Child reduction	-

In Killarney

Open: All Year

RESERVATIONS

- Confirm phone bookings in writing without delay with agreed deposit.
- To avoid misunderstandings later, check rate on booking and clarify any additional changes which may apply to your booking.
- Give details of any special requirements.
- State clearly day, date of arrival and departure date.

Killarney 2km

Mrs Kathleen McAuliffe
CARROWMORE HOUSE
Knockasarnett, Aghadoe,
Killarney, Co Kerry

Killarney Aghadoe
TEL: **064 33520**
EMAIL: **carrowmorehouse@eircom.net**

A home from home in peaceful area. Panoramic views from TV lounge and bedrooms. Off N22 (Killarney-Tralee road), take first left after Cleeney Roundabout.

B&B	4	Ensuite	€26/€27	Dinner	-
B&B	-	Standard		Partial Board	-
Single Rate			€39/€39	Child reduction	25%

Open: 1st May-31st October

In Killarney

Joan McCarthy
THE HARP
Muckross Road, Killarney,
Co Kerry

Killarney
TEL: **064 31272**
EMAIL: **ourhomeinkillarney@eircom.net**

On N71 walking distance from Town. All room ensuite TV, hairdryers. Tea/Coffee facilities in Lounge. Breakfast Menu. Private Parking. Please email for web page.

B&B	4	Ensuite	€25.50/€29	Dinner	-
B&B	-	Standard		Partial Board	-
Single Rate			€38.50/€38.50	Child reduction	-

Open: All Year

In Killarney

Mrs Kathleen McCarthy
SANCTA MARIA
53 Park Drive, Off Park Road,
Killarney, Co Kerry

Killarney Town
TEL: **064 32447**   FAX: **064 32447**

Comfortable house in residential area. Walking distance of Town, close to all amenities. Private parking. Tours arranged. Complimentary tea arrival.

B&B	3	Ensuite	€26/€28	Dinner	-
B&B	1	Standard	€23/€25	Partial Board	-
Single Rate			€36/€38.50	Child reduction	25%

Open: All Year

Killarney 1km

Mrs Margaret McCarthy
CRICKET VIEW
7 Muckross Grove,
Killarney, Co Kerry

Killarney Town
TEL: **064 32245**   FAX: **064 32245**
EMAIL: **cricketview@eircom.net**
WEB: **homepage.eircom.net/~cricketview**

Modern two storey house in quiet area, 10 min walk to Town Centre. Family run, Tours arranged. Near Gleneagle Hotel.

B&B	1	Ensuite	€25.50/€25.50	Dinner	-
B&B	2	Standard	€23/€23	Partial Board	-
Single Rate			€36/€36	Child reduction	33.3%

Open: April-September

Mrs Peggy McCarthy
DROMHALL HEIGHTS
Off Countess Road,
Killarney, Co Kerry

Killarney Countess Road Area
TEL: **064 32662**   FAX: **064 32662**
EMAIL: **peggymccarthy@eircom.net**
WEB: **homepage.eircom.net/~peggymccarthy**

Family home, quiet private location. View mountains, Lakes. Only minutes walk to Town from Countess Road through Countess Grove, to top of Hill, then left road.

B&B	2	Ensuite	€25.50/€27	Dinner	-
B&B	1	Standard	€23/€25	Partial Board	-
Single Rate			€36/€36	Child reduction	25%

In Killarney

Open: 1st March-1st November

In Killarney

Elizabeth McEnteggart
ARMAGH HOUSE
Park Road, Killarney,
Co Kerry

Killarney
TEL: **064 34346**

Purpose built B&B. 2 minutes walk from Town Centre. Adjacent to Bus and Rail services. Convenient to National Park and surrounding Lakes and Mountains.

B&B	6	Ensuite	€25.50	Dinner	-
B&B	-	Standard		Partial Board	-
Single Rate			€38.50	Child reduction	-

Open: All Year

Killarney 7km

Mrs Betty McSweeney
HILTON HEIGHTS
Glebe, Tralee Road,
Killarney, Co Kerry

Killarney Tralee Road
TEL: **064 33364**

Bungalow in pleasant restful area. All ensuite rooms, Hairdryers, TV, Tea/Coffee facilities. Sign for Hilton Heights on left on Tralee road. 7km from Killarney, turn right.

B&B	4	Ensuite	€25.50	Dinner	-
B&B	-	Standard	-	Partial Board	-
Single Rate			€38.50	Child reduction	50%

Open: 1st April-1st October

In Killarney Town

Miss Christine McSweeney
EMMERVILLE HOUSE
Muckross Drive,
Off Muckross Rd,
Killarney, Co Kerry

Killarney Muckross Road
TEL: **064 33342**

Comfortable home quiet cul-de-sac. Mins walk Town Centre/Bus/Rail. Tours arranged (Reduction low season). Personal attention. Entertainment closeby. Hairdryers all rooms. (Town end.)

B&B	4	Ensuite	€25.50/€25.50	Dinner	-
B&B	-	Standard	-	Partial Board	-
Single Rate			€38.50	Child reduction	50%

Open: All Year

Killarney 5km

Frances Moriarty
MORIARTY'S
Dunrine, Tralee Road,
Killarney, Co Kerry

Killarney
TEL: **064 36133**

Friendly home. N22 (Limerick/Tralee Rd). Convenient to Lakes, Ring of Kerry, National Park, Golf, Fishing, Riding Stables, Airport. Tours arranged.

B&B	4	Ensuite	€25.50/€28.50	Dinner	€17
B&B	-	Standard	-	Partial Board	€264
Single Rate			€38.50/€38.50	Child reduction	50%

Open: 1st March-31st October

Killarney 4km

Margaret Moriarty
BENISKA HOUSE
Lackabane, Fossa,
Killarney, Co Kerry

Killarney
TEL: **064 32200**

New luxurious home on Ring of Kerry/Dingle Road. Take N72 West 2.5 miles. Adjacent Killarney 3 Golf Courses and 5* Hotel Europe. Next to Pub and Restaurant.

B&B	4	Ensuite	€25.50/€32	Dinner	-
B&B	-	Standard	-	Partial Board	-
Single Rate				Child reduction	-

Open: March-October

Tim & Nora Moriarty
THE PURPLE HEATHER
Glencar Rd, Gap of Dunloe,
Beaufort, Killarney, Co Kerry

Killarney Gap of Dunloe

TEL: **064 44266**   FAX: **064 44266**
EMAIL: **purpleheather@eircom.net**
WEB: **homepage.eircom.net/~purpleheather**

Breakfast Conservatory panoramic view. Breakfast menu. Rooms with TV, Electric Blanket, Hairdryer, Tea/Coffee, Pool Room, Irish Music, Restaurant, Golf 1km.

B&B	5	Ensuite	€25.50/€26.50	Dinner	€20
B&B	1	Standard	€23/€24	Partial Board	
Single Rate			€36/€38.50	Child reduction	50%

Killarney 8km

Open: March-October

Mrs Maura Moynihan
KELARE LODGE
Muckross Drive,
Off Muckross Rd, Killarney,
Co Kerry

Killarney Muckross Road

TEL: **064 32895**

Luxury award winning home. Minutes walk from Town Centre. National Park, Bus, Rail station. Quiet location off Muckross road. Tours arranged.

B&B	5	Ensuite	€25.50/€26.67	Dinner	-
B&B	-	Standard	-	Partial Board	-
Single Rate			-	Child reduction	-

In Killarney

Open: 18th March-31st October

Michael & Oonagh Moynihan
KYLEMORE
Ballydowney, Killarney,
Co Kerry

Killarney

TEL: **064 31771**   FAX: **064 31771**
EMAIL: **kylemorehousekillarney@eircom.net**

Friendly home on route N72 (Ring of Kerry and Dingle road). Adjacent to Killarney, Golf and Fishing club, Riding stables and National Park.

B&B	6	Ensuite	€25.50	Dinner	-
B&B	-	Standard	-	Partial Board	-
Single Rate			€38.50	Child reduction	50%

Killarney 1km

Open: 1st January-1st December

Mrs Eileen Murphy
GREEN ACRES
Fossa, Killarney,
Co Kerry

Killarney Fossa

TEL: **064 31454**   FAX: **064 31454**

Modern family home 2km from Killarney on the main Ring of Kerry road. In the midst of three famous Golf courses, Horse riding, Fishing, 1km Walks. AA listed.

B&B	4	Ensuite	€28	Dinner	-
B&B	2	Standard	€27	Partial Board	-
Single Rate			€38.50	Child reduction	25%

Killarney 2km

Open: 1st April-30th September

Mrs Evelyn Murphy
REDWOOD
Rockfield, Tralee Road,
Killarney, Co Kerry

Killarney Tralee Road Area

TEL: **064 34754**   FAX: **064 34178**
EMAIL: **redwd@indigo.ie**
WEB: **www.kerry-insight.com/redwood**

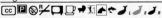

Surrounded by 15 acres. Large bedrooms include bath power showers, Multi-channel, Hairdryer, Teamakers, some with Kingsize beds, Extensive Menu. From Killarney take N22 towards Tralee.

B&B	6	Ensuite	€27/€31	Dinner	-
B&B	-	Standard	-	Partial Board	-
Single Rate			€40/€50	Child reduction	50%

Killarney 3km

Open: All Year

Mrs Sheila Murphy
SERENIC VIEW
Coolcorcoran, Killarney,
Co Kerry

Killarney Tralee Road
TEL: **064 33434**   FAX: **064 33578**
EMAIL: **serenic@eircom.net**
WEB: **homepage.eircom.net/~serenic**

Luxury ground floor accomodation. 5 min drive from Killarney, on Ring of Kerry. Signposted on Killarney/Limerick road. Quiet scenic area. Breakfast menu. Satellite TV. Tours arranged.

B&B	4	Ensuite	€25.50/€25.50	Dinner	-
B&B	-	Standard	-	Partial Board	-
Single Rate			€38.50/€38.50	Child reduction	25%

Killarney 2km

Open: 1st April-31st October

David Nash
NASHVILLE
Tralee Road, Killarney,
Co Kerry

Killarney Tralee Road
TEL: **064 32924**   FAX: **064 32924**
EMAIL: **nashville@tinet.ie**
WEB: **www.kerry-insight.com/nashville**

Modern family home on Tralee N22 road. Colour TV's, Hairdryers, Tea/Coffee facilities. Payphone for guests. Ideal centre for touring Kerry - all tours arranged. AA listed.

B&B	6	Ensuite	€25.50/€31.74	Dinner	-
B&B	-	Standard	-	Partial Board	-
Single Rate			€38.50/€38.50	Child reduction	33.3%

Killarney 3km

Open: 1st February-1st December

Mrs Triona Neilan
ROSSARNEY HOUSE
St Margaret's Road,
Killarney, Co Kerry

Killarney Town
TEL: **064 34630**

Award winning family home. Quiet area. 8 minutes walk Town. Guest TV, reading room with Tea/Coffee facilities. Golf, Riding stables, Park nearby. Itinerary planned. Reduction low season.

B&B	4	Ensuite	€25.50/€29	Dinner	-
B&B	-	Standard	-	Partial Board	-
Single Rate			-	Child reduction	-

In Killarney

Open: 1st January-20th December

Mrs Aileen O'Brien
COIS DARA
Rookery Road, Killarney,
Co Kerry

Killarney Town
TEL: **064 35567**   FAX: **064 35567**
EMAIL: **coisdara@iol.ie**

Non-smoking house in country setting. 15 mins walking distance from centre. Mountain views. Walking and fishing advised on. Golf within 2 miles. Warm welcome.

B&B	4	Ensuite	€25.50/€30	Dinner	-
B&B	-	Standard	-	Partial Board	-
Single Rate			€38.50/€38.50	Child reduction	-

Killarney 1km

Open: 1st March-31st October

Maria O'Carroll
TENTH GREEN
39 Demense Ross Road,
Killarney, Co Kerry

Killarney Ross Road
TEL: **064 37369**   FAX: **064 37369**

Luxury dormer bungalow. Award winning gardens. Walking distance Town centre, Golf course, Ross Castle, National Park. All types of tours arranged.

B&B	3	Ensuite	€25.50/€40	Dinner	-
B&B	-	Standard	-	Partial Board	-
Single Rate			€38.50/€38.50	Child reduction	25%

Killarney

Open: All Year

Mrs Rosemary O'Connell
OAKLAWN HOUSE
Muckross Drive,
Off Muckross Road,
Killarney, Co Kerry

Killarney Muckross Road

TEL: **064 32616**
EMAIL: **oaklawnhouse@eircom.net**
WEB: **www.oaklawn-house.com**

Award winning house. Winner of prestigious Killarney looking and best Town & Country Home '95 '98. Golden Circle Award '99, 2000. Two minutes to Town Centre.

B&B	6	Ensuite	€26.66/€33.01	Dinner		-
B&B	-	Standard		Partial Board		-
Single Rate			€38.50/€44.44	Child reduction		33.3%

In Killarney

Open: All Year

Mrs Anne O'Connor
CLONALIS HOUSE
Countess Road, Killarney,
Co Kerry

Killarney Countess Road Area

TEL: **064 31043**   FAX: **064 31043**
EMAIL: **clonalis@eircom.net**

Recommended Dillard Causin Guide. Luxurious home, select residential location off Muckross Road and off N22. Near Town, Lakes, Golf. Tours arranged.

B&B	6	Ensuite	€28/€31	Dinner		-
B&B	-	Standard		Partial Board		-
Single Rate			€38.50/€40	Child reduction		

Killarney 1km

Open: 6th May-30th September

Mrs Mary O'Connor
Donoghue
THE LOST BALL
Gortroe, Killarney,
Co Kerry

Killarney/Fossa

TEL: **064 37449**
EMAIL: **thelostball@eircom.net**
WEB: **www.thelostball.com**

2km west of Killarney town off N72 (Ring of Kerry). Golf club, riding stables, hotel leisure centre, national park close by. All rooms ensuite with TV, Tea/Coffee.

B&B	5	Ensuite	€25.50/€32	Dinner		-
B&B	-	Standard		Partial Board		-
Single Rate			€38.50/€38.50	Child reduction		-

Killarney 2km

Open: 1st May-30th September

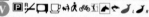

Mrs Bridie O'Donoghue
MUCKROSS DRIVE HOUSE
Muckross Drive, Off Muckross
Road, Killarney, Co Kerry

Killarney Muckross Road

TEL: **064 34290**   FAX: **064 39818**
EMAIL: **muckrossdrive@eircom.net**
WEB: **www.muckross.8m.com**

Award-winning purpose built B&B. Minutes walk Town Centre. Bus/Rail. Situated in a quiet cul-de-sac. Overlooking mountains & National Park. All tours arranged.

B&B	5	Ensuite	€26/€30	Dinner		-
B&B	-	Standard		Partial Board		-
Single Rate			€38.50/€44	Child reduction		25%

In Killarney

Open: All Year

Patrick & Julia O'Donoghue
WOODLANDS
Ballydowney, Killarney,
Co Kerry

Killarney Fossa

TEL: **064 31467**   FAX: **064 31467**
EMAIL: **stayatwoodlands@eircom.net**
WEB: **stayatwoodlands.com**

Friendly home walking distance Town. Ring of Kerry road N72. Riding stables, Golf, Fishing, Lakes/National Park nearby. Ideal walkers/climbers/cycling.

B&B	3	Ensuite	€28	Dinner		-
B&B	2	Standard		Partial Board		-
Single Rate			€36	Child reduction		33.3%

Killarney 1km

Open: January-20th December

Mrs Phil O'Donohoe
MAYWOOD
Mill Road, Killarney,
Co Kerry

Killarney Muckross Road
Tel: 064 31263

Spacious, modern bungalow in scenic area near National Park. Golf, Fishing, Mountains, Lakes nearby. Tours arranged.

B&B	3	Ensuite	€25.50	Dinner	-
B&B	2	Standard	€23	Partial Board	-
Single Rate			€36/€38.50	Child reduction	25%

Killarney 1.5km

Open: 1st March-30th September

Mrs Eileen O'Grady
FORREST HILLS
Muckross Road, Killarney,
Co Kerry

Killarney Muckross Road
Tel: 064 31844

Modern, well-heated home in scenic area, a few hundred yards from Town Centre. Spacious Parking. Home cooking.

B&B	4	Ensuite	€25.50/€28	Dinner	-
B&B	2	Standard	€23.50/€25.50	Partial Board	-
Single Rate			-	Child reduction	50%

Killarney 1km

Open: March-November

Denis & Rosaleen O'Leary
ROSS CASTLE LODGE
Ross Road, Killarney,
Co Kerry

Killarney Ross Road
Tel: 064 36942   Fax: 064 36942
Email: rosscastlelodge@killarneyb-and-b.com
Web: killarneyb-and-b.com

Luxurious house, edge of town amidst magical woodland and lakeshore walks. Golf, Lake cruising, Fishing 10 mins walk. Spacious bedrooms. RAC ◆◆◆◆ Award Winner.

B&B	4	Ensuite	€26/€35	Dinner	-
B&B	-	Standard		Partial Board	-
Single Rate			€40/€50	Child reduction	-

In Killarney

Open: 14th March-1st December

Mrs Eileen O'Leary
THE SHADY NOOK
Crohane, Fossa,
Killarney, Co Kerry

Killarney Fossa
Tel: 064 33351
Email: the-shady-nook@unison.ie

Family home in a peaceful scenic area. 4km west of Killarney, off the N72. Ideal base for touring Ring of Kerry, Dingle, Lakes. Golf, Fishing .5km arranged.

B&B	3	Ensuite	€25.50	Dinner	€17
B&B	-	Standard	-	Partial Board	-
Single Rate			€38.50	Child reduction	50%

Killarney 4km

Open: 1st May-30th September

Mrs Evelyn O'Leary
KILBROGAN HOUSE
Muckross Road, Killarney,
Co Kerry

Killarney Muckross Road
Tel: 064 31444
Email: kilbrog@indigo.ie

Family home on Ring of Kerry road adjacent National Park/Gleneagle Hotel. Log fire, home baking, spacious parking. Tours arranged. 2 single rooms.

B&B	4	Ensuite	€25.50/€26	Dinner	-
B&B	-	Standard		Partial Board	-
Single Rate			€38.50	Child reduction	50%

Killarney 1km

Open: April-October

Kerry

Killarney 2km

Miss Noreen O'Mahoney
MYSTICAL ROSE
Woodlawn Road, Killarney,
Co Kerry

Killarney Town
TEL: **064 31453**   FAX: **064 35846**
EMAIL: **mysticalr@eircom.net**

Award winning guest home. Frommer Guide recommended. Beautiful country home convenient to Mountain, Lake District. All tours arranged.

B&B	6	Ensuite	€28/€32	Dinner	-
B&B	-	Standard	-	Partial Board	-
Single Rate			€38.50/€42	Child reduction	33.3%

Open: All Year

Killarney 1km

Sean & Sheila O'Mahony
O'MAHONY'S
Cork Road, Killarney,
Co Kerry

Killarney Town
TEL: **064 32861**

Warm comfortable family run home opposite Ryan Hotel. TV, Hairdryers, Breakfast menu, Private parking. Walking distance Town centre. Tours arranged. Tea/Coffee facilities.

B&B	6	Ensuite	€25.50/€26.60	Dinner	-
B&B	-	Standard	-	Partial Board	-
Single Rate			€38.50	Child reduction	50%

Open: 1st January-1st December

Killarney 2km

Mrs Norrie O'Neill
ALDERHAVEN
COUNTRY HOME
Ballycasheen, Cork Road,
Killarney, Co Kerry

Killarney Ballycasheen
TEL: **064 31982**   FAX: **064 31982**
EMAIL: **alderhaven@eircom.net**
WEB: **www.alderhaven.com**

Secluded Tudor style house off N22 at Whitebridge. 5 acres woodlands, Private avenue. Tranquil setting. Breakfast conservatory, Menu, Hairdryers. Tours arranged.

B&B	6	Ensuite	€28/€30	Dinner	-
B&B	-	Standard	-	Partial Board	-
Single Rate			€40/€40	Child reduction	25%

Open: 1st March-1st December

In Killarney

Mrs Patricia O'Neill
LORENZO HOUSE
Lewis Road, Killarney Town,
Killarney, Co Kerry

Killarney Town
TEL: **064 31869**
EMAIL: **lorenzokillarney@hotmail.com**

Modern town house, 3 minutes walk to Town centre, Bus and Railway, National Park, Golf, Riding stables nearby. Tours arranged.

B&B	4	Ensuite	€26/€28	Dinner	-
B&B	-	Standard	-	Partial Board	-
Single Rate			-	Child reduction	-

Open: 1st April-31st October

Killarney 5km

Sheila O'Neill
ALRAN HEIGHTS
Lough Guitane Road,
Muckross, Killarney,
Co Kerry

Killarney Muckross Road
TEL: **064 32071**
EMAIL: **oneillsheila@eircom.net**

Set in quiet tranquil location with view of Mangerton Mountain. Adjacent to Killarney National Park 1km off the N71.

B&B	2	Ensuite	€26	Dinner	-
B&B	1	Standard	€23	Partial Board	-
Single Rate			-	Child reduction	-

Open: 1st May-30th September

Joan & Patrick O'Riordan
ST RITAS VILLA
Mill Road, Killarney,
Co Kerry

Killarney Muckross Road
TEL: **064 31517**   FAX: **064 37631**

House adjacent to Lakes, Muckross House, Gleneagle Hotel. Tea/Coffee served, Orthopaedic beds, Hairdryers available. Tours arranged. Private parking.

			Dinner	-
B&B	4	Ensuite	€27/€29	Partial Board	-
B&B	1	Standard	€25/€27	Child reduction	25%
Single Rate			€40/€40		

Killarney 1km

Open: 10th March-31st October

Mrs Anne O'Rourke
SILVER SPRINGS
Tralee Road, Killarney,
Co Kerry

Killarney Tralee Road
TEL: **064 31016**

Country home. 3km Killarney on Tralee-Limerick Road N22. Bedrooms ensuite, with TV, Coffee and Tea making facilities. Tours, Golf, Horse riding and Cycling near.

			Dinner	-
B&B	3	Ensuite	€25.50/€27.50	Partial Board	-
B&B	1	Standard		Child reduction	33.3%
Single Rate			€37/€40		

Killarney 3km

Open: 1st February-1st December

Mrs Kay O'Shea
SPRINGFIELD LODGE
Rookery Rd, Ballycasheen,
Killarney, Co Kerry

Killarney Cork Road Area
TEL: **064 32944**
EMAIL: **springfieldlodge@eircom.net**
WEB: **homepage.eircom.net/~springfieldlodge**

Modern, comfortable, welcoming home. Tranquil setting, adjacent to woodlands. Central location, private parking off N22. All tours arranged.

			Dinner	-
B&B	4	Ensuite	€26/€30	Partial Board	-
B&B	-	Standard	-	Child reduction	25%
Single Rate			-		

Killarney 1km

Open: 1st March-31st October

Mrs Eileen O'Sullivan
KINGDOM VIEW
Glencar Road, Kilgobnet,
Beaufort, Killarney, Co Kerry

Killarney Beaufort
TEL: **064 44343**
EMAIL: **jos@iol.ie**

On Killarney/Glencar Road, Slopes of McGillycuddy Mountains. Spectacular Countryside. Seafood speciality. Turf Fire. Cot available. Traditional musicians in family.

			Dinner	€18
B&B	5	Ensuite	€25.50/€25.50	Partial Board	€264
B&B	1	Standard	€23/€23	Child reduction	50%
Single Rate			€36/€38.50		

Killorglin 8km

Open: 1st February-1st December

Mr Eugene A O'Sullivan
NORAVILLE HOUSE
St Margarets Road, Killarney,
Co Kerry

Killarney Town
TEL: **064 36053**
EMAIL: **eugeneaosullivan@eircom.net**

Highly recommended modern townhouse. Select residential location. Tea/Coffee facilities and Hairdryers in all rooms. Tours arranged. Reduction low season. Personal attention.

			Dinner	-
B&B	5	Ensuite	€25.50/€27.31	Partial Board	-
B&B	-	Standard	-	Child reduction	25%
Single Rate			€38.50/€38.50		

In Killarney

Open: All Year

Mrs Rosaleen O'Sullivan
KILLARNEY VILLA
Cork/Mallow Road (N72),
Killarney, Co Kerry

Killarney Cork Road Area

TEL: **064 31878**   FAX: **064 31878**
EMAIL: **killarneyvilla@eircom.net**
WEB: **www.killarneyvilla.com**

AA ◆◆◆◆ Award. RAC Sparkling Diamond Award. Scenic. Providing modern comforts. We pride ourselves in our roof top conservatory that overlooks magnificent gardens.

B&B	6	Ensuite	€26/€30	Dinner	-
B&B	-	Standard		Partial Board	-
Single Rate			€40/€40	Child reduction	33.3%

Killarney 3km

Open: 15th April-31st Octobe

Mrs Phyl Perlman
ASHBROOK
Tralee Road, Dunrine,
Killarney, Co Kerry

Killarney Tralee Road

TEL: **064 39053**   FAX: **064 39053**

Luxurious home on N22. Breakfast menu and orthopaedic beds. Airport 10 mins. Ideal base for touring Killarney Lakes, Ring of Kerry and Dingle Peninsula.

B&B	4	Ensuite	€27/€29	Dinner	-
B&B	-	Standard		Partial Board	-
Single Rate			€40/€40	Child reduction	-

Killarney 5km

Open: 1st March-31st Octobe

Joan & Jerry Ryan
THE GROTTO
Fossa, Killarney,
Co Kerry

Killarney

TEL: **064 33283**
EMAIL: **the_grotto@hotmail.com**

On Ring of Kerry/Dingle, opposite Lake and Killarney Golf & Fishing Club. Tea facilities. Riding sta bles nearby. Near Castlerosse Hotel. Tours arranged.

B&B	3	Ensuite	€25.50/€28	Dinner	-
B&B	-	Standard		Partial Board	-
Single Rate			€38.50	Child reduction	50%

Killarney 2km

Open: 1st March-31st Octobe

Mrs Catherine Spillane
BEAUTY'S HOME
Cleeney, Tralee Road,
Killarney, Co Kerry

Killarney Town

TEL: **064 31567/31836** FAX: **064 34077**
EMAIL: **deroscoachtours@eircom.net**
WEB: **www.beautyshome.com**

Luxurious Bungalow. TV, Video, Movie Channel, Tea/Coffee Facilities. Electric Blankets in winter months, Orthopaedic Beds. Collection Rail/Bus Station.

B&B	3	Ensuite	€25.50/€35	Dinner	-
B&B	3	Standard	€23/€29	Partial Board	-
Single Rate			€36/€51	Child reduction	25%

Killarney 1km

Open: All Year Except Christma

Mrs Eileen Tarrant
MULBERRY HOUSE
(Off Countess Road)
Rookery Road, Killarney,
Co Kerry

Killarney Cork Road Area

TEL: **064 34112**   FAX: **064 32534**
EMAIL: **info@mulberryhousebb.com**
WEB: **www.kerry-insight.com/mulberry**

Luxurious country house backing on to Farmland. Unspoilt views Killarneys Mountain range off N22. Superb peaceful location. Tours arranged. Parking.

B&B	5	Ensuite	€27.50/€33	Dinner	-
B&B	-	Standard		Partial Board	-
Single Rate			€38.50/€50	Child reduction	33.3%

Killarney 1km

Open: 1st March-20th Novembe

Mrs Anne Teahan
FAIR HAVEN
Lissivigeen (N22), Cork Road,
Killarney, Co Kerry

Killarney Cork Road Area
TEL: **064 32542**
EMAIL: **fairhavenbb@eircom.net**

Dillard/Causin Guide recommended. Warm country home on 2 acres. Golf, Fishing locally. Tea/Coffee facilities in TV lounge. Breakfast menu. Collection point for Ring of Kerry tours.

B&B	4	Ensuite	€25.50/€25.50	Dinner	-
B&B	1	Standard	€23/€23	Partial Board	-
Single Rate			€36/€36	Child reduction	25%

Killarney 4km

Open: May-October

Mrs Mary Tuohy
FRIARY VIEW
Dennehy's, Bohereen,
Killarney, Co Kerry

Killarney Town
TEL: **064 32996**

Peaceful home in secluded area off main road. Walking distance to Town, Bus, Rail. Tours arranged. Breakfast Menu. Small road beside Friary Church.

B&B	4	Ensuite	€25.50	Dinner	-
B&B	-	Standard	-	Partial Board	-
Single Rate			-	Child reduction	-

In Killarney

Open: 1st May-30th September

Mrs Eileen Twomey
GOLDEN OAKES
Dromhale,
(Off Countess Grove),
Killarney, Co Kerry

Killarney
TEL: **064 32737**
EMAIL: **jandetwomey@eircom.net**

Excellent accommodation on private grounds. Superb view of Lakes and Mountains. 5 min from Town Centre. Tea/Coffee provided on request.

B&B	3	Ensuite	€25.50/€30	Dinner	-
B&B	-	Standard	-	Partial Board	-
Single Rate			€38.50/€40	Child reduction	25%

In Killarney

Open: 1st March-30th September

Mrs Agnes Walsh
WUTHERING HEIGHTS
Knockeenduff, Killarney,
Co Kerry

Killarney
TEL: **064 32756**
EMAIL: **wutheringheights_@hotmail.com**

Bungalow in peaceful location signposted on Killarney/Limerick Road (N22). Tea/Coffee making facilities, Orthopaedic beds, Electric blankets, Hairdryer. Low season reduction.

B&B	4	Ensuite	€25.50/€28	Dinner	€18
B&B	-	Standard	-	Partial Board	-
Single Rate			€38.50/€38.50	Child reduction	25%

Killarney 2km

Open: 31st January-15th December

Patricia Wright
SUNFLOWER COTTAGE
Cleeney, Tralee Road,
Killarney, Co Kerry

Killarney Town
TEL: **064 32101**
EMAIL: **lesw@indigo.ie**

First class accommodation close to Town. Ideal for touring Ring of Kerry, Dingle and Lakes. A warm welcome to be expected. Situated on N22.

B&B	4	Ensuite	€25.50/€33	Dinner	-
B&B	-	Standard	-	Partial Board	-
Single Rate			€38.50/€45.50	Child reduction	50%

In Killarney

Open: 1st March-31st October

Mrs Irma Clifford
FERN ROCK
Tinnahalla N70, Milltown,
Co Kerry

Killorglin
TEL: **066 9761848**   FAX: **066 9761848**
EMAIL: **fernrock@eircom.net**
WEB: **www.stayatfernrock.com**

Excellent accommodation (on N70 Tralee Rd) superb view. Tours arranged. Golf .5km. Also 10 Golf courses within 1hour drive. Central for Ring of Kerry/Dingle/Killarney. Beaches close by.

B&B	4	Ensuite	€25.50/€27	Dinner	-
B&B	-	Standard		Partial Board	-
Single Rate			€38.50	Child reduction	-

Killorglin 3km

Open: 2nd January-15th December

Mrs Marie Clifford
HILLCREST
Killarney Road, Killorglin,
Co Kerry

Killorglin Ring Of Kerry
TEL: **066 9761552**
EMAIL: **hillcrest_clifford@hotmail.com**
WEB: **www.hillcrest-bb.com**

Georgian styled residence on N72, spectacular views Irelands Highest Mountain and countryside. Orthopaedic Beds, Hairdryers. Frommer Recommended.

B&B	5	Ensuite	€25.50/€27	Dinner	-
B&B	-	Standard		Partial Board	-
Single Rate			€38.50/€38.50	Child reduction	50%

Killorglin

Open: 1st April-30th September

Mrs Bridie Evans
ORGLAN HOUSE
Killarney Road N72, Killorglin,
Co Kerry

Killorglin Ring of Kerry
TEL: **066 9761540**
EMAIL: **orglanhouse@eircom.net**

Peaceful hilltop residence with magnificent mountain views, overlooking River and Town. 5 mins walk from Town. Golf, Fishing, Beaches, Hillwalking all within 20 mins of Town centre.

B&B	3	Ensuite	€25.50/€27.50	Dinner	-
B&B	1	Standard	€23/€25	Partial Board	-
Single Rate			€36/€38.50	Child reduction	25%

In Killorglin

Open: April-October

Noreen Evans
LAUNE BRIDGE HOUSE
Killarney Rd N72, Killorglin,
Co Kerry

Killorglin Ring Of Kerry
TEL: **066 9761161**
EMAIL: **launebridgehouse@hotmail.com**
WEB: **www.launebridgehouse.com**

At the Bridge Killorglin scenic location overlooking River. Purpose built on Ring of Kerry. Walking distance high class restaurants. Golf, fishing & hillwalking.

B&B	6	Ensuite	€25.50/€27.50	Dinner	-
B&B	-	Standard		Partial Board	-
Single Rate			€36/€38.50	Child reduction	50%

In Killorglin

Open: 1st March-1st December

Mrs Christine Griffin
ARDRAHAN HOUSE
Ownagarry, Killorglin,
Co Kerry

Killorglin
TEL: **066 9762219**

Family run peaceful homely accommodation, quiet location. 2km from Town. Central for Mountain and Hill walking, Cycling, Fishing, Ring of Kerry, Dingle, Killarney, Seaside, Caragh Lake.

B&B	2	Ensuite	€25.50/€25.50	Dinner	-
B&B	1	Standard	€23/€23	Partial Board	-
Single Rate			€36/€36	Child reduction	50%

Killorglin 2km

Open: All Year Except Christmas

Killorglin

Mrs Catherine Lyons
TORINE HOUSE
Sunhill Road, Killorglin,
Ring of Kerry, Co Kerry

Killorglin Ring of Kerry

TEL: **066 9761352**   FAX: **066 9761352**
EMAIL: **torinehouse@tinet.ie**

Comfortable accommodation. Base for Ring of Kerry, Dingle, Killarney. Golf & Fishing nearby. Tea/Coffee, TV in rooms. Orthopaedic beds. Guide du Routard recommended.

B&B	5	Ensuite	€25.50/€25.50	Dinner	€17
B&B	1	Standard	€23/€23	Partial Board	-
Single Rate			€36/€36	Child reduction	50%

Open: 1st March-1st November

In Killorglin

Mrs Geraldine Mangan
RIVERSIDE HOUSE
Killorglin, Ring of Kerry,
Co Kerry

Killorglin Ring Of Kerry

TEL: **066 9761184**   FAX: **066 9761184**
EMAIL: **riversidehousebnb@eircom.net**
WEB: **www.riversidehousebnb.com**

Comfortable family home, superb view from rooms overlooking River. Golfing, Walking. Ideal touring base. Killarney, Ring/Kerry, Dingle. Information route N70.

B&B	4	Ensuite	€25.50/€27.50	Dinner	-
B&B	2	Standard	€23/€25	Partial Board	-
Single Rate			€36/€38.50	Child reduction	33.3%

Open: 1st March-1st December

In Killorglin

Christina & Jerome O'Regan
O'REGANS COUNTRY
HOME & GARDENS
Bansha, Killorglin,
Co Kerry

Killorglin Ring of Kerry

TEL: **066 9761200**   FAX: **066 9761200**
EMAIL: **jeromeoregan@eircom.net**
WEB: **www.oreganscountryhomeandgardens.com**

Luxurious modern home on award winning gardens. Golf, Fishing nearby. Ideal touring base. Home baking. AA ◆◆◆ Award. Tea/Coffee facilities. TV, Hairdryer in rooms.

B&B	3	Ensuite	€25.50/€27.50	Dinner	€25.50
B&B	1	Standard	€23/€25	Partial Board	-
Single Rate			€38.50/€38.50	Child reduction	50%

Open: 1st February-30th November

Killorglin 1km

Ms Carina O'Shea
DUIBHLEAS
Dunmaniheen, Killorglin,
Co Kerry

Killorglin Ring of Kerry

TEL: **066 9761002**

Luxurious dormer bungalow set in scenic private grounds on Ring of Kerry. Close to horseriding, golf, beaches, fishing, gourmet restaurants. Warm welcome.

B&B	3	Ensuite	€26/€32	Dinner	-
B&B	1	Standard	€26	Partial Board	-
Single Rate			€36/€38	Child reduction	25%

Open: 1st February-30th November

Killorglin 2km

Jacinta Sheehan
THE FAIRWAYS
Tinnahalla, Killorglin,
Co Kerry

Killorglin Ring of Kerry

TEL: **066 9762391**
EMAIL: **fairways@gofree.indigo.ie**

Luxurious friendly B&B. Adjacent to Golf course. Tee times arranged. Ideal base for Ring of Kerry/Dingle/Tralee/Killarney.

B&B	4	Ensuite	€25.50/€27	Dinner	-
B&B	-	Standard	-	Partial Board	-
Single Rate			€38.50/€38.50	Child reduction	33.3%

Open: 1st April-31st October

Mrs Joan Carmody
PALMGROVE HOUSE
Tarbert Rd, Listowel,
Co Kerry

Listowel
TEL: **068 21857**
EMAIL: **palmgrove@indigo.ie**

Comfortable home on Tarbert N69 Car Ferry road. Tarbert Ferry 10 min. Spacious bedrooms, laundry service, Tea/Coffee. Fishing and Golfing nearby. Permits available. Private Car park.

B&B	3	Ensuite	€26	Dinner	-
B&B	2	Standard	€23	Partial Board	-
Single Rate			€36/€36	Child reduction	50%

Listowel 2.5km

Open: 1st April-31st October

Mrs Mary Costello
ARAS MHUIRE
Ballybunion Road, Listowel,
Co Kerry

Listowel
TEL: **068 21515/23612** FAX: **068 23612**
EMAIL: **marycos@eircom.net**
WEB: **homepage.eircom.net/~doniec**

Near Town Centre on R553 opposite Convent primary school. Ideal for Ballybunion Beach and Golf and Tarbert Car Ferry. Reduction for more than 1 night. Irish Independent recommended.

B&B	4	Ensuite	€25.50/€35	Dinner	-
B&B	-	Standard	-	Partial Board	-
Single Rate			€38.50/€46	Child reduction	33.3%

In Listowel

Open: 8th January-30th December

Mrs Teresa Keane
WHISPERING PINES
Bedford, Listowel,
Co Kerry

Listowel
TEL: **068 21503**

Comfort assured in luxurious home in peaceful location on Ballylongford Road. Ballybunion and Listowel Golf Courses, Tarbert Ferry, Beaches 10 mins.

B&B	3	Ensuite	€25.50/€28	Dinner	-
B&B	1	Standard	€23/€25.50	Partial Board	-
Single Rate			€36/€38.50	Child reduction	25%

Listowel 1.5km

Open: All Year

The Lyons Family
THE HAVEN
Car Ferry Road, Cahirdown,
Listowel, Co Kerry

Listowel
TEL: **068 21992**

Purpose built to fire safety standards. Walking distance Town Centre. Breakfast menu, TV, Hairdryers, Tea making facilities in bedrooms. Laundry facilities.

B&B	5	Ensuite	€25.50/€25.50	Dinner	-
B&B	-	Standard	-	Partial Board	-
Single Rate			€38.50/€38.50	Child reduction	50%

In Listowel

Open: All Year

Mrs Breda Mahony
ASHFORD LODGE
Tarbert Road, Listowel,
Co Kerry

Listowel
TEL: **068 21280**
EMAIL: **ashfordlodge@unison.ie**

Nearest approved B&B to Town Centre on Car Ferry Road (N69). Leaving Listowel, turn right at end of bypass road. Recommended by Rough Guide to Ireland.

B&B	3	Ensuite	€26	Dinner	-
B&B	1	Standard	€24	Partial Board	-
Single Rate			€36	Child reduction	50%

In Listowel

Open: All Year

Vera & John McDermott
CLAREVILLE HOUSE
Skehenerin, Tarbert Road,
Listowel, Co Kerry

Listowel
TEL: **068 23723**   FAX: **068 23723**

Dormer bungalow. Landscaped garden. 2km from Listowel. Main N69 Tarbert Ferry Rd. Ferry 15 mins. Golf, Salmon-Trout fishing. Good bass fishing from shore in winter.

B&B	4	Ensuite	€25.50/€31.75	Dinner	-
B&B	-	Standard	-	Partial Board	-
Single Rate			€38.50	Child reduction	50%

Listowel 2km   **Open:** All Year Except Christmas

Mrs Nancy O'Neill
ASHGROVE HOUSE
Ballybunion Road, Listowel,
Co Kerry

Listowel
TEL: **068 21268/23668** FAX: **068 21268**
EMAIL: **nancy.oneill@ireland.com**
WEB: **www.dirl.com/kerry/ashgrove_house**

Luxury home near Town R553. Frommer/Sullivan Guide recommended. TV-Tea-Coffee all rooms. Golf - Car Ferry 15 mins. See www.dirl.com

B&B	3	Ensuite	€26/€30	Dinner	-
B&B	1	Standard	€24/€25	Partial Board	-
Single Rate			€40/€40	Child reduction	25%

Listowel 1km   **Open:** 1st April-30th September

Mrs Monica Quille
NORTH COUNTY HOUSE
67 Church St, Listowel,
Co Kerry

Listowel
TEL: **068 21238**   FAX: **068 22831**
EMAIL: **bryanmonica1@eircom.net**

Centre of Town. Luxurious family run home. Convenient to Ballybunion Golf Courses (fee reduction). Tarbert Car Ferry. Ideal touring base.

B&B	6	Ensuite	€26/€31	Dinner	-
B&B	2	Standard	€24/€29	Partial Board	-
Single Rate			€40/€45	Child reduction	25%

In Listowel   **Open:** All Year

Mrs Kathleen Stack
CEOL NA HABHANN
Tralee Road, Listowel,
Co Kerry

Listowel
TEL: **068 21345**   FAX: **068 21345**
EMAIL: **knstack@eircom.net**
WEB: **www.dirl.com/kerry/ceol-na-habhann.htm**

Irish National Trust Award Winner. Thatched house on wooded River bank. Frommer Guide. Elsie Dillard recommended. Superior balcony room.

B&B	4	Ensuite	€26/€32	Dinner	-
B&B	-	Standard	-	Partial Board	-
Single Rate			€45/€50	Child reduction	-

Listowel 1km   **Open:** 1st April-31st October

Mrs Majella Mangan
BALLYOUGHTRA HOUSE
Miltown, Killarney,
Co Kerry

Miltown Killarney
TEL: **066 9767502**   FAX: **066 9767502**
EMAIL: **mangansmiltown@eircom.net**

Modern comfortable welcoming home. Great location for touring Ring of Kerry, Killarney, Dingle (R563). Enjoy Pubs, Golf, Fishing, Beaches and Horse riding.

B&B	2	Ensuite	€26/€28	Dinner	-
B&B	1	Standard	€24/€26	Partial Board	-
Single Rate				Child reduction	-

Killarney 17km   **Open:** 1st March-31st October

Milltown 1km

Ms Agnes Shortt
SHORTCLIFF HOUSE
Lyre, Milltown,
Co Kerry

Milltown
TEL: **066 9767106**   FAX: **066 9767106**

Peaceful country location 1km off N70. Ring of Kerry route. Mature gardens, Riding stables on site, Golf 5 mins. Ideal for Golf, Walking, Touring & Horse riding.

B&B	3	Ensuite	€25.50/€27	Dinner	-
B&B	-	Standard	-	Partial Board	-
Single Rate			€38.50/€39	Child reduction	25%

Open: 1st April 30th-September

Portmagee 5km

Mrs Kathleen Lynch
HARBOUR GROVE
Aghadda, Portmagee,
Co Kerry

Portmagee
TEL: **066 9477116**   FAX: **066 9477116**
EMAIL: **harbourgrove@eircom.net**

Friendly home, 6km Ring of Kerry N70. Private strand. Harbour setting. Mature trees. Spacious bathrooms. Skellig tours, boat, fishing, riding, walking arranged. Restaurant, pub, music near.

B&B	3	Ensuite	€26/€26	Dinner	€17
B&B	-	Standard	-	Partial Board	€270
Single Rate			€39/€39	Child reduction	50%

Open: 1st March-30th November

In Portmagee

Christina Murphy
THE WATERFRONT
Portmagee, Co Kerry

Portmagee
TEL: **066 9477208**
EMAIL: **thewaterfront@eircom.net**

At entrance Portmagee village on scenic Skellig Ring near bridge linking Valentia Island to mainland. Adjacent to Skellig Heritage Centre.

B&B	6	Ensuite	€25.50	Dinner	-
B&B	-	Standard	-	Partial Board	-
Single Rate			€38.50	Child reduction	50%

Open: April-October

In Sneem

Ann Cronin
SNEEM RIVER LODGE
Sneem, Co Kerry

Sneem Ring of Kerry
TEL: **064 45578**   FAX: **064 45277**
EMAIL: **sneemriverlodge@eircom.net**

Newly built guesthouse with magnificent mountain views, overlooking Sneem river. Every comfort provided for our guests. Close to all amenities. Private parking.

B&B	4	Ensuite	€26/€26	Dinner	-
B&B	-	Standard	-	Partial Board	-
Single Rate			€38.50/€38.50	Child reduction	-

Open: 1st February-12th December

Sneem

Mrs Gretta Drummond
ROCKVILLE HOUSE
Sneem, Co Kerry

Sneem Ring of Kerry
TEL: **064 45135**
EMAIL: **rockville@oceanfree.net**

Luxurious dormer bungalow set in private grounds. Kerry Way walking route, Golf, Fishing nearby. Bicycle shed. Breakfast menu.

B&B	4	Ensuite	€26	Dinner	-
B&B	-	Standard	€38.50	Partial Board	-
Single Rate				Child reduction	25%

Open: 1st March-15th November

Mrs Noreen Drummond
BELLVIEW
Pier Road, Sneem,
Co Kerry

Sneem Ring Of Kerry
TEL: 064 45389

Hospitable, friendly and tranquil residence situated on the Ring Of Kerry. Beaches, Scenic Walks, Fishing, Golfing and Tennis located nearby.

B&B	2	Ensuite	€25.50/€26	Dinner	-
B&B	1	Standard	€23/€23	Partial Board	-
Single Rate			€36/€38.50	Child reduction	25%

In Sneem

Open: 2nd January-21st December

Mrs Helen Foley
HILLSIDE HAVEN
Doon, Tahilla, Sneem,
Killarney, Co Kerry

Sneem Ring Of Kerry
TEL: 064 82065   FAX: 064 82065
EMAIL: hillsidehaven@eircom.net

Spacious tastefully decorated bungalow in tranquil location with mature gardens overlooking Kenmare Bay. Caha Mountain adjacent Kerry Way walking route on N70. Sneem/Kenmare Road.

B&B	4	Ensuite	€25.50/€25.50	Dinner	€19
B&B	-	Standard	-	Partial Board	€264
Single Rate			€38.50/€38.50	Child reduction	25%

Sneem 9km

Open: 1st March-30th October

Mrs Margaret Harrington
BANK HOUSE
North Square, Sneem,
Killarney, Co Kerry

Sneem Ring of Kerry
TEL: 064 45226

Georgian house with antiques and charm situated in the heart of Ireland's most picturesque Village. Frommer and French Guide recommended. Breakfast menu.

B&B	3	Ensuite	€26	Dinner	-
B&B	2	Standard	€24	Partial Board	-
Single Rate			€38.50	Child reduction	-

In Sneem

Open: March-November

Mrs Maura Hussey
AVONLEA HOUSE
Sportsfield Road, Sneem,
Ring of Kerry, Co Kerry

Sneem Ring of Kerry
TEL: 064 45221
EMAIL: avonlea@eircom.net
WEB: www.sneem/com/avonlea

Perfect location, secluded spot beside village. Signposted. Mountain/Woodland surroundings. Frommer, Dillard/Causin, Routard recommended. Walks, Golf, Fishing, Restaurants/Pubs.

B&B	4	Ensuite	€25.50/€25.50	Dinner	-
B&B	1	Standard	€23/€23	Partial Board	-
Single Rate			€36/€36	Child reduction	-

In Sneem

Open: April-November

Mrs Alice O'Sullivan
OLD CONVENT HOUSE
Woodvale, Pier Road,
Sneem, Co Kerry

Sneem Ring of Kerry
TEL: 064 45181   FAX: 064 45181
EMAIL: conventhouse@oceanfree.net

Unique, comfortable, old world stone house (1866), on Sneem estuary. Private grounds with access to fishing river. Many recommendations. Walking enthusiasts.

B&B	6	Ensuite	€25	Dinner	-
B&B	-	Standard	-	Partial Board	-
Single Rate			€36	Child reduction	25%

In Sneem

Open: 1st January-22nd December

Kerry

Mrs Marion Barry
THE FAIRWAYS
Kerries, Fenit Road,
Tralee, Co Kerry

Tralee
TEL: **066 7127691**   FAX: **066 7127691**

Luxurious home, quiet peaceful location off R558. Tralee/Fenit road. Views of Tralee Bay/Mountains. Nearby Tralee Golf Club, Restaurants. Ideal Golf/Touring base.

B&B	4	Ensuite	€25.50/€26.50	Dinner	-
B&B	-	Standard		Partial Board	-
Single Rate			€38.50/€38.50	Child reduction	50%

Tralee 2km

Open: April-October

Mrs Patricia Canning
BRICRIU
20 Old Golf Links Road,
Oakpark, Tralee, Co Kerry

Tralee
TEL: **066 7126347**   FAX: **066 7126347**

Quiet area off N69 pass Railway. Take 1st right, left, right again (10 mins walk). Adjacent Sports Complex. Convenient Golf, Beaches.

B&B	3	Ensuite	€25.50/€27.93	Dinner	-
B&B	-	Standard	-	Partial Board	-
Single Rate			€38.50/€44.45	Child reduction	25%

In Tralee

Open: 1st June-31st October

Hazel Costello
ARDROE HOUSE
Oakpark Road, Tralee,
Co Kerry

Tralee
TEL: **066 7126050**

Period town house on N69. 5 minutes walk Bus/Train depot. Close to beach, Golf, Mountains and all local amenities. Ideal touring base. Recommended by Rough Guide To Ireland.

B&B	2	Ensuite	€26/€28	Dinner	-
B&B	2	Standard	€23/€26	Partial Board	-
Single Rate			-	Child reduction	50%

In Tralee

Open: May-September

Mrs Eileen Curley
MOUNTAIN VIEW HOUSE
Ballinorig West,
Tralee, Co Kerry

Tralee
TEL: **066 7122226**

Own grounds. Close all amenities. Ideal Golf/Touring base. Approaching Tralee on N21, turn right just before roundabout. Frommer recommended.

B&B	3	Ensuite	€25.50	Dinner	-
B&B	1	Standard	€23	Partial Board	-
Single Rate			€36/€38.50	Child reduction	25%

Tralee 2km

Open: 1st April-31st October

Mrs Gail Daly
ASHDALE
Fenit Road, Tralee,
Co Kerry

Tralee Fenit Road
TEL: **066 7128927**   FAX: **066 7128927**
EMAIL: **gaildaly@eircom.net**
WEB: **www.ashdalehouse.com**

Frommer recommended. Luxurious home on R558 overlooking Slieve Mish Mountains. Enroute to Tralee Golf club. Excellent Restaurants nearby - Ideal Touring base.

B&B	3	Ensuite	€26/€35	Dinner	-
B&B	-	Standard	-	Partial Board	-
Single Rate			€40/€50	Child reduction	33.3%

Tralee 2km

Open: 15th March-1st November

Mrs Gertie Deady
GURRANE
50 Derrylea, Tralee,
Co Kerry

Tralee
Tel: **066 7124734**

Modern two storey house on N69 Listowel Tarbert Car Ferry road. Convenient to Rail, Bus, Town, Golf, Greyhound Track, Hotel, Restaurant, Sports complex.

B&B	2	Ensuite	€26/€28	Dinner	-
B&B	2	Standard	€23/€25	Partial Board	-
Single Rate			€36/€36	Child reduction	-

Tralee 1.5km   **Open:** 8th January-20th December

Mrs Hannah Devane
EASTCOTE
34 Oakpark Demesne,
Tralee, Co Kerry

Tralee
Tel: **066 7125942**

Select accommodation in peaceful location. All facilities in rooms. Ideal touring base. 200 metres off N69 route, Tarbert Car ferry road. Warm welcome.

B&B	2	Ensuite	€25.50	Dinner	-
B&B	1	Standard	€23	Partial Board	-
Single Rate			€36/€38.50	Child reduction	-

Tralee 1km   **Open:** 2nd January-20th December

Mrs Patricia Dooley
TEACH AN PHIOBAIRE
Laharn, Listowel Rd,
Tralee, Co Kerry

Tralee
Tel: **066 7122424**   Fax: **066 7122424**
Email: **triciadooley@eircom.net**
Web: **homepage.eircom.net/~teachanphiobaire**

The Piper's House, on the N69 Ferry route. Tea/coffee on arrival. Music, golf, fishing, touring, nearby. Trad Irish Music Uilleann Pipes Workshop on site.

B&B	4	Ensuite	€25.50/€35	Dinner	-
B&B	-	Standard		Partial Board	-
Single Rate			€38.50/€48	Child reduction	50%

Tralee 2km   **Open:** All Year Except Christmas

Mrs Maura Dowling
LEESIDE
Oakpark, Tralee,
Co Kerry

Tralee
Tel: **066 7126475**   Fax: **066 7126475**
Email:**dowlingsbandb@hotmail.com**

N69 Ferry route. Near Bus/Rail. Antique Irish Furniture. Recommended Lets Go/Hachette Guides. Orthopaedic beds. TV's. Power showers. Breakfast menu. Home baking. Tea/Coffee facilities.

B&B	3	Ensuite	€25.50/€25.50	Dinner	-
B&B	-	Standard		Partial Board	-
Single Rate			€38.50/€38.50	Child reduction	25%

In Tralee   **Open:** 1st March-30th November

Mrs K Dunne
OAKDENE
53 Derrylea, Oakpark Road,
Tralee, Co Kerry

Tralee
Tel: **066 7125934**

Situated on Tralee/Listowel Road N69. Convenient to Train, Bus, Airport, Pitch & Putt, Golf, Beaches.

B&B	3	Ensuite	€25.50/€25.50	Dinner	-
B&B	1	Standard	€23/€23	Partial Board	-
Single Rate			€36/€38.50	Child reduction	25%

Tralee 1.5km   **Open:** 7th January-16th December

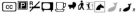

Mrs Noreen Galvin
WEST SEVEN
Tonevane, Blennerville,
Tralee, Co Kerry

TEL: **066 7129932**

Country Home on N86. Breathtaking view of Mountains. 5 minutes walk to village. Old Ship Canal, Steam Train, Horse riding, Golf, Aqua Dome, Siamsa, Theatre, Beach, Tea/Coffee at all times.

B&B	3	Ensuite	€25.50/€27	Dinner	-
B&B	-	Standard	-	Partial Board	-
Single Rate			€38.50	Child reduction	-

Tralee 3km

Open: 1st April-31st October

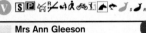

Mrs Ann Gleeson
ROSEDALE LODGE
Oakpark Road, Tralee,
Co Kerry

Tralee

TEL: **066 7125320**

On N69 Listowel (Car Ferry) Road. Luxury accommodation. Spacious bedrooms. Excellent Beaches & Restaurants nearby. Personal supervision.

B&B	3	Ensuite	€25.50/€32	Dinner	-
B&B	-	Standard	-	Partial Board	-
Single Rate			€38.50	Child reduction	-

In Tralee

Open: 1st March-1st November

Mrs Catherine Gleeson
BROOKDALE
Castlemaine Rd, Tralee,
Co Kerry

Tralee

TEL: **066 7125063**

Dormer bungalow on Killorglin/Ring of Kerry Rd (N70). Ideally located for Beaches, Golf, Fishing and Horse Riding. Complimentary Tea/Coffee. TV in all rooms.

B&B	3	Ensuite	€26/€26	Dinner	-
B&B	-	Standard	-	Partial Board	-
Single Rate			€38.50	Child reduction	25%

Tralee 1km

Open: 1st May-1st November

Mary Ann Hanafin
GLENOGUE HOUSE
Ballymakegogue, The Spa,
Tralee, Co Kerry

Tralee-Fenit Road

TEL: **066 7136476**
EMAIL: **mahanafin@eircom.net**

Newly built bungalow situated on road to famous Barrow Golf Club. Also ideally located to fishing port of Fenit.

B&B	4	Ensuite	€25.50/€26	Dinner	-
B&B	-	Standard	-	Partial Board	-
Single Rate			€38.50	Child reduction	50%

Tralee 3km

Open: 1st May-30th September

Mrs Mary Hannafin
SHANGRI-LA
The Spa, Tralee,
Co Kerry

TEL: **066 7136214**

Secluded country residence overlooking Tralee Bay. Walk to Beach, Pub & Restaurant. Golf Courses nearby. Ideal Golfing/Touring base. Walking route locally. On R558.

B&B	3	Ensuite	€25.50	Dinner	€17
B&B	2	Standard	€23	Partial Board	-
Single Rate			€36	Child reduction	25%

Tralee 4km

Open: 31st January-31st November

Mrs Eileen Hooker
SHERIDAN LODGE
Listellick, Tralee,
Co Kerry

Tralee
TEL: **066 7123272**   FAX: **066 7123272**

A warm welcome awaits you. Scenic location. Ideal Golfing/Touring base. Private Car Parking. Tea/Coffee. TV room with Log/Turf fire.

B&B	4	Ensuite	€27/€30	Dinner	-
B&B	1	Standard	€26/€28	Partial Board	-
Single Rate			€37/€39.50	Child reduction	50%

Tralee 3km

Open: 7th January-15th December

Mrs Sheila Horgan
ALVERNA
26 Liosdara, Oakpark,
Tralee, Co Kerry

Tralee
TEL: **066 7126970**

Off N69. First turn right after Swimming pool and Sports Centre. Fourth house on left. Convenient to many Golf clubs. 10 mins walk Town Centre, 5 mins walk Railway/Bus depot.

B&B	2	Ensuite	€26/€30	Dinner	-
B&B	2	Standard	€24/€26	Partial Board	-
Single Rate			€36/€36	Child reduction	50%

Tralee 1km

Open: 7th January-22nd December

Mrs Jane Hurley
SINEADS
Lios Carraig Court,
Caherslee, Tralee,
Co Kerry

Tralee
TEL: **066 7123500**   FAX: **066 7123500**
EMAIL: **sineads_gh@hotmail.com**

A warm welcome awaits you at Sineads. Ideal Touring/Golfing base. Excellent Beaches and Restaurants nearby. Power showers. Complimentary Tea/Coffee.

B&B	3	Ensuite	€25.50/€30	Dinner	-
B&B	-	Standard	-	Partial Board	-
Single Rate			€38.50/€40	Child reduction	-

In Tralee

Open: March-October

Mrs Sheila Kerins
BALLINGOWAN HOUSE
Mile Height, Killarney Road,
Tralee, Co Kerry

Tralee Killarney Road Area
TEL: **066 7127150**   FAX: **066 7120325**
EMAIL: **ballingowan@eircom.net**
WEB: **www.kerryview.com/ballingowanhouse**

All spacious rooms with TV, Tea/Coffee facilities, Hairdryer. Private parking. Approaching Tralee on N21/N22 on left before McDonalds. Tours arranged.

B&B	4	Ensuite	€26/€26	Dinner	-
B&B	-	Standard	-	Partial Board	-
Single Rate			€38.50/€38.50	Child reduction	33.3%

Tralee 1km

Open: 1st April-6th October

Mrs Eileen Lynch
ST ENDAS
Oakpark, Tralee,
Co Kerry

Tralee
TEL: **066 7126494**   FAX: **066 7126494**
EMAIL: **eileenmlynch@eircom.net**

Town house convenient Sports Complex, Aqua Dome, Golf, Beaches, Greyhound Racing. 5 mins Bus and Train Depot. Private parking. Ideal touring base. N69.

B&B	4	Ensuite	€26/€28	Dinner	-
B&B	-	Standard	-	Partial Board	-
Single Rate			€38.50/€38.50	Child reduction	50%

In Tralee

Open: All Year Except Christmas

Helen Lyons
KNOCKBRACK
Oakpark Road, Tralee,
Co Kerry

TEL: **066 7127375**
EMAIL: **knockbrackguests@eircom.net**
WEB: **www.dirl.com/kerry/knockbrack.htm**

Family home in residential area. Convenient to town centre. TV in bedrooms. Tea making facilities. Private parking. Situated on Listowel (Car Ferry) road N69.

B&B	3	Ensuite	€25.50/€32	Dinner	-
B&B	-	Standard	-	Partial Board	-
Single Rate			€38.50/€40	Child reduction	25%

In Tralee

Open: 1st March-30th November

Mrs Juliette O'Callaghan
GREEN GABLES
1 Clonmore Villas,
Ballymullen Road, Tralee,
Co Kerry

TEL: **066 7123354**   FAX: **066 7123354**
EMAIL: **info@greengablestralee.com**
WEB: **www.greengablestralee.com**

Listed Victorian period town house. Town Centre location adjacent County Library, Town park, on N70. 5 min walk Bus/Train station.

B&B	3	Ensuite	€25.50/€27	Dinner	-
B&B	1	Standard	€23/€25.50	Partial Board	-
Single Rate			€36/€44	Child reduction	-

In Tralee

Open: 1st February-10th December

Mrs Joan O'Connor
SKEHANAGH LODGE
Skehanagh,
Castlemaine Road,
Tralee, Co Kerry

TEL: **066 7124782**   FAX: **066 7124782**

Bright spacious comfortable bungalow on Killorglin/Ring of Kerry Road N70. Tea/Coffee facilities, TV in bedrooms. Guide de Routard recommended. Two large family rooms. Touring base.

B&B	4	Ensuite	€26/€27	Dinner	-
B&B	1	Standard	€23/€23	Partial Board	-
Single Rate			€36/€38.50	Child reduction	25%

Tralee 1km

Open: 1st April-1st November

Ita O'Donnell
AHAROE
Blennerville, Tralee,
Co Kerry

TEL: **066 7123108**

1 mile from Tralee towards Dingle. Right turn at T junction onto Swing bridge over canal. Quiet location. Overlooking Blennerville Village, Windmill, Steam Train, Old Ship Canal.

B&B	3	Ensuite	€25.50	Dinner	-
B&B	-	Standard	-	Partial Board	-
Single Rate				Child reduction	-

Blennerville

Open: 17th March-1st October

Rose O'Keeffe
ASHVILLE HOUSE
Ballyard, Tralee,
Co Kerry

TEL: **066 7123717**   FAX: **066 7123898**
EMAIL: **ashville@eircom.net**

Architect designed, country setting off Dingle Road (N86). Tralee 2 minutes drive, TV, Hairdryers, Power Showers, Breakfast Menu, Drying Room.

B&B	6	Ensuite	€27/€28	Dinner	-
B&B	-	Standard	-	Partial Board	-
Single Rate			€38.50/€38.50	Child reduction	50%

Tralee 1km

Open: All Year

Mrs Mary O'Neill
BEECH GROVE
Oakpark, Tralee,
Co Kerry

Tralee

TEL: **066 7126788**   FAX: **066 7180971**
EMAIL: **oneillbeechgrove@eircom.net**

On Car Ferry Rd N69. Near Railway/Bus Station, Sports Complex, Town Centre. Secure car park. Siamsa tickets. Tours arranged.

B&B	3	Ensuite	€25.50	Dinner	-
B&B	1	Standard	€23	Partial Board	-
Single Rate			€38.50	Child reduction	50%

Tralee 1km

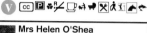

Open: 1st January-20th December

Mrs Helen O'Shea
CLUAIN MOR HOUSE
Boherbee, Tralee, Co Kerry

Tralee

TEL: **066 7125545**
EMAIL: **cluainmorguesthousetralee@eircom.net**

On 1 acre garden. 5 mins Rail Station, Aqua Dome. Golf, Angling, Beaches 5 miles. Kerry Airport 20 mins. 5 mins walk to Tralee Town. Private Car parking.

B&B	5	Ensuite	€25.50/€30.54	Dinner	-
B&B	-	Standard		Partial Board	-
Single Rate			€38.50/€41.04	Child reduction	25%

In Tralee

Open: 1st January-20th December

Mrs Catherine O'Sullivan
MARINA LODGE
Cloherbrien, (Fenit Road Area)
Tralee, Co Kerry

Tralee

TEL: **066 7123565**
EMAIL: **marinalodge@eircom.net**

Warm welcome awaits you. Family run B&B. Scenic location. Complimentary Tea/Coffee. Golf, Seafood Restaurants nearby. Private parking. Tours arranged.

B&B	4	Ensuite	€25.50/€31.74	Dinner	-
B&B	-	Standard	-	Partial Board	-
Single Rate			-	Child reduction	25%

Tralee 2km

Open: 30th March-30th September

Mrs Lena O'Sullivan
KNOCKANISH HOUSE
The Spa, Tralee,
Co Kerry

Tralee Fenit Road Area

TEL: **066 7136268**
EMAIL: **knockanishhouse@eircom.net**
WEB: **www.knockanish.mainpage.net**

Luxurious home, spacious rooms, power showers, breakfast menu. Recommended in leading guides. On R558 overlooking bay. Golf, restaurants, beaches & harbour.

B&B	5	Ensuite	€26/€33	Dinner	-
B&B	-	Standard		Partial Board	-
Single Rate			€40/€50	Child reduction	-

Tralee 3km

Open: 1st April-1st November

Mrs Colette Quinn
VILLA DE LOURDES
Brewery Road, Oakview,
Tralee, Co Kerry

Tralee

TEL: **066 7126278**

Modern house opposite Greyhound Track, convenient to Rail/Bus station, Town Centre, Churches & Sports Complex.

B&B	-	Ensuite	-	Dinner	-
B&B	4	Standard	€23/€23	Partial Board	-
Single Rate			€36/€36	Child reduction	-

In Tralee

Open: 1st March-31st October

Mrs Margaret Ryle
CRANA-LI
Greenlawn, Blennerville,
Tralee, Co Kerry

Tralee Dingle Road Area
TEL: **066 7124467**
EMAIL: **cranali@eircom.net**

Looking for a quiet and scenic place? B&B off N86 at Blennerville. Gateway to Dingle/Ring of Kerry. Landscaped gardens - Nature at its best! Only 5 mins from Tralee.

B&B	4	Ensuite	€25.50/€25.50	Dinner	-
B&B	-	Standard	-	Partial Board	-
Single Rate			€38.50/€38.50	Child reduction	33.3%

Tralee 3km

Open: 1st April-30th September

Mrs Joan Smith
BRIANVILLE
Clogherbrien,
Fenit Road Area, Tralee,
Co Kerry

Tralee Fenit Road Area
TEL: **066 7126645**   FAX: **066 7126645**
EMAIL: **michsmit@gofree.indigo.ie**

Luxurious bungalow. AA ◆◆◆◆. Frommer guide recommended, Best B&B in Ireland. Tea/Coffee, Hairdryers, TV in rooms, all on ground floor. 18 hole Golf Links. Seafood Restaurants nearby.

B&B	5	Ensuite	€30/€35	Dinner	-
B&B	-	Standard	-	Partial Board	-
Single Rate				Child reduction	50%

Tralee 1.5km

Open: All Year

Paddy & Deirdre Stack
WOODBROOK HOUSE
Laharn, Listowel Road (N69),
Tralee, Co Kerry

Tralee
TEL: **066 7180078**
EMAIL: **woodbrookhouse@esatclear.ie**
WEB: **www.esatclear.ie/~woodbrookhouse**

Luxurious hillside residence with breathtaking views of Slieve Mish mountains. Ideal base for Touring, Golfing, Hillwalking with excellent restaurants nearby. Groundfloor rooms.

B&B	4	Ensuite	€26/€32	Dinner	-
B&B	-	Standard	-	Partial Board	-
Single Rate			€38.50/€50	Child reduction	33.3%

Tralee 3km

Open: All Year

Tim & Mary Walshe
THE WILLOWS
5 Clonmore Terrace,
Moyderwell, Tralee,
Co Kerry

Tralee
TEL: **066 7123779**   FAX: **066 7123779**
EMAIL: **2thewillows@eircom.net**
WEB: **www.thewillowsbnb.com**

Friendly Victorian townhouse - Olde world charm - On N70. 5 mins walk Town/Bus/Train. Breakfast menu. TV, Tea/Coffee, Hairdryers in rooms. Ideal touring base.

B&B	3	Ensuite	€25.50/€27	Dinner	-
B&B	1	Standard	€23/€25	Partial Board	-
Single Rate			€36/€36	Child reduction	33.3%

In Tralee

Open: 1st February-18th December

Mary Lane
SHEALANE COUNTRY HOUSE
Corha-Mor, Valentia Island,
Co Kerry

Valentia Island
TEL: **066 9476354**
EMAIL: **marylane@eircom.net**
WEB: **www.kerryweb.ie**

Peaceful setting on Road bridge entrance adjacent to Skelig Experience Centre. Skelig trips, Fishing, Walking arranged. Restaurants, Traditional music nearby.

B&B	3	Ensuite	€28/€32	Dinner	-
B&B	-	Standard	-	Partial Board	-
Single Rate			€38.50/€38.50	Child reduction	-

Portmagee 1km

Open: March-October

Mrs Julie O'Sullivan
GLENREEN HEIGHTS
Knightstown Road,
Valentia Island, Co Kerry

Valentia Island

Tel: **066 9476241**   Fax: **066 9476241**
Email: **glenreen@eircom.net**
Web: **homepage.eircom.net/~glenreen**

Spectacular view Sea/Mountains. Orthopaedic beds. Breakfast Menu, local Seafood. Scenic walks, Pitch & Putt, Fishing and trips to Skellig arranged.

B&B	2	Ensuite	€25.50	Dinner	€18
B&B	1	Standard	€23	Partial Board	-
Single Rate			€36/€38.50	Child reduction	-

Knightstown 2km

Open: 1st March-1st November

Mrs Breda Barry
GOLF LINKS VIEW
Murreigh, Waterville,
Co Kerry

Waterville

Tel: **066 9474623**   Fax: **066 9474623**
Email: **jbar@eircom.net**
Web: **homepage.eircom.net/~golflinkview/**

AA ◆◆◆ recommended, luxury home downstairs bedrooms. Power showers, Hairdryers, TV, open peat fire. Golf Course, Fishing, Horse Riding, Beach, trips to Skelligs.

B&B	6	Ensuite	€25.50	Dinner	€17
B&B	-	Standard	-	Partial Board	€264
Single Rate			€38.50	Child reduction	25%

Waterville 1km

Open: 1st March-31st October

Mrs Margaret Brown
OLD CABLE HOUSE
Cable Station, Waterville,
Co Kerry

Waterville

Tel: **066 9474233**   Fax: **066 9474869**
Email: **mbrownn@iol.ie**
Web: **www.old-cable-house.com**

Interesting stay. Origins First Transatlantic Telegraph Cable from Ireland to USA - Victorian Internet, 1866. Waterville Golf Links, free Salmon - Trout fishing Lough Currane.

B&B	4	Ensuite	€25.50/€36	Dinner	-
B&B	2	Standard	€23/€31	Partial Board	-
Single Rate			€36/€50	Child reduction	25%

In Waterville

Open: All Year Except Christmas

Mrs Abbie Clifford
CLIFFORDS B&B
Waterville,
Co Kerry

Waterville

Tel: **066 9474283**   Fax: **066 9474283**
Email: **cliffordbandb@hotmail.com**

Comfortable home in Waterville village, southern end. Overlooking the Atlantic Ocean. Restaurants, Pubs, Shops walking distance. Private parking.

B&B	5	Ensuite	€25.50/€25.50	Dinner	-
B&B	1	Standard	€23/€23	Partial Board	-
Single Rate			€36/€38.50	Child reduction	-

In Waterville

Open: 1st March-31st October

Mrs Patricia Curran
ATLANTIC VIEW
Toor, Waterville,
Co Kerry

Waterville

Tel: **066 9474335**   Fax: **066 9474335**
Email: **joecurranelect@eircom.net**

Family run country home overlooking picturesque Ballinskelligs Bay and the Atlantic Ocean. Enjoy quiet country walks. Fishing, Golf, Horseriding locally.

B&B	3	Ensuite	€25.50/€28.50	Dinner	-
B&B	1	Standard	€23	Partial Board	-
Single Rate			€38.50	Child reduction	-

Waterville 4km

Open: May-September

Mrs Angela Grady
O'GRADYS TOWNHOUSE
Spunkane, Waterville,
Co Kerry

Waterville

Tel: **066 9474350**   Fax: **066 9474730**
Email: paogrady@eircom.net
Web: www.stayatogradys.com

Ideally located B&B. Close to all amenities, Golf, Fishing, trips to Skellig Rock arranged. Spacious ensuite rooms, Visitors lounge, Breakfast Menu.

B&B	6	Ensuite	€25.50/€25.50	Dinner	-
B&B	-	Standard	-	Partial Board	-
Single Rate			€38.50/€38.50	Child reduction	25%

In Waterville   **Open:** 1st March-31st October

Mrs Cirean Morris
KLONDYKE HOUSE
New Line Road, Waterville,
Co Kerry

Waterville

Tel: **066 9474119**   Fax: **066 9474666**
Email: klondykehouse@eircom.net
Web: homepage.eircom.net/~klondykehouse

Luxurious home on Ring of Kerry road N70. Bedrooms with satellite TV, Direct dial phones, Power showers. Skellig trips/Golf arranged. Baggage transfers.

B&B	6	Ensuite	€25.50/€25.50	Dinner	-
B&B	-	Standard	-	Partial Board	-
Single Rate			€38.50	Child reduction	25%

In Waterville   **Open:** All Year Except Christmas

Nora Murphy
ASHLING HOUSE
Main Street, Waterville,
Co Kerry

Waterville

Tel: **066 9474247**

Modern two-storey house situated on Main street overlooking Ballinskellig Bay. Sandy Beaches, Golf, Fishing, Trips to Skellig Rock, Mountain climbing.

B&B	4	Ensuite	€25.50/€25.50	Dinner	-
B&B	1	Standard	-	Partial Board	-
Single Rate			€36/€36	Child reduction	25%

In Waterville   **Open:** 17th March-15th October

BOOKINGS

We recommend your first and last night is pre-booked. Your hosts will make a booking for you at your next selected home for the cost of the phone call. When travelling in high season (June, July, August), it is essential to pre-book your accommodation – preferably the evening before, or the following morning to avoid disappointment.

WHEN TRAVELLING OFF-SEASON IT IS ADVISABLE TO CALL AHEAD AND GIVE A TIME OF ARRIVAL TO ENSURE YOUR HOSTS ARE AT HOME TO GREET YOU.

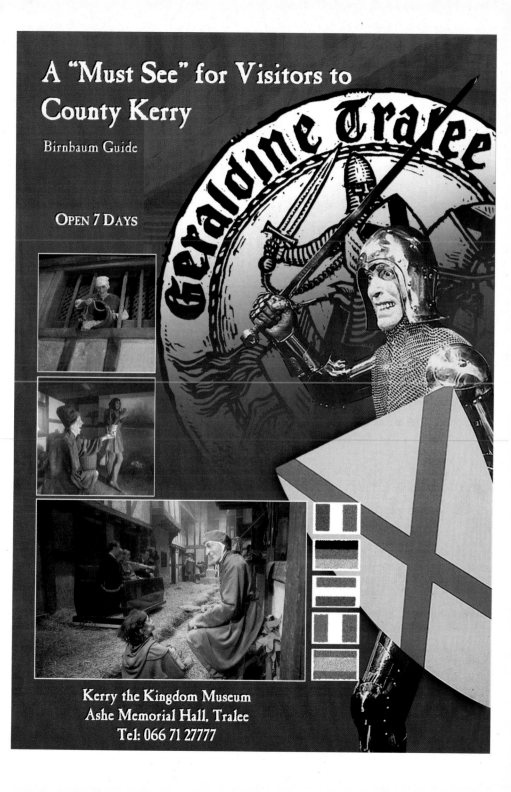

A "Must See" for Visitors to County Kerry

Birnbaum Guide

OPEN 7 DAYS

Geraldine Tralee

Kerry the Kingdom Museum
Ashe Memorial Hall, Tralee
Tel: 066 71 27777

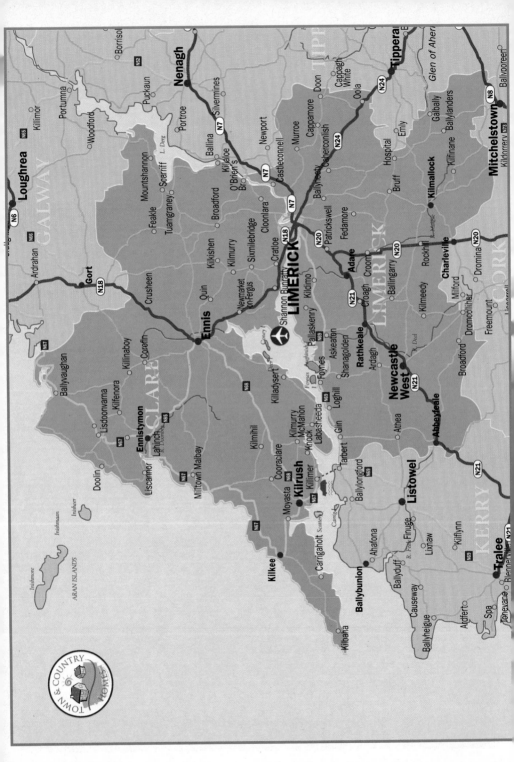

Ireland's Shannonside

The Shannon Region comprise counties Clare, Limerick, North Tipperary, North Kerry and South Offaly. It is a particularly beautiful part of Ireland and is dominated by water. The Shannon river, the longest river in Ireland or the UK flows through its centre and gives the Region its name. Shannon's Lough Derg - Ireland's pleasure lake - touches on three counties, Clare, Tipperary and Galway. The Region also boasts hundreds of smaller lakes and many rivers.

The Shannon Region has a dramatic Atlantic coastline, with beautiful beaches and a purity of air that refreshes the Region and invigorates the visitor.

Though the Shannon Region is compact, only 100 miles (166 Kms), from end to end, there is tremendous diversity in its scenery from the Slieve Bloom mountains to lakelands, golden beaches, the awesome Cliffs of Moher and the Burren District.

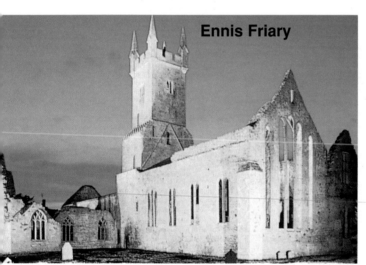

Ennis Friary

The Region offers great visitor attractions and night-time entertainment options and is also perfect for the activity enthusiast interested in Golfing, Angling, Horse Riding, Walking, Cycling or water based activities.

Area Representatives

CLARE
Mr Sean Grogan, St Patricks, Corebeg, Doora, Ennis, Co Clare
Tel: 065 6840122 Fax: 065 6840122
Mrs Teresa Petty, Sunville, Off Doolin Road, Lisdoonvarna,
Co. Clare. Tel: 065 7074065 Fax: 065 7074065
Mrs Mary Corcoran, Grange, Wood Road, Cratloe, Co Clare
Tel: 061 357389 Fax: 061 357389

LIMERICK
Ms Catherine Geary, Carnlea House, Caher Road,
Cloughkeating, Patrickswell, Co Limerick
Tel: 061 302902 Fax: 061 302902
Mrs Eileen Murphy, The Orchard, Limerick Road,
Newcastle West, Co Limerick
Tel: 069 61029 Fax: 069 61029

Tourist Information Offices
OPEN ALL YEAR

Ennis
Arthurs Road
(off O'Connell
Square)
Tel: 065 6828366

Limerick City
Arthur's Quay
Tel: 061 317522

Tralee
Ashe Hall
Denny Street
Tel: 066 7121288

Shannon Airport
Arrivals Hall
Tel: 061 471664

Website: www.shannon-dev.ie

349

Clare

Clare is renowned for traditional music, its rugged beauty with Shannon Airport at its gateway.
Attractions: Bunratty Folk Park, Ennis, The famous Burren, Cliffs of Moher, Lisdoonvarna Spa Wells & Doolin. Championship Golf at Lahinch. Great fishing, excellent beaches, walks & trails.

Ballyvaughan

Hilde & Donal O'Connell
COOLSHINE B&B
Green Road, Ballyvaughan,
Co Clare

Ballyvaughan

TEL: **065 7077163**
EMAIL: **dburren@eircom.net**
WEB: **homepage.eircom.net/~dburren**

Beautiful, quiet, friendly home. 0.1km off Galway road. Maps & Books for your use. German & French spoken. Organic homemade bread & jams. Family & 3 bedded Room.

B&B	3	Ensuite	€26/€28	Dinner	-
B&B		Standard	-	Partial Board	-
Single Rate			€45	Child reduction	**33.3%**

Open: 16th March-30th October

Bunratty 1km

Mairead Bateman
PARK HOUSE
Low Road, Bunratty,
Co Clare

Bunratty

TEL: **061 369902**   FAX: **061 369903**
EMAIL: **parkhouse@eircom.net**
WEB: **homepage.eircom.net/~parkhouse**

Luxurious peaceful home. Full menu. Home baking. Bunratty Castle 1km. Airport 10 minutes drive. Orthopaedic beds, TV, Tea/Coffee, Curling tongs, Hairdryer. AA ◆◆◆◆.

B&B	6	Ensuite	€28/€22	Dinner	-
B&B	-	Standard	-	Partial Board	-
Single Rate			€45/€45	Child reduction	**25%**

Open: 4th February-15th December

Bunratty 3km

Kathleen Browne
HEADLEY COURT
Deerpark, Bunratty,
Co Clare

Bunratty

TEL: **061 369768**
EMAIL: **headleycourt@eircom.net**
WEB: **www.headleycourt.net**

Luxurious countryside residence, spacious heated rooms with large showers. Every convenience. Sullivan, Erdvig McQuillan recommended. End Low Road go right.

B&B	5	Ensuite	€32/€32	Dinner	-
B&B		Standard	-	Partial Board	-
Single Rate			-	Child reduction	**25%**

Open: All Year

Mrs Mary Browne
BUNRATTY LODGE
Bunratty,
Co Clare

Bunratty

TEL: **061 369402**   FAX: **061 369363**
EMAIL: **reservations@bunrattylodge.com**
WEB: **www.bunrattylodge.com**

Luxurious, well heated rooms on ground floor with every convenience. Award winning breakfast. Recommended by all leading guides. Airport 10 minutes.

B&B	6	Ensuite	€32	Dinner	-
B&B	-	Standard	-	Partial Board	-
Single Rate				Child reduction	-

Open: March-November

Mrs Jackie Burns
BUNRATTY VILLA
Bunratty East,
Co Clare

Bunratty

TEL: **061 369241**   FAX: **061 369947**
EMAIL: **bunrattyvilla@eircom.net**
WEB: **www.bunrattyvilla.com**

Luxurious B&B, All rooms ensuite with tea/coffee facilities, TV & Hairdryers.Bunratty Castle 5 minutes. Recommended by Hidden Ireland.

B&B	6	Ensuite	€28/€32	Dinner	-
B&B	-	Standard	-	Partial Board	-
Single Rate			€45/€45	Child reduction	25%

Shannon 6km

Open: February-November

Mrs Mary Corcoran
GRANGE
Wood Road, Cratloe,
Co Clare

Bunratty

TEL: **061 357389**   FAX: **061 357389**
EMAIL: **alfie@iol.ie**

Off N18 at Limerick Inn Hotel. Spacious house, rooms ground floor. Shannon Airport 15 mins, Bunratty 5 mins. Frommer, Lonely Planet recommended. Electric blankets. Early arrivals welcome.

B&B	3	Ensuite	€25.50/€26.50	Dinner	€17
B&B	2	Standard	€23/€23	Partial Board	€264
Single Rate			€36/€38.50	Child reduction	25%

Limerick 6km

Open: All Year

Mrs Trish Cronin
BRIAR LODGE
Hill Road, Bunratty,
Co Clare

Bunratty

TEL: **061 363388**   FAX: **061 363161**
EMAIL: **briarlodge@eircom.net**
WEB: **www.bb-house.com/briarlodge.htm**

Turn left at corner Fitzpatricks Hotel, 1 mile on right. Tea/Coffee, Hairdryers, Curling Irons all rooms. Guest lounge. Breakfast menu. AM arrivals welcome.

B&B	6	Ensuite	€26	Dinner	-
B&B	-	Standard	-	Partial Board	-
Single Rate			€39	Child reduction	25%

Bunratty 1.5km

Open: 1st March-30th September

Mrs Patricia Darcy
BUNRATTY HEIGHTS
Low Road, Bunratty,
Co Clare

Bunratty

TEL: **061 369324**   FAX: **061 369324**
EMAIL: **bunrattyheights@eircom.net**
WEB: **www.bb-house.com/bunrattyheights.htm**

Morning guests welcome. Situated on Low Road 1 mile from Bunratty Castle/Durty Nellies. Airport 10 minutes. TV's, Hairdryers, Tea/Coffee facilities all rooms.

B&B	4	Ensuite	€26/€26	Dinner	-
B&B	-	Standard	-	Partial Board	-
Single Rate			€39/€39	Child reduction	50%

Bunratty 1.5km

Open: All Year Except Christmas

T. M. Dennehy
TUDOR LODGE
Hill Road, Bunratty,
Co Clare

Bunratty

TEL: **061 362248**   FAX: **061 362569**
EMAIL: **tudorlodge@esatclear.ie**

Tudor style residence, Sylvan setting. All rooms have private facilities, TVs, Hairdryers. Bunratty Castle 5 mins walk. Shannon Airport 10 mins drive.

B&B	5	Ensuite	€30	Dinner	-
B&B	-	Standard	-	Partial Board	-
Single Rate			€45	Child reduction	25%

In Bunratty

Open: February-November

Mrs Anne Fuller
LEAVALE
**Bunratty, Moyhill,
Cratloe, Co Clare**

TEL: **061 357439**
EMAIL: **leavale@eircom.net**
WEB: **www.leavale.com**

South of Bunratty on N18. Airport 10 mins. Inside Ireland recommended. Ground floor rooms. Orthopaedic beds, Clock Radio, Tea/Coffee in rooms. Guest garden.

B&B	2	Ensuite	€25.50/€26	Dinner	-
B&B	1	Standard	€23/€23	Partial Board	-
Single Rate			€36/€38.50	Child reduction	25%

Bunratty 1km

Open: 1st March-31st October

Mrs Teresa Grady
BUNRATTY ARMS
**Bunratty, Six Mile Bridge,
Co Clare**

TEL: **061 369 530**   FAX: **061 369 256**
EMAIL: **catherineteresa@eircom.net**
WEB: **www.bunratty.net**

R471 off N18 at Hurlers Cross 1 mile, or take road between Castle & Durty Nelly's, at end turn right.

B&B	4	Ensuite	€26	Dinner	-
B&B	-	Standard	-	Partial Board	-
Single Rate			€39	Child reduction	25%

Bunratty 3km

Open: 1st February-30th November

Denis Hegarty
DUNEDIN LODGE
**Low Road, Bunratty,
Co Clare**

TEL: **061 369966**   FAX: **061 369953**

Purpose built luxury accommodation. Rooms ensuite, Multi channel TV rooms. 1 min drive Bunratty Castle and Folk Park. 10 mins Shannon Airport.

B&B	5	Ensuite	€28/€32	Dinner	-
B&B	-	Standard	-	Partial Board	-
Single Rate			€45/€45	Child reduction	25%

Shannon 8km

Open: 15th January-15th December

Mrs Maureen McCabe
BUNRATTY HILLSIDE
**Clonmoney North (R471 Rd),
Bunratty, Co Clare**

TEL: **061 364330**   FAX: **061 364330**
EMAIL: **mccabe@bunratty.net**

Morning guests welcome. Dillard/Causin recommended. Airport 10 mins, Bunratty 2km, off N18 at Sixmilebridge R471. Guests collected from Airport & Bus Stop.

B&B	4	Ensuite	€26.66	Dinner	-
B&B	2	Standard	€24.10	Partial Board	-
Single Rate			€38.09	Child reduction	25%

Shannon 2km

Open: 1st March-1st November

Mrs Imelda McCarthy
INNISFREE
**Low Road, Bunratty,
Co Clare**

TEL: **061 369773**   FAX: **061 369926**
EMAIL: **innisfree@unison.ie**
WEB: **www.shannonheartland.ie**

Airport 10 mins. Road between Castle/Durty Nelly's. Tea/Coffee facilities, Hairdryers. Frommer Readers recommended. Breakfast menu, morning guests welcome.

B&B	4	Ensuite	€26/€28	Dinner	-
B&B	-	Standard	-	Partial Board	-
Single Rate			€39/€40	Child reduction	25%

Bunratty 1km

Open: 10th January-1st December

Freddie & Deirdre McInerney — Bunratty
AVAREST B&B
Hurlers Cross, Bunratty,
Co Clare

Tel: **061 360278**   Fax: **061 360535**
Email: **avarest@eircom.net**
Web: **www.avarest.ie**

New luxurious purpose-built home. Spacious rooms. TV, Telephones, Orthopaedic beds. Off N18 at Hurlers Cross. Bunratty/Airport 2 miles. Ideal touring base.

B&B	4	Ensuite	€28/€32	Dinner	-
B&B	-	Standard	-	Partial Board	-
Single Rate			€38.50/€40	Child reduction	25%

Shannon 3km

Open: All Year

Paula McInerney — Bunratty
RIVERSIDE B&B
Clonmoney West,
Bunratty, Co Clare

Tel: **061 364148**   Fax: **061 364148**
Email: **riverside@accommodationireland.com**

Custom built luxurious B&B. Spacious bedrooms with TV. Breakfast menu. Early Breakfast available. Situated on N18. Airport 10 mins, Bunratty 5 mins.

B&B	4	Ensuite	€26.60/€26.60	Dinner	-
B&B	1	Standard	€24.10/€24.10	Partial Board	-
Single Rate			€38/€38	Child reduction	33.3%

In Bunratty

Open: 3rd January-23rd December

Mrs Mary McKenna — Bunratty
GALLOW'S VIEW
Bunratty East,
Co Clare

Tel: **061 369125**   Fax: **061 369125**
Email: **gallowsview@eircom.net**
Web: **www.bunratty.net/gallowsview**

Warm and friendly home. Frommer Recommended. Airport 10 mins. Breakfast Menu. TV, Hairdryers, Tea/Coffee. Road between Castle/Durty Nellies, through carpark, 6th house on right.

B&B	5	Ensuite	€26	Dinner	-
B&B	-	Standard	-	Partial Board	-
Single Rate			€39	Child reduction	25%

Shannon 6km

Open: 7th March-31st October

Jan & Jim Moloney — Bunratty
HUNTING LODGE B&B
Wood Road, Cratloe,
Co Clare

Tel: **061 357216**   Fax: **061 271100**
Email: **moloneyjj@eircom.net**

Spacious house, scenic views, quiet location, Bunratty 5 minutes, Limerick 10 minutes, Airport 15 minutes. 1 mile off N18 at Limerick Inn.

B&B	2	Ensuite	€25.50	Dinner	€17
B&B	2	Standard	€23	Partial Board	€264
Single Rate			€36/€38.50	Child reduction	50%

Limerick 6km

Open: All Year

Mrs Penny O'Connor — Bunratty
DUNAREE
Low Road, Bunratty,
Co Clare

Tel: **061 369131**
Email: **dunaree@eircom.net**
Web: **www.dunaree.net**

Hillside residence with panoramic view, walking distance to Bunratty Castle. Luxurious bedrooms, all en-suite. Shannon Airport 10 minutes.

B&B	5	Ensuite	€28/€32	Dinner	-
B&B	-	Standard	-	Partial Board	-
Single Rate			€45	Child reduction	-

Bunratty Village 1km

Open: April-15th October

Mrs Rosemary Ormston
HIGHBURY HOUSE
Ballymorris, Cratloe,
Co Clare

Bunratty
TEL: 061 357212
EMAIL: cormston@iol.ie

Tudor style Country Home on N18. 2 miles from Bunratty Castle travelling south towards Limerick or 6 miles from Limerick City travelling north. Hairdryers, Electric Blankets.

B&B	4	Ensuite	€25.50/€27	Dinner	-
B&B	-	Standard	-	Partial Board	-
Single Rate			€38.50	Child reduction	50%

Bunratty 1.5km

Open: 1st January-15th December

Mrs Carmel O'Ryan
SUNNYBANK
Ballymorris, Cratloe,
Co Clare

Bunratty
TEL: 061 357108

Quiet house 400 yards Limerick-Shannon(N18) at Ballymorris. Comfortable lounge. Traditional music, Bunratty 1.5 miles. Shannon Airport 5 miles. Limerick City 6 miles.

B&B	2	Ensuite	€25.50/€25.50	Dinner	-
B&B	1	Standard	€23/€23	Partial Board	-
Single Rate			€36/€36	Child reduction	25%

Bunratty 2km

Open: 1st April-30th September

Mrs Kathleen O'Shea
MANDERLEY
Deer Park, Bunratty,
Sixmilebridge, Co Clare

Bunratty
TEL: 061 369572
EMAIL: manderley@oceanfree.net

Two storey country home with mature gardens. Take road between Durty Nellys and Castle, turn right at end of road, third house on left handside.

B&B	4	Ensuite	€27.94	Dinner	-
B&B	-	Standard	-	Partial Board	-
Single Rate			€38.50	Child reduction	25%

Shannon 8km

Open: 2nd January-30th November

Sheila Tiernan
ASHGROVE HOUSE
Lowroad, Bunratty,
Co Clare

Bunratty
TEL: 061 369332
EMAIL: frashe@eircom.net
WEB: www.ashgrovehouse.com

Take low road between Bunratty Castle and Durty Nellies. 10 min drive to Airport. Free carpark. Private entrances. 3 min drive to Bunratty. Warm rooms. Good beds. All facilities.

B&B	4	Ensuite	€26/€28	Dinner	-
B&B	-	Standard	-	Partial Board	-
Single Rate			€39/€40	Child reduction	25%

Bunratty 1.5km

Open: 1st February-30th November

Mrs Eileen Woulfe
SHANNON VIEW
Bunratty,
Co Clare

Bunratty
TEL: 061 364056   FAX: 061 364056

Bungalow on N18 Shannon - Limerick road. Galtee breakfast winner. Tea/coffee making facilities all rooms. Guests lounge.

B&B	4	Ensuite	€28.57	Dinner	-
B&B	-	Standard	-	Partial Board	-
Single Rate			€38.50	Child reduction	25%

Bunratty 1km

Open: 1st April-31st Octobe

Mrs Anne Martin
VILLA MARIA
Leagh South, Burren,
Co Clare

Burren

TEL: **065 7078019**
EMAIL: **vmaria@eircom.net**
WEB: **homepage.eircom.net/~vmaria**

Overlooking Galway Bay. Quiet area. Panoramic Burren setting. Information on Burren available. Irish Music. Excellent seafood locally. Smoke free home.

B&B	3	Ensuite	€25.50	Dinner	€17
B&B	2	Standard	€23	Partial Board	-
Single Rate			€36/€38.50	Child reduction	25%

Kinvara 4km   **Open:** 20th March-31st October

Mrs Mary Cleary
LAKEFIELD LODGE
Ennis Road, Corofin,
Co Clare

Corofin

TEL: **065 6837675**   FAX: **065 6837299**
EMAIL: **mcleary.ennis@eircom.net**

Recommended by "Le Guide du Routard". On periphery of Burren National Park. Cliffs of Moher, Shannon Airport 40 mins. Fishing locally. Tea/Coffee facilities.

B&B	4	Ensuite	€25.50/€27	Dinner	-
B&B	-	Standard	-	Partial Board	-
Single Rate			€38.50/€38.50	Child reduction	33.3%

In Corofin   **Open:** 1st April-31st October

Mrs Anne Connole
CONNOLES
Killeen, Corofin,
Co Clare

Corofin

TEL: **065 6837773**
EMAIL: **connolesbandb@eircom.ie**

A luxury family run home by Ballycullian Lake. The gateway to the Burren. 10 mins from Ennis. Leisurely activities closeby. Breakfast menu.

B&B	5	Ensuite	€27/€29	Dinner	-
B&B	-	Standard	-	Partial Board	-
Single Rate			€38.50/€38.50	Child reduction	33.3%

Corofin 2km   **Open:** 1st March-30th November

Mr Brendan Kearney
SHAMROCK & HEATHER
Station Road, Corofin,
Co Clare

Corofin

TEL: **065 6837061**
EMAIL: **bmkearney@eircom.net**

Shannon Airport 50 minutes. Lake District, Cliffs of Moher, Burren National Park, Traditional Music, Clare Heritage Centre, Museum. Hairdryer, Tea/Coffee.

B&B	2	Ensuite	€25.50	Dinner	-
B&B	1	Standard	€23	Partial Board	-
Single Rate			€36/€36	Child reduction	33.3%

Corofin   **Open:** 1st April-31st October

Thomas & Rita Kierce
BURREN HOUSE
Kilnaboy, Corofin,
Co Clare

Corofin

TEL: **065 6837143**
EMAIL: **burrenhouse@eircom.net**

Spacious house with Burren countryside views on R476 route. Close Burren National Park, Lake District, Heritage Centre. Airport 40 mins. Tea/Coffee facilities.

B&B	3	Ensuite	€25.50/€28	Dinner	€23
B&B	1	Standard	€23/€25	Partial Board	-
Single Rate			€36	Child reduction	25%

Corofin 3km   **Open:** 17th March-31st October

Mrs Kathleen Cullinan
HARBOUR VIEW
Doolin,
Co Clare

Doolin

Tel: **065 7074154**   Fax: **065 7074935**
Email: **kathlen@eircom.net**
Web: **harbourviewdoolin.port5.com**

Spacious ground floor bedrooms. Breathtaking views - Cliffs of Moher, Burren, Aran Islands.
Airport 1 hour. Hairdryers, Electric blankets. Rick Steeves.

B&B	4	Ensuite	€26/€26	Dinner	-
B&B	-	Standard		Partial Board	-
Single Rate			€38.50/€38.50	Child reduction	25%

Doolin 2km

Open: 20th February-31st October

Susan Daly
DALY'S HOUSE
Doolin,
Co Clare

Doolin

Tel: **065 7074242**   Fax: **065 7074668**
Email: **susan.daly@esatlink.com**
Web: **www.dalys-house.com**

Situated 150 yards from Doolin Village-home of Traditional Music. Panoramic views of the Sea,
Cliffs of Moher, Burren. Family run.

B&B	5	Ensuite	€28/€28	Dinner	-
B&B	-	Standard	-	Partial Board	-
Single Rate			-	Child reduction	25%

In Doolin

Open: 20th February-30th November

Ms Olive Dowling
TOOMULLIN HOUSE
Doolin Village,
Co Clare

Doolin

Tel: **065 7074723**
Email: **toomullin@eircom.net**
Web: **toomullindoolin.port5.com**

Lovely country cottage in Doolin Village. 1 mins walk to traditional music Pubs and Restaurants.
Tea/Coffee. Breakfast menu. Cliffs, Burren, Aran Ferry nearby.

B&B	3	Ensuite	€27/€28	Dinner	-
B&B	-	Standard	-	Partial Board	-
Single Rate			€45/€48	Child reduction	50%

In Doolin

Open: All Year Except Christmas

Brid & Val Egan
ATLANTIC SUNSET HOUSE
Cliffs of Moher Road,
Doolin, Co Clare

Doolin

Tel: **065 7074080**   Fax: **065 7074922**
Email: **sunsethouse@esatclear.ie**
Web: **homepage.eircom.net/~atlanticsunsetdoolin**

Warm hospitable home conveniently located on R478. Near Cliffs of Moher, Aran Ferry, Burren,
Music, Pubs. Breakfast Menu. Airport 1 hour. Highly recommended by Travel Guides.

B&B	6	Ensuite	€26/€28	Dinner	-
B&B	-	Standard	-	Partial Board	-
Single Rate			€40/€40	Child reduction	-

Doolin 2km

Open: All Year

Mrs Maeve Fitzgerald
CHURCHFIELD
Doolin,
Co Clare

Doolin

Tel: **065 7074209**   Fax: **065 7074622**
Email: **churchfield@eircom.net**
Web: **homepage.eircom.net/~churchfield**

House in Doolin Village. View - Cliffs Moher, Sea/Countryside. Traditional music. Burren. Fromme
recommended. Breakfast menu. Tea/Coffee. At bus stop.

B&B	5	Ensuite	€26/€28	Dinner	€19
B&B	1	Standard	€23/€25	Partial Board	-
Single Rate			€40/€40	Child reduction	

Doolin Village

Open: All Year Except Christmas

John D Flanagan
BALLYVARA HOUSE
Ballyvara, Doolin,
Co Clare

Doolin
Tel: **065 7074467** Fax: **065 7074868**
Email: **bvara@iol.ie**
Web: **www.ballyvarahouse.com**

19th Century Farm Cottage remodeled by owner. Panoramic Countryside views. Music, Burren. Cliffs Moher, Aran Ferry. Quiet setting on R479. Airport 1 hour.

B&B	6	Ensuite	€25.50/€30.50	Dinner	-
B&B	-	Standard		Partial Board	-
Single Rate			€38.50/€40	Child reduction	25%

In Doolin **Open:** March-October

Mrs Caitriona J Garrahy
RIVERFIELD HOUSE
Doolin,
Co Clare

Doolin
Tel: **065 7074113** Fax: **065 7074113**
Email:**riverfield@eircom.net**

Century-old reconstructed home. Five minutes walking to all Pubs and Restaurants. Family room. Credit Cards. Airport 1 hour.

B&B	3	Ensuite	€25.50/€28	Dinner	-
B&B	1	Standard	€23/€24	Partial Board	-
Single Rate			€36/€38	Child reduction	25%

In Doolin **Open:** All Year

Darra Hughes
SEA VIEW HOUSE
Fisher Street, Doolin,
Co Clare

Doolin
Tel: **065 7074826** Fax: **065 7074849**
Email: **seaviewhouse1@eircom.net**
Web: **www.kingsway.ie/seaviewhouse**

Luxury accommodation in the Village of Doolin overlooking the Atlantic Ocean. Extensive breakfast menu. Minutes walk music pubs, restaurants, Aran Ferry.

B&B	4	Ensuite	€26/€32	Dinner	-
B&B	-	Standard		Partial Board	-
Single Rate			€38/€58	Child reduction	25%

In Doolin **Open:** 1st January-22nd December

Marian & Martin McDonagh
GLASHA MEADOWS
Glasha, Doolin,
Co Clare

Doolin
Tel: **065 7074443**
Email: **glameadows@tinet.ie**

Family bungalow 1.5km from Doolin Village. Quiet location R479. Cliffs of Moher, Aran Ferries, Airport 1 hour. Breakfast menu. All guests bedrooms on ground floor.

B&B	6	Ensuite	€26/€28	Dinner	-
B&B	-	Standard	-	Partial Board	-
Single Rate			-	Child reduction	25%

Doolin 1.5km **Open:** 1st March-30th November

Mrs Josephine Moloney
HORSESHOE HOUSE
Fisher Street, Doolin,
Co Clare

Doolin/Cliffs of Moher
Tel: **065 7074006** Fax: **065 7074421**
Email: **horseshoe@eircom.net**
Web: **www.kingsway.ie/horseshoehouse**

Scenic area overlooking village beside sea. Walking distance to music, pubs, restaurants, Cliffs of Moher, boats to Aran Islands. Shannon Airport 1hr. Tennis court. R478.

B&B	4	Ensuite	€25.50/€30.50	Dinner	-
B&B	-	Standard	-	Partial Board	-
Single Rate			-	Child reduction	25%

In Doolin **Open:** 1st May-15th October

357

In Doolin

Mary Jo O'Connell
SEASCAPE B&B
Roadford, Doolin,
Co Clare

Doolin

TEL: **065 7074451**   FAX: **065 7074451**
EMAIL: **seascape@eircom.net**

Located on a quiet cul-de-sac in the heart of Doolin village. Close to Pubs, Burren, Cliffs of Moher, Aran Islands Ferries.

B&B	4	Ensuite	€26/€28	Dinner	-
B&B	-	Standard	-	Partial Board	-
Single Rate			€38.50/€44	Child reduction	25%

Open: All Year

Doolin 4km

Adrian & Bev O'Connor
CRAGGY ISLAND B&B
Ardeamush, Doolin,
Co Clare

Doolin

TEL: **065 7074595**
EMAIL: **cragisle@gofree.indigo.ie**
WEB: **homepage.eircom.net/~craggyisland/**

Peaceful, scenic location off R477 Lisdoonvarna/Ballyvaughan Coast road. Near Cliffs of Moher, Burren, Traditional music pubs. Traditional/Vegetarian breakfasts.

B&B	5	Ensuite	€25.50	Dinner	-
B&B	-	Standard	-	Partial Board	-
Single Rate			€38.50	Child reduction	33.3%

Open: All Year Except Christmas

In Doolin

Ms Lorraine Spencer
NELLIE DEE'S
Killilagh, Doolin Village,
Co Clare

Doolin/Cliffs of Moher

TEL: **065 7074020**
EMAIL: **lorspencer@eircom.net**

Located in the heart of Doolin Village. Minutes walk to music, pubs, restaurants, Burren, Cliffs, Aran Ferry nearby. Breakfast menu. Ground floor bedrooms.

B&B	4	Ensuite	€27/€28	Dinner	-
B&B	-	Standard	-	Partial Board	-
Single Rate			€44/€44	Child reduction	25%

Open: 1st February-30th November

John & Anne Sims
ISLAND VIEW
Cliffs of Moher Road (R478),
Doolin, Co Clare

Doolin

TEL: **065 7074346**   FAX: **065 7074844**
EMAIL: **sims@iol.ie**
WEB: **sites.netscape.net/islandviewdoolin/doolin**

"Lonely Planet", "Le Guide du Routard" recommended. Warm welcome. Breakfast Menu. Orthopaedic Beds. Tea, scones on arrival. Transport to pubs. Cliffs 8km.

B&B	4	Ensuite	€26/€28	Dinner	-
B&B	-	Standard	-	Partial Board	-
Single Rate			€38.50/€40	Child reduction	50%

Doolin 3km

Open: 1st February-31st October

In Ennis
358

Mrs Martina Brennan
CLONEEN
Clonroad, Ennis,
Co Clare

Ennis

TEL: **065 6829681**

Hiking, biking, driving ideal stop. Town Centre, Station 5 minutes walk. Airport, Burren, Cliffs, Castles 30 mins drive. Spacious gardens. Bicycle shed.

B&B	1	Ensuite	€25.50/€25.50	Dinner	-
B&B	2	Standard	€23/€24	Partial Board	-
Single Rate			€36/€36	Child reduction	25%

Open: 1st April-31st October

Ennis 2km

Mrs Anne Burke
CASA MARIA
Loughville, Lahinch Road,
Ennis, Co Clare

Ennis
TEL: **065 6820395**

Warm, friendly, ground floor rooms. Lovely peaceful location on N85 opposite Statoil Station. Ennis 3 minutes drive. Extensive parking.

B&B	2	Ensuite	€26/€28	Dinner	-
B&B	1	Standard	€24/€24	Partial Board	-
Single Rate			€36/€38.50	Child reduction	25%

Open: 1st April-31st October

Denis & Kathleen Cahill
RAILWAY VIEW HOUSE
Tulla Road, Ennis,
Co Clare

Ennis
TEL: **065 6821646**

Very secluded premises, 8 mins walk from Town Centre. Large private car park. No traffic noise. Shannon Airport 30 mins. Convenient to Cliffs of Moher, Burren & Castles.

B&B	3	Ensuite	€25.50	Dinner	-
B&B	-	Standard		Partial Board	-
Single Rate			€38.50	Child reduction	33.3%

Open: 1st March-30th November

Ennis 1.5km

Mrs Mary Connole
SHANLEE
Lahinch Road, Ennis,
Co Clare

Ennis
TEL: **065 6840270**
EMAIL: **mac.ennis@eircom.net**
WEB: **www.dirl.com/clare/shanlee.htm**

Comfortable home with ground floor rooms on N85 to the Burren, Cliffs of Moher, Bunratty Castle, Golf, Fishing. Traditional music. Morning guests welcome.

B&B	2	Ensuite	€25.50/€26	Dinner	-
B&B	2	Standard	€23/€24	Partial Board	-
Single Rate			€36/€38.50	Child reduction	50%

Open: All Year

Ennis 3km

Nathalie Crowe
GORT NA MBLATH
Ballaghboy, Doora,
Ennis, Co Clare

Ennis
TEL: **065 6822204**   FAX: **065 6822204**
EMAIL: **crowe.ennis@tinet.ie**

Peaceful comfortable family run home. Warm welcome. Ideal starting point for exploring the Burren. Detailed help in planning itinerary. Shannon Airport 15 mins.

B&B	2	Ensuite	€26	Dinner	-
B&B	2	Standard	€24	Partial Board	-
Single Rate			€39	Child reduction	-

Open: All Year

Ennis 2km

Teresa & Tom Crowe
SHALOM
Ballybeg, Killadysert Road,
Ennis, Co Clare

Ennis
TEL: **065 6829494**

Comfortable, warm, hospitable home. All rooms ground floor. Spacious bathrooms. Quiet location on R473 route, 2km to Ennis Town Centre. Spacious private parking. Shannon Airport 18km.

B&B	3	Ensuite	€26	Dinner	-
B&B	-	Standard		Partial Board	-
Single Rate			€38.50	Child reduction	-

Open: 1st May-1st October

Mrs Antoinette Diamond
CARRAIG MHUIRE B&B
Bearnafunshin, Barefield,
Ennis, Co Clare

TEL: **065 6827106**   FAX: **065 6827375**
EMAIL: **carraigmhuire@eircom.net**
WEB: **homepage.eircom.net/~carraigmhuire**

Country home, family friendly. Ennis/Galway Road N18. Convenient to Cliffs of Moher/Burren & beaches. TV, hairdryers, tea/coffee all rooms. Evening meals available.

B&B	3	Ensuite	€28	Dinner	€18
B&B	1	Standard	€25.50	Partial Board	€302
Single Rate			€36	Child reduction	33.3%

Ennis 8km      **Open:** 1st February-30th November

---

The Finn Family
DRUIMIN
Golf Links Road, Ennis,
Co Clare

TEL: **065 6824183**   FAX: **065 6843331**
EMAIL: **golfinn.ennis@tinet.ie**

Tranquil setting beside Ennis Golf Club on R474, with peat fire and award winning Breakfasts. We like it here, so will you.

B&B	4	Ensuite	€27/€28	Dinner	-
B&B	-	Standard	-	Partial Board	-
Single Rate			€38.50/€38.50	Child reduction	-

Ennis 1km   **Open:** 1st May-30th September

Mrs Mary Finucane
MOYVILLE
Lahinch Road, Ennis,
Co Clare

TEL: **065 6828278**
EMAIL: **moyville.ennis@eircom.net**

Spacious comfortable home on N85 to the Burren. Cliffs of Moher. Golf, Fishing, Entertainment locally. Electric Blankets, Hairdryers in rooms.

B&B	4	Ensuite	€25.50	Dinner	€17
B&B	-	Standard	-	Partial Board	-
Single Rate			€38.50	Child reduction	25%

Ennis 1km   **Open:** 1st April-31st October

Sean & Teresa Grogan
ST PATRICK'S
Corebeg, Doora,
Ennis, Co Clare

TEL: **065 6840122**   FAX: **065 6840122 (man)**

Quiet scenic area. Ideal location for Knappogue, Bunratty, Cragganowen, Burren, Cliffs of Moher, Golfing, Traditional Music. Morning visitors welcome.

B&B	3	Ensuite	€25.50	Dinner	€17
B&B	1	Standard	€23	Partial Board	€264
Single Rate			€36/€38.50	Child reduction	25%

Ennis 4km   **Open:** All Year

Mrs Maura Healy
BROOKVILLE HOUSE
Tobartaoscan,
Off Limerick Road, Ennis,
Co Clare

TEL: **065 6829802**

Tranquil location, garden. Bus station, Town 10 mins walk, adjacent West Co. Hotel, Golf Courses Airport, Cliffs, Castles 30 mins.

B&B	3	Ensuite	€26.66/€28	Dinner	-
B&B	-	Standard	-	Partial Board	-
Single Rate			€38.50/€38.50	Child reduction	25%

In Ennis   **Open:** March-Novembe

Mrs Helen Holohan
CLONRUSH
Lahinch Road, Ennis,
Co Clare

Ennis
TEL: **065 6829692**   FAX: **065 6829692**
EMAIL: **clonrushennis@eircom.net**

Easy to find, on N85, hard to leave. Ideal touring base, Cliffs of Moher, Bunratty Castle, Golf, Beaches, Burren. Restaurant and Bar 2 mins walk. 20 mins Airport.

B&B	4	Ensuite	€25.50/€26	Dinner	-
B&B	-	Standard		Partial Board	-
Single Rate			€38.50/€40	Child reduction	33.3%

Ennis 1.5km

Open: 1st March-31st October

John & Kathleen Kenneally
WILLBROOK HOUSE
Tulla Road, Ennis,
Co Clare

Ennis
TEL: **065 6820782**

A warm double glazed two storey residence within walking distance of Town Centre with central heating. Close to all amenities. Great touring base for South and West.

B&B	3	Ensuite	€25.50	Dinner	-
B&B	-	Standard	-	Partial Board	-
Single Rate			€38.50	Child reduction	33.3%

In Ennis

Open: All Year

Mr Sean Lally
SYCAMORE
Tulla Road, Ennis,
Co Clare

Ennis
TEL: **065 6821343**
EMAIL: **info@sycamore-house.com**
WEB: **www.sycamore-house.com**

Luxurious accommodation 6 mins walk town centre. TV/Radio/Tea/Coffee in bedrooms. 20 mins Shannon airport. Ideal touring base.

B&B	3	Ensuite	€25.50	Dinner	-
B&B	-	Standard		Partial Board	-
Single Rate			€38.50	Child reduction	25%

In Ennis

Open: All Year

Mrs Maureen Langan
ST ANNES
Limerick Road, Ennis,
Co Clare

Ennis
TEL: **065 6828501**
EMAIL: **jlangan.ennis@eircom.net**

On N18, Airport 20 mins. Adjacent to West County Hotel. Convenient to Cliffs of Moher, Burren, Golf. Tea/facilities, TV, Hairdryers in bedrooms.

B&B	3	Ensuite	€26/€28	Dinner	-
B&B	-	Standard	-	Partial Board	-
Single Rate				Child reduction	-

Ennis 1km

Open: 1st February-12th December

Mrs Anne McCullagh
AIN-KAREM
7 Tulla Road, Lifford,
Ennis, Co Clare

Ennis
TEL: **065 6820024**
EMAIL: **ainkaremenennis@eircom.net**

Hospitable warm home. Tea/coffee available at all times in guest lounge. Close to town centre, buses, trains and hotels. Shannon Airport 25 mins.

B&B	1	Ensuite	€25.50/€26.66	Dinner	-
B&B	2	Standard	€23/€24.13	Partial Board	-
Single Rate			€36	Child reduction	-

In Ennis

Open: All Year

Mrs Marie McDermott
BROOKE LODGE
Ballyduff, Barefield,
Ennis, Co Clare

Ennis
Tel: **065 6844830**

Luxurious country home within 5 minutes of Ennis and 20 minutes drive from Shannon Airport. An ideal base to visit Clare's tourist attractions.

B&B	3	Ensuite	€30	Dinner	-
B&B	-	Standard	-	Partial Board	-
Single Rate			€40	Child reduction	25%

Ennis 2km

Open: All Year Except Christmas

Mrs Carmel McMahon
ASHVILLE
Galway Rd, Ennis,
Co Clare

Ennis
Tel: **065 6822305**

New purpose built house on N18 Galway Road near Auburn Lodge Hotel. Ideal for touring Burren area, Cliffs of Moher & Aillwee Cave. Shannon Airport 15km.

B&B	3	Ensuite	€27	Dinner	-
B&B	-	Standard	-	Partial Board	-
Single Rate			-	Child reduction	33.3%

Ennis 1km

Open: 1st March-31st October

Tom & Rita Meaney
ASHLEIGH HOUSE
Barefield, Ennis,
Co Clare

Ennis
Tel: **065 6827187**   Fax: **065 6827331**
Email: **tommeaney@eircom.net**

Ennis/Galway Road. Shannon Airport 30 mins. Ideal touring base. Convenient to Burren, Cliffs of Moher, Castle banquets, Golf & Fishing.

B&B	5	Ensuite	€26	Dinner	€17
B&B	-	Standard	-	Partial Board	-
Single Rate			€38.50	Child reduction	33.3%

Ennis 5km

Open: 1st April-31st October

The Meere Family
FOUR WINDS
Limerick Road, Ennis,
Co Clare

Ennis
Tel: **065 6829831**
Email: **fourwinds.ennis@eircom.net**

Large home on main Airport road (N18). Private Car park at rear. Golf, Pitch/Putt nearby. 5 mins walk Town centre.

B&B	5	Ensuite	€25.50/€29	Dinner	-
B&B	-	Standard	-	Partial Board	-
Single Rate			€38.50/€40	Child reduction	33.3%

In Ennis

Open: 15th March-15th October

Mrs Mareaid O'Connor
VILLA NOVA
1 Woodlawn, Lahinch Road,
Ennis, Co Clare

Ennis
Tel: **065 6828570**

Bungalow on N85. Big Garden. Shannon 25 mins. Restaurant, Pub with music 2 mins walk. Golf, Pitch & Putt, Swimming, Cliffs of Moher, Bunratty Castle, Aillwee Caves nearby.

B&B	2	Ensuite	€26/€26	Dinner	€18
B&B	3	Standard	€24/€24	Partial Board	-
Single Rate			€36/€38.50	Child reduction	25%

Ennis 1.5km

Open: 1st February-31st October

Mr Hugh O'Donnell
RYE HILL B&B
Tulla Road, Ennis,
Co Clare

Ennis
TEL: **065 6824313**
EMAIL: **ryehillbandb@eircom.net**

Easy to find R352. Town Centre 3-4 mins by car. Ideal touring base. Golf, Fishing, Horse riding nearby. Limerick 40 mins. Shannon 25 mins. Pub and Restaurant 5 mins walk.

B&B	6	Ensuite	€26/€28	Dinner	-
B&B	-	Standard		Partial Board	-
Single Rate			€38.50/€38.50	Child reduction	50%

Ennis 2km

Open: 2nd January-18th December

Mrs Teresa O'Donohue
SANBORN HOUSE
Edenvale, Kilrush Road,
Ennis, Co Clare

Ennis
TEL: **065 6824959**
EMAIL: **sanbornbandb@eircom.net**
WEB: **www.bb-house.com/sanborn.htm**

Spacious neo-Georgian house in peaceful scenic setting on Kilrush/Car ferry road (N68). Convenient Airport, Cliffs of Moher, Burren, Castles. Early guests welcome.

B&B	4	Ensuite	€26/€28	Dinner	-
B&B	-	Standard	-	Partial Board	-
Single Rate			-	Child reduction	33.3%

Ennis 2km

Open: 2nd January-20th December

Mrs Monica O'Loughlin
MASSABIELLE
Off Quin Road, Ennis,
Co Clare

Ennis
TEL: **065 6829363**   FAX: **065 6829363**

Recommended by "Frommer", "Sullivan", "Best B&B's" Guides. Friendly, relaxed family home in peaceful rural setting with landscaped gardens, Tennis Court.

B&B	4	Ensuite	€26.50	Dinner	-
B&B	-	Standard	-	Partial Board	-
Single Rate			€39	Child reduction	25%

Ennis 3km

Open: 20th May-20th September

Mary O'Sullivan
OGHAM HOUSE
3 Abbey Court, Clare Road,
Ennis, Co Clare

Ennis
TEL: **065 6824878**
EMAIL: **oghamhouseennis@eircom.net**

On N18 opposite West County Hotel. Enjoy our warm hospitality in comfortable home. Bus/Train 10 mins walk. Shannon 20 mins drive. Ideal touring base.

B&B	2	Ensuite	€28/€30	Dinner	-
B&B	1	Standard	€28/€28	Partial Board	-
Single Rate			€38/€38	Child reduction	25%

Ennis 1km

Open: All Year

Mrs Brigid Pyne
KILMOON HOUSE
Kildysart Road,
Off Limerick Rd,
Ennis, Co Clare

Ennis
TEL: **065 6828529**

Spacious home in peaceful environment, 20 mins from Shannon Airport. Convenient to Bunratty Castle, Knappogue, Burren and Cliffs of Moher.

B&B	2	Ensuite	€25.50/€25.50	Dinner	-
B&B	1	Standard	€23/€23	Partial Board	-
Single Rate			€36/€36	Child reduction	50%

Ennis 1km

Open: 1st April-31st October

Ennis 3km

Joan & George Quinn
LAKESIDE COUNTRY LODGE
Barntick, Clarecastle,
Ennis, Co Clare

Ennis

TEL: **065 6838488** FAX: **065 6838488**
EMAIL: **lakesidecountry@eircom.net**
WEB: **www.lakesidecountry.com**

Spacious home on 3 acres. Overlooking Killone Lake and Abbey, on coast road (R473) to Car Ferry. Convenient Airport. Hairdryers. Conservatory overlooking lake.

B&B	4	Ensuite	€25.50/€27	Dinner	-
B&B	-	Standard	-	Partial Board	-
Single Rate			€38.50	Child reduction	50%

Open: 1st February-15th December

Ennis

Ms Nuala Ryan
ADOBE
21 Fernhill, Galway Road,
Ennis, Co Clare

Ennis

TEL: **065 6823919**
EMAIL: **johnryan.ennis@eircom.net**
WEB: **www.ennisbedandbreakfast.com**

Modern Detached house in quiet cul-de-sac. Breakfast menu. 5 mins walk to Town Centre, 100 metres off N18.

B&B	2	Ensuite	€25.50/€30	Dinner	-
B&B	2	Standard	€23/€26	Partial Board	-
Single Rate			€40/€40	Child reduction	25%

Open: 1st January-23rd December

In Ennis

T J & Pauline Roberts
CARBERY HOUSE
Kilrush Road/Car Ferry Rd,
Ennis, Co Clare

Ennis

TEL: **065 6824046** FAX: **065 6824046**

Route 68, morning visitors welcome. Orthopaedic beds, Electric blankets, Hospitality trays, Hairdryers. Continental breakfast reduced rate. Convenient Airport.

B&B	4	Ensuite	€26/€28	Dinner	-
B&B	-	Standard	-	Partial Board	-
Single Rate			-	Child reduction	-

Open: 1st April-25th October

Ennis 8km

Mrs Ina Troy
HAZELDENE
Barefield, Ennis,
Co Clare

Ennis

TEL: **065 6827212** FAX: **065 6827212**

Ennis/Galway Road. Morning guests welcome. Airport 30 mins distance. TV in bedrooms. Convenient Cliffs of Moher. Banquets, Golf, Fishing.

B&B	5	Ensuite	€26/€26	Dinner	-
B&B	-	Standard	-	Partial Board	-
Single Rate			€40/€40	Child reduction	25%

Open: 1st January-20th December

In Ennistymon

364

Mrs Kathleen Cahill
STATION HOUSE
Ennis Road, Ennistymon,
Co Clare

Ennistymon

TEL: **065 7071149** FAX: **065 7071709**
EMAIL: **cahilka@indigo.ie**
WEB: **www.bb-stationhouse.com**

Route 85. Spacious home. Hospitality tray, Hairdryer, Telephone, TV in bedrooms. Breakfast menu. Horse riding, Fishing, Golf, Cliffs of Moher, Burren nearby. Guide du Routard recommended.

B&B	6	Ensuite	€25.50/€25.50	Dinner	-
B&B	-	Standard	-	Partial Board	-
Single Rate			-	Child reduction	-

Open: 1st January-23rd December

Mrs Geraldine McGuane
SUNSET B&B
Kilcornan, Ennistymon,
Co Clare

Ennistymon

Tel: **065 7071527**

Situated on hill top with panoramic views of sea and countryside on R85 with peat fires and home baking. Cliffs of Moher, the Burren, Golf, Fishing.

B&B	2	Ensuite	€25.50/€25.50	Dinner	-
B&B	1	Standard	€23/€23	Partial Board	-
Single Rate			€36/€36	Child reduction	25%

Ennistymon 1km   **Open:** 1st April-30th September

Maureen Scales
CALLURA LODGE
Callura East, Kilfenora Road,
Ennistymon, Co Clare

Ennistymon

Tel: **065 7071640**
Email: **ura@eircom.net**
Web: **www.bb-house.com/calluralodge.htm**

Quiet home on R481. Nearby are Kilfenora, Cliffs of Moher, the Burren, Golf and Fishing. Tea/Coffee with home baking on arrival. TV lounge. Ideal touring base.

B&B	2	Ensuite	€25.50	Dinner	-
B&B	2	Standard	€23	Partial Board	-
Single Rate			-	Child reduction	-

Ennistymon 1.5km   **Open:** 1st May-1st November

Mary Fitzpatrick
MONTERAY
Kilrush Road,
Kilkee, Co Clare

Kilkee

Tel: **065 9056244**

Located on N68. 15 mins from Tarbert/Killimer car ferry. In a quiet and tranquil location. Close to all amenities. Secure car park at rear. Good travel base.

B&B	4	Ensuite	€25.50/€26	Dinner	-
B&B	-	Standard		Partial Board	-
Single Rate			€38.50/€38.50	Child reduction	-

Kilkee 1.5km   **Open:** 1st June-30th September

Mrs Patsy Flanagan
HARBOUR LODGE
6 Marine Parade, Kilkee,
Co Clare

Kilkee

Tel: **065 9056090**

Town Home across road from Beach in scenic area, adjacent all amenities. Recommended by "The Irish Bed & Breakfast Book".

B&B	4	Ensuite	€25.50	Dinner	-
B&B	1	Standard	€23	Partial Board	-
Single Rate			€38.50	Child reduction	-

In Kilkee   **Open:** 1st April-31st October

Mrs Maureen Haugh
DUGGERNA HOUSE
West End, Kilkee,
Co Clare

Kilkee

Tel: **065 9056152**

On seafront overlooking the Duggerna rocks. Scenic surroundings. Golf, Fishing, Scuba Diving, Pitch and Putt. Ideal Touring Centre.

B&B	4	Ensuite	€25.50/€26.50	Dinner	-
B&B	-	Standard	-	Partial Board	-
Single Rate			€38.50	Child reduction	-

In Kilkee   **Open:** 1st May-30th September

In Kilkee

Mary Hickie
BAYVIEW
O'Connell Street,
Kilkee, Co Clare

TEL: **065 9056058**
EMAIL: bayview3@eircom.net
WEB: www.bb-house.com/hickiesbayview.htm

Enjoy warm friendly hospitality in our tastefully decorated home. Magnificent view of Kilkee Bay, Cliffs. Central all amenities, Breakfast menu.

B&B	8	Ensuite	€25.50/€28	Dinner	-
B&B	-	Standard	-	Partial Board	-
Single Rate			-	Child reduction	50%

Open: 1st January-27th December

In Kilkee

Mrs Ann Nolan
NOLANS B&B
Kilrush Road, Kilkee,
Co Clare

TEL: **065 9060100**

Spacious family run accommodation in comfortable new dormer house. Breakfast menu. Private parking. Ideal touring base. Tea and Coffee available at all times.

B&B	6	Ensuite	€25.50/€26.50	Dinner	-
B&B	-	Standard	-	Partial Board	-
Single Rate			€38.50/€38.50	Child reduction	50%

Open: All Year Except Christmas

In Killaloe

Eileen Brennan
CARRAMORE LODGE
Roolagh, Ballina,
Killaloe, Co Clare

TEL: **061 376704**
EMAIL: **carramorelodge@oceanfree.net**
WEB: **www.dirl.com/clare/carramore_lodge.htm**

Spacious family home on 1.5 acres of beautiful gardens, panoramic views beside River Shannon on Lough Derg. 5 mins walk Village, Pubs, Restaurants, Churches.

B&B	4	Ensuite	€26	Dinner	-
B&B	-	Standard	-	Partial Board	-
Single Rate			€36/€39	Child reduction	33.3%

Open: 1st March-31st October

Killaloe 2km

Mrs Patricia Byrnes
RATHMORE HOUSE
Ballina, Killaloe,
Co Clare

TEL: **061 379296**
EMAIL: **rathmorebb@oceanfree.net**
WEB: **www.dirl.com/clare/rathmore-house.htm**

On R494. Comfortable, relaxing & peaceful, near Killaloe overlooking Lough Derg on River Shannon. Pubs, restaurants, heritage town, close to Shannon Airport.

B&B	5	Ensuite	€26	Dinner	-
B&B	1	Standard	€23	Partial Board	-
Single Rate			€36/€39	Child reduction	33.3%

Open: 1st March-31st October

In O'Gonnelloe

Ms Kathleen Flannery
LIG DO SCITH
O'Gonnelloe, Scarriff,
Co Clare

TEL: **061 923172**

New home with panoramic view of Lough Derg. Convenient to Shannon Airport. Timber floors throughout. Hill walking, Fishing, Water Sports, Horse Riding 5km.

B&B	4	Ensuite	€25.50/€27.50	Dinner	-
B&B	-	Standard	-	Partial Board	-
Single Rate			€38.50/€38.50	Child reduction	33.3%

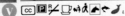

Open: 2nd January-20th December

Celine King
SHANNARRA
Killaloe,
Co Clare

Killaloe

Tel: **061 376548**
Email: **celineking@hotmail.com**
Web: **www.kingsbandb.com**

Comfortable family run accommodation 7km north of Killaloe on Scarriff road. Scenic views. Convenient to music Pubs, Restaurants, Water Sport & Hillwalking.

B&B	4	Ensuite	€25.50/€25.50	Dinner	-
B&B	-	Standard	-	Partial Board	-
Single Rate			€38.50/€38.50	Child reduction	-

Killaloe 7km

Open: 1st March-1st November

Anne O'Conner
WHITETHORN LODGE
1 Shannon View, Ballina,
Killaloe, Co Clare

Killaloe

Tel: **061 375257**
Email: **whitethornlodgebb@eircom.net**

Modern, friendly home in tranquil setting - walking distance to village pubs, shops, hotels, restaurants. Shannon Airport 20 mls. Limerick/University 14 mls.

B&B	3	Ensuite	€25.50/€25.50	Dinner	-
B&B	-	Standard	-	Partial Board	-
Single Rate			€38.50/€38.50	Child reduction	33.3%

In Killaloe

Open: 1st March-31st October

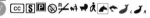

Imy Kerrigan
COIS-NA-SIONNA
Ferry Junction, Killimer,
Kilrush, Co Clare

Killimer

Tel: **065 9053073**   Fax: **065 9053073**
Email: **coisnasionna@eircom.net**
Web: **www.bb-house.com/cois-na-sionna.htm**

Spectacularly located, overlooking the beautiful Shannon Estuary and just 50 mins Shannon Airport. On the N67. Ideal touring base to tour the West of Ireland.

B&B	4	Ensuite	€25.50/€28	Dinner	-
B&B	-	Standard	-	Partial Board	-
Single Rate			€38.50	Child reduction	50%

In Killimer

Open: All Year

Michael & Mary Clarke
BRUACH NA COILLE
Killimer Road N67,
Kilrush, Co Clare

Kilrush

Tel: **065 9052250**   Fax: **065 9052250**
Email: **clarkekilrush@hotmail.com**
Web: **www.clarkekilrush.com**

On N67 opposite Vandeleur walled gardens. Rooms with views. Family run. Frommer reader recommended and AA listed. Tea/Coffee on arrival. Large car park. Comprehensive Breakfast menu.

B&B	2	Ensuite	€25.50/€30.47	Dinner	-
B&B	2	Standard	€23/€26.66	Partial Board	-
Single Rate			€36/€38.09	Child reduction	50%

Kilrush 1km

Open: All Year

Austin & Ethna Hynes
HILLCREST VIEW
Doonbeg Road (off N67),
Kilrush, Co Clare

Kilrush

Tel: **065 9051986**   Fax: **065 9051986**
Email: **ethnahynes@eircom.net**
Web: **http://kilrushclare.port5.com**

Luxurious B&B. Spacious rooms. AA ◆◆◆◆ Award. Off N67. 5 mins walk Kilrush, Killimer Ferry 8km, Airport 1 hr drive. Conservatory. Quiet area. Breakfast menu.

B&B	6	Ensuite	€25.50/€29.20	Dinner	-
B&B	-	Standard	-	Partial Board	-
Single Rate			€38.50/€43.17	Child reduction	50%

Kilrush 1km

Open: All Year

367

Kilrush 1km

Mrs Hilda Wallace
THE MOORINGS B&B
Coast Road, Cappa,
Kilrush, Co Clare

Kilrush

Tel: **065 9080997**
Email: **themooringscappa@eircom.net**

Exquisite residence situated in Cappa Village overlooking the historic Scattery Island on the Shannon Estuary and beyond to the Kerry mountains.

B&B	2	Ensuite	€26.66/€28	Dinner	-
B&B	1	Standard	-	Partial Board	-
Single Rate			€36/€36	Child reduction	-

Open: 1st February-31st October

Lahinch 1km

Mrs Joanne Barrett
EDENLANDIA
School Road, Lahinch,
Co Clare

Lahinch

Tel: **065 7081361**   Fax: **065 7081361**
Email: **xbarrett@iol.ie**

Set with panoramic views off main Lahinch - Killimer Ferry road. Golfers' 19th. Tea/Coffee, Hairdryer all rooms. Golf course 2 mins. Shannon Airport 50 mins.

B&B	3	Ensuite	€28	Dinner	-
B&B	-	Standard	-	Partial Board	-
Single Rate			€40	Child reduction	-

Open: 15th February-15th December

Lahinch 1km

Ms Rosemary Donohue
COIS FARRAIGE
Milton Malbay Road, Cregg,
Lahinch, Co Clare

Lahinch

Tel: **065 7081580**   Fax: **065 7081580**
Web: **www.bb-house.com/coisfarraige.htm**

Family run magnificent ocean views. Large family room (sleeps 5). Rooms with Electric Blankets and Hairdryers. Routard, Dillard Causin recommended.

B&B	6	Ensuite	€25.50/€25.50	Dinner	-
B&B	-	Standard	-	Partial Board	-
Single Rate			€38.50/€40	Child reduction	-

Open: 1st March-20th November

In Lahinch

Mrs Brid Fawl
MULCARR HOUSE
Ennistymon Road,
Lahinch, Co Clare

Lahinch

Tel: **065 7081123**   Fax: **065 7081123**
Email: **mulcarrhouse@esatclear.ie**
Web: **www.esatclear.ie/~mulcarrhouse**

Smoke free home, walking distance to Beach, Golf Course. Convenient Cliffs of Moher, Doolin, Burren. Tea making facilities. Hair Dryers. On N67.

B&B	4	Ensuite	€26/€27	Dinner	-
B&B	-	Standard	-	Partial Board	-
Single Rate			€38.50/€38.50	Child reduction	25%

Open: 17th March-1st November

In Lahinch
368

Mrs Anita Gallery
TUDOR LODGE
Ennistymon Road, Lahinch,
Co Clare

Lahinch

Tel: **065 7081270**

Comfortable home, personally run. Adjacent to Golf Courses. Early breakfasts if required. Rooms with electric blankets. Special rate single room.

B&B	4	Ensuite	€25.50	Dinner	-
B&B	-	Standard	-	Partial Board	-
Single Rate			€38.50	Child reduction	33.3%

Open: 15th March-1st December

Annie O'Brien
LE BORD DE MER
Milltown Malbay Rd.
Lahinch, Co Clare

TEL: **065 7081454**   FAX: **065 7081454**
EMAIL: **annieobrien@boinet.ie**
WEB: **homepage.eircom.net/~annieobrien**

Breathtaking Ocean View, Lahinch Championship Golf, French speaking, beside Beach. Ideal base Cliffs of Moher, Burren, Aran Islands, Routard recommended.

B&B	4	Ensuite	€25.50	Dinner	-
B&B	-	Standard	-	Partial Board	-
Single Rate			€38.50	Child reduction	50%

Lahinch 1km   **Open:** March-October

Mrs Frances Sarma
NAZIRA
School Road, Lahinch,
Co Clare

TEL: **065 7081362**

Architect designed, magnificent views of Bay, Golf Courses. Peaceful setting. Warm welcome. Recommended in Dillard Causin Best Bed Breakfast Guide.

B&B	4	Ensuite	€25.50	Dinner	-
B&B	-	Standard	-	Partial Board	-
Single Rate			€38.50	Child reduction	25%

Lahinch 1km   **Open:** March-November

Mrs Margaret Skerritt
MOHER VIEW
Ennistymon Road,
Lahinch, Co Clare

TEL: **065 7081206**   FAX: **065 7081206**
EMAIL: **moherview@esatclear.ie**

Elevated dormer bungalow overlooking golf course. Convenient to Cliffs of Moher, Doolin, Burren, Tea/Coffee making facilities. Route N85.

B&B	4	Ensuite	€25.50/€25.50	Dinner	-
B&B	-	Standard	-	Partial Board	-
Single Rate			€38.50/€38.50	Child reduction	25%

Lahinch 1km   **Open:** 1st May-30th September

Ita Slattery
SEAFIELD LODGE
Ennistymon Road, Lahinch,
Co Clare

TEL: **065 7081594**   FAX: **065 7081594**
EMAIL: **itaslattery@eircom.net**

Elevated dormer bungalow on N67, 5 mins walk Lahinch Beach, Golf Course. All rooms TV, Radio, & Electric Bankets, Hairdryers.

B&B	4	Ensuite	€25.50/€27	Dinner	-
B&B	-	Standard	-	Partial Board	-
Single Rate			€38.50/€38.50	Child reduction	25%

In Lahinch   **Open:** 31st March-31st October

Mrs Marian White
SEA BREEZE
Carrowgar,
Miltown Malbay Road,
Lahinch, Co Clare

TEL: **065 7081073**
EMAIL: **mariantwhite@eircom.net**

Family run bungalow on N67 in rural setting. 2km Lahinch. Convenient Beach, Cliffs of Moher, Burren, trips to Aran Islands, Golf Courses, Pony Trekking, Swimming Pools, Sauna, Jacuzzi.

B&B	3	Ensuite	€25.50/€30	Dinner	-
B&B	-	Standard	-	Partial Board	-
Single Rate			€38.50	Child reduction	-

Lahinch 2km   **Open:** 1st May-30th September

Ms Marie Dowling
CLIFF VIEW LODGE
**Lislarkin, Liscannor,
Co Clare**

Liscannor
Tel: **065 7081783**
Email: **cliffviewlodge@eircom.net**

Modern family run home, set in rural country surround. Adjacent to Cliffs of Moher, Burren. Doolin-Aran Islands Ferry.

B&B	3	Ensuite	€25.50/€25.50	Dinner	-
B&B	-	Standard	-	Partial Board	-
Single Rate				Child reduction	25%

Liscannor 2km

Open: All Year

James & Sheila Lees
SEA HAVEN
**Liscannor,
Co Clare**

Liscannor
Tel: **065 7081385**   Fax: **065 7081474**

Sea-Haven with sea views. On main Lahinch - Cliffs of Moher Road. Orthopaedic beds. 5 minutes walk to Liscannor Village.

B&B	6	Ensuite	€26/€29	Dinner	-
B&B	-	Standard	-	Partial Board	-
Single Rate			€38.50	Child reduction	25%

Open: January-November

Kevin & Ann Thynne
SEAMOUNT
Liscannor, Co Clare

Liscannor
Tel: **065 7081367**

Family run home on road to Cliffs of Moher. In quiet secluded garden. 5 minutes walk from Liscannor Village. Close to Golf, Fishing, Pubs & Restaurants.

B&B	3	Ensuite	€25.50	Dinner	-
B&B	-	Standard	€23	Partial Board	-
Single Rate			€38.50	Child reduction	-

In Liscannor

Open: 17th March-31st October

Mrs Eileen Barrett
MARCHMONT
**Lisdoonvarna,
Co Clare**

Lisdoonvarna
Tel: **065 7074050**

Town House, Car Park. TV Lounge. Hairdryers in rooms. Bicycle lock-up. Rick Steves recommended.

B&B	5	Ensuite	€26/€28	Dinner	-
B&B	-	Standard	-	Partial Board	-
Single Rate			€38.50/€40	Child reduction	33.3%

In Lisdoonvarna

Open: 1st February-30th November

Mrs Bernie Cosgrove
ST JUDES
**Coast Road, Lisdoonvarna,
Co Clare**

Lisdoonvarna
Tel: **065 7074108**

Elevated site overlooking countryside on N67 Doolin Road. Cliffs of Moher, Burren, Doolin, closeby. Hairdryer, Bicycle Shed, Electric Blankets, (1) three bedded room. Homebaking. Failte.

B&B	4	Ensuite	€26/€27	Dinner	-
B&B	-	Standard	-	Partial Board	-
Single Rate			€38.50	Child reduction	50%

Lisdoonvarna 1km

Open: 1st April-30th September

Mrs Monica Droney
CROSSWINDS
Lisdoonvarna,
Co Clare

Lisdoonvarna
TEL: 065 7074469
EMAIL: crwinds@mail.com
WEB: http://crwinds.cjb.net

Situated on Cliffs of Moher Rd, (R478). 10 mins drive Doolin, Island Ferries, Burren & Lisdoonvarna. Walking distance to nightly entertainment.

B&B	2	Ensuite	€26	Dinner	-
B&B	1	Standard	€23	Partial Board	-
Single Rate			€36/€38.50	Child reduction	33.3%

Lisdoonvarna 2km   **Open:** April-October

Mrs Mary Finn
ST ENDA'S
Church Street,
Lisdoonvarna, Co Clare

Lisdoonvarna
TEL: 065 7074066

Five minutes walk to Town Centre. Two storey house with sun lounge. Leading to main Galway Road. Welcoming tea/coffee and home baking. Bicycle lock up. Ideal base Burren, Cliffs of Moher.

B&B	3	Ensuite	€26/€27	Dinner	€17
B&B		Standard	-	Partial Board	-
Single Rate			€38.50	Child reduction	50%

In Lisdoonvarna   **Open:** 15th March-1st November

Vera Fitzpatrick
FERMONA HOUSE
Bog Road, Lisdoonvarna,
Co Clare

Lisdoonvarna
TEL: 065 7074243
EMAIL: fermona@eircom.net

Modern bungalow 10 mins walk to Town Centre. Near Doolin, Cliffs of Moher & Burren Centre. 1hr drive to Shannon Airport & Galway. Home comfort & good breakfast.

B&B	5	Ensuite	€25.50/€32	Dinner	-
B&B	-	Standard	-	Partial Board	-
Single Rate			-	Child reduction	-

In Lisdoonvarna   **Open:** 31st March-14th October

Joseph & Michelle Garrihy
LIMESTONE LODGE
Ardeamush, Lisdoonvarna,
Co Clare

Lisdoonvarna
TEL: 065 7074345   FAX: 065 7074345
EMAIL: limestone_lodge@hotmail.com
WEB: limestonelodge@freeservers.com

Family home, 3kms from the Spa town of Lisdoonvarna. Ideal base for touring the Burren, Cliffs of Moher, Doolin and the Alliwee Caves. All rooms ensuite/TV's.

B&B	4	Ensuite	€25.50/€29	Dinner	-
B&B	-	Standard	-	Partial Board	-
Single Rate			€35/€39	Child reduction	33.3%

Lisdoonvarna 4km   **Open:** 1st March-30th September

Mrs Ann Green
HILLTOP
Doolin Road,
Lisdoonvarna, Co Clare

Lisdoonvarna
TEL: 065 7074134
WEB: www.bb-house.com/hilltop.htm

Elevated site on N67, quiet location. 7 minutes walk to Village. One large family room. Convenient to Cliffs of Moher, Doolin and the Burren. Traditional music locally. Boat trips to Aran.

B&B	3	Ensuite	€25.50	Dinner	-
B&B	-	Standard	-	Partial Board	-
Single Rate			€38.50	Child reduction	33.3%

Lisdoonvarna 1km   **Open:** 15th May-1st November

Lisdoonvarna 1km

Mrs Cathleen O'Connor
Lisdoonvarna

RONCALLI
Doolin Road,
Lisdoonvarna,
Co Clare

TEL: **065 7074115**
WEB: **www.bb-house.com/roncalli.html**

7 mins walk village N67. 5 houses from Burmah Filling Station. Quiet location. "Lets Go" recommended. Close to Burren, Cliffs of Moher, Aran Ferry, Traditional Music. TV, Hairdryer.

B&B	3	Ensuite	€25.50/€25.50	Dinner	-
B&B	-	Standard	-	Partial Board	-
Single Rate			€38.50/€38.50	Child reduction	33.3%

Open: 1st April-1st November

In Lisdoonvarna

Mrs Joan O'Flaherty
Lisdoonvarna

GOWLAUN
St Brendan's Road,
Lisdoonvarna, Co Clare

TEL: **065 7074369**
EMAIL: **gowlaun@eircom.net**

Situated on a quiet location off N67. 5 mins walk from Town Centre and bus stop. One hour drive from Shannon Airport. Burren and Cliffs of Moher closeby.

B&B	3	Ensuite	€26/€27	Dinner	-
B&B	-	Standard	-	Partial Board	-
Single Rate			€38.50/€38.50	Child reduction	-

Open: 12th April-13th October

Lisdoonvarna 1km

Anne & Denis O'Loughlin
Lisdoonvarna

BURREN BREEZE
The Wood Cross,
Lisdoonvarna, Co Clare

TEL: **065 7074263**   FAX: **065 7074820**
EMAIL: **burrenbb@iol.ie**
WEB: **www.iol.ie/~burrenbb**

Rooms with Bathtub & Shower, TV, Tea/coffee, Hairdryers. 2/3/4 night Specials. NO ENSUITE SUPPLEMENT. Internet access. Junction N67/R477 - Doolin/Coast Road.

B&B	5	Ensuite	€25.50/€25.50	Dinner	€17
B&B	1	Standard	€23	Partial Board	€264
Single Rate			€36/€50	Child reduction	50%

Open: 15th January-15th December

In Lisdoonvarna

The Petty Family
Lisdoonvarna

SUNVILLE
Off Doolin Road,
Lisdoonvarna, Co Clare

TEL: **065 7074065**   FAX: **065 7074065**
EMAIL: **tpetty@gofree.indigo.ie**
WEB: **gofree.indigo.ie/~tpetty/**

Situated off N67, quiet area with private parking. Near Cliffs of Moher, Burren, Golf at Lahinch, Trips to Aran Island. Frommer recommended. Electric blankets, Hairdryers. Off season rates.

B&B	4	Ensuite	€26/€28	Dinner	-
B&B	-	Standard	-	Partial Board	-
Single Rate			€38.50/€40	Child reduction	33.3%

Open: All Year

Lisdoonvarna 1km

Mrs Helen Stack
Lisdoonvarna

ORE-A-TAVA HOUSE
Lisdoonvarna, Co Clare

TEL: **065 7074086**   FAX: **065 7074547**
EMAIL: **oreatava@eircom.net**

House in quiet area on landscaped gardens with patio for visitors use. Cliffs of Moher, Burren, Aran Islands nearby. Shannon-Galway 1 hour. Breakfast menu available. Credit cards accepted.

B&B	6	Ensuite	€25.50/€28	Dinner	-
B&B	-	Standard	-	Partial Board	-
Single Rate			€38.50/€38.50	Child reduction	33.3%

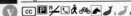

Open: 20th March-30th October

Mrs Irene Vaughan
WOODHAVEN
Doolin Coast Road,
Lisdoonvarna, Co Clare

Lisdoonvarna
TEL: **065 7074017**

Junction off N67/R477 scenic, peaceful surroundings. Near Doolin ferry. Traditional music. Cliffs of Moher. Electric Blankets, Homebaking, Private car park, Bicycle shed, Hairdryers.

B&B	4	Ensuite	€26/€27	Dinner	-
B&B	-	Standard		Partial Board	-
Single Rate			€38.50/€38.50	Child reduction	25%

Lisdoonvarna 1km

Open: All Year Except Christmas

Miltown Malbay 1km

Mary Hughes
AN GLEANN
Ennis Road, Miltown Malbay,
Co Clare

Miltown Malbay
TEL: **065 7084281**
EMAIL: **angleann@oceanfree.net**
WEB: **members.xoom.com/anglean/**

Friendly family run home, rooms ensuite, TV, Tea/Coffee. Located 1km Ennis road. Recommended "New York Times". Close to all amenities. All credit cards welcome.

B&B	5	Ensuite	€25.50/€27.94	Dinner	-
B&B	-	Standard		Partial Board	-
Single Rate			€38.50/€38.50	Child reduction	33.3%

Open: All Year Except Christmas

Miltown Malbay 4.5km

Mrs Maura Keane
SEA CREST
Rineen, Milltown Malbay,
Co Clare

Miltown Malbay
TEL: **065 7084429**   FAX: **065 7084429**
EMAIL: **seacrestguesthouse@eircom.net**

On N67 overlooking Cliffs of Moher, Golf Courses and Beaches nearby. Rooms ensuite. TV Lounge for guests, use of kitchen for Tea/Coffee facilities.

B&B	5	Ensuite	€25.50	Dinner	-
B&B	-	Standard		Partial Board	-
Single Rate			€38.50	Child reduction	50%

Open: All Year

In Mountshannon

Howe Family
OAK HOUSE
Mountshannon,
Co Clare

Mountshannon
TEL: **061 927185**   FAX: **061 927185**

Country home, panoramic view, overlooking Lough Derg. Private Beach, Boats, excellent facilities for Fishermen. Ideal base for touring. 200m village.

B&B	2	Ensuite	€25.50/€25.50	Dinner	-
B&B	1	Standard	€23/€23	Partial Board	-
Single Rate			€36	Child reduction	25%

Open: 1st April-1st November

In Newmarket on Fergus

Colette Gilbert
FERGUS LODGE
Ennis Road,
Newmarket-on-Fergus,
Co Clare

Newmarket-on-Fergus
TEL: **061 368351**   FAX: **061 368351**

On N18, beside Texaco Station. Shannon Airport, Bunratty, Knappogue, 10 minutes. Dromoland Castle and Clare Inn Hotel 2 minutes drive. Walking distance to Pubs, Restaurants.

B&B	5	Ensuite	€26.66/€27.93	Dinner	-
B&B	-	Standard		Partial Board	-
Single Rate			€38.50/€38.50	Child reduction	-

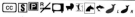

Open: All Year

Mrs Sheila Ryan
THE DORMER
Lisduff,
Newmarket-On-Fergus,
Co Clare

Newmarket-on-Fergus

TEL: **061 368354**   FAX: **061 368354**
EMAIL: gerandsheilaryan@eircom.net
WEB: www.web-ie.com/thedormer/

Peaceful rural setting, Airport side of Newmarket-on-Fergus off N18. Shannon Airport, Bunratty 15 mins. Dromoland Castle 5 mins. Fine Restaurants locally.

B&B	2	Ensuite	€25.50	Dinner —
B&B	1	Standard	€23	Partial Board —
Single Rate			€38.50	Child reduction 50%

Newmarket-on-Fergus 2km

Open: 1st March-31st October

Mrs Antoinette Fitzgerald
SCAPAFLOW
O'Brien's Bridge,
Co Clare

O'Brien's Bridge

TEL: **061 377144**
EMAIL: scapaflow@eircom.net
WEB: www.scapaflowobriensbridge.com

Scapaflow is overlooking the River Shannon. 5 minutes walk from all facilities. Bar, restaurants, Post Office, tennis, fishing.

B&B	2	Ensuite	€25.50/€27	Dinner —
B&B	1	Standard	€23/€25	Partial Board —
Single Rate			-	Child reduction 25%

Killaloe 8km

Open: 5th January-8th December

Anne & Dave Hyland
SHANNON COTTAGE
O'Brien's Bridge,
Co Clare

O'Brien's Bridge

TEL: **061 377118**   FAX: **061 377966**
EMAIL: bandb@shannoncottage.com
WEB: www.shannoncottage.com

Traditional 200 year old refurbished Cottage, on the banks of the River Shannon at O'Brien's Bridge Village. Restaurants, Fishing, Walking, Golf nearby.

B&B	6	Ensuite	€25.50/€40	Dinner —
B&B	-	Standard	-	Partial Board —
Single Rate			-	Child reduction 25%

Killaloe 8km

Open: 15th January-15th December

Mrs Joan Murphy
ROOSKA HOUSE
Quin, Co Clare

Quin

TEL: **065 6825661**

Modern house in village. Convenient Quin Abbey, Knappogue & Craggaunowen. Shannon Airport 30 mins, Ennis 15 mins, Limerick 30 mins.

B&B	2	Ensuite	€26	Dinner —
B&B	2	Standard	€24	Partial Board —
Single Rate			€40	Child reduction 33.3%

In Quin

Open: 1st April-31st October

Mr John Boland
FORT LACH
Drumline,
Newmarket-on-Fergus,
Co Clare

Shannon

TEL: **061 364003**   FAX: **061 364059**
EMAIL: johnboland@eircom.net
WEB: homepage.eircom.net/~johnboland

Modern house, rural setting, 600 yds off N18. Shannon Airport, Bunratty, Golf, Horse Riding, Fishing all 10 mins. Ideal touring centre.

B&B	6	Ensuite	€25.50	Dinner —
B&B	-	Standard	-	Partial Board —
Single Rate			€38.50	Child reduction 25%

Shannon 7km

Open: 1st February-30th November

Mrs Kathleen Collins
VALHALLA
Urlanbeg,
Newmarket-on-Fergus,
Shannon, Co Clare

Shannon
TEL: **061 368293**   FAX: **061 368660**
EMAIL: **valhalla@esatclear.ie**
WEB: **www.shannonheartland.ie**

On R472 Shannon/Newmarket-on-Fergus Rd. Bunratty/Shannon 10 mins. Early guests welcome. Tea/Coffee, hairdryers all bedrooms. All bedrooms ground floor.

B&B	3	Ensuite	€25.50	Dinner	-
B&B	-	Standard		Partial Board	-
Single Rate			€38.50	Child reduction	33.3%

Shannon 4km

Open: 5th January-20th December

Mrs Geraldine Enright
TRADAREE
Drumline,
Newmarket-on-Fergus,
Co Clare

Shannon
TEL: **061 364386**
EMAIL: **genright@gofree.indigo.ie**

Old style dormer house 100m off N18 to Ennis. Bunratty Castle, Shannon Airport 5 mins. Morning guests welcome. Visitors Garden.

B&B	1	Ensuite	€25.50	Dinner	-
B&B	2	Standard	€23	Partial Board	-
Single Rate			€36	Child reduction	25%

Shannon 4km

Open: 1st April-30th September

Mrs Phil Fleming
KNOCKNAGOW
Leimaneighmore,
Newmarket-on-Fergus,
Co Clare

Shannon
TEL: **061 368685**   FAX: **061 368685**
EMAIL: **knocknagowbandb@eircom.net**
WEB: **homepage.eircom.net/~knocknagow**

Purpose built B&B. 8km from Shannon Airport on R472 Shannon/Newmarket-on-Fergus Road. Convenient to Bunratty & Knappogue Castles. Morning guests welcome.

B&B	4	Ensuite	€25.50/€25.50	Dinner	-
B&B	-	Standard	-	Partial Board	-
Single Rate			€38.50/€38.50	Child reduction	25%

Shannon 5km

Open: 5th January-20th December

Mrs Sheila Hanrahan
THE CROOKED CHIMNEY
Hurlers Cross, Shannon,
Co Clare

Shannon
TEL: **061 364696**   FAX: **061 364696**
EMAIL: **thecrookedchimney@eircom.net**

Off main road N18 (Exit Hurlers Cross). 3 miles Shannon, 2 miles Bunratty. Private gardens for guest viewing. Tea/Coffee facilities.

B&B	5	Ensuite	€25.50/€25.50	Dinner	-
B&B	-	Standard	-	Partial Board	-
Single Rate			€38.50/€38.50	Child reduction	25%

Shannon 3km

Open: 1st January-16th December

Mrs Brede Lohan
35 Tullyglass Crescent
Shannon,
Co Clare

Shannon
TEL: **061 364268**   FAX: **061 364358**

Home overlooking River Shannon. Cul-de-sac. Airport Terminal 1.5 miles. Leisure Centre, Swimming Pool, Sauna 200 yds. Take Tullyglass Rd off Roundabout N19.

B&B	6	Ensuite	€26.67	Dinner	€26.67
B&B	-	Standard	-	Partial Board	-
Single Rate			€38.50	Child reduction	25%

In Shannon

Open: 1st January-23rd December

In Shannon

Mrs Kay Moloney
MOLONEY'S B&B
21 Coill Mhara, Shannon,
Co Clare

TEL: **061 364185**

Home situated 5 mins from Airport Terminal. Shannon Town Centre 400 yds. Third road on left after Texaco filling station.

B&B	2	Ensuite	€25.50/€25.50	Dinner	-
B&B	2	Standard	€23/€23	Partial Board	-
Single Rate			-	Child reduction	25%

Open: 10th January-20th December

Shannon 2km

Mrs Betty Nally
IVORY LODGE
Drumline,
Newmarket-on-Fergus,
Co Clare

Shannon
TEL: **061 364039**
EMAIL: **nallyivorylodge@eircom.net**

Purpose built home in Drumline, 100m off N18. Airport 12 mins, Bunratty 5 mins. TV, Hairdryer, Tea/Coffee in rooms. Morning guests welcome. Ideal base for touring.

B&B	3	Ensuite	€25.50	Dinner	-
B&B	1	Standard	€25.50	Partial Board	-
Single Rate			-	Child reduction	25%

Open: 30th January-30th November

Shannon 2km

Mrs Wiestawa O'Brien
TARA GREEN
Ballycally/Aerospace Rd,
Newmarket-on-Fergus,
Co Clare

Shannon
TEL: **061 363789**
EMAIL: **tarag@iol.ie**
WEB: **www.iol.ie/~tarag**

3 miles Shannon Airport. Welcome to Irish/Polish home. Organic garden. Home cooking. From Shannon follow signs for Ballycally and Shannon Aerospace.

B&B	4	Ensuite	€25.50/€30	Dinner	€20
B&B	1	Standard	€23/€25	Partial Board	-
Single Rate			€38.50/€45	Child reduction	-

Open: All Year

In Shannon

Mary O'Loughlin
AVALON
11 Ballycaseymore Hill,
Shannon Town, Co Clare

Shannon
TEL: **061 362032**   FAX: **061 362032**
EMAIL: **avalonbnb@eircom.net**
WEB: **www.avalonbnb.net**

Spacious modern home in quiet cul-de-sac overlooking Shannon. 5 min drive to Airport. Near Bunratty. Turn off N19 at Shannon Court Hotel.

B&B	2	Ensuite	€25.50	Dinner	-
B&B	1	Standard	€23	Partial Board	-
Single Rate			€36/€42	Child reduction	25%

Open: 2nd January-22nd December

In Shannon

Marian O'Meara
ESTUARY VIEW
20 Coill Mhara,
Shannon, Co Clare

Shannon
TEL: **061 364602**

Family home situated 5 mins from Airport. Shannon town centre 400 yards, local bus stop nearby. Third road on left after Texaco filling station.

B&B	2	Ensuite	€25.50	Dinner	-
B&B	2	Standard	€23	Partial Board	-
Single Rate			-	Child reduction	50%

Open: 2nd January-20th December

Mrs Fidelma Ryan
MAPLE VIEW
Urlanmore,
Newmarket-on-Fergus,
Shannon, Co Clare

Shannon
Tel: 061 368062

Morning guests welcome, off Shannon/Newmarket Road R472 at Ballygreen sign. 10 mins Shannon Airport, Shops & Restaurants 2km. Bunratty Castle 5 mins. Large garden.

B&B	2	Ensuite	€25.50/€25.50	Dinner	-
B&B	2	Standard	€23/€23	Partial Board	-
Single Rate			€36/€38.50	Child reduction	25%

Shannon 5km

Open: 1st February-30th November

Geraldine E Ryan
HILLCREST
Clonlohan, Shannon/
Newmarket Road, Newmarket-
On-Fergus, Co Clare

Shannon
Tel: 061 364158   Fax: 061 360582
Email: ryanhillcrest@broker.assurelink.ie

Family home. R472 back road Shannon to Newmarket-on-Fergus. Rural setting. Overlooking Airport. Morning guests, Golf, Restaurants 2km, Bunratty 4km.

B&B	2	Ensuite	€25.50/€25.50	Dinner	-
B&B	2	Standard	€23/€23	Partial Board	-
Single Rate			€36/€36	Child reduction	50%

Shannon 2km

Open: 15th January-15th December

Mrs Kathleen Ryan
ARDREE
Monument Cross,
Newmarket-on-Fergus,
Co Clare

Shannon
Tel: 061 368256   Fax: 061 368846
Email: ardree@indigo.ie
Web: indigo.ie/~ardree

Off Shannon/Newmarket Road R472, 2km from N18. Morning guests welcome. Golf, Horse Riding, Fishing. Bunratty & Shannon 10 mins.

B&B	1	Ensuite	€25.50/€25.50	Dinner	-
B&B	2	Standard	€23/€23	Partial Board	-
Single Rate			€36/€38.50	Child reduction	25%

Shannon 4km

Open: 1st April-15th October

Mrs Mary Tobin
SHANNONSIDE
Clonlohan, Shannon/
Newmarket Road R472,
Newmarket-on-Fergus, Co Clare

Shannon
Tel: 061 364191   Fax: 061 362069
Email: tobins.shannonside@oceanfree.net

Morning guests welcome, Highly recommended home offering warm hospitality for over 30 years on R472, 5 mins from Airport. Scenic area. Bunratty 10 mins.

B&B	6	Ensuite	€25.50	Dinner	-
B&B	1	Standard	€23	Partial Board	-
Single Rate			-	Child reduction	50%

Shannon 1km

Open: 7th January-20th December

SYMBOL

**LOOK OUT FOR THIS SYMBOL WHICH
ALL MEMBERS OF
TOWN & COUNTRY HOMES DISPLAY**

A pleasant county of lush green pastures, bordered by the Shannon. Adare, where you will find quaint cottages nestling in the prettiest village in Ireland.
Experience the welcome in historic Limerick. Visit King John's Castle, St. Mary's Cathedral, Hunt Museum and Georgian Pery Square. Partake of the many attractions including golf, horse-riding, fishing, festivals and evening entertainment.

In Abbeyfeale

Noreen & Tom Browne
PARK LODGE
Killarney Rd, Abbeyfeale,
Co Limerick

Abbeyfeale
TEL: **068 31312**
EMAIL: **info@parklodge.ie**
WEB: **www.parklodge.ie**

Spacious modern home, family run. Situated on N21. Ideal base for touring South West, convenient to Ballybunion, Tralee, Killarney, Dingle and Crag Cave.

B&B	4	Ensuite	€26/€28	Dinner	-
B&B	-	Standard	-	Partial Board	-
Single Rate			€38.50/€38.50	Child reduction	50%

Open: All Year

In Adare

Mrs Ann Benson
RIVERSDALE
Station Road, Adare,
Co Limerick

Adare
TEL: **061 396751**

Select modern house. 4 minutes walk to Town Centre. Tea making facilities in bedrooms. Automatic Hairdryers. Shannon Airport 30 minutes. Ideal touring base.

B&B	3	Ensuite	€28	Dinner	-
B&B	1	Standard	-	Partial Board	-
Single Rate			€36/€39	Child reduction	25%

Open: 15th March-15th December

Adare 4km

Mary Boyle
KNOCKREAD HOUSE
Croom Road, Adare,
Co Limerick

Adare
TEL: **061 396935**
EMAIL: **knockreadadare@eircom.net**
WEB: **http://www.eircom.net/~knockreadadare**

Friendly inviting home, lovely scenic countryside. Off N21, Shannon 35 mins, Adare 5 mins. Breakfast menu. Private parking, Woodland Hotel 1.5km. Near Golf, Fishing.

B&B	1	Ensuite	€25.50/€28	Dinner	-
B&B	2	Standard	€23/€23	Partial Board	-
Single Rate			€36/€38	Child reduction	33.3%

Open: 1st April-1st November

Adare 1km

Ms Deirdre Buckley
ROSSBEIGH HOUSE
Ballingarry Road, Adare,
Co Limerick

Adare
TEL: **061 395141**

Elegant Tudor-style home. Tranquil surroundings. Hairdryers, breakfast menu and orthopaedic beds. Convenient Hotels and Restaurants. Shannon Airport 30 mins.

B&B	3	Ensuite	€28/€32	Dinner	-
B&B	-	Standard	-	Partial Board	-
Single Rate			€38.50	Child reduction	-

Open: 29th March-27th October

Mrs Patsy Davis
CLONSHIRE MILL
Croagh,
Co Limerick

Adare

TEL: **069 64200**
EMAIL: **paddydavis@eircom.net**

Comfortable restored 19th Century family home. Warm welcome. Gardens, hens, donkeys. Stables available. Equestrian Centre close. Good Restaurants nearby. French spoken.

B&B	-	Ensuite	-	Dinner	€17
B&B	3	Standard	€23/€23	Partial Board	-
Single Rate			€36/€36	Child reduction	50%

Adare 5km

Open: 1st May-30th September

Mrs Anne Donegan
WESTFIELD HOUSE
Ballingarry Rd R519, Graigue,
Adare, Co Limerick

Adare

TEL: **061 396539**
EMAIL: **westfieldhouse@eircom.net**
WEB: **www.adareaccommodation.com**

Purpose built home in wooded area. Mature gardens. Just off busy N21. Airport 30 minutes. Golfers haven, touring base. Spacious rooms. Extensive menu. Highly recommended.

B&B	3	Ensuite	€26/€28	Dinner	-
B&B	-	Standard		Partial Board	-
Single Rate			€40/€40	Child reduction	25%

Adare 1km

Open: 1st April-31st October

Bridie & Pat Donegan
BERKELEY LODGE
Station Road, Adare,
Co Limerick

Adare

TEL: **061 396857**   FAX: **061 396857**
EMAIL: **berlodge@iol.ie**
WEB: **www.adare.org**

Superb warm spacious home away from home. AA ◆◆◆◆, RAC◆◆◆◆ Awards. Breakfast menu. Near Hotels Churches Golf Tour base. Turn at roundabout. Shannon 30 mins. Early arrivals welcome.

B&B	5	Ensuite	€30/€32.50	Dinner	-
B&B	1	Standard	€30/€32.50	Partial Board	-
Single Rate			€50/€58	Child reduction	25%

In Adare

Open: All Year

Mrs Geraldine Fitzgerald
SCEILIG HOUSE
Killarney Road, Adare,
Co Limerick

Adare

TEL: **061 396627**
EMAIL: **sceilig_house@ireland.com**

Welcoming family home in Adare. Convenient Hotels, Restaurants, Leisure amenities, Pitch and Putt at rear. Ideal touring base. Shannon 30 minutes.

B&B	4	Ensuite	€28/€30	Dinner	-
B&B	1	Standard	€26/€28	Partial Board	-
Single Rate			€40/€42	Child reduction	33.3%

In Adare

Open: All Year

Mrs Agnes Fitzpatrick
ADARE LODGE
Kildimo Road, Adare,
Co Limerick

Adare

TEL: **061 396629**   FAX: **061 395060**

Highly recommended AA ◆◆◆◆ award. TV, Tea & Coffee in rooms. Adjacent Dunraven Arm's Hotel. Golf, Horseriding, Churches. Shannon Airport 30 mins.

B&B	6	Ensuite	€33/€33	Dinner	-
B&B	-	Standard		Partial Board	-
Single Rate			€58/€58	Child reduction	50%

In Adare

Open: All Year

Adare

Kathleen Glavin
CASTLEVIEW HOUSE
Clonshire, Adare,
Co Limerick

Tel: **061 396394**   Fax: **061 396394**
Email: **castleview@eircom.net**

"Sullivans B&B Guide" recommended. Beautiful warm restful country home. Award winning gardens. Tea/Coffee. Excellent breakfasts including pancakes. Electric blankets. Hairdryers.

B&B	3	Ensuite	€26/€28	Dinner	€20
B&B	1	Standard	€24/€26	Partial Board	-
Single Rate			€36/€38.50	Child reduction	50%

Adare 2km

Open: All Year

Adare

Mrs Pauline Hedderman
ELM HOUSE
Mondellihy, Adare,
Co Limerick

Tel: **061 396306**

Elegant restored 1892 Georgian Home with character, enjoying sheltered garden. "Lonely Planet" recommended. Welcoming Tea/Coffee. Shannon Airport 30 mins.

B&B	1	Ensuite	€28	Dinner	-
B&B	2	Standard	€25	Partial Board	-
Single Rate			-	Child reduction	33.3%

Adare Village 1km

Open: 1st January-15th December

Adare

Nora Hennessy
DUHALLOW HOUSE
Ballingarry Road (R519),
Adare, Co Limerick

Tel: **061 395030**
Email: **duhallow@adare-ireland.com**
Web: **www.adare-ireland.com**

Charming Rustic Family home at edge of Village. Warm friendly atmosphere. Satellite TV's, Hairdryers in rooms. First on right after N21/R519 junction.

B&B	3	Ensuite	€26/€29	Dinner	-
B&B	-	Standard		Partial Board	-
Single Rate			€39/€42	Child reduction	50%

Adare 1km

Open: 1st April-1st November

Adare

Florence & Donal Hogan
COATESLAND HOUSE B&B
Tralee/Killarney Road,
Adare N21, Co Limerick

Tel: **061 396372**   Fax: **061 396833**
Email: **coatesfd@indigo.ie**
Web: **http://indigo.ie/~coatesfd/**

Modern warm home, RAC & AA ◆◆◆◆ awards. Friendly atmosphere. Nice gardens. Good restaurants. Online facilities. Also: RAC (Warm welcome & Sparkling Diamond Awards).

B&B	6	Ensuite	€31.75/€31.75	Dinner	-
B&B	-	Standard		Partial Board	-
Single Rate			€38.50/€38.50	Child reduction	25%

Adare Village 1km

Open: 1st January-23rd December

Adare

Mrs Maura Linnane
CARRIGANE HOUSE
Reinroe, Adare,
Co Limerick

Tel: **061 396778**
Email: **carrigane.house@oceanfree.net**
Web: **www.adareaccommodation.com**

Award winning luxurious spacious home just off main road. Morning guests welcome, near Woodlands Hotel. King size bed available. Extensive breakfast menu.

B&B	6	Ensuite	€25.50/€30	Dinner	-
B&B	-	Standard	-	Partial Board	-
Single Rate			€38.50/€40	Child reduction	50%

Adare 2km

Open: All Year

Mrs Margaret Liston
GLENELG
Mondellihy, Adare,
Co Limerick

Adare
TEL: **061 396077**

Luxurious superwarm home. Tranquil location. Highly recommended Karen Brown/ Erdvig. Airport 30 mins, Adare 4 mins. Tea/Coffee/Scones, TV, Hairdryers.

B&B	2	Ensuite	€29	Dinner	-
B&B	1	Standard	€29	Partial Board	-
Single Rate			€36/€36	Child reduction	50%

Adare 2km

Open: 1st January-20th December

Michael & Jennie Power
HILLCREST COUNTRY HOME
Clonshire, Croagh,
Adare, Co Limerick

Adare
TEL: **061 396534**   FAX: **061 396534**
EMAIL: **hillcrest_irl@hotmail.com**
WEB: **www.dirl.com/limerick/hillcrest.htm**

Hospitable, relaxed home. Amidst beautiful, tranquil pastures where nature abounds. Traditional farming. Forest and nature trails. Medieval ruins. Frommer recommended.

B&B	3	Ensuite	€26.50/€29.50	Dinner	-
B&B	-	Standard	-	Partial Board	-
Single Rate			€38.50/€44.50	Child reduction	25%

Adare 5km

Open: 1st March-31st October

Mrs Bridie Riordan
CHURCHVIEW HOUSE
Adare, Co Limerick

Adare
TEL: **061 396371**   FAX: **061 396371**

Warm, friendly home in Ireland's prettiest village. Tea facilities in lounge, sun lounge for guests. Adjacent Dunraven Arms Hotel, Church, Golf, Shannon, Airport 45 mins.

B&B	4	Ensuite	€25.50/€28	Dinner	-
B&B	2	Standard	€23/€24	Partial Board	-
Single Rate			€36/€38.09	Child reduction	25%

Adare

Open: All Year

Mrs Phil Clancy
DRUMINACLARA HOUSE
Pallaskenry,
Co Limerick

Askeaton Pallaskenry
TEL: **061 393148**

2km from Kilcornan House off N69, scenic route. Country setting, peaceful surroundings. 3km Curragh Chase Forest Park, Celtic Park, Animal Farm. Golf and Fishing locally. 40 mins Airport.

B&B	4	Ensuite	€25.50	Dinner	€20.32
B&B	-	Standard	-	Partial Board	€264
Single Rate			€38.50	Child reduction	25%

Askeaton 6km

Open: 3rd January-20th December

Mrs Marie Keran
KILLEEN HOUSE
Cow Park, Kilcornan,
Palaskenry, Co Limerick

Askeaton
TEL: **061 393023**

Spacious friendly home, lovely gardens on N69 scenic route. Beside Curragh Caravan Forest Park, Celtic Park. Shannon Airport 40 mins. Limerick City 15 min, Askeaton 5 min.

B&B	5	Ensuite	€25.50/€25.50	Dinner	€17
B&B	1	Standard	€23/€23	Partial Board	-
Single Rate			€38.50/€38.50	Child reduction	25%

Askeaton 5km

Open: All Year

Mrs Mary Conway Ryan
FOUR SEASONS
**Boherlode, Ballyneety,
Co Limerick**

Ballyneety
Tel: **061 351365**   Fax: **061 351643**
Email: **fourseasonsselfcatering@eircom.net**
Web: **www.fourseasonsselfcatering.ie**

Relaxing home, landscaped gardens, sandwiched between Limerick (Ballyclough) R511 & Limerick. County Golf Clubs. R512, off N20, N21, N24, N7, N18. TV, hairdryers, tea coffee rooms.

B&B	3	Ensuite	€25.50	Dinner	-
B&B	-	Standard	-	Partial Board	-
Single Rate			€38.50	Child reduction	50%

Ballyneety 2km

Open: 1st January-21st December

Mrs Margaret Ryan
GLENGROVE
**Glen, Ballyneety,
Co Limerick**

Ballyneety
Tel: **061 351399**   Fax: **061 351399**

Warm welcoming elegant home. Extensive breakfasts. Walking distance Golf, Restaurant, Pubs. On R512 parallel with N7, N24. Turn at Kilmallock roundabout on Childers Road. Ideal Shannon etc.

B&B	3	Ensuite	€25.50/€25.50	Dinner	-
B&B	1	Standard	€23/€24.13	Partial Board	-
Single Rate			€36	Child reduction	50%

Limerick 7km

Open: 10th January-18th December

William & Deirdre Guiry
SUNVILLE B&B
**Woodpark, Castleconnell,
on N7, Co Limerick**

Castleconnell
Tel: **061 377735**   Fax: **061 377735**

Modern bungalow situated on N7 with pleasant gardens, tennis court. Convenient to village, Fishing, Restaurants, Walks. University, Airport 40mins.

B&B	6	Ensuite	€25.50/€25.50	Dinner	-
B&B	-	Standard	-	Partial Board	-
Single Rate			€38.50/€38.50	Child reduction	25%

Limerick City 9km

Open: 1st January-20th December

Margaret Tyrrell
EDELWEISS
**Stradbally, Castleconnell,
Co Limerick**

Castleconnell
Tel: **061 377397**

Cosy home with lovely view beside Castle Oaks Hotel. Short walk to picturesque Village and River Shannon. Fishing, Restaurants, Pubs. Tea/coffee in lounge.

B&B	2	Ensuite	€26/€26	Dinner	-
B&B	1	Standard	€24/€24	Partial Board	-
Single Rate			€36	Child reduction	25%

Castleconnell 1km

Open: 1st April-31st October

Siobhan Moloney
BARKER HOUSE
Glin, Co Limerick

Glin
Tel: **068 34027**
Email: **wmoloney@iol.ie**

Elegant Town House on 3 acres, near Glin Castle. Offers luxury ensuite accommodation. Ideal touring base. Shannon Airport 1 hr drive. Tarbert Car Ferry 6km

B&B	3	Ensuite	€25.50/€25.50	Dinner	-
B&B	-	Standard	-	Partial Board	-
Single Rate			€38.50/€38.50	Child reduction	50%

In Glin

Open: 1st January-20th December

Estelle O'Driscoll
O'DRISCOLL'S B&B
Main Street, Glin,
Co Limerick

Glin
TEL: **068 34101**

Town house, welcoming and friendly. Glin is a picturesque Village on the N69. Near to Tarbert Car Ferry. Ballybunion Golf course 20 min.

B&B	3	Ensuite	€27	Dinner	-
B&B	1	Standard	€27	Partial Board	-
Single Rate			€36/€38.50	Child reduction	**50%**

Ⓥ 🄲🄲Ⓢ📱⤧🛏🍵✖🔦   **Open:** 10th January-18th December

Mrs Catherine Sweeney
SCENIC VIEW HOUSE
Ballyculhane, Glin,
Co Limerick

Glin Tarbert
TEL: **068 34242**
EMAIL: **scenicviewhouse@ireland.com**

Bungalow, 7 mins Tarbert Car Ferry. Panoramic view of Shannon Estuary. Enroute from Shannon to Ring of Kerry on N69.

B&B	3	Ensuite	€27	Dinner	€20
B&B	3	Standard	€27	Partial Board	-
Single Rate			€36/€38.50	Child reduction	**25%**

Tarbert 4km   Ⓥ 🄲🄲📱⤧🍵🏇⚓   **Open:** All Year

Mrs Patricia Nunan
ST ANDREW'S VILLA
Kilfinane, Kilmallock,
Co Limerick

Kilfinane
TEL: **063 91008**

Georgian Style house with interesting history. Formerly a school in rural village accessible via R517/N8/R512/N20. Organic garden, lawns, shrubs. Warm welcome.

B&B	-	Ensuite	-	Dinner	-
B&B	4	Standard	€23	Partial Board	-
Single Rate			€36	Child reduction	**33.3%**

Kilmallock 9km   Ⓥ 📱⤧🍵🏇✖   **Open:** 1st April-31st October

Mrs Anne O'Sullivan
DEEBERT HOUSE
Kilmallock, Co Limerick

Kilmallock
TEL: **063 98106**   FAX: **063 82002**
EMAIL: **deeberthouse@eircom.net**
WEB: **www.deeberthouse.com**

Splendid Georgian residence, award winning gardens. Ideal touring centre. Adjacent to historic sites, golf, hill walking, horse riding. Loughgur Heritage Centre. On R515.

B&B	4	Ensuite	€25.50	Dinner	€21
B&B	1	Standard	€23	Partial Board	€300
Single Rate			€36/€38.50	Child reduction	**25%**

In Kilmallock   Ⓥ 🄲🄲📱⤧🍵🏇✖   **Open:** 1st March-30th November

---

Agnes Callinan
MOYRHEE
Phares Road, Meelick,
Co Limerick

Limerick City
TEL: **061 326300**
EMAIL: **agnesbnb@eircom.net**

Situated on elevated site 1/2 mile off N18 South overlooking Clare Hills. Pets welcome by arrangement. Chiropractic clinic on premises.

B&B	3	Ensuite	€27/€29	Dinner	€23
B&B	-	Standard	-	Partial Board	-
Single Rate			€40/€40	Child reduction	**25%**

Limerick 5km   Ⓥ 🄲🄲📱🛏🍵🏇✖   **Open:** 1st January-1st December

Mrs Mary Dundon
ACACIA COTTAGE
2 Foxfield, Dooradoyle Road,
off N20 Dooradoyle,
Limerick, Co Limerick

Limerick City
TEL: **061 304757**   FAX: **061 304757**
EMAIL: **acaciacottage@iolfree.ie**

Warm, welcoming, cosy, friendly home, nice garden. Highly recommended. Great Breakfasts, Healthy Options. 1km from Crescent Shopping Centre roundabout (Dooradoyle - N20 link road)

B&B	3	Ensuite	€27/€29	Dinner	-
B&B	1	Standard	-	Partial Board	-
Single Rate			€36/€40	Child reduction	33.3%

Limerick 3km

Open: All Year

Elizabeth Gordon
AVONDALE B&B
Old Cratloe Road, Limerick
Co Limerick

Limerick City
TEL: **061 451697**

Warm, comfortable, country family home, peaceful surroundings. Ensuite bedrooms. Choice resturants. Leisure activities. Tea/Coffee. Bunratty 3 miles, Airport 9 miles.

B&B	2	Ensuite	€26/€28	Dinner	-
B&B	1	Standard	€25/€27	Partial Board	-
Single Rate			€38.50/€38.50	Child reduction	-

Limerick 3km

Open: All Year

Lelia & Bernard Hanly
SANDVILLA
Monaleen Road,
Castletroy, Co Limerick

Limerick City Castletroy
TEL: **061 336484**   FAX: **061 336484**
EMAIL: **sandvilla@indigo.ie**

A warm welcoming haven off N7 and N24. Landscaped gardens. Award winning breakfast menu. Orthopaedic beds, Tea/Coffee, TV in rooms. Near Castletroy, Kilmurry Hotels, University, Golf.

B&B	2	Ensuite	€25.50	Dinner	-
B&B	2	Standard	€23	Partial Board	-
Single Rate			€36/€38.50	Child reduction	-

Limerick 5km

Open: All Year

Mrs Evelyn Moore
AVONDOYLE COUNTRYHOME
Dooradoyle Road, Limerick,
Co Limerick

Limerick City
TEL: **061 301590/301501** FAX: **061 301501**
EMAIL: **avondoyl@iol.ie**
WEB: **http://welcome.to/avondoyle**

Dooradoyle exit off N20 highway. Follow golf club signs for 1km. Warm welcome. Extensive breakfast menu. TV, Tea/Coffee in rooms.

B&B	2	Ensuite	€27/€29	Dinner	-
B&B	2	Standard	€25/€27	Partial Board	-
Single Rate			€37/€40	Child reduction	25%

Limerick City 3km

Open: All Year Except Christmas

Noreen O'Farrell
DOONEEN LODGE
Caher Road, Mungret Near
Limerick, Co Limerick

Limerick
TEL: **061 301332**   FAX: **061 301332**
EMAIL: **dooneenlodge@eircom.net**

0.5 km off R526 between Limerick and Patrickswell, sign-posted. Tea/Coffee, TV all rooms. Convenient Adare, Bunratty, Shannon Airport, Limerick 5km.

B&B	2	Ensuite	€26/€28	Dinner	-
B&B	1	Standard	€23/€26	Partial Board	-
Single Rate			€36/€36	Child reduction	33.3%

Open: 1st January-30th November

Limerick 5km

Mrs Bergie Carroll
COONAGH LODGE
Coonagh, Off Ennis Rd,
Limerick, Co Limerick

Limerick City Ennis Road
Tel: **061 327050**
Email: **coonagh@iol.ie**
Web: **www.ireland-discover.com/cooaghlodge.htm**

Family run home. 10 minutes drive Shannon Airport, 5 minutes to Bunratty and Limerick City. Off Ennis Road roundabout at Travel Lodge Hotel.

B&B	6	Ensuite	€26/€28	Dinner	-
B&B	-	Standard	-	Partial Board	-
Single Rate			€38.50/€38.50	Child reduction	50%

Limerick City 3km

Open: 1st February-15th December

Martin & Patricia C Keane
SANTOLINA
Coonagh, Ennis Road,
Limerick, Co Limerick

Limerick City Ennis Road
Tel: **061 451590/328321**
Email: **patriciackeane@eircom.net**
Web: **homepage.eircom.net/~santolina**

Spacious country home. Ground floor accommodation. Coonagh is off N18 roundabout between Travelodge and Elm Garage. Convenient for City, Bunratty, Shannon.

B&B	6	Ensuite	€26/€28	Dinner	-
B&B	-	Standard	-	Partial Board	-
Single Rate			€38.50/€38.50	Child reduction	50%

Limerick 3km

Open: February-November

Mrs Joan McSweeney
TREBOR
Ennis Road, Limerick City,
Co Limerick

Limerick City Ennis Road
Tel: **061 454632**   Fax: **061 454632**
Email: **treborhouse@eircom.net**

Old fashioned Town House, short walk City Centre on Bunratty Castle/Shannon Airport road. Tea/Coffee.

B&B	5	Ensuite	€26/€28	Dinner	-
B&B	-	Standard	-	Partial Board	-
Single Rate			€38.50/€42	Child reduction	25%

In Limerick

Open: 1st April-1st November

Carole O'Toole
GLEN EAGLES
12 Vereker Gardens,
Ennis Road, Limerick,
Co Limerick

Limerick City Ennis Road
Tel: **061 455521**   Fax: **061 455521**

Quiet cul-de-sac. Nearest B&B to the City Centre, Train/Bus/Tourist Office. Off N18 beside Jurys Hotel. Frommer recommended. Hairdryers.

B&B	4	Ensuite	€27/€28	Dinner	-
B&B	-	Standard	-	Partial Board	-
Single Rate			€38.50/€38.50	Child reduction	25%

In Limerick City

Open: 1st March-9th November

Mrs Helen Quinn
ASHGROVE HOUSE
42 Rossroe Avenue,
Caherdavin, Ennis Road,
Limerick, Co Limerick

Limerick City Ennis Road
Tel: **061 453338**

Comfortable town house, 5 mins to City, RTC College. Convenient to Shannon Airport, Bunratty, off Ennis Road at Ivans Cross to N7W.

B&B	4	Ensuite	€26/€28	Dinner	-
B&B	-	Standard	-	Partial Board	-
Single Rate			€38.50/€38.50	Child reduction	-

Limerick City 2km

Open: 1st February-15th December

Mr Ken Ryan
ARMADA LODGE
1 Elm Drive, Caherdavin,
Ennis Road, Limerick,
Co Limerick

Limerick City Ennis Road
TEL: 061 326993

Modern town house, convenient to Shannon Airport, City Centre, Bunratty and King Johns Castle. Opposite Greenhills Hotel. Private car parking.

B&B	4	Ensuite	€26/€28	Dinner	-
B&B	-	Standard	-	Partial Board	-
Single Rate			€38.50	Child reduction	-

Open: 1st February-15th December

Limerick 2km

Dermot Walsh
SANTA CRUZ
10 Coolraine Terrace,
Ennis Road, Limerick,
Co Limerick

Limerick City Ennis Road
TEL: 061 454500

Spacious town house, adjacent to Ryan Hotel, Shannon bus stop. City Centre bus stop. 15 minutes to Shannon/Bunratty. 5 minutes Town. Tea/Coffee facilities.

B&B	2	Ensuite	€25.50/€27	Dinner	€17
B&B	3	Standard	€23/€24	Partial Board	€264
Single Rate			€36/€38.50	Child reduction	50%

Open: All Year

Limerick 1 km

Mrs Mary Walsh-Seaver
RINNAKNOCK
Glenstal, Murroe,
Co Limerick

Murroe
TEL: 061 386189   FAX: 061 386189
EMAIL: walshseaver@hotmail.com

Spacious bungalow beside Glenstal Abbey. Off N7 and N24. On Slieve Felim Cycling and Walking Trails.

B&B	3	Ensuite	€26/€26	Dinner	-
B&B	1	Standard	€24/€24	Partial Board	-
Single Rate			€36/€36	Child reduction	25%

Open: 1st April-31st October

Murroe 2km

Nuala Duffy
SHANAGARRY B&B
Killarney Rd, Newcastle West,
Co Limerick

Newcastle West
TEL: 069 61747
EMAIL: shanagarryb_b@yahoo.com

Welcoming home on outskirts of old market town (N21). Tea/Coffee on arrival. 13th century castle open after extensive renovation. Home of Ballygowan Spring Water.

B&B	2	Ensuite	€25.50	Dinner	-
B&B	1	Standard	€23	Partial Board	-
Single Rate			€36	Child reduction	50%

Open: All Year

Newcastle West 1km

Mrs Joan King
RANCH HOUSE
Cork Road, Newcastle West,
Co Limerick

Newcastle West
TEL: 069 62313
EMAIL: ranchhouse@eircom.net

Luxurious home on large landscape gardens, quiet peaceful setting halfway between Shannon/Killarney/Tralee, adjacent to 18 hole Golf Course.

B&B	5	Ensuite	€25.50/€25.50	Dinner	€17
B&B	-	Standard	-	Partial Board	-
Single Rate			€38.50/€38.50	Child reduction	25%

Open: All Year Except Christmas

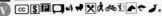
Newcastle West 1km

Mrs Eileen Murphy
THE ORCHARD
Limerick Road,
Newcastle West,
Co Limerick

Newcastle West

TEL: **069 61029**   FAX: **069 61029**
EMAIL:**eileentheorchard1@eircom.net**

Century old home with spacious rooms. Own farm produce. Breakfast menu. Homemade Breads/Jams. Near speed limit sign, on N21. Tea/Coffee on arrival.

B&B	5	Ensuite	€25.50/€25.50	Dinner	€20
B&B	-	Standard		Partial Board	-
Single Rate			€38.50	Child reduction	50%

Newcastle West 1km

Open: All Year

Mrs Carmel O'Brien
BALLINGOWAN HOUSE
Limerick Road,
Newcastle West,
Co Limerick

Newcastle West

TEL: **069 62341**   FAX: **069 62457**
EMAIL: **ballingowanhouse@tinet.ie**

Luxurious pink Georgian house with distinctive features. Dillard Causin recommended. Landscaped gardens. N21 half way stop between Shannon/Killarney. 18 hole Golf course nearby.

B&B	5	Ensuite	€25.50	Dinner	-
B&B	-	Standard	-	Partial Board	-
Single Rate			€38.50	Child reduction	25%

Newcastle West 2km

Open: All Year

Eilish Buckley
LAUREL LODGE
Adare Road, Newboro,
Patrickswell, Co Limerick

Patrickswell

TEL: **061 355059**   FAX: **061 355059**
EMAIL: **buckleyhome@yahoo.com**
WEB: **laurellodge.tourguide.net**

Secluded luxurious country home, highly recommended. Take R526 off N21 between Limerick and Adare to Patrickswell, at Church, Laurel Lodge is signposted.

B&B	3	Ensuite	€28/€28	Dinner	-
B&B	1	Standard	-	Partial Board	-
Single Rate			€38/€38	Child reduction	33.3%

Patrickswell 3km

Open: 1st April-31st October

The Geary Family
CARNLEA HOUSE
Caher Road, Cloughkeating,
Patrickswell, Co Limerick

Patrickswell

TEL: **061 302902**   FAX: **061 302902**
EMAIL: **carnleahouse@hotmail.com**

Spacious bungalow midway between Limerick City and Patrickswell on R526 (off N20/21). Ideal stopover, Cork/Kerry/Bunratty/Shannon. Friendly atmosphere. Highly recommended.

B&B	2	Ensuite	€25.50	Dinner	-
B&B	2	Standard	€23	Partial Board	-
Single Rate			€36/€38.50	Child reduction	50%

Patrickswell 3km

Open: 1st March-31st October

Mrs Margaret Kearney
BEECH GROVE
Barnakyle, Patrickswell,
Co Limerick

Patrickswell

TEL: **061 355493**

On R526 off N20/21 at Patrickswell exit. Walking distance Village, Airport 20 mins. Near horse racing, golf, greyhound track. Ideal stopover Cork/Kerry.

B&B	1	Ensuite	€25.50	Dinner	-
B&B	3	Standard	€23	Partial Board	-
Single Rate			€36	Child reduction	33.3%

Patrickswell

Open: 1st May-31st September

Mrs Deirdre O'Grady
IROKO
Caher Road, Cloughkeating,
Patrickswell, Co Limerick

Patrickswell
TEL: **061 227861/227869** FAX: **061 227861**
EMAIL: **iroko@eircom.net**
WEB: **homepage.eircom.net/~iroko/index.htm**

First class accommodation, 1/2 way between Limerick (R526) & Patrickswell. 2nd house off R526
TV, Tea/Coffee facilities, Hairdryers. Convenient Adare, Bunratty, Shannon, Golf, Cork, Kerry.

B&B	5	Ensuite	€26/€29	Dinner	-
B&B	-	Standard	-	Partial Board	-
Single Rate			€38.50/€38.50	Child reduction	25%

Limerick 2km

Open: 1st January-31st November

Noreen O'Leary
CEDAR LODGE
Patrickswell, Co Limerick

Patrickswell
TEL: **061 355137**

Situated between Limerick and Patrickswell off N20/21 on the R526. Experience quality and comfort in our friendly family-run home.

B&B	4	Ensuite	€25.50/€25.50	Dinner	-
B&B	-	Standard	-	Partial Board	-
Single Rate			€38.50/€38.50	Child reduction	-

Patrickswell 2km

Open: 1st March-31st October

Mrs Lily Woulfe
LURRIGA LODGE
Patrickswell,
Co Limerick

Patrickswell
TEL: **061 355411**   FAX: **061 355411**
EMAIL: **woulfe@esatclear.ie**

Award Winning Home, landscaped gardens. Breakfast menu. R526 off N20/N21 between
Limerick/Adare to Patrickswell. Shannon Airport 25 mins, Adare 5 mins.

B&B	4	Ensuite	€28/€28	Dinner	-
B&B	-	Standard	-	Partial Board	-
Single Rate			€38.50/€38.50	Child reduction	25%

Patrickswell Village 1km

Open: 1st May-15th October

Heritage Island

is a group of the most prestigious heritage attractions in all of Ireland...

The centres range from historic houses, castles, monuments, museums, galleries, national parks, interpretative centres, gardens and theme parks.

Visitors can avail of big savings by displaying the *Heritage Island Explorer* coupon at the following attractions, which will entitle them to reduced admission, many two for one's and special offers...

Antrim
- The Ulster Museum
- W5 whowhatwherewhenwhy

Armagh
- Armagh Planetarium
- The Argory

Cavan
- Belturbet Station
- Cavan County Museum

Cavan (cont)
- Cavan Crystal

Clare
- Bunratty Castle and Folk Park
- Clare County Museum
- Craggaunowen
- Glor Irish Music Centre

Cork
- Cork City Gaol
- Mizen Vision
- Old Midleton Distillery
- Skibbereen Heritage Centre

Derry
- Springhill House

Donegal
- Donegal County Museum

Down
- Castle Ward
- Exploris Aquarium
- Mount Stewart House and Gardens

Down (cont)
- Rowallane
- Somme Heritage Centre
- St. Patrick Centre
- Ulster Folk & Transport Museum

Dublin
- Dublinia
- Dublin's City Hall, The Story of the Capital
- GAA Museum
- Guinness Storehouse
- James Joyce Centre

Dublin (cont)
- Old Jameson Distillery
- St. Patrick's Cathedral
- Trinity College Library and Dublin Experience

Fermanagh
- Belleek Pottery Visitor Centre
- Castle Coole
- Enniskillen Castle
- Florence Court
- Marble Arch Caves

Galway
- Dartfield - Galway's Horse Museum & Park
- Galway Irish Crystal Heritage Centre
- Kylemore Abbey and Gardens

Kerry
- Crag Cave
- Kerry the Kingdom

Kildare
- Irish National Stud, Japanese Gardens & St. Fiachra's Garden
- Steam Museum

Limerick
- Adare Heritage Centre
- Croom Mills Visitor Centre
- Hunt Museum, Limerick
- King John's Castle
- Limerick County Museum

Louth
- County Museum, Dundalk

Meath
- Kells Heritage Centre
- Trim Visitor Centre

Monaghan
- Monaghan County Museum

Offaly
- Birr Castle Demesne & Ireland's Historic Science Centre
- Tullamore Dew Heritage Centre

Roscommon
- Cruachán Aí Visitor Centre
- King House
- Lough Key Forest Park
- Strokestown Park

Sligo
- Drumcliffe Church and Visitor Centre
- Michael Coleman Heritage Centre

Tipperary
- Brú Ború

Tyrone
- Ulster American Folk Park

Waterford
- Waterford Crystal Visitor Centre
- Waterford Treasures at the Granary and Reginald's Tower

Westmeath
- Athlone Castle Visitor Centre
- Belvedere House, Gardens and Park

Wexford
- Dunbrody
- Hook Lighthouse
- Irish National Heritage Park

Wicklow
- Avondale House
- National Sealife Centre
- Powerscourt House and Gardens
- Russborough
- Wicklow's Historic Gaol

Heritage Island members confirmed as at August 2002. Heritage Island can not accept responsibility for any errors or omissions.

or full details on centres, pening times, discounts nd special offers see leritage Island Touring uide 2002 available at ourist Information entres, nationwide.

eritage Island,
7 Main Street,
onnybrook, Dublin 4.
el: + 353 1 260 0055
x: + 353 1 260 0058
mail: heritage.island@indigo.ie
/eb: www.heritageisland.com

CUT ALONG DOTTED LINE

HERITAGE ISLAND EXPLORER

Display this coupon at any Heritage Island Centre to qualify for reduced admission. Touring Guide available at Tourist Information Offices throughout Ireland, or contact www.heritageisland.com

Der Führer ist in acht geographische Regionen gegliedert, die wiederum in die einzelnen Grafschaften aufgeteilt sind (Karte der Regionen und Grafschaften s. S. 3). Die Regionen sind: **Westirland, östliche Midlands, Nordwest, Nordirland, Dublin, Südost, Cork/Kerry, Shannon.**

Buchungsverfahren

Es ist empfehlenswert, die erste und letzte Übernachtung immer im voraus zu buchen.

Verfügbarkeit von Zimmern in Dublin

In der Hochsaison - Mai bis Oktober - ist es schwierig, in Dublin Zimmer zu finden, wenn man Unterkunft nicht im voraus gebucht hat.
Wir empfehlen dringend, die Unterkunft weit im voraus zu buchen, wenn Sie die Hauptstadt während dieser Monate besuchen wollen.

Verlassen Sie sich nie darauf, dass Sie in Dublin kurzfristig Zimmer finden können. Reservieren Sie immer im voraus.

Weitere Reservierungen

Wenn Sie in Irland sind und bei der Suche nach weiterer Unterkunft Probleme auftreten, dann kontaktieren Sie eine beliebige Touristen-informationsstelle oder holen Sie sich Rat oder Hilfe bei Ihrem Gastgeber/Ihrer Gastgeberin in Town and Country Homes. Sie/Er wird Ihnen gerne bei der Buchung weiterer Übernachtungen helfen (zum Preis eines Telefongesprächs).

Buchungen mit Kreditkarte

Kreditkarten werden in Pensionen akzeptiert, die das ⌐CC⌐ Symbol anzeigen.

Telefonische Reservierungen können durch Angabe einer gültigen Kreditkartennummer garantiert werden.

Reisebürogutscheine

Bitte legen Sie Ihre Unterkunftsgutscheine bei Ihrer Ankunft vor. Die Gutscheine gelten nur in Häusern, die mit dem Symbol ⓥ gekennzeichnet sind. Die Standardgutscheine beziehen sich auf Übernachtung und Frühstück in einem Zimmer ohne eigenes Bad. Der Zuschlag für ein Zimmer mit Bad/Waschgelegenheit beträgt maximal €2.00 pro Person bzw. sollte €5.00 für ein Zimmer, das von drei oder mehr Personen geteilt wird, nicht überschreiten.
"En-suite" Gutscheine beziehen sich auf ein Zimmer mit eigenem Bad. Eine zusätzliche Gebühr fällt nicht an.

Zuschlag für Dublin

In den Monaten June, Juli, August und September wird für die Stadt und die Grafschaft Dublin (Dublin City und County) ein Zimmerzuschlag in Höhe von €7.50 auf Reisebürogutscheine erhoben. Die Gebühr ist direkt an den Vermieter zu zahlen und ist nicht in dem Zimmergutschein enthalten.

Stornierungsverfahren

Bitte erkundigen Sie sich bei der Buchung nach den Bedingungen für den Fall, daß Sie eine bestätigte Reservierung absagen müssen. Die Person, die die Buchung vornimmt, haftet für die vereinbarte Stornierungsgebühr.

Bitte benachrichtigen Sie die Pension so bald möglich telefonisch, wenn Sie Ihren Aufenthalt absagen müssen. Sollte die Absage oder Änderung einer Buchung so kurzfristig erfolgen, daß eine Neuvermietung nicht möglich ist, werden folgende Gebühren in Rechnung gestellt:
• **14 Tage:** keine Gebühr
• **24 Stunden bzw. bei Nichterscheinen:** 75% der Ü/F-kosten für die erste Übernachtung

Späte Ankunft

Bitte beachten Sie, daß eine spätere **Ankunft nach 18.00 Uhr ausdrücklich mit der Pension vereinbart werden muß.**

Anzahlungen in bar / mit Kreditkarte

Bei Vorausbuchungen wird man Sie möglicherweise um Angabe einer Scheck- oder Kreditkartennummer als Sicherheit für die Ankunft bitten. Bitte erkundigen Sie sich nach den Bedingungen.

Ankunft/Abreise:

Bitte teilen Sie mit, wenn Sie sehr früh ankommen.
• Zimmer verfügbar zwischen 14.00 und 18.00 Uhr
• Die Abreise sollte nicht später als 11.00 Uhr erfolgen
• Ankunft nach Möglichkeit vor 18.00 Uhr.

Kinderermäßigung

Ermäßigung wird gewährt, wenn Kinder das Zimmer der Eltern teilen oder wenn drei oder mehr Kinder ein Zimmer teilen. Ein oder zwei Kinder in einem separaten Zimmer zahlen den vollen Preis. Bitte fragen Sie bei der Reservierung, ob das Haus für Kinder geeignet ist.
In einigen Häusern stehen Kinderbetten 🛏 zur Verfügung, für die u. U. eine kleine Gebühr erhoben wird.

Abendmahlzeiten

Können im voraus gebucht werden, nach Möglichkeit vor 12 Uhr mittags.
Imbisse ☒ werden auf Anfrage serviert.

Haustiere

Mit Ausnahme von Blindenhunden sind Haustiere aus Hygienegründen nicht im Haus erlaubt.

Ce guide est divisé en huit régions géographiques subdivisées en comtés (voir la carte des régions et comtés page 3). Les régions sont les suivantes: **(Irlande Ouest), Midlands East (Centre-Est), North West (Nord-Ouest), Northern Ireland (Irlande du Nord), Dublin, South East (Sud-Est), Cork/Kerry, Shannon.**

Réservations

Nous vous recommandons de toujours réserver l'avance votre hébergement de la premiëre et de la derniëre nuitée.

Disponibilité de chambres Dublin
En pleine saison touristique, de mai - septembre, il est difficile de trouver des chambres - Dublin ou dans l'agglomération de cette ville sans réservation préalable.

Lors d'un séjour dans la capitale au cours des mois d'été nous vous recommandons vivement de réserver votre hébergement longtemps - l'avance.

Ne comptez en aucun cas trouver des chambres - Dublin - la derniëre minute. Réservez toujours - l'avance.

Réservations pour les nuitées suivantes

En cas de difficulté - trouver un hébergement lors d'un séjour en Irlande, contactez l'office de tourisme du lieu ou demandez l'aide de voitre húte/hútesse Town and Country Homes.
Moyennant le prix de la communication téléphonique, il/elle vous aidera - réserver l'hébergement de la ou des nuitée(s) suivante (s).

Réservations par carte de crédit

Les cartes de crédit sont acceptées par les établissements affichant le symbole ⌐CC⌐.

Les réservations téléphoniques sont confirmées sur simple communication de votre numéro de carte de crédit en cours de validité.

Supplément - Dublin:

Un supplément de **€7.50** par chambre est prélevé au cours des mois de Juin, Juillet, d'Août et Sept sur les bons d'agents de voyages pour la ville et le Comté de Dublin. Ce montant est à régler directement au fournisseur de l'hébergement et n'est pas compris dans le montant du bon.

Bons d'agents de voyage

Ceux-ci sont à présenter dès l'arrivée. Les bons ne sont acceptés que par les établissements affichant le symbole Ⓥ. Les bons standard assurent l'hébergement et le petit déjeuner en chambre sans salle de bain. Supplément pour salle de bain privée:

maximum **€2.00** par personne. Le supplément par chambre pour 3 ou plus ne doit pas dépasser **€5.00** par chambre.
Les bons "en suite" concernent les chambres avec salle de bain, sans aucun supplément.

Annulations

Lors de la réservation renseignez-vous auprès de l'établissement sur ses conditions d'annulation. La personne effectuant la réservation devra régler les frais d'annulation convenus, dont la pénalité "Absence"ou, si la réservation n'a pas été honorée, une pénalité de 75% du tarif B&B pour la première nuit. Ces pénalités seront prélevées directement sur la carte de crédit.

Arrivées tardives

Arrivées tardives - <u>soit après 18.00</u> heures - avec l'accord spécifique de l'établissement.

Arrivées/départs

Prévenir de toute arrivée en avance.
- Les chambres sont mises à disposition entre 14.00h et 18.00 h.
- Les chambres sont à libérer avant 11.00 heures.
- Les réservations sont à honorer avant 18.00 heures.

Réductions pour les enfants

Celle-ci est consentie lorsque les enfants partagent la chambre des parents ou lorsqu'une chambre est occupée par trois enfants ou plus. Le tarif normal s'applique lorsqu'un ou deux enfants occupent des chambres séparées. Veuillez vérifier lors de la réservation que l'établissement convient aux enfants. Certains établissements peuvent mettre des lits ➡ d'enfant à votre disposition. Un léger supplément pourra être demandé.

Repas du soir

A réserver à l'avance, de préférence avant midi le même jour. Collations servies ✗ sur demande dans certains établissements.

Animaux domestiques

A l'exception des chiens d'aveugle et pour des raisons d'hygiène, les animaux domestiques ne sont pas admis à l'intérieur des établissements.

Personnes handicapées et utilisateurs de chaises roulantes

Le National Rehabilitation Board (NRB) a approuvé un certain nombre d'établissements adaptés aux personnes handicapées accompagnées. Ceux-ci sont repérés par le symbole ♿.

Cómo utilizar esta guía

La guía está dividida en ocho regiones geográficas que se encuentran subdivididas en condados (véase la página 3 para el mapa de regiones y condados). Las regiones son: **Oeste de Irlanda, Región central este, Noroeste, Irlanda del Norte, Dublín, Sureste, Cork/Kerry, Shannon.**

Procedimiento de reservas
Se recomienda reservar siempre con anticipación el alojamiento de la primera y última noche.

Disponibilidad de alojamiento en Dublín
A menos que se haya reservado con antelación, es difícil encontrar alojamiento en Dublín ciudad o en el condado de Dublín en plena temporada turística, de mayo a octubre.

Si se visita la capital durante estos meses, recomendamos firmemente hacer la reserva del alojamiento con mucha anticipación.

No confíe en encontrar habitaciones disponibles a corto plazo; haga siempre su reserva por anticipado

Reservas posteriores
En caso de que tenga problemas para encontrar alojamiento una vez se encuentre en Irlanda, póngase en contacto con cualquier Oficina de Turismo o pida consejo y ayuda al dueño o la dueña de la casa Town and Country Homes. Por el coste de una llamada telefónica el/ella le ayudará a hacer la reserva para la siguiente o siguientes noches. .

Reservas con tarjetas de crédito
Las casas con el símbolo [CC] aceptan tarjetas de crédito.

Se podrán garantizar las reservas realizadas mediante llamadas telefónicas indicando un número de tarjeta de crédito válido.

Vales de agencias de viaje
Le rogamos presente los vales a su llegada. Los vales sólo serán validos en aquellas casas que muestren el símbolo V. Los vales estándar cubren habitación en B&B sin servicio privado. Para elevarse a la categoría de habitaciones con baño privado (en suite) el recargo será de **€2.00** por persona. El recargo máximo para 3 personas o más compartiendo no excederá de **€5.00** por habitación.
Los vales en suite cubren la estancia en una habitación con instalaciones privadas completas. No se ha de pagar ningún recargo adicional.

Suplemento para Dublín
Se aplica un suplemento por habitación para la ciudad y el condado de Dublín de **€7.50** los meses de June, julio, agosto y September en los vales de Agencias de Viajes. Esto se paga directamente a la persona que proporciona el alojamiento y no está incluido en el vale.

Política de cancelaciones
Cuando se haya confirmado una reserva, le rogamos compruebe con le establecimiento al realizar la reserva la política de cancelaciones. La persona que realice la reserva es responsable del recargo por cancelación acordado, incluidos los recargos por "Sin aparecer" y si la reserva no se ha podido aprovechar, se deducirá un 75% de la tarjeta de crédito como recargo por no aparecer por la primera noche.

Llegadas después de las 6pm
Le rogamos que las llegadas tardías - **después de las 6pm se realizarán mediante Acuerdo especial con la casa.**

Depósitos en metálico/ depósitos mediante tarjeta de crédito
Para realizar reservas por adelantado, se le podrá pedir un número de cheque o tarjeta de crédito para garantizar la llegada. Compruebe Términos y Condiciones.

Horas de entrada/ salida
Le rogamos comunique llegadas tempranas.

- Las habitaciones están disponibles de 2pm a 6pm.
- La hora de salida no deberá realizarse más tarde de las 11am.
- Las reservas se deberán realizar antes de las 6pm. En caso de que vaya a llegar tarde, le rogamos confirme el mismo día de llegada con el/la anfitrión/a.

Descuento para niños
Se aplica cuando los niños comparten la habitación de los padres o cuando tres o más niños comparten una habitación. Se aplica la tarifa completa cuando uno o dos niños ocupan habitaciones separadas. Le rogamos compruebe que la casa es adecuada para niños cuando realice la reserva. En algunas casas se encuentran disponibles cunas - puede haber un recargo nominal.

Cenas
Reserve con antelación preferiblemente antes de las 12 del medio día de ese mismo día. Comidas ligeras disponibles a petición suya.

Animales domésticos
Con la excepción de perros-guías, por cuestiones de higiene, no se permite la entrada de animales domésticos en las casas.

La guida è divisa in otto regioni geografiche che sono a loro volta suddivise in contee (vedi pagina 3 per mappa delle regioni e contee). Le regioni sono: **Ovest, Centro Est, Nord Ovest, Irelanda del Nord, Dublino, Sud Est, Cork/Kerry, Shannon.**

Modalità di prenotazione

Si consiglia sempre di prenotare in anticipo la prima e l'ultima notte del vostro soggiorno.

Camere disponibili a Dublino

In alta stagione turistica – da maggio a ottobre – è abbastanza difficile trovare camere disponibili a Dublino e nella sua contea a meno che non si abbia già prenotato.
Se si desidera visitare la capitale irlandese durante i mesi sopracitati, vi consigliamo di prenotare il vostro alloggio con notevole anticipo.

È bene ricordare che è quasi impossibile trovare a Dublino un alloggio disponibile all'ultimo minuto.
Onde evitare spiacevoli inconvenienti si consiglia di prenotare in anticipo.

Prenotazioni successive

Se dovessero sorgere dei problemi nel trovare un alloggio una volta in Irlanda, si prega di contattare qualsiasi ufficio turistico o cercare consiglio e assistenza tramite il personale del luogo dove si alloggia (Town and Country Homes). Costoro saranno in grado di aiutarvi a trovare una sistemazione per eventuali notti successive che si necessitano e per il modico costo di una semplice telefonata.

Prenotazioni con carta di credito

Si accettano carte di credito nelle case con il simbolo cc .

Le prenotazioni telefoniche possono essere garantite comunicando un numero di carta di credito valida.

Voucher delle agenzie di viaggio

Presentare il voucher al momento dell'arrivo. I voucher sono validi solo nelle case indicate con il simbolo V . Normalmente i voucher includono pernottamento e prima colazione in camera senza servizi privati. Per le camere con servizi privati (en-suite) il supplemento massimo è di **€2.00** per persona. Il supplemento massimo per tre o più persone in condivisione non dovrebbe superare **€5.00** per camera.
I voucher "en-suite" includono una camera con servizi privati completi. Non è previsto nessun altro supplemento.

Supplemento Dublino

Un supplemento camera di **€7.50** per la città e la contea di Dublino viene applicato per i mesi di June, Luglio, Agosto ed Settembre sui vouchers delle Agenzie viaggi. Tale supplemento va pagato direttamente a chi fornisce la sistemazione e non è incluso nel voucher.

Prassi di annullamento

Una volta che la prenotazione è stata confermata, controllare la prassi di annullamento dei proprietari della casa al momento della prenotazione. La persona che effettua la prenotazione risponde della penale di annullamento convenuta, incluse le penali per "mancato arrivo" e se non ci si avvale della prenotazione una penale del 75% della tariffa per la prima notte per Mancato Arrivo verrà dedotta dalla carta di credito.

Arrivi a tarda ora

NB: arrivi dopo le **ore 18.00 solo previo accordo speciale con i proprietari della casa.**

Arrivo/Partenza:

Avvisare se si prevede di arrivare in anticipo.
• Le camere sono disponibili fra le 14.00 e le 18.00.
• Partenza: non oltre le 11.00.
• Le camere vanno occupate entro le 18.00.

Riduzione per bambini

Si applica se i bambini condividono la camera dei genitori o se tre o più bambini condividono la stessa camera. La tariffa intera si applica se uno o due bambini occupano una camera separata. Controllare al momento della prenotazione che la casa sia adatta ad ospitare bambini. In alcune case sono disponibili lettini: potrebbe esserci un addebito simbolico.

Pasti serali

Prenotare in anticipo preferibilmente non più tardi di mezzogiorno del giorno stesso. Spuntini disponibili X su richiesta.

Animali domestici

Ad eccezione dei cani guida per ciechi, per motivi igienici, gli animali non sono ammessi nei locali.

Disabili/invalidi

Il National Rehabilitation Board (NRB: ente nazionale riabilitazione) ha approvato case attrezzate per l'accoglienza di disabili con accompagnatore, indicate con il simbolo .
miglioramento del servizio.

Hoe u deze gids gebruikt

De gids is onderverdeeld in acht geografische streken die weer in graafschappen zijn onderverdeeld (zie pagina 2 voor een kaart van de streken en graafschappen). De streken zijn: **West Ierland, Centraal Ierland, het Noordwesten, Noord Ierland, Dublin, het Zuidoosten, Cork/Kerry, Shannon.**

Reserveren
U wordt geadviseerd de logies voor de eerste en laatste nacht altijd van tevoren te reserveren.

Beschikbaarheld kamers in Dublin
In de stad en het graafschap Dublin is het in het hoogseizoen (mei dot en met oktober) vaak moeilijk logies te binden, tenzij u van tevoren hebt gereserveerd. Als u de hoofdstad tijdns deze maanden bezockt, raden wij u sterk aan **vroeg te reserveren**. U kunt er niet op rekenen in Dublin op korte termijn logies te vinden. Reserveer altijd van te voren.

Voorwaarts reserveren
Indien u problemen ondervindt bij het zoeken naar logies terwijl u in Ierland bent, kunt u contact opnemen met een vreemdelingenbureau of de host/hostess van Town and Country Homes. Zij/hij helpt u vij het reserveren van logies voor ve volgende nacht(en) voor de prijs van een telefoongesprek.

Reservering voor de volgende nacht
Voor de prijs van een telefoontje helpt het huis u met de reservering voor de volgende nacht/nachten. Maak gebruik van deze service om teleurstelling te voorkomen.

Reserveringen met credit card
Credit cards worden geaccepteerd in huizen met het symbool `cc`
Telefoonreserveringen kunnen worden gegarandeerd door een geldig credit card nummer op te geven.

Bonnen van reisbureaus
Overhandig uw bon bij aankomst.
Bonnen zijn alleen geldig in huizen met het symbool V
Standaard bonnen zijn geldig voor Bed & Breakfast in een kamer zonder privé-faciliteiten. Voor opwaardering tot een kamer met badkamer betaalt u een maximale toeslag van **€2.00** per persoon.

De maximale toeslag voor 3 of meer personen op één kamer is nooit meer dan **€5.00** per kamer. Bonnen voor kamers met badkamer zijn voor kamers met volledige privé-faciliteiten. Geen extra kosten worden in rekening gebracht.

Toeslag in Dublin.
In de maanden June, Juli, Augustus et September wordt in de stad en het graafschap Dublin een kamertoeslag van **€7.50** berekend. Deze toeslag dient rechtstreeks aan de verlener van de accommodatie te worden betaald en is niet bij de bon inbegrepen.

Annuleringen
Wij adviseren u bij boeken van een reservering de annuleringsregels van het huis te controleren. De persoon die de reservering heeft gemaakt, is verantwoordelijk voor de overeengekomen annuleringskosten, inclusief de onkosten indien een gast niet verschijnt. In het geval geen gebruik wordt gemaakt van een reservering wordt 75% van de kosten voor de eerste nacht van de Credit Card afgetrokken.

Late aankomst
Een late aankomst **(na 18.00 uur) dient speciaal met het huis afgesproken te worden.**

Aankomst / Vertrek
Een vroege aankomst graag vooraf meedelen
- Kamers worden tussen 14.00 en 18.00 uur beschikbaar gesteld
- Vertrek - niet later dan 11.00 uur
- Gereserveerde kamers dienen om 18.00 uur te zijn ingenomen.

Kinderkorting
Een kinderkorting is van toepassing indien kinderen de kamer met hun ouders delen of indien 3 of meer kinderen de kamer delen. Het volle tarief is van toepassing wanneer 1 of 2 kinderen aparte kamers innemen. Controleer bij de reservering dat het huis geschikt is voor kinderen. Wiegen zijn in sommige huizen beschikbaar - soms tegen een nominaal tarief.

Avondmaaltijden
Deze dienen vooraf te worden gereserveerd, liefst voor 12.00 uur op de betreffende dag.
Lichte maaltijden zijn op verzoek beschikbaar.

Huisdieren
In het belang van hygiëne worden huisdieren niet binnenshuis toegelaten, met uitzondering van blindengeleidehonden.

Denna guidebok har indelats i atta geografiska regioner, dessa regioner har sedan indelats i landskap (se sid. 2 för kartor för regionerna och landskapen). Regionerna är: **västra Irland, östra inlandet, Nordväst, Nord Irland, Dublin, Sydöst, Cork/Kerry, Shannon.**

Bokning

Vi rekommenderar att logi för första och sista natten alltid bokas i förväg. Logi i Dublin City och länet Dublin måste reserveras minst 2/3 veckor i förväg och längre i förväg för juni/juli och augusti.

När ett resesällskap eller en resebyrå förhandsbokar logi för en kund kommer namnet på hemmet att stå på kupongen. Denna kupong gäller därför inte på något annat ställe.

Bokning kan göras genom:
- Resesällskap eller resebyrå
- Att ta direkt kontakt med individuella hem Ankomstsgaranti kan begäras, t ex handpenning eller kreditkortsnummer
- Turistinformationskontor över hela Irland hjälper dig med bokningar mot ett belopp på 3 irländska pund
- Bekräfta alltid bokningar skriftligen.

Förhandsbokning:

Värdar/värdinnor hjälper gärna till med förhandsbokningar av logi för gäster, för kostnaden av ett telefonsamtal. För att undvika besvikelse rekommenderar vi att denna service utnyttjas.

Bokning med kreditkort

Kreditkort accepteras på ställen som har symbolen cc .
Telefonbokning kan garanteras genom att ett giltigt kreditkortsnummer uppges.

RESEBYRÅKUPONGER

Var vänlig att visa kupongerna vid ankomsten. Kuponger gäller endast på de gästhus som uppvisar ❶ symbolen. Standardkuponger täcker Bed and Breakfast med rum utan privat badrum. Önskas privat badrum tillkommer en extra kostnad på €2.00 per person. Den högsta avgiften är €5.00 per rum för 3 eller fler personer som delar ett rum. Det finns kuponger som täcker kostnaden för rum med privat badrum. Inga andra kostnader tillkommer.

Extra tillägg för Dublin:

Ett extra tillägg på €7.50 per rum gäller i June, Juli, Augusti och September för Dublin City och länet Dublin, med resebyråkupongerna. Detta tillägg betalas direkt till den som hyr ut rummen och är inte § medräknat i kupongerna.

AVBESTÄLLNINGSREGLER

Var vänlig kontrollera avbeställningsreglerna med hemmet när du bokar och bekräftar bokningen. Personen som gör bokningen är ansvarig för avbeställningsavgiften samt kostnaden för "utebliven ankomst" och om bokningen inte utnyttjas tillkommer en kostnad på 75% av avgiften för "utebliven ankomst" för första natten, denna kommer att dras av på kreditkortet.

Sen ankomst

Var vänlig observera att sen ankomst, efter kl. 18.00, måste bestämmas enligt specialavtal med hemmet.

In-/Utcheckning:

Var vänlig meddela om tidigankomst.
Rummen kan intagas mellan kl. 14.00 och 18.00.
Utcheckning måste göras innan kl. 11.00.
Bokade rum måste intagas före kl. 18.00.

RABATT FÖR BARN

Gäller där barn delar rum med föräldrar, eller om 3 eller fler barn delar ett rum.
Fullt pris när 1 eller 2 barn bor i separat rum.
Kontrollera att huset är lämpligt för barn när ni bokar.
Barnsängar finns ➡på vissa ställen och kan lånas för en liten avgift.

KVÄLLSMÅLTIDER

Beställs i förväg, helst före kl. 12.00 dagen ifråga.
Lätta måltider ☒ serveras efter önskemål.

SÄLLSKAPSDJUR

Förutom guidehundar för blinda tillåts inga djur inne i husen av hygieniska skäl.

RÖRELSEHINDRAD PERSON/ RULLSTOLSBUNDEN PERSON

Det irländska rehabiliteringsförbundet (NRB) har godkänt gästhus som är lämpliga för personer med handikapp och som har ressällskap, dessa gästhus är markerade med symbolen ♿ .

Area Index

Area Index

Open your eyes to Ireland's exciting heritage...

Yearly ticket available!

Dúchas offers a guide-information service and visitor facilities at over 65 sites throughout Ireland.
For further information contact:

'Heritage Card'
Education and Visitor Service
Department of Arts, Heritage, Gaeltacht & the Islands
6 Ely Place Upper, Dublin 2, Ireland.

Tel: +353 1 6472461 Fax: +353 1 6616764
email: heritagecard@ealga.ie
web: www.heritageireland.ie

Dúchas The Heritage Service

An Roinn Ealaíon, Oidhreachta, Gaeltachta agus Oileán
Department of Arts, Heritage, Gaeltacht and the Islands

Please send me details about the Heritage Card and Dúchas sites

Name _____

Address _____

_____

Send to :

'Heritage Card',
Education & Visitor Service,
Department of Arts, Heritage, Gaeltacht & the Islands
6 Ely Place Upper,
Dublin 2, Ireland.   **T&C 2002**

Approved Accommodation

Look out for the quality shamrock approved sign whenever you're seeking accommodation and be sure of attaining the comfort you deserve when holidaying in Ireland.

This sign will be displayed at all premises which are approved to Irish Tourist Board standards by Tourism Accommodation Approvals Ltd., Coolcholly, Ballyshannon, Co. Donegal, Ireland. Tel: 072-52760 Fax: 071-52761 E-mail: taahomes@eircom.net